Conversations

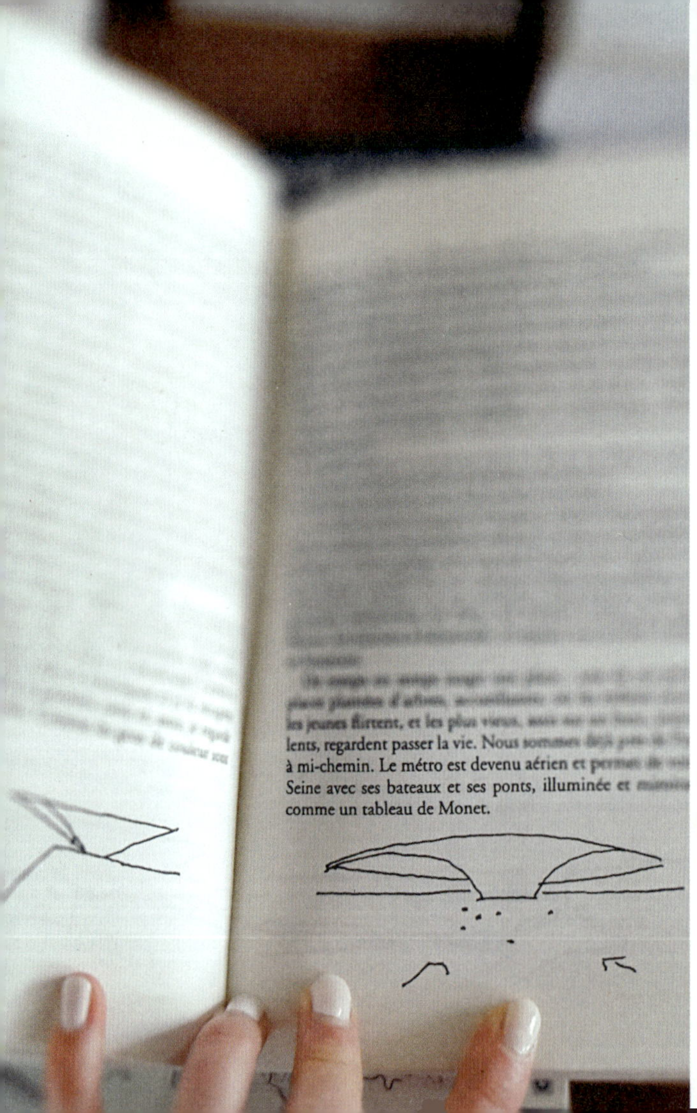
lents, regardent passer la vie. Nous
à mi-chemin. Le métro est devenu aérien et
Seine avec ses bateaux et ses ponts, illuminée et
comme un tableau de Monet.

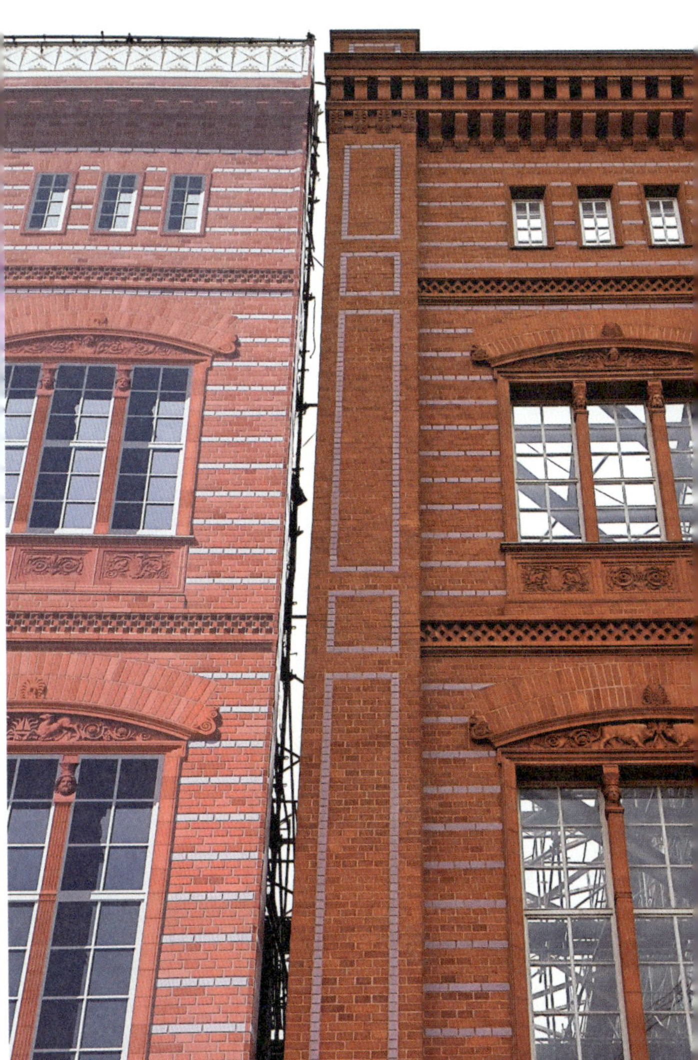

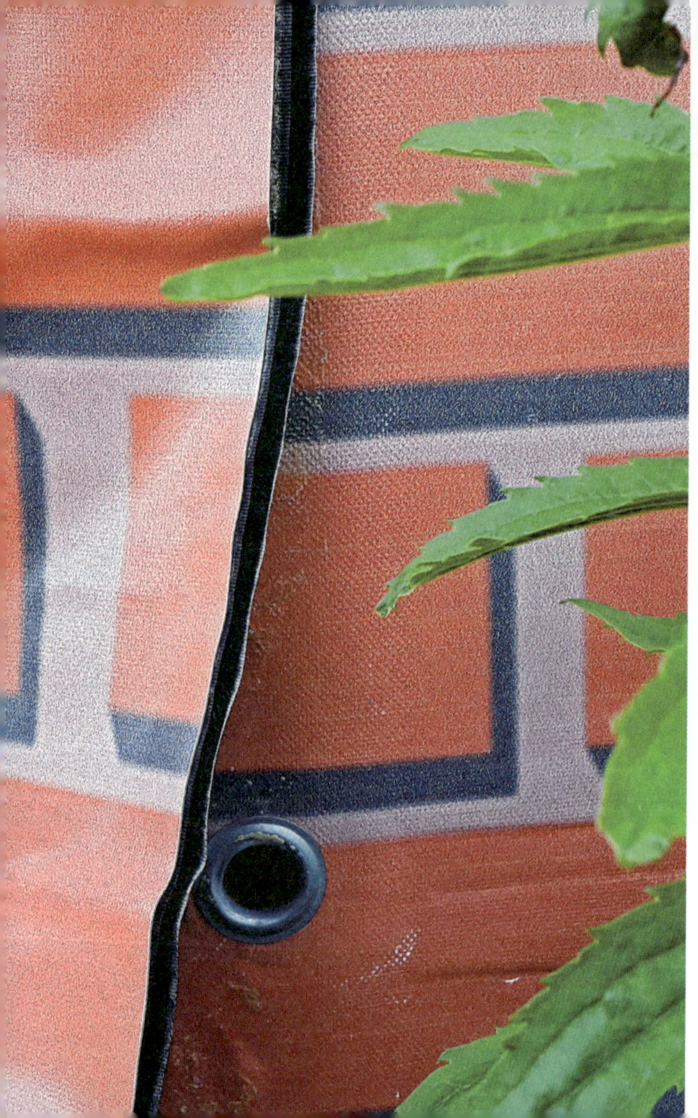

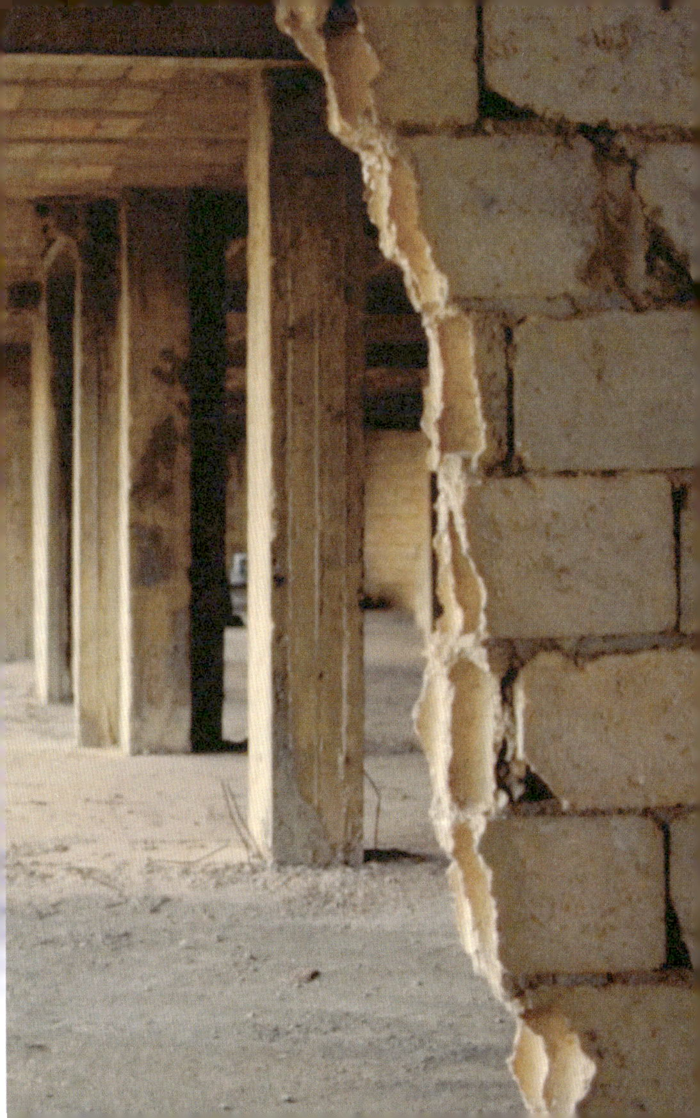

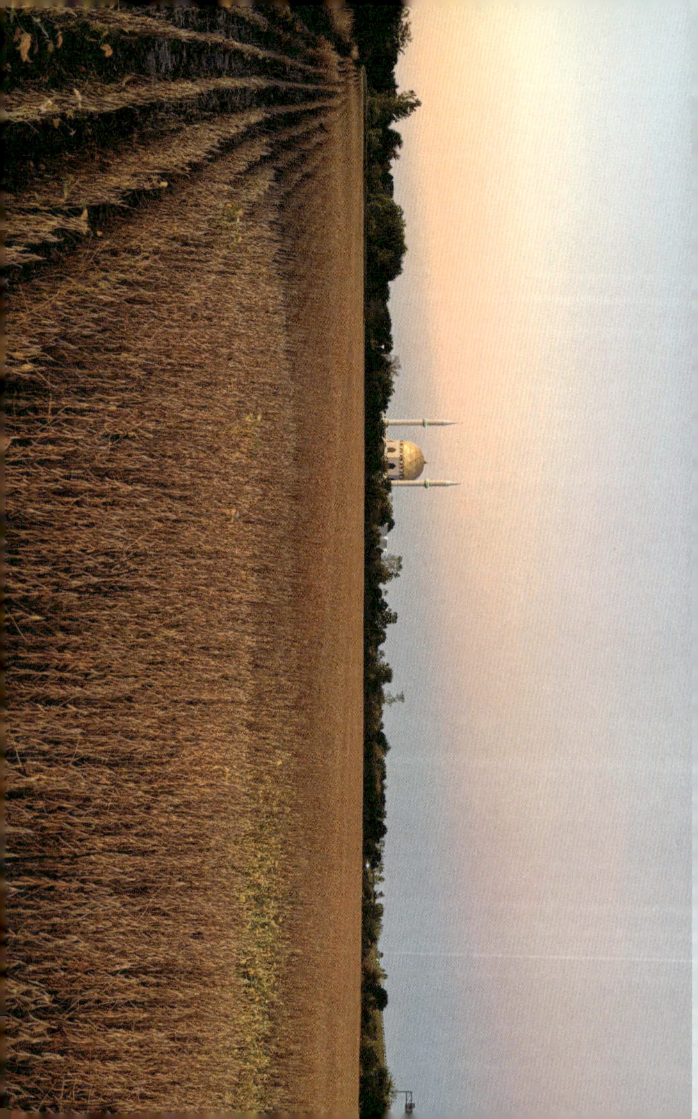

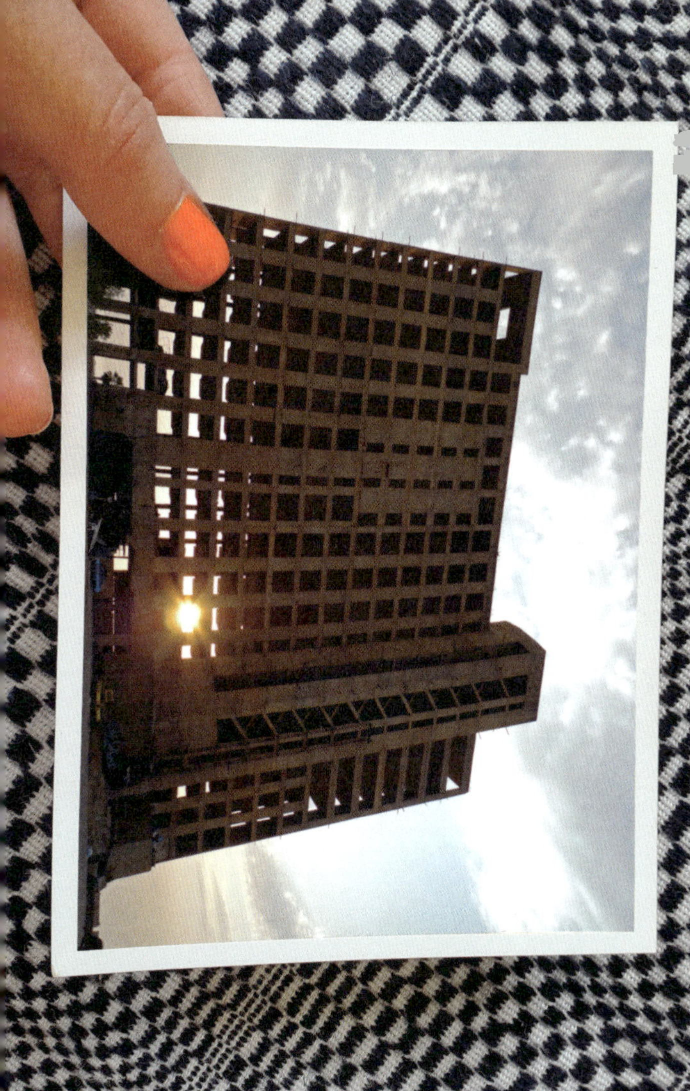

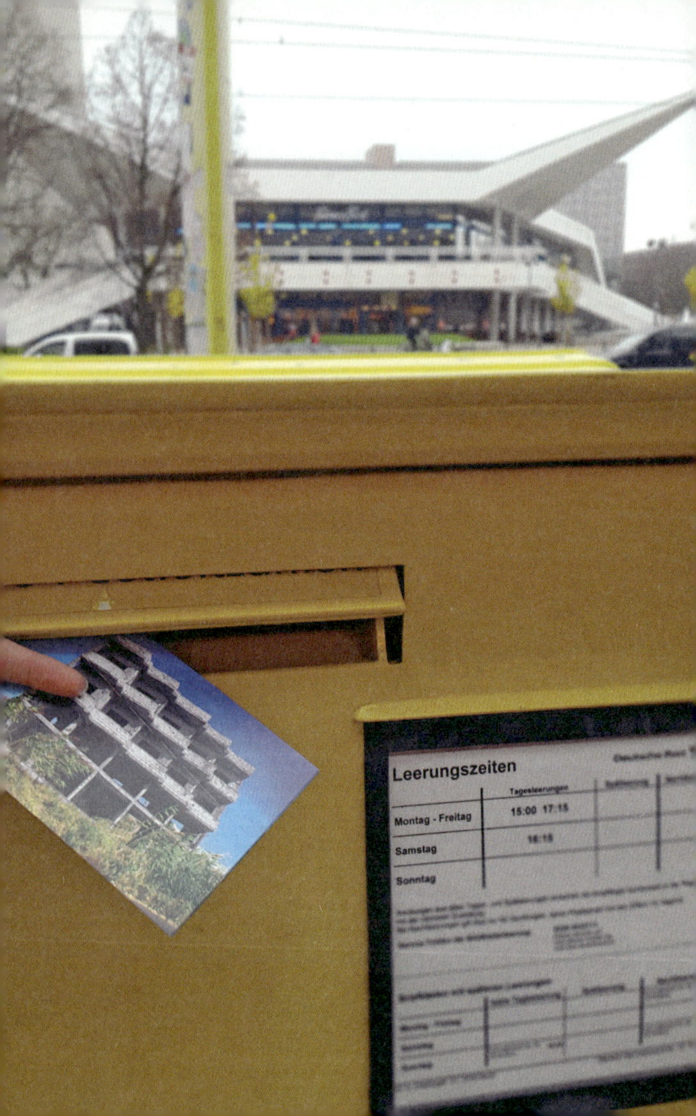
Leerungszeiten
Tagesleerungen
Montag - Freitag
15:00 17:15
Samstag
Sonntag

Researching Oscar Niemeyer's plans, 2015,
photo: Caitlin Berrigan

Bauakademie am Schinkelplatz, Berlin, 2015,
photo: Caitlin Berrigan

Bauakademie am Schinkelplatz, Berlin, 2015,
photo: Caitlin Berrigan

Video still of *Vacant Address* by Caitlin Berrigan, 2016

Islamic Center of Greater Toledo, 2025, photo: Areeb Ahmed

Reviewing Franziska's photo of Tabarja Beach Resort, 2015,
photo: Caitlin Berrigan

Alexanderplatz, Berlin, 2014,
photo: Caitlin Berrigan

Vacant Address
Caitlin Berrigan

Berlin, 2016

This is not a story of the world ending. It is a story of loose endings and loose beginnings.

A story can begin as a line on a page. Or a story can begin with a line on a page. But that is for proper narratives. Like a novel. A novel with a beginning, a middle, and an end (however arbitrary). A novel is page after page of lines assembling characters, affects, impressions, and images evoked by words that must be materialized in your own mind. You, the reader.

A novel is a volume. It takes up space. In its accumulation of lines and pages, it becomes a volume. One with density and mass. That is, of course, if it is printed on paper and bound into a codex: a block of sheets in sequence to contain a collection of words as lines on a page. They wait to be conjured into time – the time it takes – by you, the reader.

To take up space by other means is also possible. Whether it is paper pages, or data, or a haunting. Such as a novel so lucid it becomes hard to distinguish from your memories – or one whose characters you love so deeply that you miss them in your life. Maybe you are perpetually dissatisfied by an unfinished novel you lost on a train, and it wasn't worth replacing, but you still hold its incomplete narrative in your mind, where it takes up space. Or there is the possibility that you lost the line of the plot.

Here you are between one story and another. After reunification in Berlin, the future is being built since decades. A dream of the 1990s seeking occupants for its condominiums and atriums, still vacant. Empty vessels of capital. The newly rebuilt Potsdamer Platz was losing so much money that Sony pulled out of its investment years ago for a loss of 150 million Euro. The Sony Center is now owned by Merrill Lynch and a South Korean pension fund. Do the Korean pensioners worry whether the nameless doorbells will affect their investment portfolio? Do they worry about the people who should be lunching on the grass, arriving for business meetings, using the free WiFi, who should be rushing from lobby to lobby? But you are pretty sure, that these characters must have wandered off into other storylines.

What remains unfinished in Berlin is wrapped in paper façades, which means that sometimes the shadows are in the wrong places. It can be nice to have them there even on a gray day. A private wilderness grows within the scaffolding. But you notice they forgot to reflect the sky in the windows.

In 1914, Le Corbusier drew some lines on a page: the Dom-Ino House. Horizontal lines bisected with reinforced concrete columns and connected by the cascading zig-zag ofdiagonal staircases suspended on air. It was a speculation, an incomplete idea. A skeleton that could be fleshed and skinned with a variety of internal compositions and exterior façades. He said the houses could be built in three days by pouring concrete into a form like water into a bottle.

These conceptual lines were repeated into the chronicle of European modern architecture. And like a rewilded organism, the model replicates as lines in space across the globe wherever access to cheap concrete and raw steel can be found.

You go on a tour of vacancies with a woman you have invented. She is a consultant who works on a cultural redevelopment initiative between Germany and Greece. She has a partner named Dmitri who is a software engineer. He can work from anywhere.

Real estate holds a speculative value worth more than the materials and the land alone. To keep capital fluid, there is no better vessel than the construction industry.
An excess shifted from one form to another.

After an accident, you are seen by a doctor. When he tries to realign your spine, he tells you that the muscles on the left side of your body are full of sadness, and the muscles on your right are full of rage. You smile because you know it is true.
But you do not know why – it precedes the accident. It makes you think, how is it possible to move through the world in this way, one half of your body driven by sadness and the other by rage? You think there must be something else contained in that volume of bifurcated muscle
that propels you.

The optimism of Le Corbusier's architectural revolution disturbs you because people say he was a fascist. All fascists dream of the world ending. And all fascists dream of the world beginning. Fresh new lines on a page. A proper narrative. It is sloppy: this porous landscape full of plot holes that the world has produced. Wormholes, rabbit holes, black holes that irretrievably swallow the lines of a narrative of progress.

Plot holes take up space. Or rather, they define a volume.

You drive north from Beirut, looking for Batroun, where you ate the best fish sandwich in your life. You try to follow the coast, but the road that is drawn on the map is not there when you arrive. The infrastructure is erratic. There is no water in Beirut. Each morning a truck refills the tanks of individual apartments with lightly salty water – and yet here it all is, washing away the road. A distance of 30 minutes takes you three times as long, and you arrive only in Jounieh. This was a beach resort to wait out the blood, an escape from the city during the Lebanese Civil War. The old casino is rebuilt now with infinity pools overlooking the bend in the sea, and all the other half-built escape villas and hotels that slope up the mountain.

You find a perforated volume of a building with a satellite dish and a porch swing. The man who lives there puts on his pants – which he isn't wearing when you arrive – greets you and makes you coffee. He invites you to look at the view with the single request that you take photographs of his cat. He doesn't want the pictures, he just wants them to be taken.

Before he was working in Raqqa when the Syrian Civil War began. Then Daesh took over the city. It wasn't so bad for him under Daesh, he said. There was food and medicine. But the fascists wouldn't allow him to drink or smoke hash. So he came here to Jounieh to this unfinished hotel.
It has stood here for twenty years. The sea passes through to the sky on the other side in these rooms without walls. He looks over it for the owner who lives abroad, who is waiting for the right time. The time it takes.

Vacant Address, 2016, single-channel video, 12:42, shot on location in Berlin, Germany, and Beirut and Jounieh, Lebanon

Caitlin Berrigan works as a visual artist, filmmaker, and writer to explore poetics and queer science fiction as worldmaking practices, through moving images, sculptural instruments, and expanded new media. Berrigan's solo exhibitions at JOAN, Los Angeles, and Art in General, New York, were reviewed in *Artforum*, and her work has shown internationally at the Whitney, New York; Berlinale Forum Expanded; Haus der Kunst, Munich; Henry Art Gallery, Seattle; and Ashkal Alwan, Beirut; among others. Her writings have been published by *e-flux*, *Georgia*, *MARCH*, Duke University Press, Springer, and Broken Dimanche Press. Berrigan earned a PhD-in-Practice from the Akademie der bildenden Künste Wien, and a master's degree from the Art, Culture, and Technology programme at MIT.

Postscript

Suzy Halajian

Los Angeles, 2019

In a series of letters written to her friend against the backdrop of the Lebanese Civil War (1975–90), poet and artist Etel Adnan describes Beirut as a city that is not dead, but damaged. She points to its ruins: after more than fifteen years of strife, architectural remnants hint at their former stature while serving as decimated reminders of the mortal condition. This tension between death and beauty grants the artist space to reflect on the city and the state of exile. Adnan reveals Lebanon's resilient double face: on one side, it is a country whose stories are silently articulated by the skeletons of buildings exposed by destruction; on the other, it holds communities that, like its structures, have absorbed disaster and tragedy without utter collapse. Simultaneously, she rethinks the transition between *now* and *then*, describing Lebanon's capacity "to allow time to take its time, to wait patiently". Etel Adnan, *Of Cities & Women (Letters to Fawwaz)*, Post-Apollo Press, Sausalito, 1993, p. 83. Adnan meditates on her memories of a country that, when damaged, lingers in an intermediary existence before carrying on.

Caitlin Berrigan's artist book *Continual Fragments of the Now* considers Lebanon from the time of her first visit in 2010 and through subsequent journeys. Captivated by the shells of commercial and residential buildings that were never completed due to the civil war and the subsequent financial instability, Berrigan's poetic work investigates how conflict and real estate precariously move together, affecting the architecture and landscape of a place. Progress and conflict go hand in hand in Lebanon: the bullet holes that riddle façades converse with the gaping holes of unfinished structures. It is through this very absence of material that these holes narrate the construction of a country.

Berrigan documented many of these buildings while travelling from the north to the south of the country, mostly along the coast. She then made postcards, combining her photographs with excerpts of Samuel R. Delany's *Dhalgren* (1975), a speculative fiction novel composed of a multilayered narrative unconstrained by any objective measure of time and told by a young narrator who has forgotten his identity. The postcards were addressed and mailed from Berlin to the very sites depicted in each photograph. *Continual Fragments of the Now* reunites the postcards that ultimately never made it to their final destinations. Returned, marked, and full of notes made by Lebanon's unreliable postal system, the saturated postcards convey an uncanny quality of science fiction as they reassemble a novel in fragments.

This book punctuates the postcards with a series of interviews with artists, writers, and designers that concerns the relationships across architecture and capitalism, the collapse of space and time, collective imagination, and languages to build worlds. These expansive conversations seek to navigate an emptiness that contains the possibility of presence. The conversations also introduce Berlin as a site of correspondence; Berrigan maps out a relationship between the vacant slabs and gaping holes of Lebanon's incomplete structures with their unlikely German counterparts of uninhabited real estate holdings, fuelled by the capitalist desires of reconstruction since post-Soviet reunification in the 1990s.

Similar to Adnan's letters, Berrigan's postcards push against a serialised understanding of time as a succession of evenly spaced intervals. In this work titled *Unfinished State* (2010–continual), the past does not detach from the present and the future is not understood solely as what is to come. Berrigan reveals a new imaginary, which points to the potentiality of sites that have been shaped by conflict and forced into a state of unfulfilment. Appearing as both monumental and fragile, the physical structures expose the politics of property, access, and development as they have been exploited through borders and protracted wars. For those who occupied or passed through these spaces, the buildings invite continuous recollection and reflection. And for those who have not physically entered the sites, images of the buildings conjure longing and imagined experiences. Their haunting presence demands attention; speaking through vacuous and suspended states, they shift the experience of linear time. In *Ghostly Matters: Haunting and the Sociological Imagination* (University of Minnesota Press, Minneapolis, 1997), Avery F. Gordon describes haunting as a method of sociological research that confronts abusive systems of power, which are supposedly "over and done with", by paying attention to how they continue to make themselves known in everyday life. Haunting is conceived as very much alive and alters the experience of being in linear time.

A city holds the capacity to defamiliarise its narrative: unpack it of its violent histories, defragment it of its power relations, and map it in relation to precarious economic conditions. With a shift in perspective, reconstructed storytelling advances the possibility of new meanings and ways of being. Parallel to Delany's world-making of *Dhalgren*, Berrigan invites the reader into an understanding of histories of place and futurity through fractured lenses. *Continual Fragments of the Now* reconstructs a layered and fragmented narrative with the postcards, Delany's appropriated text, and conversations assembled to be in dialogue with Lebanon's coastal sites. Such a gesture emphasises that when one returns to a source – a text, a building, a photograph, a palimpsest – its references and their associations make room for alternative subjects and accounts to materialise, even if only through the holes.

Suzy Halajian is a curator and writer based in Los Angeles, where she is the executive director and chief curator of JOAN. She has curated exhibitions and programmes at Los Angeles Contemporary Archive; Hammer Museum, Los Angeles; Human Resources, Los Angeles; and Sursock Museum, Beirut; among others. She is a recipient of the Arts Writers Grant for the collaborative journal *Georgia* and the Curatorial Research Fellowship from the Andy Warhol Foundation for the Visual Arts. Halajan is co-editor with Shoghig Halajian of *A Grammar Built with Rocks* (Wendy's Subway, 2025), and her writing has been published by *ArteEast*, *BOMB*, *X-TRA*, and *Ibraaz*.

What these buildings see ...
with Franziska Pierwoss
and Caitlin Berrigan

Berlin, 2015

Franziska Who is William Dhalgren?

Caitlin This is a character from the novel *Dhalgren*. It is a speculative fiction published in 1975 by Samuel R. Delany, an author writing from a queer Black American perspective. It takes place in Bellona, a fictional city in the US, where an unknown catastrophe has occurred. There are misfits drawn to this city that has been emptied, where they cocreate a loose world together. The main character is the primary narrator, who discovers a half-written notebook while he is in the city, and he is writing within the margins and on top of the text as the novel unfolds. The narrative is fluid and unreliable. The name William Dhalgren appears in the novel and serves as the title, but it is unclear if it is connected to the main character, who cannot remember his own name.

Franziska When he finds himself in this city, he is not alone. There are others. And this was written in the early 1970s?

Caitlin Yes, around the same years as the first era of unfinished buildings in Lebanon.

Franziska The same thing came to my mind. You are sending the postcards with William Dhalgren as the sender, addressed to each unfinished building you documented. Some were returned?

Caitlin I transcribed *Dhalgren* sequentially across all of the postcards, then sent them to the buildings that are pictured in each photograph. Whatever is returned to me in the mail as “undeliverable” is compiled into a new version of the novel.

Franziska They really do return? That is incredible for the Lebanese post! I mean, we usually receive a postcard like one year and four months later.

Caitlin Yes, and because most places in Lebanon do not have systematised addresses, I described how to get to the building in relation to the other places in the landscape. Each address then becomes a narrative description of the landscape itself. I described how to get there by memory, using my photographs, maps, names of towns, remembered landmarks, and the local knowledge of friends.

Franziska Did you send particular texts to specific buildings?

Caitlin I correlated the novel with a kind of journey from north to south, along the coast. It is a wandering path, travelling north to Tripoli, then coming back to Beirut and into the south. I transcribed the novel sequentially, mapping on to that journey through space.

Franziska “Unfinished houses with banana trees”, nice. You have some buildings that are unfinished because of the civil war and some that are just due to lack of construction in the past ten years?

Caitlin It is a long range, from forty years to twenty, to fifteen, ten, and so on, during this whole period.

Franziska There is such beauty in your process, since postcards were never meant to have a serious purpose. It was always a pleasure sport to send them. And this act of sending a postcard – where you put seventy-five cents on it to send it somewhere else in the world – incurs all the labour of processing it. You deal with the body of an organisation that is working along old-fashioned patterns: things come in and they have to sort one after the other and send each one out. It is not an automated field. It does not work any other way but one thing after another.

Caitlin There is a process of translation in these postcards too. Some postcards have handwritten notes on them, which required a lot of manual labour from the postal service. My handwritten addresses in English are not machine translated into the Arabic.

Franziska Is it just my impression or did you mainly document buildings that look towards the sea in one way or another?

Caitlin Yes, they are most often on the coast.

Franziska Yes, they have big holes or big eyes that look towards the sea. There is a different story or a different character compared to the buildings in the mountains.

Caitlin Some do not face the sea, but you always have vistas: high points from the hills.

Franziska The villa with the curved staircase, I mean, what a Hollywood dream, right? Can you imagine what kind of life would take place if you had such a staircase in your hallway? I find these buildings outside of Beirut particularly interesting because they show how the country developed after the civil war. The changes in the Lebanese landscape are more obvious along the coast when compared to pictures from the '70s. These unfinished buildings spread out differently according to the decade in which they were built.

Sometimes you have one clear picture followed by another one that is blurred, which you probably took from the road?

Caitlin Yes, I am working against viewing a landscape from a single vista or one measure of distance. They are imperfect and in motion. Many of these photographs were taken in the south, where the Hezbollah and the Palestine Liberation Organization have and had strongholds. I ended up shooting from the car and leaving very quickly.

Franziska Yes, drive-by pictures in Lebanon are a matter of practical restriction because one must stay concealed in a car in order to take out the camera.

Caitlin What brought you to Lebanon and how do you live your life now between Berlin and Beirut?

Franziska Initially I was going to spend a summer holiday in Lebanon. We booked our tickets in the summer of 2006. But then I was watching the news and saw that we would not be able to fly to Lebanon as we had planned, since the airport was closed to civilians due to the outbreak of war with Israel. We had booked the tickets through a Lebanese travel agent in Munich who told us: *There is no refund in the case of war. But do not worry, it will be all over in about a month. I give you a call and then you go when it is done. It is always like this.* We thought he was insane, but then he did call us a month later and we went. Our friends told us that it would not exactly be a summer holiday, but that it was important to go and visit. I had never been anywhere in the Arab world, so I could not tell what was normal and what conditions were related to the fact that there had just been one month of war in the city. Now looking back, I understand how empty the city was. I thought it was empty because it was too hot and people did not want to go out. I was unable to identify why there was something unsettling. I could not read it. I also did not understand that the air quality back then was exceptionally bad. The big cloud lingering above Beirut for another six weeks was due to the destruction of the concrete buildings. Tons of concrete and many other particles in the air caused this crazy yellow-grey cloud.

Caitlin What did it smell like? Do you remember?

Franziska It smelled bad. A lot of buildings in Beirut were built with asbestos. Asbestos is okay unless you touch it, until you destroy it, until the very fine dust is set free. As a result of the summer war, there was asbestos in the air along with burned plastics. It was a sour, uncomfortable smell. Since Beirut was still recovering from the war, our friends suggested we go north. We visited Tripoli and the Rashid Karami International Fair, the unfinished fairground designed by Oscar Niemeyer [1907–2012] in 1962. This is how everything started. I felt the park was maybe the most special thing I had ever seen in my whole life, so I had to go back. I have been living between Berlin and Beirut since 2007. I met Siska, my husband, in Beirut in 2008. I started B/B Multiples, a publishing house in Berlin together with friends from Beirut, because all of my art projects were related to Beirut or based there. My background is that I moved to Berlin as a child in 1990, which was right after the wall came down. We moved to the eastern part of Berlin. Back then it was clearly Berlin (West) and Berlin (East), absolutely.

Caitlin You wrote a text in 2010 about the unfinished buildings in Lebanon. This is when I first took photographs of these pervasive, ghost-like structures. Do you still feel close to the subject matter?

Franziska Completely. Those spaces are also emotional. They have histories but it goes beyond facts. There is nothing as closely related to life as the spaces where people live.

Caitlin The first time I went north to Tripoli, we had driven to the coast in Batroun, swimming and eating some special seafood dishes. At the top of the mountain road, I could see the Rashid Karami Fair at the edge of the city. I was, like, *What is that?* Because it is just like what you wrote in your text, it looks like a set of building blocks for children. We had been up and down the coast and had seen structures with no signs of active construction. It was not the process of becoming. It was a suspension. Afterwards, I hitchhiked my way back north to Tripoli and wandered on to the grounds. I was checked by one of the guards because they do take care of the empty park.

Franziska On my very first trip to Lebanon, I did a performance video inside of an unfinished building. The building was also on the highway to the north. I think I was attracted to the incredible transparency. The building was on an ugly highway, but then it looks out to the sea and you have only these pillars that open up to the sea. On the one hand, you have the great concrete expanse pressing against you and at the same time, you have this vast openness.

Caitlin Weight and light.

Franziska There is something special about buildings that are not closed on top. If you leave the question of the roof open so that there could be another layer built on top, this profoundly changes how you move and feel inside ...

Caitlin … a vertical potential. I remember you said how these buildings are stages or theatres for happenings. You also wanted to organise for artists to do performances or events.

Franziska I always thought it would be amazing to invite many people to work within these spaces in different ways — not only visual artists but maybe also dancers and musicians. Back then, all of the Lebanese I met were very hesitant and did not see the point of it. I came back with a scholarship dedicated to doing a project in Tripoli inside the Rashid Karami Fair. Then I realised how difficult a project in that place would be to achieve. If you just want to walk in for a day and take two or three pictures, that is okay. But if you want to do a non-commercial project that is official, it proves difficult. Since this conversation, a few art exhibitions have been organised on the fairground, such as *Cycles of Collapsing Progress* (2018), which was curated by Studiocur/art in collaboration with BeMA-Beirut Museum of Art and Anissa Touati Corporation for Mexico.

Caitlin Was it the artists who were uninterested or was it the bureaucracy?

Franziska I think artists were hesitant to do something in Tripoli. It is a more conventional and conservative Arab city with all of the positives and negatives that come with that. I dealt with the bureaucracy myself. It took a year to get official permission to work in the fairground. I wanted to do something public inside of a space that does not know whether it is public or private. That is an official dilemma. The Ministry of Economy and Trade technically owns the Rashid Karami International Fair complex, but only if it is actively used as a fairground. Otherwise, the Ministry of Economy is obligated to give that land to another ministry. Politics play a role here. As things stand, even if it is not actively functioning as a commercial trading ground, the local people of Tripoli conceivably have a fairground, and this potential is considered one of their few local assets. Also, back then you had not only the 2006 Lebanon War but also the Nahr el-Bared Palestinian refugee camp crisis. Tripoli was not functioning well at the time, and anything they had they would protect like crazy. In addition to the politics, officials were also looking for money. Officially, I was an exchange student with the Lebanese University – the first exchange student since the 1990s – and on top of everything else, I was female. There was not a single administrative or official position in Tripoli I dealt with that was filled by a woman. It was all male. I looked at the system and realised I needed partners. The dean of the local art faculty was willing and helped me all the way through. Without him, I would have never succeeded.

Caitlin How did you manage to see Oscar Niemeyer's original drawings for the site, and where are they located?

Franziska I promised not to say. It was the personal file of somebody, and I am not even sure who the actual owner is. The drawings are super rough, just lines without a lot of information. A good engineering office, a local firm from Beirut, was brought in to turn these preliminary sketches into buildings. Niemeyer's drawings were in an oversized folio that I was allowed to keep for a few days to review. I was asked not to photocopy them and I respected that.

Caitlin In the end you created a performance.

Franziska I had two interventions that centred around the Lebanese pavilion. I was interested in this building because it was the one that Niemeyer dedicated to Lebanon, the one with which he quoted Arab architecture in the arches of his own design. It might not be the most beautiful building on the site, but I find it the most interesting. You have views from the inside and the outside: the transparency that informs all of Niemeyer's buildings is expressed most visibly in his Lebanese pavilion.

One intervention I suggested was to work with ribbons. The idea for the ribbons came from the streets, these plastic ribbons that are put up between buildings and tied between balconies to signify events like funerals, weddings, and baptisms, and also to advertise political parties and religious festivities like Ramadan. They exist in all these different colours, but almost every colour is charged with a specific meaning: white for a funeral, green and red for Ḥarakat Amal [a political party in Lebanon]. I picked red. I wanted to use them to play with the movement between the inside and outside of the building, aware that the sea nearby would always bring wind to move them slightly. Siska helped me during the whole project. I quickly realised that if I wanted to do anything in Tripoli, I could not just show up by myself. I needed a guy with me. I had permission from the director of the fair, and the guards and gardeners accepted me. I was only working with scissors and ribbon, so I tied them on everything I found inside the building. I did not fix a nail to the structure because I was not allowed to, which was ironic considering that the entire building is falling apart. I tied ribbons to everything I could find: wires and exposed steel on the inside, and trees and adjacent structures on the outside. It took me roughly a month to install.

Meanwhile, we were hosted in a small flat in Tripoli. Every morning we went to the fair and worked — sometimes from sunrise to sunset. I started to become very fond of Tripoli as a city, as well as the guys who worked at the fairground. Here is a photo of the guy with the shiny red BMW and no hair. He is one of the guards. They always came regularly to check on us. We spent all our time at the fairground; we had picnics and sometimes we ended up staying into the night. The fairground was designed for a huge public — thousands of people — and yet there was no one. The kind of silence in that vast space is very special. We also had a small friend with us: we found a turtle! In May 2008, there was a brief war with Hezbollah inside of Beirut. We thought we were fine because we were in the north, but we also knew that whenever something happens there in Tripoli, it is usually more violent than in Beirut. It took two days before the clashes reached Tripoli. We were working outdoors and we heard shooting and grenades. I was not sure how to react. Do you hide or do you just continue? We went back to Beirut the day after the conflict had calmed down to check the political situation. There was not a single car on the highway, and suddenly Siska slammed on the brakes like a maniac. I thought he must have seen somebody or there was a checkpoint because people had told us: *Be careful on the road. There might be snipers.* There were not. Siska had stopped because a big turtle was crossing the road. The turtle became our pet and each day, I arrived at the fairground carrying the turtle in a paper box. In order not to lose her, I put a plastic ribbon on her so that I would see where she walked. Even though a turtle is not quick, she managed to escape. I figured her life is much more beautiful now that she lives in the fairground.

Caitlin Did you go to the top of the helipad?

Franziska I had dinner up there and slept on the roof of another structure during the day. Each building has a different character, and the helipad is one of the few that is out in the open. It feels positive. The dome is also very special, but if you go further down there are corridors, which creates a whole system connecting everything underground. The complex was used by the Syrians during their occupation and there are rumours that it temporarily became a prison.

Caitlin The underground passageways were used as prisons?

Franziska Especially the underground passageways. Some of them are now closed, but inside the Lebanese pavilion there is one door where you could enter. They have a team of gardeners and one guy in the team is mute. What they say is that he is the only one who once dared to go in, despite all these horrifying stories about what you see when you walk those corridors. They said that he once came out running with big eyes and a shocked face, but they did not know what he saw. Since then, none of them has ever dared to go inside. You never know what is fact and what is fiction in these cases, or where in between it might be, but what we do know is that some part of the complex was used as an unofficial graveyard.

Caitlin Were the underground passageways designed by Niemeyer?

Franziska Yes. Performers were supposed to be able to go from the dome to the open-air theatre to the other stage, with underground changing rooms. You have to imagine that the outdoor spaces were supposed to be completely surrounded by water. To get offstage, you had to go underground and back up on the other side.

Caitlin And after the Syrian Civil War began, there was a moment when an aid organisation used the enclosed glass structure. The UNRWA–United Nations Relief and Works Agency for Palestine Refugees used this building to stock supplies briefly during the Syrian Civil War (2011-ongoing). Prior to this, the Lebanese army had a temporary barrack in irregular use on the site. Military presence intensified after the Nahr el-Bared crisis of 2007.

Franziska Sometimes there would be a military presence and sometimes not. The other activity inside the space was this weird, annual Arabic book fair, one of those book fairs where you could find Saddam Hussein's biography and five different editions of *Mein Kampf* in Arabic. Each of the few institutions in the city would contribute to this book fair. You would also find the Institut français doing something and the British Council, the Safadi Foundation, etc.

Caitlin All at the book fair?

Franziska Everybody would use it to present what they do. Let's say it was a very democratic approach to all opinions, where all opinions were present. We also asked the older people in Tripoli how they remembered the fairground site. They were still from the generation that said: *It was full of orange trees here before and then suddenly they come in and they construct all these buildings. They try to be modern, but then they did not finish it, so what is this? They spent so much money and, before, we had all the oranges.* [Lebanese Prime Minister] Rashid Karami [1921–1987], who wanted the fair, built a residential tower for his family not far so that he would be able to walk home after being dropped off at the fair in his famously beloved helicopter.

Caitlin On the helipad?

Franziska Yes, he ordered the helipad. He was keen on using the helicopter, an Aérospatiale Puma.

Caitlin As things go, it is a relatively modest helipad.

Franziska His idea was to land and walk home on foot to his flat. So I was told by one of his bodyguards who happened not to be riding in the helicopter with him the day it was bombed and Karami was assassinated, like so many politicians in Lebanon.

Of course, I was profiting from the fact that it is a space that is not truly public, not really accessible. Most of the time I had it to myself. Looking back, maybe all of what I did as an art intervention was just an excuse to be in that luxurious position of pretending that I lived, for a brief moment, inside a world that does not even really exist.

There is one private villa at the very end of the fairground that is beautiful, which was planned for the director of the fair. It has a little pond, a rooftop terrace, different bedrooms with adjacent bathrooms, and all of that. I liked to visit it but not ever by myself. One day I thought, *Why don't I just sit in there and have my lunch?* Then I realised that by myself I could not do it. I needed to have somebody with me.

Caitlin Because you did not deserve it all by yourself?

Franziska No, not that. Because there is always a bit of suspense with abandoned buildings. Here is a photo of the Tabarja Beach Resort with pools, chalets, and the towers. Then there is this huge unfinished building. We would always walk up to the sixth or seventh floor because there is only the sea from up there. Nothing else. Beautiful. Then it collapsed. There were people living on the ground floor, who were probably workers in the other buildings and had made their homes inside. One died and it could have been worse because the building next to it fully collapsed. I remember all of the pictures we had taken inside the resort, jumping around, sitting in there, drinking and watching the sunset.

Caitlin One of the things I find interesting about the unfinished buildings is this tension between monumentality and banality. It changes depending on the scale. If you are far away from the buildings, they become sculptures or sketches – pure architectonic forms in the landscape. But then, when you are close to them, you encounter smells and see dirt. These are textures and details I enjoyed reading in your text, along with the irrational discomfort with other people using the spaces. There is a distance between that monumental, pure form and that intimate proximity of lived reality.

Franziska It is romantic because, after all, if these buildings were finished, we would likely have no access to them.

Caitlin It is the potential.

Franziska It is the endless potential of the unfinished. It allows us to make up stories when we encounter these structures. It is the same as falling in love. It is the stage where you still focus only on what you want to see. I still believe that those buildings, because they were left alone for so long, developed their own character and desires. Perhaps because they were never finished and never used by inhabitants, they had time to decide on what they wanted to be. They are a pure form of architecture because they do not have to deal with the daily routine of occupants riding elevators and using the stairs. They can function without a staircase.

Caitlin They accumulate stories from their temporary uses, but they resist being defined by these incursions. They are still owned by people with money and there are restrictions on their use. But at the same time, they cannot function as symbols of ambient power because their social potential remains unrealised. Your writing identifies these moments of flux that have been sporadic in Lebanon for over forty years, in which someone who might be dispossessed and excluded can temporarily possess the most luxurious spatial moments. One can take pleasure in witnessing patriarchy and capitalism remain suspended and unfulfilled.

Franziska I see what you mean, although I would say that capitalism and politics in Lebanon take four or five dimensions rather than two. Think of the Lebanese Civil War, all of the different layers of religion, and so on.

This country has rarely had a moment when it existed outside of a state of emergency, confusion, or tragedy. Look at the wars before the civil war: each created its own cosmos that allowed alternative realities to exist. Think, for example, of the workers that squatted in the Tabarja building. They built walls on all sides but their magnificent view of the sea was left open except for curtains. They were absolutely aware of their privilege in that space. Some things, of course, need money – if you want to own that view, you have to buy it. But you can also still have it in this other context, even with a very humble occupation.

Caitlin There is one see-through complex of condominiums, built on a hill overlooking the sea and the Rashid Karami Fair. There was a woman who lived there on the ground floor, in the centre, with just one furnished room, a little garden, a satellite dish, and a generator – surrounded by this vast concrete frame and an incredible view on to the Mediterranean. There is a desire to have these things that otherwise only luxury affords.

I really liked what you wrote along these lines: "Der Friedhof der Moderne ist ein Spielplatz. Die Bauten auf dem Messegelände in Tripoli und das Hotel in Tabarja produzieren Plätze, die keiner Funktion dienen und nichts als puren Raum bieten. Das ist ein Luxus – in einer Region, in der jeder Platz religiös oder politisch besetzt und umkämpft wird, stellt das Messegelände eine Ausnahmeerscheinung dar. Der Messerohbau bietet also neben dem physischen

Freiraum und zeitlichen Zwischenraum auch den Spielraum für Ideen und beherbergt Scheitern und Sehnsucht". [The cemetery of modernism is a playground. The buildings in the fairground of Tripoli and the hotel in Tabarja are sites that serve no function and offer nothing but pure space. In a region where every inch is occupied or contested for religious or political reasons, the fairground is a luxurious exception. The unfinished buildings in the fairground thus offer not only physical and temporal space, but also room for ideas – harbouring failure and longing simultaneously.] Franziska Pierwoß, "Der Rohbau als Überbleibsel moderner Bauten in Nahost", diploma thesis, Hochschule für Grafik und Buchkunst Leipzig, 2010, p. 53.

Franziska I think what is important in that quote is that all of these places live in a fascinating and constant ambivalence. I have known Berlin for a long time, since the 1990s. The face of the city has changed in strange ways. I once did a small work on the colour of buildings from the DDR [Deutsche Demokratische Republik; East Germany]. It was a specific colour that was probably ubiquitous in the DDR because it was very cheap. You always had only one choice and then you had the car pollution and the coal heating. All of these buildings have a patina that you cannot recreate elsewhere because it was a colour that existed only in that specific system. A colour that is full of melancholia and maybe also a questionable nostalgia, but still it is a valid something that vanished.

Caitlin What did this colour look like?

Franziska A very dirty grey-brown. It is such a specific shade. Now there is a trend of putting other colours on top of it: rose, greens, mint, or baby blue. Why would you cover a colour that is charged with so much history with a baby blue?

Caitlin You conceived of and organise Sundowner, a series of events on Tuesdays at sunset at the Neue Nationalgalerie in Berlin, which was designed by Mies van der Rohe. In its own way that modernist museum is like an unfinished building too: an architectural drawing in space – a silhouette. While the museum building is closed for renovation and in an in-between state, you curate these unofficial happenings on the grounds, using it again as a stage for a different kind of public, outside of the official museum programming. In a sense, you are taking back a luxurious playground of space, unfixing it from normalised structures of ownership and access.

Franziska The Neue Nationalgalerie is never as perfect as when it is empty. This is what takes you somewhere: the full potential of the outline. They should leave the ground level empty permanently, and the sculpture garden should be open to the public again. There is also so much of the rebuilt Potsdamer Platz that has minimal character and no authenticity. This is where I lived when we were first in Berlin. I saw how there was nothing, how it was a no-man's-land, and then suddenly Potsdamer Platz started going up. It used to be a centre in the 1920s and ’30s, but later it became a place charged with negativity. You cannot just erase that. After all, Germany is a very sad country if you look at it closely. It still has a lot of sombre traces. It cannot be eliminated.

Caitlin There are different kinds of ghosts.

Franziska I feel that there is something to the unfinished buildings in your postcards. They exist within a system where you are constantly reminded of the fact that nothing runs smoothly. Every other day in Lebanon, there is a huge cloud of a fire somewhere and daily power cuts. Now, due to the unprecedented influx of refugees in addition to the existing chronic misuse of water, there are water shortages. Even if you have money, you cannot order water anymore because all the delivery trucks are busy. This kind of turn into absurdity is probably precisely that which allows for these unfinished buildings to exist. That is what is beautiful in postcards like the one where there is a villa with a Saudi-style staircase. I wonder what these buildings see as their future. The pillars and the balcony – a balcony where no one will ever stand and look out because it is on a very ugly road, where trucks pass by, making a lot of dust. Who would they greet?

Franziska Pierwoss works as an artist through performance and installation. She creates solo and collaborative projects around food systems and waste management as both political symbols and materials that can be instrumentalised within social and financial spheres. She studied at the Hochschule für Grafik und Buchkunst in Leipzig and at the Lebanese University, Beirut. Her performances have been featured at the Fast Forward Festival, Athens; Sharjah Biennial 13; Literaturforum im Brecht-Haus, Berlin; and nGbK–neue Gesellschaft für bildende Kunst, Berlin; among others. Pierwoss has shown her work at Kunsthal Extra City, Antwerp; Jameel Arts Centre, Dubai; and Urbane Künste Ruhr, Bochum.

To view a common imaginary ...
with Mirene Arsanios
and Caitlin Berrigan

Berlin, 2015

Caitlin Language is a form of spatial movement in Samuel Delany's *Dhalgren*. At the beginning he writes: "And someone might pick the night up by its edge, tear it along the perforations, crumple it, and toss it away." Samuel R. Delany, *Dhalgren* [1975], Vintage Books, New York, 2001, p. 36. The implication is that space and time are material, like paper. He creates worlds in the novel and forges journeys through language, accompanied by an internal reflection on writing as the central process of world creation.

Mirene What is interesting in your *Unfinished State* is that there are two levels of worldmaking: material and conceptual. The postcards in your book materialise the novel in the form of objects that are simultaneously your subject of inquiry. Your postcards are all stamped, stickered, and perforated; some are lost. A book is a world, so what kind of world is the writer creating? Do you want to reproduce a world we are living in or speculate on a different one? Books are able to offer a meta understanding of the writer's approach that is not purely conceptual. In *Dhalgren*, the meta is woven into the fiction itself so that abstraction and narrative come together. The meta does not reside outside the writing, which is also why it is such a difficult book to read. It is as if the protagonist has written over the text of someone else's notebook, inscribing the margins.

Caitlin In *Dhalgren*, the emergence of language is both cerebral and visceral. Like this passage: "He read.

What had come to him as images (among which he had pecked with tongue tip and pen point) returned, shocked, luminous — sometimes more, sometimes less vivid than memory, but so rich he thrust them out with his tongue to keep from trying to eat them." Delany, p. 262. There is an oscillation between the neurological process of creating words and images in the mind and their materialisation in the world through language. Words that make spatial shapes that slide through the mouth; words that populate the pages in marginalia. It is about articulation itself and the process of imagination.

Mirene Right. It is also a way of distancing the reader from the text while simultaneously pulling in. A phrase like "he read" embodies the protagonist's position as a reader while reflecting one's own; a reminder of one's own body while reading.

Caitlin When a writer works with language and imagery, there is desire to evoke an indirect bodily experience or presence in the world. Optimistic visions for future spaces beyond the present world are more about evocations than prescriptions. Visions do not have to be interpreted literally, but somehow the process of evocation itself gives more energy than representational designs and systems.

Mirene I do feel that there is plenty to say about the future, with a renewed interest in the universe and discoveries that lend urgency to multiple questions.

Whatever image or conception of the future we have is always revealing of the present we are living in. The genre of the future, in and of itself, crystallises expectations, desires, and identity crises that are very much part of the present tense. Futuristic literature can produce the rhetoric of ecstasy, but I sometimes feel that it does not take on the challenge of rigorously examining what it would mean to experience alternate worlds. In fact, I rarely think about the future.

Caitlin Thinking about the future can also be a wish to deny the past. This is one of the reasons why I was interested in these buildings that are locked in a moment of potential. Here in Berlin, in the time it takes for all these spaces to be built for a city of the future, they arrive already too old for the present. Where is the future in the crevices of what already exists? And how can we occupy those crevices? Again, with *Dhalgren*, it is a book that is very much about a kind of presence rather than projection.

Mirene Yes, presence. The work of actually staying with something is more interesting than the gesture of imaginative projection. I am thinking about presence in relation to the buildings you photographed and how they become part of the landscape. They are present but you stop noticing them. You forget about them. They constitute an affective, sensorial knowledge, but not an institutionalised or historical one. There is no history written about them. They are remnants of a moment in the development of a landscape, what that moment was going towards and where it stopped. They all come from different periods with different sources of injected capital and different conflicts arresting their construction.

Beirut has developed so chaotically; the urban space was only partially planned. You always feel that something is about to erupt – yet another tower or skyscraper is being built – in addition to all of the other unfinished ones. The new ones grow so quickly. There are different rhythms and speeds. In a year, a street can become completely unrecognisable. It is like you are hallucinating the landscape, while in fact it is very real – already there and irreversible. When I see these buildings as images on advertisement panels separating the construction sites from the street, I think, *This is never actually going to be built like this.*

Caitlin I think of them as empty vessels of capital. It is a speculation that money can be held in the form of real estate, which will materialise into something that generates income down the line. But often it is not about the social activation of the site itself, it is just about the fluidity of capital.

Mirene Yes. In Beirut, most of the buildings remain empty. Politics in Lebanon are linked to land and territory, and different neighbourhoods are occupied by opposing political groups. One could think capital transcends this but it does not. Maybe that is a good thing? Many of these coastal buildings were built during the civil war. When the Christian population fled Beirut, they started constructing beach resorts on the northern coast. See Karine Wehbé, *Stop Here for Happy Holiday: An investigation into the beach resorts of the north littoral of Lebanon*, self-published, 2017. All of these construction projects were illegal, but it was safer than the city. The alternative to the war in the city of Beirut was to have these chalets with palm trees and swimming pools. After the war ended, people migrated back to Beirut and abandoned the coastal settlements. These beach resorts are very much connected to the civil war.

I wanted to ask you about your decision to choose to use the contrasting, saturated colours, and artificial-looking landscapes. Is it a postcard aesthetic?

Caitlin Yes, it is an aesthetic of tourism, and I used it to signal my position as a travelling outsider in this landscape.

Mirene There is something very surreal in your artwork: addressing these buildings in the first person. I was also thinking about the relationship between postcards and sci-fi, which are almost opposites. The postcard is supposed to represent the shared image of a known place. Sci-fi is this other completely different trope that, by definition, wants to escape visual familiarity. So I was thinking about how your work held sci-fi and tourism together, which are very different ways of being in space.

Caitlin Sci-fi and tourism often share the experiences of travel, discovery, and speculative projection.

Mirene Or tourism and something apocalyptic.

Caitlin Rather than the apocalypse, I want to evoke the idea that we are at a turning point, where one kind of space can then become something else entirely. All of these ghost buildings are reassembled into one landscape: the spatial codex of the book. Whenever aspects of the present world are isolated in order to examine it closely, there are qualities of surrealism. I also want to evoke tensions between a common and an uncommon imaginary. In other words, there is no singular vista from which to view a common imaginary.

Mirene There is a clear methodology to *Unfinished State* through the organisation of these postcards into a narrative. Did that create a new narrative for you? Did it shift something in your understanding of buildings and landscapes and language?

Caitlin Initially, I started taking photographs of the buildings as visual research. Then, I wanted to engage with them in some way, perhaps in a performative way, but there were so many barriers to understanding their narratives. Like you said, the histories and financial transactions of these buildings are not well documented, and I am ultimately not doing a geographic catalogue.
I see them as part of a pattern repeating itself in different material forms all over the planet.

Mirene Going back to this idea of language, I think that the relationship between image and text on your postcards occupies multiple dimensions and spaces; for example, in the little handwritten marginalia. Otherwise, image and text can remain hermetically enclosed in their own representations: the novel is complete as a text, and the postcard is a saturated image. A postcard has a front and a back, but they are never going to interact. I feel like there is something happening for me in these stamps and notations. When the person addressed is not available, they might be deceased or no longer live at that particular location, the postcards are returned and annotated in the process.

Caitlin Journey is in the material gesture. The text and image cross together through space, and they are handled and inscribed there and back.

Mirene The postal system in Lebanon is dysfunctional, and one never knows if something is going to be delivered. It is amazing that you actually received anything back. The postal system belongs to a colonial legacy.

Caitlin Yes, after the civil war was officially over, Canada Post partnered with an investment company to rebuild the Lebanese postal system through LibanPost [est. 1998]. This initiative only lasted for three years before falling apart, and since then the postal sector has never been properly rehabilitated.

Mirene Exactly. These addresses are also signifiers for a system that has collapsed. For example, I often see how locations in Beirut are organised into coded districts, but we as citizens do not have access to these codes. So they are not socially activated through lived experience. We navigate space with a completely different understanding of what an address represents. It is like the way that you describe the building; it is a description rather than an address.

Caitlin I grew up in the rural woods without proper street names and infrastructure. Wayfinding required a narrative and image-rich description of space. My mother gives directions to her house based on the evolution of dirt to pavement and back to dirt, or which way to turn when you find a pile of dirt in relation to a particular species of tree. It is not a codified urban system like in New York City, where directions are given based on the grid system of numbered streets and avenues. Or when I lived in Chicago, people would give directions in degree coordinates instead of referring to intersections of main streets, because they are so long and the city is so huge that it is better to navigate by longitude and latitude. But then in Beirut, there is the added dimension of time and memory. People say things like *it is where the old Italian bank used to be*. There is a reference to something that is no longer there, a spatial reference for a ghost. Space itself can be made into a relational narrative. In her song "Big Science" [1982], Laurie Anderson has these wonderful lines: "take a left at what's going to be the new sports center / and keep going until you hit the place where / they're thinking of building that drive-in bank".

It is all about what is coming next. Speaking of, I wanted to talk to you about an institution like 98weeks in Beirut as an exercise in future-making.

Mirene Yes. 98weeks is a temporal platform I cofounded with my cousin and artist, Marwa Arsanios. And it is about time! Ninety-eight weeks, which is almost two years. We dedicate two years to researching a topic before we shift to a new one. So far, we had the topic of the city, then publications, and then feminisms. I guess I never thought of 98weeks as an initiative that creates futures. It was always a response to the present conditions in Beirut. It also has a very uncertain relationship to time because of the lack of regular funding. Whatever we do addresses concerns on the ground. It is about engaging with issues alongside other people and worldbuilding to think about our concerns.

With 98weeks, the future keeps changing because it is also something that is very related to Marwa's and my own interests. For example, because I am interested in writing and publishing, I started the magazine *Makhzin*. The programming of 98weeks is always connected to us as individuals, and the structure itself is not strong enough to survive without us, meaning that we will have no institutional legacy unless we work on it. Should we publish our research by investing in a publication? How do we present work when it is so specific to certain situations and people? We lost our space, as you know, and when that happened, we questioned whether we should give the project up altogether or pass it on to other people. No one wanted to take it because the structure was so connected to us.

Caitlin When I suggest that 98weeks could be a future-making enterprise, it is because there is a practice of being and thinking together that also becomes externalised. Culture is doing this, too, but then there is another practice of future-making where you are conducting research together and sharing in a process of discovery and thinking through ideas. There is a generosity that does not have to have a predetermined form of an artwork, a publication, or a curated system. Being together is a practice in creating bonds and methodologies that serve everyone for different purposes, like political solidarity. If you do not actually spend the time to build that organisational base, then you find yourself alone and restless when you truly need solidarity or action. There is a real need for international cultural dialogue that is not dominated by elite interest. Where small groups of people in different places are each saying: *I know that it exists over there! And we are over here!* Even sharing some traces of this activity is a general act of resistance. It is planning and creating the base for something else, for another kind of system.

Mirene Definitely, it is built on a network of affinities. We come together because we are moved by the same things. It can be difficult because we deal with a lot of personal inclinations, which are often linked to the ego. There are a lot of things that get in the way of creating a support structure. But overall, that is how it should ideally operate: bringing people together who are moved by a same collective desire. I think that the ethos of 98weeks is engaging people in the present, because we are not conditioned by an ideal form of programming or vision of cultural space. We never had that kind of curatorial ambition or strategic way of decision-making, and I think that is why we created very special situations.

Caitlin Does the research for 98weeks feed into your own writing?

Mirene I was asking myself this question. We did a reading group on experimental female writers, and we have been reading a lot of theory. It is hard to translate theory into fiction, unless you are Samuel Delany! I had to unlearn the language of theory, references, and name-dropping. I have not read a lot of theory lately. I try to express certain ideas through the writing itself, which is extremely difficult.

Caitlin Very hard.

Mirene It is super hard. Even while thinking about feminism or the body — the female body specifically. How should I think of the writing subject and the relationship between the narrator and the author? For example, right now, I am working on chronic pain, the different sets of techniques we use to shape and treat the body — yoga, acupuncture, hormones, etc. — and the relationship between pain management and global capital. I am still searching for ways of writing fiction that spark an experiential critique through the writing itself. It is very hard, and I suspect I will be working on that for the rest of my life!

Caitlin We were talking about feminist practice and the issue of feminisms. The thing about alliances is that they are not representations. If it is merely a representation of an alliance, then it is false. I do not make much work explicitly about queer or feminist subjectivity. For me, it is the methodology rather than the subject. It is meaningful to represent alliances and subjectivities, but the practice of it is very different. You can represent a queer subjectivity while reinscribing patriarchy in the making of the work.

Mirene It is interesting that you talk about alliances, because I think there are alliances in literature and particularly in poetry. A book can do a lot of things. I have faith in fiction. There are other ways of being together that do not rely on articulating a certain position or a cause. It can be ambivalent. I am thinking about the writers that I like. Their writing is political through the perception it creates in its reordering of reality and experience. This is why, also, I very much believe in a practice that incorporates parallel interests and languages that do not necessarily intersect. I know that when I am writing, I am not talking specifically about the female body and capital, but in a way, there is the presence of that "other thing" in the writing.

Caitlin That is why the fiction, or the world, that evokes materialisations of capital draws me in. In *Unfinished State*, I wanted to evoke the fluidity of the life of capital and stories through space.

Mirene I believe in processes. Rather than deciding explicitly that my work is going to be about that, or I am going to talk about that, I let the process take me there. Which is very hard and sometimes it does not produce anything, but it is necessary. We live in an economy that always demands an outcome, a product.

Caitlin Which is also why a platform for research is necessary because they are ways of creating a kind of openness to experimentation that does not necessarily have to result in something. They can be their own kind of unfinished states.

Mirene Arsanios is the author of *The Autobiography of a Language* (Futurepoem books, 2022), *Notes on Mother Tongues* (Ugly Duckling Presse, 2020), and *The City Outside the Sentence* (Ashkal Alwan, 2015). She has contributed her essays and short stories to *e-flux*, *Hyperallergic*, *VIDA–Women in Literary Arts*, *The Brooklyn Rail*, *Lit Hub*, and *Guernica*, among others. Arsanios is the programme director of the Poetry Project in New York City and the founding editor of the bilingual English-Arabic magazine *Makhzin*. She teaches at Pratt Institute and holds an MFA in writing from the Milton Avery Graduate School of the Arts at Bard College.

A city built for a people who left …
with Marwan Abou Dib
and Caitlin Berrigan

Cambridge, Massachusetts, 2016

Caitlin You write about the relationship between people and the forces of real estate, and how this shapes landscapes and the fabric of a city. As someone who is involved in both real estate development and architecture, you have experience with the way people move in and out of Lebanon and how that affects a shifting and fractured public. You have an understanding of lived spatial reality and how it is influenced by both architectural and financial forces.

Marwan That is true. My point of view is both from real estate and architecture. I love the authenticity of a city but at the same time, I also understand the corporate capitalist approach to urbanism.

Caitlin In my work, I am interested in the unseen forces of capitalism, as well as landscape and site. The alliance of financial phenomena with the landscape and history of Lebanon is a compelling dynamic. Could you outline some of the broad financial flows in real estate in Lebanon?

Marwan After the end of the civil war, downtown Beirut was mostly uninhabited. It was where everything had happened; where the fighting was concentrated for fifteen years. When the war ended, who was going to come in and fix the heart of the city? The scars were there. A lot of people who owned the real estate in downtown Beirut had abandoned the city. The buildings were deserted and they were crumbling. There were bullet holes everywhere, stray dogs roaming across the street. I did not live through this. This is what I heard.

Caitlin Are your parents from Beirut?

Marwan Yes. My dad lived and worked downtown at the Hotel St. Georges. It is so sad when I hear his stories. No one wanted to come back. The downtown area was very emotional as a space for the Lebanese people, but the city needed to invest in it. The government – the public sector – would not fix downtown Beirut due to the corruption that existed and the lack of funds. Prime Minister Rafik al-Hariri and a lot of the politicians had real estate backgrounds. So they set up Solidere, a private entity that would be in charge of the reconstruction of the city. Solidere forced the owners of all these downtown properties, many of whom had died or left the country, to sell. This was a big controversy.

Caitlin And they made the owners sell not for cash but for stock holdings in Solidere. In many cases, it was also hard to figure out who still maintained the property rights, which were often shared across scattered families. The World Bank then the International Monetary Fund financed reconstruction, but of course, with all of the strings that are attached to such international support. Solidere was a novel financing structure.

Marwan Yes. It was a promised dream of the future. They were going to own part of the city. It became the world's first privatised downtown. It was an interesting coup. There is no city like Beirut where the downtown, which before the war had been all about public space, became owned by a private company. There is no more public space at all. Solidere promised gardens and public spaces. Today, such areas are private, marked off by signs that say so. At the Hotel St. Georges, where my father worked, there was a big fight to maintain their independent ownership from Solidere and they won. Many people disagree, but still, I sympathise with Solidere, because no one was going to fix this city. Today, anything outside Solidere is unplanned chaos. And today we have no president. Thank god the downtown is still operating!

Caitlin Just in the last few years, Solidere has privatised some of the public beaches I went to before. What is it like to be downtown? Who goes there?

Marwan I grew up in Dubai, a city that had no context. It was a city rising from the desert, and for me, I am addicted to economic growth. I love seeing progress. Human progress, economic progress. It is not about the forces of capitalism, I like seeing cities being created. But Dubai lacks culture and history – bland, soulless, just like an airport, a generic city without authenticity. Beirut, on the other hand, is such a beautiful city. The Roman temples ... There is so much history ... All these civilisations that passed through the city ... They say Beirut was rebuilt seven times and that now this is the eighth time. I love looking at the construction sites. I am very proud as a Lebanese to go to my country and see construction. The saddest thing, though, is that it looks good to photograph but it needs people. This is where capitalism comes in. Who are they, rebuilding the city this time? Are they just doing it because they need to build a city?

Solidere was focused on bringing in international starchitects. It was this idea that Beirut could return as a globalised city, as a hub in the Middle East. It is the cookie cutter approach: *We need skyscrapers. We need famous architects. We need marketing campaigns. We need to sell the slogan.* What I bring is the fact that I grew up in Dubai and I worked in Dubai, but I know that Beirut is a different city and needs a different approach.

Caitlin You called Beirut a "city built for a population that left". Marwan Abou Dib, "Downtown Beirut", master's thesis, Massachusetts Institute of Technology, 2014.

Marwan Solidere was trying to create an image for the outside world. That is how they got investment from the outside. The wealthy Lebanese who are living in Brazil and Mexico and the United Arab Emirates, they do not go back to Lebanon, but they want to own a part of Lebanon. They want to invest in Lebanon. If I sell them the dream of the city's recovery, even though they are not going to come back, they will still invest. But what about the Lebanese inside the country?

Caitlin Is there a real class divide in terms of who stayed and who left?

Marwan Yes. My dad's family is still in Lebanon. There is a lot of poverty. My own family left, but we still have Lebanese citizenship. Then there is a diaspora that still has Lebanese citizenship, but they do not come back as often. Most who left were Christians, and this is now where class divides: the rich Lebanese who stayed were more political and they had better connections. But it is impressive how successful the Lebanese diaspora is, because there has always been the sense of community, of supporting each other.

Caitlin This is what I find interesting about the financial strokes you laid out — the diaspora is the primary source of real estate investment in Lebanon. Something like 15 to 20 million Lebanese diaspora live abroad, whereas only roughly 6 million people live inside of Lebanon.

Marwan Yes, the main clusters of the diaspora are in Latin America and the Caribbean with about 8.5 million; North America has 2.5 million; and only 300,000 in the Arab world.

Caitlin I am stunned that one-fifth of the total gross domestic product of Lebanon comes from foreign direct investments and remittances from the diaspora?

Marwan Yes. It is amazing. Lebanon is so small, but you always want to keep part of your country, right? It is a sense of ownership and political currency. My father never went to university. He lived a very poor life and when he moved to the desert in Dubai, he was offered asylum in the United States, in Alabama. It was part of this whole plan to move Christians out of Lebanon. My dad did not want political asylum. The hospitality sector was growing in this new country called the United Arab Emirates and his friend told him he should go. My dad was a waiter at St. Georges, and because the Lebanese speak three languages – English, Arabic, and French – they were being hired in the Gulf. Now, there is so much investment from the Gulf into Lebanon. My dad will never invest in Dubai. We own nothing in Dubai.

We own land next to the Syrian border. I told my dad, *What is wrong with you?* He was, like, *Real estate will never go down*. He was right. Prices stabilised, and for the past seven years, they have always gone up. So you do not put your money in a bank, you invest in Lebanon. The church owns most of the real estate in Lebanon. It is part of an effort to keep the land "Christian". There is not that much supply and there is more demand than supply, way more demand. Even if there is a war in Lebanon, there is more demand. I do not know how that happens. There is always money coming into the country in the form of real estate investment. I am not informed about the laws that enable secrecy and sheltering, but the Lebanese banking industry is one of the strongest. That is why they call it the Switzerland of the Middle East. A lot of people store their money in banks there, which is also counted as part of the remittances.

Caitlin Does most of the money coming into real estate from foreign direct investments come from the UAE

[United Arab Emirates], or is it from across the whole global diaspora?

Marwan Most of it is from the oil countries. There are two waves of the Lebanese diaspora. The first wave was a result of the 1860 conflict with Syria under the Ottoman Empire. Those are the ones that went to Latin America. Then there was a second wave that began with the Lebanese Civil War in 1975. These people went largely to Canada, Australia, and the United States, but also to the Middle East and the countries in the Gulf Cooperation Council – Saudi Arabia, Kuwait, Oman, Bahrain, Qatar, and the UAE. In those countries, so much wealth is being created because of oil. New cities sprang up from the desert, such as Dubai and Abu Dhabi, and the Lebanese became very successful in industries there. Because they were so close to Lebanon and they all still held Lebanese citizenship, they were the ones who were investing. The wealth was going back to Lebanon even though it was generated in another country.

But also, the wealthy Saudis, not the Lebanese diaspora, used to spend their vacations in Europe or go to the US before 9/11. After that, it became more difficult to travel. It was, like, *We want to go to a place where the weather is nice that has a European feel*, so Lebanon became a destination. Solidere was Saudi-affiliated, so this was also the source of the major money.

Caitlin Also Saudi medical tourism to the hospital in Beirut.

Marwan Yes. After 9/11, that is really when the foreign direct investment happened. The timing was perfect. With travel more difficult and financial investments under more scrutiny, Lebanon offered an attractive tourist destination and banking location rolled into one. It was like Monte Carlo in Monaco. If you remove all of the politics and the problems, Beirut is one of the best cities because it has everything. It has the history, the people, the food, the mountains, and the weather. No one wants to be in Dubai, in the desert, during the summer months. Saudi princes were building huge, beautiful mansions. If you called from a Saudi number, the nightclubs would give you the best table. If you called from a Lebanese number, they would not let you in. This is where it started to frustrate me. I was, like, *Wow, you are just catering to the foreigners, the Saudis*. What happens when they leave or stop coming? In Lebanon, hospitality and tourism are a big part of our GDP, along with the banking industry.

Caitlin You wrote in your research: "Downtown Beirut is experiencing a unique situation where the increasing housing stock although owned are not occupied. This leaves the polished city center devoid of much life or activity. The fear of a spillover from the Syrian civil war has prevented expats from visiting causing a major hit to the tourism sector. In addition, travel warnings and bans have been put into effect by most of the rich oil-petroleum producing countries. Within this context, residential property demand has slowed down and new sales reflect a new reality for the Lebanese market, one of a consolidation phase following years of frenetic activity." Abou Dib, p. 14.

Marwan Did you go downtown when you were last in Beirut? It is sad. Many restaurants shut down. The Saudis are not coming. No one is coming. This is the first time in memory that the real estate sector is struggling. The problem of so many Syrian refugees, the travel ban issue, Israel, ISIS, municipal garbage not being collected – because of these things, no one is investing.

Caitlin I know that some of these luxury high-rises in downtown Beirut do not have any occupants. A few wealthy Syrians could manage to pay for that kind of craziness, but in general, if the Saudis are not coming, who can possibly afford those places? Ordinary Lebanese certainly cannot.

Marwan That is what is sad. Even downtown they were building large houses and four-bedroom apartments for Saudi families, because Lebanese families are usually small. Then they realised they needed to start building micro units for the Lebanese. So there was some shift in the real estate culture, but Solidere never budged. They would rather sell fewer apartments for $5 million than get $300,000 for more. It was enough to sell ten apartments. This was their mentality. But there is some good architecture that is well built and needs people. The residential skyscraper Beirut Terraces was designed by Herzog & de Meuron. That is why I studied real estate.

It is not just about the return; it is about investing in good design and great public spaces. But no one is living there. They are struggling to sell units in those towers. Even the Herzog & de Meuron building will probably be empty. They are monuments that are just ghosts. This is where the power of capitalism reaches its limits.

Caitlin In Berlin, there is the beautiful Atrium Tower by Renzo Piano. It has been empty for nearly twenty years. What kind of market forces would be required for such a building to be occupied? Or is it social forces?

Marwan It is not possible to lower the cost because the Lebanese are obsessed with things that are expensive, which they equate to status, right? They always have this hope that wealthy enough people will come. Even for the Lebanese living in Lebanon, they go there to shop and drink, but they will never live there. It is not just that it is too expensive: they do not want to live there.
The scars have not healed. That is what I meant about the downtown being built for a population that will never come back. Who is going to come? Are we going to wait for the Saudis to come back? I think the Saudis just moved on. My dad has been saying he would go back for thirty, forty years. Has he gone back? He has not gone back. If all of the educated Lebanese abroad were to go back, I think Lebanon would be one of the best countries in the world, but we cannot deal with the politics. There is no public sector in Lebanon. And the politicians are real estate developers and they want to make a return.

I have this dream of becoming the minister of tourism one day. I hate politics but I love my country so much that I just want to get people who live abroad to come back and for tourists to come. My friends and family, they say: *Even if you were to be a minister of tourism, they would not let you do anything, so then you will just hate yourself or they will assassinate you.* Which did happen, you know that part.

Caitlin Don't get assassinated …

Marwan That is a joke but also true …

Caitlin I think it is interesting that you did a joint degree in real estate development and architecture. How did your studies in both programmes at MIT [Massachusetts Institute of Technology] give you perspective?

Marwan Growing up in Dubai, I saw the city grow, but they did not care about people or public space, it was just about money. Since I was ten, I knew I wanted to study architecture. I was fascinated by real estate development, but I did not know how that worked. After my undergrad, I went to work for Bernard Khoury. He is a well-known Lebanese architect. Living in Beirut, I started to understand what architecture and good design were about. It is about the people, the urban context. For the first time I was living in a city where the architect's role and responsibility were to take into consideration the history and the people. How does one design for people? I realised that what I wanted was the authenticity of that city. Comparing my experience of growing up in Dubai with my professional experience in Beirut, these were two cities that were rising; Beirut was in a renaissance, while Dubai was created from scratch with no soul. Both cities had their problems, and I wanted to understand how to fix them.

In the Middle East, there are only corporate architecture firms. I wanted to wake up from the dreamy bubble of architecture school and understand my client: the real estate developer. I wanted to create value out of real estate through good design. I wanted to combine the two. The real estate programme wants more architects, people who care about these cities. I now see things differently: I think of numbers, I think of returns, of percentages. A good architect is someone who can think like a real estate developer, while at the same time understanding that it is not just about money. These are cities that people will inhabit and that is priceless.

Caitlin Where does your family own real estate in Lebanon?

Marwan We are not very active in real estate. I live in Jeita [20 km north of Beirut]; do you know the grotto and the caves? That is where my house is. My dad lived in Beirut growing up, but my family is originally from Zaḥlah in the Beqaa [Al-Biqāʿ] Valley. Because my dad is from there, he buys land there. It is also because it is cheaper and it appreciates in value. I go there once a year.

Caitlin Have you built anything?

Marwan No, no. This is undeveloped land. When you build on it, then the value becomes concrete. It is about the idea of real estate, the speculative property exchange that it could be worth more.

Caitlin What would you want for the Burj el Murr, the unfinished sniper tower between downtown Beirut and the district of Hamra?

Marwan You know, when I was living in Lebanon, I sketched the tower. I wanted to revitalise it and encase it in glass; this is the architect in me speaking. It is an artefact, a monument. I wanted to light it up at night so it could become a beacon.

Caitlin The army still occupies the bottom of the tower, and they do not want anyone to go up inside of it.

Marwan It would be extremely difficult to demolish because of the way the core was engineered and constructed. So why not make it into public space, like a maze or a labyrinth? That is what makes Beirut such a beautiful city, right? An invasion of ghostly monuments ...

Caitlin Accepting them as part of the landscape is also accepting that we are not starting from scratch. I am not interested in the logic of apocalyptic ends.

Marwan Neither am I. It is more about the forces of capitalism. How can architects both accept them and find alternatives?

Marwan Abou Dib is a founding partner of Tekuma Frenchman, an urban design firm. His research focuses on the intersection of real estate, design, and technology, through which he works in collaboration with Dennis Frenchman and laboratories at MIT. His passion for city-making stems from having witnessed the rapid transformation of Dubai, at an early age, and the renaissance of postwar Beirut. Abou Dib has been invited as a featured speaker by the United Nations, McKinsey & Company, and the Boston Consulting Group. He holds dual master's degrees in architecture and real estate development from MIT.

Marginal forms …
with Caleb Waldorf
and Caitlin Berrigan

Berlin, 2015

Caitlin Speculative fiction never appealed to me because it appeared to be dominated by techno-fetishistic fantasies of white male melancholy and post-apocalyptic defeatism, all wrapped in a flat level of prose. So I was stunned some years ago when I read Ursula LeGuin's *The Dispossessed* [1974]. At the time, we were all navigating the Occupy movement, which was unfolding and changing every day with all kinds of inventions and disturbing hang-ups. *The Dispossessed* was a revelation of how an author could model worlds – gender relations, capitalism, socialist anarchism, the benefits and detriments of two opposing ideological and economic systems – and articulate these worlds without drawing hard conclusions and prophecies or judgments. She allows room for the reader's own thinking with literary mastery.

I feel like I am still discovering the novelists I need to read, even though much of my work in the visual arts has taken on what could be called forms of speculative fiction that model and play with biopolitical realms. I want to explore forms of speculative fiction and literature as alternatives to the overly patriarchal genre of political theory. Politics can be both loose and lucid in speculative fiction, and this offers a lot to the imagination.

Caleb The question that I would put to you, about *Unfinished State* and also generally: What is it about worldbuilding that you find important to engage with? It is often asserted that speculative fiction is not about the future but the present. While this is true, at least to a certain extent, we do have past examples of speculative work having a direct impact on shaping the future. For instance, take *Atlas Shrugged* [1957] by Ayn Rand. This book prefigured our current reality – our notion of rationality, individual decision-making, laissez-faire capitalism. The thrust of her focus in objectivism was, at the time of her writing, a very experimental and marginal idea that rational decision-making based on individual self-interest must drive everything, and that society must be organised around a particular form of capitalism. Rand worked through political theory within speculative fiction. That fiction, as well as her other writings, inspired many actors who, in the last decades, have been at the levers of power: from Alan Greenspan, an American economist and former chairman of the Federal Reserve – under both Republican and Democratic presidents – who was part of Rand's inner circle, to influential figures in Silicon Valley like Peter Thiel, the German American cofounder of PayPal and an early investor in Facebook. My question is whether there is speculative work being done today that will be so influential on our reality in fifty years.

Political theory is trying to map out how politics function – what are the mechanics, how do they affect people, how do they relate to economics. It is a form of mapping the world, but it is generally limited to mapping existing conditions. This contrasts with speculative fiction, which is also mapping and worldbuilding based on similar ideas or observations, while also being required to present ideas in a way that political theory does not need nor have to. I think we are both drawn to this notional, worldbuilding aspect of speculative fiction.

It necessitates attention to all of the little details that make a fictional world compelling.

One could do a similar type of thinking within political theory, but it is far more difficult to address emotion, affect, and the texture of lived experience in that discursive space. Theory is not charged with building a narrative. If I am reading someone who is writing *about* subjectivity, it is much more challenging for me to position myself within the viewpoint of what is being discussed. If I am reading a novel, and the narrator and main protagonist is a ship, as in the *Imperial Radch* trilogy [2013–15] by Ann Leckie, I am more likely to find a way to inhabit that specific subjectivity. The narrative system allows a kind of intimacy that is unavailable in many forms of cultural production.

Caitlin Yes, and although it is impossible for authors to shed entirely all of the social constructs that every individual comes with, they can shape-shift the subjectivities of characters into objects, other-bodied beings, or an alien life form and allow the reader to enter more easily into different subjective roles. With philosophy the problem is ... I mean, I love it and I read a lot of it ...

Caleb The problem with philosophy ...

Caitlin The problem with the philosophical proof is cutting out the inconsistencies and contingencies of lived reality. Those are, I think, essential to understanding and problematising discontinuous power relations.

The thing I appreciated most about Octavia Butler's *Xenogenesis Series* [1987–89] is the ambivalent and myriad ways people choose to express human dignity and to effectuate the continuation of the species under hardship. How do people react to kidnapping, violent occupation, and colonisation? Some people resist with violence, others co-operate, others become suicidal. If it becomes clear that total resistance is de facto accompanied by annihilation, what are the complexities contained within frameworks of co-operation and resistance? How does dignity survive under coercion? In particular, Butler's main character, Lilith, closely models the moral dilemmas of dignity and survival faced by African and Indigenous women enslaved in the Americas. In the novel, the survival of the whole human species depends upon this woman's skilful yet self-compromising co-operation under coercion with the colonising aliens, which she combined with intelligent modes of resistance in order to maintain her own, and humanity's own, dignity. Butler's speculative fiction illuminates how these kinds of struggle play out in the "real" space of contemporary history and politics. Contrary to a hermetic, proof-like theory, she can address and experiment with the full variety of affect and subjectivity.

Caleb Yes. In George R. R. Martin's novel *A Game of Thrones* [1996] from the series *A Song of Ice and Fire*, he spends an inordinate amount of time describing what people are eating. Finely detailed tastes and smells of individual banquets activate the reader's senses, while also sketching the agricultural, economic, and distribution systems that are involved in bringing all of these foods, and the sensations they produce, together. Through this thing that is very familiar and that can quickly trigger physical reactions like hunger or disgust, he is effectively mapping out a region and a culture without overtly describing either directly. In good speculative fiction, much of the contextual work happens in such moments.

Caitlin Sociological depth through lived textures. I want to discuss what you said about the idea that we are living in a speculative future, which is true on various levels. The reason I wanted to send a novel from the genre of speculative fiction to these unfinished buildings was because, when you gather all of the buildings themselves together to constitute a landscape of their own, they are a kind of speculative fiction. When you draw them out of their quotidian environment and look closely, they appear otherworldly. And yet, this landscape of exception exists.

Similarly, so many new buildings here in Berlin over the last two decades – built with the promise of a transformative society to fill a still underpopulated city – are left empty. Buildings left unfinished for so many years are speculative social futures that never quite arrived and remain unfulfilled. This is true at least for the owners, even if the original investors made out with their capital. And yet, in and of themselves, they constitute a landscape apart that is hard to integrate with the rest of the contemporary moment.

Caleb I feel like the drive towards articulating a future is incompatible with certain orientations in philosophy, due in large part to the hangover from postmodernism and deconstruction. With the discourse around the Anthropocene, there is an actual horizon speeding towards us that must be discussed concretely. There is an end to humanity in sight. It is quite easy to see that. I think this changes how one would write a speculative fiction today. We have that which seems so unimaginable – human extinction – up against these retrofutures that were never realised. We have a lot of competing temporalities. If a typical future in a speculative fiction book forecasts 200 to 2,000 years into the future, and we might only have 50 years or so left on this planet, how does contemporary speculative fiction account for this reality?

I want to change subjects slightly. You were initially talking about speculative fiction versus political theory or philosophy. I wonder what there is to say about speculative fiction versus contemporary art. The international art world that you and I orbit within appears to do very little to challenge our imaginations of the future. It maintains its own conventions and is a very safe space. What does it do to insert a speculative fiction into a context that tends to diminish or abate transformative experiences and evacuate rather than expand?

Caitlin [*Laughs*]

Caleb Sorry, I do not mean to sound so pessimistic. In this work, you are exploring the structure of a novel and I am wondering just how that structure can operate within a different mode of display, circulation, and temporality. The durational aspect of reading is crucial here. It takes a long time to read a book like *Dhalgren*, which I am ashamed to say I have never finished!

Caitlin Yes, it is a good question: What does it do within this specific circuit of the production of professionalised visual art? I guess two of the most formative art-making experiences for me, when I was very young, were poetry and photography. Just before digital photography became a viable alternative to film, I had an existential crisis about what a single image was. I lost faith in the singularity of an image and all of the effort one puts into decoding it.

My lack of faith in the unique image, or instant, is reflected in *Unfinished State*. These are plural and imperfect photographs. I did not want the expansive lens of traditional architectural photography. Sometimes the image is blurred or incomplete. Multiple perspectives produce a refracted vision of space; in other words, a time-based experience of moving through space. Perceptual vision needs to be read differently from the symbolic weights of representation and art history.

I realise in my own practice that I am less motivated to dialogue directly with the conservative genealogies of art history. I love art history, but I want to dialogue with broader visual and interdisciplinary cultures. My friend, who reads art reviews for sport, sent me some criticism from *Artforum* that made my eyes roll. The critic searches throughout the review to anchor the artist's paintings in a patrilineal version of art history. This quest for filial provenance feels impoverishing, as does a minutely innovative formal shift within a canon of micro shifts. I seek dialogue with other forms that may not be visual and express themselves in a spatial language.

Caleb Art history functions to make things legible as art; art criticism does this as well, it is what galleries and institutions do. There are obviously forms of legibility that serve different interests, which we do not need to get into here, but maybe it is interesting to think about the postcards within an art historical lineage. I am thinking specifically about mail art, which created a way to bypass existing networks of circulation. It became a means to share art amongst groups of people who were not necessarily connected, in order to map and reinforce existing networks and to create new ones. But the network you created is with ghosts. The aesthetic is of cheap, high-contrast tourist postcards. It is a familiar device that anchors people's perspective. Those photographs can be printed badly, not taken well, blurry, or with false colour. People can relate them to a context and yet there is a bit of mystery. Is there a relationship between your artwork and the work done within mail art?

Caitlin Yes, of course. I did not mean to imply that I have no relationship with art history, but this is perhaps an investigation of its minor and marginal forms. Historically, mail art practices are concerned with relationality and evading luxury markets. Currently, there is also a lot of experimentation with platforms of sociality in communities of visual art, and it is possible to connect these emergent forms of social relations within a lineage. Your work, such as with pedagogy and publishing, could be seen as experimental sites where sociality hooks into other forms of practising, being, and thinking together in ways not afforded by capitalist structures built around the establishment of an individual artist. Interconnected distribution was part of my interest in thinking about the novel as a conceptual form. A whole narrative is dispersed and moved over space, from one site to another and back, so that its travels enact a distance and then reassemble in an incomplete form. Mail art is a relational form with an object, intimate interlocutors, and unintended audiences. There is a conceptual motion to the dispersion of mail art and this motion is a form of art. Books are also a reproducible form of art that is time-based and relational. Do you think of publishing as a way to enact different social relations?

Caleb Yes. Practically speaking, in collaborative publishing, you have contributors, editors, designers, technologists, and producers who have a connection together while orbiting around a work. Those relationships are tied to historical, educational, and infrastructural formations that facilitate the distribution, circulation, and legibility of a text. So before anything arrives at a reader, there is an array of dynamic elements and complex relationships at play.

One area that I have continually been drawn towards, across a number of different projects, has todo with the impact that comes with serial publishing. Specifically, I am interested in how to create rhythms of content production that are regular and ongoing, in contrast with the more "exceptional" examples such as exhibitions, conferences, festivals, etc., which tend to fracture time but remain tightly bounded in duration and physical location. Things that we experience simultaneously with others, even if we are doing so privately, can sometimes produce a stronger foundation for a relationship than an event, a form that has become a dominant framework for the production and consumption in contemporary cultural practices. That being said, the internet continues to get more and more awful, which increases the difficulty in trying to engender the kind of sociality I have been pursuing.

Publication is happening all of the time. Finished products are put into the world, but there is always something next, and always something preceding, that gives it meaning. I like this aspect because each person is afforded a continuous relationship with the work over time. As you said, books and other media are minor forms. You can have them as can others, which I think is nice. You can also simply access them and not just possess them.

Caitlin You have other ongoing projects like the Public School, where the classes are in dialogue with each other. The ability to archive class materials and conversations online, across continents, creates a relationality of ideas, as well as the possibility to return. The urgency of a discussion on say, languages of revolution, can reemerge in a different time or a different location. I find it difficult that artists are either expected to stick to a single subject, which can be explored through different media, or to stick to a single medium through which various subjects are explored. It also assumes a repetitive focus of a relatively short time scale of a year or two. I find that I often return to media and subjects, but it may be several years later. With classes at the Public School, it is interesting that there is no particular time scale. A class could be revived and led at a different time by a totally different person. It loosens things up. It is an interpretive idea of culture.

This question of ways to think together that resist traditional forms of end-product creative work also came up in our class about Afrofuturism at the Public School. We talked about how the Sun Ra Arkestra lived, rehearsed, and improvised together constantly, such that the rehearsal was a method of being together, a collective occupation of time and space. But to maintain that social cohesion of creative coexistence, is it necessary to be led by a gentle despot like Sun Ra [1914–1993]?

Caleb It is also related to scale and scalability. Not everything needs to be scalable. Some things just work with two people, and some work with thousands of people, but one has to make a realistic assessment of where the work lives and circulates and how transformative it can be. With something like the Public School or A Public Library or *Triple Canopy*, the scale goes from a small, intimate network, to tens of thousands of people, to potentially hundreds of thousands of people. The biggest challenge right now, politically and artistically, is how to think in a scalable way about the experiments that we are working on, whether structurally or with new forms of subjectivity. How are different kinds of work politically reproducible, how can they operate at the scale of politics?

Caitlin Scalability is one of the major issues in the political project to resist neoliberal capitalism. Localised oppressions can be very specific, yet share some global patterns. Can resistance that makes sense in one context be replicable and scalable across the world? The Occupy movement took a lot of cues from the Arab Spring and there was a real dialogue happening between two extremely different contexts. There were militarised responses to both of them, especially harsh and murderous in Egypt, that were largely accountable for breaking them up. There was a desire for forms of social cohesion that have nothing to do with traditional leftist organisation. It was not about rejecting them, but rather recognising the need for other models. This is where the necessity arises for practices in modelling and building alternative forms of scalable bases and scalable relations. These practices may be unrelated, and they may not be tasked to do anything specific, but they can be drawn upon when a moment of urgency arises.

Caleb I also wonder if Occupy and Arab Spring are like your buildings. They are forgotten dreams, right? And they are ...

Caitlin Unfulfilled.

Caleb Unfulfilled, yes, they are unfulfilled futures. Like the postcards, they are shells one no longer sees.

Caitlin What can we do with this unfulfilled desire and speculations for the future? The desire is not always to create something totally new, but instead to create points of departure. We must acknowledge everything in the past and work from it. There is no escape hatch or fresh start. We must attempt to turn that unfulfillment and dissatisfaction into something transformative, instead of into cynicism.

Caleb It is interesting that you sent messages to buildings. How do you think the buildings felt about getting postcards from overseas?

Caitlin [*Laughs*]

Caleb I am totally serious. You were writing to the buildings, and you were showing them a photo of themselves. What kind of response do you think the buildings could have?

Caitlin To address the buildings is both about speaking and seeing. One question for me was how to acknowledge an informal architectural phenomenon, which is more of a landscape than a typology. I wanted to acknowledge each building in its individuality, to see it, and call it back into the fold. Each building is a plot hole in the narrative of an emergent landscape. It was a way to reach into the holes.

When I first encountered these spaces, my impulse was to inhabit them performatively with limited duration. Part of their allure is their vacancy, whereas most buildings are filled with layers upon layers of accumulated histories. The gesture of an epistolary performance is to offer a narrative to inhabit the structures temporarily and to call all of these lost buildings back into another storyline. The process itself creates new holes in the narrative, and the work reassembles only fragments. I never got the sense that these buildings were failures. They might be failures of capitalism, but they have the best views. They look out at the sea and are filled by the sky behind them.

Caleb People have intimacy with structures and space. We walk around barefoot, we are naked in it: the space sees us in some way. It feels our presence. It works on a temporality with different nerves and notions of touch. You are acknowledging that these buildings exist and have a life unto themselves. I wonder what kind of relationship there is between you and those buildings. Postcards are not sent to strangers. We send them to family, to lovers, to friends. Here, you enter a familiar relationship with a structure, sending them excerpts you think will be relevant to them. You are reconfiguring the notion of intimacy or sexuality in relation to nonhuman entities.

Caitlin Yes, I would say that there is a sensual intimacy with these unfinished buildings. Artists and architects have a profound relationship with space and material. The artist Lars Laumann did a documentary about people who identify as sexual lovers of objects and architectures and who call themselves *objectum sexuals*. There is Erika Eiffel, who married the Eiffel Tower, and was so in love with the Berlin Wall that she moved into a condo on Bernauer Straße, just opposite a memorialised portion of the wall, so that she could be with it every day. She came down the street to PROGRAM for a screening and discussion along with some others who identify as objectum sexuals. PROGRAM Initiative for Art and Architecture Collaborations (2006–12) was co-directed by Carson Chan and Fotini Lazaridou-Hatzigoga. The nonprofit project occupied the ground level of the legendary Russian hotel Newa on Invalindenstraße in Berlin and offered a discursive platform through exhibitions, performances, workshops, lectures, and residencies. Among them was a woman in a relationship with her DDR-era Plattenbau [prefabricated concrete social housing]. It was the first public discussion this group held for an audience full of architects and artists. They were astonished by how many in the audience understood and shared a similarly intimate relationship to objects and sites, except for the point at which such intimacy might constitute a categorical sexual identification. Such a radical configuration of sexuality speaks to your point about the idea of alien relationality.

After the discussion at PROGRAM, Carson Chan said something like, *Did you ever notice that they mostly fall in love with rock stars, with starchitectures: the Berlin Wall, the Eiffel Tower?* Capital "A" architecture. Partly what drew me to these unfinished spaces in Lebanon is that they are phenomena that encompass both major and minor architectures. Here in Berlin, Renzo Piano's buildings at Potsdamer Platz are vacant for the same reasons as those out-of-the-box, drafted-in-Google-SketchUp luxury condos on the waterfront in Rummelsburg. They are all materialised under similar forces of capital. In Lebanon, some of the buildings are just a few lines in space. Maybe it was supposed to be a shed, or perhaps it was supposed to be a house and then it never made it past being a shed. And then there is one of Oscar Niemeyer's few projects in the Arab region, the Rashid Karami International Fair: monumental buildings alongside totally minor structures, both affected by flows and withdrawals of capital.

Caleb The other thing that has happened, and this is deliberate because you knew that the postcards would come back ...

Caitlin I did not know they would come back.

Caleb Did you want them to come back? What is being traced in *Unfinished State*? It does not feel like nostalgia, but it seems to map infrastructures that may become obsolete. Another layer is when the work takes the form of a printed book, it will reenter the network as a bounded publication. Books travel. Printed books have to travel through the traditional network infrastructure of the postal system.

Caitlin We may anticipate the obsolescence of extensive spatial networks to accompany the rise of digital networks. The idea that we can exist without forms of embodiment is disturbing, right? As if the body is an anachronism. Anachronism is particularly clear with domestic labour. The issue is not a technological one, but a question of power. We may have the technological future of privatised space travel existing alongside the continuous, present anachronism of enslaved domestic workers all over the world.

However, I think to pit digital and spatial communication networks against each other is a false dichotomy. These infrastructures of circulation reinscribe the way that bodies move through landscapes and sites. To move through a novel can also be a spatial experience. I do not think my engagement in this work is nostalgic, even if it acknowledges ruptures in space and time. It employs anachronistic language and yet those anachronisms exist currently. Concurrently.

Caleb Concurrently. It is a good time to be alive!

Caleb Waldorf is an artist living in Berlin. His practice operates at the intersection of publication, pedagogy, and technology, with a focus on designing, developing, and maintaining collaborative systems on- and offline. He served on the committee for the Public School, an open framework for self-organised learning. In 2007, he cofounded the magazine *Triple Canopy*, for which he worked as Creative Director until 2022. He has collaborated on developing a number of publishing platforms including the editorial collective "and/or Evacuate" (established as Occupy Everything), magazine *East of Borneo*, and *post: notes on art in the global context* (MoMA–Museum of Modern Art). Waldorf received an MFA from the University of California San Diego.

Murmuring of the void ...
with Marwa Arsanios
and Caitlin Berrigan

Berlin, 2019

Caitlin In your work, Marwa, you have looked at architecture and buildings as vessels that communicate contested narratives of violence, war, and ideology. Sometimes these histories are told through visible marks or traces, and other times the stories orbit around an object in immaterial, affective modes. Unfoldings of war, land, statecraft, and capitalist-driven real estate can share familiar patterns around the world, even if the granularity of these histories differs from place to place. You have looked at the post-1990s transformation of downtown Beirut, as well as at experiments in emancipatory violence and radical autonomy in feminist settlements in Rojava, on border zones in northeastern Syria. I am wondering if you can speak about how you theorise the voids that have been facilitated by war and dispossession. Could we call these "material metabolisms" of real estate?

Marwa The 1990s were a particular historical moment in terms of the expansion of global neoliberal economies. Today things have changed, and these economies have accelerated. It is tragic that there is apparently a bid to rebuild downtown Aleppo by Solidere – the development company that rebuilt downtown Beirut after the civil war. They have established their model of rebuilding city centres under the company Solidere International, which is headquartered in Dubai.

Caitlin In the case of Beirut, Solidere was very much embedded within the state.

Marwa Yes, it started in the early '90s by Rafik al-Hariri, who had just become the prime minister of Lebanon. His political position allowed him to work around the legal system in order to transform properties into shares and rebuild the downtown. You have mentioned your position as a tourist in relation to these sites. But in fact, these places could be located anywhere, right? The city centres of neoliberal cities are the same in almost every place. This is how generic Beirut's downtown is.

Caitlin Yes, they share formations and perforations of the modernist project in unfinished structures throughout the world. At the same time, there is a historical specificity to the circumstances that account for why sites drop out of modernist teleology – whether a site booms and busts or whether it is complicated by layers of urban legal structures, as in the unprecedented and layered case of downtown Beirut.

Marwa Right. On another level, I would like to think about these buildings in Lebanon as a part of a more universal heritage, in order to make strategic claims about their belonging within the history of modernism, which extends throughout the world. My personal experience of this moment in the '90s was growing up on the Green Line of demarcation between East and West Beirut. From the balcony of our kitchen, we could see the ring. The ring was where you could cross from one side to the other. At that time, it was a no-man's-land. The downtown was very close to it. I grew up with this void that is very material. In fact, the void is never completely void, because it was populated by all kinds of humans and nonhumans and trees and animals. It was very dangerous to live there, but a lot of people squatted offices and abandoned buildings. After the war ended, they cleared these people out to start Solidere's big construction project. There was a lot of wilderness in this area. The trees grew in the buildings. It had been a political territory dividing the city. When they removed the containers and all of the rubble that divided the city, I remember going to the downtown and walking in this ghostly place.

A deal was put on the table in 1985 for a form of possible reconciliation and reconstruction but it failed. In the '90s, the deal that ended up being made was not only political amnesty, it also included the reconstruction. We knew that this was going to happen. My adolescent years were spent within this construction site. There was a void formed and facilitated by the destruction of war that allowed real estate to come in. But this kind of void is not really a void. The concept of "the void" has been used as the ultimate colonial-capitalist, expansionist excuse in order to reclaim, expropriate, and appropriate land. It is similarly used in urban contexts, where it takes the name of "the wasteland". The downtown was growing in financial value throughout the fifteen years of civil war. Of course, when you are in the midst of civil war, you are not thinking about that. The first land reclamation consisted of shoving into the sea the so-called Normandy garbage dump, which was the main dump of Beirut during the ’80s. All kinds of waste had been thrown in there – medical, industrial, and probably human bodies. The rubble from the destroyed downtown buildings and other construction material was used to reclaim land from the sea in the downtown area. The new ideological structure of the ’90s, on to which the reconstruction project after the civil war was to be built, materialised in this process of land extension. It was a literal mattering of the void.

Caitlin Can you talk about how you relate Karen Barad’s theories of voids and materiality to the land reclamation in downtown Beirut?

Marwa The void in Newtonian physics is where matter is absent, where, according to Barad, there is an absence of property and laws, which entails that it has no energy. Then they explain that in quantum physics, the vacuum is where particles are created. Therefore, the void and matter are inseparable. The vacuum is not silent. It is murmuring, Barad argues, so it is a space of energy countering the concept of Newtonian physics. It is a way to think about the process of how the void of downtown Beirut was transformed into legal and financial abstractions of shares that no longer corresponded to property parcels. In connecting this to Barad, I was trying to think about the waste and the rubble in its relation to legality and financial value. And to think about how energy, life, and matter werevcreated within this no-man’s-land *before* the very high noise of the reconstruction and real estate machine.

Caitlin I also like how Barad says that people find the abstractions of quantum physics to be relatable and allegorical at so many levels because they are, in fact, the very basis of reality. The way that you are abstracting the formation of matter and reproductive potential in postconflict territories is in the murmuring of what may come. In these unfinished buildings, there is a murmuring of their intended direction. But then in their failure to materialise their intended form, there is also a murmuring of some other potential. It is a kind of oscillating thrill between what was emptied out and its potential futurity. The ideology that comes in to fill the void influences the direction of its future. You have a film series titled *Who is Afraid of Ideology?* [2017–ongoing]. So, who is afraid of ideology? Fascism and colonialism love to create a void and a blank slate in order to fill it with ideology. But critical liberational politics also have an ideological agenda, even if we do not like to talk about it that way.

Marwa I think the '90s were afraid of ideology. The time of the reconstruction of Beirut coincided with this historical moment of the so-called end of history. A lot of intellectuals and artists in Beirut in the '90s fought the amnesia of the tabula rasa with the discourse of memory. They discovered that it was not a strong enough discourse to fight neoliberalism. They also recognised that, in the end, they were defeated by this soft discourse of memory. Something else is needed to fight this. I do not know what.

Caitlin Now you have also been observing separatist feminist collectives on the Syrian-Turkish border. It is a moment of formulating ideology, of radical imaginary murmuring, and matter-making. Once this moment takes on a denser form of practical ideology, it perhaps loses its appeal for those with stakes in theoretical emancipatory politics.

Marwa In the case of rebuilding in northern Syria, some towns were destroyed and others were newly constructed on reappropriated state lands. I noticed that there is never an ideological void because what you have is a layering of ideologies that is shaping this space, this matter, and their subjectivities. Ideology seeps in, and in some sense, it is enunciated. It is still there, of course, even if the Assad regime has left. The formations of radical thinking are very beautiful, but there is a survival mechanism that can take over and rigidly occupy power vacuums in a precarious situation.

Caitlin Yes, I am interested in trying to imagine futurity from within the deep layering of the past. Within building and layering, what forms of futurity might take place? To practise futurity, one does have to commit to certain ideological premises and formations.

Marwa I think what is necessary is to acknowledge that you are never talking from a nonideological place. It is always ideologies that are speaking through you. It is not about you.

Caitlin And in fact, we are always working backwards when we are trying to build the future. I love how in your film the Kurdish feminists declare that no men are allowed in their community.

Marwa No men in.

Caitlin Yes, I love that.

Marwa That is the future.

Marwa Arsanios is an artist, filmmaker, and researcher who reconsiders mid-twentieth-century politics from a contemporary perspective, with a particular focus on gender relations, spatial practices, and land struggles. Arsanios approaches research collaboratively and seeks to work across disciplines. She is a cofounder, with Mirene Arsanios, of the research project 98weeks in Beirut. She has exhibited at documenta fifteen and held solo exhibitions at the Beirut Art Center; Hammer Museum, Los Angeles; Kunstinstituut Melly, Rotterdam; Kunsthalle Lissabon; and Art in General, New York. Arsanios holds a PhD-in-Practice from the Akademie der bildenden Künste Wien and teaches at the Dutch Art Institute.

To embody holes in time ...
with Haseeb Ahmed
and Caitlin Berrigan

Brussels, 2019

Caitlin I want to talk about the way time manifests in architecture, and the instances where buildings embody holes in time, or wormholes through chronopolitics; forms of architecture as resistance to linear time and historical time. Did your interest in geometric patterns of architectural form come prior to your interest in Islamic architecture? Or did encountering Islamic architecture generate your interest in geometries? Did your interest originate from a loose beginning or a specific instance?

Haseeb First came the experience of growing up in the Midwest [US] and visiting an Ottoman-style mosque that was built in the middle of cornfields every Sunday. The building was extremely familiar to me, but I recognised it as something that existed entirely outside of the vernacular architecture that surrounded it. It is on an extremely prominent site because it is built right at the interstate junction, in the vicinity of Toledo, where the major north-south and east-west highways in Ohio converge. You see the mosque as a volume while passing through.

Caitlin You can see it from the highways as you drive by? Can you also see the highways and the cars moving past when you are at the mosque?

Haseeb Absolutely. The highways surround it, so in fact and you have a kind of tracking or travelling shot of the mosque from the interchange overpass. It appears on the horizon for quite some distance before that moment. You have the image of the two large minarets and a central dome built on an octagonal base, following Ottoman-style architecture. It was the biggest mosque in North America for ten years or more, called the Islamic Center of Greater Toledo.

Caitlin When was it built?

Haseeb It was finished in 1983, two years before I was born. Historically, the Ottomans tried to lay claim to the whole of the Muslim world by asserting that they maintained the last caliphate and producing similar mosques throughout their empire. Almost all American mosques are based on the Ottoman typology, which is itself modelled on the Dome of the Rock shrine [within the Al-Aqsa mosque compound] in Jerusalem that houses the rock from which the prophet ascended to the heavens on the Night of Power [Laylat al-Qadr]. There is actually no proof that the rock is *that* rock, which could possibly undermine the religious – but never the historical – significance of the Dome of the Rock. Following the assassinations of the first four caliphates, there was a power struggle and the Dome of the Rock was created to mark a new, unified centre of power, which was shifted eastward to the Levant instead of Baghdad. So the Dome of the Rock became a model for forging a relationship between form and identity, up to and including its use in the context of the Midwest, long after the fall of the Ottoman Empire [c. 1299–1922].

Caitlin Do you know why the mosque was built at that highway interchange?

Haseeb People were very conscious of it being a symbol. That community is old, from the early 1900s, made up of Lebanese and Syrians who came to work in the automobile factories in Detroit and the Jeep plants that are still operating in Toledo. Originally the mosque was located in the inner city on Bancroft Street. After many years of saving money, they bought land in a suburb called Perrysburg, outside of Toledo. In some ways it was a step up, being out in the countryside, but it demanded access. Most people lived in the city of Toledo, so they arrived from the highway, which suited the infrastructure of a region centred around the automotive industry. There was no reason to build it as big as they did except for symbolic presence. There is a colossal sign facing the highway. A truck driver tried to burn down the mosque a few years ago. He drove on this highway all the time while listening to conservative radio and seeing the mosque. Having these two things in his mind for years got him to the point where eventually he set fire to the mosque. U.S. Attorney's Office, Northern District of Ohio, "Indiana Man Sentenced to 20 Years in Prison for Religiously Motivated Attack on Toledo-Area Mosque", 16 April 2013.

Caitlin Racialised violence is also a subtext in *Dhalgren*, with allusions to race riots such as in Detroit [1967] and the tumultuous and complex transformations of a city crumbling under white supremacy. On the one hand, it is possible that land near a highway intersection would not have a whole lot of real estate value, since infrastructural zones are often cheaper land. But the mosque was made with automobile culture in mind, influenced by that expanse of space. They took advantage of a vista created exclusively by highway infrastructure in a presumably flat geography. Are you thinking the decision to build there was more in connection to vehicular culture than to being on the periphery?

Haseeb I think it is a combination of the two. In this part of Ohio, architecture functions with a duration, and the duration is that of the car. One learns how to experience a building while moving past it at seventy miles an hour. That is the primary experience of architecture in Midwestern Ohio. The point of purchase is where one enters, which is more important than where that place actually is.

Caitlin The mosque did not have anything to do with Black Islam?

Haseeb No, because the mosque was built by and for a primarily immigrant community. Probably before my time, there was more mixing in its original Bancroft St. location. When they moved out to the suburbs, they left the underprivileged African American communities in the inner city, who do not always have the ability to drive twenty-five miles in a car to a mosque. The Nation of

Islam has a whole separate mosque. It is a cordial relationship, but they are not always recognised as Muslims.

Caitlin I took photographs of an unfinished Ottoman-style mosque located in the south of Beirut, but those postcards were never returned to me in the mail, so they will not be in the book. Maybe the mosque received them! But let's go back to how your interest in pattern evolved.

Haseeb I was finding a way to deal with the history I was brought up with, including identities with which I did not identify. There had to be worlds outside of narratives and iconic forms, forms with so much semiotic value. Pattern, especially concerning Islamic architecture, still has that. At the same time, geometry always only describes itself or its function. Like when you make compass constructions or geometric forms as a pattern, it does not relate to anything outside of itself and only describes the rules of its own making.

Caitlin This creates an uneasy relationship between architectural form and ideology. There is a deep love for form because it can be made to embody ideologies, but can it be detached? Ideologies can be oppressive, but they are not unchangeable. Is it possible to reinterpret form if it is reappropriated for another purpose? Can one live among multiple layers of meanings? This has something to do with why I am drawn to these ageing, unfinished buildings in Lebanon, as well as to nonspaces, these empty volumes of newly built constructions in Berlin. Some of the structures I photographed were designed by Oscar Niemeyer and possess the hopeful futurism of modernity. But most are nameless, formal replicas of modernism. Rather than erasing evidence and starting anew – trying to circumnavigate history and its unpalatable parts – do you think there are ways to interpret these sites as places where it is possible to acknowledge the failures of capitalism and to deal with history differently?

Haseeb Oscar Niemeyer was a lifelong communist. He was invested in the question of what a communist architecture should look like. But defining this question stylistically and positively, identifying it so strongly with a set of formal manoeuvres, actually reduces its potency. It eliminates imagination. The potency of Niemeyer's work is its capacity to create moments of alienation between oneself and one's environment by breaking with vernacular architecture. This alienation opens space for reconstitution of subjectivity, but it only lasts for a short while until the work also becomes reduced to formalisation and vernacularisation. How can we distinguish, now, between Niemeyer's work and the string of corporate headquarters that surround most major airports? The city plan of Niemeyer's Brasília is shaped like an airplane, so perhaps he anticipated this relationship and prolonged the alienation that occurs through overdetermination. However, by identifying left-wing ideology with set forms, one is setting the stage for a false assumption that the form itself has the power to change people. Forms can produce certain kind of experiences, but they cannot enact ideological programmes. They are the product of ideologies rather than their instigators as they exist in historically specific contexts of time.

Caitlin That is why I think these sites offer possibilities to be occupied by new models of sociality, rather than representing social formations on their own. I had hoped this could be the strategy in Berlin, with the Palast der Republik [built 1973–76, demolished 2008] that the DDR built on top of the destroyed Berliner Stadtschloß [city palace]. Instead, the Palast der Republik was demolished amid controversy and is being replaced by a replica of the old Prussian palace. It was controversial, partly because the claims about asbestos and toxicity of the site were questionable, and partly due to the decision to replace it with a symbol of royal power. The Palast embodied the Soviet era in Germany and it was ideologically toxic to some, but whether or not it had to be torn down was debatable. I found the Palast to be horrifying and beautiful at the same time. I loved it. It had these copper-tinted windows and the reflective surfaces offered something different than the mirror reflections of glass: they were shiny and opaque, with an almost machinic bug-like body. I do not understand why the city could not find a way to occupy these histories without repeating them. If you learn to live with these husks, you can create new narratives for them. They could have started a new story for this building rather than demolishing it and substituting it with another defunct narrative of nostalgic value. I prefer a strategy of accumulating narratives in these spaces rather than attempting to delete them and pretend a fragment of history never existed.

Haseeb In my opinion, that would have been the smarter thing to do politically. The erasure antagonises the histories you mentioned while providing no way of addressing them, which the "husk", as you say, could do.

Caitlin Your work with wind tunnels explores how to model the ideal within defined conditions. The condition of a wind tunnel is a model environment within which to develop optimised forms that can be replicated with scientific methods. Architecture is pervaded by quests for ideal, optimised forms and by the quest for ideal conditions. Every time a developed form seems to meet the requirements of a particular set of conditions, it calls the parameters into question. Processes of replication and repetition can quickly become adaptive. Replication increases the potential and tendency for aberration, for pathological things to emerge – a kind of cancerous excess. It could be evolutionary or pathological, innovative or self-destructive.

Haseeb That is true. On the one hand, a wind tunnel is supposed to recreate an outside atmospheric reality, but on the other, that outside reality is understood primarily through the conditions modelled in the controlled wind tunnel. There is an intimate relationship between the test frame and the outside world; they are cocreating one another, but they are never going to be identical. It might be impossible for a wind tunnel to match the reality it is meant to model. However, one wind tunnel and another wind tunnel can be identically constructed. It then becomes possible to quite literally experience the same thing, outside of the infinite nuances of so-called reality.

Caitlin That is what is so interesting about pathology and aberrant replication. A utopian realm without porosity is a dictatorial and closed system. Ideals are not spaces, they are movements. They are fluid strategies that shift as they move through time. So ideals are not forms, but there is a critical formal question about how to create the conditions for those strategies to manifest when thinking about political future-making.

Haseeb Yes. A wind tunnel is used to study fluid dynamics, and as you say, it is a closed system. In a certain sense, it is necessary to standardise and simplify in order to understand complex systems of movement. Scale models of buildings and airplanes that are tested within wind tunnels shape industrially produced realities. However, the conditions of reproduction, not only production, should be questioned. For instance, wind tunnels are designed to create laminar flow — straight-moving air — in order to observe natural conditions. However, nowhere in nature does the wind blow straight. This redundancy created by the reliance on verifiability in the scientific method can be a liability and undermine its insights; it can allow for the recognition of multiple realities existing at once and how they may or may not interact with one another. But with architecture, how do you make sense of the fluidity and multiplicity of forces that occur in buildings? At the end of the day, buildings are different from people. You have to consider what a person can do that a building cannot. It is about having a type of intimacy that we all desire — that you are never alone. You are always with an entity; you are always with this building.

Caitlin I grew up in a big wooden house that was hand built out of rough-hewn, unfinished redwood in a redwood forest. It was like living in a tree. We could not touch the house because it would sting us with splinters, which would become infected from the natural resin in redwood that repels fire. And being a temperate rainforest, it was very damp. Everything was covered in mould, including me, covered in a fine hair of imperceptible mould that could only be noticed by its odour.

Haseeb The house was digesting you?

Caitlin Yes. And in turn, it was being digested by a number of insects: scorpions, termites, sow bugs, centipedes, millipedes, black ants, and carpenter ants. And mice. The scorpions were the worst. It was so quiet the redwood forest at night that you could hear the scorpions climbing up the walls of the house on their little arachnid legs.

Haseeb Scary!

Caitlin There is also the question of having an environment that anticipates your needs, rather than being able to project your desires into the construction of space. The soulless nature of much architecture derives from a kind of paternalistic, capitalist order. It presumes and anticipates a normative circuit of what your needs should be, the ways you are to circulate, keep moving, work, or take leisure. On the flip side of adaptability is design for control and violence.

One of the reasons why I chose to work with *Dhalgren* is because it involves strategies of experimentation and coexistence with other people. It has a story without plot. It is a novel that creates a world in itself, while simultaneously being a novel about worldmaking strategies. The suspension of time is another theme of the novel. The main character is unable to remember his own name. He has amnesia, experiences blackouts, and is generally unreliable when it comes to memory and time, both as a character and as a narrator. The reader is eventually led to question whether he is the narrator at all. There is also cultural amnesia about what catastrophe actually occurred in the city of Bellona to cause most people to abandon it. Only the poor people, megalomaniacs, and misfits have remained or moved in, scraping together a scene from the ashes.

All of this is accompanied by beautiful descriptions of what it means to move through space, to move through architecture, and the experience of time through a city.

Haseeb What I found interesting about Bellona is that it sounds as though the city is constantly undergoing its own destruction, and at the same time, it is not being renewed. He describes quite explicitly in this passage: "What makes it terrible is that in this timeless city, in this spaceless preserve where any slippage can occur, these closing walls, laced with fire-escapes, gates, and crenellations, are too unfixed to hold it in, so that, from me as a moving node, it seems to spread, by flood and seepage, over the whole uneasy scape. He had a momentary image of all these walls on pivots controlled by subterranean machines, so that, after he had passed, they might suddenly swing to face another direction, parting at this corner, joining at that one, like a great maze – forever adjustable, therefore unlearnable –". Samuel R. Delany, *Dhalgren* [1975], Vintage Books, New York, 2001, p. 382–83. There is a collapse of time and space, which means that there is no way to move outside of it because movement relies on speed, which is distance over time, and one is only able to move through time in Bellona. Conversely, if there is no aspect of time, one only has distance, and the city consumes the entirety of distance. I like that it describes this as terror. If *horror vacui* is the fear of empty space, this novel describes the opposite: a dread of the too full and the all-consuming.

Caitlin Yes, like being digested by your own house. There is also an attraction to emptiness that contains the possibility of presence. As well as the presence of absence. It does not have to be filled with anything in particular. It could also be filled with something that moves through it and disappears – a shifting occupancy, or as you were saying, a movement that exists over time, which goes back to the experience of nonchronological time or nonhistorical time in architecture. Including future speculations and retrofuturistic projections, like the condominiums at Potsdamer Platz that anticipated late twentieth-century dotcom dreams and the Soviet architecture of the Palast der Republik. Being with architecture is a way of being present with something that stretches beyond the present moment. I remember in another conversation we had, you said something about the condensation of time into space. It regarded your investigations into 3D printing the inversions of Islamic *muqarnas* [layered niches] and your work in taking moulds of parts of buildings all over the world, with your project *Has the World Already Been Made?* [2011–18].

Haseeb Indeed, architecture is not just architecture: it is ruin; it is the historical preservation of competing moments in time; it is everything around it. For this reason, I like the strategy of replication. One root of "replication" is *plico*, which means "to fold" [in Latin]. You can create a multiplicity out of a single entity by folding it up. When you fold a piece of paper, the two sides meet one another, and at that moment, there is replication.

Caitlin There is an uncanny quality to replication, too, the artificial feeling that no time has passed between now and then.

Haseeb Yes. Maybe something comes out of literally inhabiting the past: if you make an architectural replica at a 1:1 scale, then you are in it. You are experiencing the programmatic qualities of the past and not just as it has been received through textuality. Something I liked about *Dhalgren* was the way that he wrote about architecture, especially its disappearances. It is an architecture that exists on the page as literary architecture.

Caitlin *Dhalgren* is over 800 pages long. You have to be present with it because you forget where you were. Like you are saying, you have to become a moving node through the text. The plot is not like grid architecture that orients, so you immediately forget where you were just before. This is why I felt that the text was suited to what I wanted to do with the postcard images, because a book is itself a time-based medium as you move from page to page. The postcards imperfectly represent space and they are multiple.

Haseeb That is a point where I found the novel linked up with your postcards. This protagonist is an anonymous person and he is experiencing architecture in its passing. Which makes sense for the postcards, where you are having a kind of anonymous experience of an architecture you encountered in passing. Some of the photos I like the most are the blurred photos taken from a moving car. Typically, one sends a postcard to somebody else so that they can have an experience of a place they have not been themselves.

Caitlin These buildings exist like texts in space. They are concrete drawings against the sky, a conceptual architecture that is more linguistic than it is inhabitable.

Haseeb Rarely does a person just go to a building to confront the building itself. Usually, they have a list of things to do when visiting a city, and this list functions as a text introducing the buildings before the motion of entering and exiting them. Maybe that is why it is fitting that we are sitting in an airport. We are passing through this building that is only a portal. It is a building that only exists in a traveller's experience, in the moment of passing.

On 22 March 2016, the airport terminal in which this conversation had taken place a few months prior was bombed in an attack claimed by ISIS, killing 32 people and injuring over 300. The Belgian state reacted with extensive police raids within immigrant neighbourhoods in Brussels.

Your work is a funny way to experience a book, I have to say. It is a completely new experience of texts, which are scattered across multiple postcards, through passages and through conversations, as opposed to a linear, unbroken perusal. It is another model for reading. It is productive for me because I am trying to understand the wind tunnels in my own work as wormholes that reproduce the same thing across distance. For me, your postcards are producing something similar.

Caitlin There is another way that I like thinking about these buildings: as surface growths on a plane of the relationship between territory and capital.

Haseeb A lot of these notions in my work about time and space come out of a close reading of just one essay, György Lukács's "Reification and the Class Consciousness of the Proletariat" from the early 1920s. He is talking about how capitalism creates a collapse between space and time, and how that relates to ideas of credit and jurisprudence. It is almost one hundred years old, but it is pretty good.

Caitlin That is another thing I like about text: it only generates more text.

Haseeb Endless reading.

Caitlin Yeah, endless reading.

Haseeb Ahmed produces objects, site-specific installations, and films, and writes for various publications. Often working collaboratively, Ahmed integrates methodologies from the fields of science and technology into his art production. He received his PhD in practice-based arts from Universiteit Antwerpen and Sint Lucas Antwerpen, and his master's from the Art, Culture, and Technology programme at MIT. Ahmed has exhibited at the 15th Gwangju Biennale; Museum Bärengasse, Zurich; and de Appel, Amsterdam; among others. He is represented by Harlan Levey Projects and is an assistant professor at the University of Toronto.

Acknowledgements

The materialisation of this experiment as a book mirrored the protracted time of the built world it aims to explore. Throughout its fitful production, the work was touched by a beautiful assembly of people to whom I owe much gratitude. Many thanks to Randa Mirza, my partner in innocent crimes, whose wayward and queer photographic record of Beirut is a world of its own. To my admired interlocutors: Mirene Arsanios, Marwa Arsanios, Caleb Waldorf, Haseeb Ahmed, Marwan Abou Dib, and Franziska Pierwoss. To Suzy Halajian for the beautiful introduction, and for carrying forward with Noah Simblist the fervour for the Rashid Karami International Fair of Tripoli. To Samuel "Chip" Delany for building a world in *Dhalgren* that my imagination continues to inhabit, and for the generous permission to republish its fragments and refractions here. To those who supported *Unfinished State* in its many stages: Fotini Lazaridou-Hatzigoga, Melanie Sehgal, Nicola Guy, Ashkal Alwan, Imogen Heath, Omar Dewachi, Jules Gaffney, Tara Dominguez, Benji Mauer, Lauren Harrison Lentz, Anya Bitkina, and Gary Berrigan. I wish to offer much gratitude to those whose encouragement and patience helped me to persist and finalise this form despite seemingly insurmountable challenges. To Mika Hayashi Ebbesen for bringing new clarity, style, and virtuosic attention to detail. To Márcia Novais for the brilliant design. To Matthias Kliefoth and the warm team at DISTANZ for giving it a home among celebrated company. To the Graham Foundation for Advanced Studies in the Fine Arts and the Alexander von Humboldt-Stiftung for their enduring support. To Siska, Franziska, redeem ميدر, and our extended communities in and through Beirut and Berlin and Palestine, whose beautiful resistance to the violence of statecraft and ethnonationalisms is the future, is the past, is the continual now that insists upon being and creating worlds together.

Concept, photography, editing
Caitlin Berrigan

Editorial consultancy
Mika Hayashi Ebbesen

Graphic design
Márcia Novais

Proofreading
Mika Hayashi Ebbesen, Dan Koh

Typography
Knif by A is for, ABC Marist and
ABC Monument Grotesk by Dinamo

Printing, binding
Gráfica Maiadouro

All images by Caitlin Berrigan

Excerpts of *Dhalgren* by Samuel R.
Delany reproduced with permission
of the author

ISBN 978-3-95476-822-6

Legal Deposit 559839/26

Printed in Gráfica Maiadouro,
Portugal

Published by
DISTANZ Verlag
www.distanz.de
DISTANZ

Production of this publication
was made possible through
generous grants provided by the
Graham Foundation for Advanced
Studies in the Fine Arts and
the Alexander von Humboldt-
Stiftung, and through an artist
residency at Archive Books, Berlin.

Excerpts of *Unfinished State*
were previously published in
Architecture Is All Over, edited
by Esther Choi and Marrikka Trotter,
Columbia Books on Architecture
and the City, New York, 2017.

ontinual
ragments
f the Now

itlin
erigan

ANZ

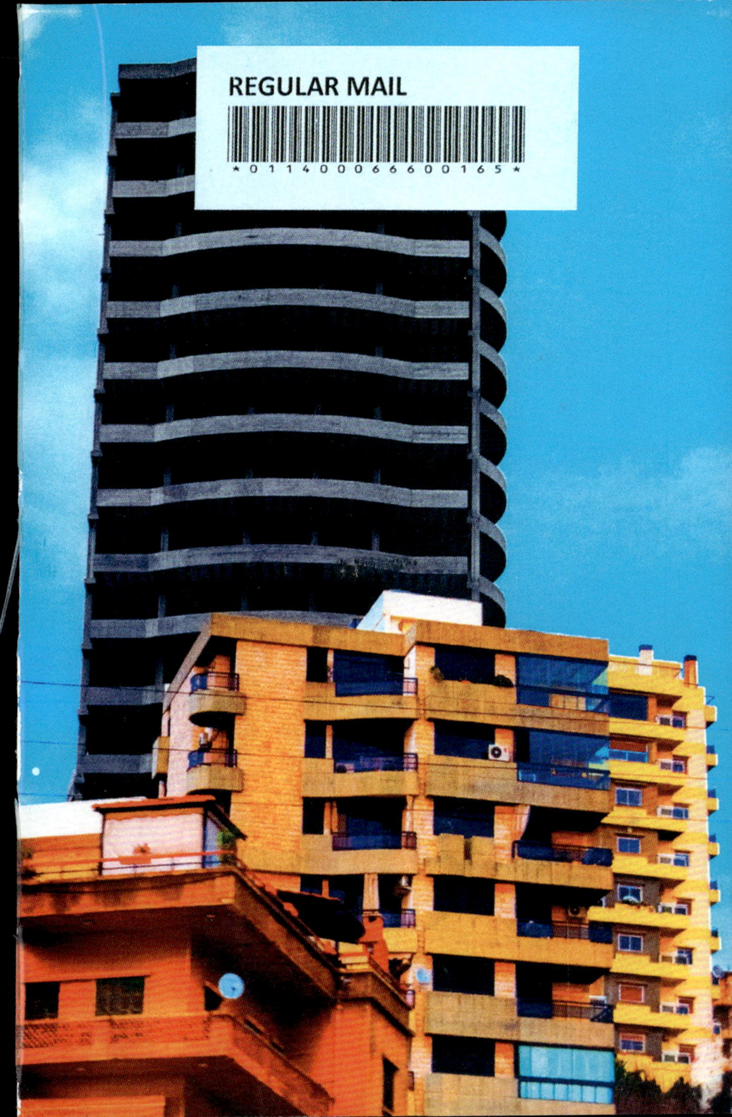
REGULAR MAIL
01140006600165

SHADOW FOR CEILING, NEXT STEP.

BEYOND A DEAD LIMB, A DISH OF BRASS WIDE AS A CAR TIRE HAD NEARLY BURNED TO EMBERS. SOMETHING IN THE REMAINING FIRE SNAPPED, SPILLING SPARKS ON WET STONE.

AHEAD, WHERE THE FLICKER LEAKED HIGH UP INTO THE NARROWING SLASH, SOMETHING CAUGHT AND FLUNG BACK FLASHINGS.

HE CLIMBED AROUND ONE BOULDER, PAUSED; THE ECHO FROM BREATH AND BURNING CAST UP INTIMATIONS OF THE CAVERN'S SIZE. HE GAUGED A CREVICE, LEAPED THE METER, AND SCRAMBLED ON THE FAR SLOPE. THINGS LOOSENED UNDER HIS FEET. HE HEARD PEBBLES IN THE GASH COMPLAINING DOWN ROCKS, AND STUTTERING, AND WHISPERING—AND SILENCE.

THEN: A SPLASH!

HE PULLED IN HIS SHOULDERS; HE HAD ASSUMED IT WAS ONLY A YARD OR SO DEEP.

HE HAD TO CLIMB A LONG TIME. ONE FACE, FIFTEEN FEET HIGH, STOPPED HIM A WHILE. HE WENT TO THE SIDE AND CLAMBERED UP THE MORE UNEVEN OUTCROPPINGS. HE FOUND A THICK RIDGE THAT, HE REALIZED AS HE PULLED HIMSELF UP IT, WAS A ROOT. HE WONDERED WHAT IT WAS A ROOT TO, AND GAINED THE LEDGE.

SOMETHING WENT EEEK! SOFTLY, SIX INCHES FROM HIS NOSE, AND SCURRIED OFF AMONG OLD

UNFINISHED STATE // 1D.012

FROM: WILLIAM DHALGREN
ARCHIVE BOOKS
DIEFFENBACHSTRAßE 31
10967 BERLIN, GERMANY

TO:

THE UNFINISHED HIGH RISE

SEA SIDE RD., SOUTH EAST SIDE

ANTELIAS

LEBANON

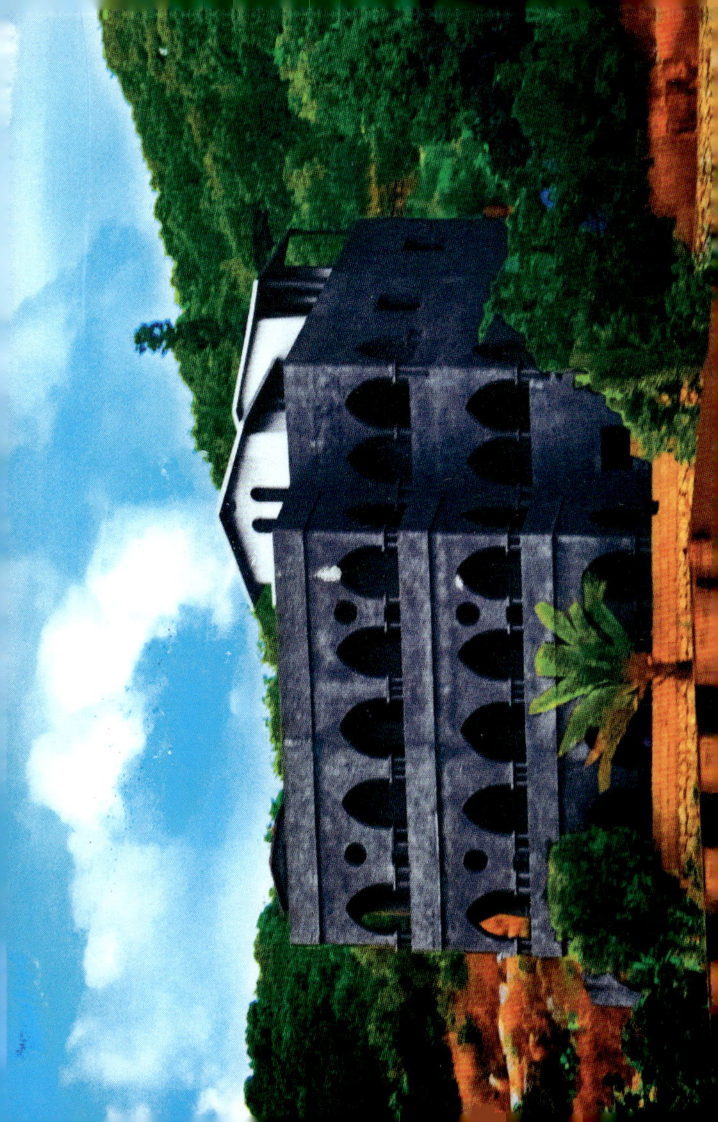

WAS OPAQUE. TILTING IT, HE SAW PASS, DIM AND INCHES DISTANT IN THE CIRCLE, HIS OWN EYE, QUIVERING IN THE QUIVERING GLASS.

EVERYTHING WAS QUIET.

HE PULLED THE CHAIN ACROSS HIS HAND. THE RANDOM ARRANGEMENT WENT ALMOST NINE FEET. ACTUALLY, THREE LENGTHS WERE ATTACHED. EACH OF THE THREE ENDS LOOPED ON ITSELF. ON THE LARGEST LOOP WAS A SMALL METAL TAG.

HE STOOPED FOR MORE LIGHT.

THE CENTIMETER OF BRASS (THE LINKS BRADDED INTO THE OPTICAL BITS WERE BRASS) WAS INSCRIBED: PRODUCTO DO BRAZIL. HE THOUGHT: WHAT THE HELL KIND OF PORTUGUESE IS THAT?

HE CROUCHED A MOMENT LONGER LOOKING ALONG THE GLITTERING LINES.

HE TRIED TO PULL IT ALL TOGETHER FOR HIS JEAN POCKET, BUT THE THREE TANGLED YARDS SPILLED HIS PALMS. STANDING, HE FOUND THE LARGEST LOOP AND LOWERED HIS HEAD. POINTS AND EDGES NIPPED HIS NECK. HE GOT THE TINY RINGS TOGETHER UNDER HIS CHIN AND FINGERED (THINKING: LIKE DAMNED CLUBS) THE CATCH CLOSED.

HE LOOKED AT THE CHAIN IN LOOPS OF LIGHT BETWEEN HIS FEET. HE PICKED UP THE SHORTEST

UNFINISHED STATE // 1D.014

Schützt die Natur

WWF

www.wwf.de

50 Jahre Fehmarnsundbrücke

Deutschland

75

FROM: ~~WILLIAM DHALGREN~~
~~ARCHIVE BOOKS~~
~~DIEFFENBACHSTRAßE 31~~
~~10967 BERLIN, GERMANY~~

TO:

TIERED ARCADE BUILDING

ON THE HILL ABOVE SEA SIDE RD.

ZELHMAYA

LEBANON

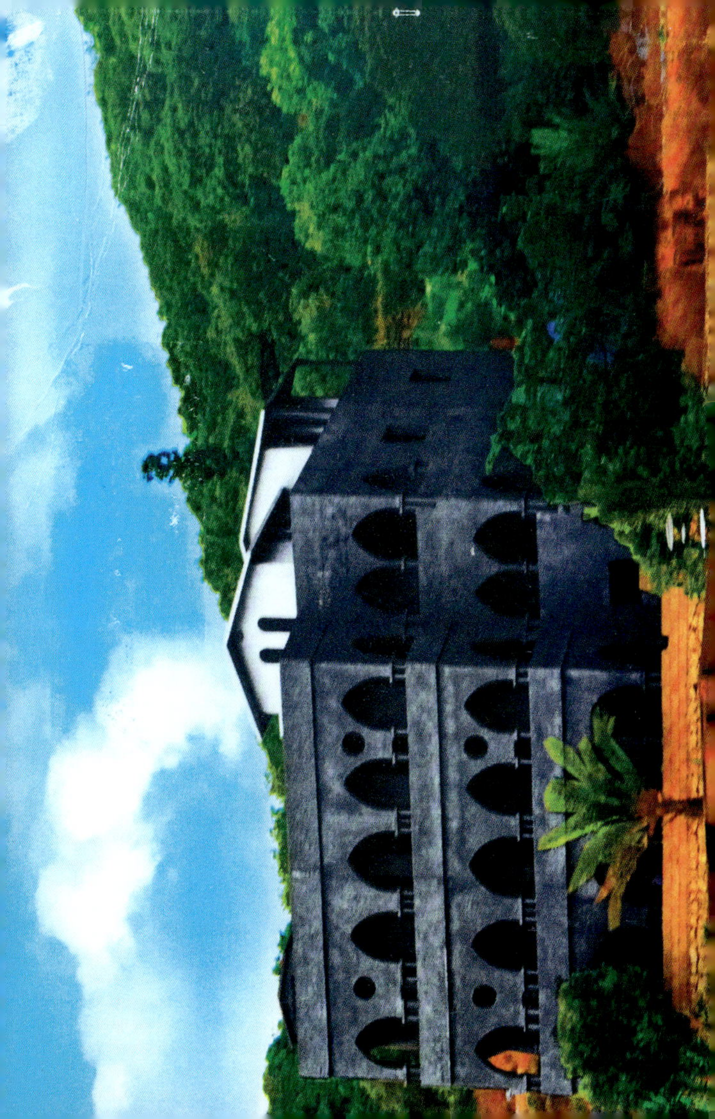

END FROM HIS THIGH. THE LOOP THERE WAS SMALLER.

HE WAITED, HELD HIS BREATH EVEN—THEN WRAPPED THE LENGTH TWICE AROUND HIS UPPER ARM, TWICE AROUND HIS LOWER, AND FASTENED THE CATCH AT HIS WRIST. HE FLATTENED HIS PALM ON THE LINKS AND BAUBLES HARD AS PLASTIC OR METAL. CHEST HAIR TICKLED THE CREASING BETWEEN JOINT AND JOINT.

HE PASSED THE LONGEST END AROUND HIS BACK: THE BITS LAY OUT COLD KISSES ON HIS SHOULDER BLADES. THEN ACROSS HIS CHEST; HIS BACK ONCE MORE; HIS BELLY. HOLDING THE LENGTH IN ONE HAND (IT STILL HUNG DOWN ON THE STONE), HE UNFASTENED HIS BELT WITH THE OTHER.

PANTS AROUND HIS ANKLES, HE WOUND THE FINAL LENGTH ONCE AROUND HIS HIPS; AND THEN AROUND HIS RIGHT THIGH; AGAIN AROUND; AND AGAIN. HE FASTENED THE LAST CATCH AT HIS ANKLE. PULLING UP HIS TROUSERS, HE WENT TO THE LEDGE, BUCKLED THEM, AND TURNED TO CLIMB DOWN.

HE WAS AWARE OF THE BINDINGS. BUT, CHEST FLAT ON THE STONE, THEY WERE MERELY LINES AND DID NOT CUT.

THIS TIME HE WENT TO WHERE THE CREVICE WAS ONLY A FOOT WIDE AND STEPPED FAR OF

UNFINISHED STATE // 1D.015

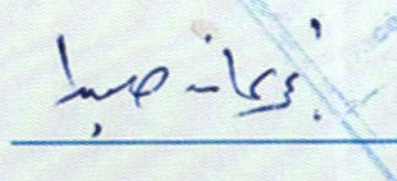

FROM: WILLIAM DHALGREN
ARCHIVE BOOKS
DIEFFENBACHSTRAßE 31
10967 BERLIN, GERMANY

TO:

TIERED ARCADE BUILDING

ON THE HILL ABOVE SEA SIDE RD.

زلحمايا، ZELHMAYA

LEBANON

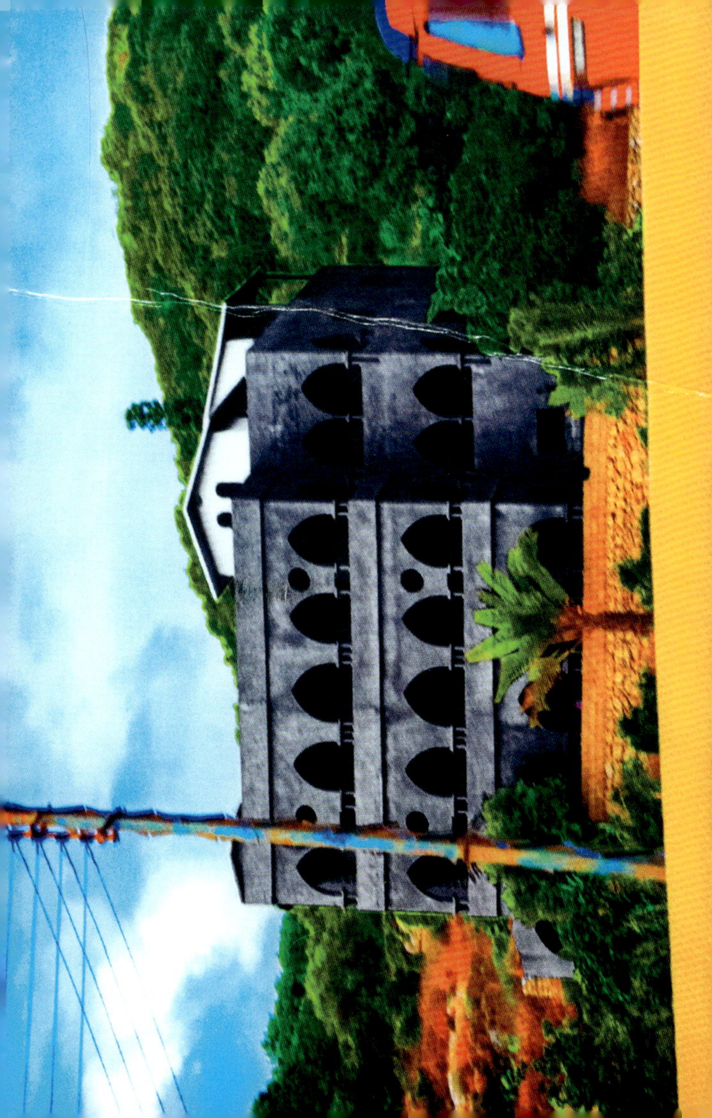

INTO MUD. HIS BARE ONE SWUNG TO THE GRAVELED SHOULDER. HE STAGGERED OUT ON THE ASPHALT, ONE FOOT SLIDING ON FLOODED LEATHER, TOOK A HISSING BREATH, AND GAZED AROUND.

LEFT, THE ROAD SLOPED UP BETWEEN THE TREES. HE STARTED RIGHT. DOWNWARD WOULD TAKE HIM TOWARD THE CITY.

ON ONE SIDE WAS FOREST. ON THE OTHER, HE REALIZED AFTER A DOZEN SLIPPERY JOGS, IT WAS ONLY A HEDGE OF TREES. TREES DROPPED AWAY WITH ANOTHER DOZEN. BEHIND, THE GRASS WHISPERED AND SHUSHED HIM.

SHE WAS STANDING AT THE MEADOW'S CENTER.

HE BROUGHT HIS FEET—ONE STRAPPED AND MUDDY, ONE BARE AND DUSTY—TOGETHER; SUDDENLY FELT HIS HEART BEATING; HEARD HIS SURPRISED BREATH SHUSH THE GRASS BACK. HE STEPPED ACROSS THE DITCH TO ILL-MOWED STUBBLE.

SHE'S TOO TALL, HE THOUGHT, NEARING.

HAIR LIFTED FROM HER SHOULDERS; GRASS WHISPERED AGAIN.

SHE HAD BEEN TALLER THAN HE WAS, BUT NOT LIKE... "HEY, I GOT THE... I" SHE WAS HOLDING HER ARMS OVER HER HEAD. WAS SHE STANDING ON SOME STUMPY PEDESTAL? "HEY...?"

SHE TWISTED FROM THE WAIST: "WHAT THE HELL

Return / Retour CN 15
Inconnu à l'adresse indiquée / Unknown at this address
Déménagé sans laisser d'adresse / Moved without leaving an address
Adresse insuffisante pour la distribution / Insufficient address for delivery
Nom s'applique à plusieurs personnes / Duplicate addressee names
Refusé / Refused
Destinataire n'est pas présent / Addressee not present
Personne n'est à l'adresse / No one available at the address
Décédé / Deceased / متوفى
مركز بيروت للفرز

UNFINISHED STATE / 1D.017

FROM: WILLIAM DHALGREN
ARCHIVE BOOKS
DIEFFENBACHSTRAßE 31
10967 BERLIN, GERMANY

TO:
TIERED ARCADE BUILDING
ON THE HILL ABOVE SEA SIDE RD.
ZELHMAYA
LEBANON

Deutschland 75
50 Jahre Fehmarnsundbrücke

Schützt die Natur

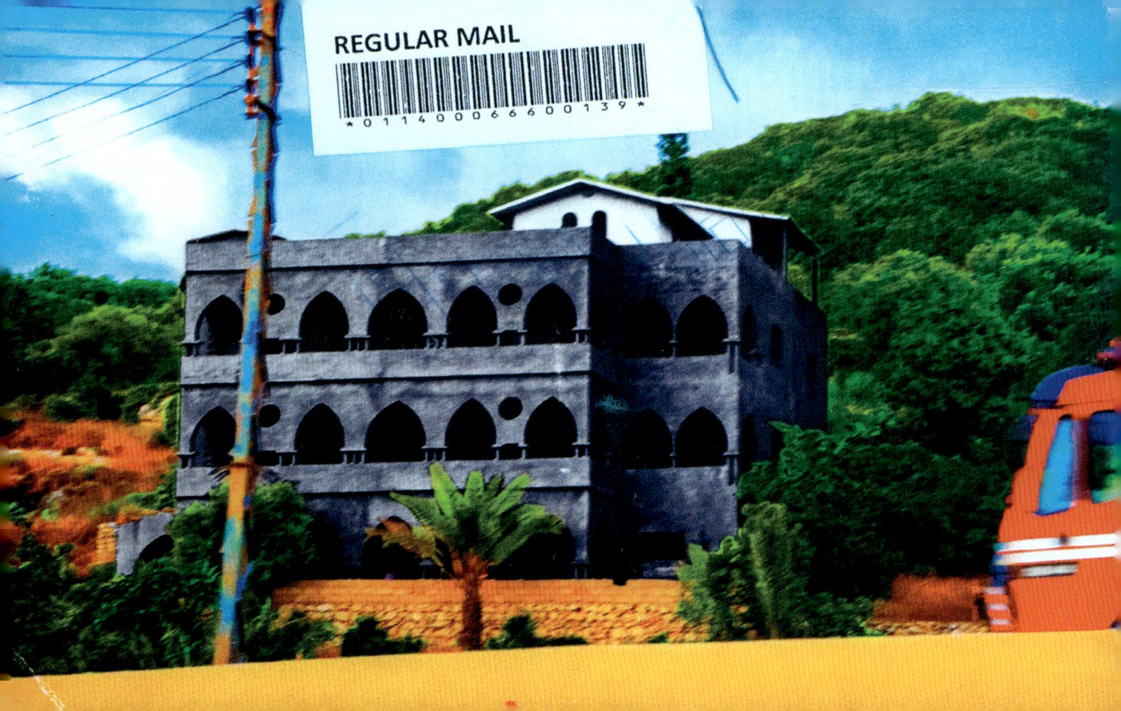
REGULAR MAIL
01140006600139

ARE YOU DOING HERE?"

AT FIRST HE THOUGHT SHE WAS SPLATTERED WITH MUD ALL UP HER THIGH. "I THOUGHT YOU...?" BUT IT WAS BROWN AS DRIED BLOOD.

SHE GAZED DOWN AT HIM WITH BATTING EYES.

MUD? BLOOD? IT WAS THE WRONG COLOR FOR EITHER.

"GO AWAY!"

HE TOOK ANOTHER, ENTRANCED STEP.

"WHAT ARE YOU DOING HERE? GO AWAY!"

WERE THE BLOTCHES UNDER HER BREASTS SCABS? "LOOK, I GOT IT! NOW, CAN'T YOU TELL ME MY...?"

LEAVES WERE CLUTCHED IN HER RAISED HANDS. HER HANDS WERE RAISED SO HIGH! LEAVES DROPPED ABOUT HER SHOULDERS. HER LONG, LONG FINGERS SHOOK, AND BRITTLE DARKNESS COVERED ONE FLANK. HER PALE BELLY JERKED WITH A BREATH.

"NO!" SHE BENT AWAY WHEN HE TRIED TO TOUCH HER; AND STAYED BENT. ONE ARM, BRANCHED AND BRANCHING TEN FEET OVER HIM, PULLED A WEB OF SHADOW-ACROSS THE GRASS.

"YOU...!" WAS THE WORD HE TRIED; BREATH WAS ALL THAT CAME.

HE LOOKED UP AMONG THE TWIGS OF HER EARS. LEAVES SHUCKED FROM HER EYEBROWS. HER MOUTH WAS A THICK, TWISTED BOLE, AS

UNFINISHED STATE // 1D.018

FROM: WILLIAM DHALGREN
ARCHIVE BOOKS
DIEFFENBACHSTRAßE 31
10967 BERLIN, GERMANY

TO:

TIERED ARCADE BUILDING

ON THE HILL ABOVE SEA SIDE RD.

ZELHMAYA

LEBANON

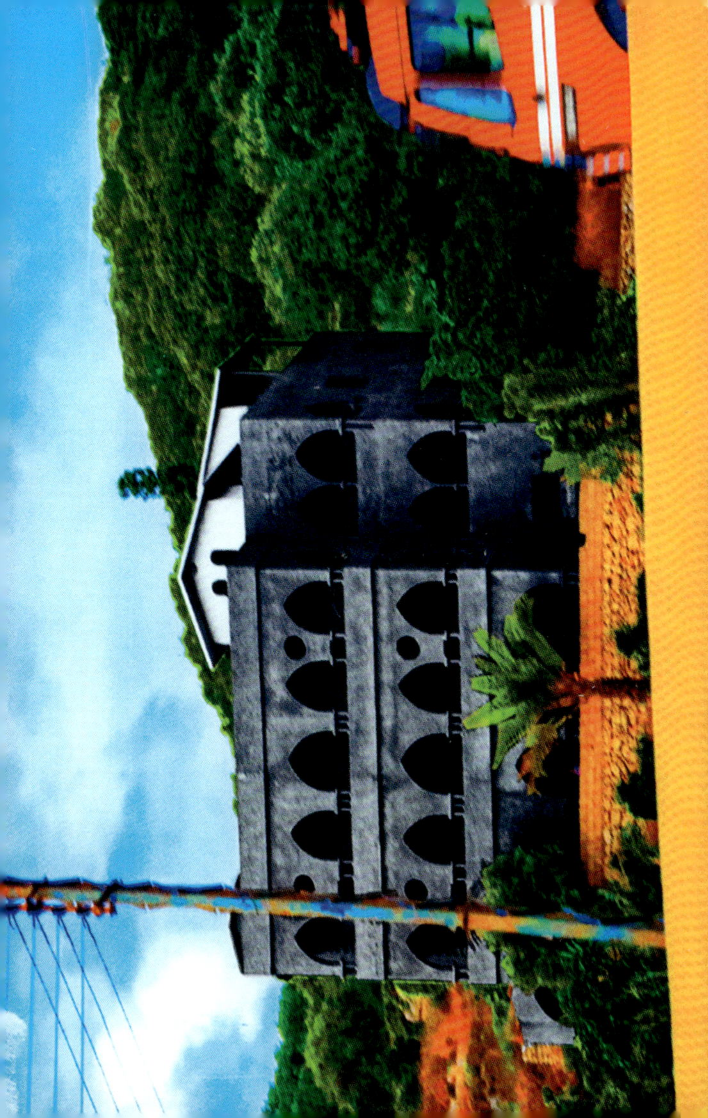

THOUGH SOME FOOTWIDE BRANCH HAD BEEN LOPPED OFF BY LIGHTNING. HER EYES—HIS MOUTH OPENED AS HE CRANED TO SEE THEM—DISAPPEARED, FIRST ONE, UP THERE, THEN THE OTHER, WAY OVER THERE: SCABBY LIDS SEALED.

HE BACKED THROUGH STIFF GRASS.

A LEAF CRASHED HIS TEMPLE LIKE A CHARRED MOTH.

ROUGH FINGERS BLUDGEONING HIS LIPS, HE STUMBLED, TURNED, RAN TO THE ROAD, GLANCED ONCE MORE WHERE THE TWISTED TRUNK RAKED FIVE BRANCHES AT THE MOON, LOPED UNTIL HE HAD TO WALK, WALKED—GASPING—UNTIL HE COULD THINK. THEN HE RAN SOME MORE.

IT IS NOT THAT I HAVE NO PAST. RATHER, IT CONTINUALLY FRAGMENTS ON THE TERRIBLE AND VIVID EPHEMERA OF NOW. IN THE LONG COUNTRY, CUT WITH RAIN, SOMEHOW THERE IS NOWHERE TO BEGIN. LOPING AND LIMPING IN THE RUTS, IT WOULD BE EASIER NOT TO THINK ABOUT WHAT SHE DID (WAS DONE TO HER, DONE TO HER, DONE), TRYING INSTEAD TO RECONSTRUCT WHAT IT IS AT A DISTANCE. OH, BUT IT WOULD NOT BE SO TERRIBLE HAD ONE CALF, NOT BORNE (IF I'D LOOKED CLOSE, IT WOULD HAVE BEEN A CHAIN OF TINY WOUNDS WITH MOMENTS OF FLESH BETWEEN;

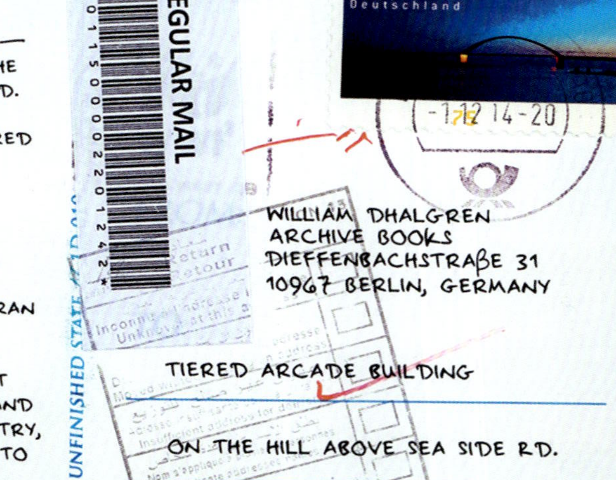

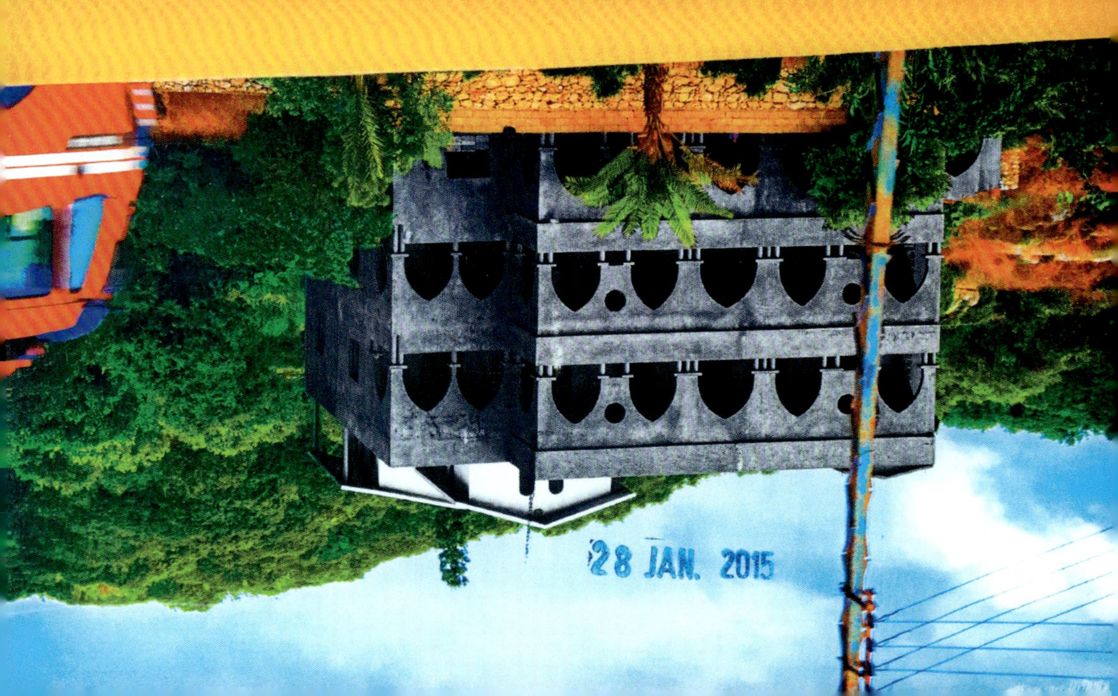
28 JAN. 2015

I'VE DONE THAT MYSELF WITH A SWIPE IN A GARDEN PAST A ROSE) THAT SCRATCH.

THE ASPHALT SPILLED HIM ONTO THE HIGHWAY'S SHOULDER. THE PAVING'S CHIPPED EDGES FILED VISIONS OFF HIS EYES. A ROAR CAME TOWARD HIM HE HEARD ONLY AS IT PASSED. HE GLANCED BACK: THE TRUCK'S RED, REAR EYES SANK TOGETHER. HE WALKED FOR ANOTHER HOUR, SAW NO OTHER VEHICLE.

A MACK WITH A DOUBLE VAN BELCHED TWENTY FEET BEHIND HIM, SAGGED TO A STOP TWENTY FEET AHEAD. HE HADN'T EVEN BEEN THUMBING. HE SPRINTED TOWARD THE OPENING DOOR, HAULED HIMSELF UP, SLAMMED IT. THE DRIVER, TALL, BLOND, AND ACNED, LOOKING BLANK, RELEASED THE CLUTCH.

HE WAS GOING TO SAY THANKS, BUT COUGHED. MAYBE THE DRIVER WANTED SOMEBODY TO RAP AT? WHY ELSE STOP FOR SOMEONE JUST WALKING THE ROAD!

HE DIDN'T FEEL LIKE RAPPING. BUT YOU HAVE TO SAY SOMETHING:

"WHAT YOU LOADING?"

"ARTICHOKES."

APPROACHING LIGHTS SPILLED PIT TO PIT IN THE DRIVER'S FACE.

THEY SHOOK ON DOWN THE HIGHWAY.

HE COULD THINK OF NOTHING MORE, EXCEPT:

UNFINISHED

Deutschland

50 Jahre Fehmarnsundbrücke

WILLIAM DHALGREN
ARCHIVE BOOKS
DIEFFENBACHSTRAẞE 31
10967 BERLIN, GERMANY

TIERED ARCADE BUILDING

ON THE HILL ABOVE SEA SIDE RD.

ZELHMAYA

LEBANON

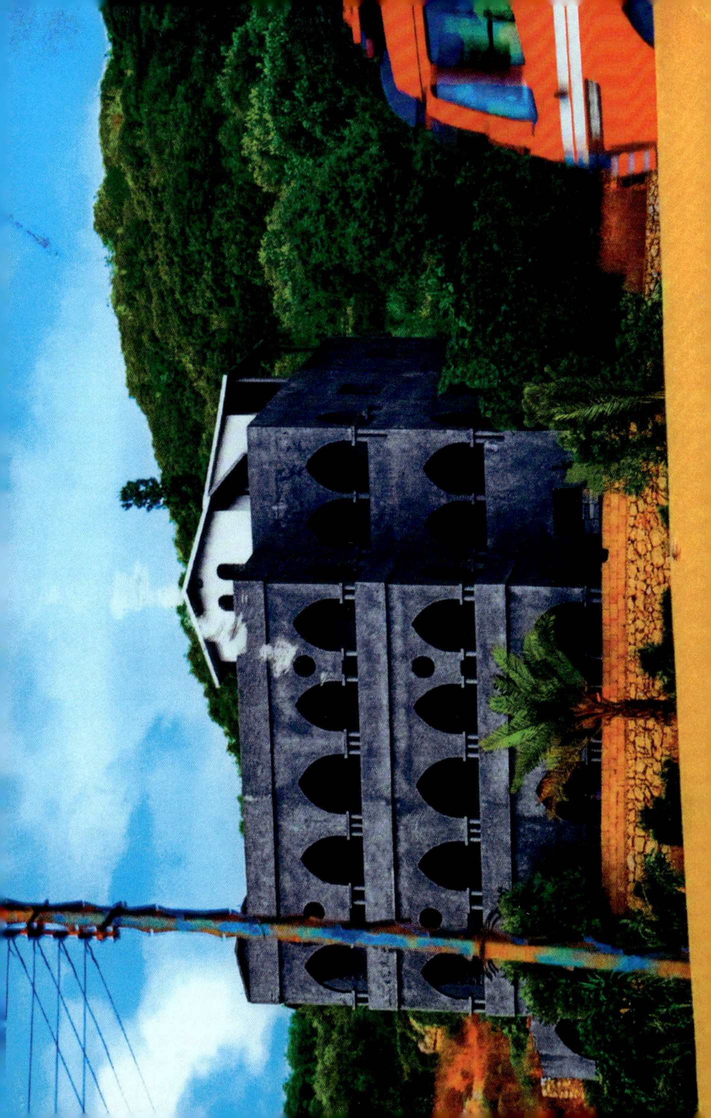

I WAS JUST MAKING LOVE TO THIS WOMAN, SEE, AND YOU'LL NEVER GUESS... NO, THE DAPHNE BIT WOULD NOT PASS—

IT WAS HE WHO WANTED TO TALK! THE DRIVER WAS CONTENT TO DISPENSE WITH PHATIC THANKS AND CHATTER. WESTERN INDEPENDENCE. HE HAD HITCHED THIS SECTOR OF COUNTRY ENOUGH TO DECIDE IT WAS ALL MANIC TERROR.

HE LEANED HIS HEAD BACK. HE WANTED TO TALK AND HAD NOTHING TO SAY.

FEAR PAST, THE ARCHNESS OF IT FORCED THE ARCHITECTURE OF A SMILE HIS LIPS [illegible].

HE SAW THE RANKED HIGHWAY LIGHTS [illegible] MINUTES LATER AND SAT FORWARD TO SEE THE TURNOFF. HE GLANCED AT THE DRIVER WHO WAS JUST GLANCING AWAY. THE BRAKES [illegible] AND THE CAB SLOWED BY LURCHES.

THEY STOPPED. THE DRIVER SUCKED IN THE SIDES OF HIS MINED CHEEKS, LOOKED OVER, STILL BLANK.

HE NODDED, SORT OF SMILED, FUMBLED THE DOOR, DROPPED TO THE ROAD; THE DOOR SLAMMED ARID THE TRUCK STARTED WHILE HE WAS STILL PREPARING THANKS; HE HAD TO DUCK THE VAN CORNER.

THE VEHICLE GRUMBLED DOWN THE TURNOFF. WE ONLY SPOKE A LINE APIECE.

WHAT AN ODD RITUAL EXCHANGE TO EXHAUST.

50 Jahre Fehmarnsundbrücke

Deutschland 75

REGULAR MAIL

* 0 [illegible] 0 0 6 8 4 0 0 0 1 3 *

WILLIAM DHALGREN
ARCHIVE BOOKS
DIEFFENBACHSTRAẞE 31
10967 BERLIN, GERMANY

TIERED ARCADE BUILDING

ON THE HILL ABOVE SEA SIDE RD.

Anschrift überprüft durch Deutsche Post / BZ 10 /G

ZURÜCK:

10967

CN 18

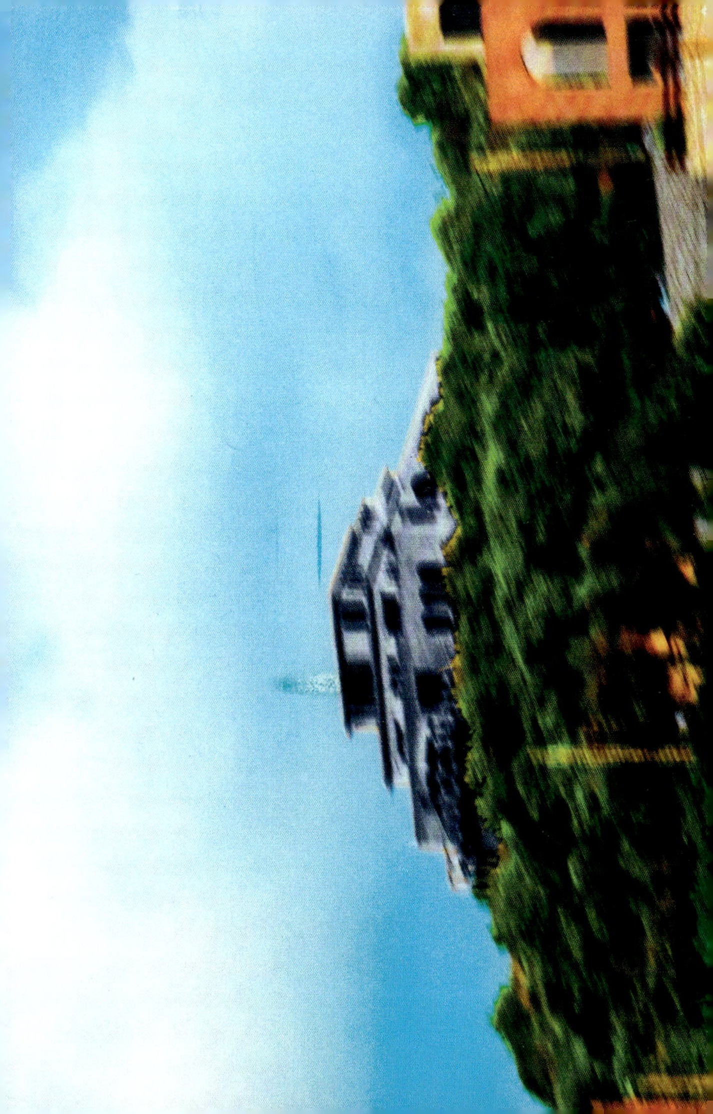

COMMUNICATION. (IS THAT TERROR?) WHAT AMAZING AND ENGAGING RITUALS ARE WE PRACTICING NOW? (HE STOOD ON THE ROAD SIDE, LAUGHING.) WHAT TORQUE AND TENSION IN THE MOUTH TO LAUGH SO IN THIS WINDY, WINDY, WINDY...

UNDERPASS AND OVERPASS KNOTTED HERE. HE WALKED... PROUDLY? YES, PROUDLY BY THE LOW WALL. ACROSS THE WATER THE CITY FLICKERED. ON ITS DOCKFRONT, DOWN HALF A MILE, FLAMED ROILED SMOKE ON THE SKY AND REFLECTIONS ON THE RIVER. HERE, NOT ONE CAR CAME OFF THE BRIDGE. NOT ONE WENT ON.

THIS TOLL BOOTH, LIKE THE RANK OF BOOTHS, WAS DARK. HE STEPPED INSIDE: FRONT PANE SHATTERED, STOOL OVERTURNED, NO DRAWER IN THE REGISTER—A THIRD OF THE KEYS STUCK DOWN; A FEW BENT. SOME WERE MISSING THEIR HEADS. SMASHED BY A MACE, A MALLET, A FIST? HE DRAGGED HIS FINGERS ACROSS THEM, LISTENED TO THEM CLICK, THEN STEPPED FROM THE GLASS-FLECKED, RUBBER MAT, OVER THE SILL TO THE PAVEMENT.

METAL STEPS LED UP TO THE PEDESTRIAN WALKWAY. BUT SINCE THERE WAS NO TRAFFIC, HE SAUNTERED ACROSS TWO EMPTY LANES—A METAL GRID SUNK IN THE BLACKTOP GLEAMED WHERE TIRES HAD POLISHED IT—TO AMBLE THE

UNFINISHED STATE // 1D.022

50 Jahre Fehmarnsundbrücke
Deutschland

FROM: WILLIAM DHALGREN
ARCHIVE BOOKS
DIEFFENBACHSTRAßE 31
10967 BERLIN, GERMANY

TO:
SKINNY ARCADE BUILDING
OVERLOOKING HALAT SUR MER
BEIT AL BOUME
LEBANON

Empfänger/Firma unter der angegebenen Anschrift nicht zu ermitteln.
Empfänger verzogen.
Einwilligung zur Weitergabe der neuen Anschrift liegt nicht vor.
Annahme verweigert.

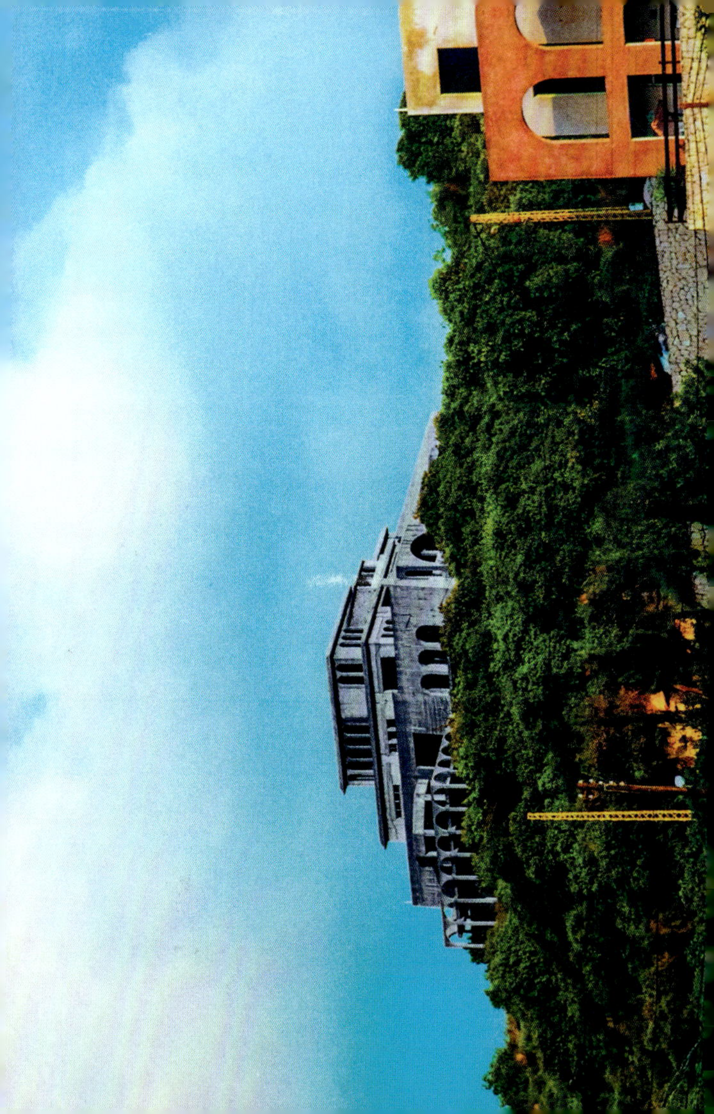

BROKEN WHITE LINE, SANDALED FOOT ONE SIDE, BARE FOOT THE OTHER. GIRDERS WHEELED BY HIM, LEFT AND RIGHT. BEYOND, THE BURNING CITY SQUATTED ON WEAK, INVERTED IMAGES OF ITS FIRES.

HE GAZED ACROSS THE WALE OF NIGHT WATER, ALL WIND-RUNNELED, AND SNIFFED FOR BURNING. A GUST PARTED THE HAIR AT THE BACK OF HIS NECK; SMOKE WAS MOVING OFF THE RIVER.

"HEY, YOU!"

HE LOOKED UP AT THE SURPRISING FLASHLIGHT. "HUH...?" AT THE WALKWAY RAIL, ANOTHER AND ANOTHER PUNCTURED THE DARK.

"YOU GOING INTO BELLONA?"

"THAT'S RIGHT." SQUINTING, HE TRIED TO SMILE. ONE, AND ANOTHER, THE LIGHTS MOVED A FEW STEPS, STOPPED. HE SAID: "YOU'RE... LEAVING?"

"YEAH. YOU KNOW IT'S RESTRICTED IN THERE."

HE NODDED. "BUT I HAVEN'T SEEN ANY SOLDIERS OR POLICE OR ANYTHING. I JUST HITCH-HIKED DOWN."

"HOW WERE THE RIDES?"

"ALL I SAW WAS TWO TRUCKS FOR THE LAST TWENTY MILES. THE SECOND ONE GAVE ME A LIFT."

"WHAT ABOUT THE TRAFFIC GOING OUT?"

HE SHRUGGED. "BUT I GUESS GIRLS SHOULDN'T

UNFINISHED STATE // 1D.023

Schützt die Natur. WWF www.wwf.de Schützt die Natur

50 Jahre Fehmarnsundbrücke
Deutschland 75

FROM: WILLIAM DHALGREN
ARCHIVE BOOKS
DIEFFENBACHSTRAßE 31
10967 BERLIN, GERMANY

TO:

SKINNY ARCADE BUILDING

OVERLOOKING HALAT SUR MER

BEIT AL BOUME

LEBANON

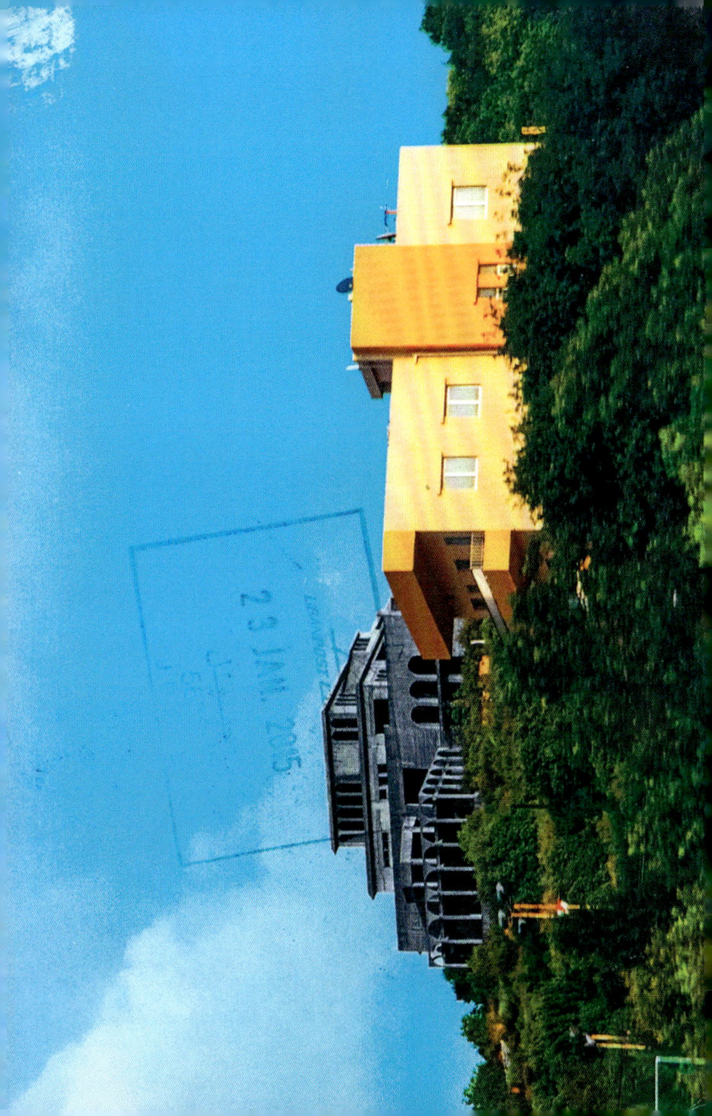

HAVE TOO HARD A TIME, THOUGH.
A CAR PASSES, YOU'LL PROBABLY G
WHERE YOU HEADING?"
"TWO OF US WANT TO GET TO A
JUDY WANTS TO GO TO SAN FRANC
"I JUST WANT TO GET SOME PLA
VOICE CAME DOWN. "I'VE GOT A FI
BE IN BED. I WAS IN BED FOR THE
DAYS."
HE SAID: "YOU'VE GOT A WAYS TO
DIRECTION."
"NOTHING'S HAPPENED TO SAN FR
"—OR NEW YORK?"
"NO." HE TRIED TO SEE BEHIND TH
"THE PAPERS DON'T EVEN TALK ABO
HAPPENING HERE, ANY MORE."
"BUT, JESUS! WHAT ABOUT THE TE
THE RADIO—"
"STUPID, NONE OF IT WORKS OUT
HOW ARE THEY GONNA KNOW?"
"BUT—OH, WOW...!"
HE SAID: "THE NEARER YOU GET,
LESS AND LESS PEOPLE. AND THE ON
ARE... FUNNIER. WHAT'S IT LIKE INSID
ONE LAUGHED.
ANOTHER SAID: "IT'S PRETTY ROUG
THE ONE WHO'D SPOKEN FIRST SAI
YOU SAY, GIRLS HAVE AN EASIER TIME
01150000450164I
REGULAR MAIL
50 Jahre Fehmarnsundbrücke
Deutschland
75
Schützt die Natur
CN
Return
WILLIAM DHALGREN
ARCHIVE BOOKS
DIEFFENBACHSTRAßE 31
10967 BERLIN, GERMANY
Inconnu / Unknown
Déménagé sans laisser d'adresse / Moved without leaving address
Insuffisance d'adresse / Insufficient address for delivery
Duplicate addresse
Refusé / Refused
Destinataire n'est pas présent / Addressee not present
Personne n'est à l'adresse / No one at the address
Décédé / Deceased
LIBANPOST
KINNY ARCADE BUILDING
RLOOKING HALAT SUR MER
BEIT AL BOUME
LEBANON
مرفوض
متوفى
كتب بريد

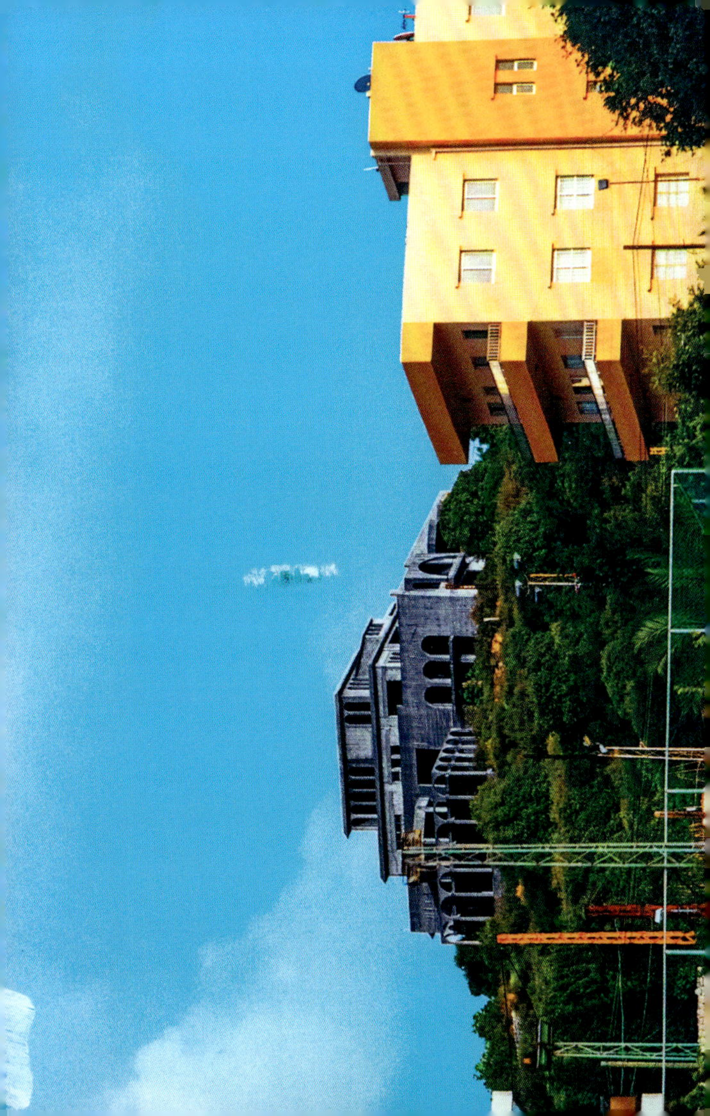

THEY LAUGHED.

HE DID TOO. "IS THERE ANYTHING YOU CAN TELL ME? I MEAN THAT MIGHT BE HELPFUL? SINCE I'M GOING IN?"

"YEAH. SOME MEN CAME BY, SHOT UP THE HOUSE WE WERE LIVING IN, TORE UP THE PLACE, THEN BURNED US OUT."

"SHE WAS MAKING THIS SCULPTURE," THE WHINY VOICE EXPLAINED; "THIS BIG SCULPTURE. OF A LION. OUT OF JUNK METAL AND STUFF. IT WAS BEAUTIFUL...! BUT SHE HAD TO LEAVE IT."

"WOW," HE SAID. "IS IT LIKE THAT?"

ONE SHORT, HARD LAUGH: "YEAH. WE GOT IT REAL EASY."

"TELL HIM ABOUT CALKINS? OR THE SCORPIONS?"

"HE'LL LEARN ABOUT THEM." ANOTHER LAUGH. "WHAT CAN YOU SAY?"

"YOU WANT A WEAPON TO TAKE IN WITH YOU?"

THAT MADE HIM AFRAID AGAIN. "DO I NEED ONE?"

BUT THEY WERE TALKING AMONG THEMSELVES:

"YOU'RE GONNA GIVE HIM THAT?"

"YEAH, WHY NOT? I DON'T WANT IT WITH ME ANY MORE."

"WELL, OKAY. IT'S YOURS."

METAL SOUNDED ON CHAIN, WHILE ONE ASKED: "WHERE YOU FROM?" THE FLASHLIGHTS TURNED

50 Jahre Fehmarnsundbrücke

Deutschland

-1.12.14-20

1D.025

FROM: WILLIAM DHALGREN
ARCHIVE BOOKS
DIEFFENBACHSTRAßE 31
10967 BERLIN, GERMANY

Absender

Adresse!

REGULAR MAIL

01140006840042 8

...LINNY ARCADE BUILDING

...LOOKING HALAT SUR MER

BEIT AL BOUME

LEBANON

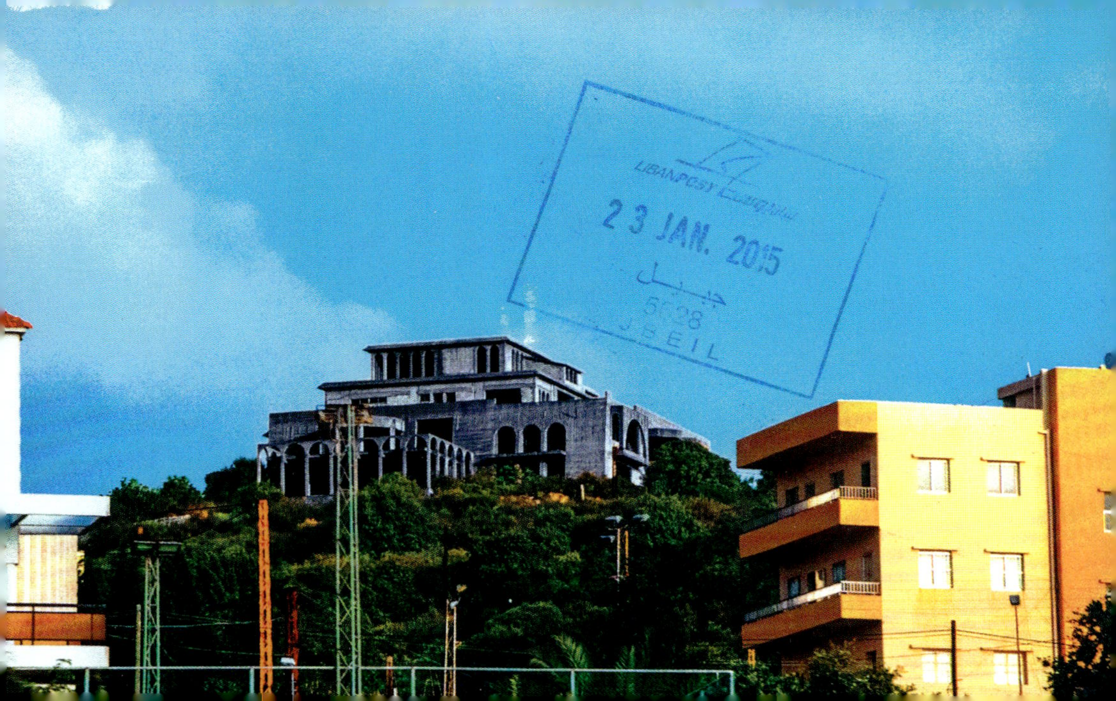
LIBANPOST
23 JAN. 2015
جبيل
JBEIL

AWAY, GHOSTING THE GROUP. O
NEAR THE RAIL WAS MOMENTARII
ENOUGH TO SEE SHE WAS VERY
BLACK, AND VERY PREGNANT.
"UP FROM THE SOUTH."
"YOU DON'T SOUND LIKE YOU'
SOUTH," ONE SAID WHO DID.
"I'M NOT FROM THE SOUTH. BU
MEXICO."
"OH, HEY!" THAT WAS THE PREC
"WHERE WERE YOU? I KNOW MEXI
THE EXCHANGE OF HALF A DO
ENDED IN DISAPPOINTED SILENCE
"HERE'S YOUR WEAPON."
FLASHLIGHTS FOLLOWED THE FL
AIR, THE CLATTER ON THE GRIDT
WITH THE BEAMS ON THE GROU
HIS EYES), HE COULD MAKE OUT
WOMEN ON THE CATWALK.
"WHAT—" A CAR MOTOR THRU
END OF THE BRIDGE; BUT THERE
HEADLIGHTS WHEN HE GLANCED.
ON SOME TURNOFF—"IS IT?"
"WHAT'D THEY CALL IT?"
"AN ORCHID."
"YEAH, THAT'S WHAT IT IS."
HE WALKED OVER, SQUATTED IN
BEAM.

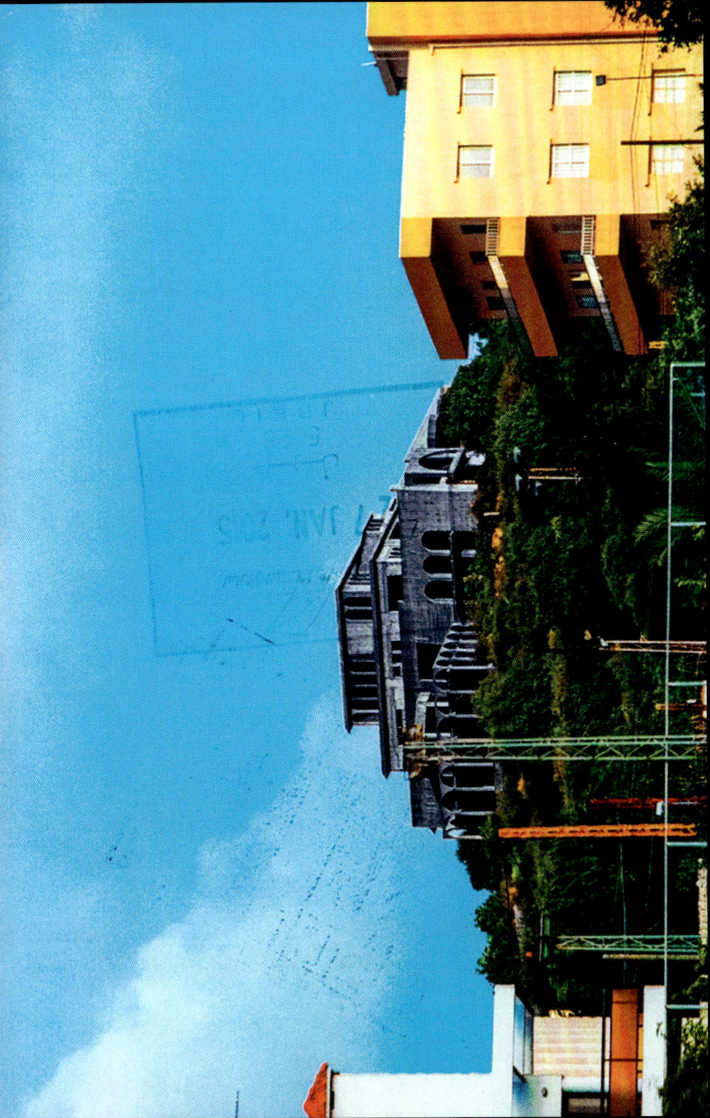

"YOU WEAR IT AROUND YOUR WRIST. WITH THE
BLADES STICKING OUT FRONT. L
FROM AN ADJUSTABLE METAL
SEVEN BLADES, FROM EIGHT TO
CURVED SHARPLY FORWARD. TH
CHAIN-AND-LEATHER HARNESS
IT STEADY ON THE FINGERS. TH
SHARPENED ALONG THE OUTSI
HE PICKED IT UP.
"PUT IT ON."
"ARE YOU RIGHT OR LEFT H
"AMBIDEXTROUS..." WHICH, I
CLUMSY WITH BOTH. HE TURN
"BUT I WRITE WITH MY LEFT.
"OH."
HE FITTED IT AROUND HIS
SNAPPED IT. "SUPPOSE YOU
THIS ON A CROWDED BUS.
SOMEBODY," AND FELT THE
MADE A FIST WITHIN THE BL
SLOWLY AND, BEHIND CURV
TWO BLUNT AND HORNY C
UNDERSIDE OF HIS GREAT
"THERE AREN'T TOO MA
THINKING: DANGEROUS,
ABOUT SOME KNOBBED, H
"UGLY THING," HE TOLD
DON'T NEED YOU."

0115000004501508

REGULAR MAIL

Deutschland 75

50 Jahre Fehmarnsundbrücke

Return / Retour

FROM: WILLIAM DHALGREN
ARCHIVE BOOKS
DIEFFENBACHSTRAßE 31
10967 BERLIN, GERMANY

TO:
SKINNY ARCADE BUILDING
OVERLOOKING HALAT SUR MER
BEIT AL BOUME
جبيل
LEBANON

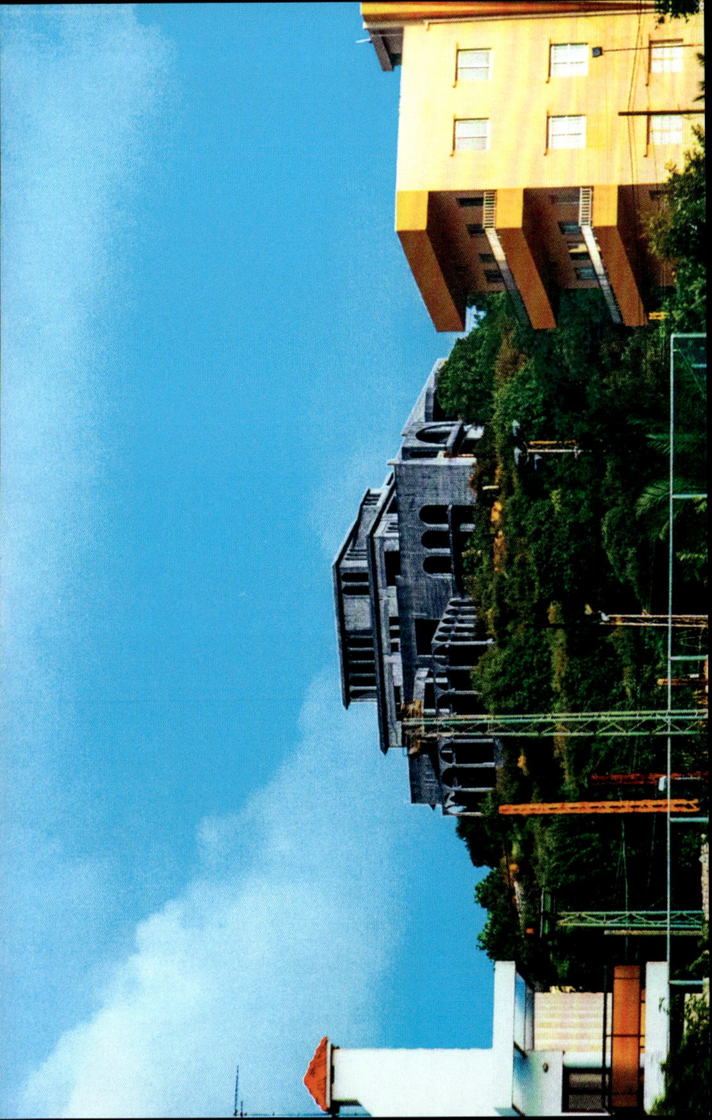

"HOPE YOU DON'T EITHER," ONE SAID ABOVE. "I GUESS YOU CAN GIVE IT TO SOMEBODY ELSE WHEN YOU LEAVE."

"YEAH." HE STOOD UP. "SURE."

"IF HE LEAVES," ANOTHER SAID, GAVE ANOTHER LAUGH.

"HEY, WE BETTER GET GOING."

"I HEARD A CAR. WE'RE PROBABLY GONNA HAVE TO WAIT LONG ENOUGH ANYWAY. WE MIGHT AS WELL START."

SOUTH: "HE DIDN'T MAKE IT SOUND LIKE WE WERE GONNA GET ANY RIDES."

"LET'S JUST GET GOING. HEY, SO LONG!"

"SO LONG." THEIR BEAMS SWEPT BY. "AND THANKS." ARTICHOKES? BUT HE COULD NOT REMEMBER WHERE THE WORD HAD COME FROM TO RING SO BRIGHTLY. HE RAISED THE ORCHID AFTER THEM. HIS GNARLED HAND, CAGED IN BLADES, WAS SILHOUETTED WITH RIVER GLITTER STRETCHING BETWEEN THE BRIDGE STRUTS. WATCHING THEM GO, HE FELT THE VAGUEST FLUTTER OF DESIRE. ONLY ONE OF THEIR FLASHLIGHTS WAS ON. THEN ONE OF THEM BLOCKED THAT. THEY WERE FOOTSTEPS ON METAL PLATES; SOME LAUGHTER DRIFTING BACK; RUSTLINGS...

HE WALKED AGAIN, HOLDING HIS HAND FROM HIS SIDE.

UNFINISHED STATE // 1D.028

Schützt die Natur WWF www.wwf.de Schützt die Natur

50 Jahre Fehmarnsundbrücke Deutschland 75

FROM: WILLIAM DHALGREN
ARCHIVE BOOKS
DIEFFENBACHSTRAßE 31
10967 BERLIN, GERMANY

TO:

SKINNY ARCADE BUILDING

OVERLOOKING HALAT SUR MER

BEIT AL BOUME

LEBANON

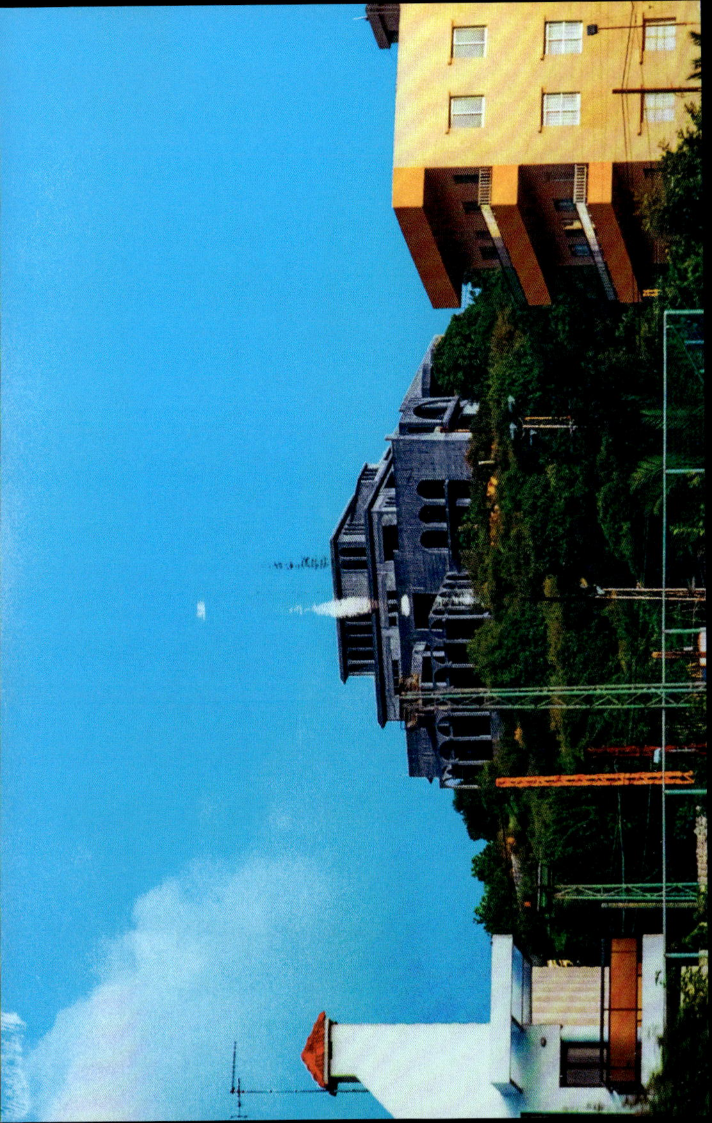

THIS PARCHED EVENING SEASONS THE NIGHT WITH REMEMBRANCES OF RAIN. VERY FEW SUSPECT THE EXISTENCE OF THIS CITY. IT IS AS IF NOT ONLY THE MEDIA BUT THE LAWS OF PERCEPTION THEMSELVES HAVE REDESIGNED KNOWLEDGE AND PERCEPTION TO PASS IT. RUMOR SAYS THERE IS PRACTICALLY NO POWER HERE. NEITHER TELEVISION CAMERAS NOR ON-THE-SPOT BROADCASTS FUNCTION: THAT SUCH A CATASTROPHE AS THIS SHOULD BE OPAQUE, AND THEREFORE DULL, TO THE ELECTRIC NATION! IT IS A CITY OF INNER DISCORDANCES AND RETINAL DISTORTIONS.

BEYOND THE BRIDGE-MOUTH, THE PAVEMENT SHATTERED.

ONE LIVE STREET LAMP LIT FIVE DEAD ONES—TWO WITH BROKEN GLOBES. CLIMBING A TEN-FOOT, TILTED, ASPHALT SLAB THAT JERKED ONCE UNDER HIM, RUMBLING LIKE A LIVE THING, HE SAW PEBBLES ROLL OFF THE EDGE, HEARD THEM CLINK ON FUGITIVE PLUMBING, THEN SPLASH SOMEWHERE IN DARKNESS... HE RECALLED THE CAVE AND VAULTED TO A MORE SOLID STRETCH, WHOSE CRACKS WERE MORTARED WITH NUBBY GRASS.

NO LIGHTS IN ANY NEAR BUILDINGS; BUT DOWN THOSE WATERFRONT STREETS, BEYOND THE VEILS OF SMOKE—WAS THAT FIRE? ALREADY USED TO THE SMELL, HE HAD TO BREATHE DEEPLY TO

UNFINISHED STATE // 1D.029

50 Jahre Fehmarnsundbrücke

Deutschland

Schützt die Natur

WWF

www.wwf.de

FROM: WILLIAM DHALGREN
ARCHIVE BOOKS
DIEFFENBACHSTRAßE 31
10967 BERLIN, GERMANY

TO:

SKINNY ARCADE BUILDING

OVERLOOKING HALAT SUR MER

BEIT AL BOUME

LEBANON

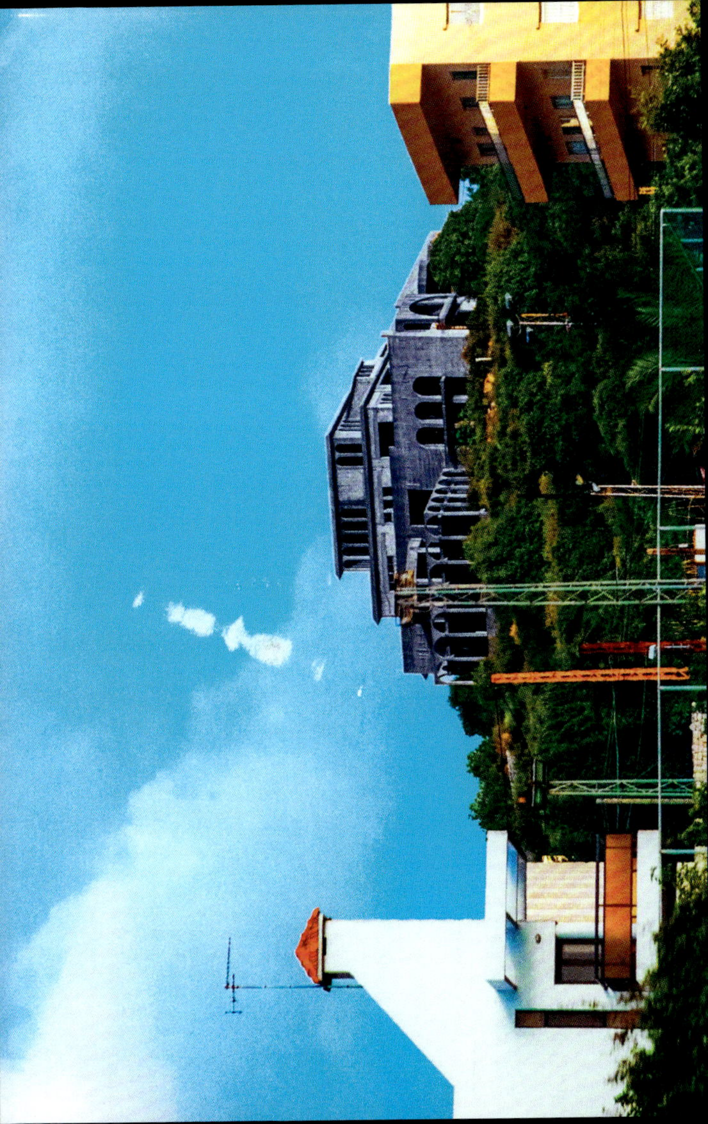

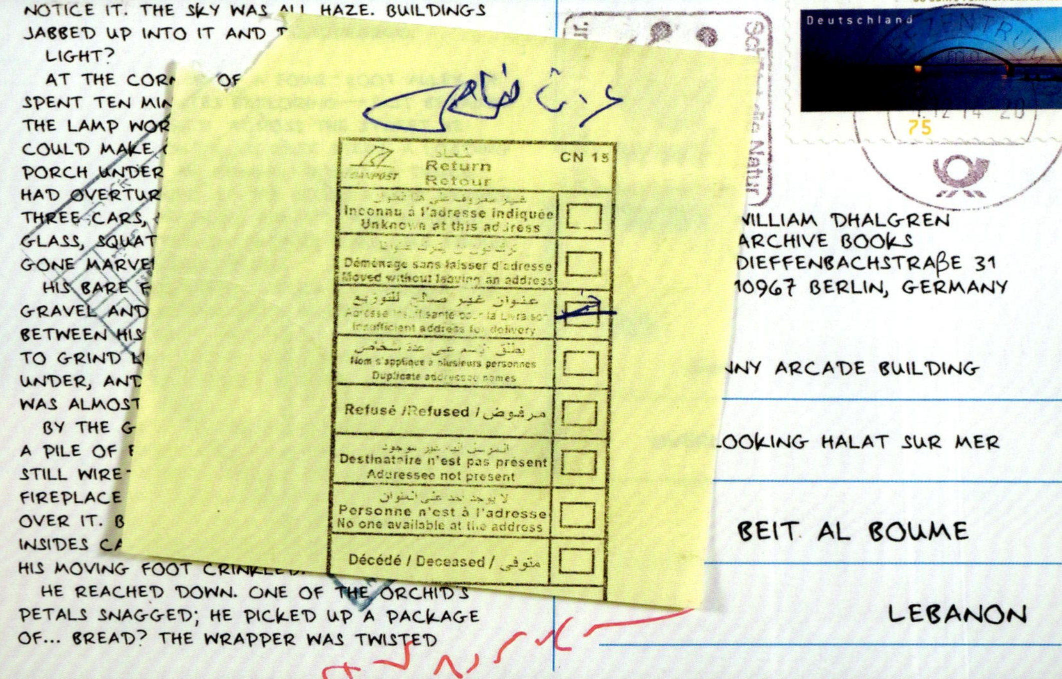
NOTICE IT. THE SKY WAS ALL HAZE. BUILDINGS
JABBED UP INTO IT AND T
LIGHT?
AT THE CORN OF
SPENT TEN MIN
THE LAMP WOR
COULD MAKE
PORCH UNDER
HAD OVERTUR
THREE CARS,
GLASS, SQUAT
GONE MARVE
HIS BARE F
GRAVEL AND
BETWEEN HIS
TO GRIND
UNDER, AND
WAS ALMOST
BY THE G
A PILE OF
STILL WIRE
FIREPLACE
OVER IT. B
INSIDES CA
HIS MOVING FOOT CRINKLED.
HE REACHED DOWN. ONE OF THE ORCHID'S
PETALS SNAGGED; HE PICKED UP A PACKAGE
OF... BREAD? THE WRAPPER WAS TWISTED
Return
Retour
CN 15
Inconnu à l'adresse indiquée
Unknown at this address
Déménage sans laisser d'adresse
Moved without leaving an address
عنوان غير صالح للتوزيع
Insufficient address for delivery
Nom s'applique à plusieurs personnes
Duplicate addressee names
Refusé /Refused / مرفوض
Destinataire n'est pas présent
Addressee not present
Personne n'est à l'adresse
No one available at the address
Décédé / Deceased / متوفى
50 Jahre Fehmarnsundbrücke
Deutschland
75
WILLIAM DHALGREN
ARCHIVE BOOKS
DIEFFENBACHSTRAßE 31
10967 BERLIN, GERMANY
NY ARCADE BUILDING
LOOKING HALAT SUR MER
BEIT AL BOUME
LEBANON

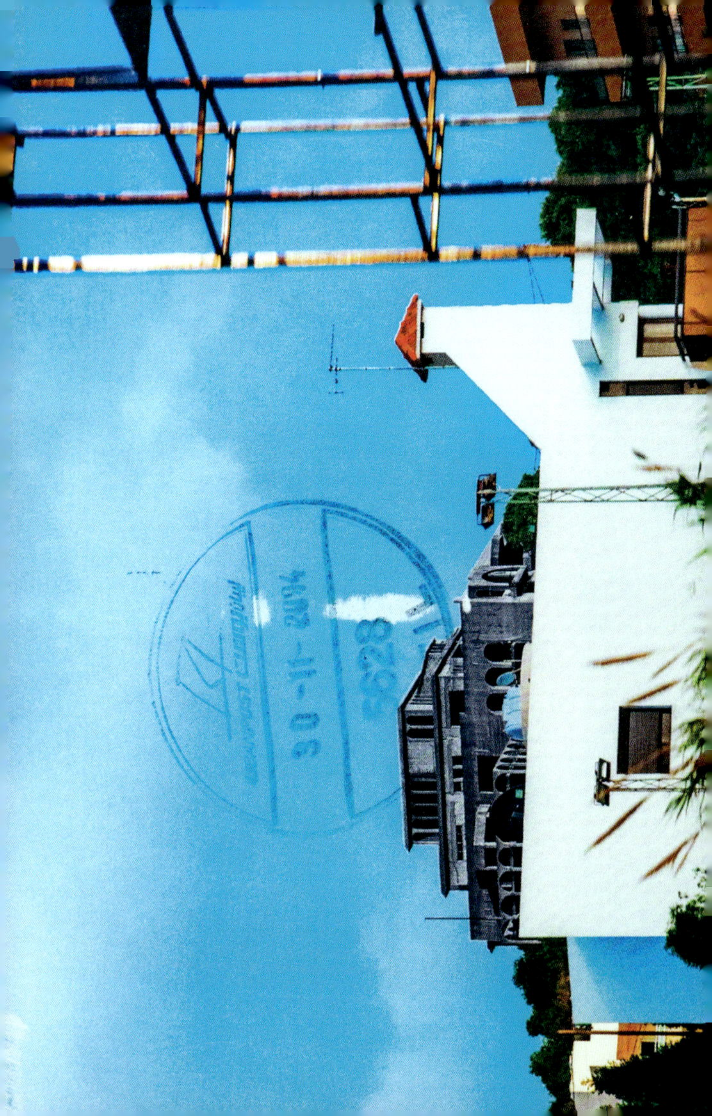

HE SPRINTED TO THE NEAREST WALL, MOVED ALONG IT REHEARSING HIS APPREHENSIONS OF ALL TERRIBLE THAT MIGHT HAPPEN. HE PASSED A DOORWAY, NOTED IT FOR DUCKING, AND KEPT ON TO THE CORNER. VOICES NOW. AND MORE GLASS.

HE PEERED AROUND THE BUILDING EDGE.

THREE PEOPLE VAULTED FROM A SHATTERED DISPLAY WINDOW TO JOIN TWO WAITING. BARKING, A DOG FOLLOWED THEM TO THE SIDEWALK. ONE MAN WANTED TO CLIMB BACK IN; DID. TWO OTHERS TOOK OFF DOWN THE BLOCK.

THE DOG CIRCLED, LOPED HIS WAY—

HE PULLED BACK, FREE HAND GRINDING ON THE BRICK.

THE DOG, CROUCHED AND DANCING TEN FEET OFF, BARKED, BARKED, BARKED AGAIN.

DIM LIGHT SLATHERED CANINE TONGUE AND TEETH. ITS EYES (HE SWALLOWED, HARD) WERE GLISTENING RED, WITHOUT WHITE OR PUPIL, SMOOTH AS CRIMSON GLASS.

THE MAN CAME BACK OUT THE WINDOW. ONE IN THE GROUP TURNED AND SHOUTED: "MURIEL! (IT COULD HAVE BEEN A WOMAN.) THE DOG WHEELED AND FLED AFTER.

ANOTHER STREET LAMP, BLOCKS DOWN, GAVE THEM MOMENTARY SILHOUETTE.

AS HE STEPPED FROM THE WALL, HIS BREATH

50 Jahre Fehmarnsundbrücke

Deutschland

-1.12.14-20

.032

REGULAR MAIL

0114000684004 84

FROM: WILLIAM DHALGREN
ARCHIVE BOOKS
DIEFFENBACHSTRAßE 31
10967 BERLIN, GERMANY

SKINNY ARCADE BUILDING

VERLOOKING HALAT SUR MER

BEIT AL BOUME

LEBANON

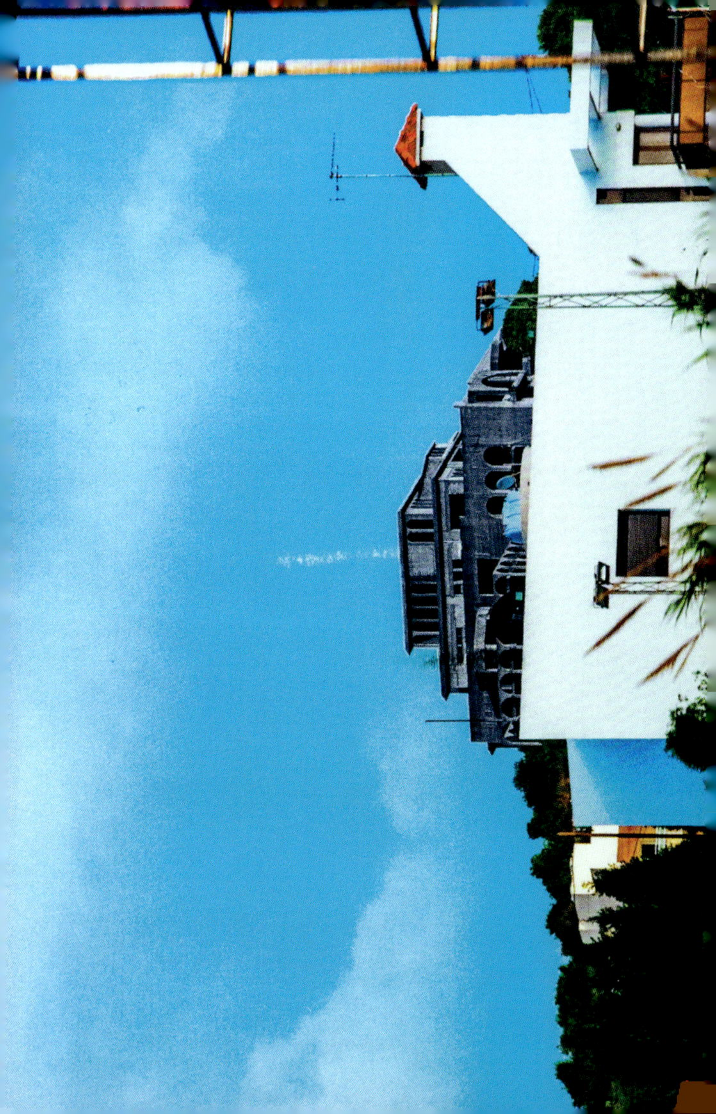

"WHERE'D YOU GET THE ORCHID?"

"HUH?" HE RAISED HIS HAND AGAIN. THE STREET LAMP DRIBBLED LIGHT DOWN A BLADE. "THIS?"

"YEAH."

"SOME WOMEN GAVE IT TO ME. WHEN I WAS CROSSING THE BRIDGE."

"I SAW YOU LOOKING AROUND THE CORNER AT THE HUBBUB. I COULDN'T TELL FROM UP HERE— WAS IT SCORPIONS?"

"HUH?"

"I SAID, WAS IT SCORPIONS?"

"IT WAS A BUNCH OF PEOPLE TRYING TO BREAK INTO A STORE, I THINK. THEY HAD A DOG WITH THEM."

AFTER SILENCE, GRAVELLY LAUGHTER GREW. "YOU REALLY HAVEN'T BEEN HERE LONG, KID."

"I—" AND REALIZED THE REPETITION—"JUST GOT HERE."

"YOU OUT TO GO EXPLORING BY YOURSELF? OR YOU WANT COMPANY FOR A BIT."

THE GUY'S EYES, HE REFLECTED, MUST BE AWFULLY GOOD. "COMPANY... I GUESS."

"I'LL BE THERE IN A MINUTE."

HE DIDN'T SEE THE FIGURE GO; THERE WAS TOO MUCH SMOKE. AND AFTER HE'D WATCHED SEVERAL DOORWAYS FOR SEVERAL MINUTES, HE FIGURED THE MAN HAD CHANGED HIS MIND.

"HERE YOU GO," FROM THE ONE HE'D SET

UNFINISHED STATE // 1D.034

50 Jahre Fehmarnsundbrücke

Deutschland

-1.12 14-20

schützt die Natur

WWF

www.wwf.de

Deutsche Post

Empfänger/Firma unter der angegebenen Anschrift nicht zu ermitteln.

Empfänger verzogen. Einwilligung zur Weitergabe der neuen Anschrift liegt nicht vor.

FROM: WILLIAM DHALGREN
ARCHIVE BOOKS
DIEFFENBACHSTRAßE 31
10967 BERLIN, GERMANY

?

TO: SKINNY ARCADE BUILDING
OVERLOOKING HALAT SUR MER
BEIT AL BOUME
LEBANON

26 | B

23 JAN 2015
جبيل

ASIDE FOR DUCKING.

"NAME IS LOUFER. TAK LOUFER. Y… WHAT THAT MEANS, LOUFER? RED W… WOLF."

"OR IRON WOLF." HE SQUINTED. "H…

"IRON WOLF? WELL, YEAH…" THE M… DIM ON THE TOP STEP. "DON'T KNOW… THAT ONE SO MUCH. RED WOLF. THA… FAVORITE." HE WAS A VERY BIG MAN.

HE CAME DOWN TWO MORE STEPS; … ENGINEER'S BOOTS, HITTING THE BOAR… SOUNDED LIKE DROPPED SANDBAGS. … BLACK-JEANS WERE HALF STUFFED IN… BOOT TOPS. THE WORN CYCLE JACKET… SCARRED WITH ZIPPERS. GOLD STUBBL… AND JAW SNAGGED THE STREET LIGHT… AND BELLY, BARE BETWEEN FLAPPING Z… TEETH, WERE A TANGLE OF BRASS HAIR. … FINGERS WERE MASSIVE, MATTED—"WHA… NAME?"—BUT CLEAN, WITH NEAT AND C… FOR NAILS.

"URN… WELL, I'LL TELL YOU: I DON'T K… IT SOUNDED FUNNY, SO HE LAUGHED. "I… KNOW."

LOUFER STOPPED, A STEP ABOVE THE SIDEWALK, AND LAUGHED TOO. "WHY THE… DON'T YOU?" THE VISOR OF HIS LEATHER BLOCKED HIS UPPER FACE WITH SHADOW.

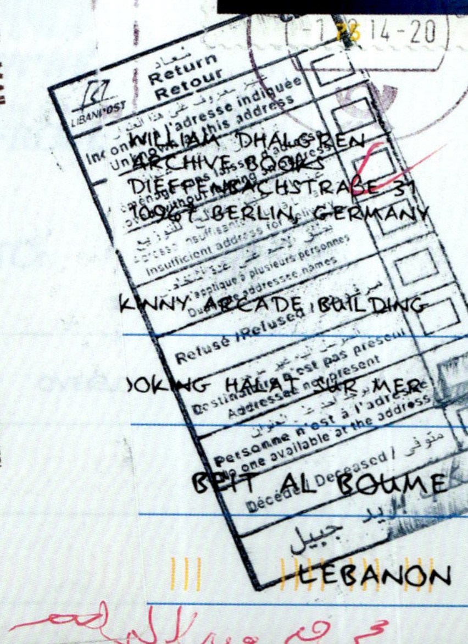

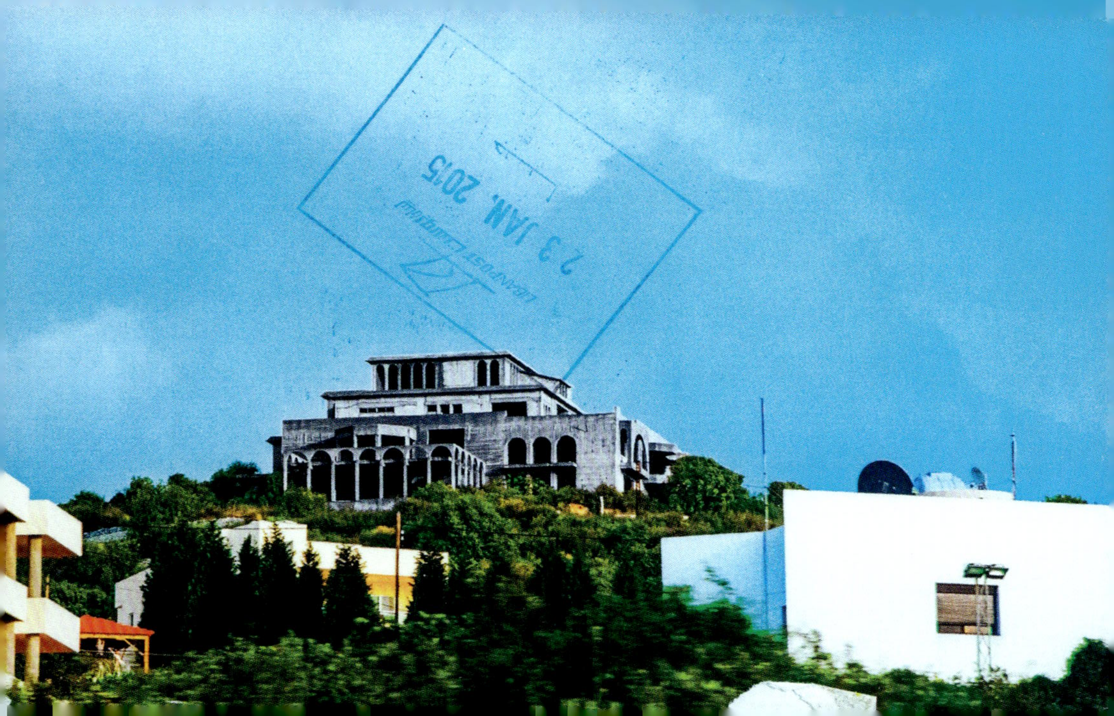
23 JAN. 2015

HE SHRUGGED. "I JUST DON'T. I HAVEN'T FOR... A WHILE NOW."

LOUFER CAME DOWN THE LAST STEP, TO THE PAVEMENT "WELL, TAK LO[illegible]
HERE WITH STRANGER STO[illegible]
SOME KIND OF NUT, OR S[illegible]
A MENTAL HOSPITAL, MAYB[illegible]

"YES..." HE SAW THAT L[illegible]
A NO.

TAK'S HEAD COCKED. [illegible]
SHOW THE RIMS OF NEGR[illegible]
AN EXTREMELY CAUCASIA[illegible]
LOOKED LIKE ROCKS IN [illegible]

"JUST FOR A YEAR. A[illegible]
AGO."

LOUFER SHRUGGED. "[illegible]
MONTHS... ABOUT SIX OR [illegible]
BUT THAT'S AS CLOSE A[illegible]
NO-NAME KID? WHAT A[illegible]
EIGHTEEN? NO, I BET Y[illegible]

"TWENTY-SEVEN."

TAK'S HEAD COCKET[illegible]
TOPPED HIS CHEEK BO[illegible]
DO IT EVERY TIME. YO[illegible]
PEOPLE WITH SERIOUS [illegible]
THAT SLEEP ALL DAY? [illegible]
MEAN. THEY ALWAYS L[illegible]
THAN THEY ARE."

REGULAR MAIL

*0115000[illegible]150[illegible]

Natur. WWF www.wwf.de Schützt die Natur

50 Jahre Fehmarnsundbrücke

Deutschland 75

CN 15

Return / Retour

LIBANPOST

Inconnu à l'adresse / Unknown at the address

Déménagé sans laisser d'adresse / Moved without leaving an address

Insuffisant adresse / Insufficient address

Refusé / Refused

Destinataire n'est pas présent / Addressee not present

Personne n'est à l'adresse / No one available at the address

Décédé / Deceased

FROM: WILLIAM DHALGREN
ARCHIVE BOOKS
DIEFFENBACHSTRAßE 31
10967 BERLIN, GERMANY

TO: SKINNY ARCADE BUILDING
OVERLOOKING HALAT SUR MER
BEIT AL BOUME
LEBANON

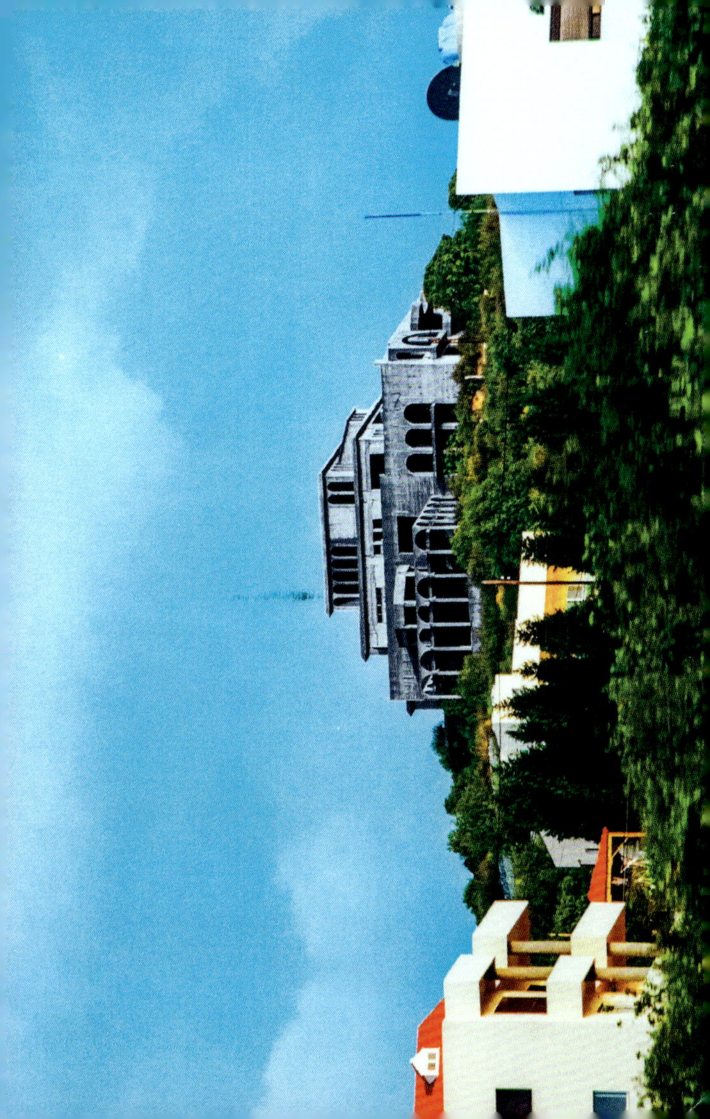

HE NODDED.

"I'M GOING TO CALL YOU KID, THEN. THAT'LL DO YOU FOR A NAME. YOU CAN BE—THE KID, HEY?"

THREE GIFTS, HE THOUGHT: ARMOR, WEAPON, TITLE (LIKE THE PRISMS, LENSES, MIRRORS ON THE CHAIN ITSELF). "OKAY..." WITH THE SUDDEN CONVICTION THIS THIRD WOULD COST, BY FAR, THE MOST. REJECT IT, SOMETHING WARNED: "ONLY I'M NOT A KID. REALLY; I'M TWENTY-SEVEN. PEOPLE ALWAYS THINK I'M YOUNGER THAN I AM. I JUST GOT A BABY FACE, THAT'S ALL. I'VE EVEN GOT SOME WHITE HAIR, IF YOU WANT TO SEE—"

"LOOK, KID—" WITH HIS MIDDLE FINGERS, TAK PUSHED UP HIS VISOR— "WE'RE THE SAME AGE." HIS EYES WERE LARGE, DEEP, AND BLUE. THE HAIR ABOVE HIS EARS, NO LONGER THAN THE WEEK'S BEARD, SUGGESTED A SEVERE CREW UNDER THE CAP. "ANY SIGHTS YOU PARTICULARLY WANT TO SEE AROUND HERE? ANYTHING YOU HEARD ABOUT? I LIKE TO PLAY GUIDE. WHAT DO YOU HEAR ABOUT US, OUTSIDE, ANYWAY? WHAT DO PEOPLE SAY ABOUT US HERE IN THE CITY?"

"NOT MUCH."

"GUESS THEY WOULDN'T." TAK LOOKED AWAY. "YOU JUST WANDER IN BY ACCIDENT, OR DID YOU COME ON PURPOSE?"

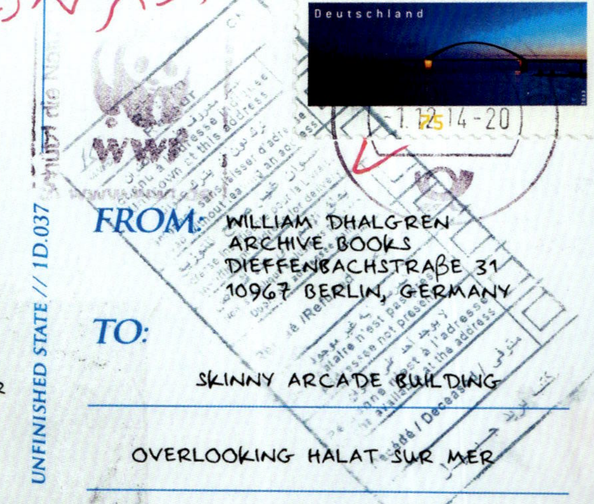

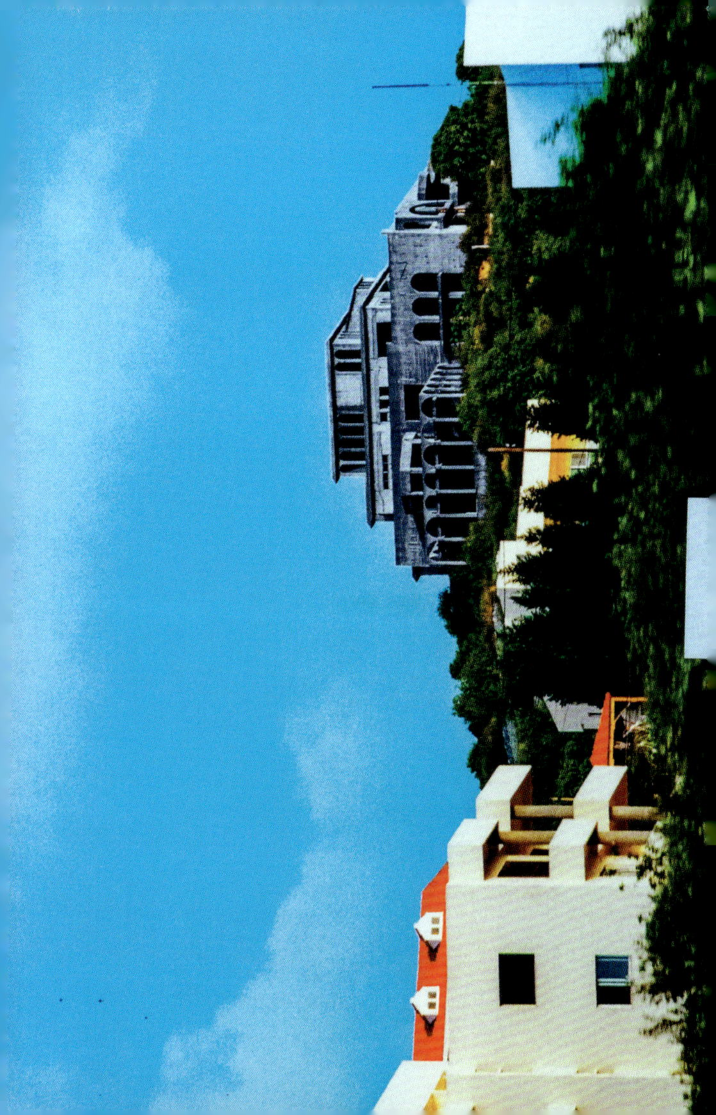

"PURPOSE."

"GOOD KID! LIKE A MAN WITH A PURPOSE. COME ON UP HERE. THIS STREET TURNS INTO BROADWAY SOON AS IT LEAVES THE WATERFRONT."

"WHAT IS THERE TO SEE?"

LOUFER GAVE A GRUNT THAT DID FOR A LAUGH. "DEPENDS ON WHAT SIGHTS ARE OUT." THOUGH HE HAD THE BEGINNING OF A GUT, THE RIDGES UNDER THE BELLY HAIR WERE MUSCLE DEEP. "IF WE'RE REALLY LUCKY, MAYBE—" THE ASHY LEATHER, SWINGING AS LOUFER TURNED, WINKED OVER A CIRCULAR BRASS BUCKLE THAT HELD TOGETHER A TWO-INCH-WIDE GARRISON—"WE WON'T RUN INTO ANYTHING AT ALL! COME ON." THEY WALKED.

"...KID. THE KID..."

"HUH?" ASKED LOUFER.

"I'M THINKING ABOUT THAT NAME."

"WILL IT DO?"

"I DON'T KNOW."

LOUFER LAUGHED. "I'M NOT GOING TO PRES FOR IT, KID. BUT I THINK IT'S YOURS."

HIS OWN CHUCKLE WAS PART DENIAL, PART FRIENDLY.

LOUFER'S GRUNT IN ANSWER ECHOED THE FRIENDLY.

THEY WALKED BENEATH LOW SMOKE.

REGULAR MAIL

01140006600415

TATE // 1D.038

Schützt die Natur.

WWF

www.wwf.de

50 Jahre Fehmarnsundbrücke

Deutschland

75

FROM: WILLIAM DHALGREN
ARCHIVE BOOKS
DIEFFENBACHSTRAßE 31
10967 BERLIN, GERMANY

TO:
SKINNY ARCADE BUILDING
OVERLOOKING HALAT SUR MER
BEIT AL BOUME
LEBANON

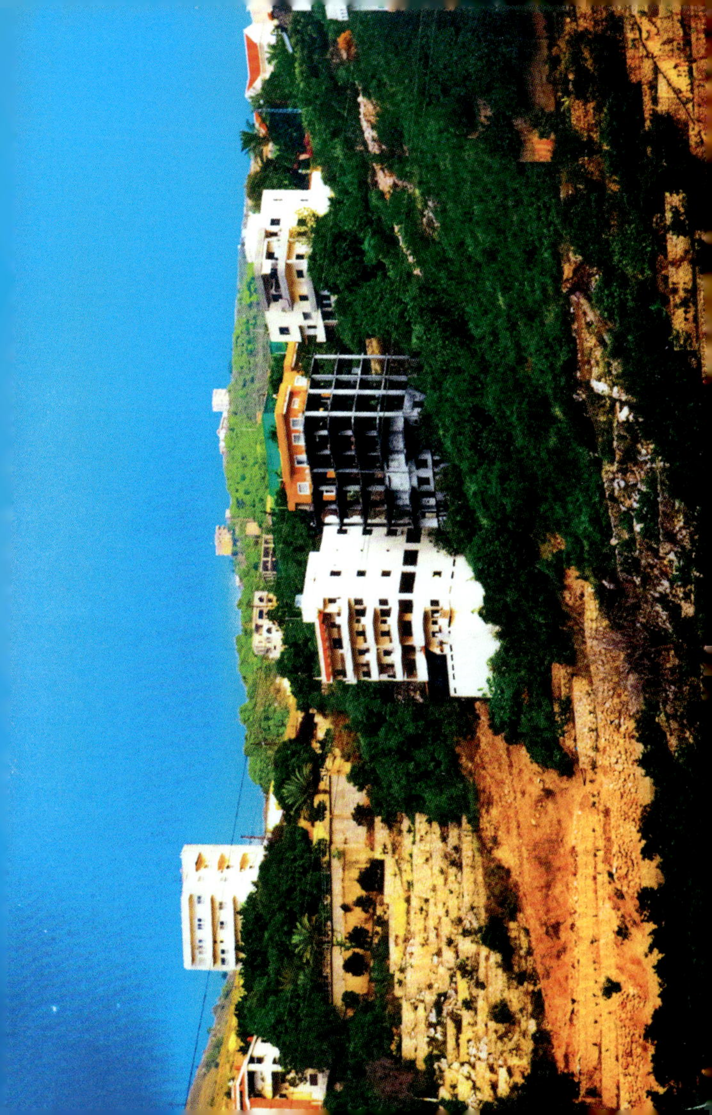

THERE IS SOMETHING DELICATE ABOUT THIS IRON WOLF, WITH HIS FACE LIKE A PUG-NOSED, GERMANIC GORILLA. IT IS NEITHER HIS SPEECH NOR HIS CARRIAGE, WHICH HAVE THEIR ROUGHNESS, BUT THE WAY IN WHICH HE ASSUMES THEM, AS THOUGH THE SURFACE WHERE SPEECH AND CARRIAGE ARE FLUSH WERE SOMEHOW INFLAMED.

"HEY, TAK?"

"YEAH?"

"HOW LONG HAVE YOU BEEN HERE?"

"IF YOU TOLD ME TODAY'S DATE, I COULD FIGURE IT OUT. BUT I'VE LET IT GO. IT'S BEEN A WHILE." AFTER A MOMENT, LOUFER ASKED, IN A STRANGE, LESS BLUSTERY VOICE: "DO YOU KNOW WHAT DAY IT IS?"

"NO, I..." THE STRANGENESS SCARED HIM. "I DON'T." HE SHOOK HIS HEAD WHILE HIS MIND RUSHED AWAY TOWARD SOME OTHER SUBJECT. "WHAT DO YOU DO? I MEAN, WHAT DID YOU WORK AT?"

TAK SNORTED. "INDUSTRIAL ENGINEERING."

"WERE YOU WORKING HERE, BEFORE... ALL THIS?"

"NEAR HERE. ABOUT TWELVE MILES DOWN, AT HELMSFORD. THERE USED TO BE A PLANT THAT JARRED PEANUT BUTTER. WE WERE CONVERTING IT INTO A VITAMIN C FACTORY. WHAT DO YOU

50 Jahre Fehmarnsundbrücke

Deutschland 75

Schützt die Natur. WWF www.wwf.de

UNFINISHED STATE // 1D.039

FROM: WILLIAM DHALGREN
ARCHIVE BOOKS
DIEFFENBACHSTRAẞE 31
10967 BERLIN, GERMANY

TO: CONDOMINIUMS

LOWER HALAT HILLS

HALAT

LEBANON

Retour / Return

Inconnu à l'adresse indiquée / Unknown at this address

Déménagé sans laisser d'adresse / Moved without leaving an address

Adresse insuffisante / Insufficient address

Non réclamé / Unclaimed

Refusé / Refused

CN 15

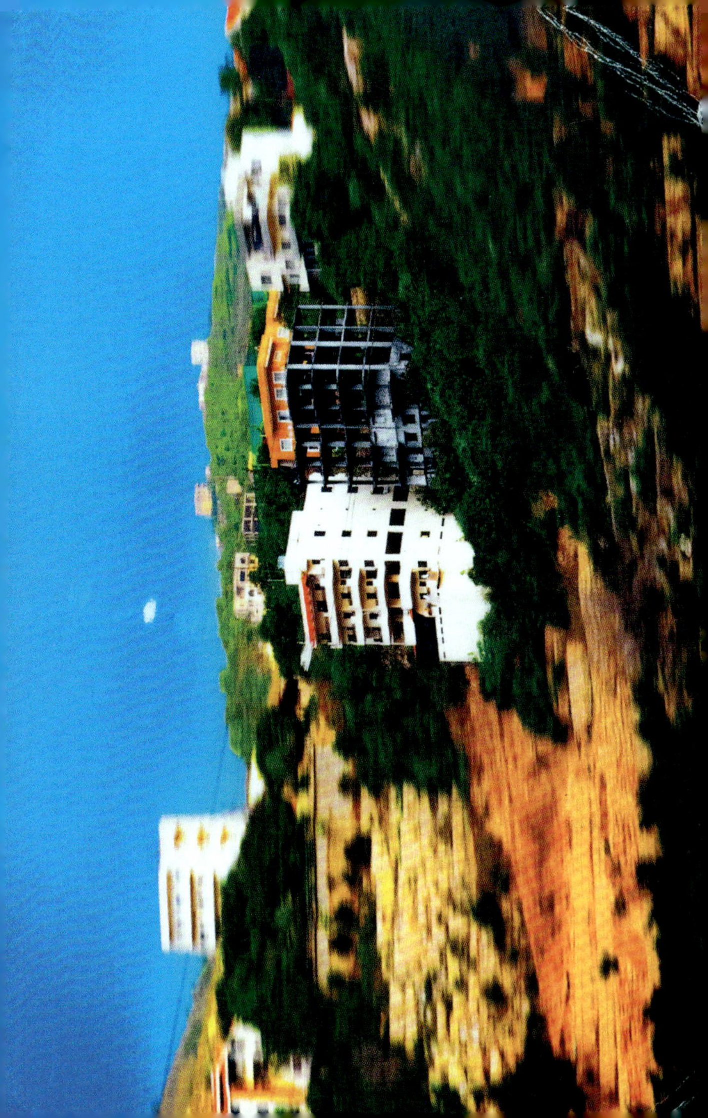

OR LESS LIKE IT DOES NOW."

"WHERE'S YOUR CAR?"

"SITTING ON THE STREET WITH THE WINDSHIELD BUSTED, THE TIRES GONE—ALONG WITH MOST OF THE MOTOR. I LET A LOT OF STUPID THINGS HAPPEN, AT FIRST. BUT I GOT THE HANG OF IT AFTER A WHILE." TAK MADE A SWEEPING GESTURE WITH BOTH HANDS—AND DISAPPEARED BEFORE IT WAS FINISHED: THEY'D PASSED INTO COMPLETE BLACKNESS. "A THOUSAND PEOPLE ARE SUPPOSED TO BE HERE NOW. USED TO BE ALMOST TWO MILLION."

"HOW DO YOU KNOW, I MEAN THE POPULATION?"

"THAT'S WHAT THEY PUBLISH IN THE PAPER."

"WHY DO YOU STAY?"

"STAY?" LOUFER'S VOICE NEARED THAT OTHER, UPSETTING TONE. "WELL, ACTUALLY, I'VE THOUGHT ABOUT THAT ONE A LOT. I THINK IT HAS TO DO WITH—I GOT A THEORY NOW—FREEDOM. YOU KNOW, HERE—" AHEAD, SOMETHING MOVED— "YOU'RE FREE. NO LAWS: TO BREAK, OR TO FOLLOW. DO ANYTHING YOU WANT. WHICH DOES FUNNY THINGS TO YOU. VERY QUICKLY, SURPRISINGLY QUICKLY, YOU BECOME—" THEY NEARED ANOTHER HALF-LIT LAMP; WHAT MOVED …AME SMOKE, LOBLING FROM A WINDOW SILL …ITH GLASS TEETH LIKE AN EXTINGUISHED

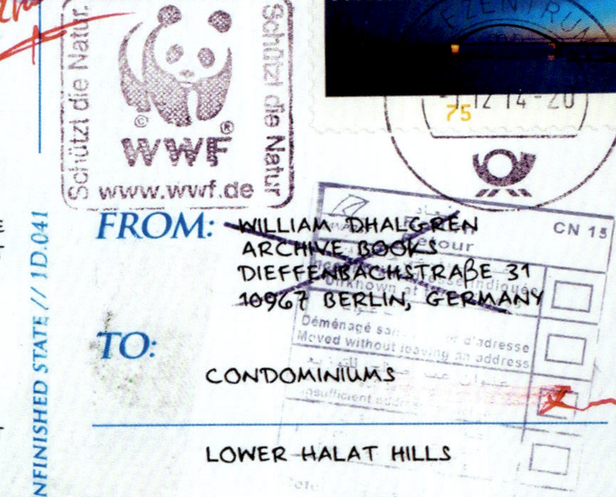

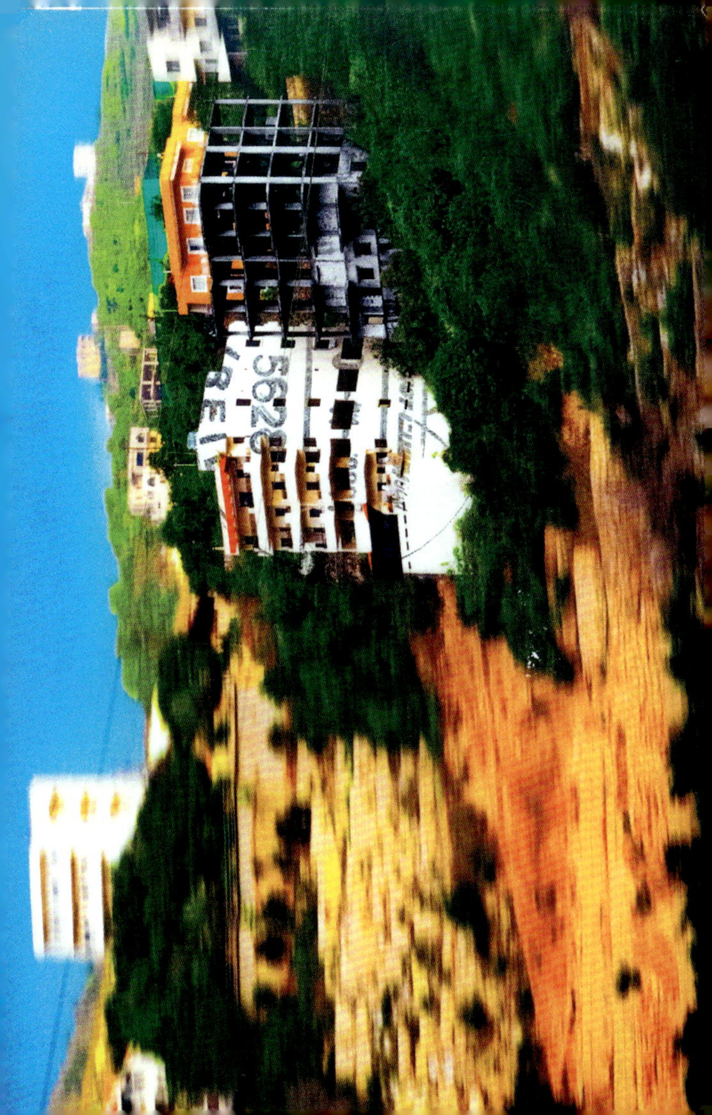

JACK-O-LANTERN- "EXACTLY WHO YOU ARE." AND TAK WAS VISIBLE AGAIN. "IF YOU'RE READY FOR THAT, THIS IS WHERE IT'S AT."

"IT MUST BE PRETTY DANGEROUS. LOOTERS AND STUFF."

TAK NODDED. "SURE IT'S DANGEROUS."

"IS THERE A LOT OF STREET MUGGING?"

"SOME." LOUFER MADE A FACE. "DO YOU KNOW ABOUT CRIME, KID? CRIME IS FUNNY. FOR INSTANCE, NOW, IN MOST AMERICAN CITIES—NEW YORK, CHICAGO, ST. LOUIS—CRIMES, NINETY-FIVE PER CENT I READ, ARE COMMITTED BETWEEN SIX O'CLOCK AND MIDNIGHT. THAT MEANS YOU'RE SAFER WALKING AROUND THE STREET AT THREE O'CLOCK IN THE MORNING THAN YOU ARE GOING TO THE THEATER TO CATCH A SEVEN-THIRTY CURTAIN. I WONDER WHAT TIME IT IS NOW. SOMETIME AFTER TWO I'D GATHER. I DON'T THINK BELLONA IS MUCH MORE DANGEROUS THAN ANY OTHER CITY. IT'S A VERY SMALL CITY, NOW. THAT'S A SORT OF PROTECTION."

A FORGOTTEN BLADE SCRAPED HIS JEANS. "DO YOU CARRY A WEAPON?"

"MONTHS OF DETAILED STUDY ON WHAT IS GOING ON WHERE, THE MOVEMENTS AND VARIATIONS OF OUR TOWN. I LOOK AROUND A LOT. THIS WAY."

THAT WASN'T BUILDINGS ON THE OTHER SIDE

UNFINISHED STATE // 1D.042

Return / Retour / Inconnu à l'adresse indiquée / Unknown at this address / Déménagé sans laisser d'adresse / Moved without leaving an address / Adresse insuffisante / Insufficient address for delivery / Refusé / Refused / Destinataire n'est pas présent / Décédé / Deceased

CN 15

Deutschland 75

FROM: WILLIAM DHALGREN
ARCHIVE BOOKS
DIEFFENBACHSTRAßE 31
10967 BERLIN, GERMANY

TO:

CONDOMINIUMS

LOWER HALAT HILLS

HALAT

LEBANON

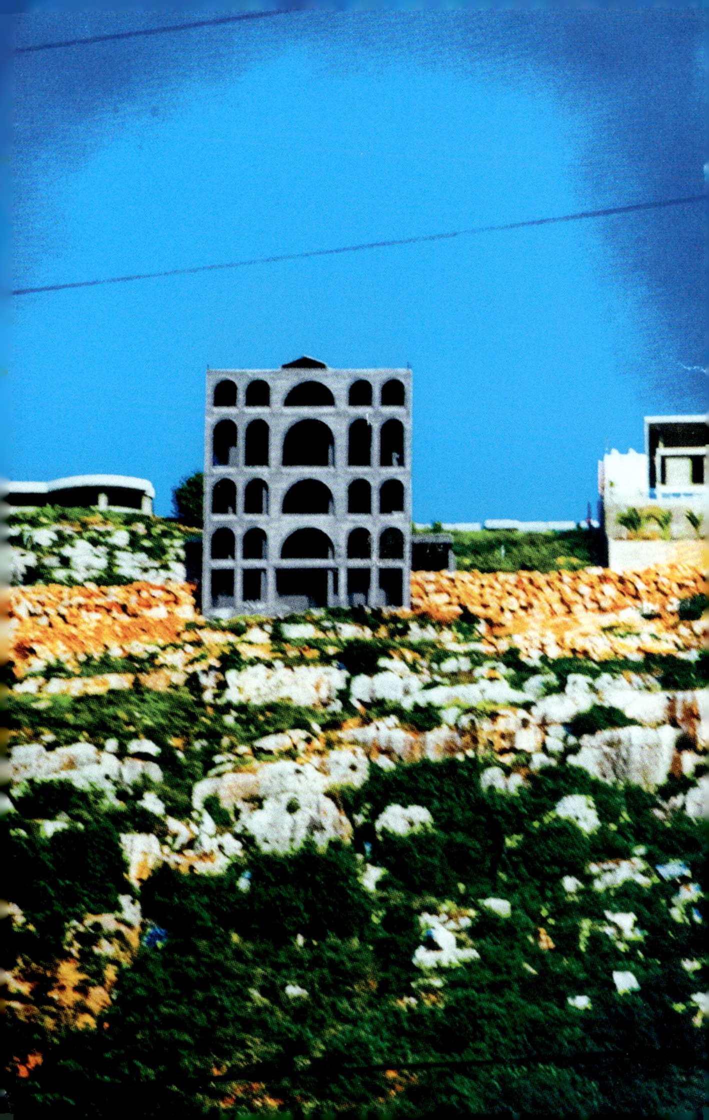

OF THE STREET: TREES ROSE ABOVE THE PARK WALL, BLACK AS SHALE. LOUFER HEADED TOWARD THE ENTRANCE.

"IS IT SAFE IN THERE?"

"LOOKS PRETTY SCARY." TAK NODDED. "PROBABLY KEEP ANY CRIMINAL WITH A GRAIN OF SENSE AT HOME. ANYBODY WHO WASN'T A MUGGER WOULD BE OUT OF HIS MIND TO GO IN THERE." HE GLANCED BACK, GRINNED. "WHICH PROBABLY MEANS ALL THE MUGGERS HAVE GOTTEN TIRED OF WAITING AND GONE HOME TO BED A LONG TIME AGO. COME ON."

STONE LIONS FLANKED THE ENTRANCE.

"IT'S FUNNY," TAK SAID; THEY PASSED BETWEEN. "YOU SHOW ME A PLACE WHERE THEY TELL WOMEN TO STAY OUT OF AT NIGHT BECAUSE OF ALL THE NASTY, EVIL MEN LURKING THERE TO DO NASTY, EVIL THINGS; AND YOU KNOW WHAT YOU'LL FIND?"

"QUEERS."

TAK GLANCED OVER, PULLED HIS CAP VISOR DOWN. "YEAH."

THE DARK WRAPPED THEM UP AND BUOYED THEM ALONG THE PATH.

THERE IS NOTHING SAFE ABOUT THE DARKNESS OF THIS CITY AND ITS STINK. WELL, I HAVE ABROGATED ALL CLAIM TO SAFETY, COMING HERE. IT IS BETTER TO DISCUSS IT AS THOUGH I HAD CHOSEN. THAT KEEPS THE SCRIM OF SANITY

UNFINISHED STATE // 1D.043

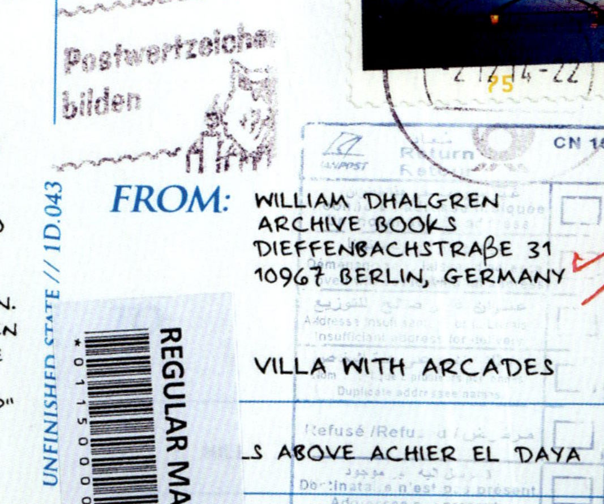

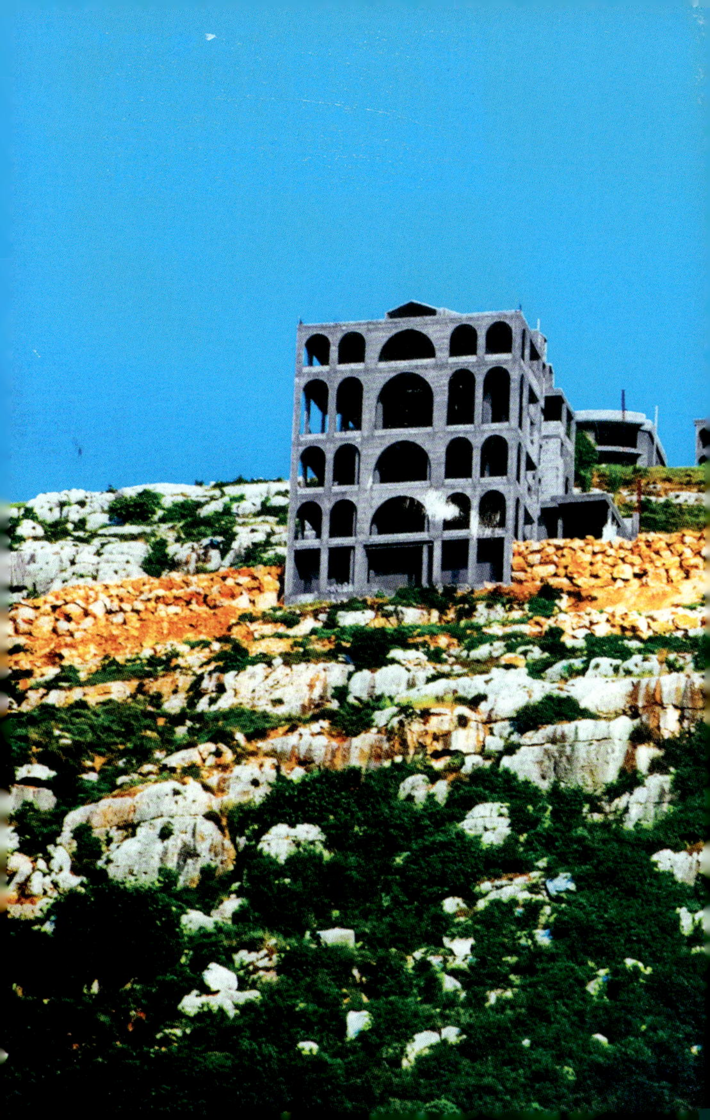

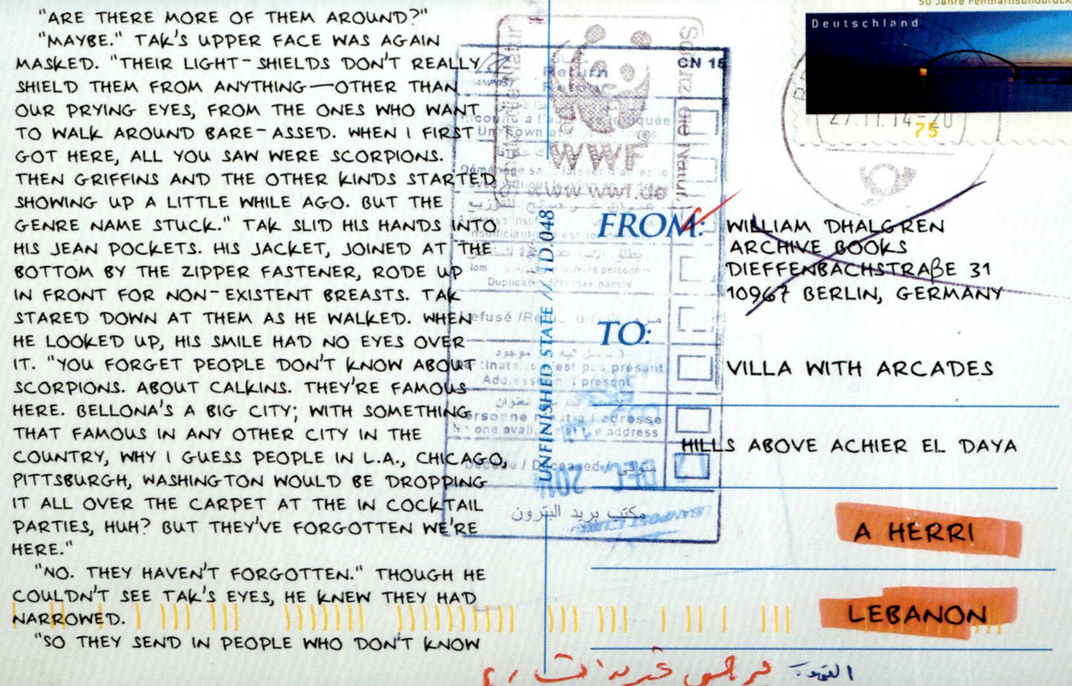

"ARE THERE MORE OF THEM AROUND?"
"MAYBE." TAK'S UPPER FACE WAS AGAIN MASKED. "THEIR LIGHT-SHIELDS DON'T REALLY SHIELD THEM FROM ANYTHING—OTHER THAN OUR PRYING EYES, FROM THE ONES WHO WANT TO WALK AROUND BARE-ASSED. WHEN I FIRST GOT HERE, ALL YOU SAW WERE SCORPIONS. THEN GRIFFINS AND THE OTHER KINDS STARTED SHOWING UP A LITTLE WHILE AGO. BUT THE GENRE NAME STUCK." TAK SLID HIS HANDS INTO HIS JEAN POCKETS. HIS JACKET, JOINED AT THE BOTTOM BY THE ZIPPER FASTENER, RODE UP IN FRONT FOR NON-EXISTENT BREASTS. TAK STARED DOWN AT THEM AS HE WALKED. WHEN HE LOOKED UP, HIS SMILE HAD NO EYES OVER IT. "YOU FORGET PEOPLE DON'T KNOW ABOUT SCORPIONS. ABOUT CALKINS. THEY'RE FAMOUS HERE. BELLONA'S A BIG CITY; WITH SOMETHING THAT FAMOUS IN ANY OTHER CITY IN THE COUNTRY, WHY I GUESS PEOPLE IN L.A., CHICAGO, PITTSBURGH, WASHINGTON WOULD BE DROPPING IT ALL OVER THE CARPET AT THE IN COCKTAIL PARTIES, HUH? BUT THEY'VE FORGOTTEN WE'RE HERE."
"NO. THEY HAVEN'T FORGOTTEN." THOUGH HE COULDN'T SEE TAK'S EYES, HE KNEW THEY HAD NARROWED.
"SO THEY SEND IN PEOPLE WHO DON'T KNOW
50 Jahre Fehmarnsundbrücke
Deutschland
75
CN 15
Return
WWF
www.wwf.de
UNFINISHED STATE // ID.048
FROM:
WILLIAM DHALGREN
ARCHIVE BOOKS
DIEFFENBACHSTRAßE 31
10967 BERLIN, GERMANY
TO:
VILLA WITH ARCADES
HILLS ABOVE ACHIER EL DAYA
A HERRI
LEBANON
Refusé / Refused
Décédé / Deceased
مكتب بريد البترون

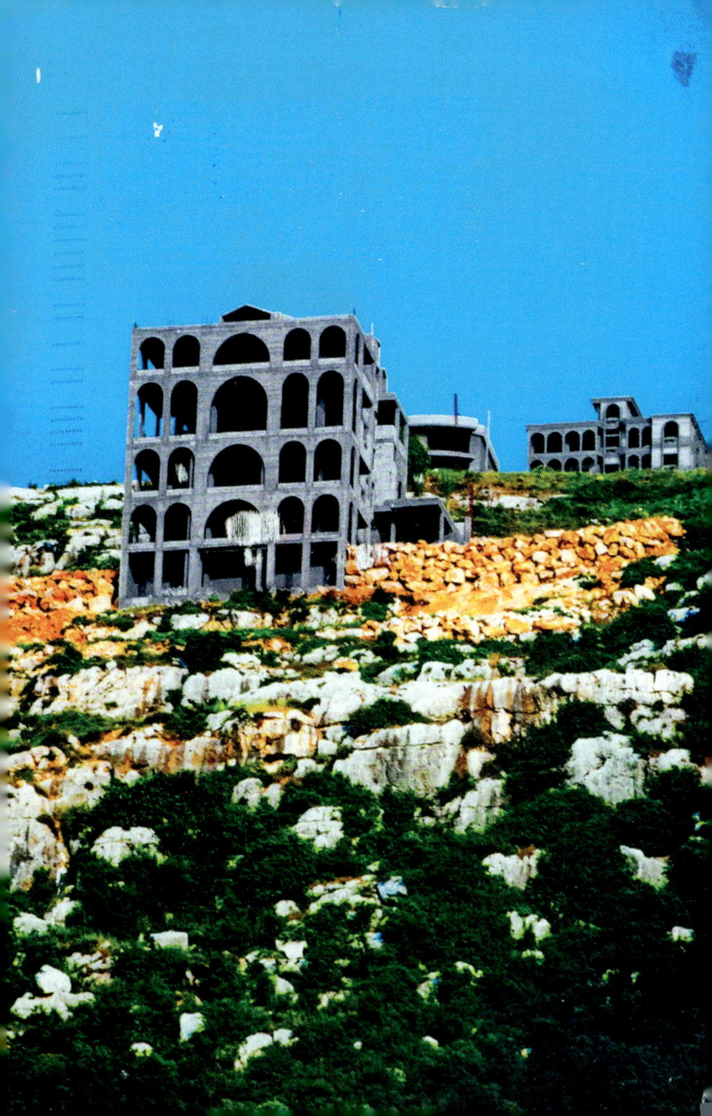

THEIR OWN NAME. LIKE YOU?"

HE LAUGHED, SHARPLY; IT FELT LIKE A BARK.

TAK RETURNED THE HOARSE SOUND THAT WAS HIS OWN LAUGHTER. "OH, YEAH! YOU'RE QUITE A KID." LAUGHTER TRAILED ON.

"WHERE WE GOING NOW?"

BUT TAK LOWERED HIS CHIN, STRODE AHEAD.

FROM THIS PLAY OF NIGHT, LIGHT, AND LEATHER, CAN I LET MYSELF TAKE IDENTITY? HOW CAN I RECREATE THIS ROASTED PARK IN SOME MEANINGFUL MATRIX? EQUIPPED WITH CONTRADICTORY VISIONS, AN UGLY HAND CAGED IN PRETTY METAL, I OBSERVE A NEW MECHANICS. I AM THE WILD MACHINIST, PAST DESTROYED, RECONSTRUCTING THE PRESENT.

"TAK!" SHE CALLED ACROSS THE FIRE, ROSE, AND SHOOK BACK FIRE-COLORED HAIR. "WHO'D YOU BRING?" SHE SWUNG AROUND THE CINDERBLOCK FURNACE AND CAME ON, A SILHOUETTE NOW, STEPPING OVER SLEEPING BAGS, BLANKET ROLLS, A LAWN OF REPOSING FORMS. TWO GLANCED AT HER, THEN TURNED OVER. TWO OTHERS SNORED AT DIFFERENT PITCHES.

A GIRL ON A BLANKET, WITH NO SHIRT AND REALLY NICE BREASTS, STOPPED PLAYING HER HARMONICA, BANGED IT ON HER PALM FOR SPIT, AND BLEW ONCE MORE.

UNFINISHED STATE N° LD.049

FROM: WILLIAM DHALGREN
ARCHIVE BOOKS
DIEFFENBACHSTRAẞE 31
10967 BERLIN, GERMANY

TO:

VILLA WITH ARCADES

HILLS ABOVE ACHIER EL DAYA

A HERRI

LEBANON

Deutschland
50 Jahre Fehmarnsundbrücke
75

Insufficient address for delivery
Nom s'applique à plusieurs personnes
Duplicate addressee names
Refused / مرفوض
... présent
... not present
... address
... sed / متوفى

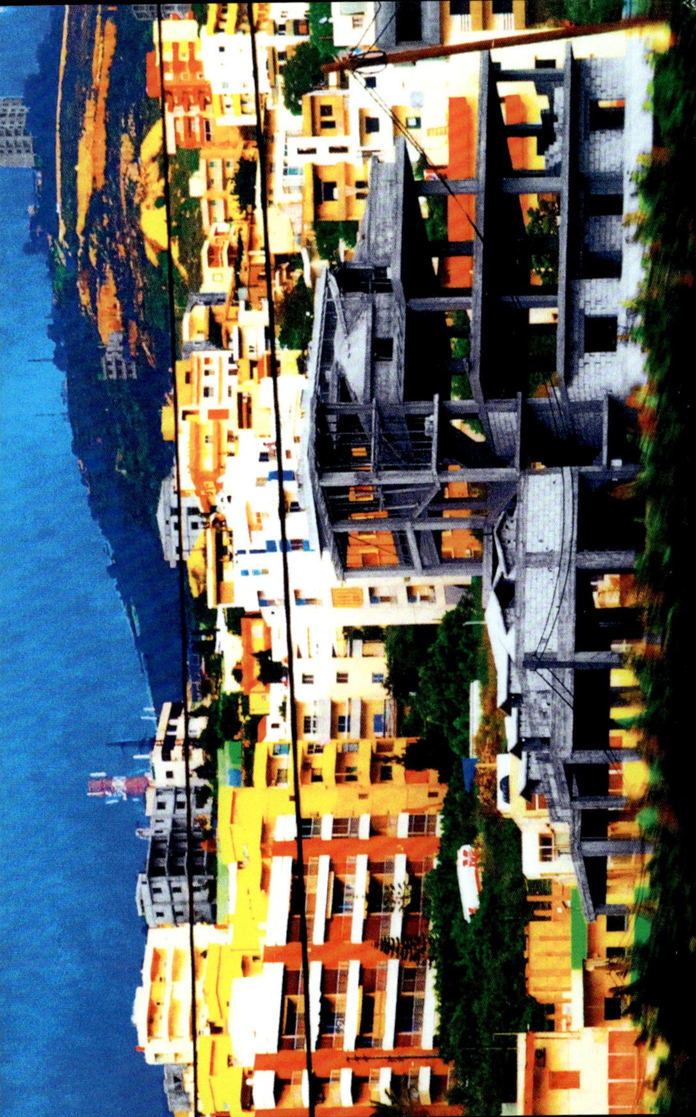

HAVEN'T SEEN STARS SINCE I'VE BEEN HERE—MOONS OR SUNS EITHER."

"YEAH, BUT—"

"I'VE THOUGHT, MAYBE: IT'S NOT THE SEASON THAT CHANGES. IT'S US. THE WHOLE CITY SHIFTS, TURNS, REARRANGES ITSELF. ALL THE TIME. AND REARRANGES US..." HE LAUGHED. "HEY, I'M PULLING YOUR LEG, KID. COME ON." TAK RUBBED HIS STOMACH AGAIN. "YOU TAKE IT ALL TOO SERIOUSLY." STEPPING UP THE CURB, TAK PUSHED HIS HANDS INTO HIS LEATHER POCKETS. "BUT I'M DAMNED IF I WOULDN'T HAVE SWORN MORNING USED TO START OVER THERE."

AGAIN HE NODDED, WITH PURSED LIPS. "ALL THAT MEANS IS I WASN'T PAYING ATTENTION, DOESN'T IT?" AT THE NEXT CORNER HE ASKED: "WHAT WERE YOU IN A MENTAL HOSPITAL FOR?"

"DEPRESSION. BUT IT WAS A LONG TIME AGO."

"YEAH?"

"I WAS HEARING VOICES; AFRAID TO GO OUT; I COULDN'T REMEMBER THINGS; SOME HALLUCINATIONS—THE WHOLE BIT. IT WAS RIGH AFTER I FINISHED MY FIRST YEAR OF COLLEGE. WHEN I WAS NINETEEN. I USED TO DRINK A LOT TOO."

"WHAT DID THE VOICES SAY?"

HE SHRUGGED. "NOTHING. SINGING... A LOT, BUT IN SOME OTHER LANGUAGE. AND CALLING

UNFINISHED STATE // 2D.061

FROM: WILLIAM DHALGREN
ARCHIVE BOOKS
DIEFFENBACHSTRAßE 31
10967 BERLIN, GERMANY

TO: العنوان ناقص

UNFINISHED BUILDING WITH DORMERS

STANDING ABOVE THE BANANA FIELDS

BYBLOS

LEBANON

REGULAR MAIL

7870078900040110

50 Jahre Fehmarnsundbrücke

Deutschland 75

CN 15

Unknown at this address

Déménagé sans laisser d'adresse

Moved, left no address

Adresse insuffisante pour la livraison

Insufficient address for delivery

wwf.de

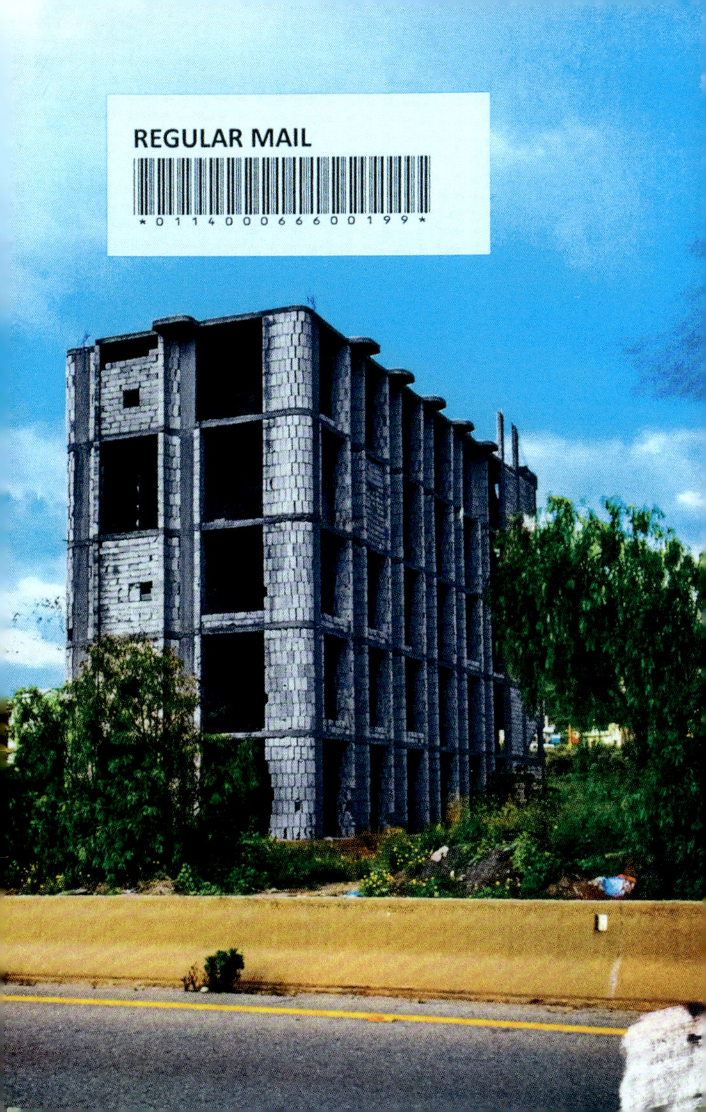
REGULAR MAIL
011400066600199

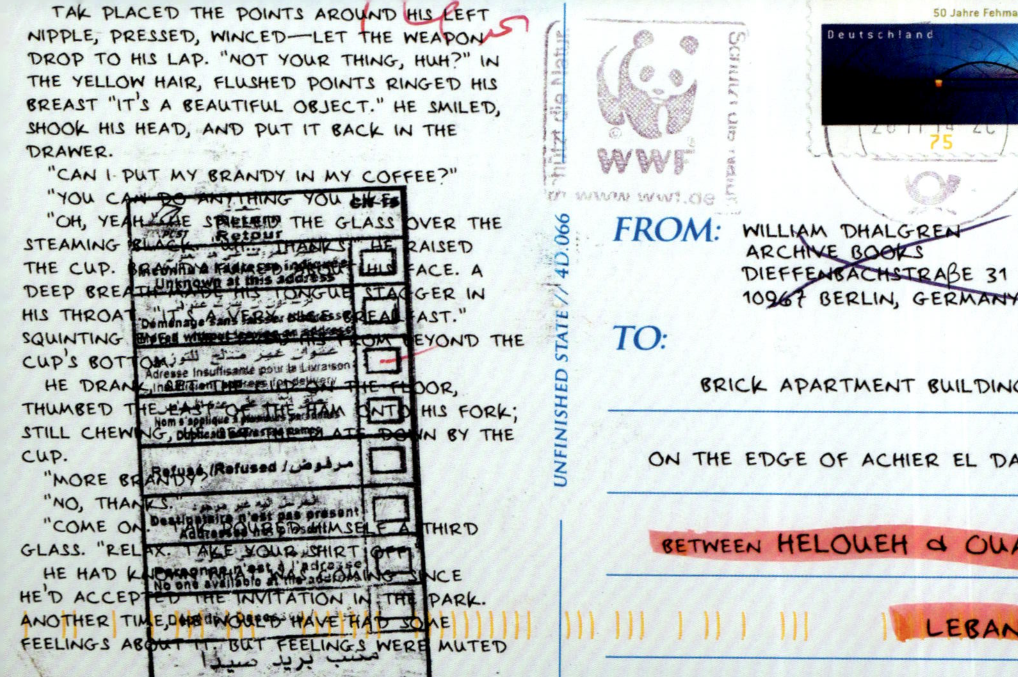

TAK PLACED THE POINTS AROUND HIS LEFT NIPPLE, PRESSED, WINCED—LET THE WEAPON DROP TO HIS LAP. "NOT YOUR THING, HUH?" IN THE YELLOW HAIR, FLUSHED POINTS RINGED HIS BREAST "IT'S A BEAUTIFUL OBJECT." HE SMILED, SHOOK HIS HEAD, AND PUT IT BACK IN THE DRAWER.
"CAN I PUT MY BRANDY IN MY COFFEE?"
"YOU CAN DO ANYTHING YOU LIKE."
"OH, YEAH." HE SPILLED THE GLASS OVER THE STEAMING BLACK. "THANKS." HE RAISED THE CUP. BRANDY FLARED ABOUT HIS FACE. A DEEP BREATH MADE HIS TONGUE STAGGER IN HIS THROAT. "IT'S A VERY NICE BREAKFAST."
SQUINTING
FROM BEYOND THE CUP'S BOTTOM.
HE DRANK
ON THE FLOOR, THUMBED THE LAST OF THE HAM ONTO HIS FORK; STILL CHEWING,
DOWN BY THE CUP.
"MORE BRANDY?"
"NO, THANKS."
"COME ON."
HIMSELF A THIRD GLASS. "RELAX. TAKE YOUR SHIRT OFF."
HE HAD KNOWN
SINCE HE'D ACCEPTED THE INVITATION IN THE PARK. ANOTHER TIME, HE WOULD HAVE HAD SOME FEELINGS ABOUT IT. BUT FEELINGS WERE MUTED
Retour
Inconnu à l'adresse indiquée
Unknown at this address
Déménagé sans laisser d'adresse
Moved without leaving an address
Adresse Insuffisante pour la Livraison
Insufficient address for delivery
Nom s'applique à plusieurs personnes
Duplicate addresses names
Refusé /Refused / مرفوض
Destinataire n'est pas présent
Addressee not present
Personne n'est à l'adresse
No one available at the address
مكتب بريد صيدا
50 Jahre Fehmarnsundbrücke
Deutschland
75
WWF
Schützt die Natur
www.wwf.de
UNFINISHED STATE // 4D.066
FROM: WILLIAM DHALGREN
ARCHIVE BOOKS
DIEFFENBACHSTRAßE 31
10967 BERLIN, GERMANY
TO:
BRICK APARTMENT BUILDING
ON THE EDGE OF ACHIER EL DAYA
BETWEEN HELOUEH & OUATA
LEBANON

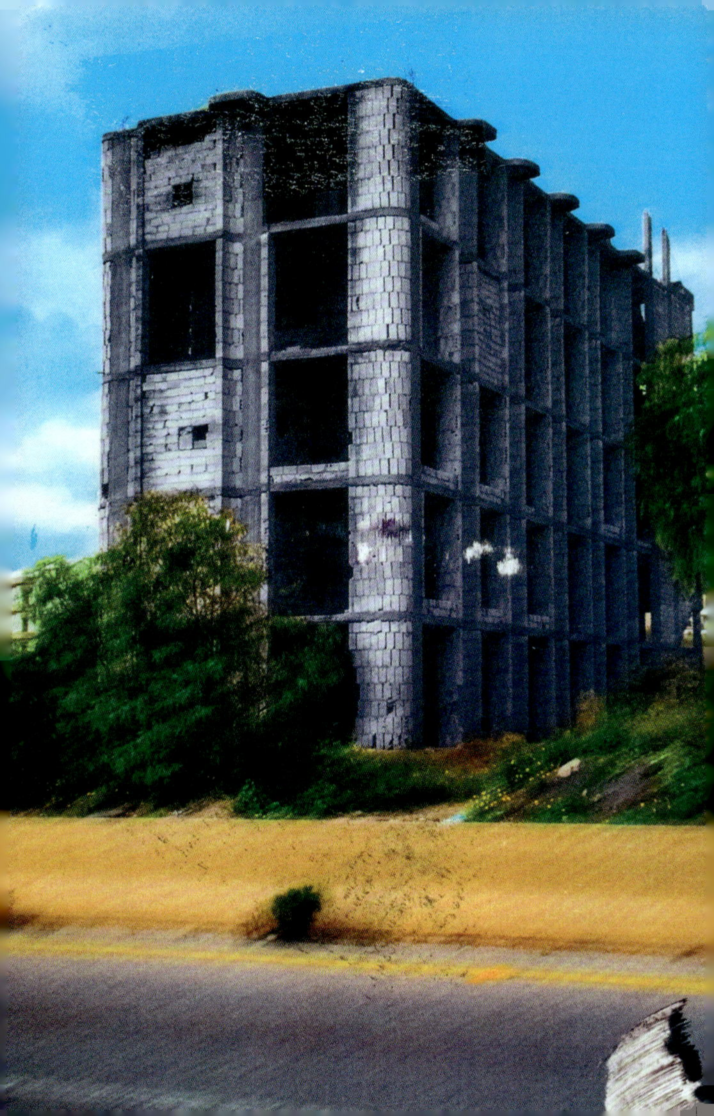

IN HIM; THINGS HAD DRIFTED TO THIS WITHOUT HIS REALLY CONSIDERING. HE TRIED TO THINK OF SOMETHING TO SAY, COULDN'T, SO UNBUTTONED THE THREE BUTTONS, PULLED THE TAILS FROM HIS PANTS.

TAK RAISED HIS EYEBROWS AT THE OPTICAL CHAIN. "WHERE'D YOU GET THAT?"

"ON MY WA[illegible]"

"OUTSIDE THE CITY."

"IT SAYS MADE IN BRAZIL, I THINK."

TAK SHOOK HIS HEAD. "BELLONA HAS BECOME A CITY OF ST[illegible]." HE BURLESQUED THE WORD WITH A DRA[illegible] AH [illegible] NOTIONS THAT ARE EN[illegible] HERE. ORCHIDS, LIGHT-SHIELDS, THAT CHAIN YOU'RE WEARING—OUR LOCAL FOLK ART."

"I'M NOT GOING TO TAKE IT OFF!" THE CONVICTION SURPRISED HIM; ITS ARTICULATION ASTOUNDED HIM.

TAK LAUGHED. "I WASN'T GOING TO ASK YOU TO." HE LOOKED DOWN AT HIS CHEST, RAN HIS FOREFINGER, IN THE HAIR, FROM ONE D[illegible]K DOT TO THE NEXT—STILL VISIBLE WHERE HE'D PRESSED THE ORCHID PRONGS. "YOU'VE GOT SOME NERVE THINKING YOU WERE EVER ANY CRAZIER THAN ANYBODY ELSE."

HIS SHIRT LAY BESIDE HIM ON THE BED. HE PULLED HIS HANDS TOGETHER INTO HIS LAP,

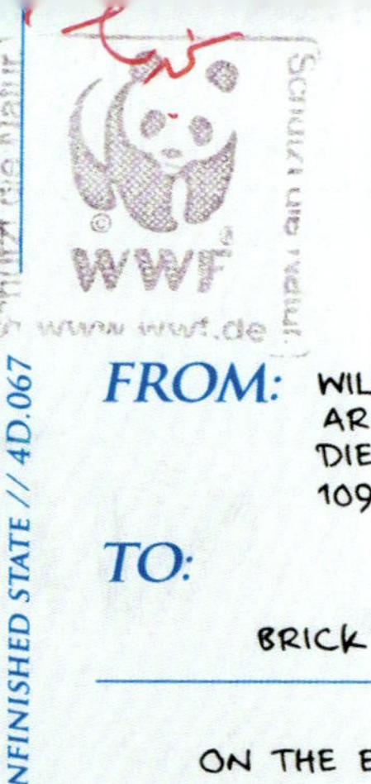

UNFINISHED STATE // 4D.067

FROM: WILLIAM DHALGREN
ARCHIVE BOOKS
DIEFFENBACHSTRAßE 31
10967 BERLIN, GERMANY

TO:

BRICK APARTMENT BUILDING

ON THE EDGE OF ACHIER EL DAYA

BETWEEN HELOUEH & OUATA

LEBANON

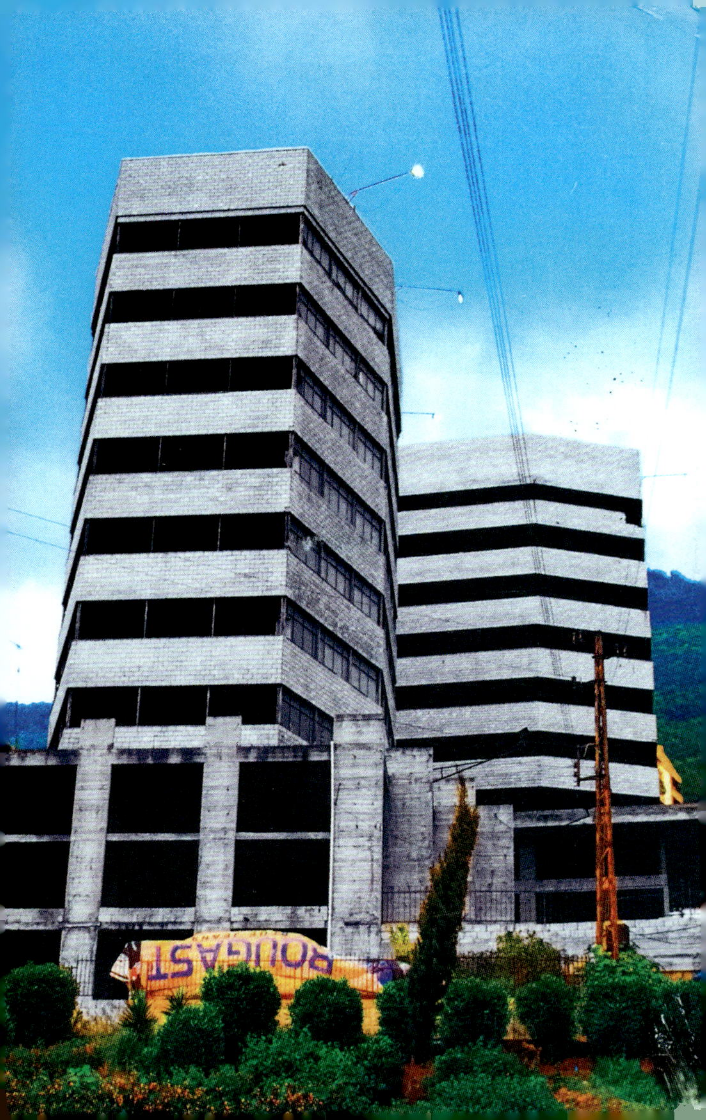

LAUGHED AND PRESSED HIS PALM ON THE STONE JAW; MOVED HIS HAND. STAIN PASSED BETWEEN HIS FINGERS. THE SKY—HE'D LAUGHED, FLUNG UP HIS HEAD—DID NOT LOOK INFINITELY FAR; A SOFT CEILING, RATHER, AT SOME DECEPTIVE TWENTY, A HUNDRED TWENTY FEET. OH YES, LAUGHTER WAS GOOD. HIS EYES FILLED WITH THE BLURRY SKY AND TEARS; HE MOVED HIS HAND ON THE PITTED JAW. WHEN HE TOOK HIS PALM FROM THE DENSE BRAILLE HE WAS BREATHING HARD.

NO GUSHING BREEZE OVER THIS GRASS. HIS BREATH WAS THIN, HOARSE, SUGGESTIVE OF PHLEGM AND OBSTACLES AND VEINS. STILL HE'D LAUGHED.

THE SCULPTOR HAD DUG HOLES FOR EYES TOO DEEP TO SPOT BOTTOM.

HE DUG HIS FINGER IN HIS NOSE AGAIN, SUCKED IT, GNAWED IT, A GUSTY CHUCKLE, AND HE TURNED THROUGH THE LEONINE GATE. IT'S EASY, HE THOUGHT, TO PUT SOUNDS WITH EITHER WHITE (MAYBE THE PURE TONE OF AN AUDIO GENERATOR; AND THE OTHER, ITS OPPOSITE THAT WAS CALLED WHITE NOISE), BLACK (LARGE GONGS, LARGER BELLS), OR THE PRIMARY COLORS (THE VARIETY OF THE ORCHESTRA). PALE GREY IS SILENCE.

A GOOD WIND COULD WAKE THIS CITY. AS HE—WANDERED IN, BUILDINGS DROPPED BEHIND

Schützt die Natur

REGULAR MAIL

0114000684002O7

50 Jahre Fehmarnsundbrücke

Deutschland

75

WILLIAM DHALGREN
ARCHIVE BOOKS
DIEFFENBACHSTRAßE 31
10967 BERLIN, GERMANY

HEXAGON TOWER

SEA SIDE RD., SOUTH EAST SIDE

JUST NORTH OF DAOURA

BEIRUT, LEBANON

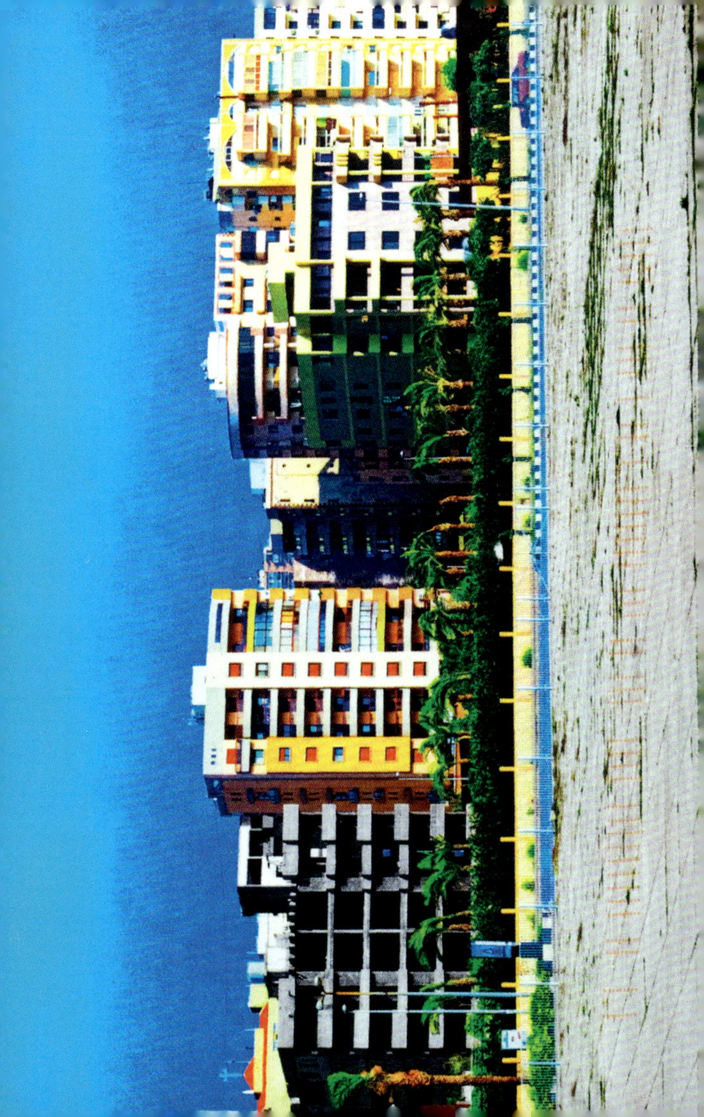

PUT ON THE OTHER 'D'. BUT IT ISN'T MY NAME. I DON'T REMEMBER MY GOD-DAMN NAME."

THE TURNING HALTED.

"THAT'S LIKE BEING CRAZY. I FORGET LOTS OF OTHER THINGS. TOO. WHAT DO YOU THINK ABOUT THAT:" AND DIDN'T KNOW HOW HE WOULD HAVE INTERPRETED HIS FALLING INFLECTION EITHER.

SHE SAID: "I DON'T REALLY KNOW."

HE SAID, AFTER THE SILENT BRIDGE: "WELL, YOU HAVE TO THINK SOMETHING!"

SHE REACHED INTO THE COILED BLANKET AND LIFTED OUT... THE NOTEBOOK? HE RECOGNIZED THE CHARRED COVER.

BITING AT HER LIP, SHE BEGAN RUFFLING PAGES. SUDDENLY SHE STOPPED, HANDED IT TO HIM – "ARE ANY OF THESE NAMES YOURS?"

THE LIST, NEATLY PRINTED IN BALLPOINT, FILLED TWO COLUMNS:

GEOFF RIVERS	ARTHUR PEARSON
KIT DARKFEATHER	EARLTON RUDOLPH
DAVID WISE	PHILLIP EDWARDS
MICHAEL ROBERTS	VIRGINIA COLSON
JERRY SHANK	HANK KAISER
FRANK YOSHIKAMI	GARRY DISCH
HAROLD REDWING	ALVIN FISCHER
MADELEINE TERRY	SUSAN MORGAN
PRISCILLA MEYER	WILLIAM DHALGREN
GEORGE NEWMAN	PETER WELDON
ANN HARRISON	LINDA EVERS
THOMAS SASK	PRESTON SMITH

Return / Retour CN
Inconnu à l'adresse indiquée / Unknown at this address
Déménagé sans laisser d'adresse / Moved without leaving an address
Adresse insuffisante pour la livraison / Insufficient address for delivery
Nom s'applique à plusieurs personnes / Duplicate addressee names
Refusé / Refused / مرفوض
Destinataire n'est pas présent / Addressee not present
Personne n'est à l'adresse / No one available at the address
Décédé / Deceased / متوفى
مكتب بريد طرابلس البلد

UNFINISHED STATE // SD.076

FROM: WILLIAM DHALGREN
ARCHIVE BOOKS
DIEFFENBACHSTRAßE 31
10967 BERLIN, GERMANY

TO:
BOXY APARTMENT BUILDING
EAST ENTRY TO RACHID KARAMI
INTERNATIONAL FAIR PARK
AL MARAAD CIRCLE
TRIPOLI, LEBANON

Deutschland 75
50 Jahre Fehmarnsundbrücke
ZENTRUM

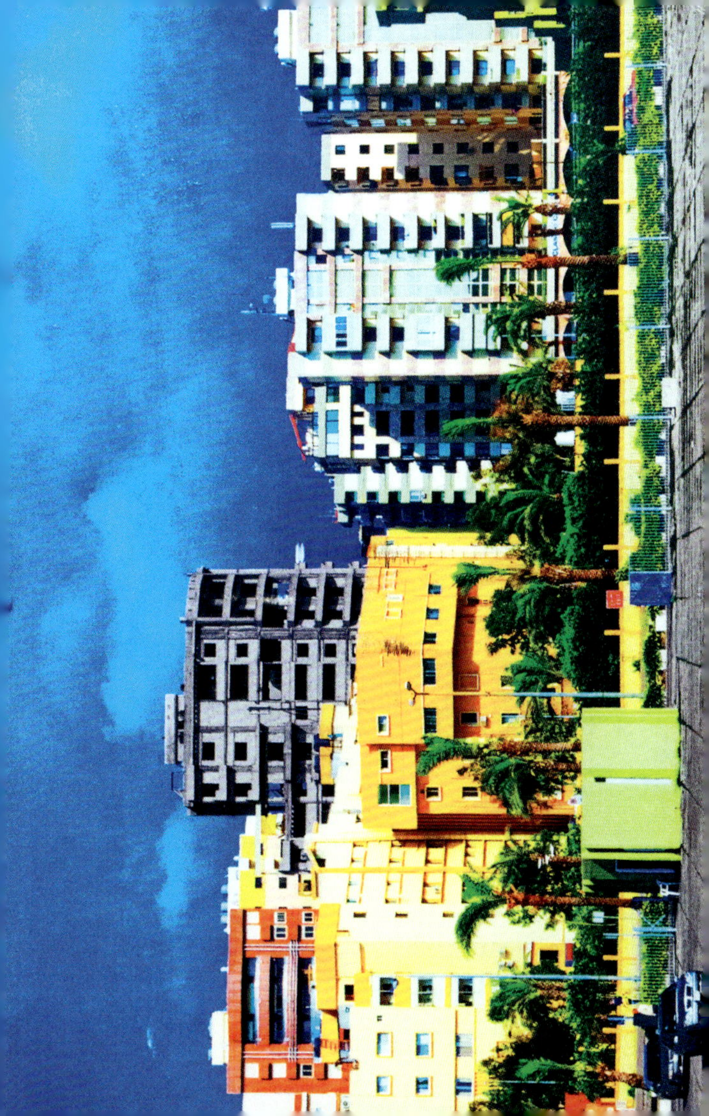

WHAT WAS IN THE BLOCK OF WRITING BELOW THE LISTS—"THAT WE'RE IN A CITY, AN ABANDONED CITY. IT'S BURNING, SEE. ALL THE POWER'S OUT. THEY CAN'T GET TELEVISION CAMERAS AND RADIOS IN HERE, RIGHT? SO EVERYBODY OUTSIDE'S FORGOTTEN ABOUT IT. NO WORD COMES OUT. NO WORD COMES IN. WE'LL PRETEND IT'S ALL COVERED WITH SMOKE, OKAY? BUT NOW YOU CAN'T EVEN SEEN THE FIRE."

"JUST THE SMOKE," SHE SAID. "LET'S PRETEND—"

HE BLINKED.

"—YOU AND I ARE SITTING IN A GREY PARK ON A GREY DAY IN A GREY CITY." SHE FROWNED AT THE SKY. "A PERFECTLY ORDINARY CITY. THE AIR POLLUTION IS TERRIBLE HERE." SHE SMILED. "I LIKE GREY DAYS, DAYS LIKE THIS, DAYS WITHOUT SHADOWS—" THEN SHE SAW HE HAD JABBED HIS ORCHID AGAINST THE LOG.

PINIONED TO THE BARK, HIS FIST SHOOK AMONG THE BLADES.

SHE WAS ON HER KNEES BESIDE HIM: "I'LL TELL YOU WHAT LET'S DO. LET'S TAKE THAT OFF!" SHE TUGGED AT THE WRIST SNAP. HIS ARM SHOOK IN HER FINGERS. "HERE." THEN HIS HAND WAS FREE.

HE WAS BREATHING HARD. "THAT'S—" HE LOOKED AT THE WEAPON STILL FIXED BY THREE POINTS—"A PRETTY WICKED THING. LEAVE IT

مرسوم على سر ١٢٨٧

50 Jahre Fehmarnsundbrücke
Deutschland
75

Return
Retour
CN
غير معروف على هذا العنوان
Inconnu à l'adresse indiquée
Unknown at this address
Déménagé sans laisser d'adresse
Moved without leaving an address
عنوان غير كاف للتوزيع
Adresse insuffisante pour la livraison
Insufficient address for delivery
Nom s'applique à plusieurs personnes
Duplicate addressee names
Refusé / Refused
Destinataire n'est pas présent
Addressee not present
Personne n'est à l'adresse
No one available at the address
Décédé / Deceased / متوفى
مكتب بريد طرابلس البلد

UNFINISHED STATE // SD 078

FROM: WILLIAM DHALGREN
ARCHIVE BOOKS
DIEFFENBACHSTRAßE 31
10967 BERLIN, GERMANY

TO:
UNFINISHED APARTMENT COMPLEX
EAST ENTRY TO RACHID KARAMI
INTERNATIONAL FAIR PARK
AL MARAAD CIRCLE
TRIPOLI, LEBANON

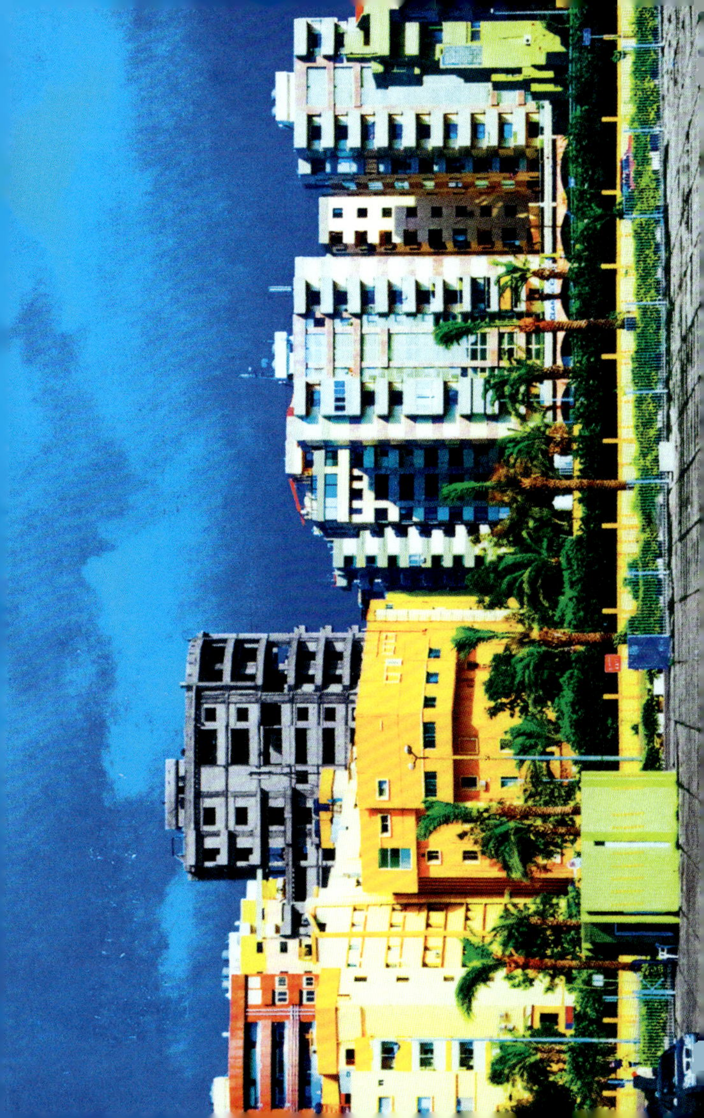

THE FUCK ALONE."

"IT'S A TOOL," SHE SAID. "YOU MAY NEED IT. JUST KNOW WHEN TO USE IT." SHE WAS RUBBING HIS HAND.

HIS HEART WAS SLOWING. HE TOOK ANOTHER, VERY DEEP BREATH. "YOU OUGHT TO BE AFRAID OF ME, YOU KNOW?"

SHE BLINKED. "I AM." AND SAT BACK ON HER HEELS. "BUT I WANT TO TRY OUT SOME THINGS I'M AFRAID OF. THAT'S THE ONLY REASON TO BE HERE. WHAT," SHE ASKED, "HAPPENED TO YOU JUST THEN?"

"HUH?"

SHE PUT THREE FINGERS ON HIS FOREHEAD, THEN SHOWED HIM THE GLISTENING PADS. "YOU'RE SWEATING."

"I WAS... VERY HAPPY ALL OF A SUDDEN."

SHE FROWNED. "I THOUGHT YOU WERE SCARED TO DEATH!"

HE CLEARED HIS THROAT, TRIED TO SMILE. "IT WAS LIKE A... WELL, SUDDENLY BEING VERY HAPPY. I WAS HAPPY WHEN I WALKED INTO THE PARK. AND THEN ALL OF A SUDDEN IT JUST..." HE WAS RUBBING HER HAND BACK.

"OKAY." SHE LAUGHED. "THAT SOUNDS GOOD."

HIS JAW WAS CLAMPED. HE LET IT LOOSEN, AND GRUNTED: "WHO... WHAT KIND OF A PERSON ARE YOU?"

UNFINISHED STATE // 5D 079

FROM: WILLIAM DHALGREN
ARCHIVE BOOKS
DIEFFENBACHSTRAẞE 31
10967 BERLIN, GERMANY

TO:
UNFINISHED APARTMENT COMPLEX
EAST ENTRY TO RACHID KARAMI
INTERNATIONAL FAIR PARK
AL MARAAD CIRCLE
TRIPOLI, LEBANON

Return / Retour
Refusé / Refused
Décédé / Deceased

Deutschland 75
50 Jahre Fehmarnsundbrücke

Schützt die Natur
WWF
www.wwf.de

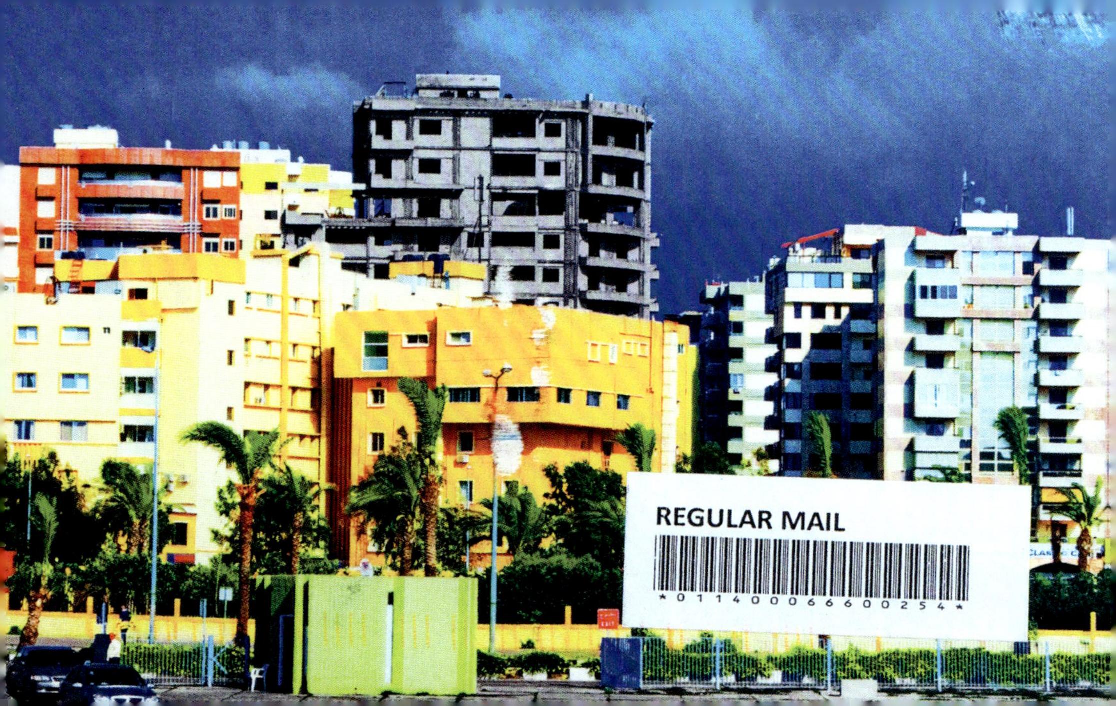
REGULAR MAIL
01140006660254

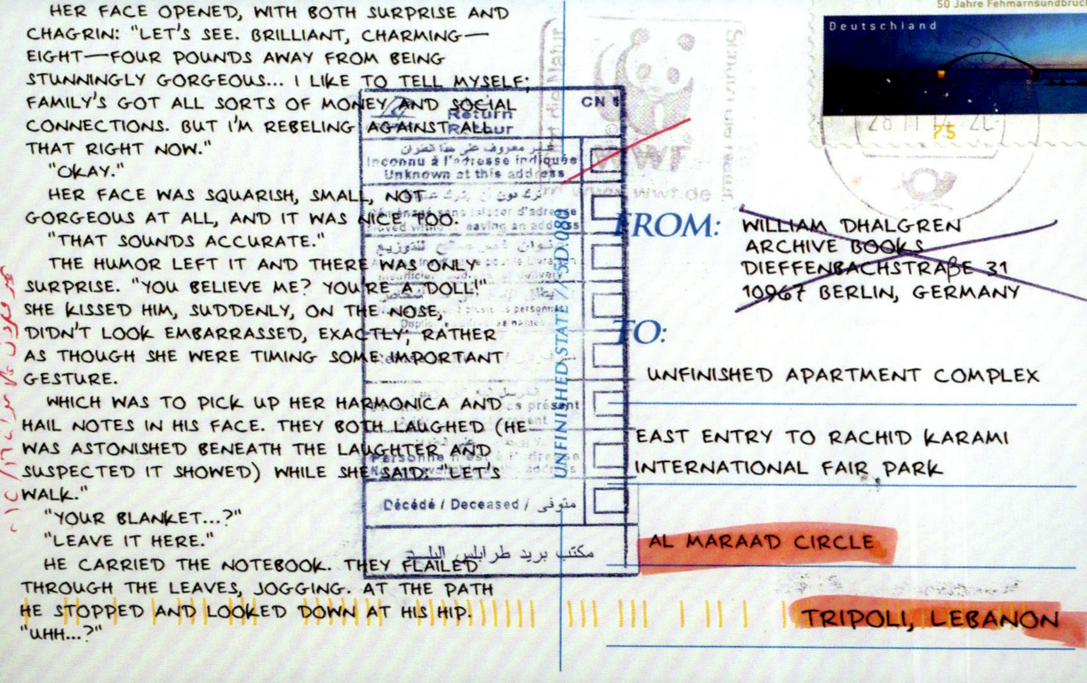
HER FACE OPENED, WITH BOTH SURPRISE AND CHAGRIN: "LET'S SEE. BRILLIANT, CHARMING—EIGHT—FOUR POUNDS AWAY FROM BEING STUNNINGLY GORGEOUS... I LIKE TO TELL MYSELF; FAMILY'S GOT ALL SORTS OF MONEY AND SOCIAL CONNECTIONS. BUT I'M REBELING AGAINST ALL THAT RIGHT NOW."
"OKAY."
HER FACE WAS SQUARISH, SMALL, NOT GORGEOUS AT ALL, AND IT WAS NICE TOO.
"THAT SOUNDS ACCURATE."
THE HUMOR LEFT IT AND THERE WAS ONLY SURPRISE. "YOU BELIEVE ME? YOU'RE A DOLL!" SHE KISSED HIM, SUDDENLY, ON THE NOSE, DIDN'T LOOK EMBARRASSED, EXACTLY, RATHER AS THOUGH SHE WERE TIMING SOME IMPORTANT GESTURE.
WHICH WAS TO PICK UP HER HARMONICA AND HAIL NOTES IN HIS FACE. THEY BOTH LAUGHED (HE WAS ASTONISHED BENEATH THE LAUGHTER AND SUSPECTED IT SHOWED) WHILE SHE SAID: "LET'S WALK."
"YOUR BLANKET...?"
"LEAVE IT HERE."
HE CARRIED THE NOTEBOOK. THEY FLAILED THROUGH THE LEAVES, JOGGING. AT THE PATH HE STOPPED AND LOOKED DOWN AT HIS HIP.
"UHH...?"
50 Jahre Fehmarnsundbrücke
Deutschland
75
CN
Return
Inconnu à l'adresse indiquée
Unknown at this address
Décédé / Deceased / متوفى
مكتب بريد طرابلس البلد
UNFINISHED STATE // 5D.080
FROM:
WILLIAM DHALGREN
ARCHIVE BOOKS
DIEFFENBACHSTRAßE 31
10967 BERLIN, GERMANY
TO:
UNFINISHED APARTMENT COMPLEX
EAST ENTRY TO RACHID KARAMI
INTERNATIONAL FAIR PARK
AL MARAAD CIRCLE
TRIPOLI, LEBANON

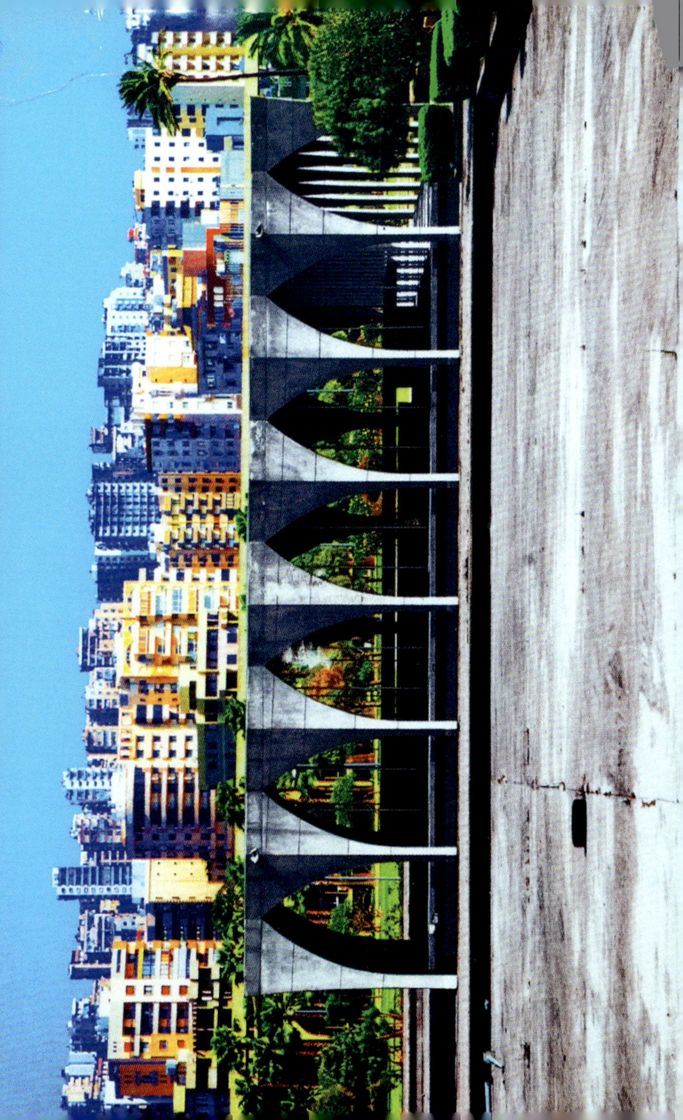

SHE LOOKED OVER.

"DO YOU," HE ASKED SLOWLY, "REMEMBER MY PICKING UP THE ORCHID AND PUTTING IT ON BELT HERE?"

"I PUT IT ON THERE." SHE THUMBED SOME BLEMISH ON THE HARMONICA. "YOU WERE GOIN TO LEAVE IT BEHIND, SO I STUCK A BLADE THROUGH YOUR BELT LOOP. REALLY. IT CAN BE DANGEROUS AROUND HERE."

MOUTH SLIGHTLY OPEN, HE NODDED AS, SIDE BY SIDE, THEY GAINED THE SHADOWLESS PATHS.

HE SAID: "YOU STUCK IT THERE." SOMEWHERE A BREEZE, WITHOUT FORCE, MADE ITS EASY WA IN THE GREEN. HE WAS AWARE OF THE SMOKY ODOR ABOUT THEM FOR TWO BREATHS BEFORE IT FADED WITH INATTENTION. "ALL BY YOURSELF YOU JUST FOUND THOSE PEOPLE IN THE PARK?"

SHE GAVE HIM A YOU-MUST-BE-OUT-OF-YOUR-MIND LOOK. "I CAME IN WITH QUITE A PARTY, ACTUALLY. FUN; BUT AFTER A COUPLE OF DAYS THEY WERE GETTING IN THE WAY. I MEAN IT'S NICE TO HAVE A CAR. BUT IF YOU'RE RENDERED HELPLESS BY LACK OF GASOLINE..." SHE SHRUGGED. "BEFORE WE GOT HERE, PHIL AND I WERE TAKING BETS WHETHER THIS PLACE REALLY EXISTED OR NOT." HER SUDDEN AND SURPRISING SMILE WAS ALL EYES AND VERY LITTLE MOUTH. "I WON. I STAYED WITH THE GROUP I CAME IN WITH

REGULAR MAIL

0115000022009 32

50 Jahre Fehmarnsundbrücke

Deutschland 75

26 JAN 2015

TRIPOLI CENTER

UNFIN

OM: WILLIAM DHALGREN
ARCHIVE BOOKS
DIEFFENBACHSTRAßE 31
10967 BERLIN, GERMANY

OPEN PAVILION

RACHID KARAMI INTERNATIONAL FAIR PARK

AL MARAAD CIRCLE

TRIPOLI, LEBANON

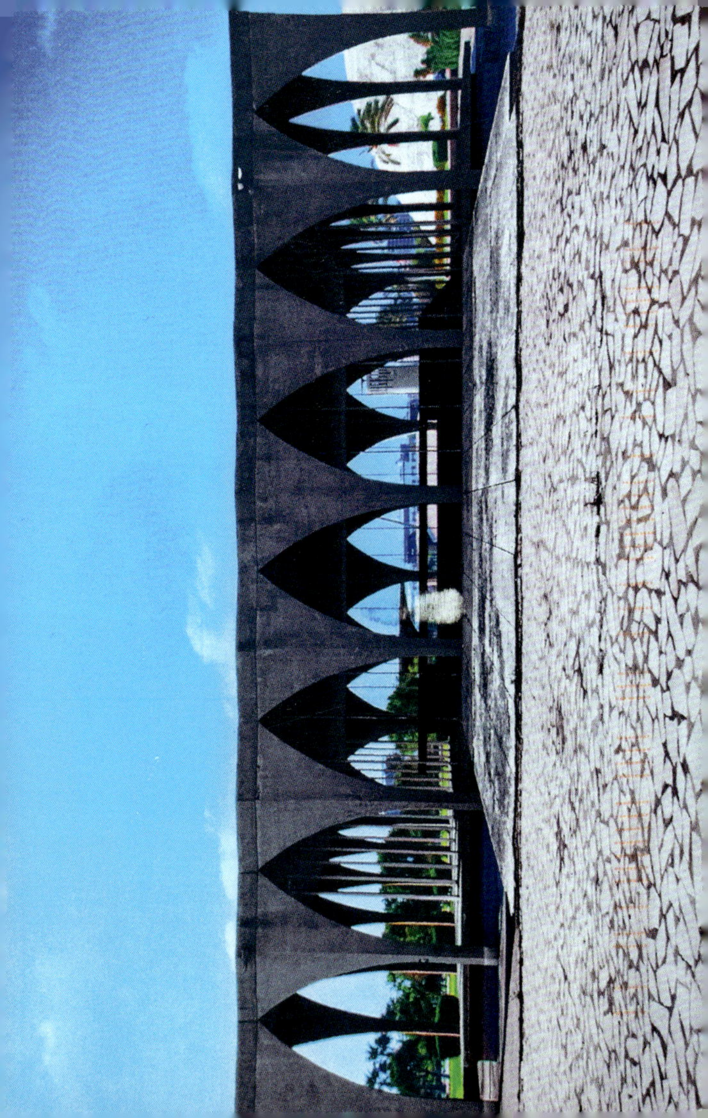

LOOKED AT HIM CURIOUSLY, LAUGHED, AND HIT AT THE HIGH STEMS. HE LOOKED; AND HER EYES, WAITING FOR HIM TO SPEAK, WERE GREENER THAN THE HAZE ALLOWED ANY LEAF AROUND.

"IT'S LIKE A SMALL TOWN," HE SAID. "IS THERE ANYTHING ELSE TO DO BUT GOSSIP?"

"NOT REALLY." SHE HIT THE STEMS AGAIN. "WHICH IS A RELIEF, IF YOU LOOK AT IT THAT WAY."

"WHERE DOES CALKINS LIVE?"

"OH, YOU LIKE TO GOSSIP! I WAS SCARED FOR A MOMENT." SHE STOPPED KNOCKING THE STALKS. "HIS NEWSPAPER OFFICE IS AWFUL! HE TOOK SOME OF US THERE, RIGHT TO WHERE THEY PRINT IT. GREY AND GLOOMY AND DISMAL AND ECHOING." SHE SCREWED UP HER FACE AND HER SHOULDERS AND HER HANDS. "AHHHH! BUT HIS HOUSE—" EVERYTHING UNSCREWED. "JUST FINE. RIGHT ABOVE THE HEIGHTS. LOTS OF GROUNDS. YOU CAN SEE THE WHOLE CITY. I IMAGINE IT MUST HAVE BEEN QUITE A SIGHT WHEN ALL THE STREET LIGHTS WERE ON AT NIGHT." A SMALL SCREWING, NOW. "I WAS TRYING TO FIGURE OUT WHETHER HE'S ALWAYS LIVED THERE, OR IF HE JUST MOVED IN AND TOOK IT OVER TOO. BUT YOU DON'T ASK QUESTIONS LIKE THAT."

HE TURNED AND SHE FOLLOWED.

"WHERE IS HIS HOUSE?"

UNFINISHED STATE // 5D.084

FROM: WILLIAM DHALGREN
ARCHIVE BOOKS
DIEFFENBACHSTRAẞE 31
10967 BERLIN, GERMANY

TO:

OPEN PAVILION

RACHID KARAMI INTERNATIONAL FAIR PARK

AL MARAAD CIRCLE

TRIPOLI, LEBANON

Return Retour

Deutschland 75

50 Jahre Fehmarnsundbrücke

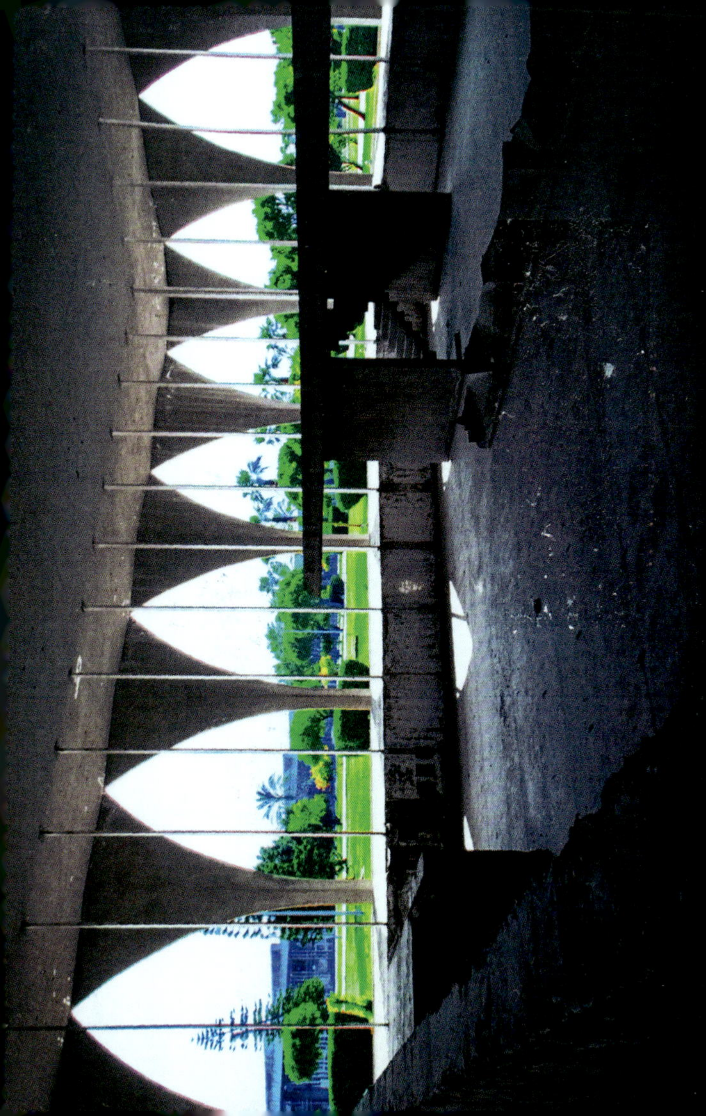

"I THINK THE ACTUAL ADDRESS IS ON BRISBAIN SOUTH."

"HOW'D YOU GET TO MEET HIM?"

"THEY WERE HAVING A PARTY. I WAS WANDERING BY. SOMEONE I KNEW INVITED ME IN. PHIL, ACTUALLY."

"THAT SOUNDS EASY."

"AH, IT WAS VERY DIFFICULT. YOU WANT TO GO UP THERE AND MEET CALKINS?"

"WELL, EVERYTHING LOOKS PRETTY SCROUNGY DOWN AROUND HERE. I COULD WANDER UP AND SEE IF SOMEBODY WOULD INVITE ME IN." HE PAUSED. "OF COURSE, YOU'RE A GIRL. YOU'D HAVE AN EASIER TIME, WOULDN'T YOU? TO BE... DECORATIVE?"

SHE RAISED HER EYEBROWS. "NOT NECESSARILY."

HE GLANCED AT HER IN TIME TO CATCH HER GLANCING BACK. THE IDEA STRUCK HIM AS AMUSING.

"YOU SEE THAT PATH BEHIND THE SOCCER POSTS?"

"YEAH."

"IT EXITS RIGHT ON TO BRISBAIN NORTH. WHICH TURNS INTO BRISBAIN SOUTH AFTER A WHILE."

"HEY!" HE GRINNED AT HER, THEN LET HIS HEAD FALL TO THE SIDE. "WHAT'S THE MATTER?"

"I'M SAD YOU'RE GOING. I WAS ALL SET FOR A DANGEROUS, EXCITING AFTERNOON, WANDERING

Deutschland 75

LIBANPOST Return Retour

UNFINISHED STATE ANNO 1985

FROM: WILLIAM DHALGREN
ARCHIVE BOOKS
DIEFFENBACHSTRAẞE 31
10967 BERLIN, GERMANY

TO: OPEN PAVILION
RACHID KARAMI INTERNATIONAL
FAIR PARK
AL MARAAD CIRCLE
TRIPOLI, LEBANON

Inconnu à l'adresse indiquée / Unknown at the address
Déménagé sans laisser d'adresse / Moved without leaving an address
Refusé / Refused
Destinataire n'est pas présent / Addressee not present
Personne n'est à l'adresse / No one available at the address
Décédé / Deceased / متوفى
مكتب بريد طرابلس البلد

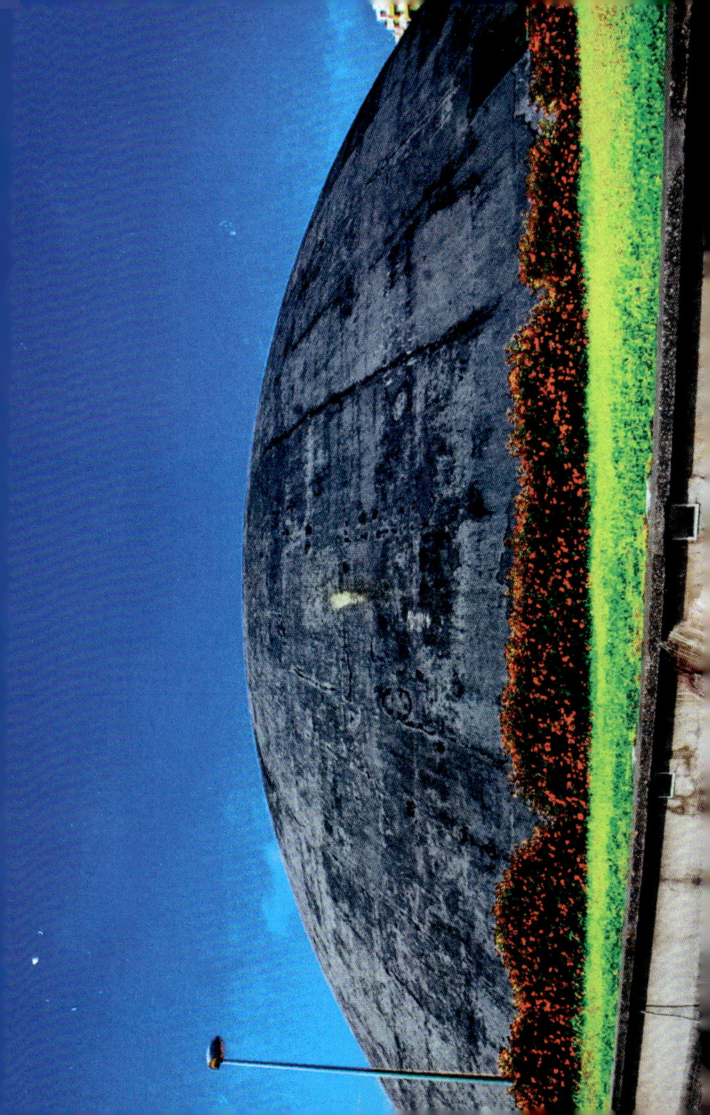

STRAIGHT. SOMETHING FELL."

"HUH?"

"SOME PEOPLE SAY A HOUSE COLLAPSED. SOME OTHERS SAY A PLANE CRASHED RIGHT THERE IN THE MIDDLE OF JACKSON. SOMEBODY ELSE WAS TALKING ABOUT SOME KID WHO GOT ON THE ROOF OF THE SECOND CITY BANK BUILDING AND GUNNED SOMEBODY DOWN."

"SOMEBODY GOT KILLED?"

"VERY. IT WAS SUPPOSED TO BE A WHITE KID ON THE ROOF AND A NIGGER THAT GOT SHOT. SO THEY STARTED A RIOT."

"WHAT DID THE PAPER SAY?"

"ABOUT EVERYTHING I DID. NOBODY KNOWS WHICH ONE HAPPENED FOR SURE."

"IF A PLANE CRASHED, SOMEBODY WOULD HAVE KNOWN."

"THIS WAS BACK AT THE BEGINNING. THINGS WERE A HELL OF A LOT MORE CONFUSED THEN. A LOT OF BUILDINGS WERE BURNING. AND THE WEATHER WAS SOMETHING ELSE. PEOPLE WERE STILL TRYING TO GET OUT. THERE WERE A HELL OF A LOT MORE PEOPLE HERE. AND THEY WERE SCARED."

"YOU WERE HERE THEN?"

JOAQUIM PRESSED HIS LIPS TILL MUSTACHE MERGED WITH BEARD. HE SHOOK HIS HEAD. "I JUST HEARD ABOUT THE NEWSPAPER ARTICLE.

UNFINISHED STATE // 5D.094

Return / Retour — Inconnu à l'adresse indiquée / Unknown at this address — Décédé / Deceased / متوفى

مكتب بريد طرابلس البلد

FROM: WILLIAM DHALGREN
ARCHIVE BOOKS
DIEFFENBACHSTRAßE 31
10967 BERLIN, GERMANY

TO: HALF-MOON DOME
RACHID KARAMI INTERNATIONAL FAIR PARK
AL MARAAD CIRCLE
TRIPOLI, LEBANON

Deutschland — 50 Jahre Fehmarnsundbrücke

28.9 14-22

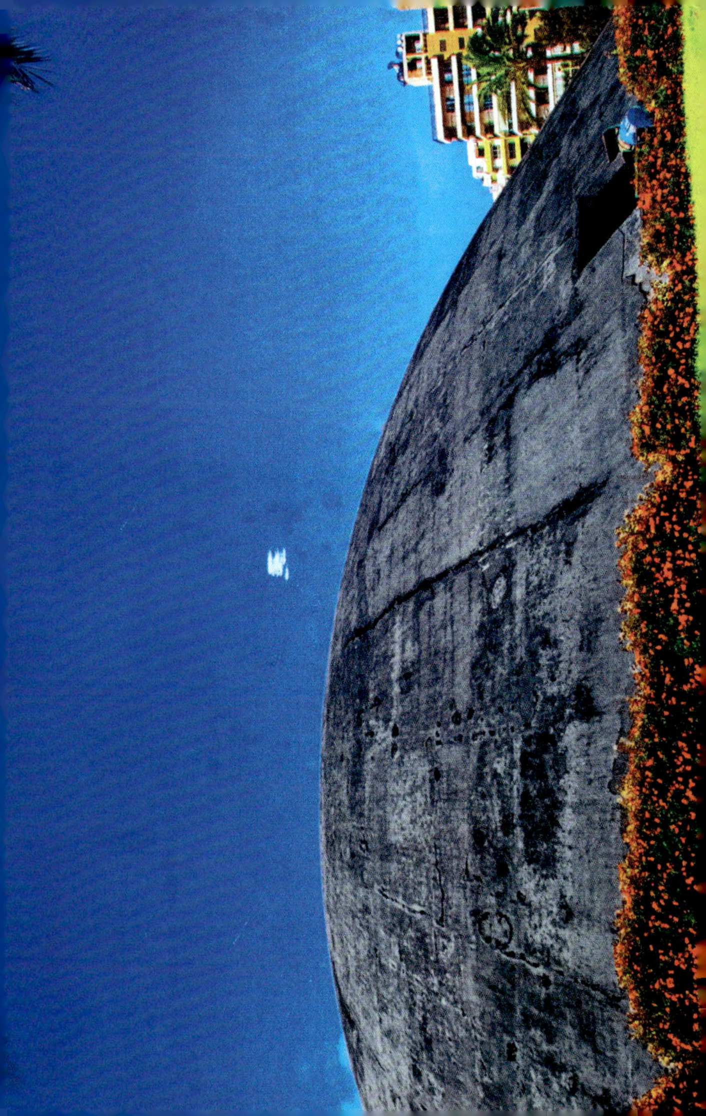

AND THE PICTURES."

"WHERE'D YOU COME FROM?"

"AHHHHH!" FAUST WAGGLED A FREE FINGER IN MOCK REPROVAL. "YOU HAVE TO LEARN NOT TO ASK QUESTIONS LIKE THAT. IT'S NOT POLITE. I DIDN'T ASK NOTHING ABOUT YOU, DID I? I TOLD YOU MY NAME, BUT I DIDN'T ASK YOURS."

"I'M SORRY." HE WAS TAKEN BACK.

"YOU GOING TO MEET A LOT OF PEOPLE WHO'LL GET ALL KINDS OF UPSET IF YOU GO ASKING THEM ABOUT BEFORE THEY CAME TO BELLONA. I MIGHT AS WELL TELL YOU, SO YOU DON'T GET YOURSELF IN TROUBLE. ESPECIALLY—" FAUST RAISED HIS BEARD AND PUT A THUMB BENEATH HIS CHOKER— "PEOPLE WEARING ONE OF THESE. LIKE US. I BET IF I ASKED YOUR NAME, OR MAYBE YOUR AGE, OR WHY YOU GOT AN ORCHID ON YOUR BELT... ANYTHING LIKE THAT, I COULD REALLY GET YOUR DANDER UP. NOW COULDN'T I?"

HE FELT THE DISCOMFORT, VAGUE AS REMEMBERED PAIN, IN HIS BELLY.

"I COME FROM CHICAGO, MOST RECENTLY. FRISCO BEFORE THAT." FAUST REACHED DOWN TO HOLD OUT ONE LEG OF HIS BELLED PANTS. "A GRANDPA YIPPIE, YEAH? I'M A TRAVELING PHILOSOPHER. IS THAT GOOD ENOUGH FOR YOU?"

"I'M SORRY I ASKED."

50 Jahre Fehmarnsundbrücke

Deutschland

28-1 14-22

LIBANPOST

Return
Retour

CN

Inconnu
Unknown

Refusé
Refused

Décédé / Deceased

UNFINISHED STATE // 5D 095

FROM: WILLIAM DHALGREN
ARCHIVE BOOKS
DIEFFENBACHSTRAßE 31
10967 BERLIN, GERMANY

TO:

HALF MOON DOME

RACHID KARAMI INTERNATIONAL
FAIR PARK

AL MARAAD CIRCLE

TRIPOLI, LEBANON

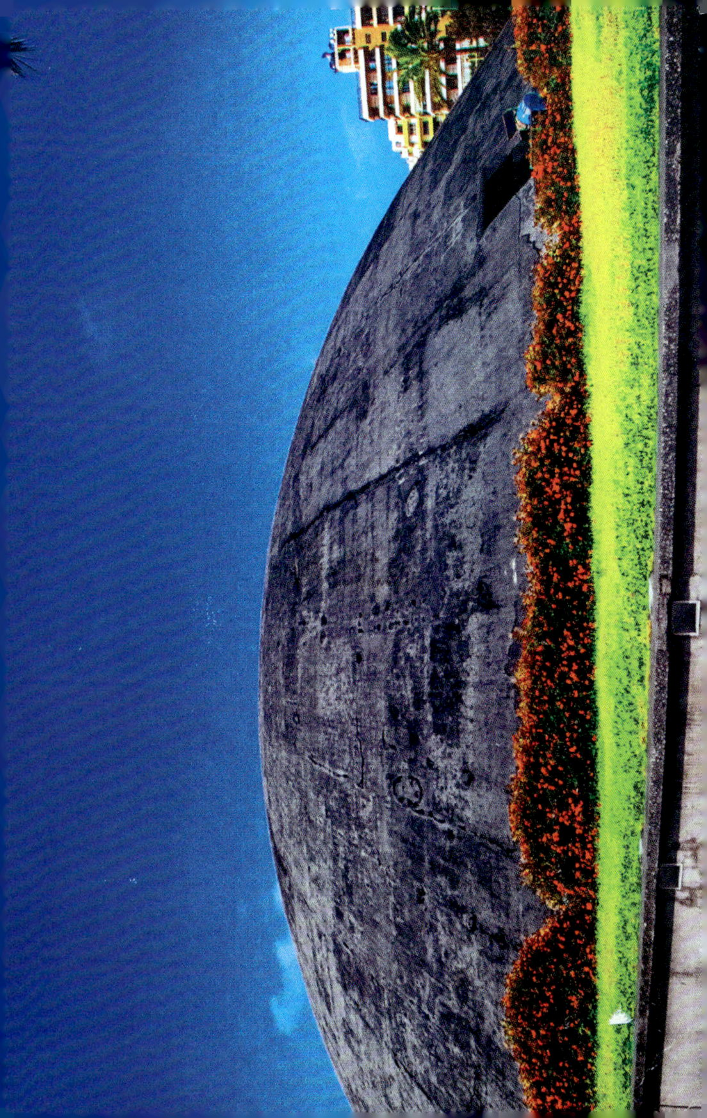

THINK NOTHING OF IT. I HEARD BELLONA WAS WHERE IT WAS AT. IT MUST BE, NOW. I'M HERE. IS THAT GOOD ENOUGH?"

HE NODDED AGAIN, DISCONCERTED.

"I GOT A GOOD, HONEST JOB. SOLD THE TRIBE ON THE COMER OF MARKET AND VAN NESS. HERE I'M BELLONA'S OLDEST NEWSPAPER BOY. IS THAT ENOUGH?"

"YEAH. LOOK, I DIDN'T MEAN—"

"SOMETHING ABOUT YOU, BOY. I DON'T LIKE IT. SAY—" EYELIDS WRINKLED BEHIND GOLD-RIMMED LENSES— "YOU'RE NOT COLORED, ARE YOU? I MEAN YOU'RE PRETTY DARK. SORT OF FULL-FEATURED. NOW, I COULD SAY 'SPADE' LIKE YOU YOUNGSTERS. BUT WHERE I WAS COMIN' UP, WHEN I WAS COMIN' UP, THEY WERE NIGGERS. THEY'RE STILL NIGGERS TO ME AND I DON'T MEAN NOTHING BY IT. I WANT ALL THE BEST FOR THEM."

"I'M AMERICAN INDIAN," HE DECIDED, WITH RESIGNED WRATH.

"OH." JOAQUIM TILTED HIS HEAD ONCE MORE TO APPRAISE. "WELL, IF YOU'RE NOT A NIGGER, YOU MUST BE PRETTY MUCH IN SYMPATHY WITH THE NIGGERS." HE CAME DOWN HEAVY ON THE WORD FOR ANY DISCOMFORT VALUE IT STILL HELD. "SO AM I. SO AM I. ONLY THEY WON'T EVER BELIEVE IT OF ME. I WOULDN'T EITHER IF I WAS THEM. BOY, I GOT TO DELIVER MY PAPERS. GO

UNFINISHED STATE // 5D.096

FROM:
WILLIAM DHALGREN
ARCHIVE BOOKS
DIEFFENBACHSTRAẞE 31
10967 BERLIN, GERMANY

TO:
HALF-MOON DOME
RACHID KARAMI
INTERNATIONAL FAIR PARK
AL MARAAD CIRCLE
TRIPOLI, LEBANON

Return / Retour
Inconnu à l'adresse indiquée / Unknown at this address
Déménagé sans laisser d'adresse / Moved without leaving an address
Adresse insuffisante pour la Livraison / Insufficient address for delivery
Nom s'applique à plusieurs personnes / Duplicate addressee names
Refusé / Refused
Destinataire n'est pas présent / Addressee not present
Personne n'est à l'adresse / No one available at the address
Décédé / Deceased

Deutschland 75

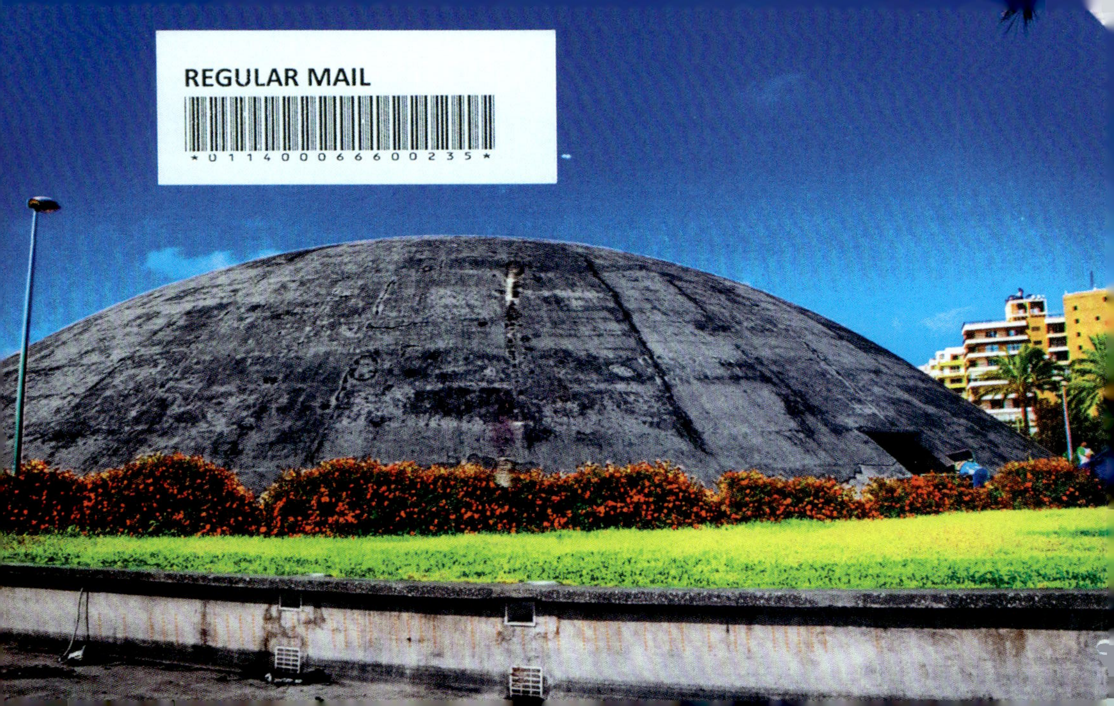
REGULAR MAIL
011400066600235

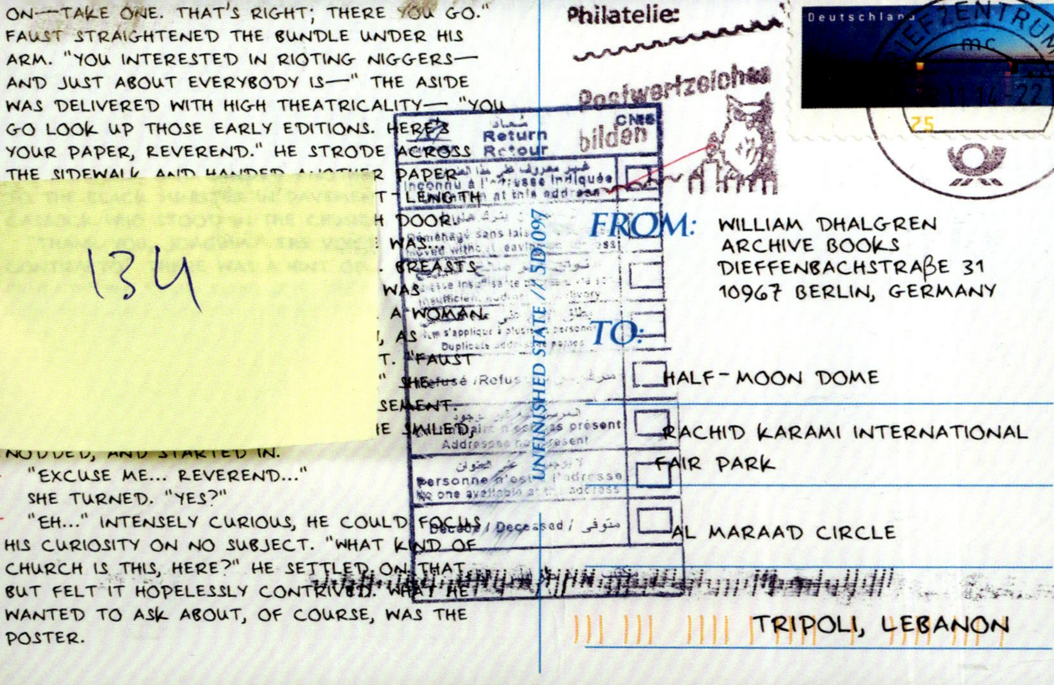
ON—TAKE ONE. THAT'S RIGHT; THERE YOU GO." FAUST STRAIGHTENED THE BUNDLE UNDER HIS ARM. "YOU INTERESTED IN RIOTING NIGGERS—AND JUST ABOUT EVERYBODY IS—" THE ASIDE WAS DELIVERED WITH HIGH THEATRICALITY— "YOU GO LOOK UP THOSE EARLY EDITIONS. HERE'S YOUR PAPER, REVEREND." HE STRODE ACROSS THE SIDEWALK AND HANDED ANOTHER PAPER
LENGTH
DOOR.
WAS.
BREASTS
WAS
A WOMAN.
, AS
T. "FAUST
" SHE
SEMENT.
HE SMILED,
NODDED, AND STARTED IN.
"EXCUSE ME... REVEREND..."
SHE TURNED. "YES?"
"EH..." INTENSELY CURIOUS, HE COULD FOCUS HIS CURIOSITY ON NO SUBJECT. "WHAT KIND OF CHURCH IS THIS, HERE?" HE SETTLED ON THAT BUT FELT IT HOPELESSLY CONTRIVED. WHAT HE WANTED TO ASK ABOUT, OF COURSE, WAS THE POSTER.
134
Philatelie:
Postwertzeichen
bilden
Deutschland
25
BRIEFZENTRUM
Return
Retour
Inconnu à l'adresse indiquée
Déménagé sans laisser d'adresse
Refusé / Refused
Décédé / Deceased / متوفى
UNFINISHED STATE // SD.097
FROM:
WILLIAM DHALGREN
ARCHIVE BOOKS
DIEFFENBACHSTRAßE 31
10967 BERLIN, GERMANY
TO:
HALF-MOON DOME
RACHID KARAMI INTERNATIONAL
FAIR PARK
AL MARAAD CIRCLE
TRIPOLI, LEBANON

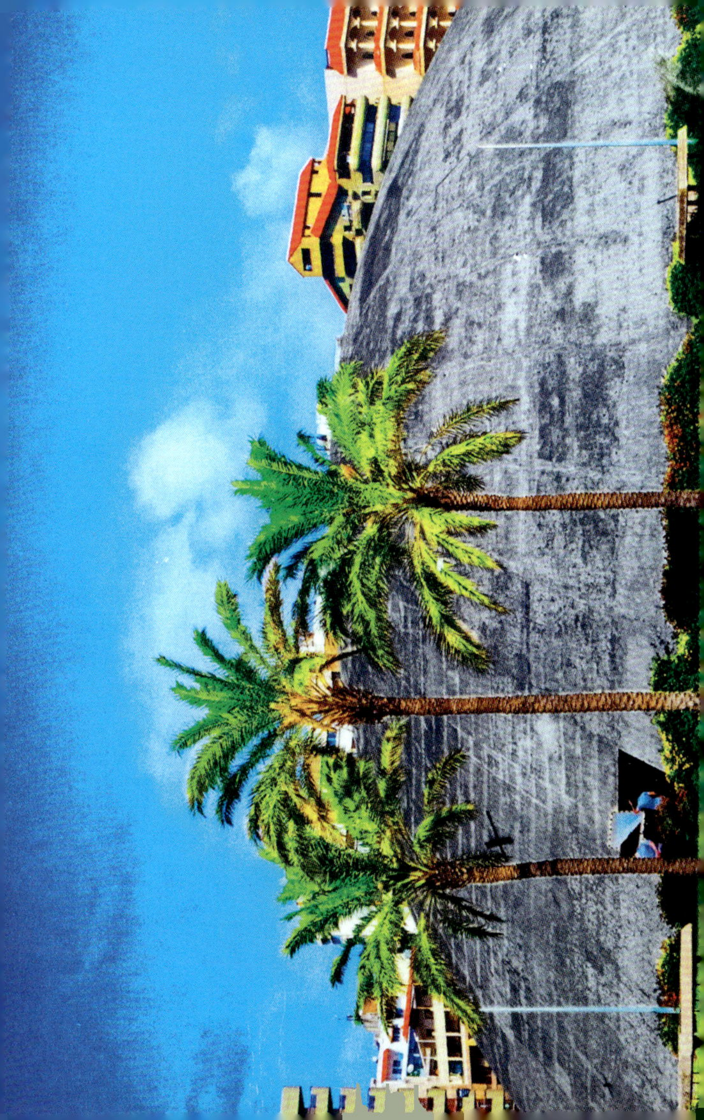

SHE SMILED. "INTERFAITH, INTERRACIAL. WE'VE BEEN MANAGING TO HAVE SERVICES THREE TIMES A WEEK FOR A WHILE NOW. WE'D BE VERY HAPPY IF YOU WERE INTERESTED IN COMING. SUNDAY MORNING, OF COURSE. THEN AGAIN, TUESDAY AND THURSDAY EVENINGS. WE DON'T HAVE A VERY LARGE CONGREGATION, YET. BUT WE'RE GATHERING OUR FLOCK."

"YOU'RE REVEREND...?"

"AMY TAYLOR. I'M A LAY PREACHER, ACTUALLY. THIS IS A PROJECT I'VE TAKEN ON MYSELF. WORKING OUT QUITE WELL, TOO, EVERYTHING CONSIDERED."

"YOU JUST SORT OF MOVED INTO THE CHURCH AND TOOK IT OVER?"

"AFTER THE PEOPLE WHO WERE HERE ABANDONED IT." SHE DID NOT BRUSH HER HANDS OFF. SHE EXTENDED ONE. IT MIGHT HAVE BEEN THE SAME GESTURE. "I'M GLAD TO MEET YOU."

HE SHOOK. "GLAD TO MEET YOU."

"I HOPE YOU COME TO OUR SERVICES. THIS IS A TIME OF STRESS FOR EVERYBODY. WE NEED ALL THE SPIRITUAL HELP WE CAN GET... DON'T YOU THINK?"

HER GRIP (LIKE JOAQUIM'S) LINGERED. AND IT WAS FIRMER. "HEY, DO YOU KNOW WHAT DAY IT IS?"

SHE LOOKED DOWN AT THE PAPER.

UNFINISHED STATE // 5D.098

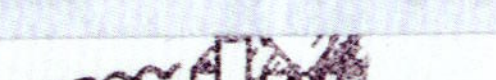

REGULAR MAIL

0114000684004 21

FROM: WILLIAM DHALGREN
ARCHIVE BOOKS
DIEFFENBACHSTRAßE 31
10967 BERLIN, GERMANY

TO:

HALF-MOON DOME

RACHID KARAMI INTERNATIONAL
FAIR PARK

AL MARAAD CIRCLE

TRIPOLI, LEBANON

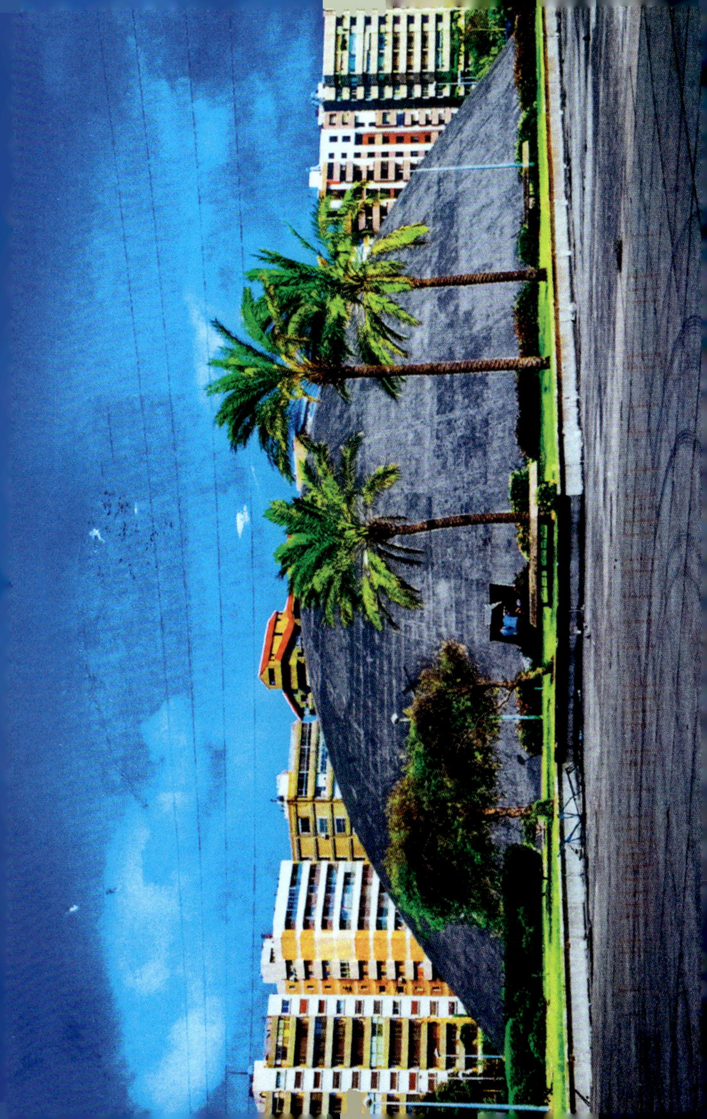

TREK BETWEEN CORNER AND CORNER TO WATCH HIM WATCHING. THOUGH IT WAS AN ARBITRARY WEDNESDAY AFTERNOON, THE FEEL WAS OF SOME OMINOUS SUNDAY MORNING.

THERE IS NO ARTICULATE RESONANCE. THE COMMON PROBLEM, I SUPPOSE, IS TO HAVE MORE TO SAY THAN VOCABULARY AND SYNTAX CAN BEAR. THAT IS WHY I AM HUNTING IN THESE DESICCATED STREETS. THE SMOKE HIDES THE SKY'S VARIETY, STAINS CONSCIOUSNESS, COVERS THE HOLOCAUST WITH SOMETHING SAFE AND INSUBSTANTIAL. IT PROTECTS FROM GREATER FLAME. IT INDICATES FIRE, BUT OBSCURES THE SOURCE. THIS IS NOT A USEFUL STREET. VERY LITTLE HERE APPROACHES ANY EIDOLON OF THE BEAUTIFUL.

THIS IS WHAT A GOOD NEIGHBORHOOD IN BELLONA LOOKS LIKE?

THE GROUND FLOOR WINDOWS WERE BROKEN IN THE WHITE HOUSE THERE; CURTAINS HUNG OUT

THE STREET WAS CLEAN.

BARE FOOT AND SANDAL, BARE FOOT AND SANDAL: HE WATCHED THE PAVEMENT'S GRAIN SLIP BENEATH THEM.

A DOOR BESIDE HIM STOOD WIDE.

HE KEPT WALKING. EASIER TO THINK THAT ALL THESE BUILDINGS ARE INHABITED, THAN THAT THEIR VACANCY GIVES ME LICENSE TO LOOT

UNFINISHED STATE / ASD.101

Return / Retour
Refuse / Refu
Personne n'est à l'adresse / No one available at the address
Décédé / Deceased / متوفى

FROM: WILLIAM DHALGREN
ARCHIVE BOOKS
DIEFFENBACHSTRAßE 31
10967 BERLIN, GERMANY

TO: HALF-MOON DOME
RACHID KARAMI INTERNATIONAL
FAIR PARK
AL MARAAD CIRCLE

TRIPOLI, LEBANON

Deutschland 75
50 Jahre Fehmarnsundbrücke

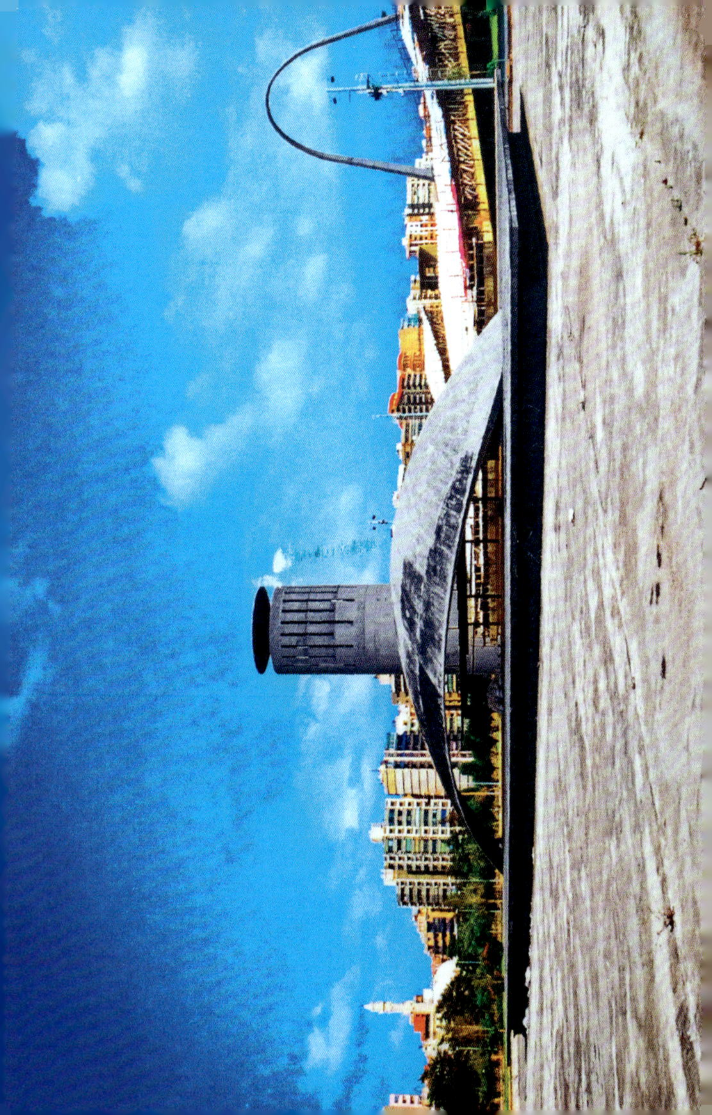

HE LOOKED UP AT CREAKINGS. BUT IT WAS ONLY SOME SLIGHT ARCHITECTURAL SHIFT. NOBODY, HE SUBVOCALIZED, LIVES HERE NOW. (THE KITCHEN WAS VERY CLEAN.) WITHOUT PARTICULARLY UNDERSTANDING WHAT HE'D READ (OR NOT UNDERSTANDING IT, FOR THAT MATTER) THE NOTES BY THE ABSENT JOURNALIST, COUPLED WITH THE CREAK, MADE THE BACK OF HIS NECK TINGLE.

DEJA VU IS A THING OF THE EYE.

THIS WAS LIKE READING LINES THAT ECHOED SOME CONVERSATION HE MIGHT HAVE FOLLOWED IDLY ONCE ON A CROWDED STREET. THE BOOK HINTED HE PAY ATTENTION TO PART OF HIS MIND HE COULD NOT EVEN LOCATE.

LABILITY, NOT AFFECTATION; A TRUE AND COMMON TRAIT. BUT IF I TRIED TO WRITE DOWN WHAT I SAY AS I MOVE FROM SPEECH

HE FLIPPED MORE PAGES. THERE WAS ONLY WRITING ON THE RIGHT-HAND ONES. THE LEFT-HAND ONES WERE BLANK. HE CLOSED THE BOOK. HE PUT THE COFFEE CUP IN THE SINK, THE CAN IN THE EMPTY GARBAGE PAIL: WHEN HE CAUGHT HIMSELF DOING IT, HE LAUGHED OUT LOUD, THEN TRIED SILENT JUSTIFICATION: HE COULD ALWAYS STAY HERE, MAKE THIS PLACE NICER THAN TAK'S.

REGULAR MAIL

0114000684000017

UNFINISHED

Deutschland 75

Schützt die Natur.

1: WILLIAM DHALGREN
ARCHIVE BOOKS
DIEFFENBACHSTRAßE 31
10967 BERLIN, GERMANY

.ACHID KARAMI
INTERNATIONAL FAIR PARK
AL MARAAD CIRCLE
TRIPOLI
LEBANON

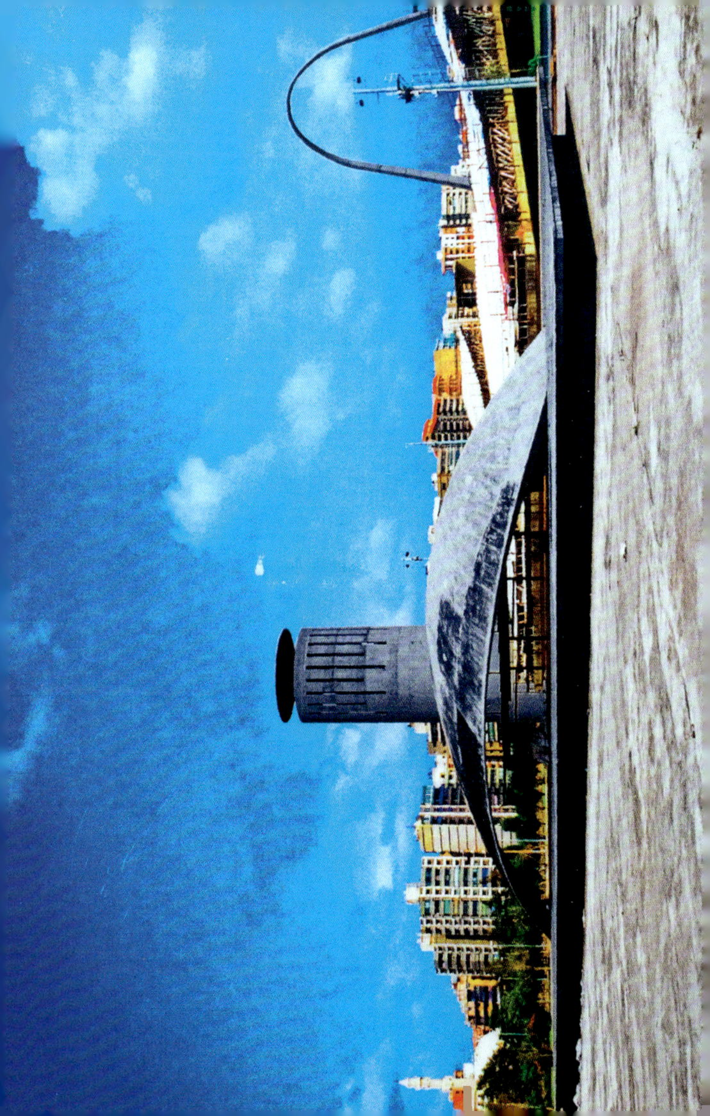

THAT MADE THE BACK OF HIS NECK TINGLE AGAIN.

HE CLOSED THE NOTEBOOK AND, WITH THE PAPER RUCKED BESIDE IT, CLIMBED BACK OUT THE WINDOW.

HE SCRATCHED HIMSELF ON BROKEN GLASS, BUT ONLY NOTICED IT A BLOCK AWAY WHEN HE LOOKED DOWN TO SEE A DROP OF BLOOD HAD TRICKLED ACROSS THE NOTEBOOK COVER, RED-BROWN ON THE CHAR. HE NUDGED AT THE NEW, PURPLE-RED SCAB WITH THE BLUNT OF HIS THUMB, WHICH JUST MADE IT ITCH. SO HE FORGOT ABOUT IT AND HURRIED ON UP BRISBAIN. IT WAS ONLY... A SCRATCH.

DISTANCE? OR DESTINATION?

HE HAD NO IDEA WHAT TO EXPECT OF EITHER. THESE LAWNS AND FACADES NEEDED SUNLIGHT, OR AT LEAST LIGHT RAIN, TO BE BEAUTIFUL. THE CORNER TREES MIGHT BE CLEAR GREEN. BUT MIST BLURRED THEM NOW.

ODD THAT THE ELEMENTS OF PLEASURE WERE SO MANY GREYS, SO MUCH FEAR, SO MANY SILENCES. THAT HOUSE THERE, GAPING THROUGH DREAR DRAPES WITH INTIMATIONS OF RUGS STIL OUT IN JULY—SOMEONE HAD LIVED THERE. A DOCTOR SIGN HUNG BESIDE, THE DOOR OF THA ONE: HE MULLED ON THE DRUGS CLOSETED BEHIND THE VENETIAN BLINDS. WELL, MAYBE ON

UNFINISHED STATE // 5D.104

FROM: WILLIAM DHALGREN
ARCHIVE BOOKS
DIEFFENBACHSTRAßE 31
10967 BERLIN, GERMANY

TO: RACHID KARAMI
INTERNATIONAL FAIR PARK
AL MARAAD CIRCLE
TRIPOLI
LEBANON

Deutschland 75

Schützt die Natur WWF www.wwf.de

28 JAN 2013
TRIPOLI CENTER 5697

REGULAR MAIL
0115000022009939

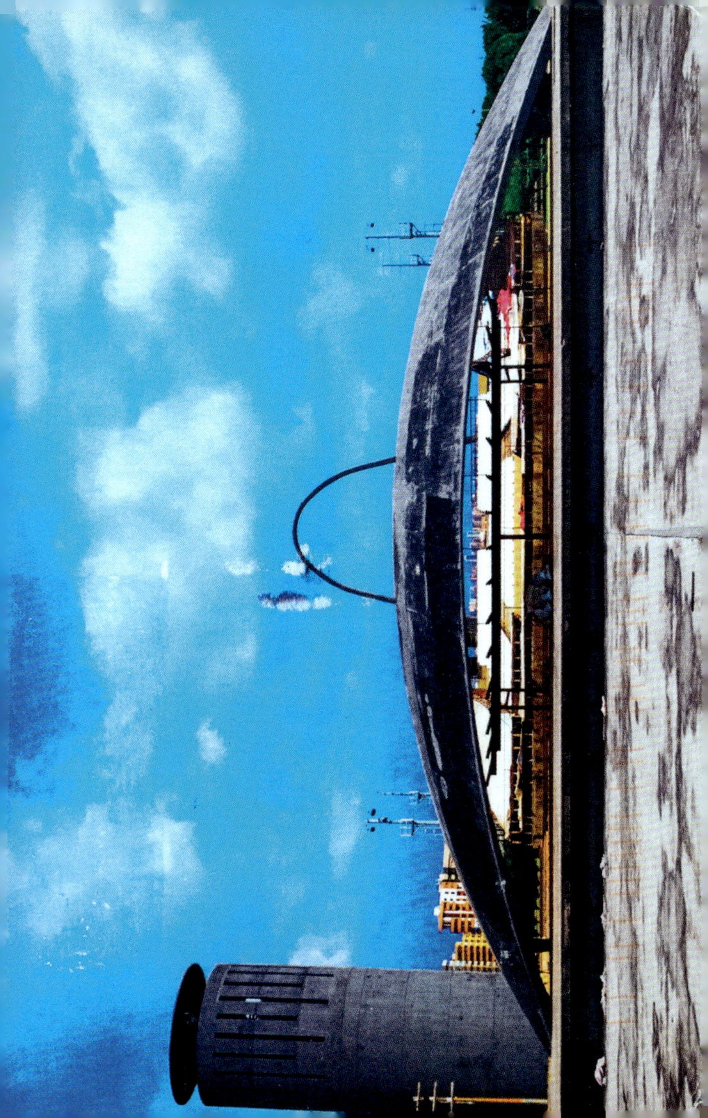

OF SOUND AMONG HIS BODY'S CAVITIES. HE SLAPPED THE PAPER AND BLOODY NOTEBOOK ON HIS THIGH, THINKING OF LANYA, OF MILLY, OF JOHN. FROM HIS OTHER HIP THE ORCHID SWUNG. CHAINED IN POINTS OF VIEW, HE LOPED ALONG, AN UNEASY VANDAL, SUFFERING FOR THE PILLAGE HIS MIND WREAKED AMONG THE FABULOUS FACADES. HE MOVED, A POINT OF TENSION, BY HOMES THAT WOULD HAVE BEEN LUXURIOUS IN SUNLIGHT.

HE WAS NOT SURE WHY HE DECIDED TO EXPLORE OFF THE AVENUE.

IN THE CENTER OF THE ALLEY WAS AN OAK, SET IN A CIRCLE OF COBBLES, RINGED IN A DECORATIVE FENCE. HIS HEART BEAT FAST.

HE PASSED IT.

THE BACKSIDE OF THE TRUNK WAS ASH. INSTEAD OF HEAVY GREENERY, THE REAR LEAVES WERE SHRIVELED BLACK.

EYES WIDE AT THE VISION, HE TURNED AS HE PASSED IT, TO BACK AWAY. THEN HE LOOKED AT THE HOUSES.

ON BOTH SIDES OF HIM WALLS WERE SUNDERED ON SMASHED FURNITURE, BEAMS, AND PILED MASONRY. THE DEMARCATION BETWEEN LAWN AND STREET VANISHED BENEATH JUNK. TWENTY FEET ON, THE COBBLES WERE UPTURNED. HE FELT HIS FACE SQUINCH AGAINST THE DESTRUCTION.

FROM: WILLIAM DHALGREN
ARCHIVE BOOKS
DIEFFENBACHSTRAßE 31
10967 BERLIN, GERMANY

TO: AMPHITHEATER SHELL
RACHID KARAMI INTERNATIONAL
FAIR PARK
AL MARAAD CIRCLE
TRIPOLI, LEBANON

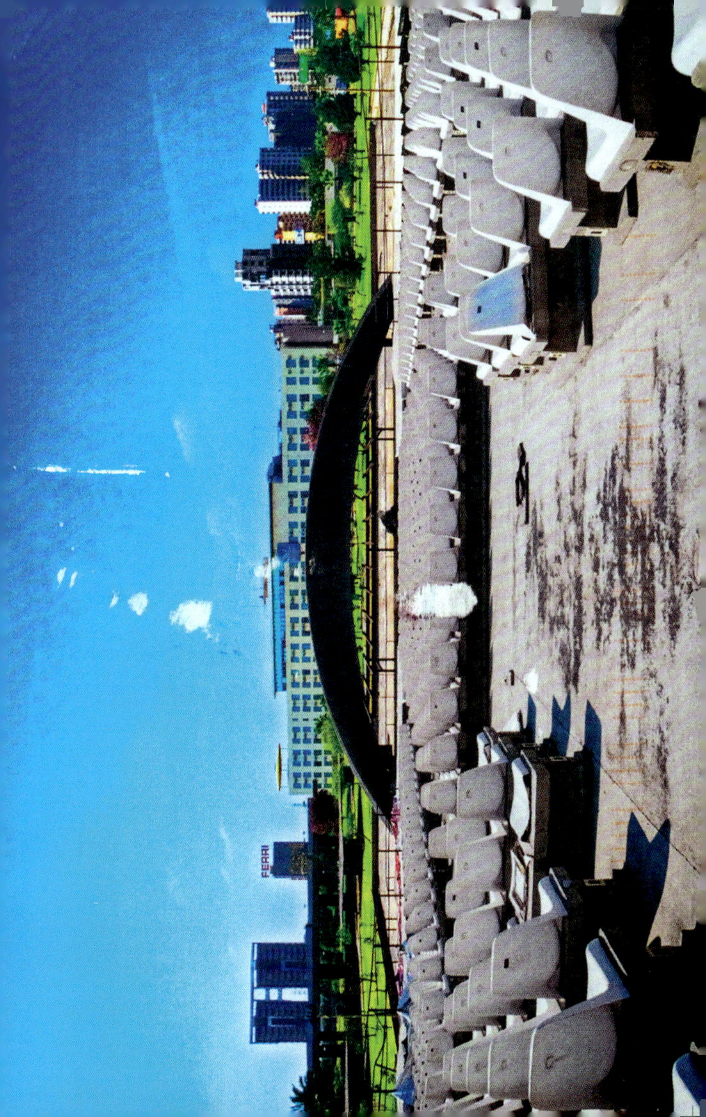

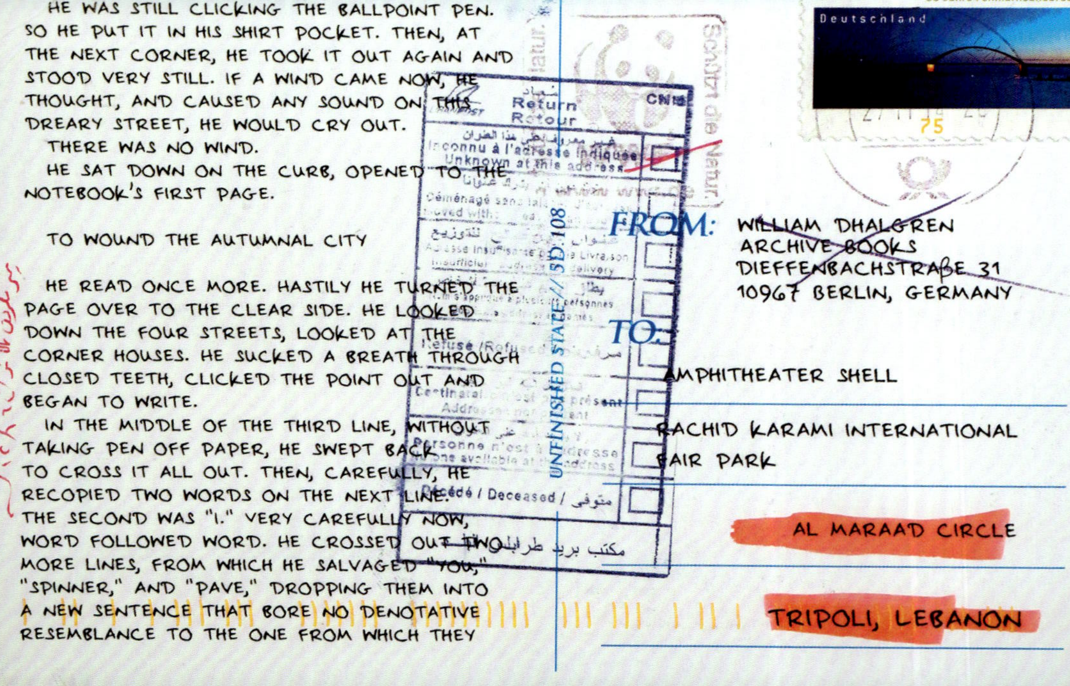
HE WAS STILL CLICKING THE BALLPOINT PEN. SO HE PUT IT IN HIS SHIRT POCKET. THEN, AT THE NEXT CORNER, HE TOOK IT OUT AGAIN AND STOOD VERY STILL. IF A WIND CAME NOW, HE THOUGHT, AND CAUSED ANY SOUND ON THIS DREARY STREET, HE WOULD CRY OUT.
THERE WAS NO WIND.
HE SAT DOWN ON THE CURB, OPENED TO THE NOTEBOOK'S FIRST PAGE.
TO WOUND THE AUTUMNAL CITY
HE READ ONCE MORE. HASTILY HE TURNED THE PAGE OVER TO THE CLEAR SIDE. HE LOOKED DOWN THE FOUR STREETS, LOOKED AT THE CORNER HOUSES. HE SUCKED A BREATH THROUGH CLOSED TEETH, CLICKED THE POINT OUT AND BEGAN TO WRITE.
IN THE MIDDLE OF THE THIRD LINE, WITHOUT TAKING PEN OFF PAPER, HE SWEPT BACK TO CROSS IT ALL OUT. THEN, CAREFULLY, HE RECOPIED TWO WORDS ON THE NEXT LINE. THE SECOND WAS "I." VERY CAREFULLY NOW, WORD FOLLOWED WORD. HE CROSSED OUT TWO MORE LINES, FROM WHICH HE SALVAGED "YOU," "SPINNER," AND "PAVE," DROPPING THEM INTO A NEW SENTENCE THAT BORE NO DENOTATIVE RESEMBLANCE TO THE ONE FROM WHICH THEY
Return
Retour
Inconnu à l'adresse indiquée
Unknown at this address
Refusé / Refused
Décédé / Deceased / متوفى
مكتب بريد طرابلس
UNFINISHED STATE // SD.108
FROM:
WILLIAM DHALGREN
ARCHIVE BOOKS
DIEFFENBACHSTRAßE 31
10967 BERLIN, GERMANY
TO:
AMPHITHEATER SHELL
RACHID KARAMI INTERNATIONAL
FAIR PARK
AL MARAAD CIRCLE
TRIPOLI, LEBANON
Deutschland
75
Schützt die Natur.

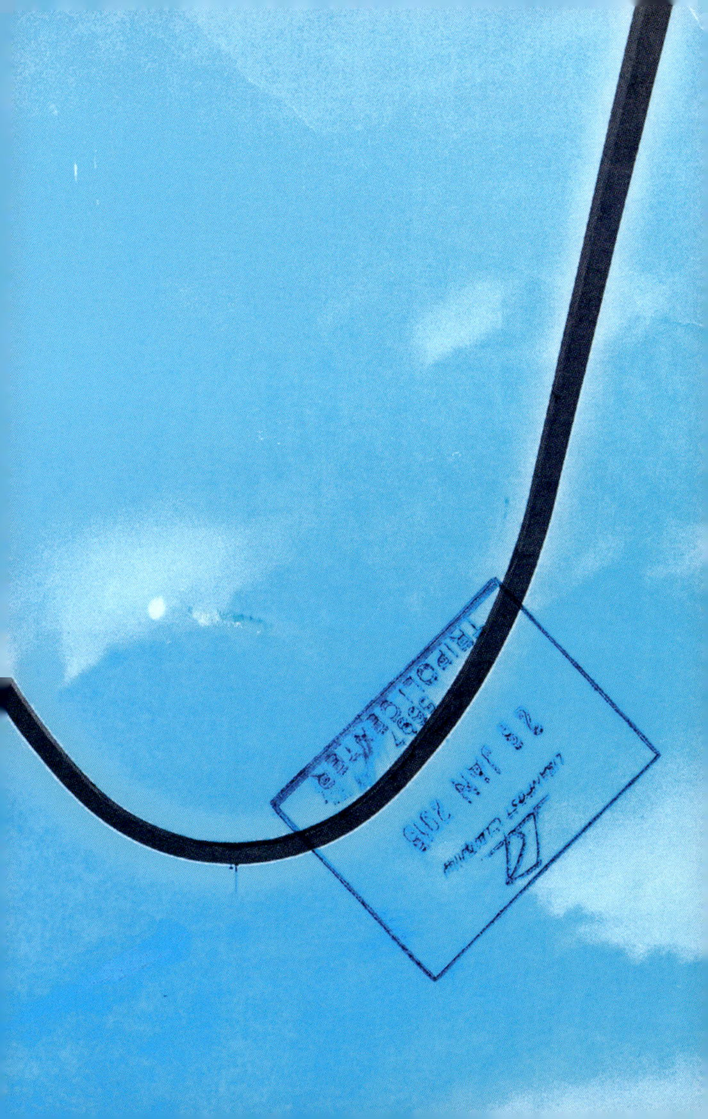

"NO, I DON'T THINK WE SHOULD." THE BLACK PUT HIS HANDS IN THE POCKETS OF HIS SLACKS.

HE SHOOK HIS HEAD—ONLY ONCE, BECAUSE IT HURT THAT MUCH.

"WERE YOU ATTACKED, YOUNG MAN?"

HE SAID, "YES," VERY THICKLY. A NOD WOULD HAVE MADE IT CYNICAL, BUT HE DIDN'T DARE.

THE WHITE COLLAR BETWEEN THE SERGE LAPELS WAS KNOTTED WITH AN EXTRAORDINARILY THIN TIE. WHITE TEMPLES, BELOW GREY HAIR: THE MAN HAD AN ACCENT THAT WAS DISTURBINGLY NEAR BRITISH. HE PICKED UP THE NOTEBOOK. (THE NEWSPAPER SLID OFF ONTO THE LEAVES.) "IS THIS YOURS?"

ANOTHER THICK, "YES."

"ARE YOU A STUDENT? IT'S TERRIBLE, PEOPLE ATTACKING PEOPLE RIGHT OUT IN THE OPEN LIKE THIS. TERRIBLE!"

"I THINK WE'D BETTER GET INSIDE," THE BLACK MAN SAID. "THEY'LL BE WAITING FOR US."

"JUST A MINUTE!" CAME OUT WITH SURPRISING AUTHORITY. THE GENTLEMAN HELPED HIM TO SITTING POSITION. "MR FENSTER, I REALLY THINK WE SHOULD TAKE THIS POOR YOUNG MAN INSIDE. MR CALKINS CAN'T POSSIBLY OBJECT. THIS IS SOMETHING OF AN EXCEPTIONAL CIRCUMSTANCE."

FENSTER TOOK DARK BROWN HANDS FROM HIS POCKETS AND CAME OVER. "I'M AFRAID IT ISN'T

UNFINISH

REGULAR MAIL.

0114000684007709

50 Jahre Fehmarnsundbrücke

Deutschland

75

WILLIAM DHALGREN
ARCHIVE BOOKS
DIEFFENBACHSTRAßE 31
10967 BERLIN, GERMANY

HE ARC

RACHID KARAMI
INTERNATIONAL FAIR PARK

AL MARAAD CIRCLE

TRIPOLI, LEBANON

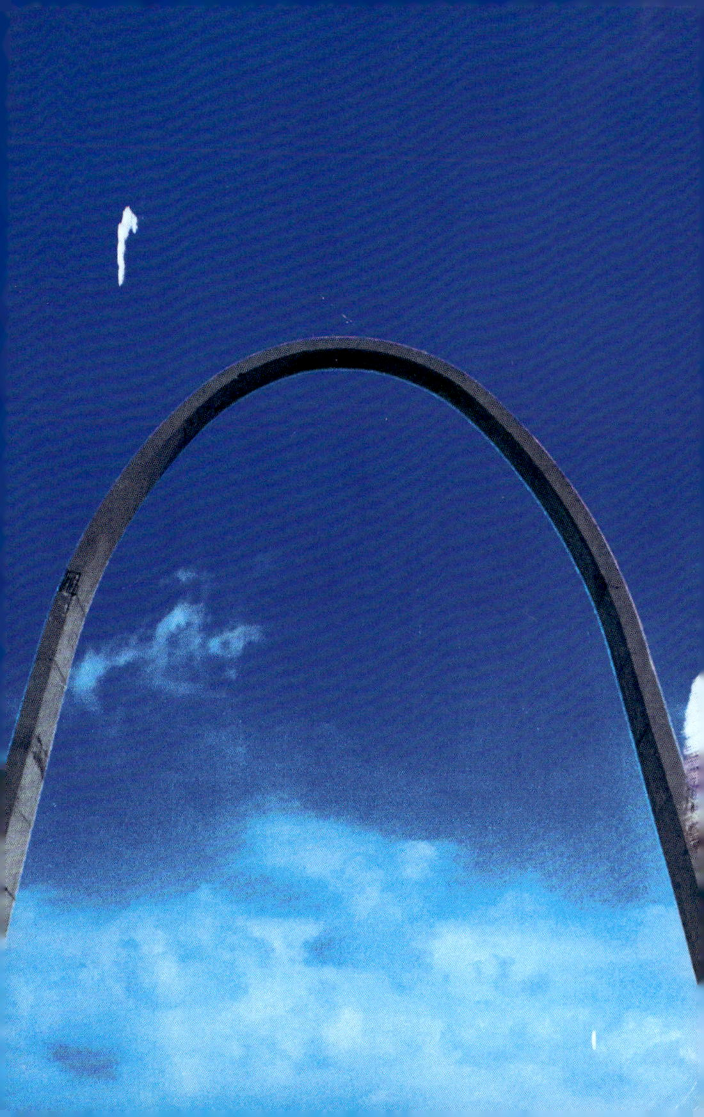

LOOK FOR SHADOW IN THIS DOUBLE-LIT MIST. A DARK COMMUNION IN THE BURNING STREETS BETWEEN THE LANDSCAPE AND THE SMARTING SENSES SUGGESTS MORE STERILE AGONIES. CLOUDS OUT OF CONTROL DECOCT ANTICIPATION. WHAT USE CAN ANY OF US HAVE FOR TWO MOONS? THE MIRACLE OF ORDER HAS RUN OUT AND I AM LEFT IN AN UNMIRACULOUS CITY WHERE ANYTHING MAY HAPPEN. I DON'T NEED MORE INTIMATIONS OF DISORDER. IT HAS TO BE MORE THAN THAT! SEARCH THE SMOKE FOR THE FIRE'S BASE. READ FROM THE COALS NEITHER SUCCESS NOR DESPAIR. THIS EDGE OF BOREDOM IS AS BRIGHT. I PASS IT, INTO THE DARK RIM. THERE IS THE DECEIVING WARMTH THAT ASKS NOTHING. THERE ARE OBJECTS LOST IN DOUBLE-LIGHT.

WITH THE JOLLITY OF THEIR PROGRESS THROUGH THE NIGHT STREETS, THE REPEATED EXCLAMATIONS AND SPECULATIONS AT THE TWINNED SATELLITES, MOMENTS INTO TAK'S DARK STAIRWAY—FOOTSTEPS PUMMELING AROUND HIM, DOWN, ACROSS, THEN PUMMELING UP—HE REALIZED HE HAD NO MEMORY OF THE DOORWAY THROUGH WHICH THEY'D JUST ENTERED OUT OF THE NIGHT, SAVE THE MEMORY OF HIS EXIT THAT LINGERED FROM THE MORNING.

"A GREAT IDEA!" LANYA, BEHIND, WAS

UNFINISHED STATE // 6D.123

Deutschland 75

50 Jahre Fehmarnsundbrücke

BRIEFZENTRUM

FROM: WILLIAM DHALGREN
ARCHIVE BOOKS
DIEFFENBACHSTRAßE 31
10967 BERLIN, GERMANY

TO: THE ARC

RACHID KARAMI
INTERNATIONAL FAIR PARK

AL MARAAD CIRCLE

TRIPOLI, LEBANON

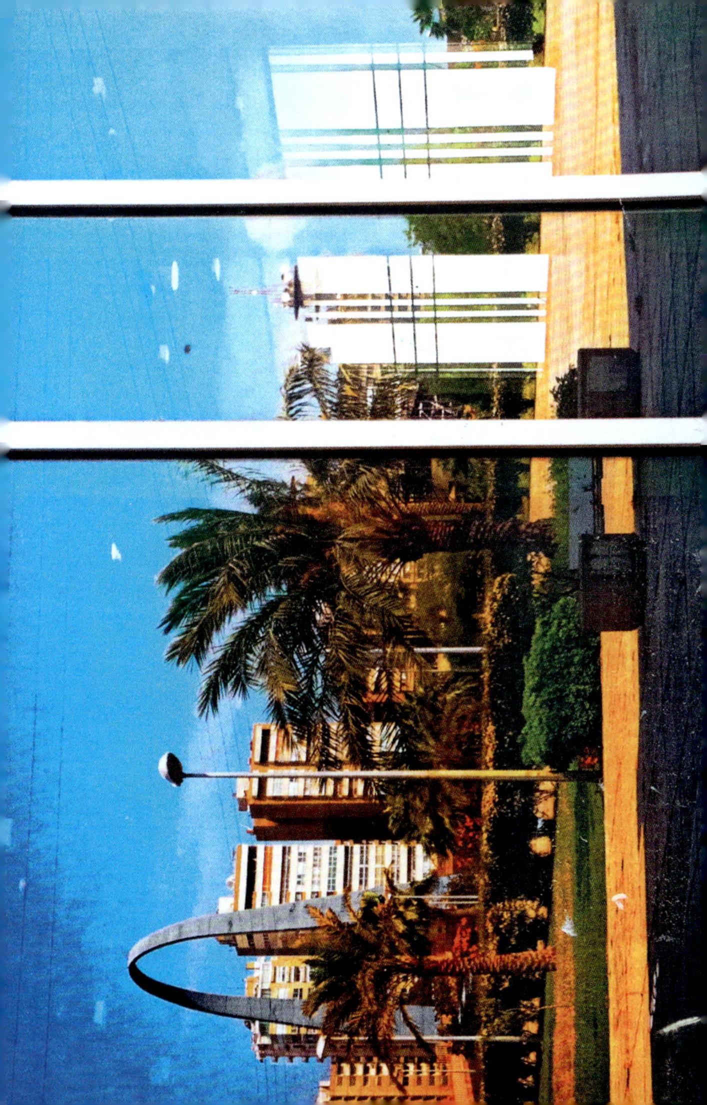

BREATHING HEAVILY. "A FULL GEORGE PARTY!"

"IF GEORGE WAS THE FULL ONE," TAK SAID. "EXCUSE ME; GIBBOUS."

"HOW FAR UP DO YOU LIVE?" JACK ASKED, AHEAD.

THE ORCHID JOGGED ON HIS HIP. NOTEBOOK AND NEWSPAPER—HE'D READ NONE OF THE PAPER YET—WERE STILL CLAMPED IN CLAMMY FINGERS.

"WE'LL BE THERE IN ONE MORE—NOPE. I MISCOUNTED," TAK CALLED DOWN. "WE'RE HERE ALREADY! COME ON! IT'S PARTY TIME!"

METAL CREAKED ON METAL.

BOTH LANYA, BEHIND, AND JACK, AHEAD, WERE LAUGHING.

ABOVE IS LIGHT. WHAT ELSE DOES THIS CITY CAST UP ON ITS CLOUDY COVER, FROM ILL-FUNCTIONING STREETLIGHTS, FROM WHAT LEAKS TENTATIVELY OUT OF BADLY SHADED DOORS AND WINDOWS, FROM FLAME? IS IT ENOUGH TO ILLUMINATE ANOTHER BRIGHT, BRIEF, CAREENING, BUT LESS-THAN-STANDARD BODY?

HE PUT THE WINE BOTTLE ON THE ROOF'S THIGH-HIGH WALL. BELOW, THE STREET LAMP WAS A BLURRED PEARL. HE SEARCHED THE DENSE AND FOGGY DISTANCES, WAS LOST IN THEM.

"WHAT ARE YOU LOOKING AT?" SHE CAME UP, SURPRISING, BEHIND.

Philatelie:

Postwertzeichen bilden

50 Jahre Fehmarnsundbrücke

Deutschland 75

Return

Inconnu à l'adresse indiquée
Unknown at this address

UNFINISHED STATE // ED-124

FROM: WILLIAM DHALGREN
ARCHIVE BOOKS
DIEFFENBACHSTRAßE 31
10967 BERLIN, GERMANY

TO:

BENDING ENCLOSED PAVILION

RACHID KARAMI

INTERNATIONAL FAIR PARK

AL MARAAD CIRCLE

TRIPOLI, LEBANON

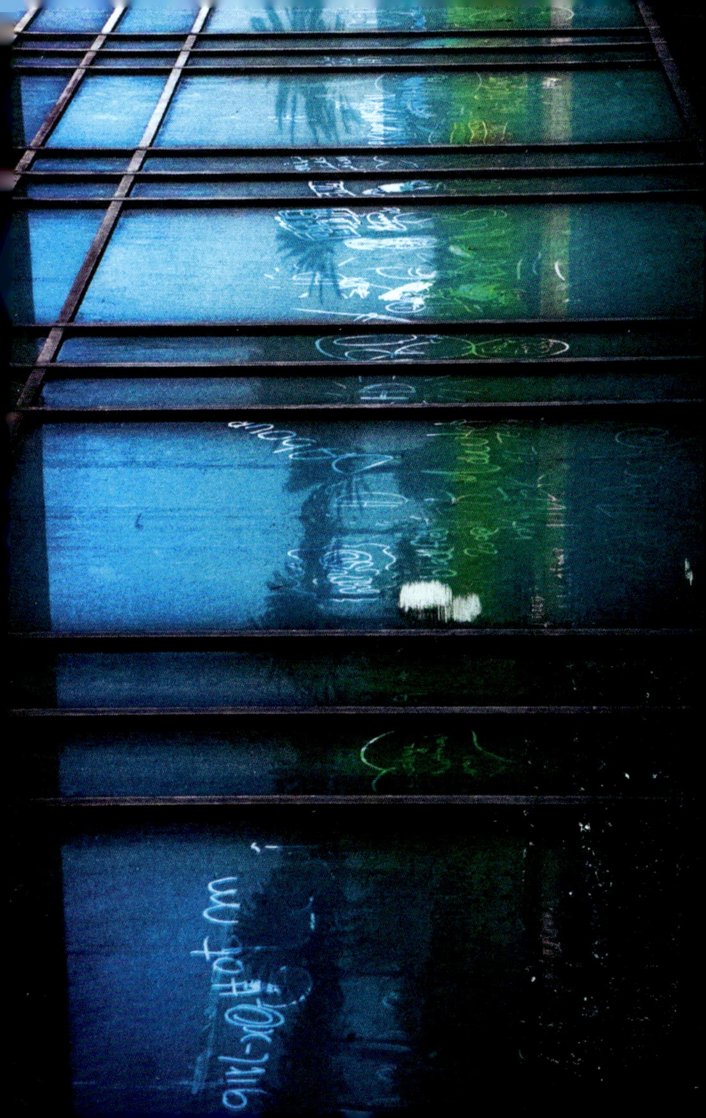

[illegible]ERIOUS RUMORS!
MYSTERIOUS LIGHTS!

WOULD YOUR EDITOR EVER LIKE SOME PICTURES WITH THIS ONE! WE, UNFORTUNATELY, WERE ASLEEP. BUT FROM WHAT WE CAN GATHER, SHORTLY AFTER MIDNIGHT LAST NIGHT – SO FAR TWENTY-SIX VERSIONS OF THE STORY HAVE COME IN, WITH CONTRADICTIONS ENOUGH TO OBLIGE OUR REGISTERING AN OFFICIAL EDITORIAL DOUBT—THE FOG AND SMOKE BLANKETING BELLONA THESE LAST MONTHS WAS TORN BY A WIND AT TOO GREAT AN ALTITUDE TO FEEL AT STREET LEVEL. PARTS OF THE SKY WERE CLEARED, AND THE FULL—OR NEAR FULL—MOON WAS, ALLEGEDLY, VISIBLE—AS WELL AS A CRESCENT MOON, ONLY SLIGHTLY SMALLER (OR SLIGHTLY LARGER?) THAN THE FIRST!

THE EXCITED VERSIONS FROM WHICH WE HAVE CULLED OUR OWN REPORT CONTAIN MANY DISCREPANCIES. HERE ARE SOME: THE FULL ORB WAS THE USUAL MOON, THE CRESCENT WAS THE INTRUDER.

THE CRESCENT WAS THE REAL MOON, THE FULL, THE IMPOSTOR… A YOUNG STUDENT SAYS THAT, IN THE FEW MINUTES THESE DOWNRIGHT ELIZABETHAN PORTENTS WERE REVEALED, HE MADE OUT MARKINGS ON THE FULL DISK THAT

UNFINISHED ST[…]

FROM: WILLIAM DHALGREN
ARCHIVE BOOKS
DIEFFENBACHSTRAßE 31
10967 BERLIN, GERMANY

TO:
BENDING ENCLOSED PAVILION
RACHID KARAMI INTERNATIONAL
FAIR PARK
AL MARAAD CIRCLE
TRIPOLI, LEBANON

Retour
Return
Inconnu à l'adresse indiquée
Unknown at this address
Refusé
Décédé / Deceased / متوفى

50 Jahre Fehmarnsundbrücke
Deutschland
75

REGULAR MAIL
0114000666000274

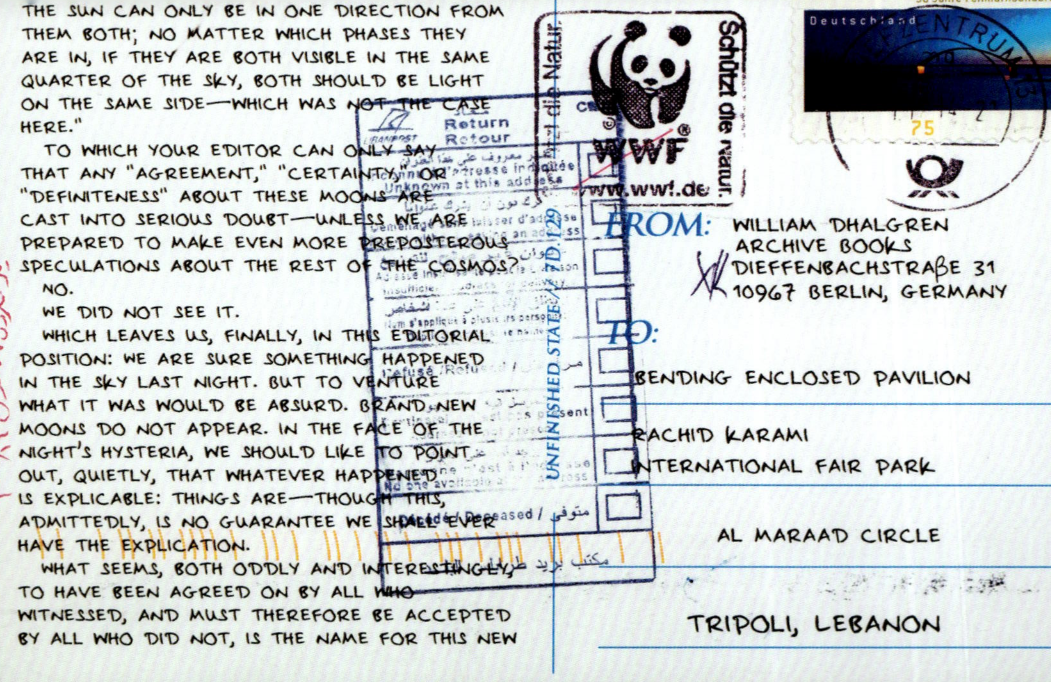

THE SUN CAN ONLY BE IN ONE DIRECTION FROM THEM BOTH; NO MATTER WHICH PHASES THEY ARE IN, IF THEY ARE BOTH VISIBLE IN THE SAME QUARTER OF THE SKY, BOTH SHOULD BE LIGHT ON THE SAME SIDE—WHICH WAS NOT THE CASE HERE."

TO WHICH YOUR EDITOR CAN ONLY SAY THAT ANY "AGREEMENT," "CERTAINTY," OR "DEFINITENESS" ABOUT THESE MOONS ARE CAST INTO SERIOUS DOUBT—UNLESS WE ARE PREPARED TO MAKE EVEN MORE PREPOSTEROUS SPECULATIONS ABOUT THE REST OF THE COSMOS?

NO.

WE DID NOT SEE IT.

WHICH LEAVES US, FINALLY, IN THIS EDITORIAL POSITION: WE ARE SURE SOMETHING HAPPENED IN THE SKY LAST NIGHT. BUT TO VENTURE WHAT IT WAS WOULD BE ABSURD. BRAND NEW MOONS DO NOT APPEAR. IN THE FACE OF THE NIGHT'S HYSTERIA, WE SHOULD LIKE TO POINT OUT, QUIETLY, THAT WHATEVER HAPPENED IS EXPLICABLE: THINGS ARE—THOUGH THIS, ADMITTEDLY, IS NO GUARANTEE WE SHALL EVER HAVE THE EXPLICATION.

WHAT SEEMS, BOTH ODDLY AND INTERESTINGLY, TO HAVE BEEN AGREED ON BY ALL WHO WITNESSED, AND MUST THEREFORE BE ACCEPTED BY ALL WHO DID NOT, IS THE NAME FOR THIS NEW

UNFINISHED STATE // 7D.129

FROM: WILLIAM DHALGREN
ARCHIVE BOOKS
DIEFFENBACHSTRAẞE 31
10967 BERLIN, GERMANY

TO: BENDING ENCLOSED PAVILION
RACHID KARAMI
INTERNATIONAL FAIR PARK
AL MARAAD CIRCLE
TRIPOLI, LEBANON

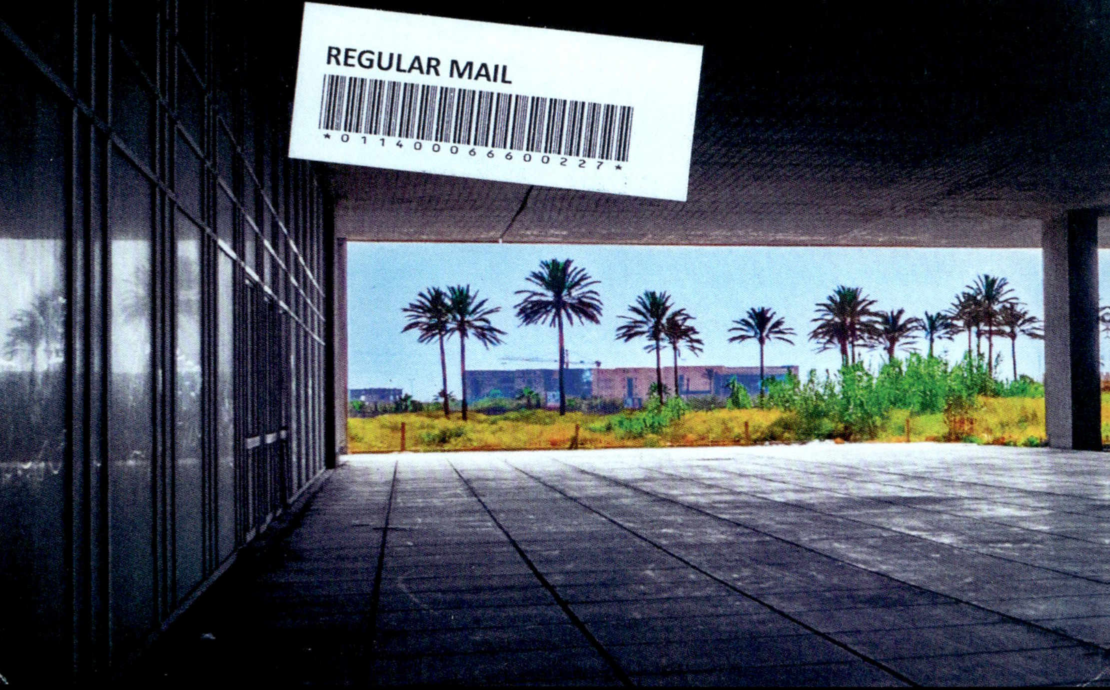
REGULAR MAIL
011400066600227

NEWBOY SWIRLED BLUNTED ICE. "EVERYONE KNOWS EVERYONE. YES, YOU'RE RIGHT." HE NODDED. "I WONDER SOMETIMES IF THE PURPOSE OF THE ARTISTIC COMMUNITY ISN'T TO PROVIDE A CONCERNED SOCIAL MATRIX WHICH SIMULTANEOUSLY ASSURES THAT NO MEMBER, REGARDLESS OF HONORS OR APPROBATION, HAS THE SLIGHTEST IDEA OF THE WORTH OF HIS OWN WORK."

KIDD DRANK HIS BEER, RESENTFUL AT THE LONG-WINDED-NESS BUT CURIOUS ABOUT THE MAN INDULGING IT.

"THE AESTHETIC EQUATION," NEWBOY MUSED. "THE ARTIST HAS SOME INTERNAL EXPERIENCE THAT PRODUCES A POEM, A PAINTING, A PIECE OF MUSIC. SPECTATORS SUBMIT THEMSELVES TO THE WORK, WHICH GENERATES AN INNER EXPERIENCE FOR THEM. BUT HISTORICALLY IT'S A VERY NEW, NOT TO MENTION VULGAR, IDEA THAT THE SPECTATOR'S EXPERIENCE SHOULD BE IDENTICAL TO, OR EVEN HAVE ANYTHING TO DO WITH, THE ARTIST'S. THAT IDEA COMES FROM AN OVER-INDUSTRALIZED SOCIETY WHICH HAS LEARNED TO DISTRUST MAGIC—"

"YOU'RE HERE!" LANYA SEIZED HIS ARM. "YOU LOOK SO BRIGHT AND SHINY AND POLISHED I DIDN'T RECOGNIZE YOU!"

HE PULLED HER AGAINST HIS SHOULDER. "THIS

-Retoure- -Zurück-

Return
Retour
Inconnu à l'adresse indiquée
Unknown at this address
Refusé / Refused / مرفوض
Destinataire n'est pas présent
Addressee not present
Personne n'est à l'adresse
No one available at the address
Décédé / Deceased / متوفى

UNFINISHED STATE 7D 134

FROM: WILLIAM DHALGREN
ARCHIVE BOOKS
DIEFFENBACHSTRAßE 31
10967 BERLIN, GERMANY

TO: BENDING ENCLOSED PAVILION
RACHID KARAMI
INTERNATIONAL FAIR PARK
AL MARAAD CIRCLE
TRIPOLI, LEBANON

Deutschland
50 Jahre Fehmarnsundbrücke
BRIEFZENTRUM

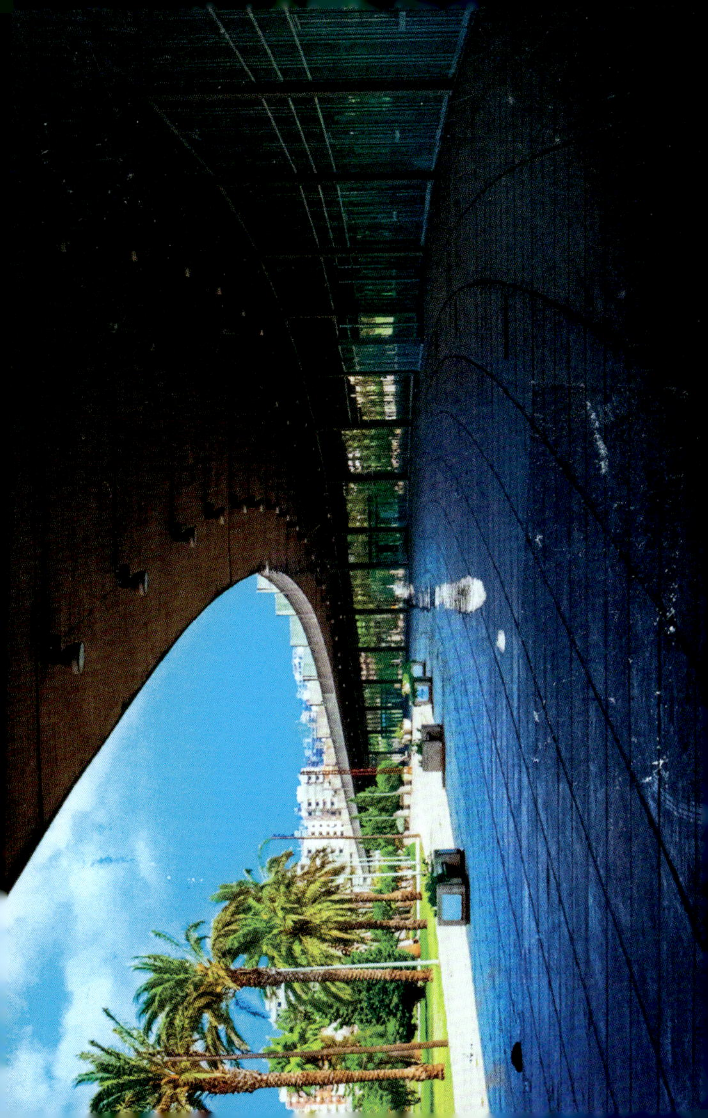

IS ERNEST NEWBOY," GLAD OF THE INTERRUPTION. "THIS IS MY FRIEND LANYA."

SHE LOOKED SURPRISED. "KIDD TOLD ME YOU HELPED HIM UP AT MR CALKINS'." SHE AND NEWBOY SHOOK HANDS ACROSS KIDD'S CHEST.

"I'M STAYING THERE. BUT I WAS LET OUT FOR THE EVENING."

"I WAS THERE FOR DAYS BUT I DON'T THINK I EVER GOT A NIGHT OFF."

NEWBOY LAUGHED. "THERE IS THAT TO IT, YES. AND WHERE DO YOU STAY NOW?"

"WE LIVE IN THE PARK. YOU MUSTN'T LOOK ASTONISHED. LOTS OF PEOPLE DO. IT'S PRACTICALLY AS POSH AN ADDRESS AS ROGER'S, TODAY."

"REALLY? DO THE TWO OF YOU LIVE THERE TOGETHER?"

"WE LIVE IN A LITTLE PART ALL BY OURSELVES. WE VISIT PEOPLE. WHEN WE'RE HUNGRY. NOBODY'S COME TO VISIT US YET. BUT IT'S BETTER THAT WAY."

NEWBOY LAUGHED AGAIN.

KIDD WATCHED THE POET SMILE AT HER BANTER.

"I WOULDN'T TRUST MYSELF TO HUNT YOU OUT OF YOUR HIDDEN SPOT. BUT YOU MUST CERTAINLY COME AND SEE ME, SOME DAY DURING THE AFTERNOON." THEN TO KIDD: "AND

UNFINISHED STATE // 8D.135

Philatelie Postwertzeichen bilden

Deutschland 75 50 Jahre Fehmarnsundbrücke

Return Retour

Décédé / Deceased / متوفى

مكتب بريد طرابلس البلد

FROM: WILLIAM DHALGREN
ARCHIVE BOOKS
DIEFFENBACHSTRAßE 31
10967 BERLIN, GERMANY

TO: BENDING ENCLOSED PAVILION
RACHID KARAMI
INTERNATIONAL FAIR PARK
AL MARAAD CIRCLE
TRIPOLI, LEBANON

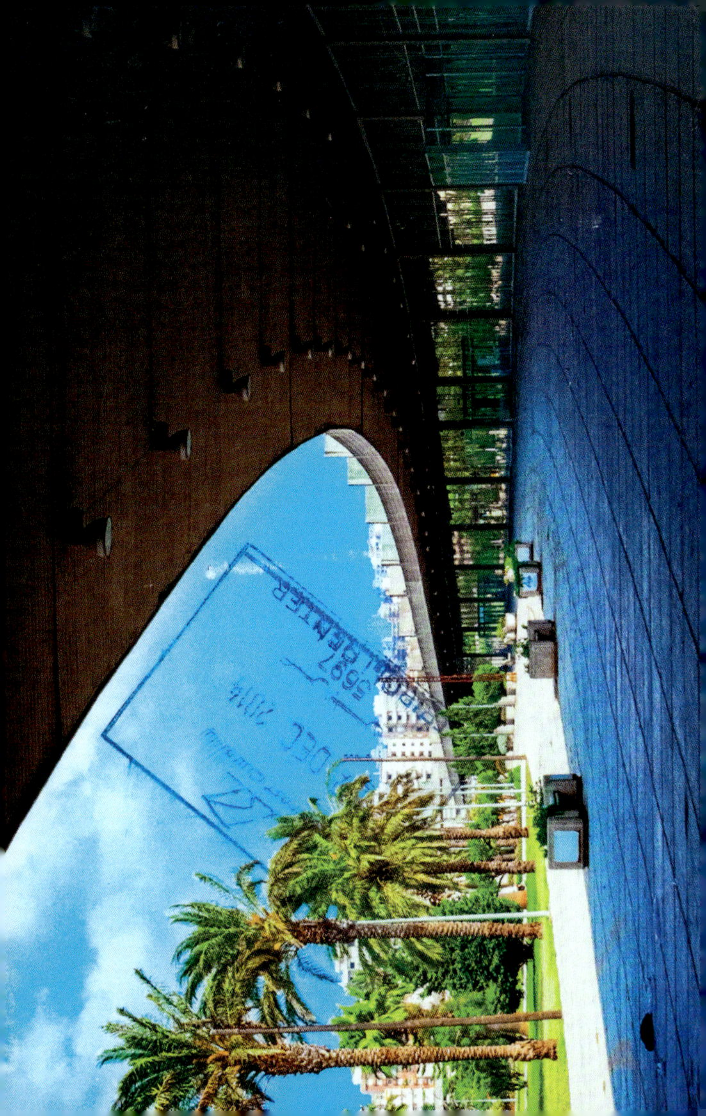

YOU CAN BRING YOUR POEMS."

"SURE." KIDD WATCHED LANYA BE DELIGHTEDLY SILENT. "WHEN?"

"THE NEXT TIME ROGER DECIDES IT'S TUESDAY, WHY DON'T YOU BOTH COME AROUND? I PROMISE YOU WON'T HAVE THE SAME PROBLEM AGAIN."

HE NODDED VIGOROUSLY. "ALL RIGHT."

MR NEWBOY SMILED HUGELY. "THEN I'LL EXPECT YOU." HE NODDED, STILL SMILING, TURNED, AND WALKED AWAY.

"CLOSE YOUR MOUTH." LANYA SQUINTED ABOUT. "OH, I GUESS IT'S OKAY. I DON'T SEE ANY FLIES." THEN SHE SQUEEZED HIS HAND.

IN THE CAGE, NEON FLICKERED. MUSIC RASPE[D] FROM A SPEAKER.

"OH, QUICK, LET'S GO!"

HE CAME WITH HER, ONCE GLANCED BACK: T[HE] SACK OF NEWBOY'S BLUE SERGE WAS WEDGED ON BOTH SIDES WITH LEATHER, BUT HE COULD NOT TELL IF THE POET WAS TALKING OR JUST STANDING.

"WHAT HAVE YOU BEEN DOING ALL DAY?" HE ASKED ON THE COOL STREET.

SHE SHRUGGED CLOSER. "HANGING OUT WITH MILLY. I ATE A LOT OF BREAKFAST. JOMMY IS COOKING THIS WEEK SO I REALLY HAD MORE TH[AN] I WANTED. IN THE MORNING I ADVISED JOHN O[N] A WORK PROJECT. KIBITZED ON SOMEBODY'S

CN 15 Return Inconnu / Unknown Refusé / Refused Décédé / Deceased

REGULAR MAIL

0114000068400456

Philatelie

Postwertzeichen bilden

50 Jahre Fehmarnsundbrücke

Deutschland 75

E // 8D.136

FROM: WILLIAM DHALGREN
ARCHIVE BOOKS
DIEFFENBACHSTRAßE 31
10967 BERLIN, GERMANY

BENDING ENCLOSED PAVILION

RACHID KARAMI
INTERNATIONAL FAIR PARK

AL MARAAD CIRCLE

TRIPOLI, LEBANON

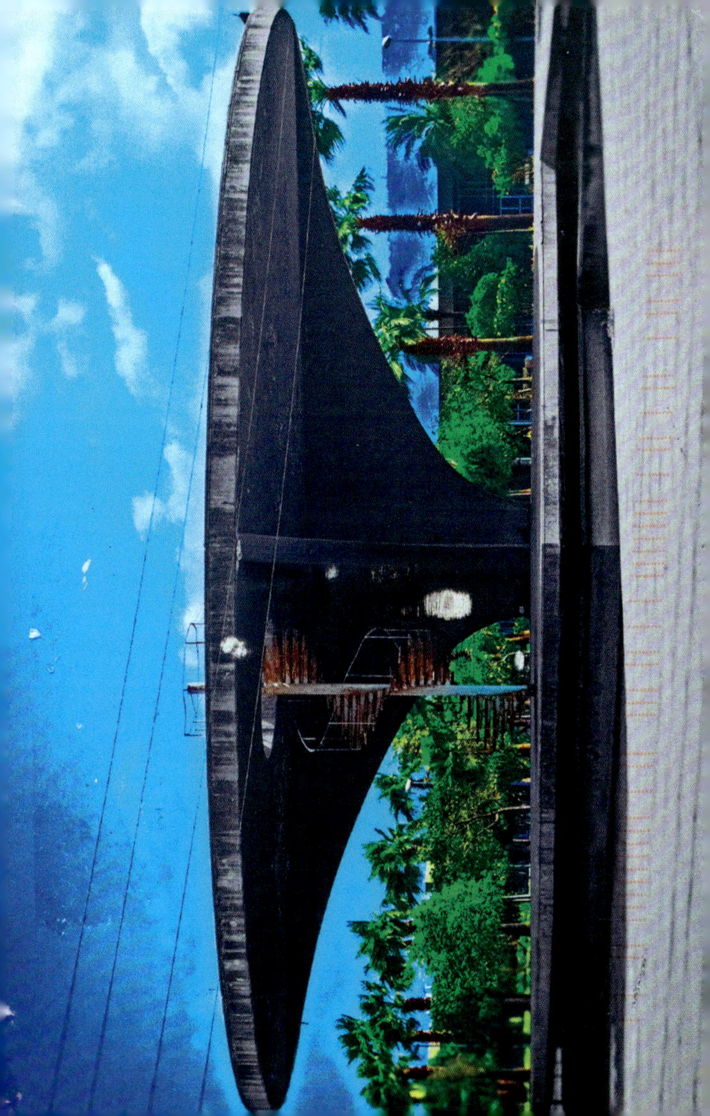

TO MEASURE, BUT COME AWAY WITH ONLY THE PERPETUAL ANGLE OF DISTORTION, THE FREQUENCY OF AN AMAZED DEFRACTION.

IN THE HALF—OR RATHER FOUR-FIFTHS DARK—THE LIONS LOOKED WET. HE BRUSHED HIS RIGHT KNUCKLES AGAINST THE STONE FLANK IN PASSING: IT WAS EXACTLY AS WARM AS LANYA'S WRIST, BRUSHING HIS KNUCKLES ON THE LEFT.

HOW DOES SHE FIND HER WAY? HE WONDERED, BUT THIRTY STEPS ON REALIZED HE HAD ANTICIPATED THE LAST DARK TURN HIMSELF.

DISTANT FIRELIGHT FILIGREED THROUGH NEAR LEAVES. LANYA PUSHED THEM ASIDE AND SAID, "HI!"

A SHIRTLESS MAN, HOLDING A SHOVEL, STOOD KNEE DEEP IN A... HALF-DUG GRAVE?

ANOTHER MAN IN A DENIM SHIRT, UNBUTTONED, STOOD ON THE LIP. A YOUNG WOMAN IN A SCRAPE, HER CHIN BALANCED ON BOTH FISTS, SAT ON A LOG, WATCHING.

"ARE YOU STILL AT THIS?" LANYA ASKED. "YOU WERE THIS FAR ALONG WHEN I WAS HERE THIS MORNING."

"I WISH YOU'D LET ME DIG," THE YOUNG WOMAN SAID.

"SURE," THE BARE-CHESTED MAN WITH THE SHOVEL SAID. HE SHOOK BLOND HAIR FROM HIS SHOULDERS. "JUST AS SOON AS WE GET IT GOING

UNFINISHED STATE // 8D.138

FROM: WILLIAM DHALGREN
ARCHIVE BOOKS
DIEFFENBACHSTRAßE 31
10967 BERLIN, GERMANY

TO:
HELICOPTER PAD
RACHID KARAMI
INTERNATIONAL FAIR PARK
AL MARAAD CIRCLE
TRIPOLI, LEBANON

Retour / Return
Inconnu / Unknown
Déménagé sans laisser d'adresse / Moved without leaving an address
Adresse insuffisante / Insufficient address
Refusé / Refused
Destinataire n'est pas présent / Addressee not present
Personne n'est à l'adresse / No one available at the address
Décédé / Deceased / متوفى
مكتب بريد طرابلس البلد

50 Jahre Fehmarnsundbrücke
Deutschland
75
-1.12.14-20

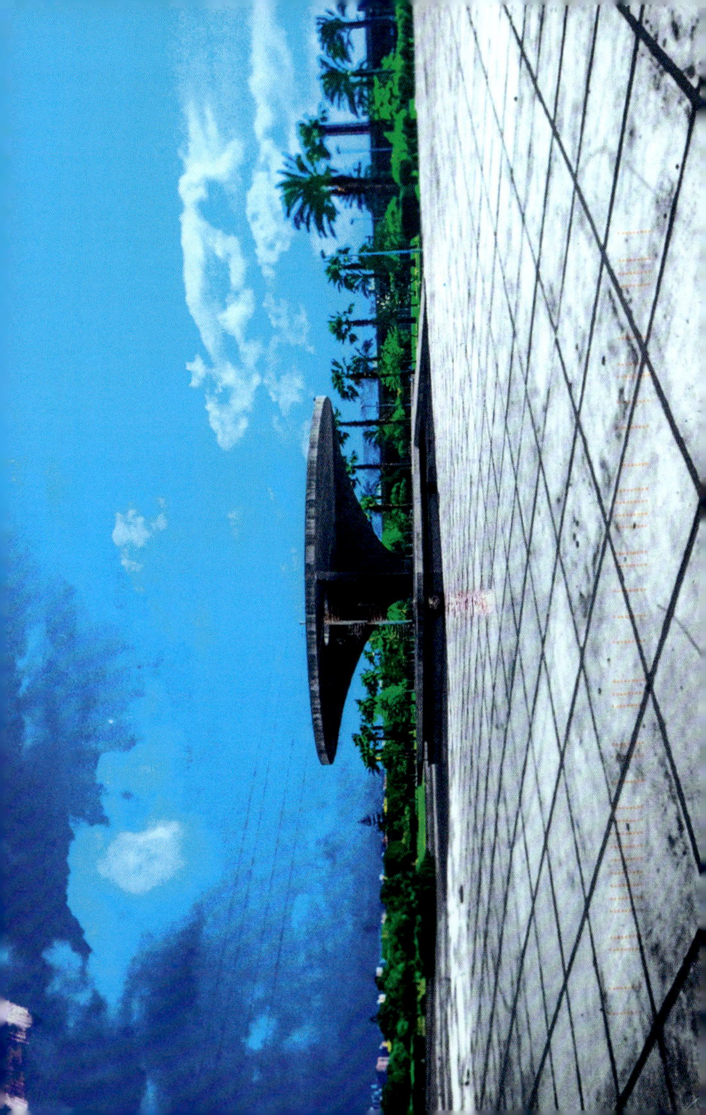

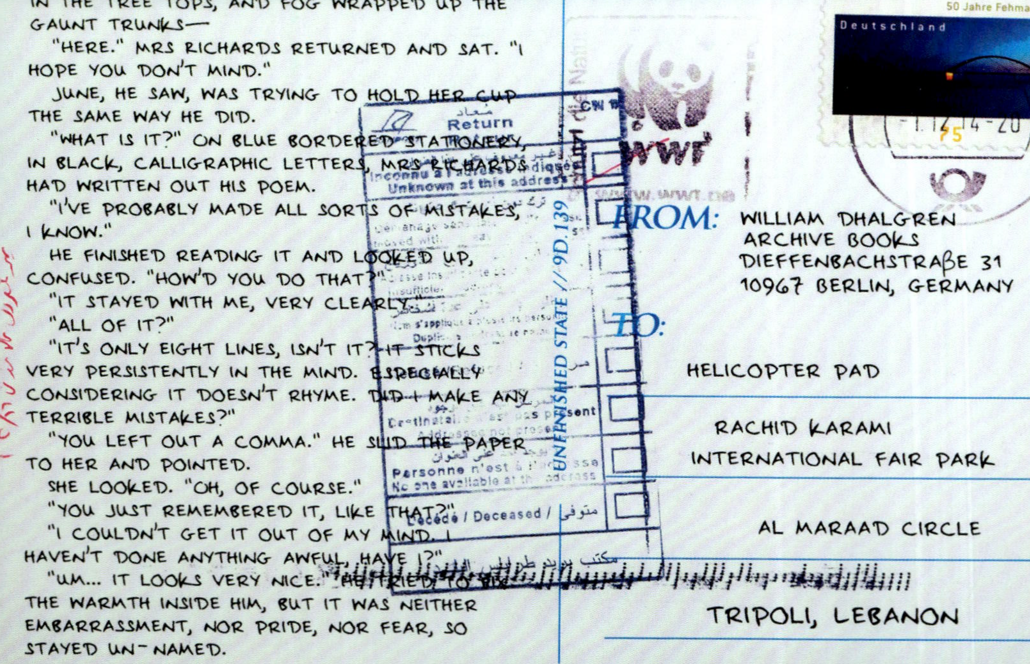
IN THE TREE TOPS, AND FOG WRAPPED UP THE GAUNT TRUNKS—
"HERE." MRS RICHARDS RETURNED AND SAT. "I HOPE YOU DON'T MIND."
JUNE, HE SAW, WAS TRYING TO HOLD HER CUP THE SAME WAY HE DID.
"WHAT IS IT?" ON BLUE BORDERED STATIONERY, IN BLACK, CALLIGRAPHIC LETTERS, MRS RICHARDS HAD WRITTEN OUT HIS POEM.
"I'VE PROBABLY MADE ALL SORTS OF MISTAKES, I KNOW."
HE FINISHED READING IT AND LOOKED UP, CONFUSED. "HOW'D YOU DO THAT?"
"IT STAYED WITH ME, VERY CLEARLY."
"ALL OF IT?"
"IT'S ONLY EIGHT LINES, ISN'T IT? IT STICKS VERY PERSISTENTLY IN THE MIND. ESPECIALLY CONSIDERING IT DOESN'T RHYME. DID I MAKE ANY TERRIBLE MISTAKES?"
"YOU LEFT OUT A COMMA." HE SLID THE PAPER TO HER AND POINTED.
SHE LOOKED. "OH, OF COURSE."
"YOU JUST REMEMBERED IT, LIKE THAT?"
"I COULDN'T GET IT OUT OF MY MIND. I HAVEN'T DONE ANYTHING AWFUL, HAVE I?"
"UM... IT LOOKS VERY NICE." HE TRIED TO FIX THE WARMTH INSIDE HIM, BUT IT WAS NEITHER EMBARRASSMENT, NOR PRIDE, NOR FEAR, SO STAYED UN-NAMED.
Return
Inconnu à l'adresse indiquée
Unknown at this address
Personne n'est à l'adresse
No one available at this address
Décédé / Deceased / متوفى
UNFINISHED STATE // 9D.139
FROM:
WILLIAM DHALGREN
ARCHIVE BOOKS
DIEFFENBACHSTRAßE 31
10967 BERLIN, GERMANY
TO:
HELICOPTER PAD
RACHID KARAMI
INTERNATIONAL FAIR PARK
AL MARAAD CIRCLE
TRIPOLI, LEBANON
50 Jahre Fehmarnsundbrücke
Deutschland
75

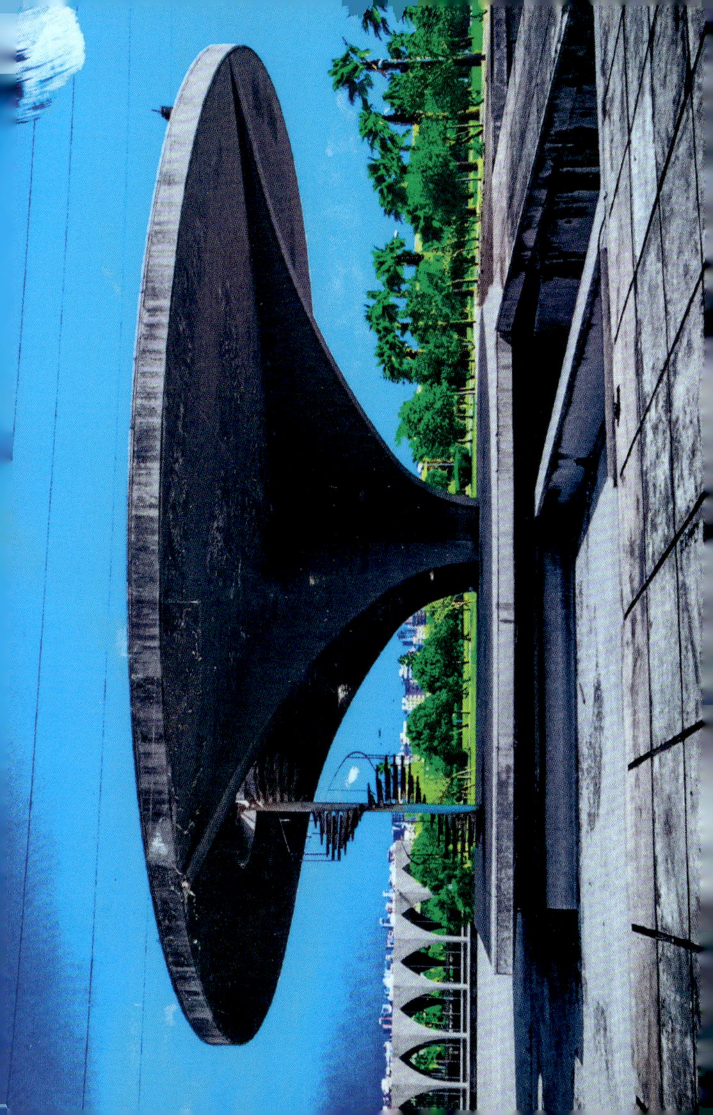

SAID. "NEVER IN MY LIFE. SOMETIMES I THOUGHT I WAS GOING TO—BECAUSE I'D GOTTEN SOME CRAZY COMPULSION, TO JUMP OFF A BUILDING OR THROW MYSELF UNDER A TRAIN, JUST TO SEE WHAT DYING WAS LIKE. BUT I NEVER THOUGHT THAT LIFE WASN'T WORTH LIVING, OR THAT THERE WAS ANY SITUATION SO BAD WHERE JUST SITTING IT OUT WOULDN'T FIX IT UP—THAT'S IF I COULDN'T GET UP AND GO SOMEWHERE ELSE. BUT NOT WANTING TO KILL MYSELF DOESN'T STOP ME THINKING ABOUT DEATH. SAY, HAS THIS EVER HAPPENED TO YOU? YOU'RE WALKING ALONG A STREET, OR SITTING IN A ROOM, OR LYING DOWN ON THE LEAVES, OR EVEN TALKING TO PEOPLE, AND SUDDENLY THE THOUGHT COMES—AND WHEN IT COMES, IT COMES ALL THROUGH YOU LIKE A STOP-ACTION FILM OF A CRYSTAL FORMING OR AN OPENING BUD: 'I AM GOING TO DIE.' SOMEDAY, SOMEWHERE, I WILL BE DYING, AND FIVE SECONDS AFTER THAT, I WILL BE DEAD. AND WHEN IT COMES IT COMES LIKE—" HE SMASHED CUPPED PALMS TOGETHER IN THE AIR SO SHARPLY SHE JUMPED—"THAT! AND YOU KNOW IT, KNOW YOUR OWN DEATH, FOR A WHOLE SECOND, THREE SECONDS, MAYBE FIVE OR TEN... BEFORE THE THOUGHT GOES AND YOU ONLY REMEMBER, THE WORDS YOU WERE MUMBLING, LIKE 'SOMEDAY I WILL DIE,' WHICH ISN'T THE

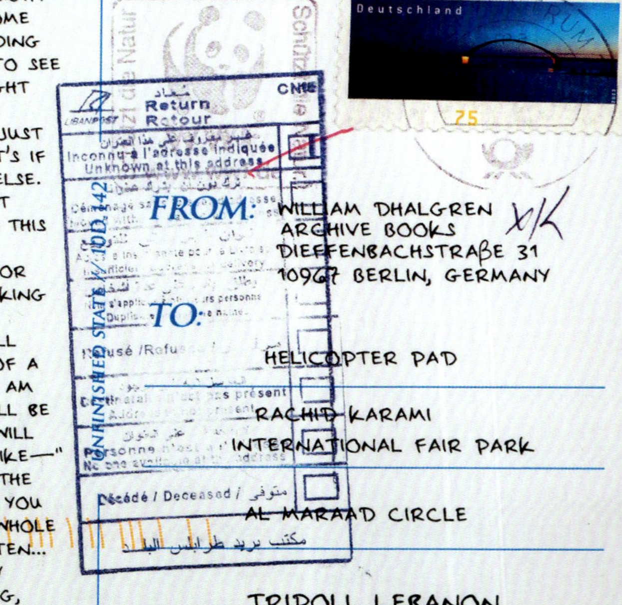

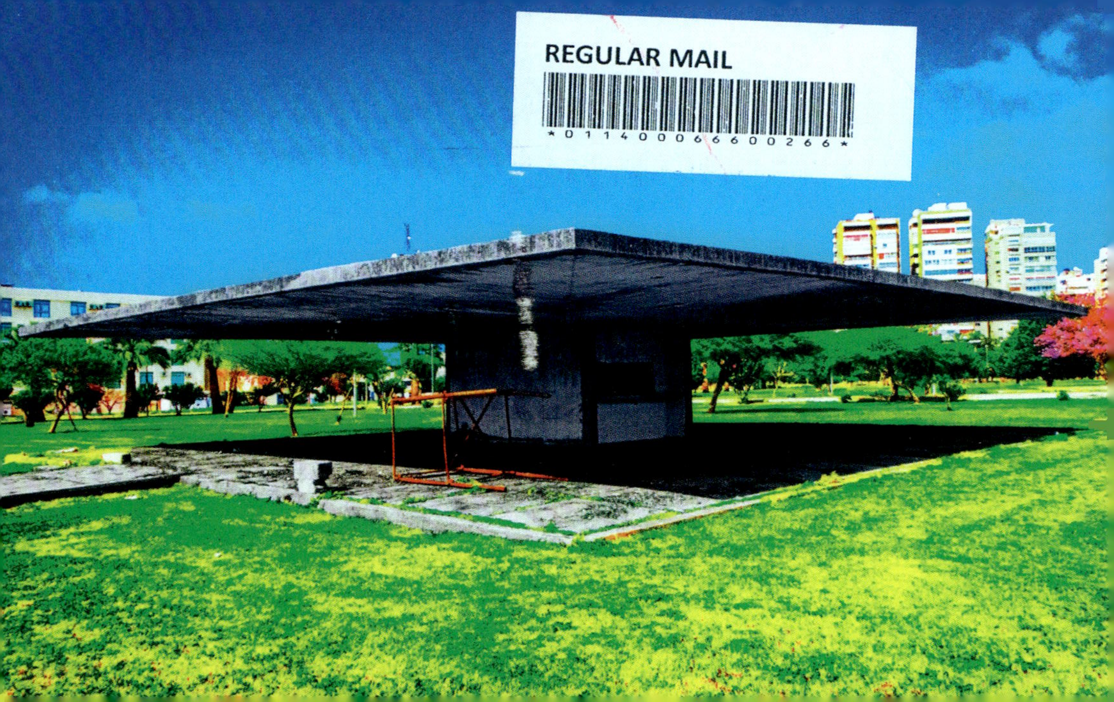
REGULAR MAIL
01140006600266

THOUGHT AT ALL, JUST ITS ASHES."

"YES... YES, THAT'S HAPPENED TO ME."

"WELL, I THINK ALL THE BUILDINGS AND THE BRIDGES AND THE PLANES AND THE BOOKS AND THE SYMPHONIES AND THE PAINTINGS AND THE SPACESHIPS AND THE SUBMARINES AND THE POEMS: THEY'RE JUST TO KEEP PEOPLE'S MINDS OCCUPIED SO IT DOESN'T HAPPEN AGAIN."

AFTER A WHILE HE SAID: "GEORGE HARRISON..."

SHE SAID: "JUNE RICHARDS..." AND GLANCED AT HIM. WHEN HE SAID NOTHING, SHE SAID: "I HAVE THIS PICTURE, OF US GOING DOWN TO THE BAR ONE NIGHT, AND YOU SAYING, 'HEY, MAN, COME ON WITH ME. I WANT YOU TO MEET A FRIEND OF MINE,' AND GEORGE SAYS, 'WHY SURE!'—AND HE PROBABLY WOULD, TOO; HE KNOWS HOW SMALL THE WORLD IS HE'S ACTING MOON FOR—SO YOU TAKE HIM, IN ALL HIS BIG, BLACK, BEAUTIFUL PERSON UP TO THAT PINK BRICK HIGH-RISE WITH ALL THE BROKEN WINDOWS AND YOU GET A-HOLD OF MISS DEMENTED SWEETNESS-AND-LIGHT, AND YOU SAY, 'HEY, LADY, I'VE JUST BROUGHT YOU HIS MIDNIGHT EMINENCE, IN THE FLESH. JUNE, MEET GEORGE. GEORGE, MEET JUNE.' I WONDER WHAT THEY'D TALK ABOUT—ON HER TERRITORY?"

HE CHUCKLED. "OH, I DON'T KNOW. HE MIGHT EVEN SAY, THANK YOU. AFTER ALL, SHE MADE

UNFINISHED STATE // 10D.143

FROM: WILLIAM DHALGREN
ARCHIVE BOOKS
DIEFFENBACHSTRAẞE 31
10967 BERLIN, GERMANY

TO:
EASTERNMOST QUADRILATERAL
MINI PAVILION

RACHID KARAMI
INTERNATIONAL FAIR PARK

AL MARAAD CIRCLE

TRIPOLI, LEBANON

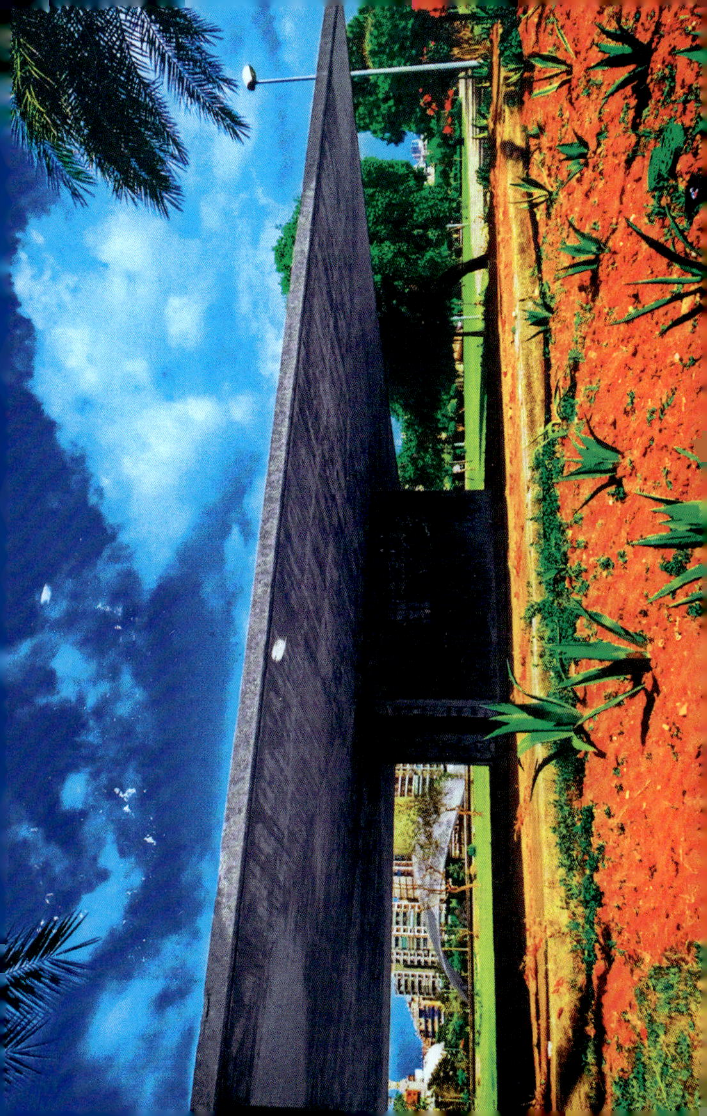

HIM WHAT HE IS TODAY." HE BLINKED AT THE LEAVES. "IT'S FASCINATING, LIFE THE WAY IT IS; THE WAY EVERYTHING SITS TOGETHER, COLORS, SHAPES, POOLS OF WATER WITH LEAVES IN THEM, REFLECTIONS ON WINDOWS, SUNLIGHT WHEN THERE'S SUN, CLOUDLIGHT WHEN IT'S CLOUDY; AND NOW I'M SOMEWHERE WHERE, IF THE SMOKE PULLS BACK AT MIDNIGHT AND GEORGE AND THE MOON ARE UP, I MIGHT SEE TWO SHADOWS INSTEAD OF ONE!" HE STRETCHED HIS HANDS BEHIND HIM ON THE BLANKET. HE KNOCKED SOMETHING—WHICH WAS HIS ORCHID, ROLLING ACROSS HIS NOTEBOOK COVER.

"WHEN I WAS AT ART SCHOOL," SHE SAID, "I REMEMBER AN INSTRUCTOR OF MINE SAYING THAT IT WAS ONLY ON DAYS LIKE YOU HAVE HERE THAT YOU KNOW THE TRUE COLOR OF ANYTHING. THE WHOLE CITY, ALL OF BELLONA, IT'S UNDER PERPETUAL NORTH LIGHT."

"MMM," HE SAID.

WHAT IS THIS PART OF ME THAT LINGERS TO OVERHEAR MY OWN CONVERSATION? I LIE RIGID IN THE RIGID CIRCLE. IT REGARDS ME FROM DIAMETRIC POINTS, WITHOUT SEX, AND WISE. WE LIE IN A RIGID CITY, ANTICIPATING WINDS. IT CIRCLES ME, INTIMATING ONLY ITS POSITION THAT IT KNOWS MORE THAN I WANT TO. THERE, IT MAKES A GESTURE TOO MASCULINE

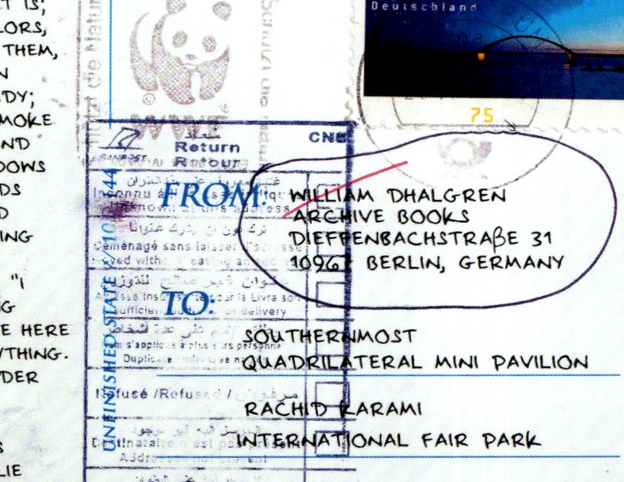

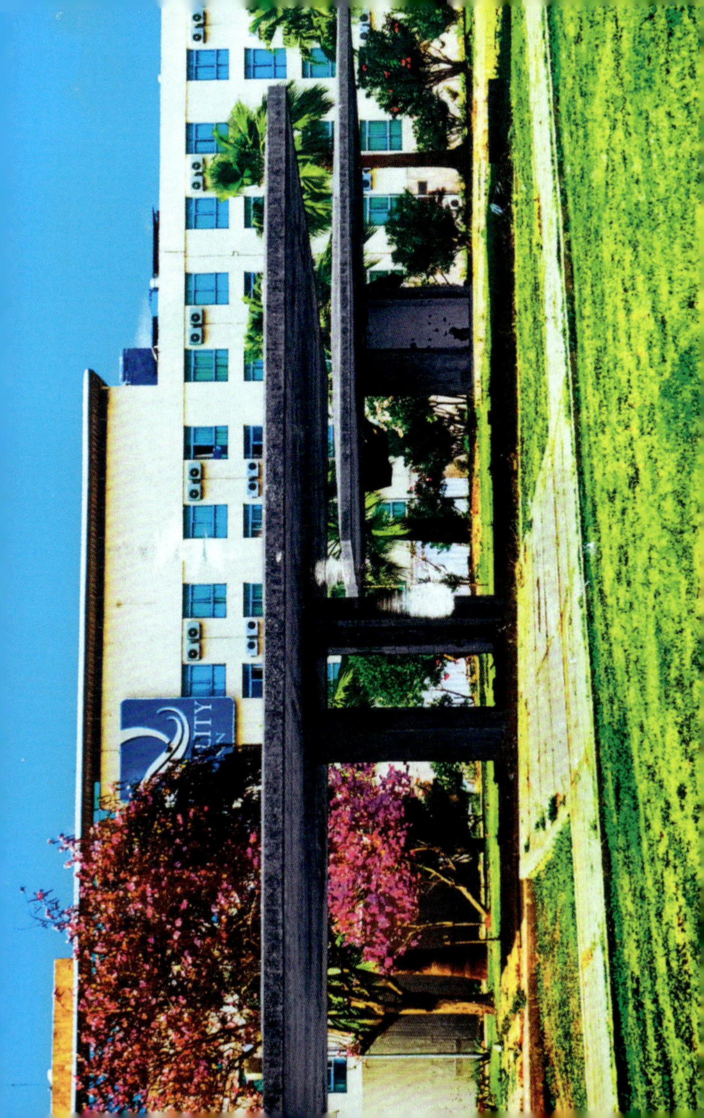

BEFORE ECSTATIC SCENERY. HERE, IT SUGGESTS FEMININITY, PAUSING AT GORE AND BONE. IT DITHERS AND STAMMERS, CONFRONTED BY LOVE. IT BOWS A BLUNT, MUMBLING HEAD BEFORE INJUSTICE, RAGE, OR EVEN ITS LIKE IGNORANCE. STILL, I AM CONVINCED THAT AT THE PROPER SHOCK, IT WOULD TURN AND CALL ME, USING THOSE HERMETIC SYLLABLES I HAVE ABANDONED ON THE CRAGS OF A BROKEN CONSCIENCE, ON THE PLANES OF CHARRED CONSCIOUSNESS, AT THE ENTRANCE TO THE GANGLIAL CITY. AND I WOULD RAISE MY HEAD.

"YOU..." HE SAID, SUDDENLY. IT WAS DARK. "ARE YOU HAPPY, I MEAN, LIVING LIKE THAT?"

"ME?" SHE BREATHED A LONG BREATH. "LET ME SEE... BEFORE I CAME HERE, I WAS TEACHING ENGLISH TO CANTONESE CHILDREN WHO'D JUST ARRIVED IN NEW YORK'S CHINATOWN. BEFORE THAT, I WAS MANAGING A PORNOGRAPHIC BOOKSTORE ON 42ND STREET. AND BEFORE THAT, FOR QUITE A WHILE, I WAS A SELF-TAUGHT TAPE-JOCKEY AT WBAI, FM, IN NEW YORK, AND BEFORE THAT, I WAS DOING A STINT AT HER SISTER STATION KPFA, IN BERKELEY, CAL. BABES, I AM SO BORED HERE THAT I DON'T THINK, SINCE I'VE COME, I'VE EVER BEEN MORE THAN THREE MINUTES AWAY FROM SOME REALLY ASTONISHING ACT OF VIOLENCE." AND SUDDENLY, IN THE DARK, SHE ROLLED AGAINST HIM.

UNFINISHED STATE // 10D.145

FROM: WILLIAM DHALGREN
ARCHIVE BOOKS
DIEFFENBACHSTRAßE 31
10967 BERLIN, GERMANY

TO:
QUADRILATERAL MINI PAVILIONS
NEXT TO THE QUALITY INN

RACHID KARAMI
INTERNATIONAL FAIR PARK

AL MARAAD CIRCLE

TRIPOLI, LEBANON

مكتب بريد طرابلس البلد

Deutschland 75

Schützt die Natur WWF www.wwf.de

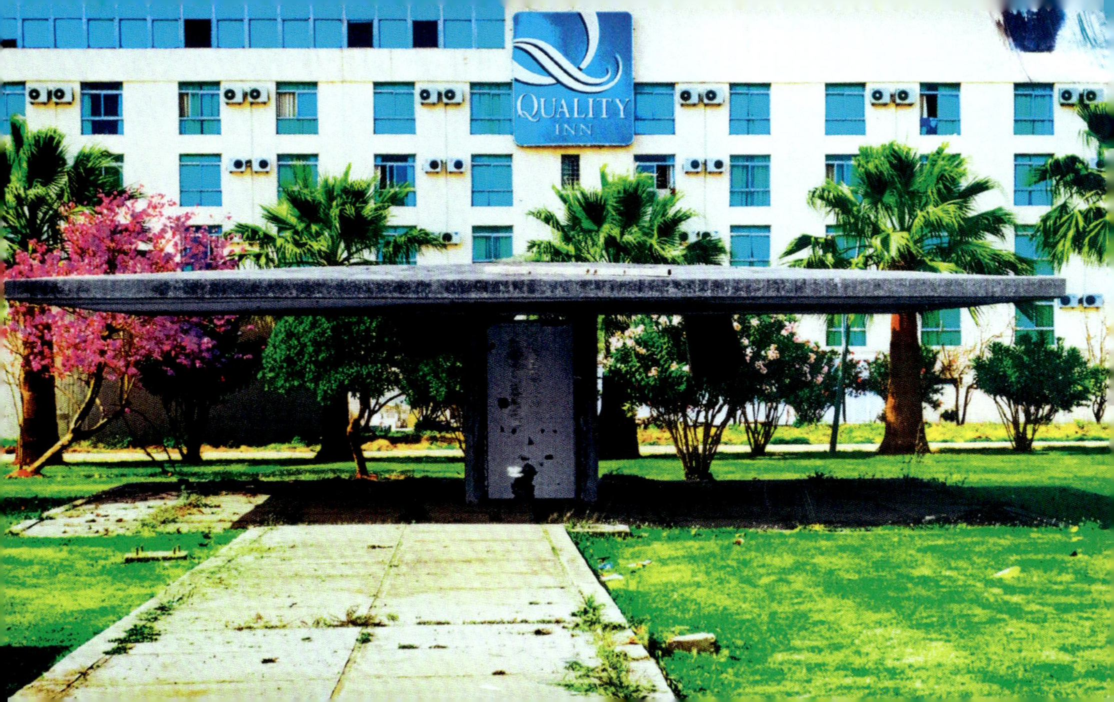
QUALITY
INN

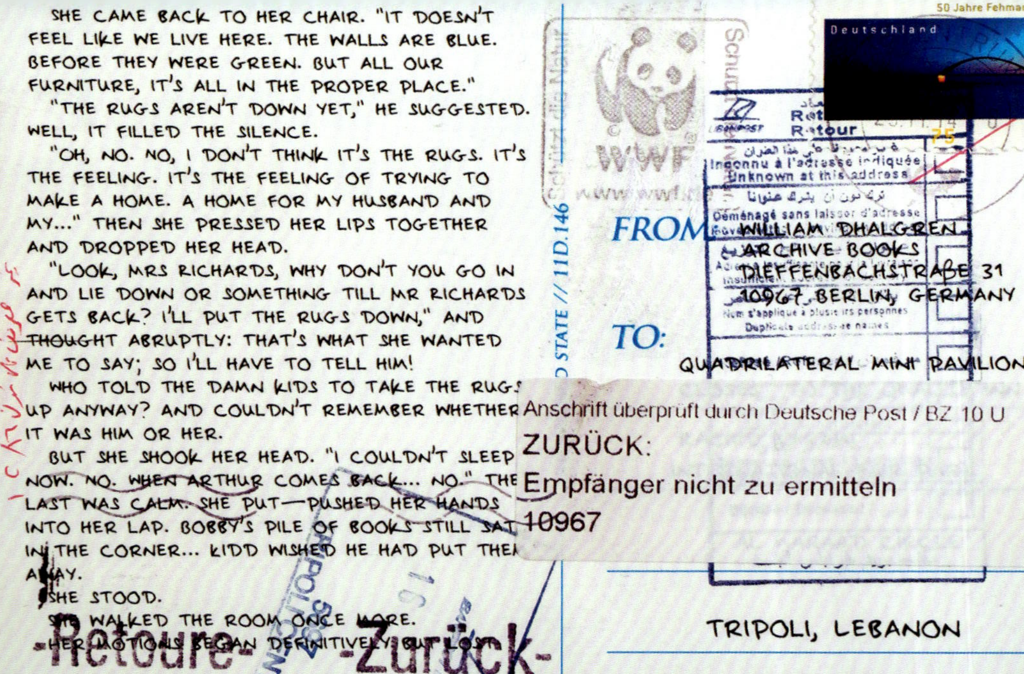

SHE CAME BACK TO HER CHAIR. "IT DOESN'T FEEL LIKE WE LIVE HERE. THE WALLS ARE BLUE. BEFORE THEY WERE GREEN. BUT ALL OUR FURNITURE, IT'S ALL IN THE PROPER PLACE."

"THE RUGS AREN'T DOWN YET," HE SUGGESTED. WELL, IT FILLED THE SILENCE.

"OH, NO. NO, I DON'T THINK IT'S THE RUGS. IT'S THE FEELING. IT'S THE FEELING OF TRYING TO MAKE A HOME. A HOME FOR MY HUSBAND AND MY..." THEN SHE PRESSED HER LIPS TOGETHER AND DROPPED HER HEAD.

"LOOK, MRS RICHARDS, WHY DON'T YOU GO IN AND LIE DOWN OR SOMETHING TILL MR RICHARDS GETS BACK? I'LL PUT THE RUGS DOWN," AND THOUGHT ABRUPTLY: THAT'S WHAT SHE WANTED ME TO SAY; SO I'LL HAVE TO TELL HIM!

WHO TOLD THE DAMN KIDS TO TAKE THE RUGS UP ANYWAY? AND COULDN'T REMEMBER WHETHER IT WAS HIM OR HER.

BUT SHE SHOOK HER HEAD. "I COULDN'T SLEEP NOW. NO. WHEN ARTHUR COMES BACK... NO." THE LAST WAS CALM. SHE PUT—PUSHED HER HANDS INTO HER LAP. BOBBY'S PILE OF BOOKS STILL SAT IN THE CORNER... KIDD WISHED HE HAD PUT THEM AWAY.

SHE STOOD.

SHE WALKED THE ROOM ONCE MORE.

HER MOTIONS BEGAN DEFINITIVELY, BUT LOST

-Retoure- -Zurück-

50 Jahre Fehmarnsundbrücke

Deutschland 75

Schützt die Natur WWF www.wwf.de

Retour

Inconnu à l'adresse indiquée
Unknown at this address

Déménagé sans laisser d'adresse

Nom s'applique à plusieurs personnes
Duplicate addressee names

…D STATE // 11D.146

FROM: WILLIAM DHALGREN
ARCHIVE BOOKS
DIEFFENBACHSTRAßE 31
10967 BERLIN, GERMANY

TO: QUADRILATERAL MINI PAVILION

TRIPOLI, LEBANON

Anschrift überprüft durch Deutsche Post / BZ 10 U
ZURÜCK:
Empfänger nicht zu ermitteln
10967

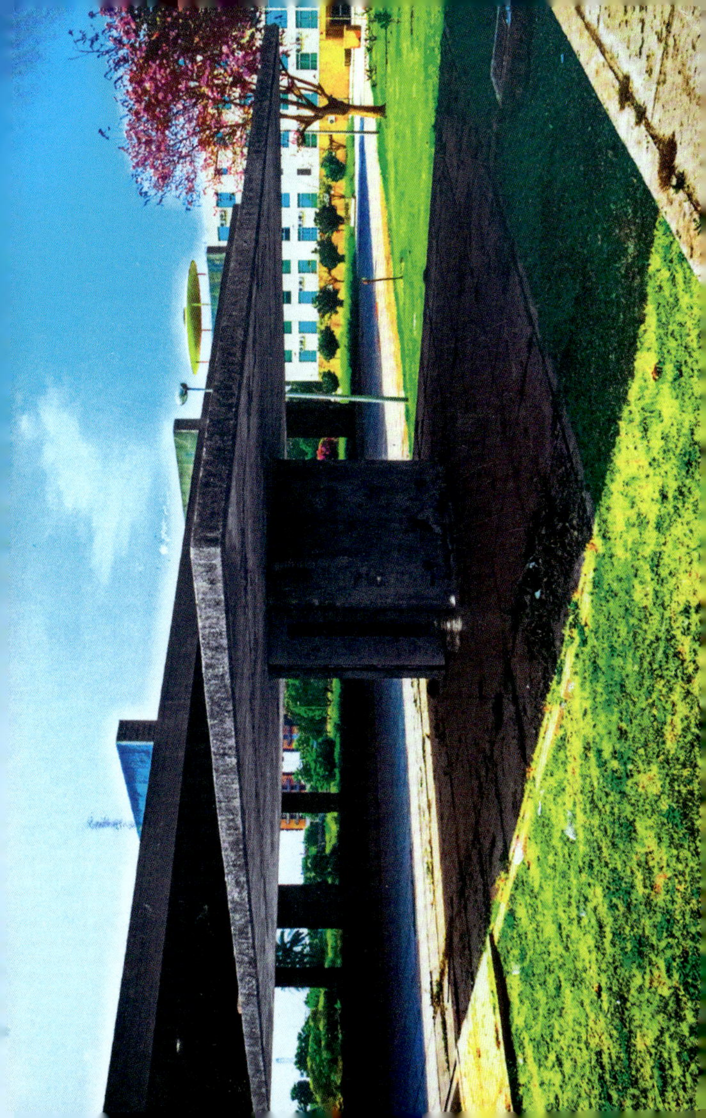

FOCUS IN A GLANCE—FIRST OUT THE BALCONY DOORS, NEXT INTO THE DINING ROOM, NOW TOWARD THE HALL.

SHE STOPPED BEHIND HER CHAIR.

"ARTHUR," SHE SAID, FOLLOWED BY WHAT SOUNDED MORE LIKE A COMMA OF ADDRESS THAN OF APPOSITION, "HE'S OUTSIDE."

"MA'AM?"

"ARTHUR IS OUTSIDE, IN THAT." SHE SAT. "HE GOES OUT EVERY DAY. I CAN WATCH HIM FROM THE WINDOW TURN DOWN FORTY-FOURTH THERE AND DISAPPEAR. INTO THE SMOKE. LIKE THAT." OUTSIDE THE BALCONY DOOR, BUILDINGS WERE BLURRED. "WE'VE MOVED." SHE WATCHED THE FOG FOR THE LENGTH OF FIVE BREATHS. "THIS BUILDING, IT'S LIKE A CHESSBOARD. NOW WE OCCUPY A DIFFERENT SQUARE. WE HAD TO MOVE. WE HAD TO. OUR POSITION BEFORE WAS TERRIBLE." SMOKE PULLED FROM THE WINDOW, UNCOVERING MORE SMOKE—"BUT I DIDN'T KNOW THE MOVE WOULD COST SO MUCH."—AND MORE. "I AM NOT PREPARED FOR THIS. I'M REALLY NOT. ARTHUR GOES OUT THERE, EVERY DAY, AND WORKS IN SYSTEMS. MAITLAND SYSTEMS ENGINEERING. THEN HE COMES HOME." SHE LEANED FORWARD. "DO YOU KNOW, I DON'T BELIEVE ALL THAT OUT THERE IS REAL. ONCE THE SMOKE COVERS HIM, I DON'T BELIEVE HE

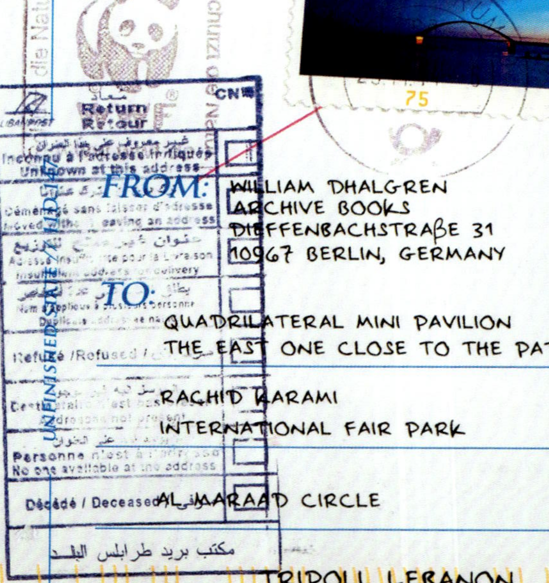

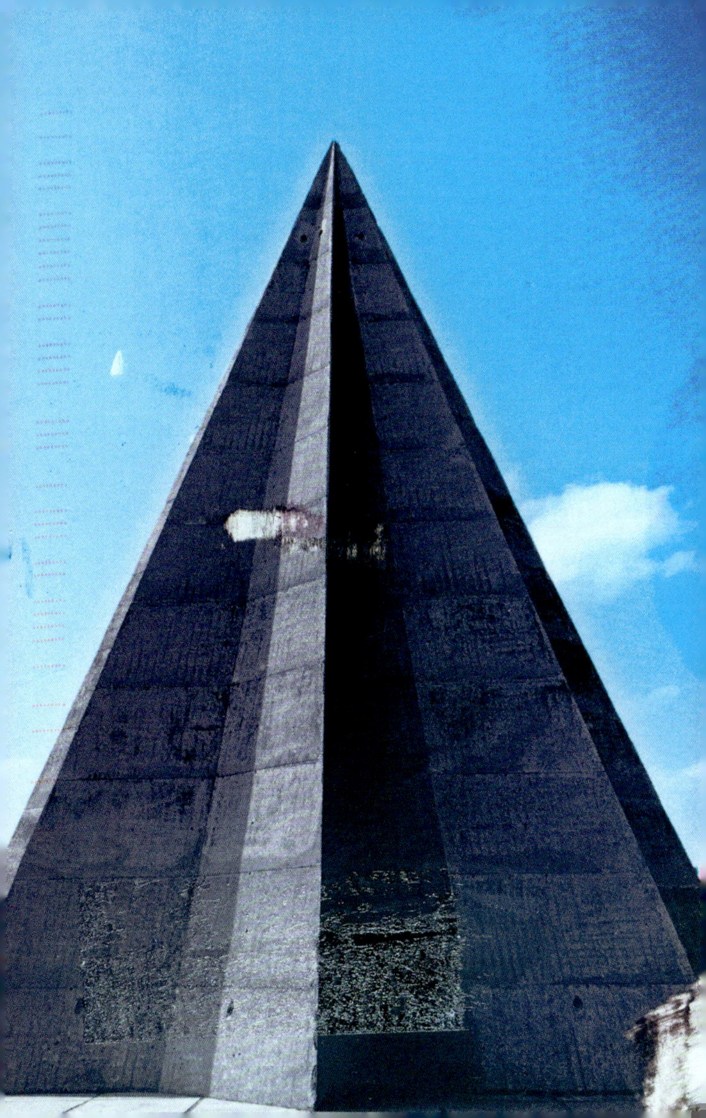

THE BALCONY DOORS. "I'VE SUSPECTED, OH, I'VE SUSPECTED THAT WHATEVER WAS THERE WASN'T REALLY WHAT HE NEEDED, WHAT WOULD MAKE HIM—HAPPY? OH, I LEARNED A LONG TIME AGO YOU DON'T LOOK FOR THAT. BUT THE THING YOU DO TRY FOR—EXCELLENCE? CONTENTMENT? OH NO, OH NO: NOT IN A GREAT EMPTY OFFICE BUILDING, WHERE THE LIGHTS DON'T WORK, WHERE THE WINDOWS ARE BROKEN, WHERE THERE AREN'T ANY PEOPLE."

"THERE'RE PROBABLY PEOPLE THERE," KIDD SAID, UNCOMFORTABLY. "PROBABLY A SKELETON STAFF. MADAME BROWN AND I WERE TALKING ABOUT THAT. IT'S PROBABLY LIKE AT... THE MANAGEMENT OFFICE."

"AH." HER HANDS MET IN HER LAP. "YES." SHE SAT BACK. "BUT I'M ONLY TELLING YOU HOW IT FEELS. TO ME. WHEN THE SMOKE THINS, I CAN LOOK ACROSS AT THE OTHER BUILDINGS. SO MANY OF THE WINDOWS ARE BROKEN. MAYBE THE MAINTENANCE MEN IN ARTHUR'S OFFICE HAVE ALREADY STARTED PUTTING IN NEW PANES. THE MAINTENANCE IS ALWAYS BETTER IN A PLACE OF BUSINESS. WELL, THERE'S MORE MONEY INVOLVED. I JUST WONDER WHEN WE CAN EXPECT SOME SORT OF REASONABLE RETURN TO NORMAL HERE. THERE'S A CERTAIN MINIMUM STANDARD THAT MUST BE KEPT UP. THEY SHOULD SEND SOMEBODY

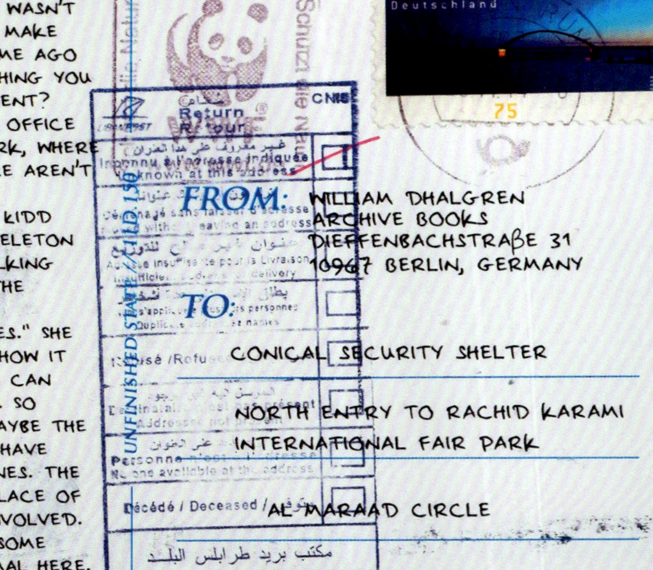

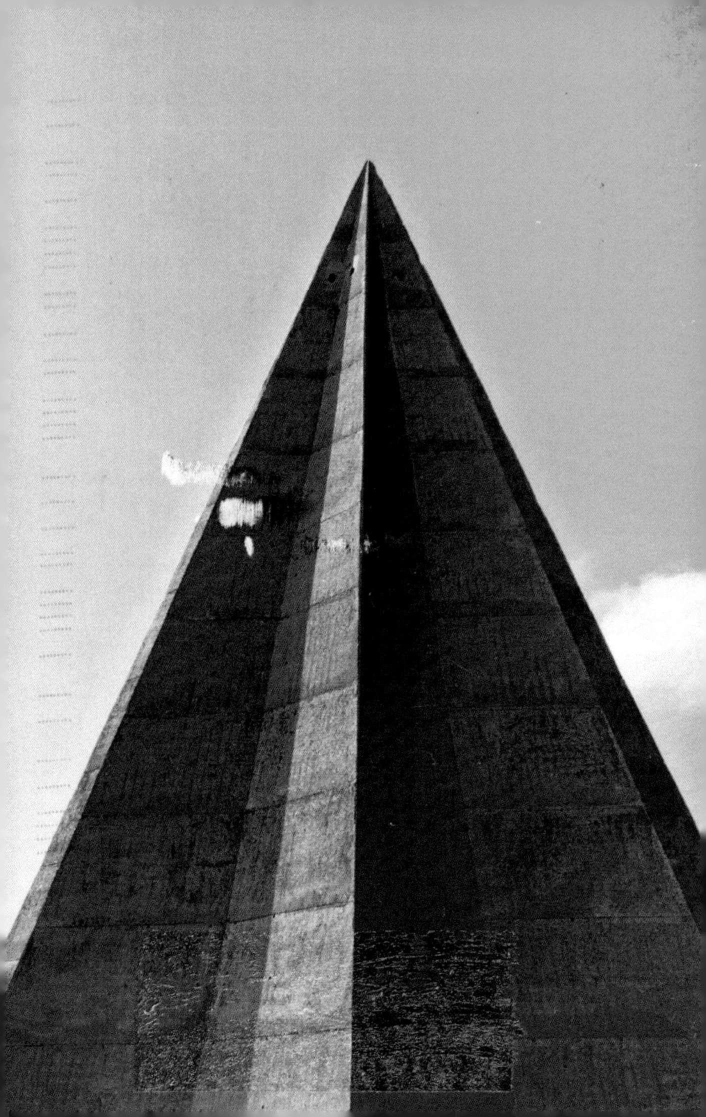

AROUND, IF ONLY TO LET US KNOW WHAT THE SITUATION IS. NOT KNOWING, THAT'S THE WORST. IF I DID KNOW SOMETHING, SOMETHING FOR SURE ABOUT PLANS FOR REPAIRING THE DAMAGES, FOR RESTORING SERVICE, LIGHTS, AND THINGS, WHEN WE COULD EXPECT THEM TO START..." SHE LOOKED ODDLY ANNOYED.

"MAYBE THEY WILL," HE SUGGESTED, "SEND SOMEBODY AROUND."

"YOU'D THINK THEY WOULD. WE HAVE HAD TROUBLE WITH THEM BEFORE; THERE WAS A HUGE CRACK, IT OPENED UP IN JUNE'S CEILING. IT WASN'T OUR FAULT. SOMETHING UPSTAIRS LEAKED. IT TOOK THEM THREE MONTHS TO SEND SOMEBODY. BUT THEY ANSWERED MY LETTER RIGHT AWAY. MEANWHILE, I JUST HAVE TO MUDDLE, MUDDLE ON. AND EVERY MORNING I SEND ARTHUR OUT OF HERE, OUT INTO THAT." SHE NODDED. "THAT'S THE CRIME. OF COURSE I COULDN'T KEEP HIM BACK; HE WOULDN'T STAY. I'D TELL HIM HOW DANGEROUS I THOUGHT IT WAS OUT THERE, ALL THE AWFUL THINGS I'M AFRAID MIGHT HAPPEN, AND HE'D— OH, I WISH HE'D LAUGH. BUT HE WOULDN'T. HE'D SCOWL. AND GO. HE GOES AWAY, EVERY MORNING, JUST DISAPPEARS, DOWN FORTY-FOURTH. THE ONLY THING I CAN DO FOR HIM IS TRY AND KEEP A GOOD HOME, WHERE NOTHING CAN HURT HIM, AT

UNFINISHED STATE // 11D.151

Schützt die Natur. WWF www.wwf.de

Deutschland 50 Jahre Fehmarnsundbrücke 75

Return Retour
غير معروف على هذا العنوان
Inconnu à l'adresse indiquée
Unknown at this address
Nom s'applique à plusieurs personnes
Duplicate addressee names
المرسل اليه غير موجود
Destinataire n'est pas présent
Personne n'est à l'adresse
No one available at this address
Décédé / Deceased
مكتب بريد طرابلس البلد

FROM: WILLIAM DHALGREN
ARCHIVE BOOKS
DIEFFENBACHSTRAßE 31
10967 BERLIN, GERMANY

TO: CONICAL SECURITY SHELTER
NORTH ENTRY TO RACHID KARAMI
INTERNATIONAL FAIR PARK
AL MARAAD CIRCLE
TRIPOLI, LEBANON

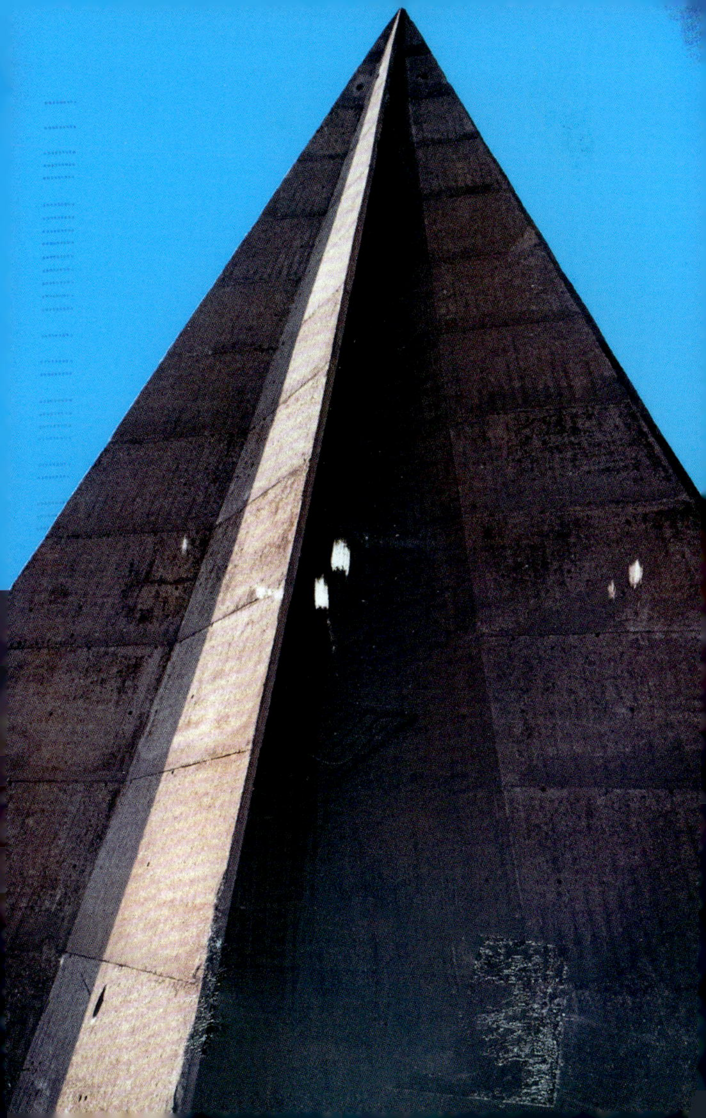

LEAST HERE, A HAPPY, SAFE AND—"

HE THOUGHT SHE'D SEEN SOMETHING BEHIND HIM, AND WAS ABOUT TO TURN AROUND. BUT HER EXPRESSION WENT ON TO SOMETHING MORE VIOLENT THAN RECOGNITION.

SHE BENT HER HEAD. "I GUESS I HAVEN'T DONE THAT VERY WELL. I HAVEN'T DONE THAT AT ALL."

HE WISHED SHE WOULD LET HIM LEAVE.

"MRS RICHARDS, I'M GOING TO SEE ABOUT THAT STUFF IN—THE BACK." HE THOUGHT THERE WAS SOME STUFF IN THE BACK STILL TO BE PUT IN PLACE. "YOU JUST TRY AND TAKE IT EASY NOW." HE GOT UP, THINKING: WHEN I COME BACK I CAN PUT DOWN THE LIVING-ROOM RUG.

THERE'S NOTHING I CAN DO, HE JUSTIFIED, TO SPONGE UP HER GRIEF. AND I CAN'T DO NOTHING.

HE OPENED THE DOOR TO BOBBY'S ROOM WHERE THE FURNITURE HAD STILL NOT BEEN PUT AGAINST THE WALLS.

AND JUNE'S FISTS CRASHED THE EDGES OF THE POSTER TOGETHER.

"HEY, I'M SORRY... I DIDN'T REALIZE THIS WAS YOUR—"

BUT IT WAS BOBBY'S ROOM. KIDD'S APOLOGETIC SMILE DROPPED BEFORE HER ASTONISHED DESPAIR. "LOOK, I'LL LEAVE YOU ALONE..."

"HE WAS GOING TO TELL!" SHE WHISPERED,

CN15
Return / Retour
Inconnu à l'adresse indiquée / Unknown at this address
Déménagé sans laisser d'adresse / Moved without leaving address
Adresse insuffisante pour la Livraison / Insufficient address for delivery
S'applique à plusieurs personnes / Duplicate address names
Refusé / Refused
Destinataire n'est pas présent / Addressee not present
Personne n'est à l'adresse / No one available at the address
Décédé / Deceased

UNFINISHED STATE / 2 11 152

Deutschland 25

Schützt die Natur. WWF www.wwf.de

FROM: WILLIAM DHALGREN
ARCHIVE BOOKS
DIEFFENBACHSTRAßE 31
10967 BERLIN, GERMANY

TO: CONICAL SECURITY SHELTER
NORTH ENTRY TO RACHID KARAMI
INTERNATIONAL FAIR PARK
AL MARAAD CIRCLE
TRIPOLI, LEBANON

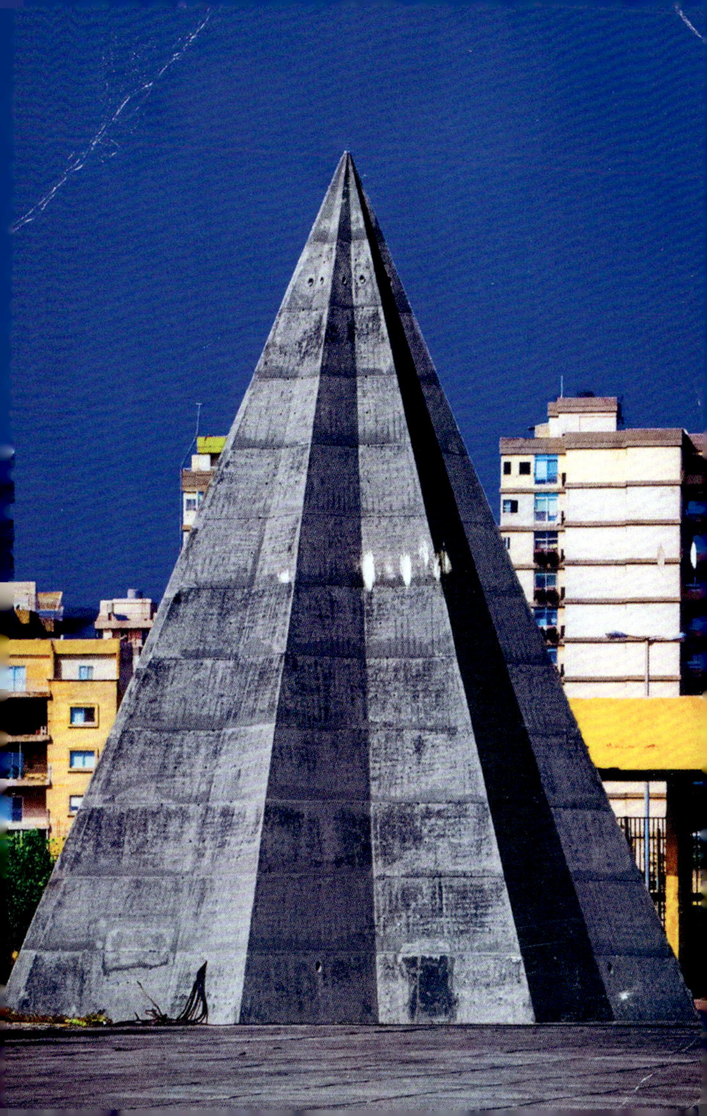

ALL OVER ME, LIKE A FLAYED CARCASS OFF A BUTCHER HOOK... YOU KNOW, I HAD HALF A HARD-ON? THAT'S TOO MUCH, HUH?"

SHE REACHED BETWEEN HIS LEGS. "YOU STILL DO." SHE MOVED HER FINGERS THERE; HE MOVED IN HER FINGERS.

"MAYBE THAT'S WHAT I WAS DREAMING ABOUT?" HE LAUGHED SHARPLY. "DO YOU THINK THAT'S WHAT I WAS—?"

HER HAND CONTRACTED, RELEASED, MOVED FORWARD, MOVED BACK.

HE SAID: "I DON'T THINK THAT'S GOING TO DO ANY GOOD..."

AGAINST HIS CHEST HE FELT HER SHRUG. TRY. NOT SO MUCH TO HIS SURPRISE, BUT SOMEHOW AGAINST HIS WILL, HIS WILL CEASED, AND IT DID.

I LET MY HEAD FALL BACK IN THIS ANGRY SEASON. THERE, TENSIONS I HAD HOPED WOULD RESOLVE, MERELY SHIFT WITH THE BODY'S MACHINERY. THE ACT IS CLUMSY, HALTING, AND WITHOUT GRACE OR REASON. WHAT CAN I READ IN THE SMELL OF HER, WHAT MESSAGE IN THE CODE OF HER BREATH? THIS MOUNTAIN OPENS PASSAGES OF LIGHT. THE LINES ON SQUEEZED LIDS CAGE THE BURSTING BALLS. ALL EFFORTS DYING HERE, COALESCE IN THE BLOCKAGE OF EAR AND THROAT, TO AN A-CORPORAL LUCENCE, A PATTERNING RELEASED FROM PLEASURE, THE RETAINED SHADOW OF PURE IDEA.

UNFINISHED STATE // 12D.155

FROM: WILLIAM DHALGREN
ARCHIVE BOOKS
DIEFFENBACHSTRAßE 31
10967 BERLIN, GERMANY

TO: CONICAL SECURITY SHELTER
NORTH ENTRY TO RACHID KARAMI
INTERNATIONAL FAIR PARK
AL MARAAD CIRCLE
TRIPOLI, LEBANON

Return
Retour
Inconnu à l'adresse indiquée
Unknown at this address
Déménagé sans laisser d'adresse
Adresse insuffisante pour la Livraison
Refusé
n'est pas présent
Décédé / Deceased / متوفى
مكتب بريد طرابلس البلد

mal wieder

50 Jahre Fehmarnsundbrücke
Deutschland
75

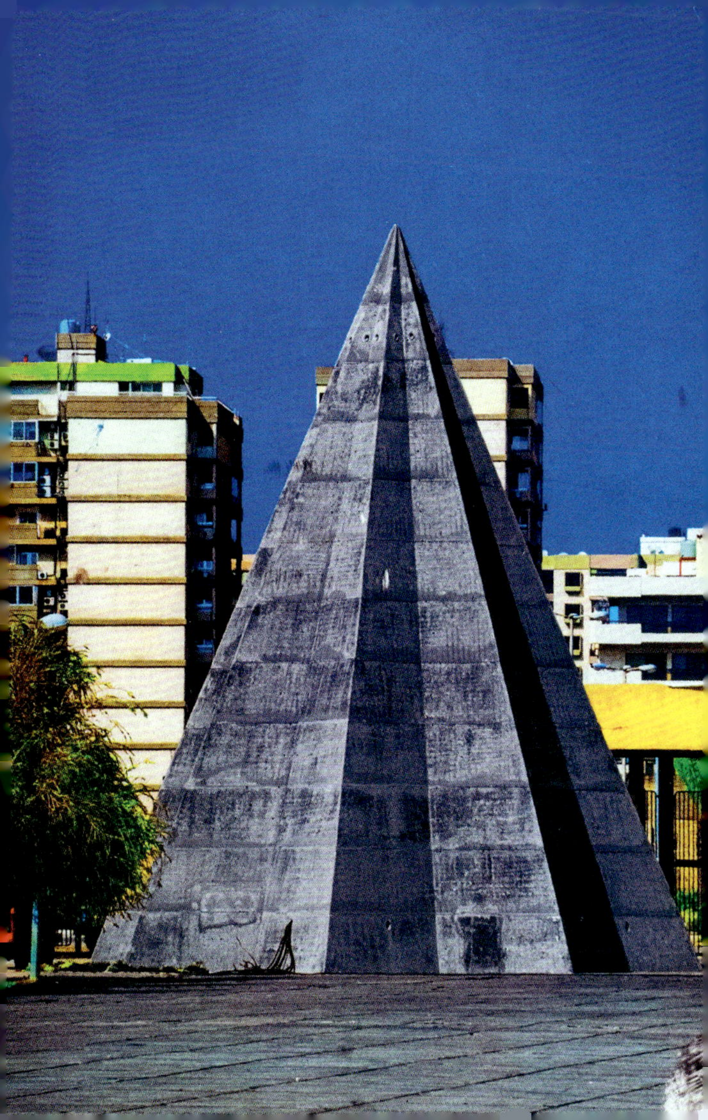

HARP."

"WHERE DID HE GET VIOLINS HERE IN BELLONA?"

"HE DID. AND PEOPLE WITH LOTS AND LOTS OF GORGEOUS CLOTHES."

KIDD WAS GOING TO SAY SOMETHING ABOUT PHIL.

LANYA TURNED. "IF MY DRESSES ARE STILL HERE, I KNOW EXACTLY WHERE THEY'D BE."

MR NEWBOY PUSHED THROUGH THE GLASS DOORS WITH A TEAWAGON. URN AND CUPS RATTLED TWICE AS THE TIRES CROSSED THE SILL. THE LOWER TRAY HELD DISHES OF PASTRY. "YOU CAUGHT MRS ALT RIGHT AFTER A DAY OF BAKING."

"HEY," KIDD SAID. "THOSE LOOK GOOD."

"HELP YOURSELF." HE POURED STEAMING COFFEE INTO BLUE PORCELAIN. "SUGAR, CREAM?"

KIDD SHOOK HIS HEAD; THE CUP WARMED HIS KNEE. HE BIT. COOKIE CRUMBS FELL AND ROLLED ON HIS NOTEBOOK.

LANYA, SITTING ON THE WALL AND SWINGING HER TENNIS SHOES AGAINST THE STONE, MUNCHED A CRISP CONE FILLED WITH BUTTER-CREAM.

"NOW," MR NEWBOY SAID. "HAVE YOU BROUGHT SOME POEMS?"

"OH." KIDD BRUSHED CRUMBS AWAY. "YEAH BUT THEY'RE HANDWRITTEN. I DON'T HAVE ANY TYPEWRITER. I PRINT THEM OUT NEAT, AFTER I

UNFINISHED STATE // 13D 157

FROM:
WILLIAM DHALGREN
ARCHIVE BOOKS
DIEFFENBACHSTRAßE 31
10967 BERLIN, GERMANY

TO:
CONICAL SECURITY SHELTER
NORTH ENTRY TO RACHID KARAMI
INTERNATIONAL FAIR PARK
AL MARAAD CIRCLE
TRIPOLI, LEBANON

Return / Retour CN15
Inconnu à l'adresse indiquée / Unknown at this address
Décédé / Deceased / متوفى
مكتب بريد طرابلس البلد

50 Jahre Fehmarnsundbrücke
Deutschland 75

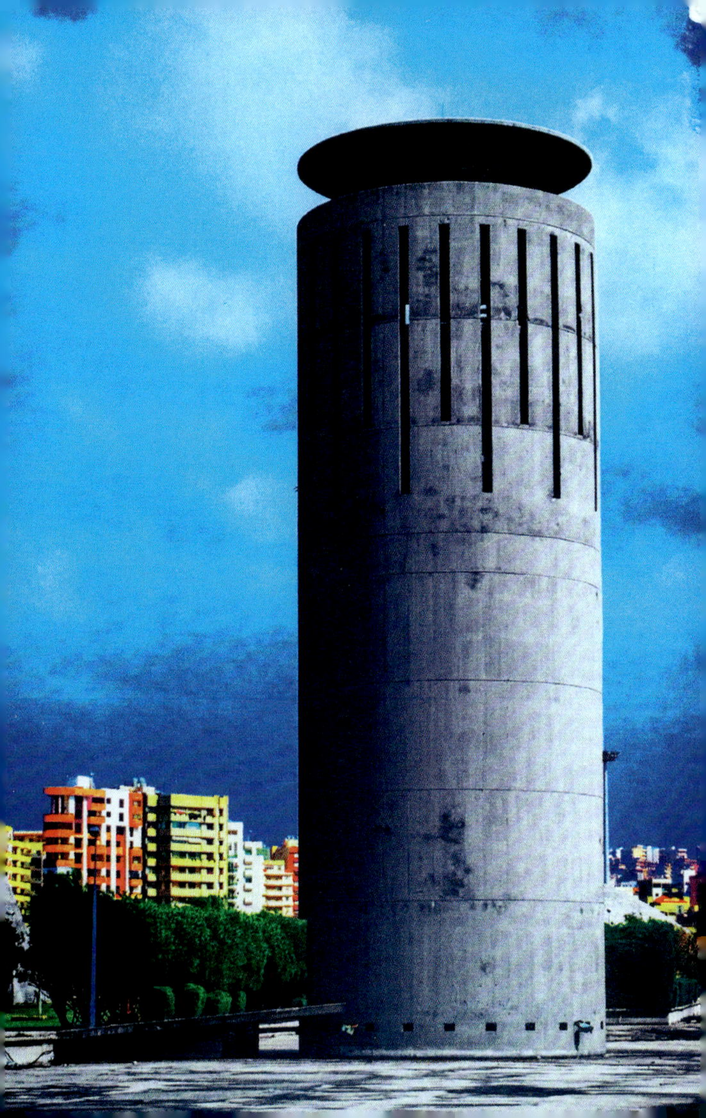

DISCARDED AND GLITTERING ABOUT IN THAT SPIKY LANDSCAPE. NOT TO MENTION ALL THOSE NAKED PEOPLE DOING ALL THOSE STRANGE THINGS ON THE TOPS OF THEIR VARIOUS HILLS, OR DOWN IN THEIR SEVERAL DELLS, SOME OF THEM—LORD, HOW MANY?—BEYOND DOUBT OUT OF THEIR MINDS! AT THE SAME TIME—" HE TURNED ANOTHER PAGE—"NOTHING IS QUITE AS HUMBLING, AFTER A VERY LITTLE WHILE, AS REALIZING HOW CLOSE ONE HAS ALREADY COME TO DROPPING IT A DOZEN TIMES ONESELF, HAVING BEEN DISTRACTED—HEAVENS, NO!—NOT BY WEALTH—OR FAME, BUT BY THOSE ENDLESS STRUCTURES OF LOGIC AND NECESSITY THAT GO SO TEDIOUSLY ON BEFORE THEY REACH THE INEVITABLE FLAW THAT CAUSES THEIR JOINTS TO SHATTER AND ALLOW YOU PASSAGE. ONE PICKS ONE'S WAY ABOUT THROUGH THE GLASS AND ALUMINUM DOORS, THE RECEPTIONISTS' SMILES, THE LUNCHES WITH TOO MUCH ALCOHOL, THE OPENINGS WITH MORE, THE MOBS OF PEOPLE DESPERATELY TRYING TO DEFINE GOOD TASTE IN SUCH LOUD VOICES ONE CAN HARDLY HEAR ONESELF GIGGLE, WHILE THE SHEBANG IS LIT BY FLASHES AND FLARES THROUGH THE PAINT-STAINED WINDOW, GLIMMERS UNDER THE POLICE-LOCKED DOOR, OR, IF ONE IS TAKING A RARE WALK OUTSIDE THAT DAY, BY A LIGHT

UNFINISHED STATE // 13D.160

50 Jahre Fehmarnsundbrücke

Deutschland 75

Schützt die Natur

WWF

www.wwf.de

FROM: WILLIAM DHALGREN
ARCHIVE BOOKS
DIEFFENBACHSTRAẞE 31
10967 BERLIN, GERMANY

TO:

TOWER WITH SLITS

NORTH ENTRY TO RACHID KARAMI
INTERNATIONAL FAIR PARK

AL MARAAD CIRCLE

TRIPOLI, LEBANON

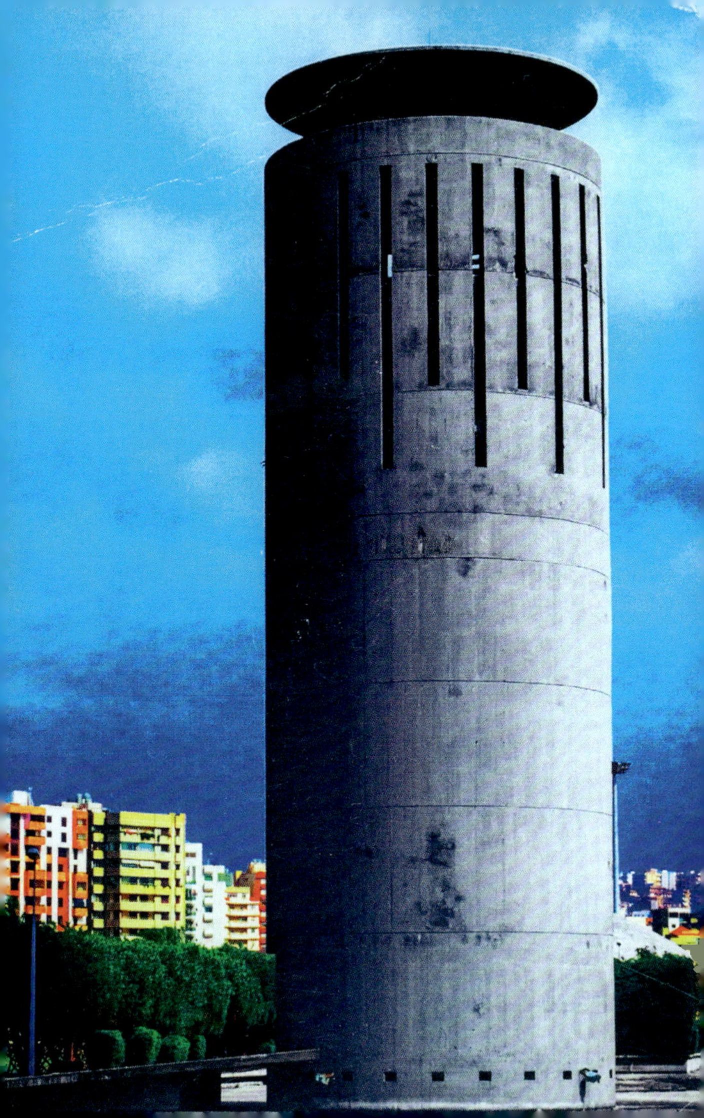

SUFFUSING THE WHOLE SKY, COMPLEX AS THE NORTHERN AURORA. AT ANY RATE, THEY MAKE EVERY OBJECT FROM AXLETREES TO ZARFS AND FINJONS CAST THE MOST ASTONISHING SHADOWS." MR NEWBOY GLANCED UP AGAIN. "PERHAPS YOU'VE FOLLOWED SOME DOZEN SUCH LIGHTS TO THEIR SOURCE?" HE HELD THE PAGE BETWEEN HIS FINGERS. "ADMIT IT—SINCE WE ARE TALKING AS EQUALS—MOST OF THE TIME THERE SIMPLY WASN'T ANYTHING THERE. THOUGH TO YOUR JOURNAL—" HE LET THE PAGE FALL BACK TO WHAT HE'D BEEN PERUSING BEFORE—"OR IN A LETTER TO A FRIEND YOU FEEL WILL TAKE CARE TO PRESERVE IT, YOU WILL ALSO ADMIT THE WHOLE EXPERIENCE WAS RATHER MARVELOUS AND FILLED YOU WITH INADMISSIBLE LONGINGS THAT YOU WOULD BE MORE THAN A LITTLE CURIOUS TO SEE SETTLE DOWN AND, AFTER ALL, ADMITS. SOMETIMES YOU SIMPLY FOUND A PLAQUE WHICH READ, 'HERE MOZART MET DA PONTI,' OR 'RODIN SLEPT HERE.' THREE OR FOUR TIMES YOU DISCOVERED A STRANGE GROUP HEATEDLY DISCUSSING SOMETHING THAT HAPPENED ON THAT VERY SPOT A VERY LONG TIME BY, WHICH, THEY ASSURE YOU, YOU WOULD HAVE THOROUGHLY ENJOYED HAD YOU NOT ARRIVED TOO LATE. IF YOU CAN BEAR THEM, IF YOU CAN LISTEN, IF YOU CAN LEARN WHY THEY ARE STILL THERE, YOU

UNFINISHED STATE // 13D.161

Deutschland 75
50 Jahre Fehmarnsundbrücke

Schützt die Natur
www.wwf.de

FROM: WILLIAM DHALGREN
ARCHIVE BOOKS
DIEFFENBACHSTRAßE 31
10967 BERLIN, GERMANY

TO:

TOWER WITH SLITS

NORTH ENTRY TO RACHID KARAMI
INTERNATIONAL FAIR PARK

AL MARAAD CIRCLE

TRIPOLI, LEBANON

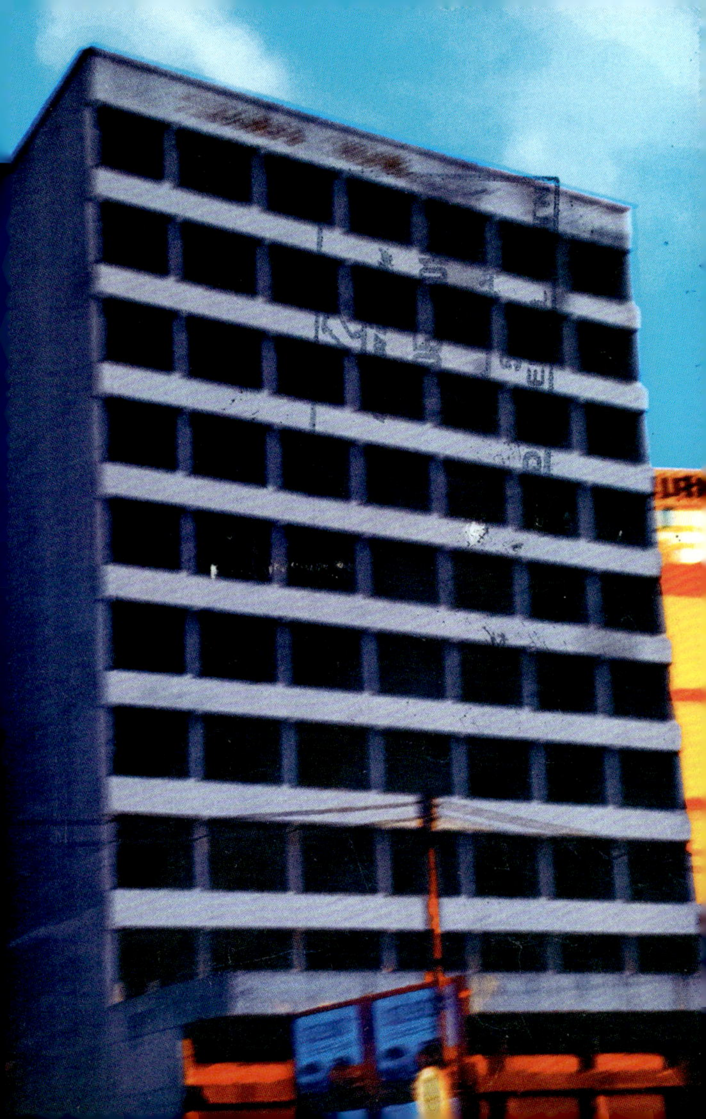

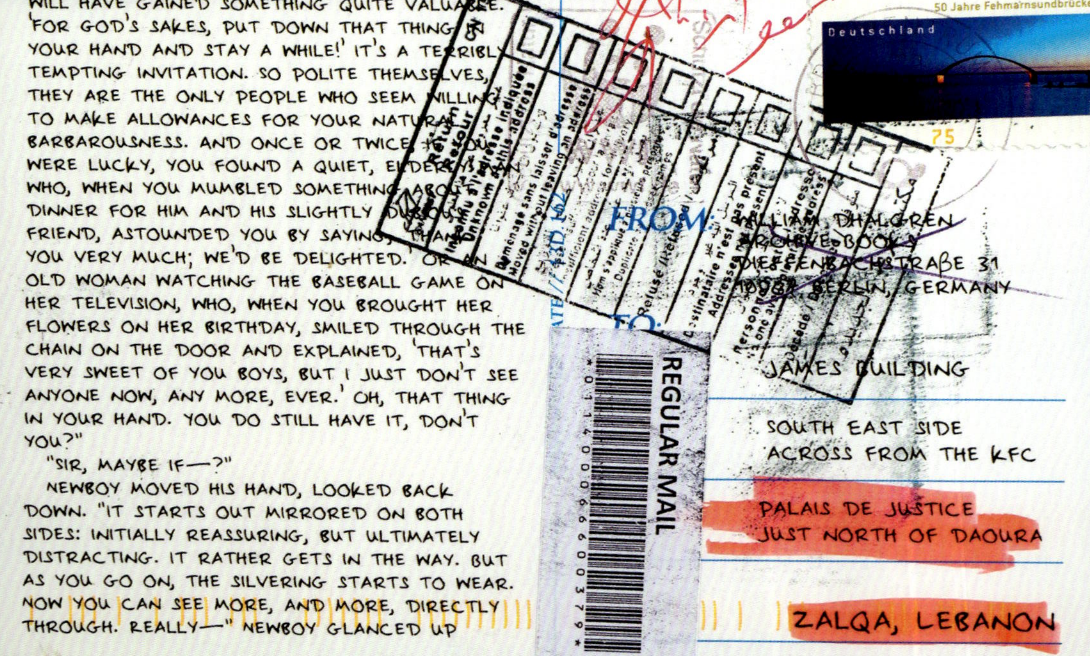
WILL HAVE GAINED SOMETHING QUITE VALUABLE. 'FOR GOD'S SAKES, PUT DOWN THAT THING IN YOUR HAND AND STAY A WHILE!' IT'S A TERRIBLY TEMPTING INVITATION. SO POLITE THEMSELVES, THEY ARE THE ONLY PEOPLE WHO SEEM WILLING TO MAKE ALLOWANCES FOR YOUR NATURAL BARBAROUSNESS. AND ONCE OR TWICE, IF YOU WERE LUCKY, YOU FOUND A QUIET, ELDERLY MAN WHO, WHEN YOU MUMBLED SOMETHING ABOUT DINNER FOR HIM AND HIS SLIGHTLY DUBIOUS FRIEND, ASTOUNDED YOU BY SAYING, 'THANK YOU VERY MUCH; WE'D BE DELIGHTED.' OR AN OLD WOMAN WATCHING THE BASEBALL GAME ON HER TELEVISION, WHO, WHEN YOU BROUGHT HER FLOWERS ON HER BIRTHDAY, SMILED THROUGH THE CHAIN ON THE DOOR AND EXPLAINED, 'THAT'S VERY SWEET OF YOU BOYS, BUT I JUST DON'T SEE ANYONE NOW, ANY MORE, EVER.' OH, THAT THING IN YOUR HAND. YOU DO STILL HAVE IT, DON'T YOU?"

"SIR, MAYBE IF—?"

NEWBOY MOVED HIS HAND, LOOKED BACK DOWN. "IT STARTS OUT MIRRORED ON BOTH SIDES: INITIALLY REASSURING, BUT ULTIMATELY DISTRACTING. IT RATHER GETS IN THE WAY. BUT AS YOU GO ON, THE SILVERING STARTS TO WEAR. NOW YOU CAN SEE MORE, AND MORE, DIRECTLY THROUGH. REALLY—" NEWBOY GLANCED UP

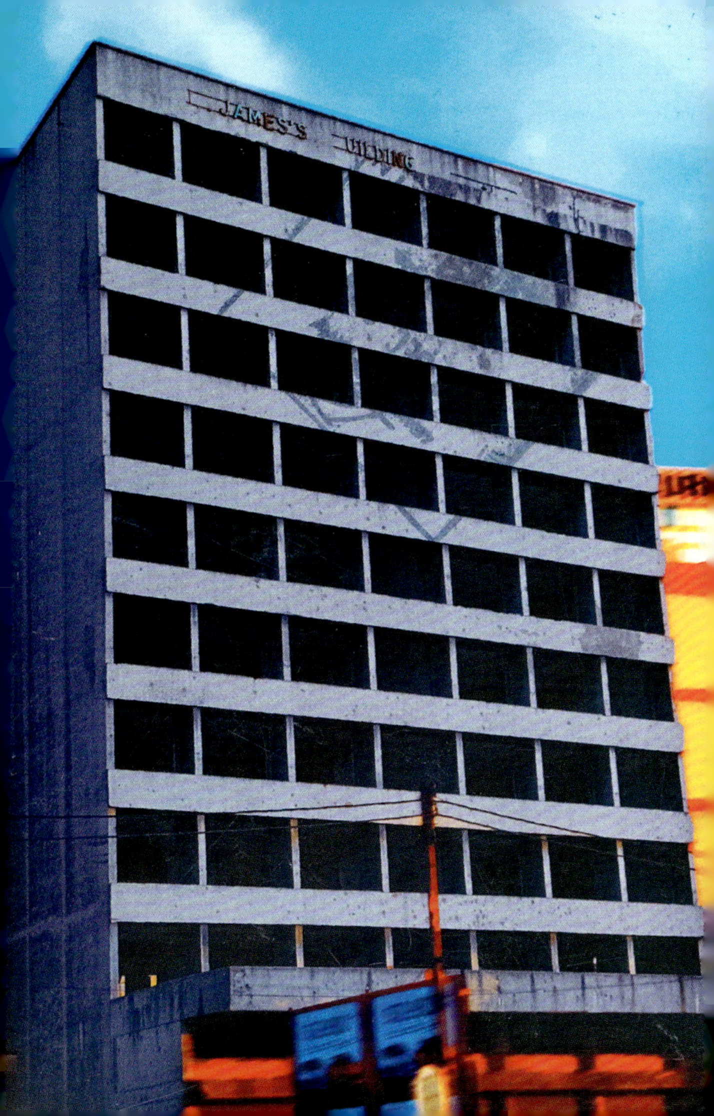
JAMES'S

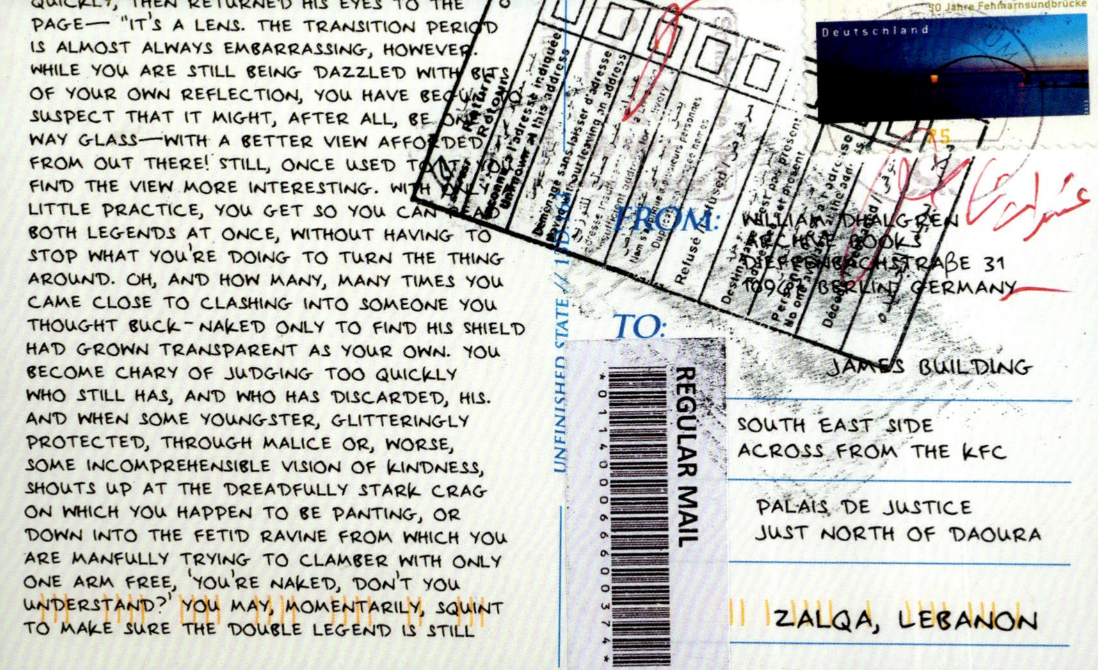

QUICKLY, THEN RETURNED HIS EYES TO THE PAGE— "IT'S A LENS. THE TRANSITION PERIOD IS ALMOST ALWAYS EMBARRASSING, HOWEVER. WHILE YOU ARE STILL BEING DAZZLED WITH BITS OF YOUR OWN REFLECTION, YOU HAVE BEGU[illegible] SUSPECT THAT IT MIGHT, AFTER ALL, BE ON[illegible] WAY GLASS—WITH A BETTER VIEW AFFORDED FROM OUT THERE! STILL, ONCE USED TO IT, YOU FIND THE VIEW MORE INTERESTING. WITH [illegible] LITTLE PRACTICE, YOU GET SO YOU CAN READ BOTH LEGENDS AT ONCE, WITHOUT HAVING TO STOP WHAT YOU'RE DOING TO TURN THE THING AROUND. OH, AND HOW MANY, MANY TIMES YOU CAME CLOSE TO CLASHING INTO SOMEONE YOU THOUGHT BUCK-NAKED ONLY TO FIND HIS SHIELD HAD GROWN TRANSPARENT AS YOUR OWN. YOU BECOME CHARY OF JUDGING TOO QUICKLY WHO STILL HAS, AND WHO HAS DISCARDED, HIS. AND WHEN SOME YOUNGSTER, GLITTERINGLY PROTECTED, THROUGH MALICE OR, WORSE, SOME INCOMPREHENSIBLE VISION OF KINDNESS, SHOUTS UP AT THE DREADFULLY STARK CRAG ON WHICH YOU HAPPEN TO BE PANTING, OR DOWN INTO THE FETID RAVINE FROM WHICH YOU ARE MANFULLY TRYING TO CLAMBER WITH ONLY ONE ARM FREE, 'YOU'RE NAKED, DON'T YOU UNDERSTAND?' YOU MAY, MOMENTARILY, SQUINT TO MAKE SURE THE DOUBLE LEGEND IS STILL

UNFINISHED STATE // 13D.163

FROM: WILLIAM DHALGREN
ARCHIVE BOOKS
DIEFFENBACHSTRAßE 31
10967 BERLIN GERMANY

TO: JAMES BUILDING
SOUTH EAST SIDE
ACROSS FROM THE KFC
PALAIS DE JUSTICE
JUST NORTH OF DAOURA
ZALQA, LEBANON

REGULAR MAIL
0114000660374

Deutschland
50 Jahre Fehmarnsundbrücke

Retour / Return
Inconnu à l'adresse indiquée / Unknown at this address
Déménagé sans laisser d'adresse / Moved without leaving an address
Adresse insuffisante / Insufficient address for delivery
Nom s'applique à plusieurs personnes / Duplicated or ... names
Refusé / Refused
Destinataire n'est pas présent / Addressee not present
Personne ... à l'adresse / No one available at the address
Décédé / Deceased

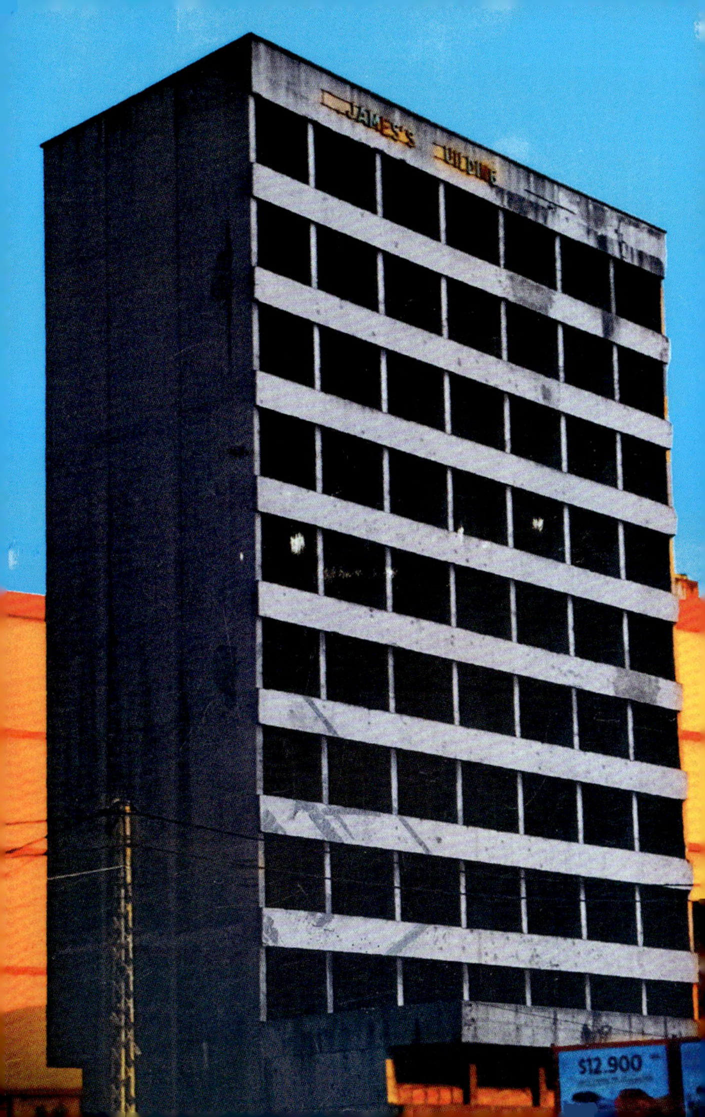
$12.900

CEASELESSLY ABOUT POETRY AND TRUTH. AFTER
ALL, THEY WERE NICE IN A USELESS SORT OF
WAY, WHICH IS, AFTER ALL, THE ONLY WAY TO BE
TRULY NICE. YOU EVEN COULD DISCERN TWO
OR THREE OF THE PROPER LETTERS AMONG
THE FOIL FOLDS, ADMITTEDLY CUT FROM
CARDBOARD AND TAPED THERE WITH STICKING
PLASTER. ARE ALL THESE HUMBLING FIREWORKS
SOME SORT OF CRUEL SECOND CHILDHOOD, A
DEFECT IN THE EYE? YOU BEGIN TO SUSPECT,
AS YOU GAZE THROUGH THIS YOU-SHAPED HOLE
OF INSIGHT AND FIRE, THAT THOUGHT IS THE
MOST IMPORTANT THING YOU OWN—NEVER DENY
THAT FOR AN INSTANT. IT HAS NOT SHIELDED
YOU FROM ANYTHING TERRIBLY IMPORTANT. THE
ONLY CONSOLATION IS THAT THOUGH ONE COULD
HAVE THROWN IT AWAY AT ANY TIME, MORNING
OR NIGHT, ONE DIDN'T. ONE CHOSE TO ENDURE
WITHOUT ANY ASSURANCE OF IMMORTALITY, OR
EVEN COMPETENCE, ONE ONLY KNOWS ONE HAS
NOT BEEN CHEATED OUT OF THE CONSOLATIONS
OF CARPENTERS, ACCOUNTANTS, DOCTORS,
DITCH-DIGGERS, THE ORDINARY PEOPLE WHO
MUST DO USEFUL THINGS TO BE HAPPY. MEANDER
ALONG, THEN, HALF BLIND AND A LITTLE MAD,
WONDERING WHEN YOU ACTUALLY LEARNED—WAS
IT BEFORE YOU BEGAN?—THE TERRIFYING FACT
THAT HAD YOU THROWN IT AWAY, YOUR WOUND
Return
Retour
Schützt die Natur
WWF
www.wwf.de
50 Jahre Fehmarnsundbrücke
Deutschland
75
FROM:
WILLIAM DHALGREN
ARCHIVE BOOKS
DIEFFENBACHSTRAßE 31
10967 BERLIN, GERMANY
TO:
ATE // 13D.165
Anschrift überprüft durch Deutsche Post / BZ 05
ZURÜCK:
Empfänger nicht zu ermitteln
10967
JUST NORTH OF DAOURA
ZALQA, LEBANON

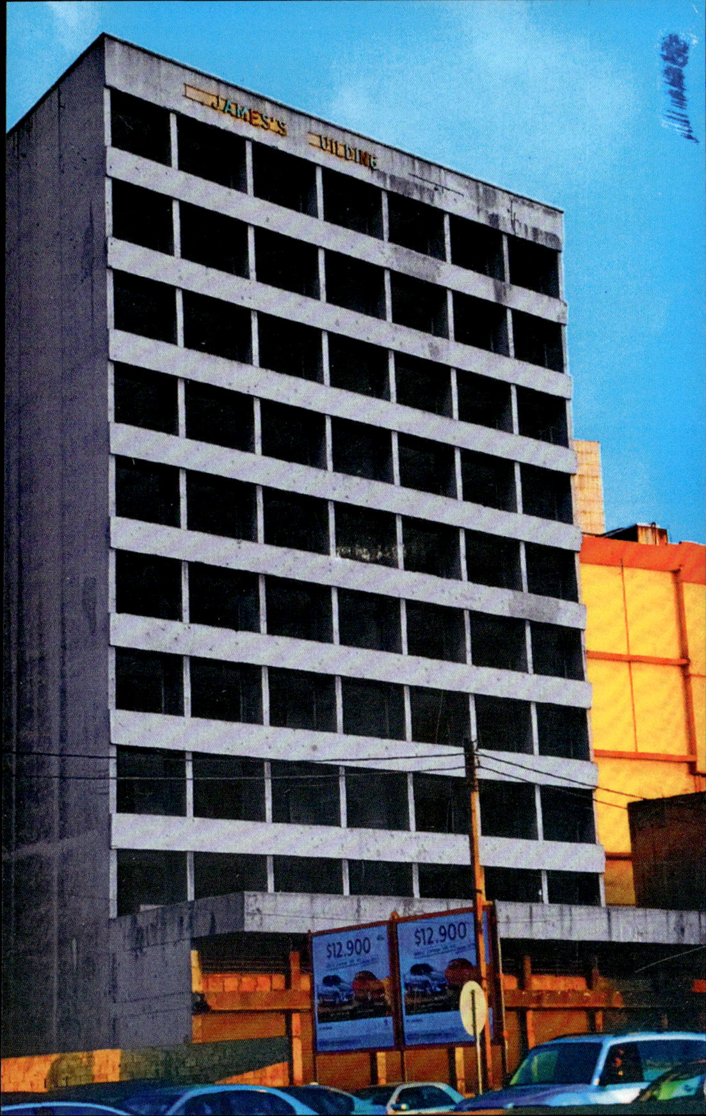
JAMES'S
UILDING
$12.900
$12.900

WOULD HAVE BEEN NO MORE LIKELY TO HEAR. INDEED, IN AN AFFLUENT SOCIETY SUCH AS THIS, YOU MIGHT EVEN HAVE GONE ON MAKING SONGS, POEMS, PICTURES, AND GETTING PAID. THE ONLY DIFFERENCE WOULD HAVE BEEN—AND YOU LEARNED IT LISTENING TO ALL THOSE BRUTAL, UNHAPPY PEOPLE WHO DID THROW AWAY THEIRS—AND THEY DO, AFTER ALL, COMPRISE THE VAST AND TERRIFYING MAJORITY—THAT WITHOUT IT, THERE PLAINLY AND STARKLY WOULD HAVE BEEN NOTHING THERE; NO, NOTHING AT ALL."

NEWBOY FIXED HIS EYES ON KIDD'S. KIDD SMILED AND FELT UNCOMFORTABLE. THEN HE FELT BELLIGERENT, WHICH MAYBE TAINTED THE SMILE. HE WAS GOING TO SAY, DO YOU ALWAYS RAP LIKE THIS WHEN SOMEBODY...

THE NOTEBOOK SUDDENLY SLIPPED FROM NEWBOY'S KNEES. THE POET BENT, BUT KIDD SNATCHED IT UP FIRST.

ITS BACK COVER HAD FALLEN OPEN. KIDD FROWNED AT THE FINAL BLOCK OF HANDWRITING THAT RAN OFF THE PAGE BOTTOM:

...THE SKY IS STRIPPED. I AM TOO WEAK TO WRITE MUCH. BUT I STILL HEAR THEM WALKING IN THE TREES; NOT SPEAKING. WAITING HERE, AWAY FROM THE TERRIFYING WEAPONRY, OUT OF THE

Return / Retour

Inconnu à l'adresse indiquée / Unknown at this address

Déménagé sans laisser d'adresse / Moved without leaving an address

Refusé / Refused

Destinataire n'est pas présent / Addressee not present

Personne n'est à l'adresse / No one available at the address

Décédé / Deceased

50 Jahre Fehmarnsundbrücke

Deutschland 75

FROM: WILLIAM DHALGREN
ARCHIVE BOOKS
DEFFENBACHSTRAβE 31
10967 BERLIN, GERMANY

REGULAR MAIL

01140006840 0115

JAMES BUILDING

SOUTH EAST SIDE
ACROSS FROM THE KFC

PALAIS DE JUSTICE
JUST NORTH OF DAOURA

ZALQA, LEBANON

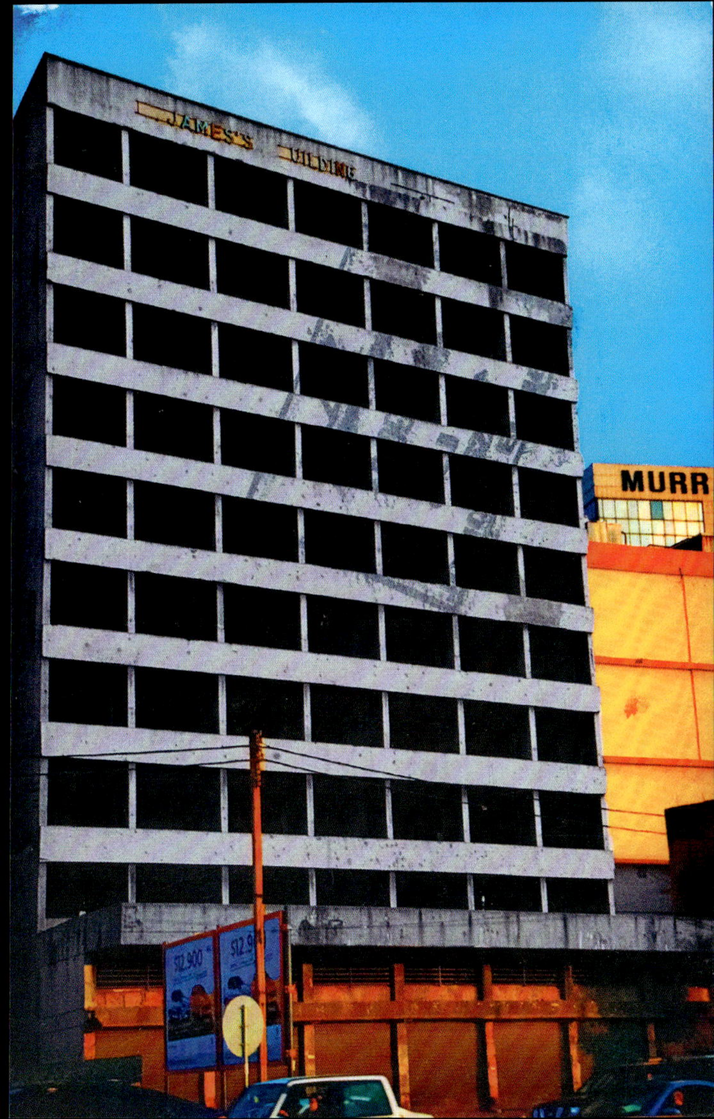
JAMES'S
MURR
$12.900

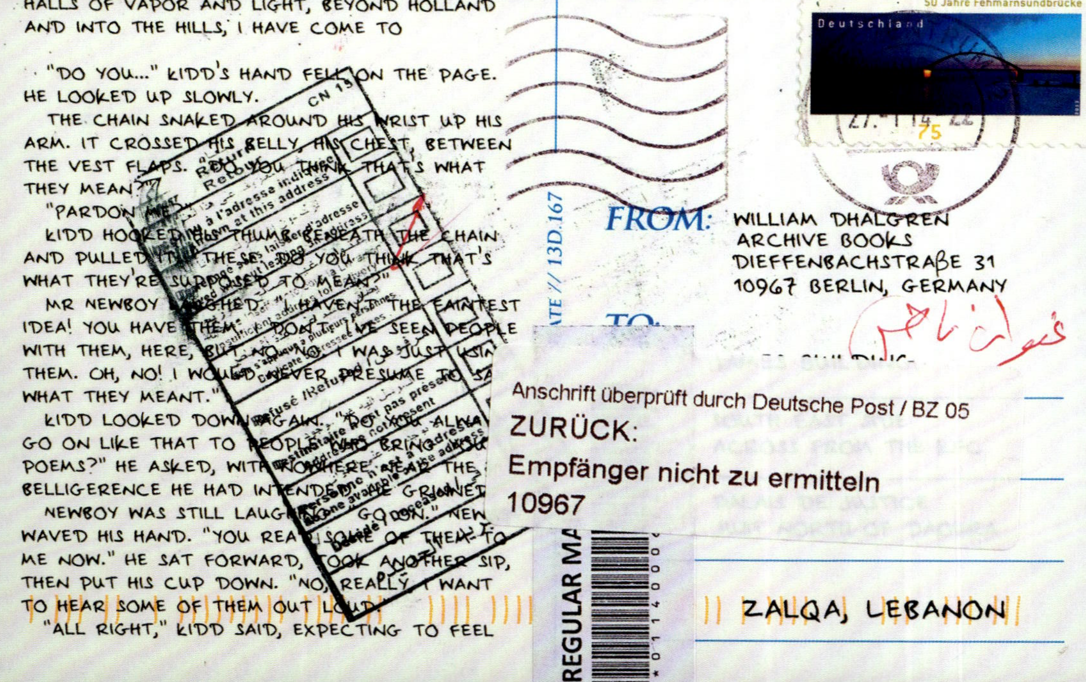
HALLS OF VAPOR AND LIGHT, BEYOND HOLLAND
AND INTO THE HILLS, I HAVE COME TO
"DO YOU..." KIDD'S HAND FELL ON THE PAGE.
HE LOOKED UP SLOWLY.
THE CHAIN SNAKED AROUND HIS WRIST UP HIS
ARM. IT CROSSED HIS BELLY, HIS CHEST, BETWEEN
THE VEST FLAPS. "DO YOU THINK THAT'S WHAT
THEY MEAN?"
"PARDON ME?"
KIDD HOOKED HIS THUMB BENEATH THE CHAIN
AND PULLED IT. "THESE. DO YOU THINK THAT'S
WHAT THEY'RE SUPPOSED TO MEAN?"
MR NEWBOY LAUGHED. "I HAVEN'T THE FAINTEST
IDEA! YOU HAVE THEM. DON'T I'VE SEEN PEOPLE
WITH THEM, HERE, BUT NO, NO. I WAS JUST
THEM. OH, NO! I WOULD NEVER PRESUME TO
WHAT THEY MEANT."
KIDD LOOKED DOWN AGAIN. "DO YOU ALWA
GO ON LIKE THAT TO PEOPLE WHO BRING YOU
POEMS?" HE ASKED, WITH NOWHERE NEAR THE
BELLIGERENCE HE HAD INTENDED. HE GRINNED.
NEWBOY WAS STILL LAUGHING. "GO ON." NEW
WAVED HIS HAND. "YOU READ SOME OF THEM TO
ME NOW." HE SAT FORWARD, TOOK ANOTHER SIP,
THEN PUT HIS CUP DOWN. "NO, REALLY, I WANT
TO HEAR SOME OF THEM OUT LOUD."
"ALL RIGHT," KIDD SAID, EXPECTING TO FEEL
CN 15
Retour
à l'adresse indiquée
Return at this address
Refusé
Refused
Décédé
ATE // 13D.167
FROM:
WILLIAM DHALGREN
ARCHIVE BOOKS
DIEFFENBACHSTRAßE 31
10967 BERLIN, GERMANY
TO:
Anschrift überprüft durch Deutsche Post / BZ 05
ZURÜCK:
Empfänger nicht zu ermitteln
10967
REGULAR MA
ZALQA, LEBANON
50 Jahre Fehmarnsundbrücke
Deutschland
75

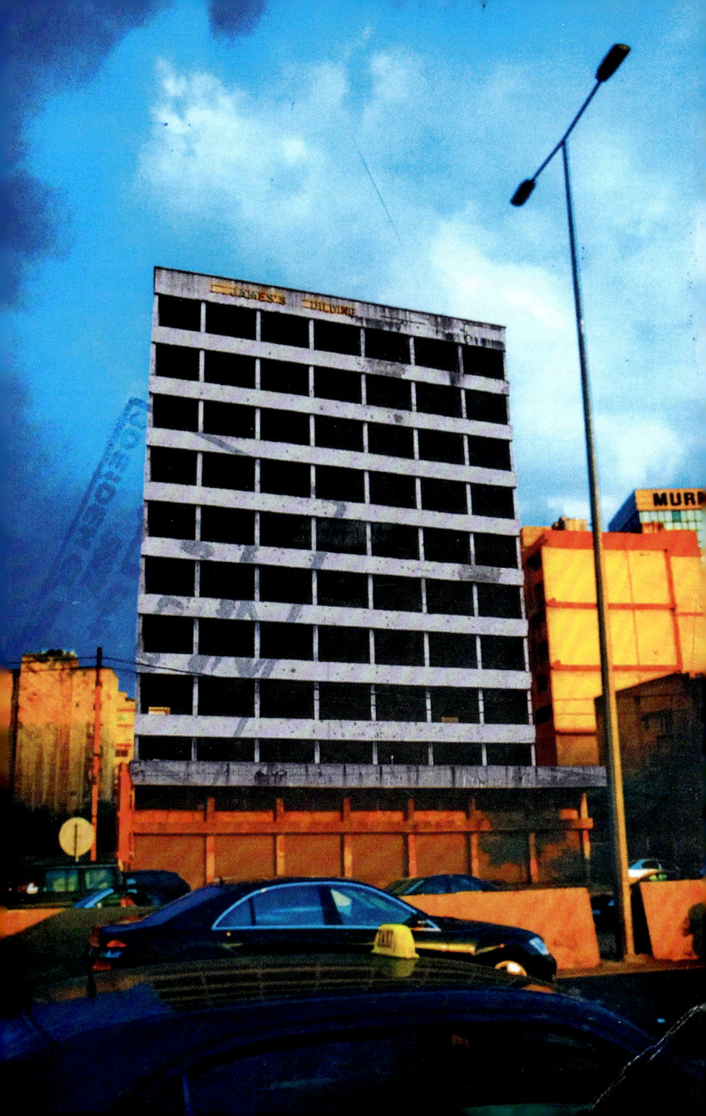

RESENTMENT, BUT EXPERIENCING A DIFFERENT ANXIETY ALTOGETHER. HE NOTED, WITH CONCERN ONCE MORE, THE NUMBER OF PAGES LEFT WITH FREE SIDES.

"READ THE ONE ABOUT. THE DOG THING. I LIKED THAT ONE."

"MURIELLE?"

NEWBOY NODDED, HANDS TOGETHER IN HIS LAP.

KIDD TURNED TOWARD THE FRONT OF THE BOOK.

HE BEGAN TO READ.

BREATHLESSNESS LEFT ABOUT THE THIRD LINE. SOMEWHERE, SOMETHING LIKE ENJOYMENT BLOOMED UNDER HIS TONGUE AND, RATHER THAN TRIPPING IT, SOMEHOW MADE IT MORE SENSITIVE, SO THAT, WITHOUT PAUSE HE REALIZED HOW THE VOWELS IN BOTH LOOM AND FLOW TOOK OFF FROM THE SAME POINT BUT WENT DIFFERENT PLACES. HE FOUND HIS FACE HOLLOWING FOR THE MORE RESONANT TONES. HE LET THEM MOVE THE MUSCLES ABOUT HIS MOUTH TILL STACCATO T'S AND K'S RIDDLED THE FINAL LINE AND MADE HIM SMILE.

"LOVELY," NEWBOY SAID. "IN A RATHER HORRIFYING WAY. READ THE ONE IN FRONT OF IT."

HE READ, AND LOST HIMSELF IN THE MOVEMENTS OF HIS MOUTH, TILL A MOMENTARY

FROM: WILLIAM DHALGREN
ARCHIVE BOOKS
DIEFFENBACHSTRAßE 31
10967 BERLIN, GERMANY

TO:
JAMES BUILDING
SOUTH EAST SIDE
ACROSS FROM THE KFC
PALAIS DE JUSTICE
JUST NORTH OF DAOURA
ZALQA, LEBANON

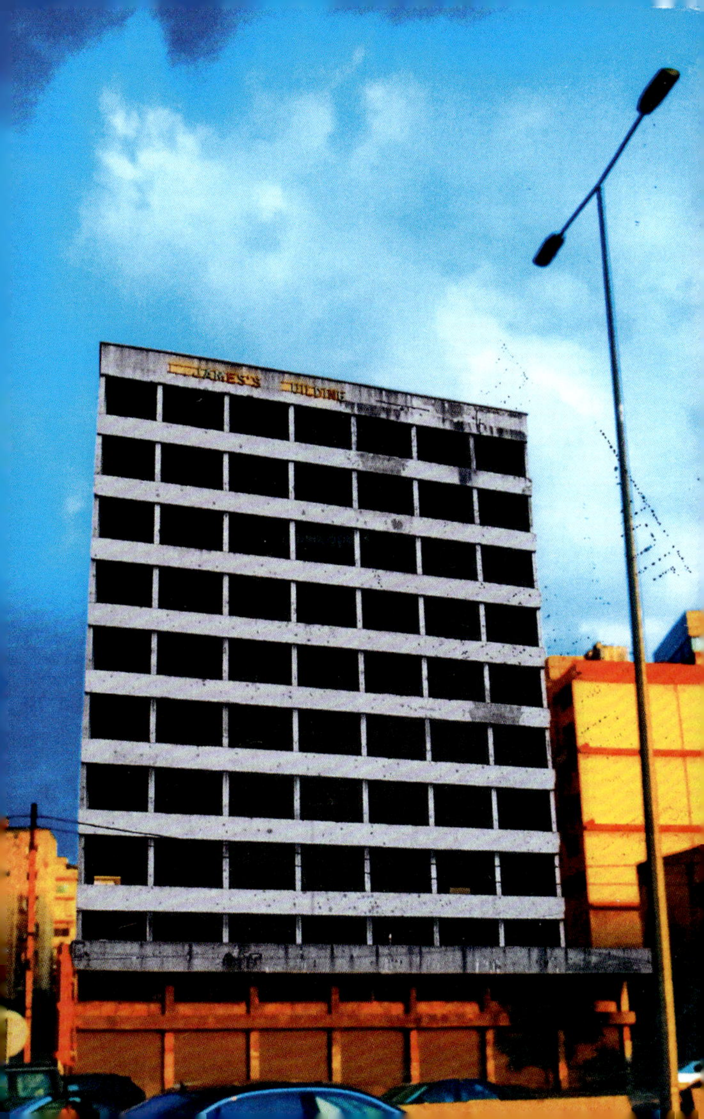
JAMES'S

CONVOCATION IN THE EAR STUNNED HIM INTO A SHRILLER VOICE. THEN THE LONG SOUNDS QUIETED THE ANSWER.

"THERE ARE TWO VOICES IN DIALOGUE IN THAT ONE, AREN'T THERE," NEWBOY COMMENTED AT THE FINISH. "I DIDN'T PICK IT UP JUST GLANCING AT IT."

"HUH? OH, YEAH. MAYBE I SHOULD SET THEM APART ON THE PAGE—"

"NO, NO!" MR NEWBOY SAT UP AND MOTIONED. "NO, BELIEVE ME, IT ISN'T NECESSARY. IT WOULD BE PERFECTLY CLEAR IN A PAGE OF PRINT. IT WAS MY ATTENTION READING, BELIEVE ME. JUST GO ON."

HE READ.

WHAT HAD COME TO HIM AS IMAGES AMONG WHICH HE HAD PECKED WITH TONGUE TIP AND PEN POINT, RETURNED, SHOCKED, LUMINOUS, SOMETIMES MORE, SOMETIMES LESS LUMINOUS THAN MEMORY, BUT SO RICH HE THRUST THEM OUT WITH HIS TONGUE TO KEEP FROM TRYING TO EAT THEM.

"IT'S SO MUCH FUN," NEWBOY SAID, "THAT YOU ENJOY YOUR OWN POEMS SO MUCH. HAVE YOU EVER NOTICED HOW FREE VERSE TENDS TO TURN INTO IAMBIC PENTAMETER ALL BY ITSELF, ESPECIALLY BY PEOPLE WHO HAVEN'T WRITTEN MUCH POETRY."

Return / Retour
Adresse indiquée / Unknown at this address
Déménagé sans laisser d'adresse / Moved without leaving address
Refusé / Refused
Destinataire n'est pas présent / Addressee not present
Personne n'est à l'adresse / No one available at the address
Décédé / Deceased

UNFINISHED STATE // 13D 169

REGULAR MAIL
0114000684001 14

50 Jahre Fehmarnsundbrücke
Deutschland 75

WILLIAM DHALGREN
ARCHIVE BOOKS
DIEFFENBACHSTRAßE 31
10967 BERLIN, GERMANY

JAMES BUILDING

SOUTH EAST SIDE
ACROSS FROM THE KFC

PALAIS DE JUSTICE
JUST NORTH OF DAOURA

ZALQA, LEBANON

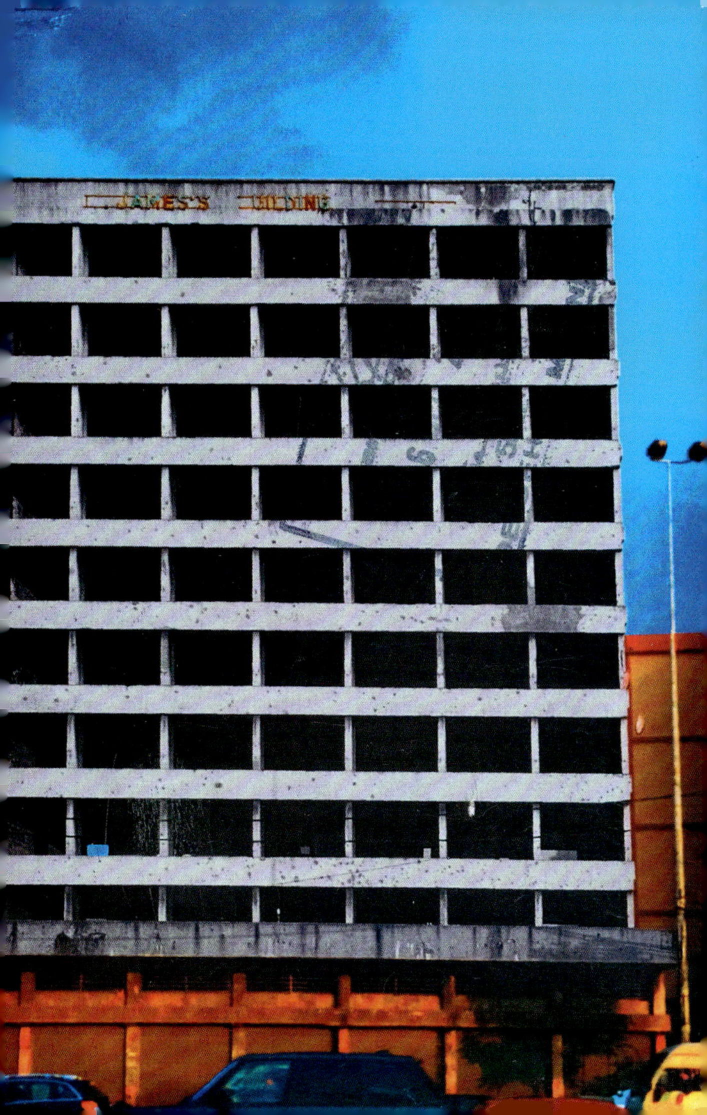
JAMES'S

"SIR?"

"WELL, IT'S ONLY NAUTRAL. IT'S THE NATURAL RHYTHM OF ENGLISH SPEECH. YOU KNOW, WHEN THE LINE GOES BA-DA, BA-DA, BA-DA, BA-DA, BA-DA? OH, NOW DON'T SIT THERE AND LOOK CONFUSED. READ SOME MORE. I'M NOT GOING TO GET PEDANTIC AGAIN. I AM ENJOYING THIS, REALLY."

KIDD WAS HAPPILY EMBARRASSED. HIS EYES DROPPED– TO THE PAGE. KIDD READ; TURNED; READ... SEVERAL TIMES HE THOUGHT HE MUST BE GOING ON AWFULLY LONG. BUT NEWBOY MOTIONED FOR ANOTHER, AND ONCE ASKED TO HEAR BOTH VERSIONS ("I SAW THAT YOU HAD TWO WHEN I WAS LOOKING THROUGH..." AND, AFTER THE EARLIER VERSION: "WELL, MOST OF YOUR REVISIONS ARE IN THE RIGHT DIRECTION.") AND HAD HIM REREAD SEVERAL MORE. MORE CONFIDENT, KIDD CHOSE OTHERS NOW, WENT BACK TO ONE HE HAD LEFT OUT, THEN SKIPPED AHEAD, GATHERING SOME ENJOYMENT THAT WAS NOT PRIDE, WAS GREATEST WHEN HE WAS LEAST AWARE OF THE MAN EATING COOKIES BEFORE HIM, WAS A SUPPORTIVE PATTERN IN THE CAVERNS UNDER THE TONGUE.

HE STOPPED TO GLANCE AT NEWBOY—

THE POET WAS FROWNING AT SOMETHING NOT HIM.

Return / Retour
Inconnu à l'adresse / Unknown at this address
Déménagé sans laisser d'adresse / Moved without leaving an address
Adresse insuffisante / Insufficient address for delivery
Nom s'applique à plusieurs personnes / Duplicate names
Refusé / Refused
Destinataire n'est pas présent / Addressee not present
Personne n'est à l'adresse / No one available at the address
Décédé / Deceased

50 Jahre Fehmarnsundbrücke
Deutschland
75

E // 13D.170

FROM: WILLIAM DHALGREN
ARCHIVE BOOKS
DIEFFENBACHSTRAßE 31
10967 BERLIN, GERMANY

REGULAR MAIL
011400066600377

JAMES BUILDING

SOUTH EAST SIDE
ACROSS FROM THE KFC

PALAIS DE JUSTICE
JUST NORTH OF DAOURA

ZALQA, LEBANON

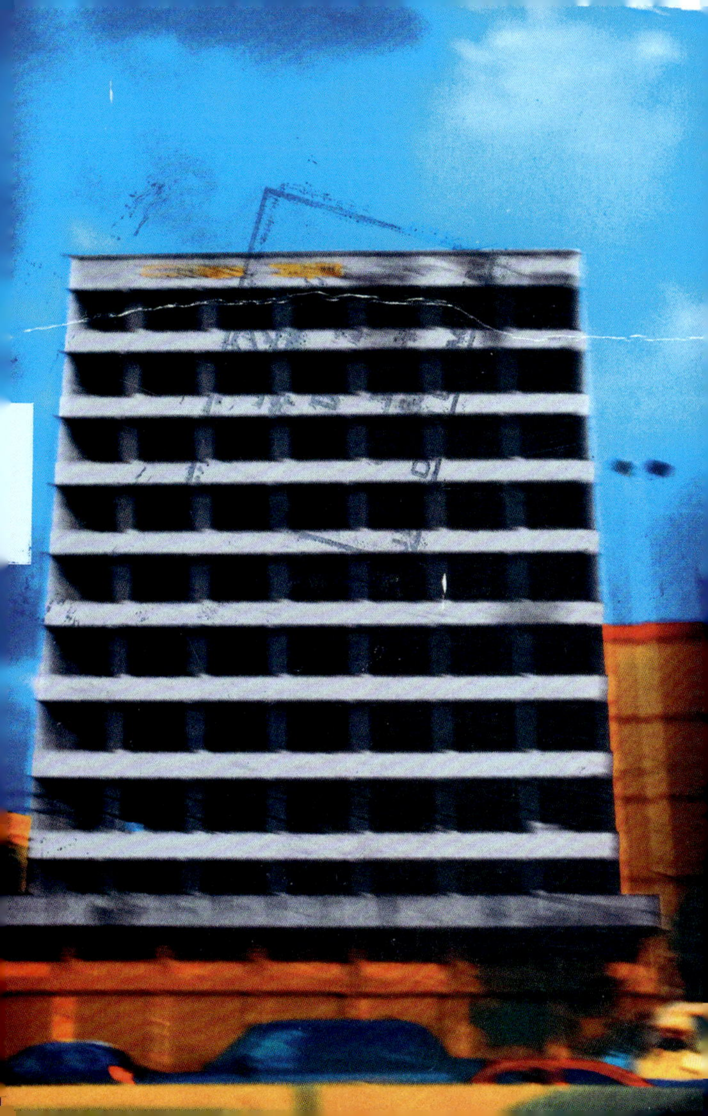

LANYA SAID (IN A VOICE THAT MADE KIDD TURN, FROWNING) TEN FEET DOWN THE TERRACE: "I... I DIDN'T MEAN TO INTERRUPT." IT WAS BLUE, IT WAS SHREDDED, IT WAS SILK.

"WHAT'S THAT?"

"MY... DRESS." SHE CAME FORWARD CARRYING IT OVER HER ARM. "I LOOKED UPSTAIRS IN THE OBSERVATORY WING... FOR MY DRESS, WHILE YOU WERE READING. CHRIST, IT'S A MESS UP THERE!"

MR NEWBOY FROWNED. "I DIDN'T EVEN KNOW ANYBODY WAS STAYING THERE."

"IT DOESN'T LOOK LIKE ANYBODY IS," SHE SAID, "NOW."

"IS THAT ON THE THIRD FLOOR?"

LANYA NODDED.

"ROGER SAID SOMETHING ABOUT NOT USING THAT SECTION—THE DOORS WERE CLOSED, WEREN'T THEY? I THOUGHT IT WAS SOMETHING ABOUT PLUMBING REPAIRS."

"THEY WERE CLOSED BUT THEY WEREN'T LOCKED." LANYA SAID. "I JUST WENT RIGHT IN. THEY WERE USING IT WHEN I WAS HERE—I WAS JUST LOOKING FOR THE ROOM I STAYED IN. BUT... THE CARPETS HAVE BEEN PULLED UP OFF THE FLOOR; AND TORN. LOOKS LIKE SOMEBODY YANKED THE LIGHT FIXTURES OUT OF THE CEILING, WITH ABOUT A FOOT OF PLASTER...

UNFINISHED STATE // 13D.171

50 Jahre Fehmarnsundbrücke

Deutschland 75

FROM: WILLIAM DHALGREN
ARCHIVE BOOKS
DIEFFENBACHSTRAßE 31
10967 BERLIN, GERMANY

TO:

JAMES BUILDING

SOUTH EAST SIDE
ACROSS FROM THE KFC

PALAIS DE JUSTICE
JUST NORTH OF DAOURA

ZALQA, LEBANON

REGULAR MAIL

0314000660 0380

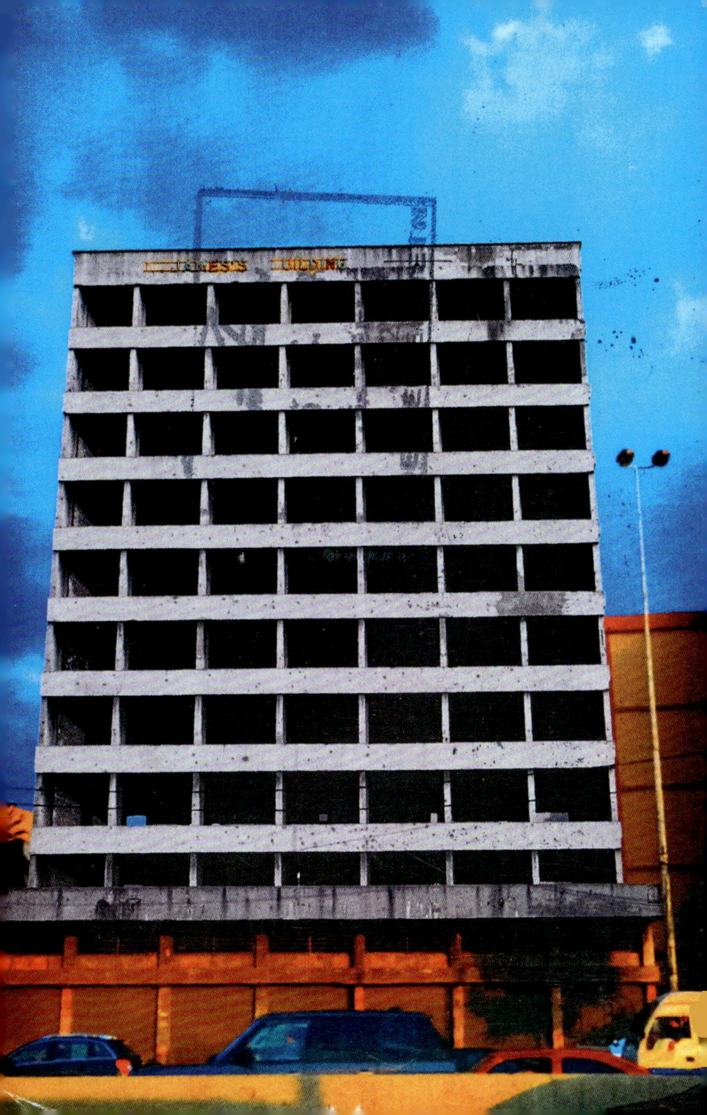

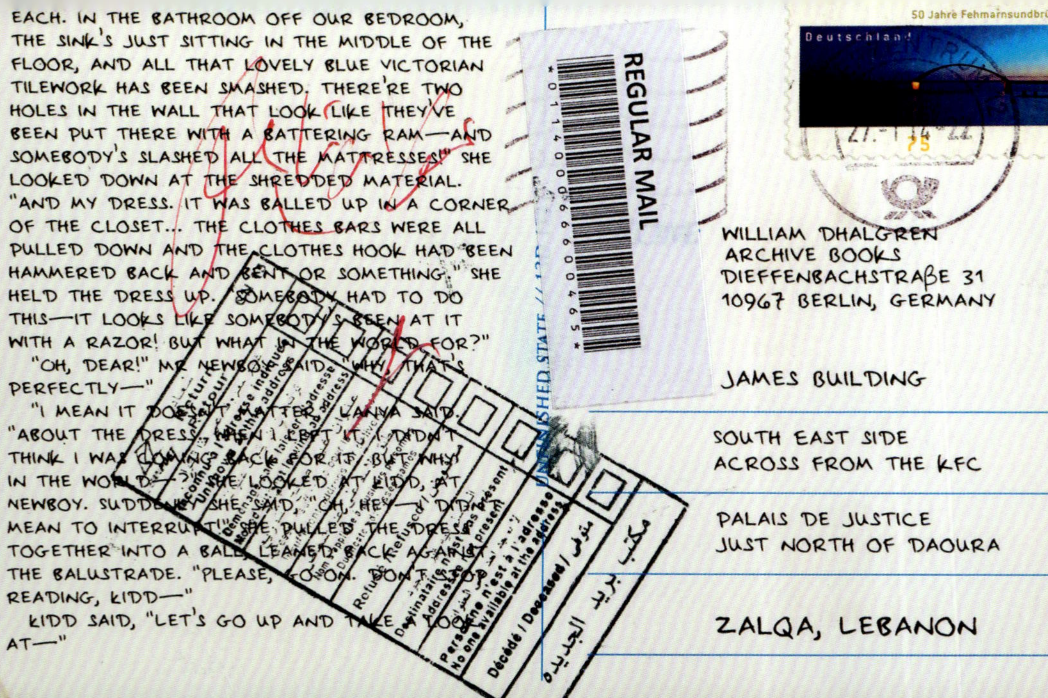

EACH. IN THE BATHROOM OFF OUR BEDROOM, THE SINK'S JUST SITTING IN THE MIDDLE OF THE FLOOR, AND ALL THAT LOVELY BLUE VICTORIAN TILEWORK HAS BEEN SMASHED. THERE'RE TWO HOLES IN THE WALL THAT LOOK LIKE THEY'VE BEEN PUT THERE WITH A BATTERING RAM—AND SOMEBODY'S SLASHED ALL THE MATTRESSES!" SHE LOOKED DOWN AT THE SHREDDED MATERIAL. "AND MY DRESS. IT WAS BALLED UP IN A CORNER OF THE CLOSET... THE CLOTHES BARS WERE ALL PULLED DOWN AND THE CLOTHES HOOK HAD BEEN HAMMERED BACK AND BENT OR SOMETHING." SHE HELD THE DRESS UP. "SOMEBODY HAD TO DO THIS—IT LOOKS LIKE SOMEBODY'S BEEN AT IT WITH A RAZOR! BUT WHAT IN THE WORLD FOR?"
"OH, DEAR!" MR NEWBOY SAID. "WHY, THAT'S PERFECTLY—"
"I MEAN IT DOESN'T MATTER," LANYA SAID. "ABOUT THE DRESS. WHEN I LEFT IT, I DIDN'T THINK I WAS COMING BACK FOR IT. BUT WHY IN THE WORLD—" SHE LOOKED AT KIDD, AT NEWBOY. SUDDENLY SHE SAID, "OH, HEY—I DIDN'T MEAN TO INTERRUPT!" SHE PULLED THE DRESS TOGETHER INTO A BALL, LEANED BACK AGAINST THE BALUSTRADE. "PLEASE, GO ON. DON'T STOP READING, KIDD—"
KIDD SAID, "LET'S GO UP AND TAKE A LOOK AT—"
50 Jahre Fehmarnsundbrücke
Deutschland
75
REGULAR MAIL
0114000666004665
UNFINISHED STATE // 13D
Retour
Inconnu à l'adresse indiquée
Unknown at this address
Déménagé sans laisser d'adresse
Moved, left no address
Refusé / Refused
Destinataire n'est pas présent
Addressee not present
Personne n'est à l'adresse
No one available at the address
Décédé / Deceased / متوفى
مكتب بريد الجديدة
WILLIAM DHALGREN
ARCHIVE BOOKS
DIEFFENBACHSTRAßE 31
10967 BERLIN, GERMANY
JAMES BUILDING
SOUTH EAST SIDE
ACROSS FROM THE KFC
PALAIS DE JUSTICE
JUST NORTH OF DAOURA
ZALQA, LEBANON

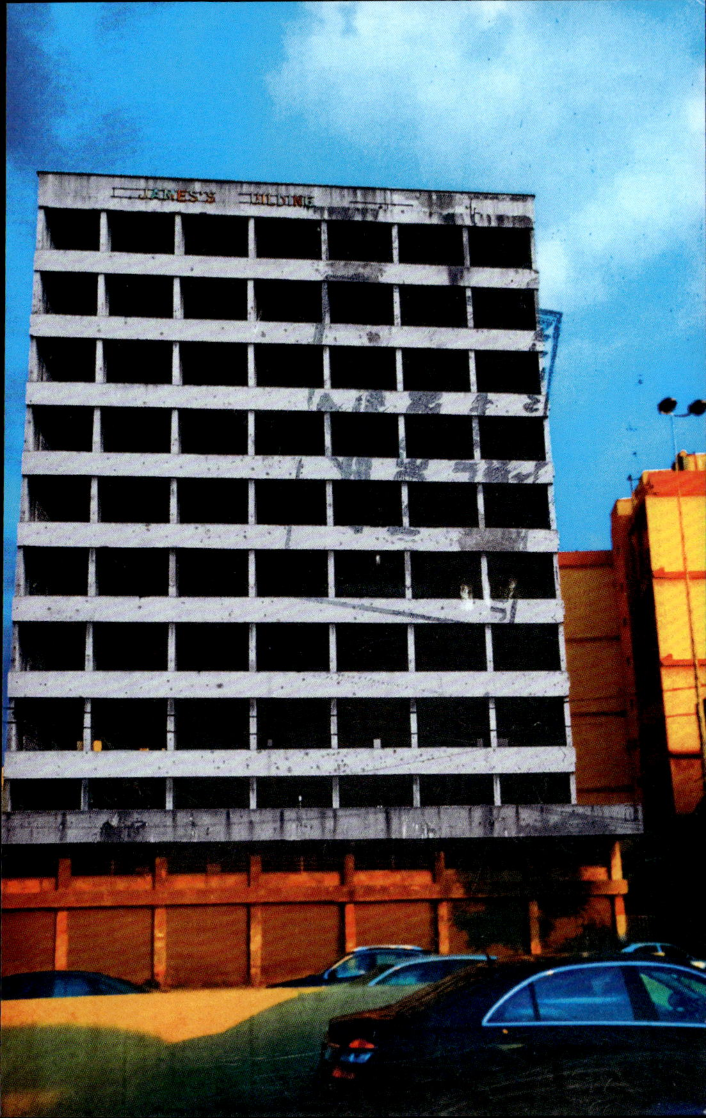
JAMES'S

"NO," LANYA SAID, SURPRISINGLY LOUD.

NEWBOY BLINKED.

"NO, I REALLY DON'T WANT TO GO BACK UP THERE."

"BUT...?" KIDD FROWNED.

"ROGER DID ASK US ALL NOT TO GO IN THAT WING," NEWBOY SAID, UNCOMFORTABLY. "BUT I HAD NO IDEA IT WAS—"

"I CLOSED THE DOORS." LANYA LOOKED AT THE BLUE SILK IN HER FIST. "I SHOULD HAVE LEFT THIS UP THERE."

"MAYBE SOME WILD PARTY GOT OUT OF HAND?" KIDD ASKED.

LANYA SAID: "IT DIDN'T LOOK LIKE ANY PARTY TO ME."

NEWBOY, KIDD SUDDENLY SAW (AND REALIZ[ED] AT THE SAME TIME THAT LANYA SAW IT TOO) [WAS] UPSET. LANYA'S RESPONSE WAS: "IS THE COFF[EE] HOT? I THINK I'D LIKE A CUP."

"CERTAINLY." NEWBOY STOOD, WENT TO THE URN.

"GO ON, KIDD," LANYA SAID. "READ ANOTHER POEM," AS NEWBOY BROUGHT HER THE CUP.

"YES." THE ELDERLY POET, COLLECTING HIMSELF, RETURNED TO HIS CHAIR. "LET'S HEAR ANOTHER ONE."

"ALL RIGHT." KIDD PAGED THROUGH: THEY WERE ALL IN SOME CONSPIRACY TO OBLITERATE,

Return / Retour

Inconnu à l'adresse indiquée / Unknown at this address

Déménagé sans laisser d'adresse / Moved without leaving an address

Nom s'appliquant à plusieurs personnes

Refusé / Refused

Destinataire n'est pas présent / Addressee not present

Personne n'est à l'adresse / No one available at the address

Décédé / Deceased

50 Jahre Fehmarnsundbrücke

Deutschland

75

FROM:

WILLIAM DHALGREN
ARCHIVE BOOKS
DIEFFENBACHSTRAẞE 31
10967 BERLIN, GERMANY

REGULAR MAIL

0114000666003378

TO:

JAMES BUILDING

SOUTH EAST SIDE
ACROSS FROM THE KFC

PALAIS DE JUSTICE
JUST NORTH OF DAOURA

ZALQA, LEBANON

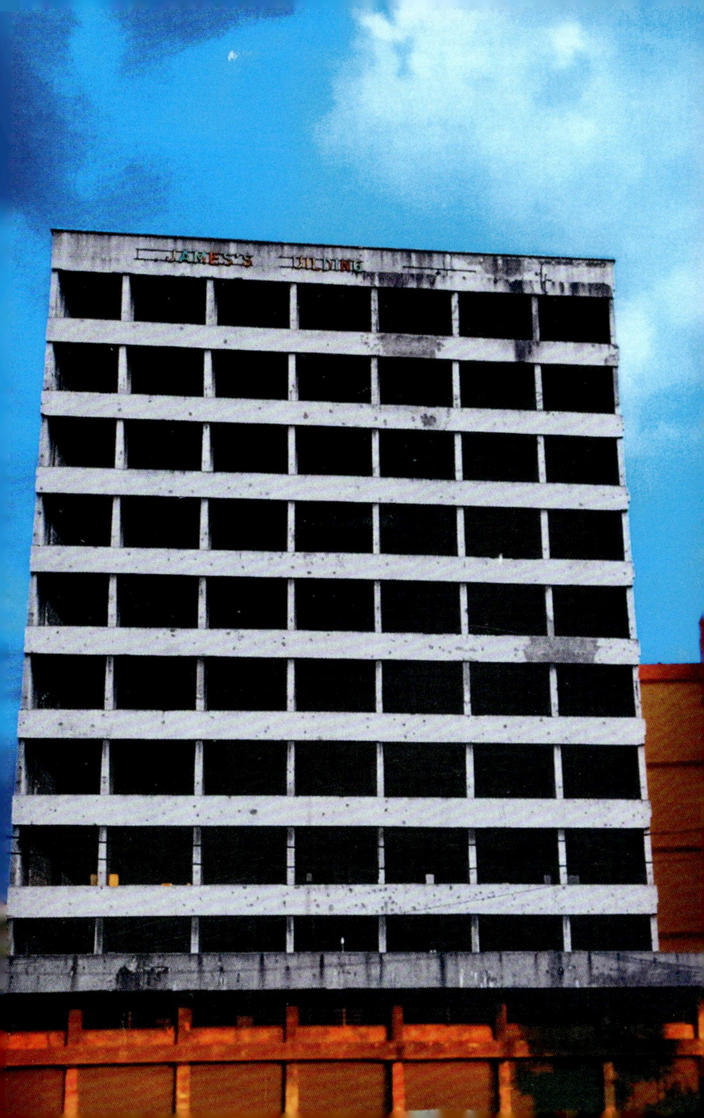
JAMES'S UILDING

IF NOT LANYA'S NEWS ITSELF, AT LEAST ITS UNSETTLING EFFECT. AND HE'S GOT TO LIVE HERE, KIDD THOUGHT. THERE WERE ONLY THREE MORE POEMS.

AFTER THE SECOND, LANYA SAID: "THAT ONE'S ONE OF MY FAVORITES." HER HAND MOVED OVER TORN BLUE, FOLDED OVER THE WALL.

AND HE READ THE THIRD. "SO NOW," KIDD SAID, PRIMARILY TO KEEP SOMETHING GOING, "YOU'VE GOT TO GIVE ME SOME IDEA OF WHAT YOU THINK OF THEM, WHETHER THEY'RE GOOD OR BAD," A THOUGHT WHICH HADN'T OCCURRED TO HIM ONCE SINCE HE'D COME; ONLY PREVIOUS MENTAL REHEARSAL BROUGHT IT OUT NOW.

"I THOROUGHLY ENJOYED HEARING YOU READ THEM," NEWBOY SAID. "BUT FOR ANYTHING ELSE YOU SIMPLY HAVE TO SAY TO YOURSELF, WITH MANN: I CANNOT KNOW AND YOU CANNOT TELL ME."

KIDD SMILED, REACHED FOR THREE MORE COOKIES ON THE TEA-WAGON, TRIED TO THINK OF SOMETHING ELSE.

NEWBOY SAID: "WHY DON'T WE TAKE A STROLL AROUND THE GROUNDS? IF IT WERE A BRIGHT SUNNY DAY, IT WOULD BE QUITE SPECTACULAR I'M SURE. BUT IT'S STILL NICE, IN AN AUTUMNAL SORT OF WAY."

LANYA, WHO WAS LOOKING INTO HER CUP,

50 Jahre Fehmarnsundbrücke
Deutschland
75

LAR MAIL
4000684002O3*

WILLIAM DHALGREN
ARCHIVE BOOKS
DIEFFENBACHSTRAßE 31
10967 BERLIN, GERMANY

Anschrift überprüft durch Deutsche Post / BZ 05
ZURÜCK:
Empfänger nicht zu ermitteln
10967

Retour
Return
Inconnu à l'adresse indiquée
Unknown at this address
Refusé / Refused
Destinataire n'est pas présent
Addressee not present
Personne n'est à l'adresse
No one available at the address
Décédé / Deceased / متوفى
مكتب بريد

PALAIS DE JUSTICE
JUST NORTH OF DAOURA
ZALQA, LEBANON

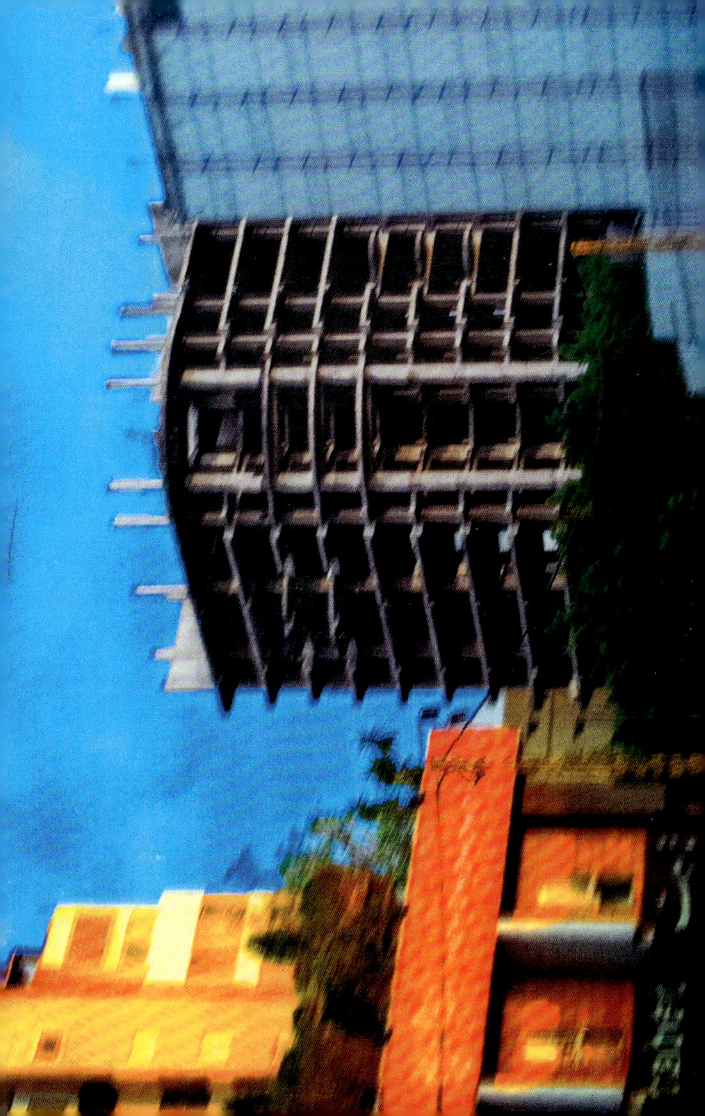

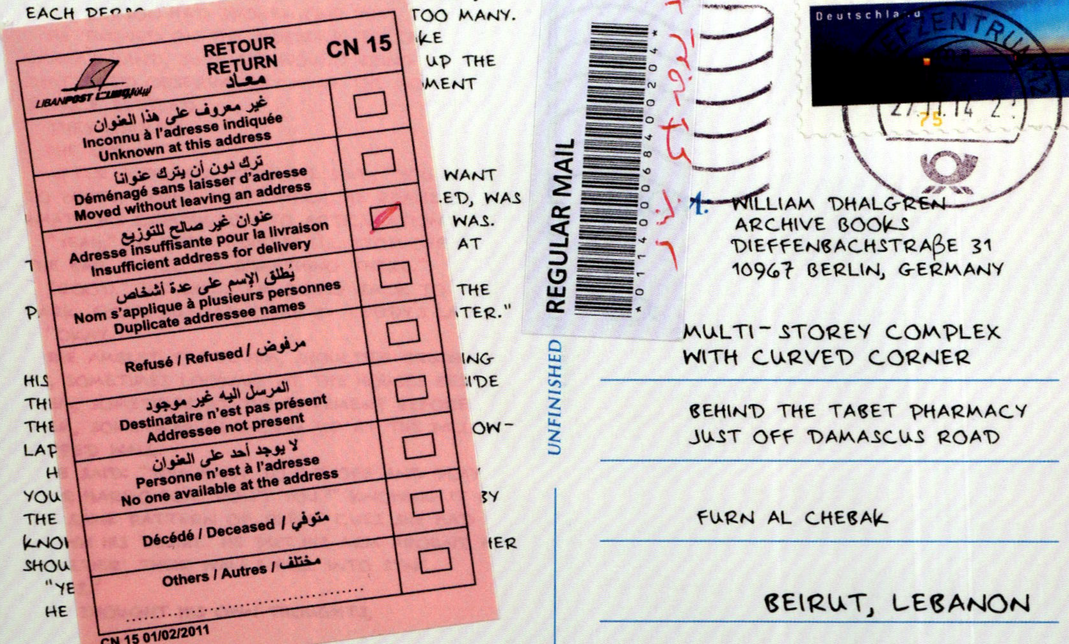
RETOUR
RETURN
معاد
CN 15
LIBANPOST
غير معروف على هذا العنوان
Inconnu à l'adresse indiquée
Unknown at this address
ترك دون أن يترك عنواناً
Déménagé sans laisser d'adresse
Moved without leaving an address
عنوان غير صالح للتوزيع
Adresse insuffisante pour la livraison
Insufficient address for delivery
يُطلق الإسم على عدة أشخاص
Nom s'applique à plusieurs personnes
Duplicate addressee names
Refusé / Refused / مرفوض
المرسل اليه غير موجود
Destinataire n'est pas présent
Addressee not present
لا يوجد أحد على العنوان
Personne n'est à l'adresse
No one available at the address
Décédé / Deceased / متوفي
Others / Autres / مختلف
CN 15 01/02/2011
REGULAR MAIL
01140006840020 4
UNFINISHED
50 Jahre Fehmarnsundbrücke
Deutschland
WILLIAM DHALGREN
ARCHIVE BOOKS
DIEFFENBACHSTRAẞE 31
10967 BERLIN, GERMANY
MULTI-STOREY COMPLEX
WITH CURVED CORNER
BEHIND THE TABET PHARMACY
JUST OFF DAMASCUS ROAD
FURN AL CHEBAK
BEIRUT, LEBANON

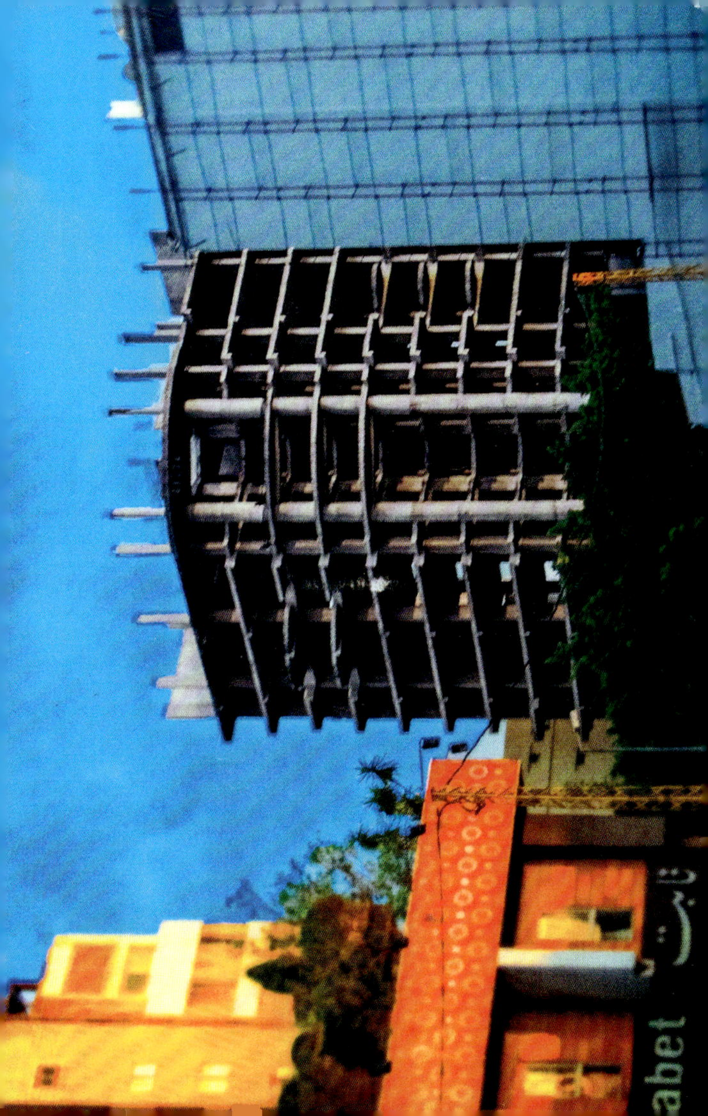

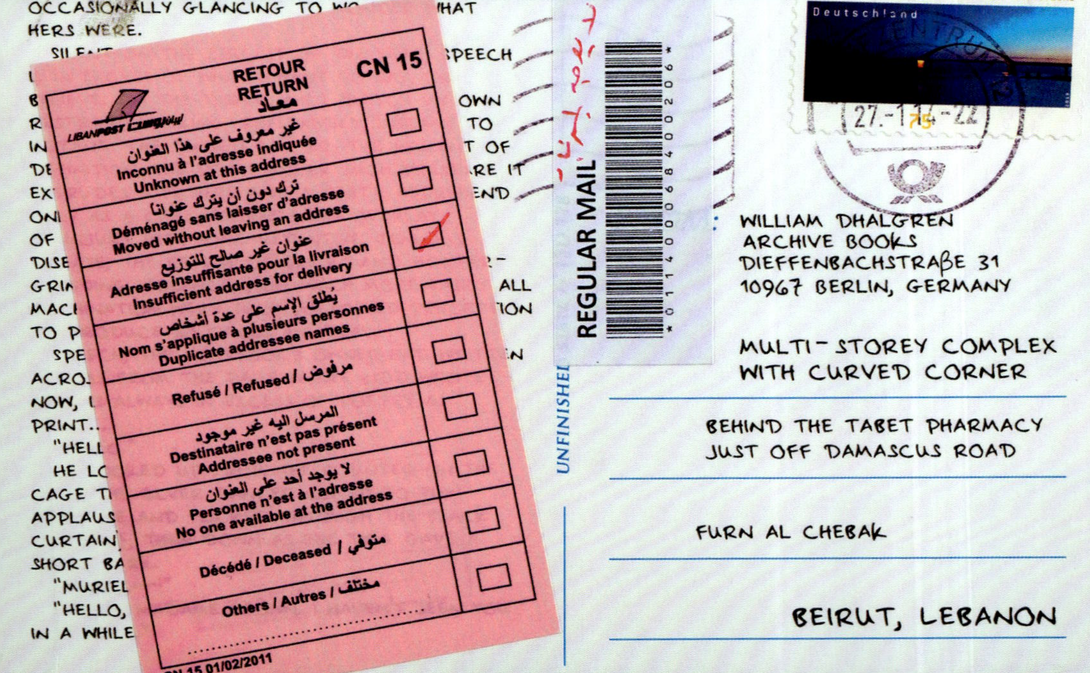
OCCASIONALLY GLANCING TO
HERS WERE.
SPEECH
OWN
TO
T OF
RE IT
END
ALL
TION
RETOUR
RETURN
معاد
CN 15
LIBANPOST
غير معروف على هذا العنوان
Inconnu à l'adresse indiquée
Unknown at this address
ترك دون أن يترك عنوانا
Déménagé sans laisser d'adresse
Moved without leaving an address
عنوان غير صالح للتوزيع
Adresse insuffisante pour la livraison
Insufficient address for delivery
يُطلق الإسم على عدة أشخاص
Nom s'applique à plusieurs personnes
Duplicate addressee names
Refusé / Refused / مرفوض
المرسل اليه غير موجود
Destinataire n'est pas présent
Addressee not present
لا يوجد أحد على العنوان
Personne n'est à l'adresse
No one available at the address
Décédé / Deceased / متوفي
Others / Autres / مختلف
CN 15 01/02/2011
REGULAR MAIL
* 0 1 1 4 0 0 0 6 8 4 0 0 2 0 6 *
UNFINISHED
50 Jahre Fehmarnsundbrücke
Deutschland
75
27.-1.17-22
WILLIAM DHALGREN
ARCHIVE BOOKS
DIEFFENBACHSTRAßE 31
10967 BERLIN, GERMANY
MULTI-STOREY COMPLEX
WITH CURVED CORNER
BEHIND THE TABET PHARMACY
JUST OFF DAMASCUS ROAD
FURN AL CHEBAK
BEIRUT, LEBANON

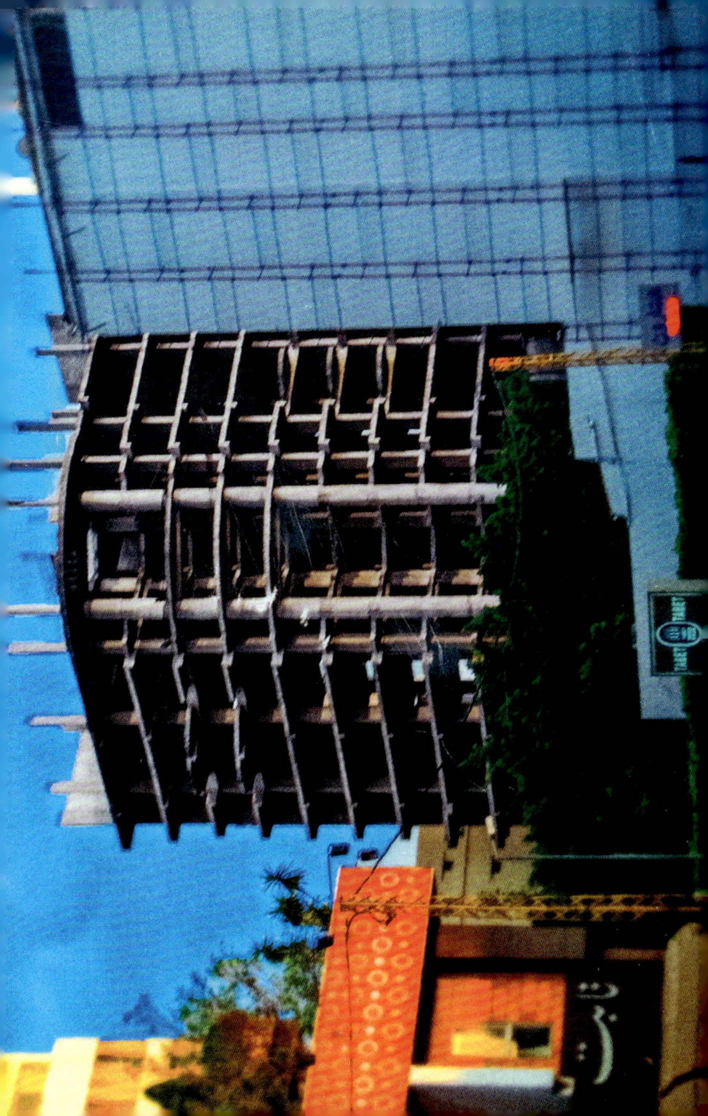

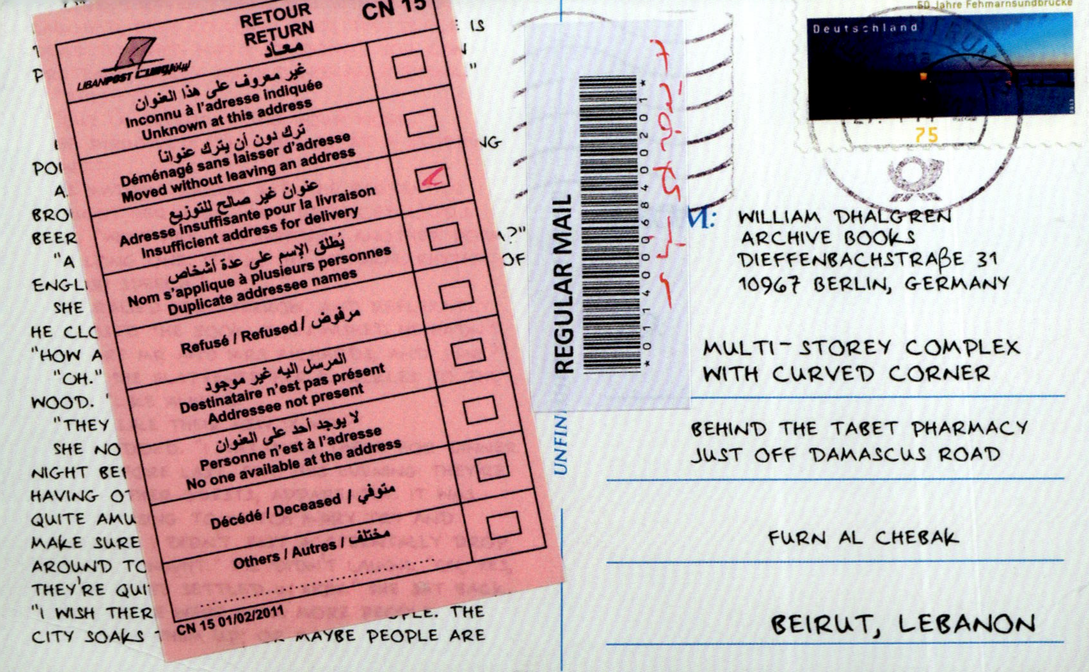
RETOUR
RETURN
معاد
CN 15
LIBANPOST
غير معروف على هذا العنوان
Inconnu à l'adresse indiquée
Unknown at this address
ترك دون أن يترك عنوانا
Déménagé sans laisser d'adresse
Moved without leaving an address
عنوان غير صالح للتوزيع
Adresse insuffisante pour la livraison
Insufficient address for delivery
يُطلق الإسم على عدة أشخاص
Nom s'applique à plusieurs personnes
Duplicate addressee names
Refusé / Refused / مرفوض
المرسل اليه غير موجود
Destinataire n'est pas présent
Addressee not present
لا يوجد أحد على العنوان
Personne n'est à l'adresse
No one available at the address
Décédé / Deceased / متوفي
Others / Autres / مختلف
CN 15 01/02/2011
REGULAR MAIL
0114000684002201
50 Jahre Fehmarnsundbrücke
Deutschland
75
WILLIAM DHALGREN
ARCHIVE BOOKS
DIEFFENBACHSTRAßE 31
10967 BERLIN, GERMANY
MULTI-STOREY COMPLEX
WITH CURVED CORNER
BEHIND THE TABET PHARMACY
JUST OFF DAMASCUS ROAD
FURN AL CHEBAK
BEIRUT, LEBANON

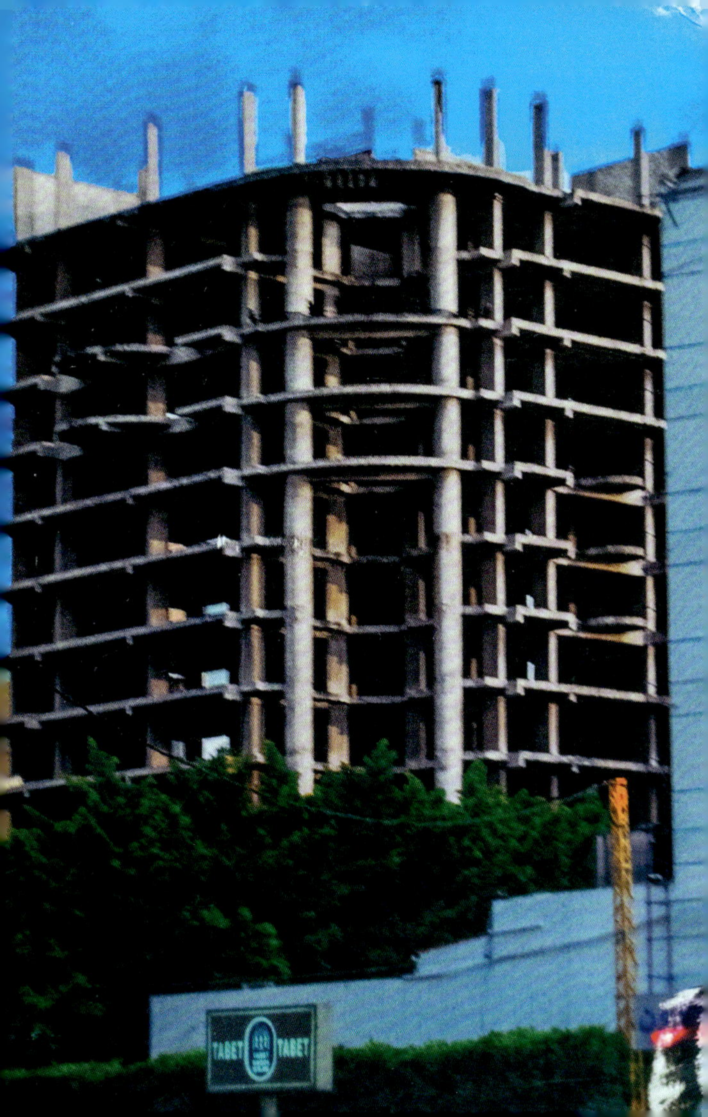
TABET
TABET

JUST... LEAVING?"

LIBANPOST	RETOUR RETURN معاد	CN 15
غير معروف على هذا العنوان Inconnu à l'adresse indiquée Unknown at this address		☐
ترك دون أن يترك عنواناً Déménagé sans laisser d'adresse Moved without leaving an address		☐
عنوان غير صالح للتوزيع Adresse insuffisante pour la livraison Insufficient address for delivery		☒
يُطلق الإسم على عدة أشخاص Nom s'applique à plusieurs personnes Duplicate addressee names		☐
Refusé / Refused / مرفوض		☐
المرسل اليه غير موجود Destinataire n'est pas présent Addressee not present		☐
لا يوجد أحد على العنوان Personne n'est à l'adresse No one available at the address		☐
Décédé / Deceased / متوفي		☐
Others / Autres / مختلف		☐

CN 15 01/02/2011

UNFINISHED

WILLIAM DHALGREN
ARCHIVE BOOKS
DIEFFENBACHSTRAßE 31
10967 BERLIN, GERMANY

MULTI-STOREY COMPLEX
WITH CURVED CORNER

BEHIND THE TABET PHARMACY
JUST OFF DAMASCUS ROAD

FURN AL CHEBAK

BEIRUT, LEBANON

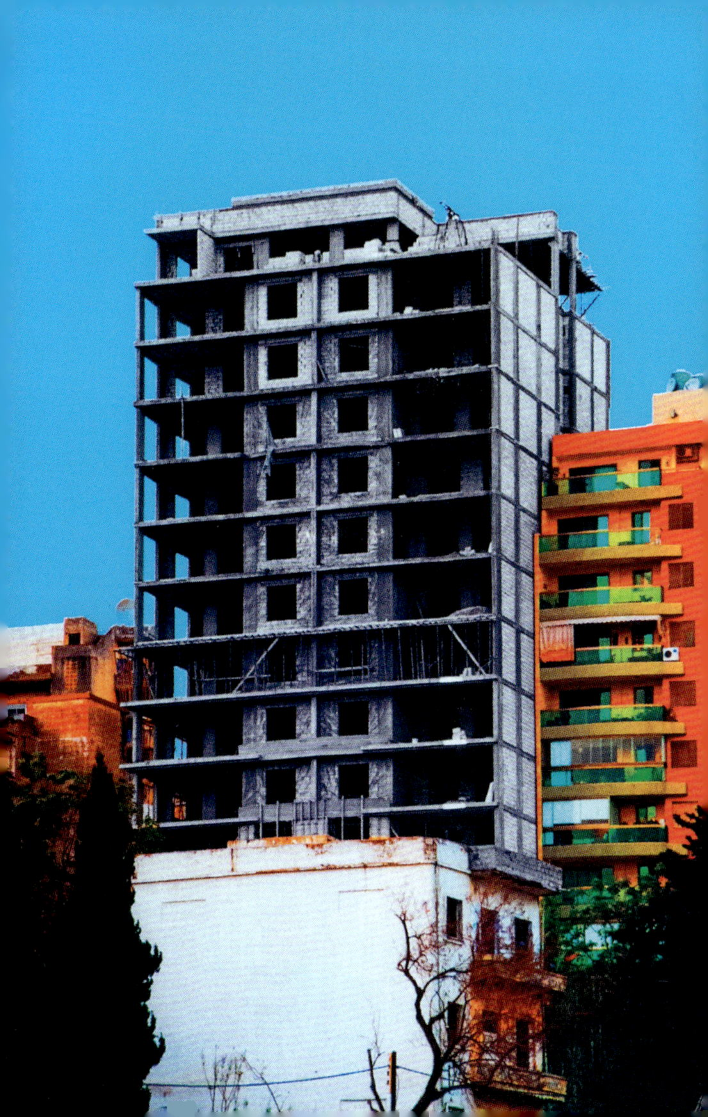

LIBANPOST لبنان بوست

RETOUR
RETURN
معاد

CN 15

غير معروف على هذا العنوان Inconnu à l'adresse indiquée Unknown at this address	☐
ترك دون أن يترك عنوانا Déménagé sans laisser d'adresse Moved without leaving an address	☐
عنوان غير صالح للتوزيع Adresse insuffisante pour la livraison Insufficient address for delivery	☑
يُطلق الإسم على عدة أشخاص Nom s'applique à plusieurs personnes Duplicate addressee names	☐
Refusé / Refused / مرفوض	☐
المرسل اليه غير موجود Destinataire n'est pas présent Addressee not present	☐
لا يوجد أحد على العنوان Personne n'est à l'adresse No one available at the address	☐
Décédé / Deceased / متوفي	☐
Others / Autres / مختلف	☐

CN 15 01/02/2011

AN WHO
SHOULD
LLARS AN

E JOB.
D IT HERE.
RE DOING,

E'D HAVE

D HE WAS
HAT LAST

DD."
D TALK
OOK. "I
NOW,

E." SHE

FOUND:

WANT
TO WRITE; BUT CAN FIX WITH WORDS ONLY

50 Jahre Fehmarnsundbrücke
Deutschland
75

Schützt die Natur
WWF
www.wwf.de

ATE // 13D.181

FROM: WILLIAM DHALGREN
ARCHIVE BOOKS
DIEFFENBACHSTRAßE 31
10967 BERLIN, GERMANY

TO

TALL BUILDING
WITH SQUARE WINDOWS

NEAR THE BEIRUT MALL
OLD SAIDA ROAD

CHIYAH

BEIRUT, LEBANON

REGULAR MAIL

0114000666600386

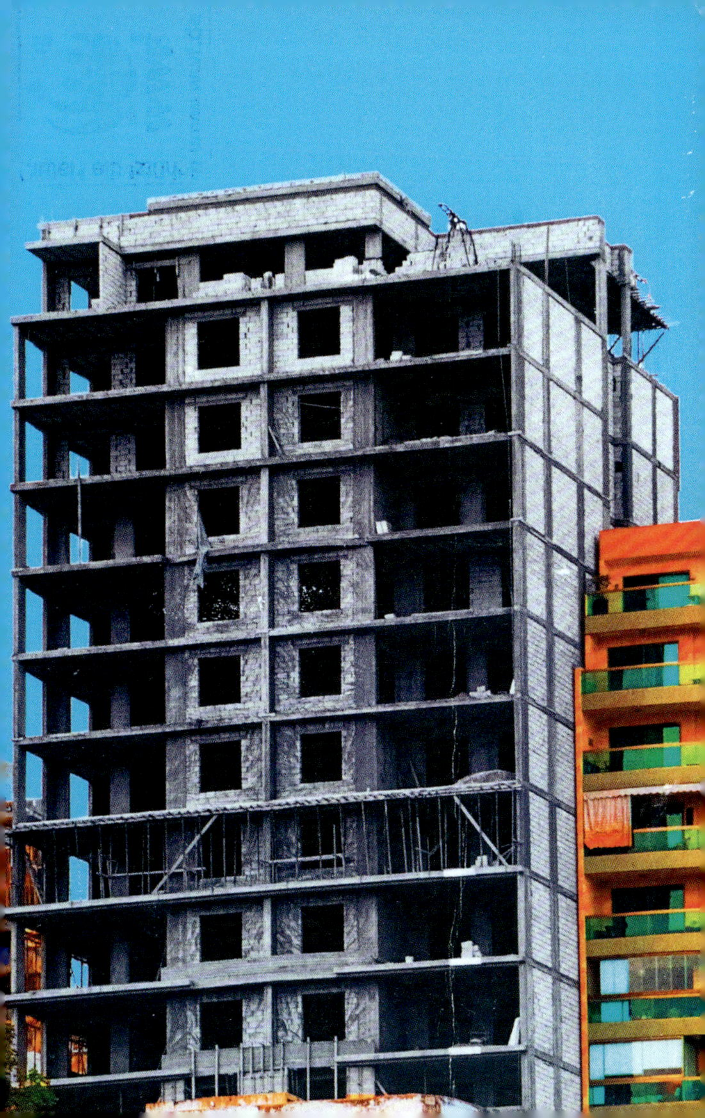

THE DESIRE ITSELF. I SUPPOSE I SHOULD TAKE SOME SMALL COMFORT IN THE FACT THAT, FOR THE FEW WRITERS I HAVE ACTUALLY KNOWN, PUBLICATION, IN DIRECT PROPORTION TO THE TALENT OF EACH, SEEMS TO HAVE BEEN AN OCCURRENCE ALWAYS CONNECTED WITH CATASTROPHE. THEN AGAIN, PERHAPS THEY WERE SIMPLY A STRANGE GROUP OF...

"BA-DA," HE WHISPERED AND TURNED OVER THE NOTEBOOK TO THE BLANK PAGE, "BA-DA, BA-DA, BA-DA, BA-DA."

THE LETTER WAS STILL IN THE MAILBOX.

AMONG THE BENT AND BROKEN DOORS, RED, WHITE, AND BLUE EDGING CROSSED THIS ONE, INTACT GRILLE. HE THOUGHT HE COULD SEE THE INKING OF A RETURN ADDRESS. I CAN PRETEND, HE THOUGHT, IT SAYS EDWARD RICHARDS, FROM A HOTEL IN SEATTLE, WASHINGTON, OFF FREEMONT AVENUE, ON THIRD. HE COULD MAKE SOME THINGS APPEAR LIKE THAT, WHEN IT WAS THIS DIM... HE TURNED AND WENT TO THE ELEVATOR.

SOMEONE, AT LEAST, HAD MOPPED THE LOBBY.

HE PRESSED THE BUTTON.

WIND HISSED FROM THE EMPTY SHAFT. HE STEPPED INTO THE OTHER.

HE'D COME OUT IN THE PITCH-DARK HALL BEFORE—AS THE DOOR WENT K-CHUNK—HE REALIZED HABIT HAD MADE HIM PUSH SEVENTEEN,

UNFINISHED STATE // 13D.182

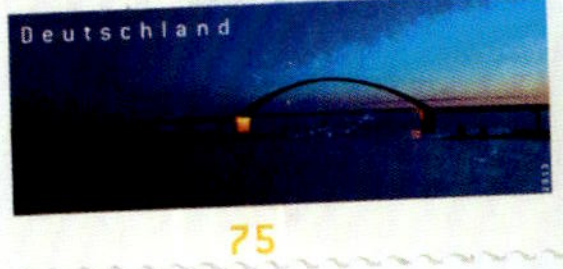

FROM: WILLIAM DHALGREN
ARCHIVE BOOKS
DIEFFENBACHSTRAßE 31
10967 BERLIN, GERMANY

TO: TALL BUILDING
WITH SQUARE WINDOWS

NEAR THE BEIRUT MALL
OLD SAIDA ROAD

CHIYAH

BEIRUT, LEBANON

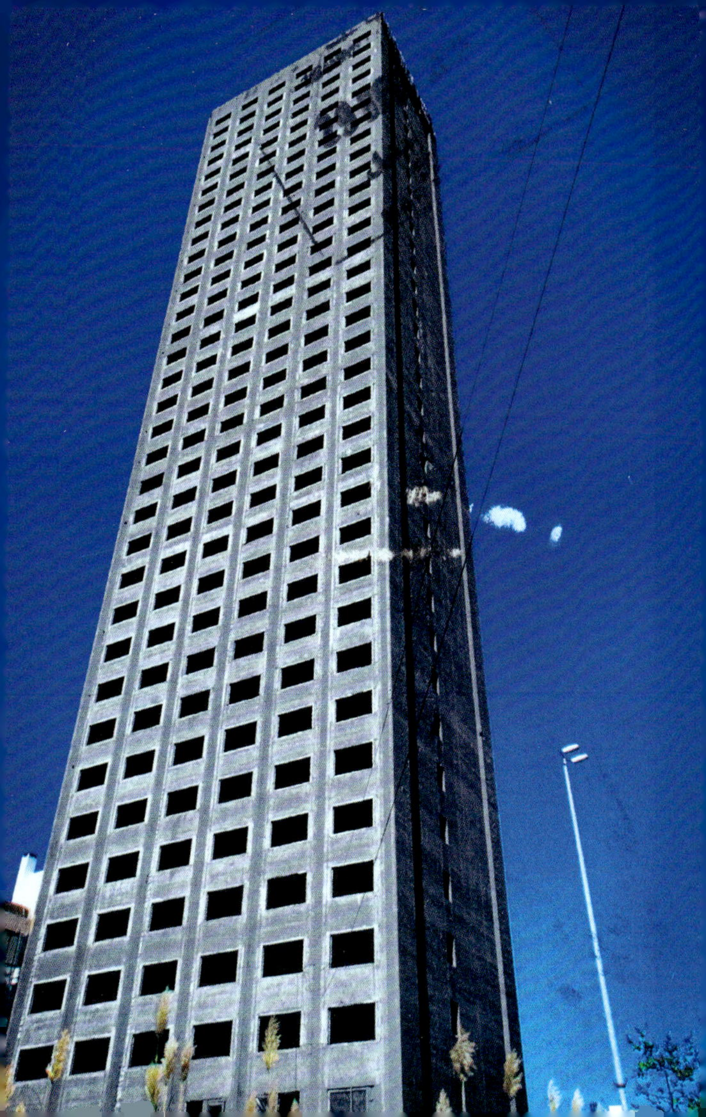

HE NODDED AND SWALLOWED. HE HAD TRIED TO TELL HER EVERYTHING IMPORTANT, ABOUT THE RICHARDS, ABOUT NEWBOY. HE SAID, "THAT SCRATCH..."

.."

ONE,
AND JUST
HE TOOK
CUT THERE
GETS HIS
RSTAND THAT.

SENSE WHEN I

HAVE ANY CUT ON
H OUT; AND COULD
WN IN HER CHEST. "BUT

IG YOU SAW?"

UNFINISHED

1: WILLIAM DHALGREN
ARCHIVE BOOKS
DIEFFENBACHSTRAßE 31
10967 BERLIN, GERMANY

BURJ EL MURR TOWER

ON THE CORNER OF ARMY
AND GENERAL FOAAD CHEHAB

MINAT AL HOSN, BEIRUT

LEBANON

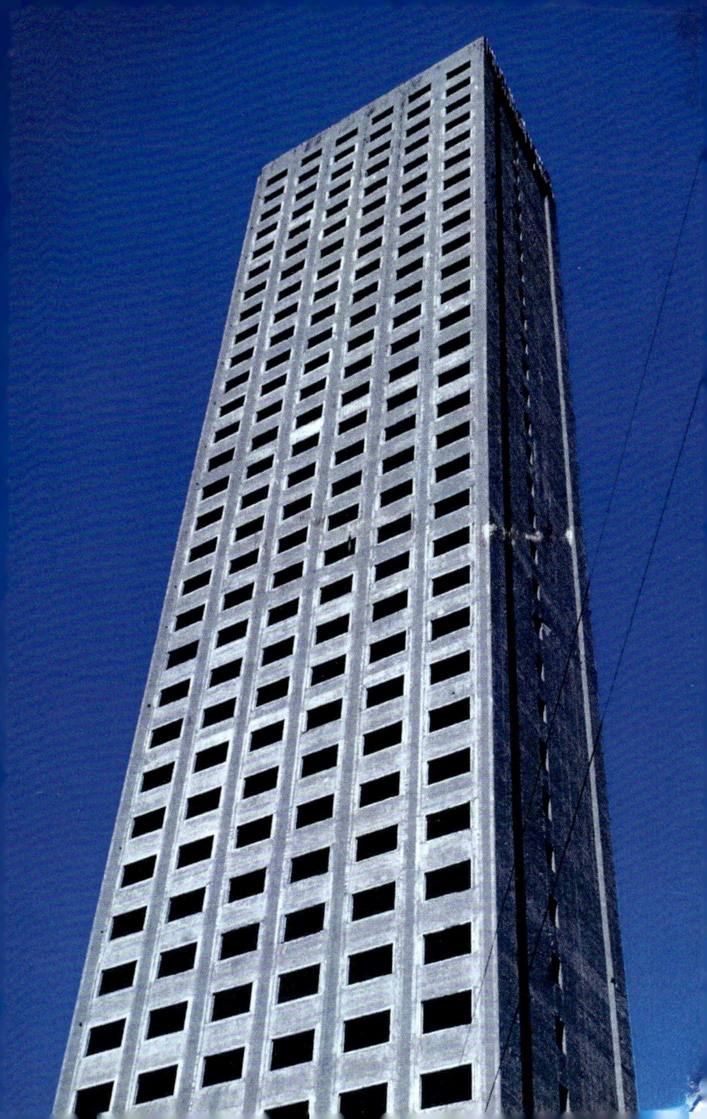

"SHE WAS STANDING UP. AND HE WAS SITTING DOWN. AND SUDDENLY HE REACHED OVER AND JUST SLASHED DOWN HER LEG. PROBABLY IT WASN'T A VERY BIG CUT. HE'D DONE IT BEFORE.

Schützt die Natur.

Deutschland
50 Jahre Fehmarnsundbrücke
75

M: WILLIAM DHALGREN
ARCHIVE BOOKS
DIEFFENBACHSTRAßE 31
10967 BERLIN, GERMANY

BURJ EL MURR TOWER

ON THE CORNER OF ARMY
AND GENERAL FOAAD CHEHAB

MINAT AL HOSN, BEIRUT

LEBANON

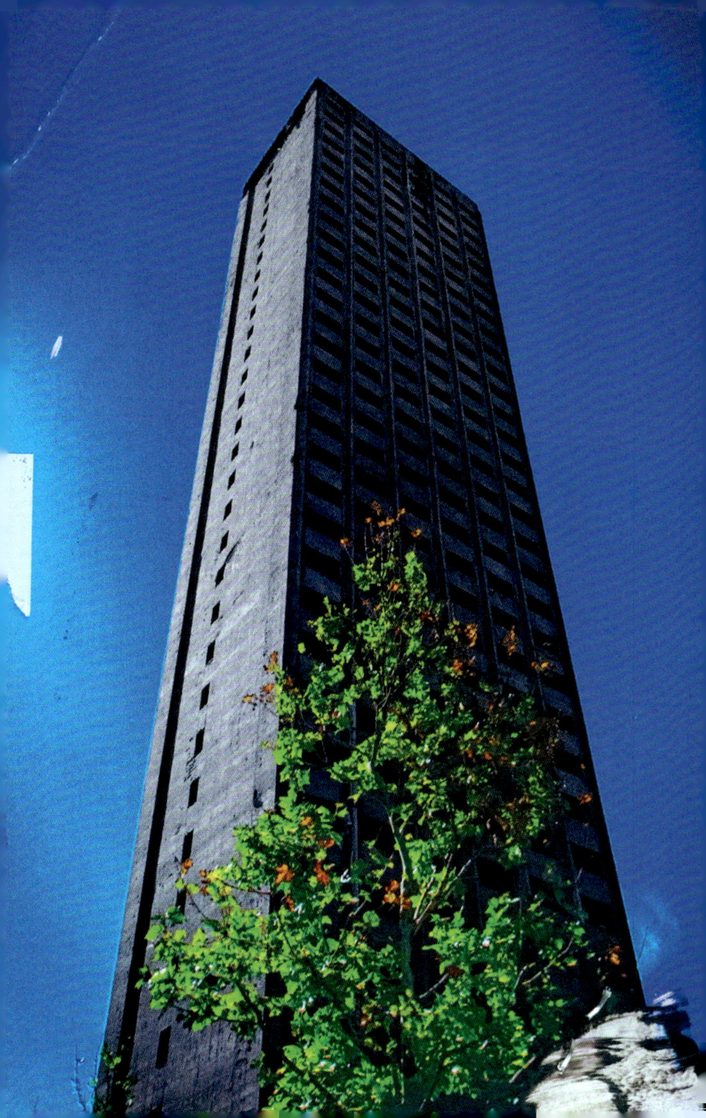

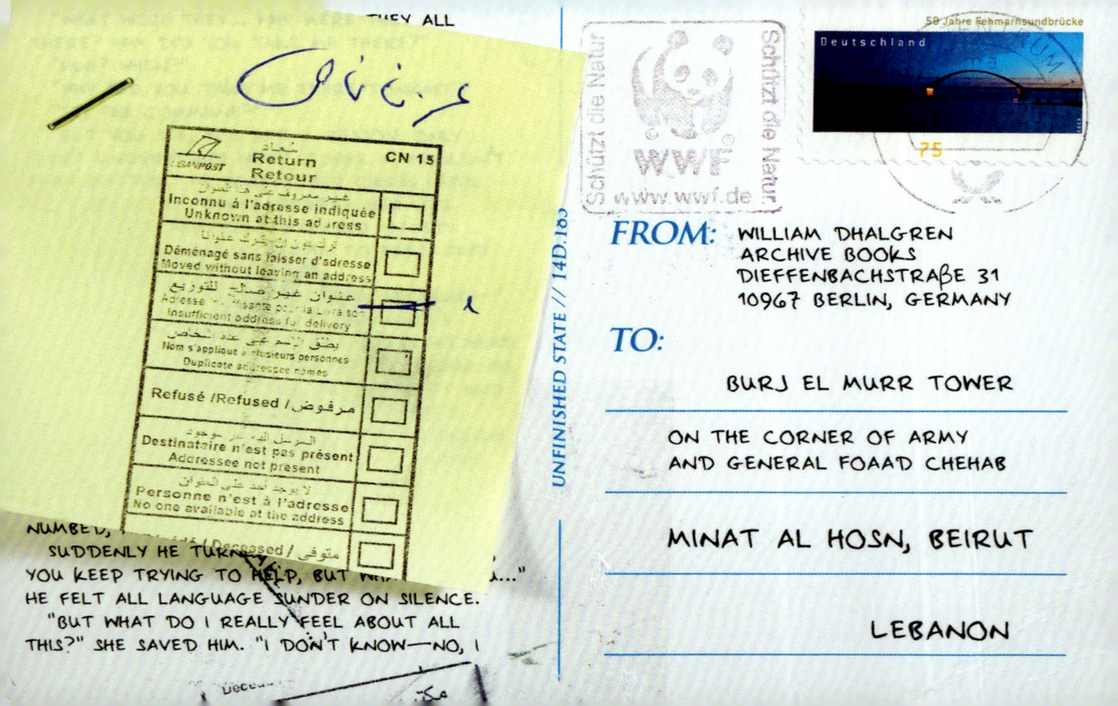

... THEY ALL

NUMBE...

SUDDENLY HE TU...

YOU KEEP TRYING TO HELP, BUT ...…"

HE FELT ALL LANGUAGE SUNDER ON SILENCE.

"BUT WHAT DO I REALLY FEEL ABOUT ALL THIS?" SHE SAVED HIM. "I DON'T KNOW—NO, I

LIBANPOST Return / Retour	CN 15
Inconnu à l'adresse indiquée / Unknown at this address	☐
Déménagé sans laisser d'adresse / Moved without leaving an address	☐
Adresse insuffisante pour la livraison / Insufficient address for delivery	☐
Nom s'applique à plusieurs personnes / Duplicate addressee names	☐
Refusé / Refused / مرفوض	☐
Destinataire n'est pas présent / Addressee not present	☐
Personne n'est à l'adresse / No one available at the address	☐
Décédé / Deceased / متوفى	☐

UNFINISHED STATE // 14D.183

Schützt die Natur WWF www.wwf.de Schützt die Natur

Deutschland 75 — 50 Jahre Fehmarnsundbrücke

FROM: WILLIAM DHALGREN
ARCHIVE BOOKS
DIEFFENBACHSTRAßE 31
10967 BERLIN, GERMANY

TO:

BURJ EL MURR TOWER

ON THE CORNER OF ARMY
AND GENERAL FOAAD CHEHAB

MINAT AL HOSN, BEIRUT

LEBANON

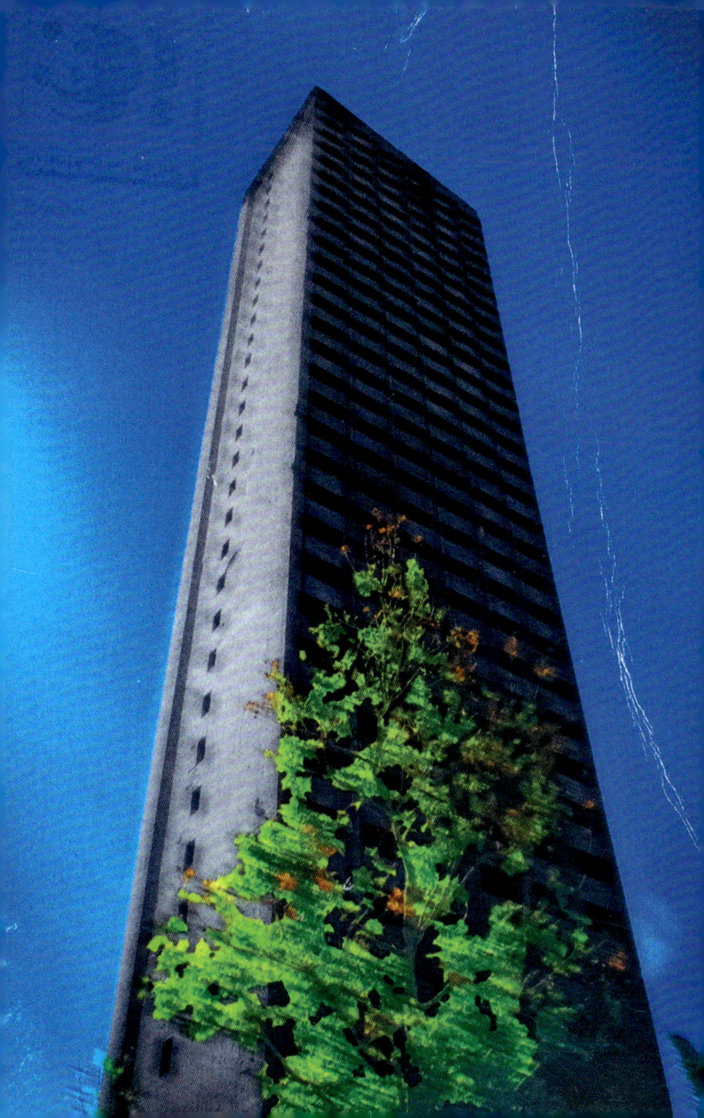

DO." SHE SIGHED. "LOTS OF IT ISN'T TOO NICE. MAYBE YOU'RE IN REALLY BAD SHAPE. AND SINCE I'VE ONLY KNOWN YO... ...E.

LIBANPOST	RETOUR RETURN معاد	CN 15
غير معروف على هذا العنوان Inconnu à l'adresse indiquée Unknown at this address		☐
ترك دون أن يترك عنواناً Déménagé sans laisser d'adresse Moved without leaving an address		☐
عنوان غير صالح للتوزيع Adresse insuffisante pour la livraison Insufficient address for delivery		☒
يُطلق الإسم على عدة أشخاص Nom s'applique à plusieurs personnes Duplicate addressee names		☐
Refusé / Refused / مرفوض		☐
المرسل اليه غير موجود Destinataire n'est pas présent Addressee not present		☐
لا يوجد أحد على العنوان Personne n'est à l'adresse No one available at the address		☐
Décédé / Deceased / متوفي		☐
Others / Autres / مختلف		☐

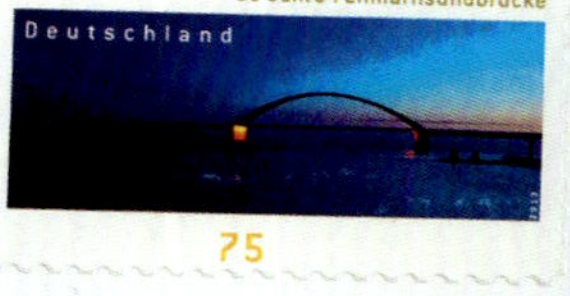

FROM: WILLIAM DHALGREN
ARCHIVE BOOKS
DIEFFENBACHSTRAßE 31
10967 BERLIN, GERMANY

TO:

BURJ EL MURR TOWER

ON THE CORNER OF ARMY
AND GENERAL FOAAD CHEHAB

MINAT AL HOSN, BEIRUT

LEBANON

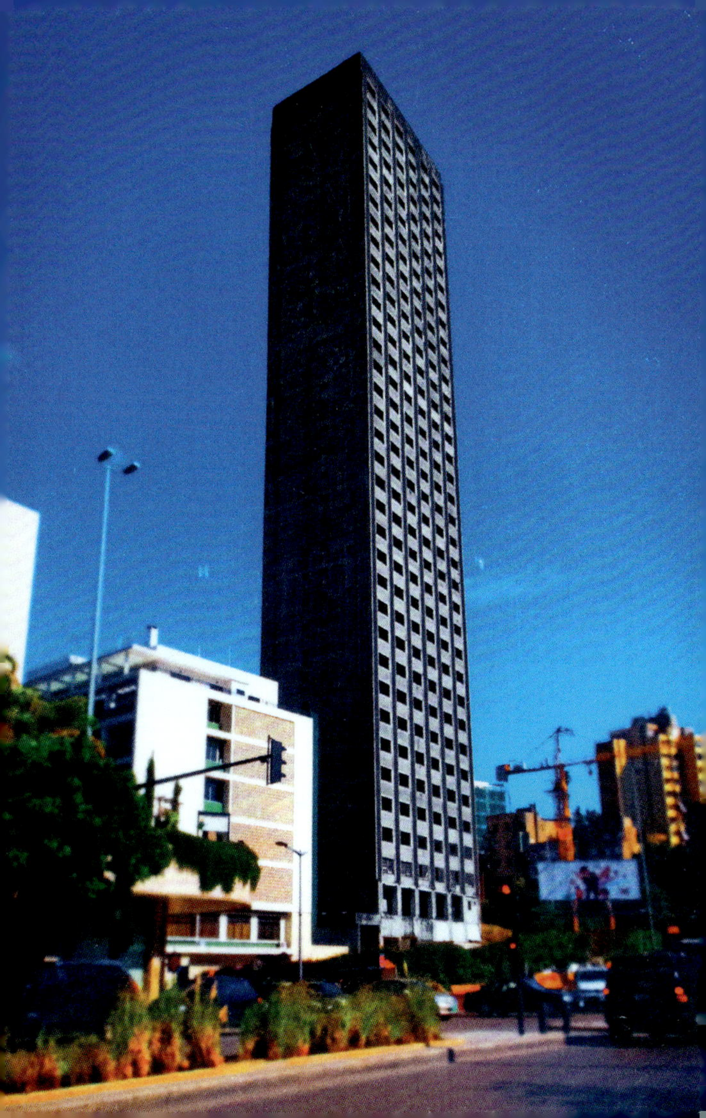

PART. BUT WE DO OTHER THINGS. REMEMBER THOSE TOO. THAT'S CRUEL OF ME TO ASK WHEN YOU'RE GOING THROUGH THIS, ISN'T IT? BUT THERE'S SO MUCH YOU DON'T SEE. YOU WALK AROUND IN A WORLD WITH HOLES IN IT; YOU STUMBLE INTO THEM.

WILLIAM DHALGREN
ARCHIVE BOOKS
DIEFFENBACHSTRAßE 31
10967 BERLIN, GERMANY

RJ EL MURR TOWER

ON THE CORNER OF ARMY
AND GENERAL FOAAD CHEHAB

MINAT AL HOSN, BEIRUT

LEBANON

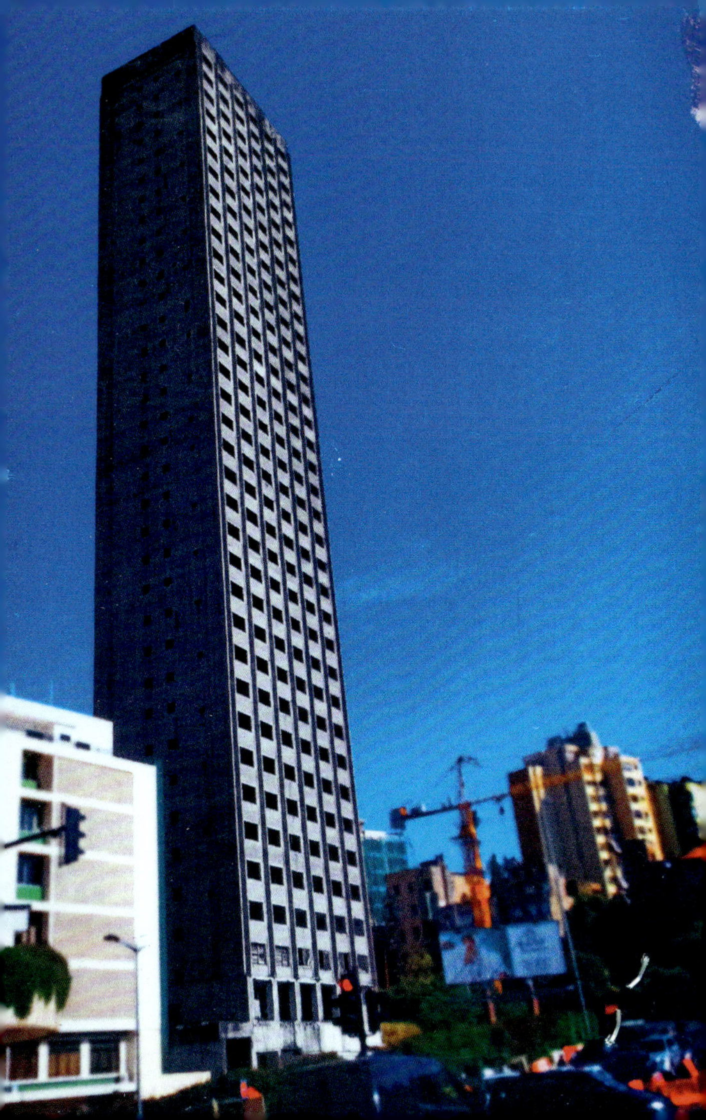

DARK. "I LEFT HIS OFFICE IN THE MORNING AND GOT STARTED THAT AFTERNOON. I WAS VERY EXCITED. I FELT I MIGHT GET INTO ALL SORTS OF AREAS OF MY UNCONSCIOUS IN MY PAINTING THAT WAY... WHATEVER THAT MEANT. I DIDN'T FALL BEHIND UNTIL THE THIRD DAY. AND THEN ONLY TWENTY MINUTES. BUT I COULDN'T BRING MYSELF TO DO TWO HOURS OF DISH WASHING."

"HOW MANY DISHES DID YOU HAVE?"

"I WAS SUPPOSED TO WASH CLEAN ONES IF I RAN OUT OF DIRTY ONES. THE NEXT DAY I WAS OKAY. ONLY I DIDN'T LIKE THE PAINTING THAT WAS COMING OUT. THE DAY AFTER THAT I DON'T THINK I PAINTED AT ALL. THAT'S RIGHT, SOMEBODY CAME OVER AND WE WENT UP TO POE'S COTTAGE."

"EVER BEEN TO ROBERT LOUIS STEVENSON'S HOUSE IN MONTEREY?"

"NO."

"HE ONLY RENTED A ROOM IN IT FOR A COUPLE OF MONTHS AND FINALLY GOT THROWN OUT BECAUSE HE COULDN'T PAY THE RENT. NOW THEY CALL IT STEVENSON'S HOUSE AND IT'S A MUSEUM ALL ABOUT HIM."

SHE LAUGHED. "ANYWAY, I WAS SUPPOSED TO SEE THE DOCTOR THE NEXT DAY. AND REPORT ON HOW IT WAS GOING. THAT NIGHT I STARTED LOOKING AT THE PAINTINGS—I TOOK THEM

REGULAR MAIL

0114000669004040

50 Jahre Fehmarnsundbrücke

Deutschland 75

1: WILLIAM DHALGREN
ARCHIVE BOOKS
DIEFFENBACHSTRAßE 31
10967 BERLIN, GERMANY

UNFINISHED

BURJ EL MURR TOWER

ON THE CORNER OF ARMY
AND GENERAL FOAAD CHEHAB

MINAT AL HOSN, BEIRUT

LEBANON

Destinataire n'est pas présent
Addressee not present

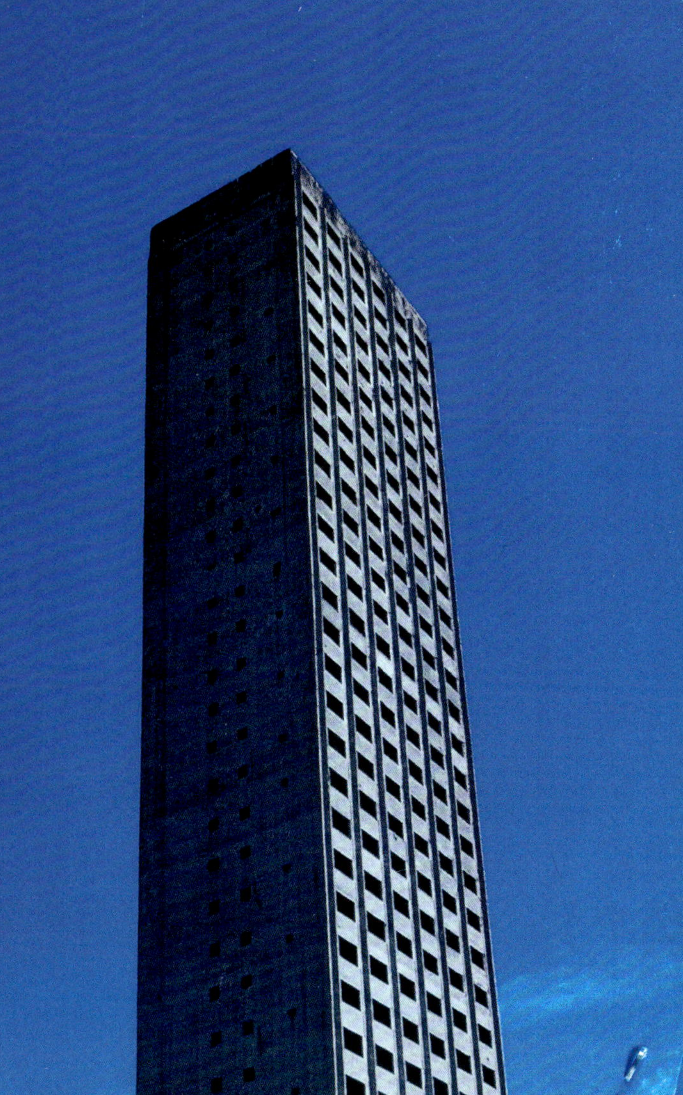

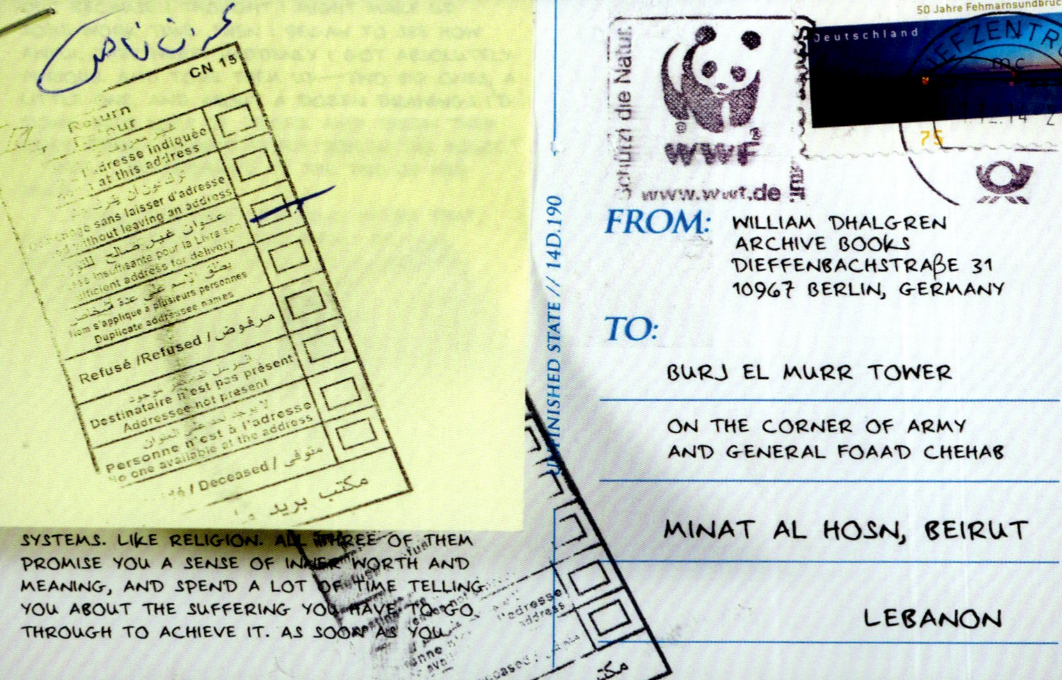
CN 15
Return
Retour
l'adresse indiquée
at this address
sans laisser d'adresse
without leaving an address
Insuffisante pour la Livraison
insufficient address for delivery
Nom s'applique à plusieurs personnes
Duplicate addressee names
Refusé /Refused / مرفوض
Destinataire n'est pas présent
Addressee not present
Personne n'est à l'adresse
No one available at the address
/ Deceased / متوفى
مكتب بريد
SYSTEMS. LIKE RELIGION. ALL THREE OF THEM
PROMISE YOU A SENSE OF INNER WORTH AND
MEANING, AND SPEND A LOT OF TIME TELLING
YOU ABOUT THE SUFFERING YOU HAVE TO GO
THROUGH TO ACHIEVE IT. AS SOON AS YOU
UNFINISHED STATE // 14D.190
50 Jahre Fehmarnsundbrücke
Deutschland
75
Schützt die Natur.
WWF
www.wwf.de
FROM:
WILLIAM DHALGREN
ARCHIVE BOOKS
DIEFFENBACHSTRAßE 31
10967 BERLIN, GERMANY
TO:
BURJ EL MURR TOWER
ON THE CORNER OF ARMY
AND GENERAL FOAAD CHEHAB
MINAT AL HOSN, BEIRUT
LEBANON

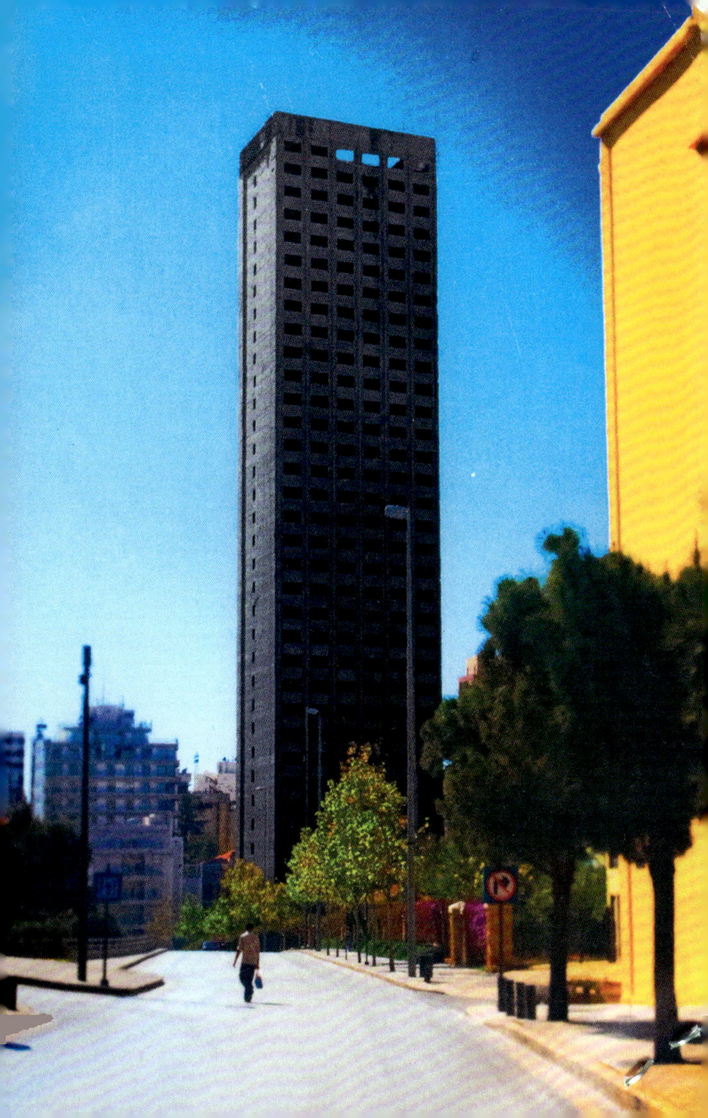

GET A PROBLEM IN ANY ONE OF THEM, THE SOLUTION IT GIVES IS ALWAYS TO GO DEEPER INTO THE SAME SYSTEM. THEY'RE ALL IN RATHER UNEASY TRUCE WITH ONE ANOTHER IN WHAT'S ACTUALLY A MORTAL BATTLE. LIKE ALL SELF-REINFORCING SYSTEMS. AT BEST, EACH IS TRYING TO ENCOMPASS THE OTHER TWO AND DEFINE THEM AS SUB-GROUPS. YOU KNOW: RELIGION AND ART ARE BOTH FORMS OF MADNESS AND MADNESS IS THE REALM OF PSYCHIATRY. OR, ART IS THE STUDY AND PRAISE OF MAN AND MAN'S IDEALS, SO THEREFORE A RELIGIOUS EXPERIENCE BECOMES JUST A BRUTALIZED AESTHETIC RESPONSE AND PSYCHIATRY IS JUST ANOTHER TOOL FOR THE ARTIST TO OBSERVE MAN AND RENDER HIS PORTRAITS MORE ACCURATELY. AND THE RELIGIOUS ATTITUDE I GUESS IS THAT THE OTHER TWO ARE ONLY USEFUL AS LONG AS THEY PROMOTE THE GOOD LIFE. AT WORST, THEY ALL TRY TO DESTROY ONE ANOTHER. WHICH IS WHAT MY PSYCHIATRIST, WHETHER HE KNEW IT OR NOT, WAS TRYING, QUITE EFFECTIVELY, TO DO TO MY PAINTING. I GAVE UP PSYCHIATRY TOO, PRETTY SOON. I JUST DIDN'T WANT TO GET ALL WOUND UP IN ANY SYSTEMS AT ALL.

"YOU LIKE WASHING DISHES?"

"I HAVEN'T HAD TO IN A LONG, LONG TIME." SHE SHRUGGED AGAIN. "AND WHEN I HAVE TO

UNFINISHED STATE // 14D.191

Schützt die Natur
WWF
www.wwf.de

Deutschland
50 Jahre Fehmarnsundbrücke
75

FROM: WILLIAM DHALGREN
ARCHIVE BOOKS
DIEFFENBACHSTRAßE 31
10967 BERLIN, GERMANY

TO:

BURJ EL MURR TOWER

ON THE CORNER OF ARMY
AND GENERAL FOAAD CHEHAB

MINAT AL HOSN, BEIRUT

LEBANON

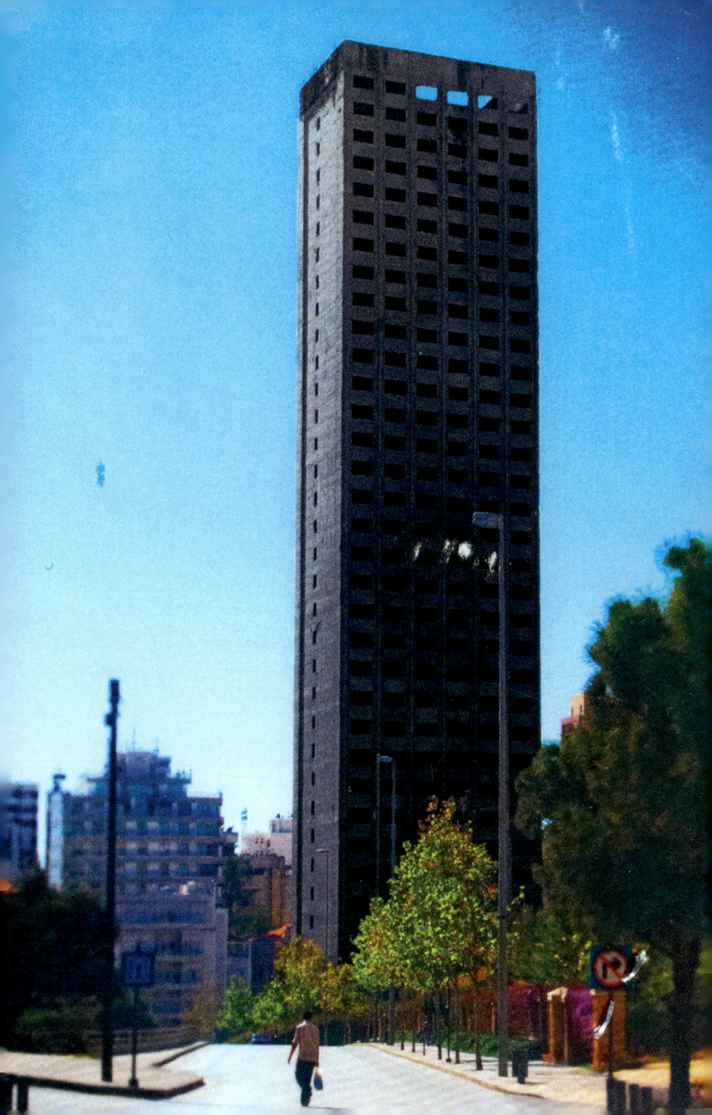

NOW, ACTUALLY I FIND IT RATHER RELAXING."

HE LAUGHED. "I GUESS I DO TOO." THEN: "BUT YOU SHOULDN'T HAVE TORN UP THOSE PAINTINGS. I MEAN, SUPPOSE YOU CHANGED YOUR MIND. OR MAYBE THERE WAS SOMETHING GOOD IN THEM THAT YOU COULD HAVE USED LATER—"

"IT WAS BAD IF I WANTED TO BE AN ARTIST. BUT I WASN'T AN ARTIST. I DIDN'T WANT TO BE."

"YOU GOT A SCHOLARSHIP."

"SO DID A LOT OF OTHER PEOPLE. THEIR PAINTINGS WERE TERRIBLE, MOSTLY. BY THE LAWS OF CHANCE, MINE WERE PROBABLY TERRIBLE TOO. NO, IT WASN'T BAD IF I DIDN'T WANT TO PAINT AT ALL."

BUT HE WAS STILL SHAKING HIS HEAD.

"THAT REALLY UPSETS YOU, DOESN'T IT? WHY?"

HE TOOK A BREATH AND MOVED HIS ARM FROM UNDER HER. "IT'S LIKE EVERYTHING YOU— ANYBODY SAYS TO ME... IT'S LIKE THEY'RE TRYING TO TELL ME A HUNDRED AND FIFTY OTHER THINGS AS WELL. BESIDES WHAT THEY'RE SAYING DIRECT."

"OH, PERHAPS I AM, JUST A BIT."

"I MEAN, HERE I AM, HALF NUTS AND TRYING TO WRITE POEMS, AND YOU'RE TRYING TO TELL ME I SHOULDN'T PUT MY FAITH IN ART OR PSYCHIATRY."

"OH NO!" SHE FOLDED HER HANDS ON HIS

UNFINISHED STATE // 14D.192

Deutschland 75

50 Jahre Fehmarnsundbrücke

FROM: WILLIAM DHALGREN
ARCHIVE BOOKS
DIEFFENBACHSTRAßE 31
10967 BERLIN, GERMANY

TO:

BURJ EL MURR TOWER

ON THE CORNER OF ARMY
AND GENERAL FOAAD CHEHAB

MINAT AL HOSN, BEIRUT

LEBANON

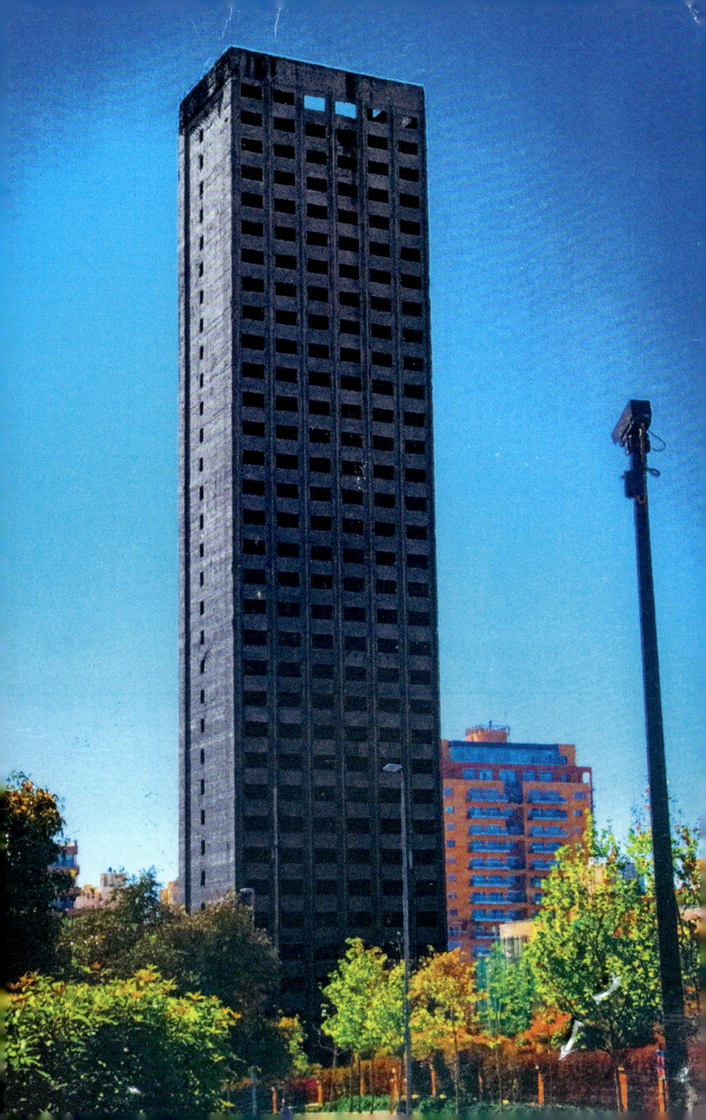

CHEST, AND PUT HER CHIN THERE. "I'M SAYING I DECIDED NOT TO. BUT I WASN'T NUTS. I WAS JUST LAZY. THERE IS A DIFFERENCE, I HOPE. AND I WASN'T AN ARTIST. A TAPE EDITOR, A TEACHER, A HARMONICA PLAYER, BUT NOT AN ARTIST." HE FOLDED HIS ARMS ACROSS HER NECK AND PUSHED HER HEAD FLAT TO ITS CHEEK. "I SUPPOSE THE PROBLEM," SHE WENT ON, MUFFLED IN HIS ARMPIT, "IS THAT WE HAVE AN INSIDE AND AN OUTSIDE. WE'VE GOT PROBLEMS BOTH PLACES, BUT IT'S SO HARD TO TELL WHERE THE ONE STOPS AND OTHER TAKES UP." SHE PAUSED A MOMENT, MOVING HER HEAD. "MY BLUE DRESS..."

"THAT REMINDS YOU OF THE PROBLEMS WITH THE OUTSIDE?"

"THAT, AND GOING UP TO CALKINS'. I DON'T MIND LIVING LIKE THAT—EVERY ONCE IN A WHILE. WHEN I'VE HAD THE CHANCE, I'VE ALWAYS DONE IT RATHER WELL."

"WE COULD HAVE A PLACE LIKE CALKINS'. YOU CAN HAVE ANYTHING YOU WANT IN THIS CITY. MAYBE IT WOULDN'T BE AS BIG, BUT WE COULD FIND A NICE HOUSE; AND I COULD GET STUFF LIKE EVERYBODY ELSE DOES. TAK'S GOT AN ELECTRIC STOVE THAT COOKS A ROAST BEEF IN TEN MINUTES. WITH MICROWAVES. WE COULD HAVE ANYTHING—"

"THAT—" SHE WAS SHAKING HER HEAD—

UNFINISHED STATE // 14D.193

Schützt die Natur WWF www.wwf.de Schützt die Natur

50 Jahre Fehmarnsundbrücke Deutschland 75

FROM: WILLIAM DHALGREN
ARCHIVE BOOKS
DIEFFENBACHSTRAßE 31
10967 BERLIN, GERMANY

TO:

BURJ EL MURR TOWER

ON THE CORNER OF ARMY
AND GENERAL FOAAD CHEHAB

MINAT AL HOSN, BEIRUT

LEBANON

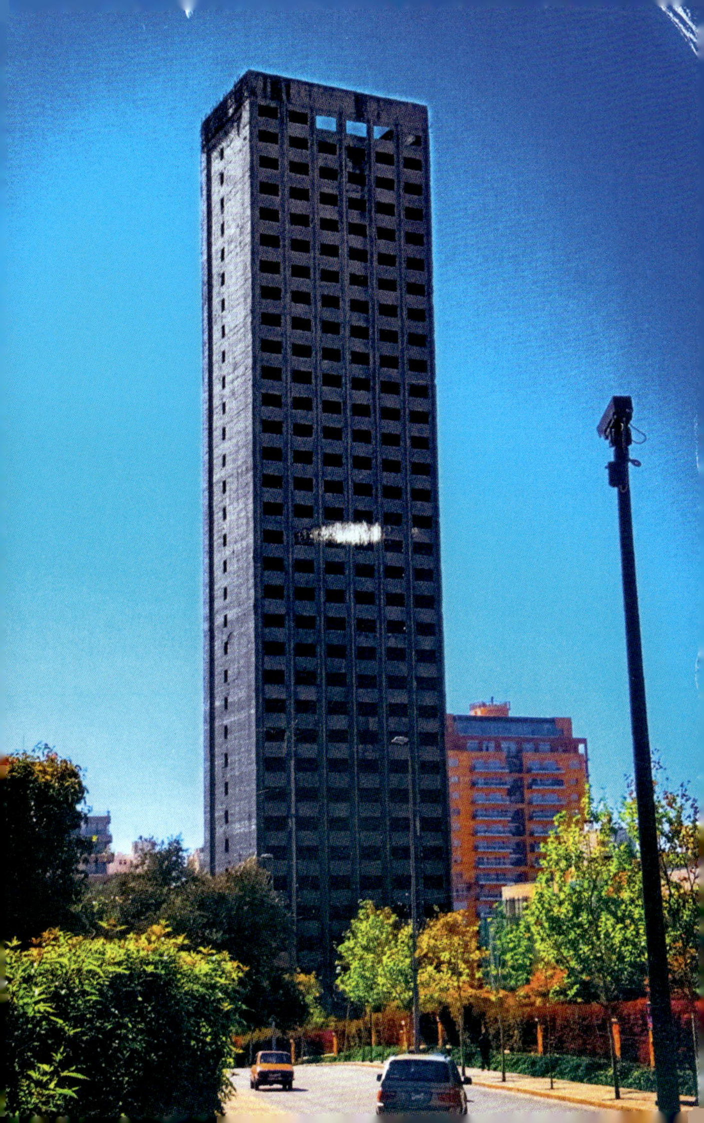

"HOWEVER, IS WHEN THE INSIDE PROBLEMS START. OR START TO BECOME PROBLEMS, ANYWAY. SOMETIMES, I DON'T THINK I HAVE ANY INSIDE PROBLEMS AT ALL. I THINK I'M JUST GIVING MYSELF SOMETHING TO WORRY ABOUT. I'M NOT SCARED OF HALF THE THINGS HALF THE PEOPLE I KNOW ARE. I'VE GONE LOTS OF PLACES, MET LOTS OF PEOPLE, HAD LOTS OF FUN. MAYBE IT IS ALL A MATTER OF GETTING THE OUTSIDE PROBLEMS SOLVED. ANOTHER NOT NICE THING: WHEN I LOOK AT YOU, SOMETIMES I DON'T THINK I HAVE A RIGHT TO THINK I HAVE ANY PROBLEMS, INSIDE OR OUT."

"DON'T YOU WANT TO DO ANYTHING? CHANGE ANYTHING; PRESERVE ANYTHING; FIND ANY..." HE STOPPED BECAUSE HE FELT DISTINCTLY UNCOMFORTABLE.

"NO." SHE SAID IT VERY FIRMLY.

"I MEAN, MAYBE THAT WOULD MAKE IT EASIER TO SOLVE SOME OF THE OUTSIDE PROBLEMS, ANYWAY. YOU KNOW, MAYBE YOU'D FEEL HAPPIER IF YOU COULD GET ANOTHER DRESS."

"NO," SHE REPEATED. "I WANT WONDERFUL AND FASCINATING AND MARVELOUS THINGS TO HAPPEN TO ME AND I DON'T WANT TO DO ANYTHING TO MAKE THEM HAPPEN. NOTHING AT ALL. I SUPPOSE THAT MAKES YOU THINK I'M A SUPERFICIAL PERSON... NO, YOU'RE TOO INTELLIGENT. BUT A

UNFINISHED STATE

REGULAR MAIL

011400068400121

Schützt die Natur

.de

50 Jahre Fehmarnsundbrücke

Deutschland

75

WILLIAM DHALGREN
ARCHIVE BOOKS
DIEFFENBACHSTRAßE 31
10967 BERLIN, GERMANY

BURJ EL MURR TOWER

ON THE CORNER OF ARMY
AND GENERAL FOAAD CHEHAB

MINAT AL HOSN, BEIRUT

LEBANON

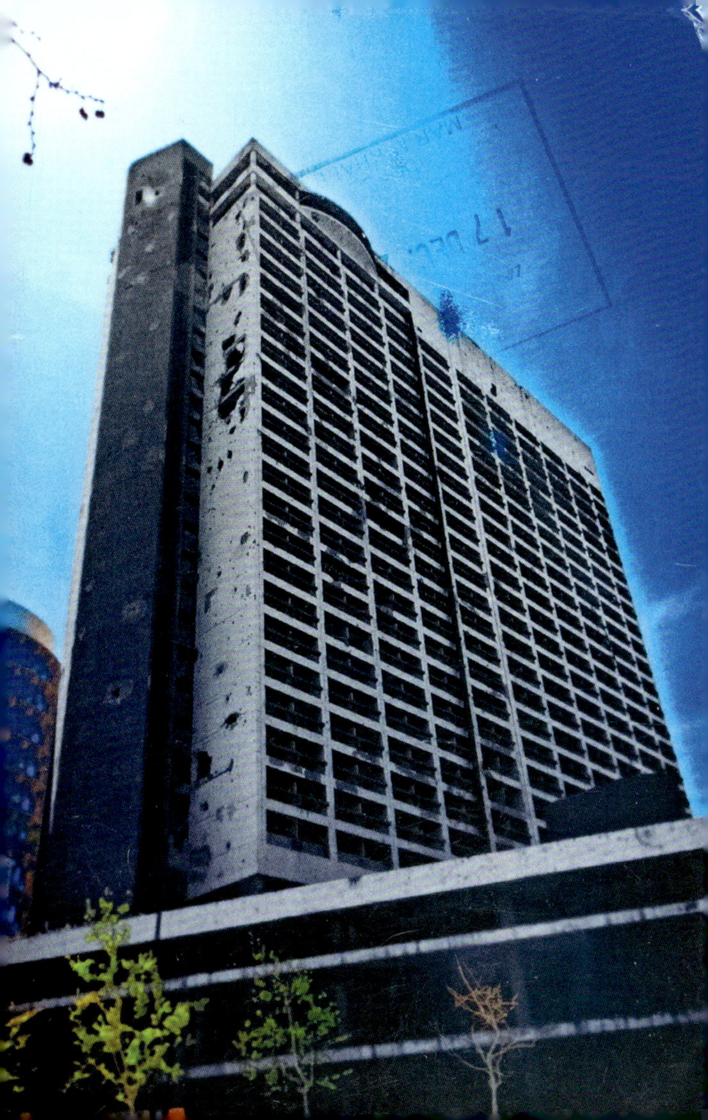

ON MORE THAN FIVE MINUTES."

"NO..." LANYA GIGGLED AGAINST HIS NECK.

"SHE BOUGHT ME A BUS TICKET AND A PAIR OF JEANS AND A NEW SHIRT."

HER GIGGLING TH...

Inconnu à l'adresse indiquée Unknown at this address	☐
غير معروف بالعنوان Déménagé sans laisser d'adresse Moved without leaving an address	☐
عنوان غير صالح للتوزيع Adresse insuffisante pour la Livraison Insufficient address for delivery	☒
يطلق الاسم على عدة أشخاص ...plusieurs personnes ...names	☐
Refusé /Refused	☐
...t pas ... ...present	☐
Personne ... à l'adresse No one ava... at the address	☐
Décédé ...ceased / متوفى	☐
مكتب بريد ما: مخايل	

OUT TO BE ONE OR TWO PEOPLE WHO CAME UP TO MY PARTY IN NOVA SCOTIA WHO WERE

UNFINISHED STATE // 14D.203

Schützt die Natur www.wwf.de WWF

Deutschland 75 50 Jahre Fehmarnsundbrücke

FROM: WILLIAM DHALGREN
ARCHIVE BOOKS
DIEFFENBACHSTRAẞE 31
10967 BERLIN, GERMANY

TO:

SEAFRONT HOLIDAY INN

ACROSS FROM THE PHOENICIA HOTEL
FAKHREDDINE

MINAT AL HOSN, BEIRUT

LEBANON

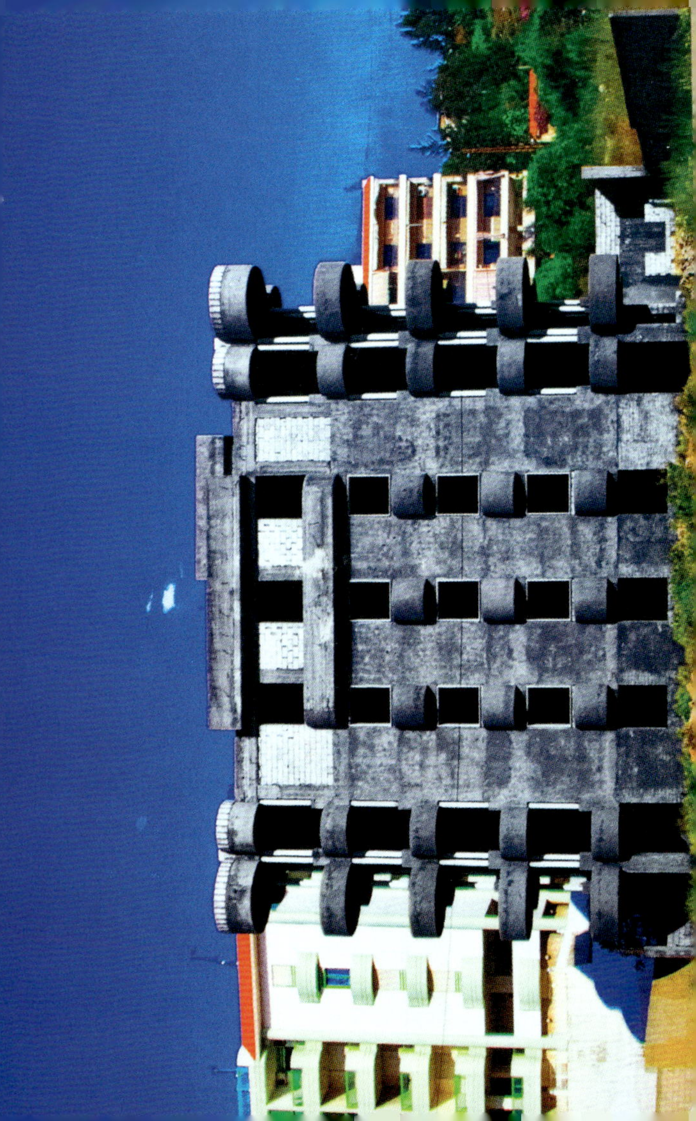

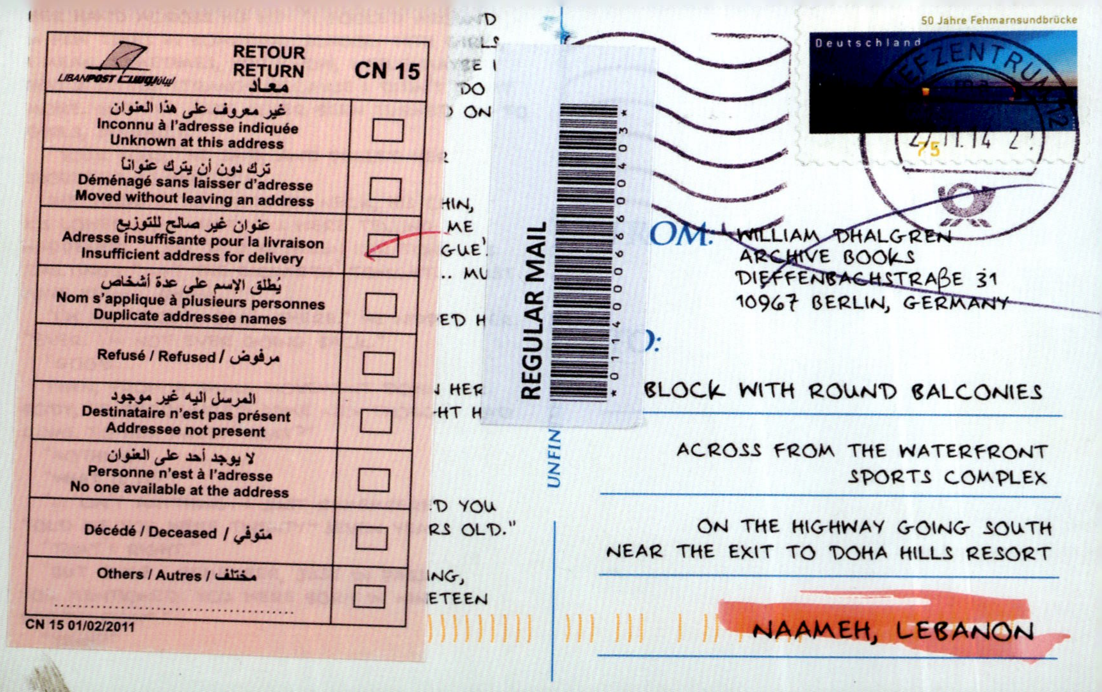

LIBANPOST ليبان بوست

RETOUR
RETURN
معاد

CN 15

غير معروف على هذا العنوان Inconnu à l'adresse indiquée Unknown at this address	☐
ترك دون أن يترك عنواناً Déménagé sans laisser d'adresse Moved without leaving an address	☐
عنوان غير صالح للتوزيع Adresse insuffisante pour la livraison Insufficient address for delivery	☑
يُطلق الإسم على عدة أشخاص Nom s'applique à plusieurs personnes Duplicate addressee names	☐
Refusé / Refused / مرفوض	☐
المرسل اليه غير موجود Destinataire n'est pas présent Addressee not present	☐
لا يوجد أحد على العنوان Personne n'est à l'adresse No one available at the address	☐
Décédé / Deceased / متوفي	☐
Others / Autres / مختلف	☐

CN 15 01/02/2011

REGULAR MAIL

0114000066600403

50 Jahre Fehmarnsundbrücke

Deutschland 75

FROM: WILLIAM DHALGREN
ARCHIVE BOOKS
DIEFFENBACHSTRAßE 31
10967 BERLIN, GERMANY

TO: BLOCK WITH ROUND BALCONIES

ACROSS FROM THE WATERFRONT
SPORTS COMPLEX

ON THE HIGHWAY GOING SOUTH
NEAR THE EXIT TO DOHA HILLS RESORT

NAAMEH, LEBANON

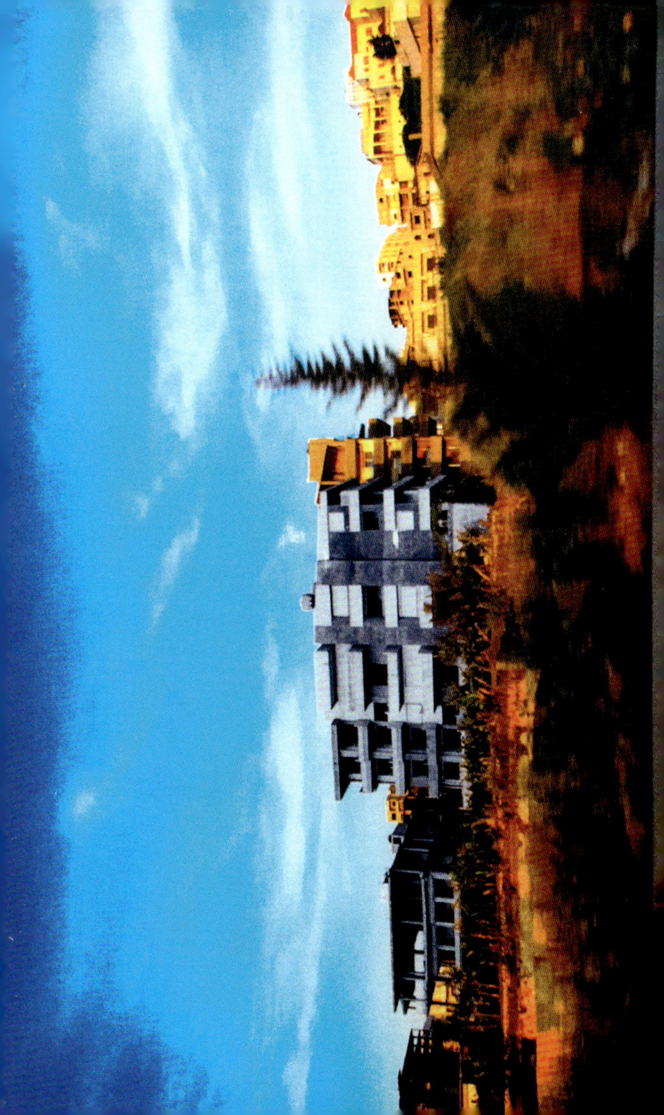

"WELL, THAT'S IMPOSSIBLE... HEY, WHAT'S THE MA... GOING ALL GOOSEFLESH."

LIBANPOST ليبان بوست

RETOUR
RETURN
معاد

CN 15

غير معروف على هذا العنوان Inconnu à l'adresse indiquée Unknown at this address	☐
ترك دون أن يترك عنواناً Déménagé sans laisser d'adresse Moved without leaving an address	☐
عنوان غير صالح للتوزيع Adresse insuffisante pour la livraison Insufficient address for delivery	☑
يُطلق الإسم على عدة أشخاص Nom s'applique à plusieurs personnes Duplicate addressee names	☐
Refusé / Refused / مرفوض	☐
المرسل اليه غير موجود Destinataire n'est pas présent Addressee not present	☐
لا يوجد أحد على العنوان Personne n'est à l'adresse No one available at the address	☐
Décédé / Deceased / متوفي	☐
Others / Autres / مختلف	☐

CN 15 01/02/2011

REGULAR MAIL

011400066600441

50 Jahre Fehmarnsundbrücke

Deutschland 75

...M: WILLIAM DHALGREN
ARCHIVE BOOKS
DIEFFENBACHSTRAẞE 31
10967 BERLIN, GERMANY

UNFINISHED HOUSES

WITH BANANA TREES

ALONG THE COASTAL HIGHWAY

NAAMEH, LEBANON

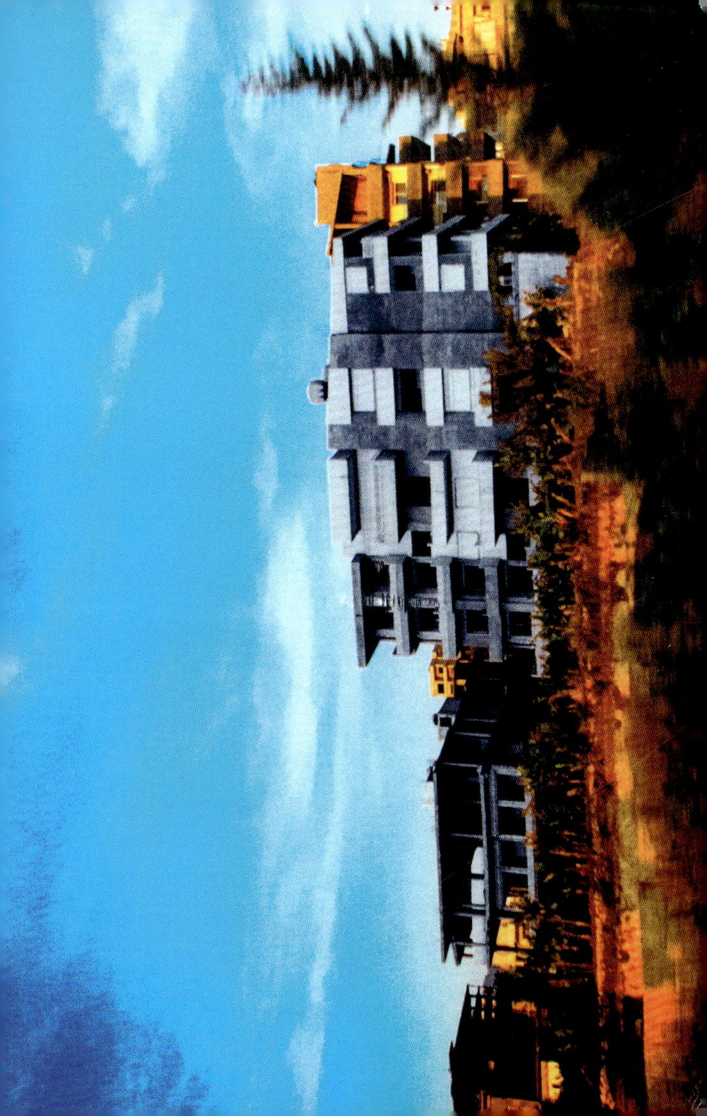

TERROR IS EXPERIENCED AS TERROR AND RAGE

LIBANPOST ليبان بوست	RETOUR RETURN معـاد	CN 15
غير معروف على هذا العنوان Inconnu à l'adresse indiquée Unknown at this address		☐
ترك دون أن يترك عنواناً Déménagé sans laisser d'adresse Moved without leaving an address		☐
عنوان غير صالح للتوزيع Adresse insuffisante pour la livraison Insufficient address for delivery		☑
يُطلق الإسم على عدة أشخاص Nom s'applique à plusieurs personnes Duplicate addressee names		☐
Refusé / Refused / مرفوض		☐
المرسل اليه غير موجود Destinataire n'est pas présent Addressee not present		☐
لا يوجد أحد على العنوان Personne n'est à l'adresse No one available at the address		☐
Décédé / Deceased / متوفي		☐
Others / Autres / مختلف		☐

CN 15 01/02/2011

REGULAR MAIL

0114000684002 10

Deutschland 75

50 Jahre Fehmarnsundbrücke

WILLIAM DHALGREN
ARCHIVE BOOKS
DIEFFENBACHSTRAßE 31
10967 BERLIN, GERMANY

UNFINISHED HOUSES

WITH BANANA TREES

ALONG THE COASTAL HIGHWAY

NAAMEH, LEBANON

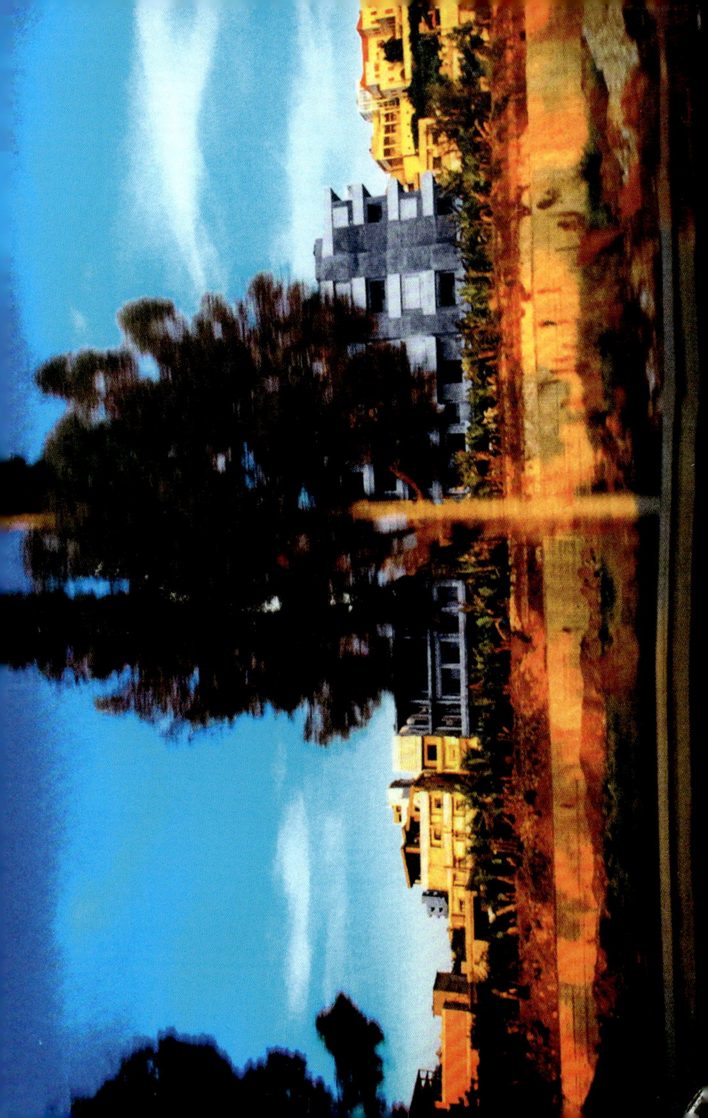

...ACE.

...HINK

...E MOVED
...ED IT
...CIOUS.
...BLACK)
...ORNING
...NE BOM
...ONE.

...GAINS
...D OF

...F THE
...KEPT

...END OF

...MARE H

...WERE
...ALL
...THE

LIBANPOST ليبان بوست

RETOUR RETURN معـاد	CN 15
غير معروف على هذا العنوان Inconnu à l'adresse indiquée Unknown at this address	☐
ترك دون أن يترك عنواناً Déménagé sans laisser d'adresse Moved without leaving an address	☐
عنوان غير صالح للتوزيع Adresse insuffisante pour la livraison Insufficient address for delivery	☑
يُطلق الإسم على عدة أشخاص Nom s'applique à plusieurs personnes Duplicate addressee names	☐
Refusé / Refused / مرفوض	☐
المرسل اليه غير موجود Destinataire n'est pas présent Addressee not present	☐
لا يوجد أحد على العنوان Personne n'est à l'adresse No one available at the address	☐
Décédé / Deceased / متوفي	☐
Others / Autres / مختلف	☐

CN 15 01/02/2011

REGULAR MAIL

0114000666003 99

50 Jahre Fehmarnsundbrücke
Deutschland
75

...OM. WILLIAM DHALGREN
ARCHIVE BOOKS
DIEFFENBACHSTRAßE 31
10967 BERLIN, GERMANY

UNFINISHED HOUSES

WITH BANANA TREES

ALONG THE COASTAL HIGHWAY

NAAMEH, LEBANON

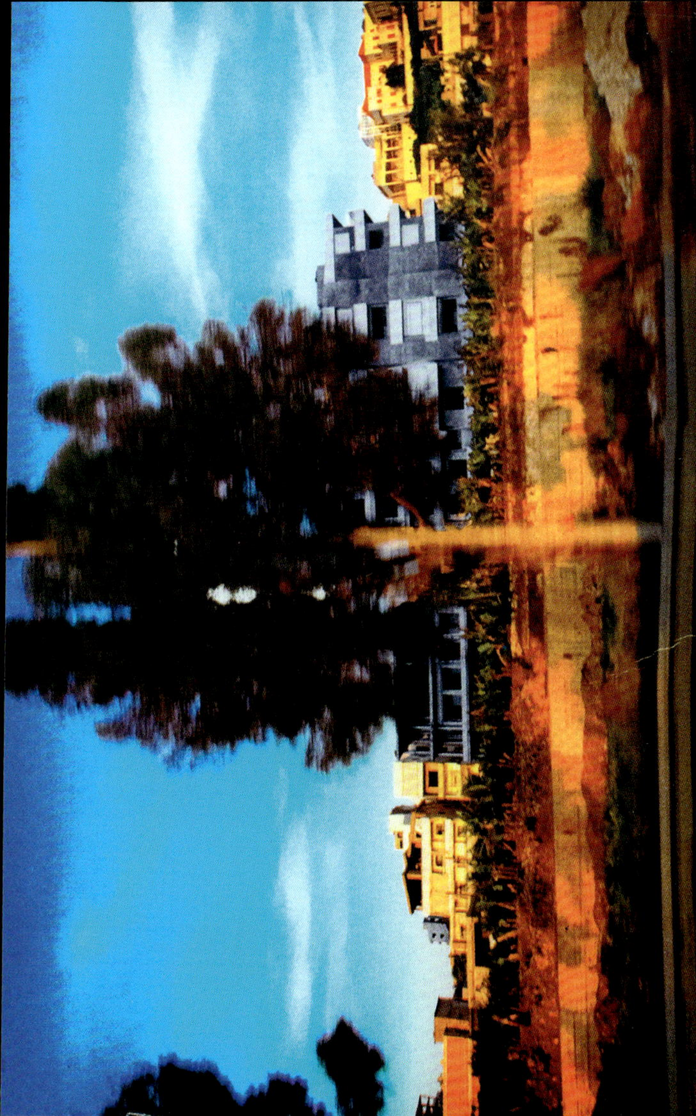

LIBANPOST ليبان بوست	RETOUR RETURN معاد	CN 15
غير معروف على هذا العنوان Inconnu à l'adresse indiquée Unknown at this address		☐
ترك دون أن يترك عنواناً Déménagé sans laisser d'adresse Moved without leaving an address		☐
عنوان غير صالح للتوزيع Adresse insuffisante pour la livraison Insufficient address for delivery		☑
يُطلق الإسم على عدة أشخاص Nom s'applique à plusieurs personnes Duplicate addressee names		☐
Refusé / Refused / مرفوض		☐
المرسل اليه غير موجود Destinataire n'est pas présent Addressee not present		☐
لا يوجد أحد على العنوان Personne n'est à l'adresse No one available at the address		☐
Décédé / Deceased / متوفي		☐
Others / Autres / مختلف		☐

CN 15 01/02/2011

...ED BY

EL...

...LEC...

CA...

HI...

...D, AND

...; HER

...S AND

...THER

HUH?

REGULAR MAIL

01140006660042 5

50 Jahre Fehmarnsundbrücke

Deutschland

75

...EFZENTRUM...

27.11.14 2...

FROM: WILLIAM DHALGREN
ARCHIVE BOOKS
DIEFFENBACHSTRAßE 31
10967 BERLIN, GERMANY

TO: UNFINISHED HOUSES
WITH BANANA TREES
ALONG THE COASTAL HIGHWAY
NAAMEH, LEBANON

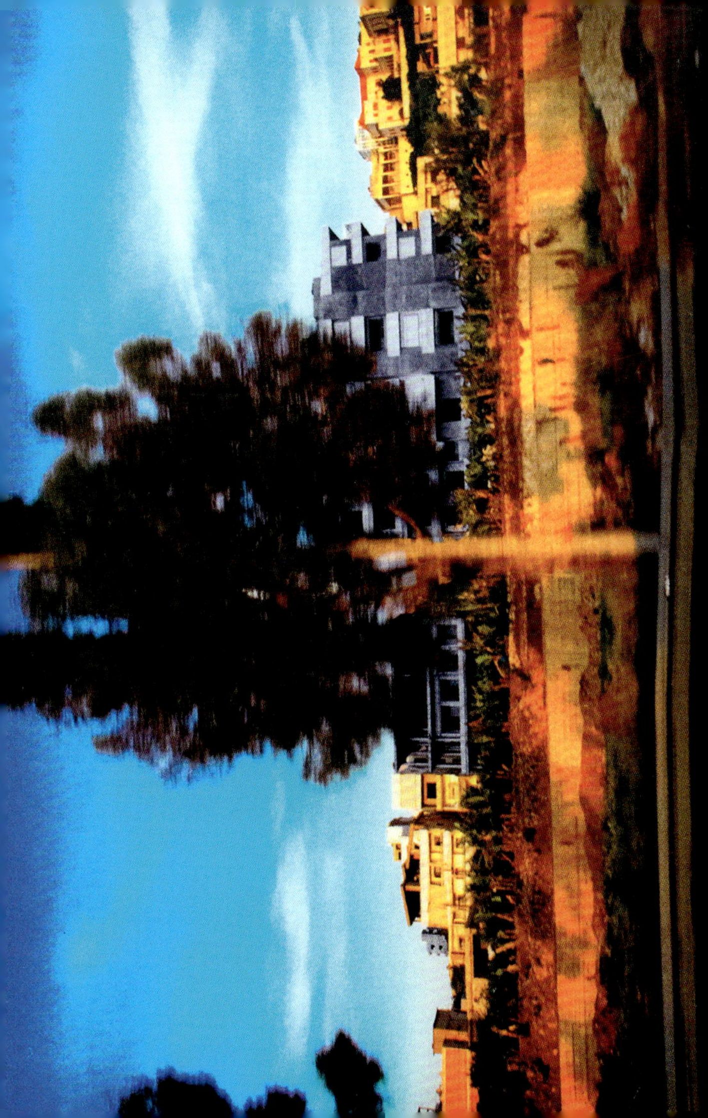

LIBANPOST

RETOUR
RETURN
معاد

CN 15

غير معروف على هذا العنوان Inconnu à l'adresse indiquée Unknown at this address	☐
ترك دون أن يترك عنواناً Déménagé sans laisser d'adresse Moved without leaving an address	☐
عنوان غير صالح للتوزيع Adresse insuffisante pour la livraison Insufficient address for delivery	☑
يُطلق الإسم على عدة أشخاص Nom s'applique à plusieurs personnes Duplicate addressee names	☐
Refusé / Refused / مرفوض	☐
المرسل اليه غير موجود Destinataire n'est pas présent Addressee not present	☐
لا يوجد أحد على العنوان Personne n'est à l'adresse No one available at the address	☐
Décédé / Deceased / متوفي	☐
Others / Autres / مختلف	☐

CN 15 01/02/2011

THAT
MOVED
VED
DON'T
ASKED
HEAD
BRAIDED
OF
ED IT
FROM
LINKS
ONE FIST
NST HIS
KLED,
ALLER
FOR
LED
ANYA'S
HER.
SHE

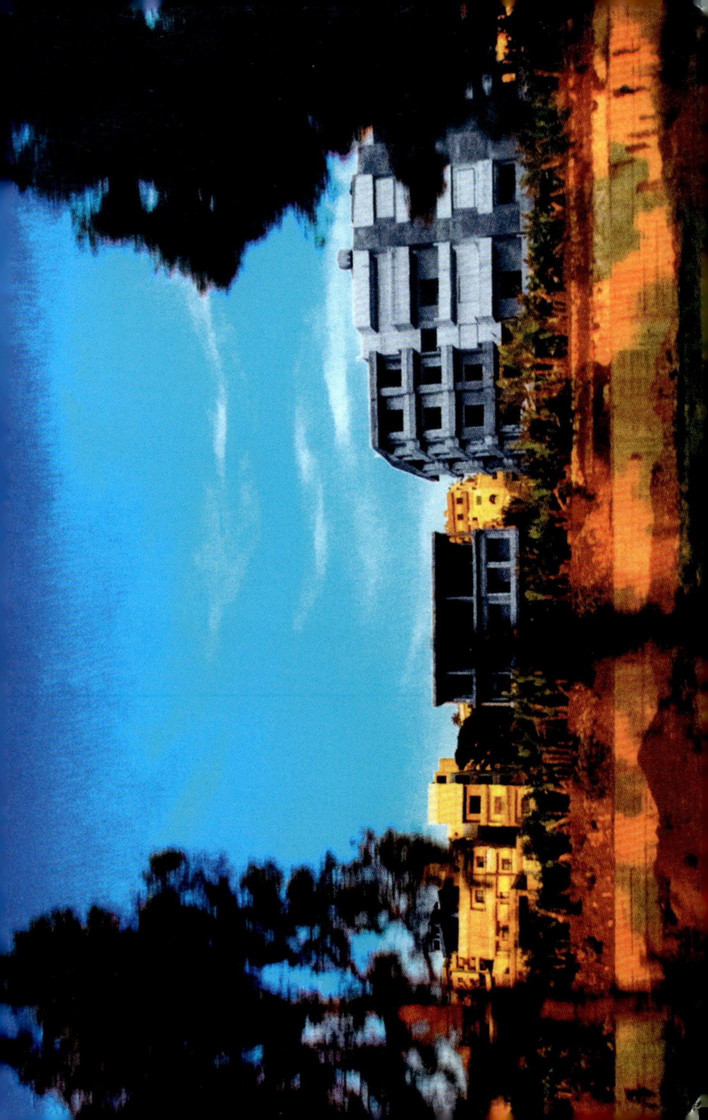

TOOK HER HAND FROM KIDD'S KNEE, PUT BOTH
FISTS AROUND THE CHAIN, UP NEAR HER NECK,
AN ... ONE
PU ... KE
IT ... ON'T
... ARE
... ND
... SE
... ND
... DO
... ITH US,
... D.
... NG HE
... M HIS
... WANT IT
... DON'T
... AUGH.
... DDY."
... N THE
... RS?"
... FTED
... OM THE

LIBANPOST لبنانبوست	RETOUR RETURN معاد	CN 15
غير معروف على هذا العنوان Inconnu à l'adresse indiquée Unknown at this address		☐
ترك دون أن يترك عنواناً Déménagé sans laisser d'adresse Moved without leaving an address		☐
عنوان غير صالح للتوزيع Adresse insuffisante pour la livraison Insufficient address for delivery		☐
يُطلق الإسم على عدة أشخاص Nom s'applique à plusieurs personnes Duplicate addressee names		☐
Refusé / Refused / مرفوض		☐
المرسل اليه غير موجود Destinataire n'est pas présent Addressee not present		☐
لا يوجد أحد على العنوان Personne n'est à l'adresse No one available at the address		☐
Décédé / Deceased / متوفي		☐
Others / Autres / مختلف		☐

CN 15 01/02/2011

Schützt die Natur
WWF
www.wwf.de
Schützt die Natur

/ 14D.212

REGULAR MAIL

0114000660042 9

50 Jahre Fehmarnsundbrücke
Deutschland
75

FROM: WILLIAM DHALGREN
ARCHIVE BOOKS
DIEFFENBACHSTRAẞE 31
10967 BERLIN, GERMANY

UNFINISHED HOUSES

WITH BANANA TREES

ALONG THE COASTAL HIGHWAY

NAAMEH, LEBANON

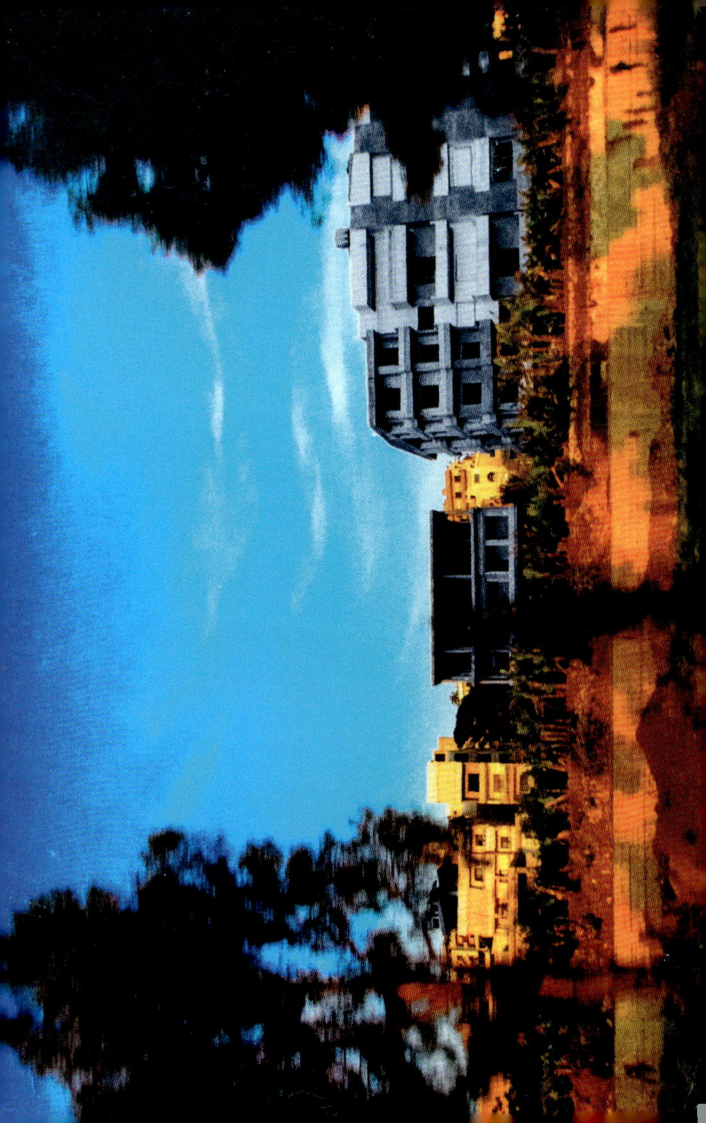

THEN THE SCORPION SWIVELED, BOOT TOES

RETOUR RETURN معاد	CN 15
غير معروف على هذا العنوان Inconnu à l'adresse indiquée Unknown at this address	☐
ترك دون أن يترك عنواناً Déménagé sans laisser d'adresse Moved without leaving an address	☐
عنوان غير صالح للتوزيع Adresse insuffisante pour la livraison Insufficient address for delivery	☑
يُطلق الإسم على عدة أشخاص Nom s'applique à plusieurs personnes Duplicate addressee names	☐
Refusé / Refused / مرفوض	☐
المرسل اليه غير موجود Destinataire n'est pas présent Addressee not present	☐
لا يوجد أحد على العنوان Personne n'est à l'adresse No one available at the address	☐
Décédé / Deceased / متوفي	☐
Others / Autres / مختلف	☐

CN 15 01/02/2011

OVER
CED
OME
NAS
PPLE.
EFT
TMARE
WITH
NTLY.
KIDD
AN?"
GO.
LAND
CK AND
ERS
PIONS
FEET
E OR
O LAUGH
FAST
NOUSLY,
A
NS

Schützt die Natur

UNFINISHED STATE // 14D 213

REGULAR MAIL

0114000068400205

Deutschland 75 50 Jahre Fehmarnsundbrücke

WILLIAM DHALGREN
ARCHIVE BOOKS
DIEFFENBACHSTRAßE 31
10967 BERLIN, GERMANY

UNFINISHED HOUSES

WITH BANANA TREES

ALONG THE COASTAL HIGHWAY

NAAMEH, LEBANON

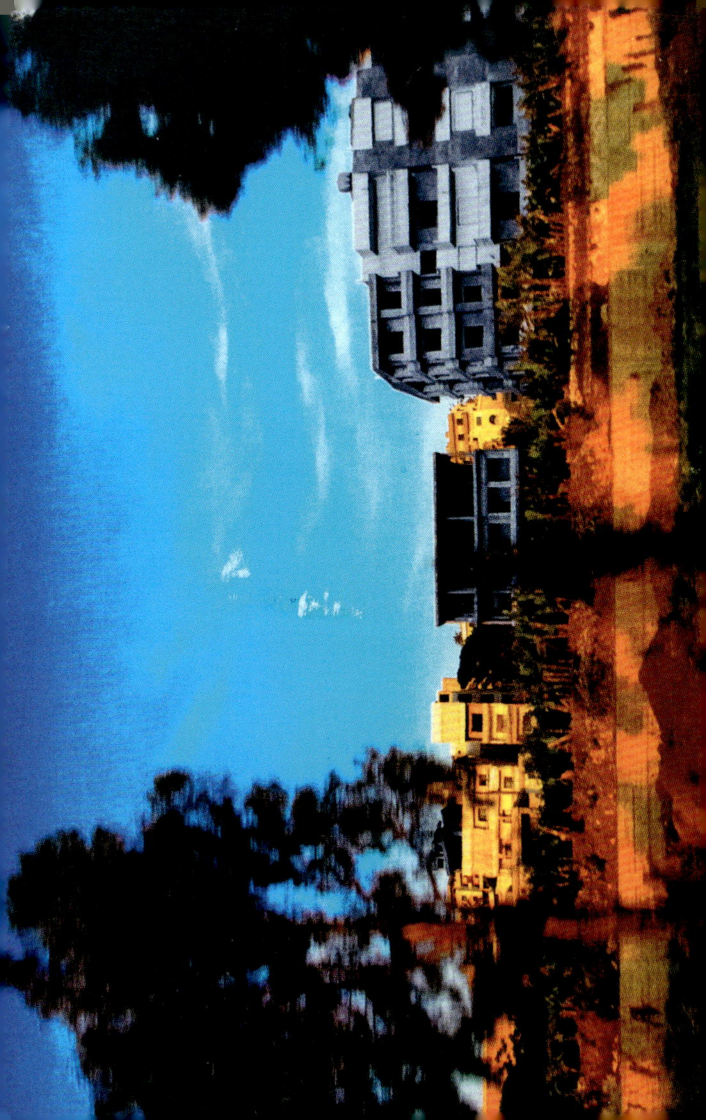

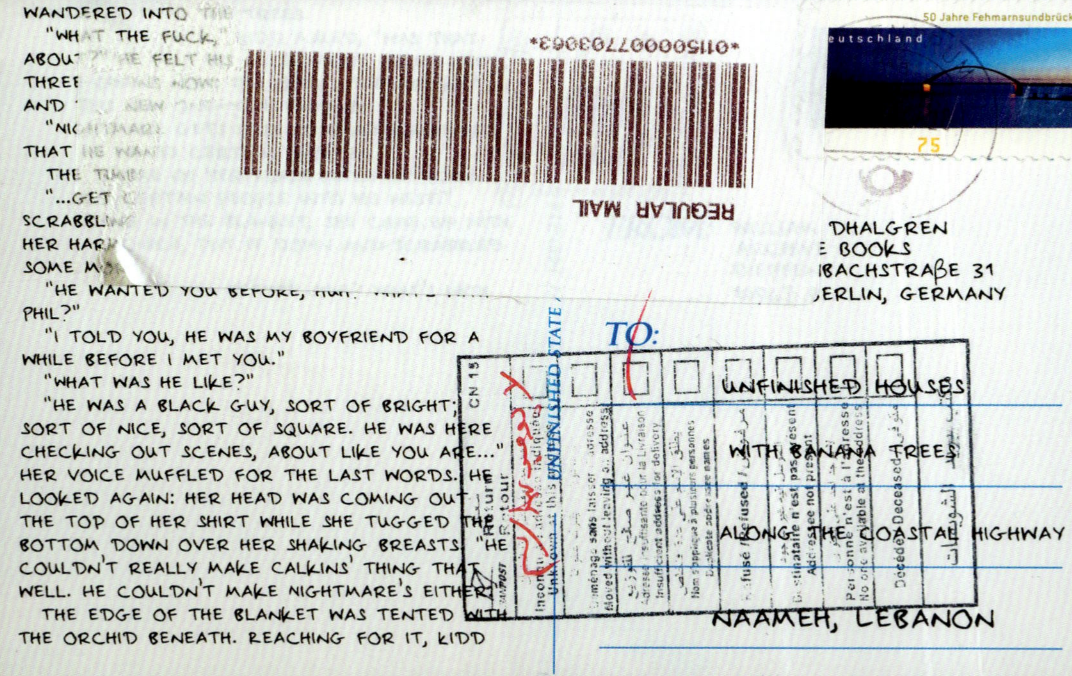

WANDERED INTO
"WHAT THE FUCK,"
ABOU
THREE
AND
"NIG
THAT
THE
"...GET
SCRABBL
HER HAR
SOME M
"HE WANTED YOU BEFORE,
PHIL?"
"I TOLD YOU, HE WAS MY BOYFRIEND FOR A WHILE BEFORE I MET YOU."
"WHAT WAS HE LIKE?"
"HE WAS A BLACK GUY, SORT OF BRIGHT; SORT OF NICE, SORT OF SQUARE. HE WAS HERE CHECKING OUT SCENES, ABOUT LIKE YOU ARE..." HER VOICE MUFFLED FOR THE LAST WORDS. HE LOOKED AGAIN: HER HEAD WAS COMING OUT THE TOP OF HER SHIRT WHILE SHE TUGGED THE BOTTOM DOWN OVER HER SHAKING BREASTS. "HE COULDN'T REALLY MAKE CALKINS' THING THAT WELL. HE COULDN'T MAKE NIGHTMARE'S EITHER."
THE EDGE OF THE BLANKET WAS TENTED WITH THE ORCHID BENEATH. REACHING FOR IT, KIDD
0115000770303063
REGULAR MAIL
50 Jahre Fehmarnsundbrücke
Deutschland
75
DHALGREN
BOOKS
BACHSTRAßE 31
ERLIN, GERMANY
TO:
UNFINISHED STATE
CN 15
Retour
Unknown at this address
Déménagé sans laisser d'adresse
Moved without leaving an address
Adresse insuffisante pour la Livraison
Insufficient address for delivery
Nom s'applique à plusieurs personnes
Duplicate addressee names
Refusé / Refused
Destinataire n'est pas présent
Addressee not present
Personne n'est à l'adresse
No one available at the address
Décédé / Deceased
UNFINISHED HOUSES
WITH BANANA TREES
ALONG THE COASTAL HIGHWAY
NAAMEH, LEBANON

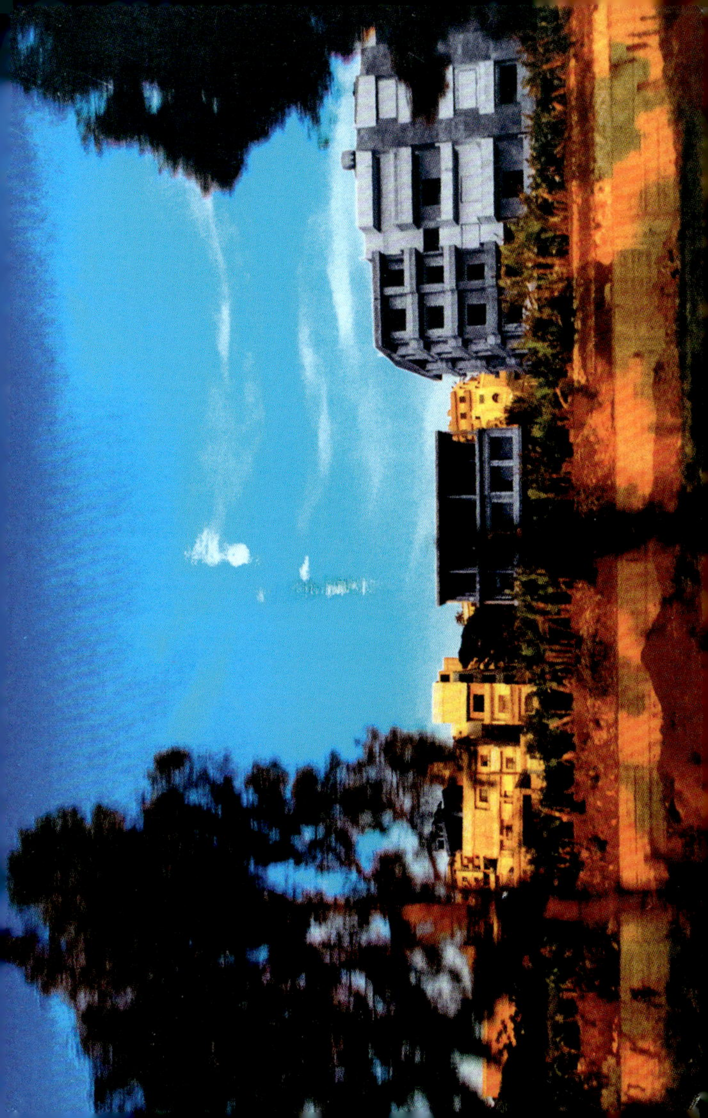

NOTICED NEARLY AN ACRE OF CHARRED GRASS
A... THE MEADOW. SMOKE WISPED ALONG THE
E... ...WNED.

LIBANPOST لبنانبوست	RETOUR RETURN معاد	CN 15
غير معروف على هذا العنوان Inconnu à l'adresse indiquée Unknown at this address		☐
ترك دون أن يترك عنواناً Déménagé sans laisser d'adresse Moved without leaving an address		☐
عنوان غير صالح للتوزيع Adresse insuffisante pour la livraison Insufficient address for delivery		☑
يُطلق الإسم على عدة أشخاص Nom s'applique à plusieurs personnes Duplicate addressee names		☐
Refusé / Refused / مرفوض		☐
المرسل اليه غير موجود Destinataire n'est pas présent Addressee not present		☐
لا يوجد أحد على العنوان Personne n'est à l'adresse No one available at the address		☐
Décédé / Deceased / متوفي		☐
Others / Autres / مختلف		☐

CN 15 01/02/2011

...UNE,
...E YOU
...THE
...NNY.
...I'M
...E."
...G
...D HIS
...ED.
...O
...NG
...K,
...SOME
...S AND
...ROSSED
...E GREW

Schützt die Natur
WWF
www.wwf.de

Deutschland
50 Jahre Fehmarnsundbrücke
75

14D.215

REGULAR MAIL

011400068400217

FROM: WILLIAM DHALGREN
ARCHIVE BOOKS
DIEFFENBACHSTRAßE 31
10967 BERLIN, GERMANY

UNFINISHED HOUSES

WITH BANANA TREES

ALONG THE COASTAL HIGHWAY

NAAMEH, LEBANON

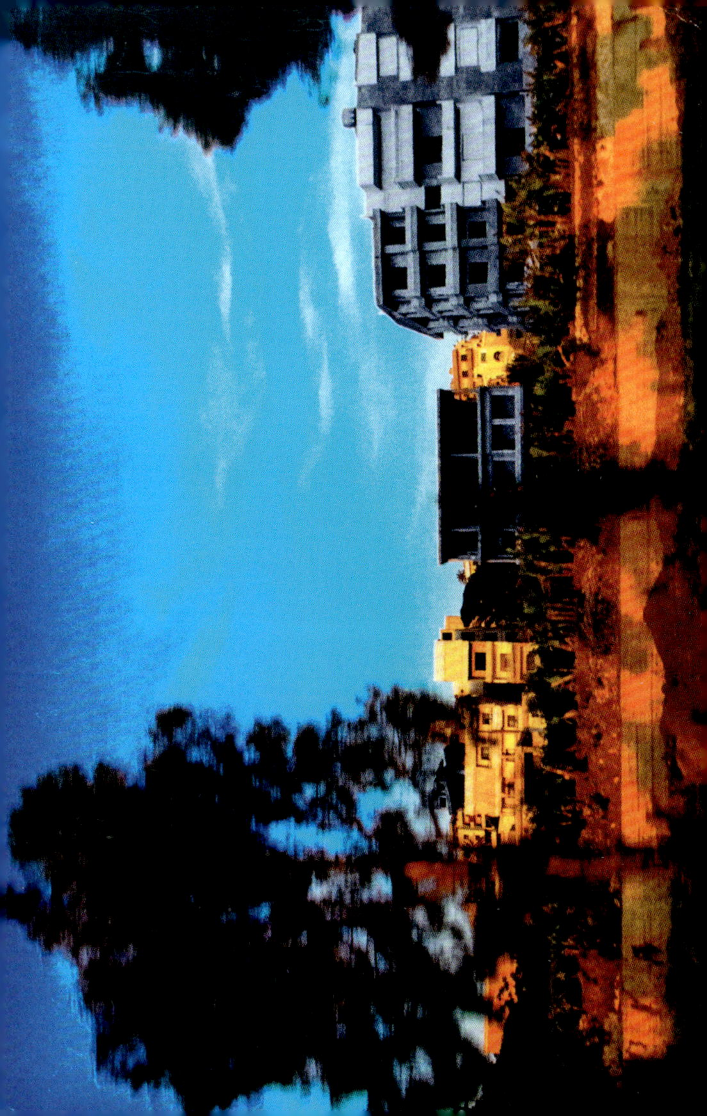

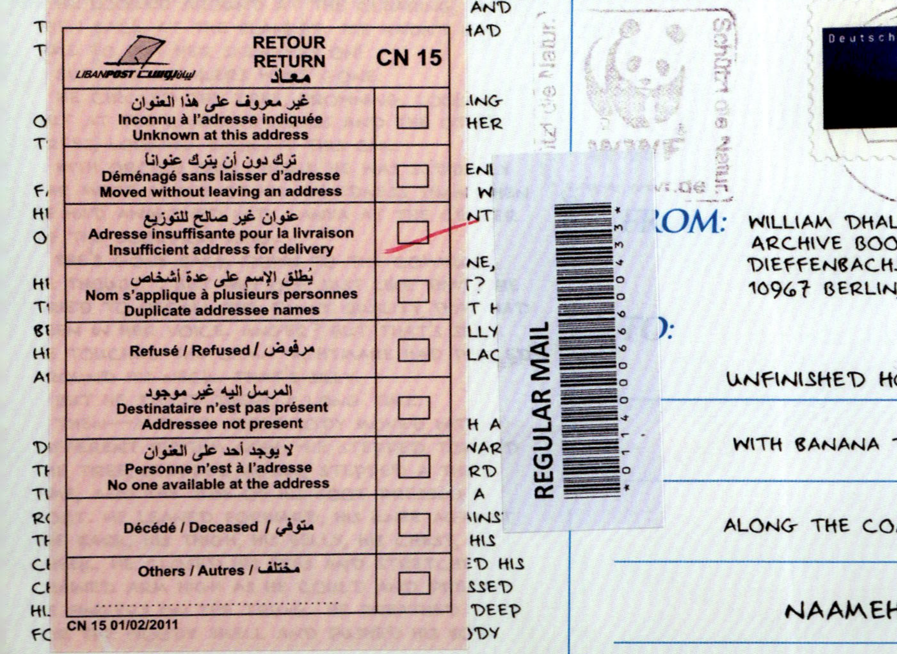

LIBANPOST
RETOUR
RETURN
معاد
CN 15
غير معروف على هذا العنوان
Inconnu à l'adresse indiquée
Unknown at this address
ترك دون أن يترك عنواناً
Déménagé sans laisser d'adresse
Moved without leaving an address
عنوان غير صالح للتوزيع
Adresse insuffisante pour la livraison
Insufficient address for delivery
يُطلق الإسم على عدة أشخاص
Nom s'applique à plusieurs personnes
Duplicate addressee names
Refusé / Refused / مرفوض
المرسل اليه غير موجود
Destinataire n'est pas présent
Addressee not present
لا يوجد أحد على العنوان
Personne n'est à l'adresse
No one available at the address
Décédé / Deceased / متوفي
Others / Autres / مختلف
CN 15 01/02/2011
REGULAR MAIL
01140006660043 3
50 Jahre Fehmarnsundbrücke
Deutschland
75
WILLIAM DHALGREN
ARCHIVE BOOKS
DIEFFENBACHSTRAßE 31
10967 BERLIN, GERMANY
UNFINISHED HOUSES
WITH BANANA TREES
ALONG THE COASTAL HIGHWAY
NAAMEH, LEBANON

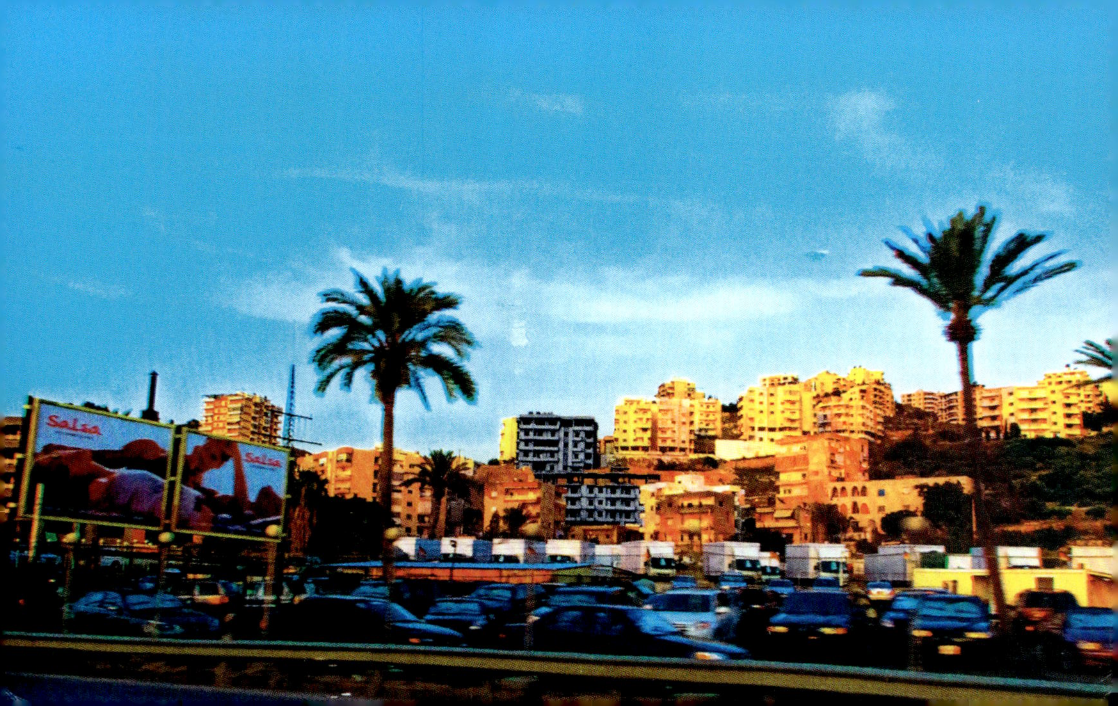
Salsa
Salsa

LIBANPOST لبنان بوست	RETOUR RETURN معاد	CN 15
غير معروف على هذا العنوان Inconnu à l'adresse indiquée Unknown at this address		☐
ترك دون أن يترك عنوانًا Déménagé sans laisser d'adresse Moved without leaving an address		☐
عنوان غير صالح للتوزيع Adresse insuffisante pour la livraison Insufficient address for delivery		☐
يُطلق الإسم على عدة أشخاص Nom s'applique à plusieurs personnes Duplicate addressee names		☐
Refusé / Refused / مرفوض		☐
المرسل اليه غير موجود Destinataire n'est pas présent Addressee not present		☐
لا يوجد أحد على العنوان Personne n'est à l'adresse No one available at the address		☐
Décédé / Deceased / متوفي		☐
Others / Autres / مختلف		☐

CN 15 01/02/2011

THEN SAT TO STRAP ON (WONDERING ... HE

Schützt die Natur

WWF

www.wwf.de

50 Jahre Fehmarnsundbrücke

Deutschland

75

REGULAR MAIL

0114000066600396

...OM: WILLIAM DHALGREN
ARCHIVE BOOKS
DIEFFENBACHSTRAẞE 31
10967 BERLIN, GERMANY

...:

INCOMPLETE APARTMENTS

BEHIND THE CAR SALES LOT

ALONG THE COASTAL HIGHWAY

DAMOUR, LEBANON

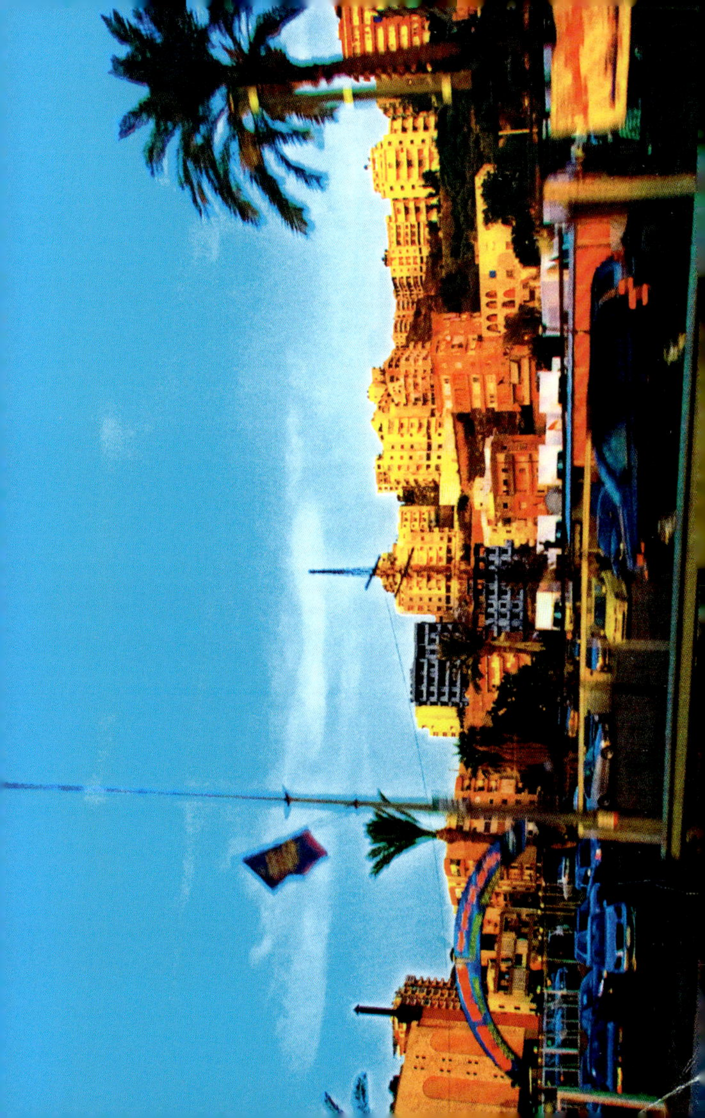

STILL BOTHERED) HIS ONE SANDAL.

LIBANPOST ليبانبوست	RETOUR RETURN معاد	CN 15
غير معروف على هذا العنوان Inconnu à l'adresse indiquée Unknown at this address		☐
ترك دون أن يترك عنواناً Déménagé sans laisser d'adresse Moved without leaving an address		☐
عنوان غير صالح للتوزيع Adresse insuffisante pour la livraison Insufficient address for delivery		☑
يُطلق الإسم على عدة أشخاص Nom s'applique à plusieurs personnes Duplicate addressee names		☐
Refusé / Refused / مرفوض		☐
المرسل اليه غير موجود Destinataire n'est pas présent Addressee not present		☐
لا يوجد أحد على العنوان Personne n'est à l'adresse No one available at the address		☐
Décédé / Deceased / متوفي		☐
Others / Autres / مختلف		☐

CN 15 01/02/2011

SEE
D THE
HE
. IT
OF
KED
EN SO
REW)
THE
AWLED
XT SINK
TS, AND
HED
IDDLE
OSE
UND
E
ANDS,

UNFINISHED

50 Jahre Fehmarnsundbrücke

Deutschland

M: WILLIAM DHALGREN
ARCHIVE BOOKS
DIEFFENBACHSTRAßE 31
10967 BERLIN, GERMANY

INCOMPLETE APARTMENTS

BEHIND THE CAR SALES LOT

ALONG THE COASTAL HIGHWAY

DAMOUR, LEBANON

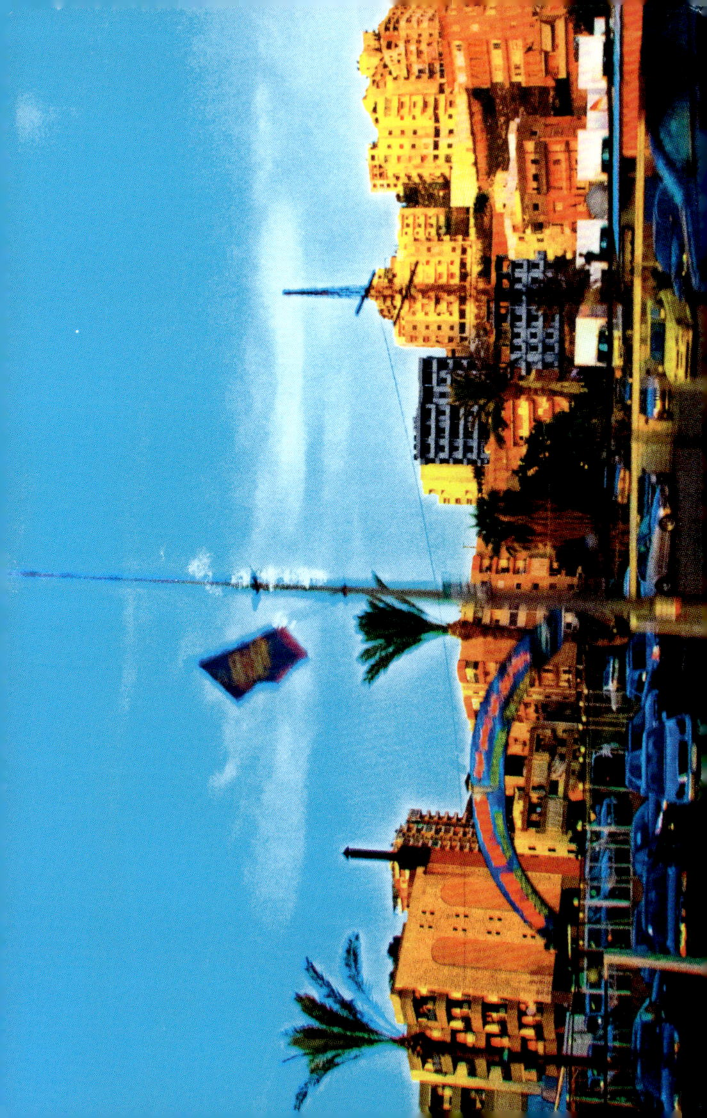

FILL AGAIN. BARK CRUMBS FLECKED HIM, NECK

RETOUR
RETURN
معاد

LIBANPOST ليبان بوست

CN 15

غير معروف على هذا العنوان Inconnu à l'adresse indiquée Unknown at this address	☐
ترك دون أن يترك عنواناً Déménagé sans laisser d'adresse Moved without leaving an address	☐
عنوان غير صالح للتوزيع Adresse insuffisante pour la livraison Insufficient address for delivery	☑
يُطلق الإسم على عدة أشخاص Nom s'applique à plusieurs personnes Duplicate addressee names	☐
Refusé / Refused / مرفوض	☐
المرسل اليه غير موجود Destinataire n'est pas présent Addressee not present	☐
لا يوجد أحد على العنوان Personne n'est à l'adresse No one available at the address	☐
Décédé / Deceased / متوفي	☐
Others / Autres / مختلف	☐

CN 15 01/02/2011

RE IN MENTS. ACK NG, HAT ET AND FAN THE NEADED WATER. CED R, IS SY. MUCH . THE D THE ONK- ED. ALL R-

UNFINISHED STATE // 14D 219

50 Jahre Fehmarnsundbrücke
Deutschland
75

WILLIAM DHALGREN
ARCHIVE BOOKS
DIEFFENBACHSTRAßE 31
10967 BERLIN, GERMANY

INCOMPLETE APARTMENTS

BEHIND THE CAR SALES LOT

ALONG THE COASTAL HIGHWAY

DAMOUR, LEBANON

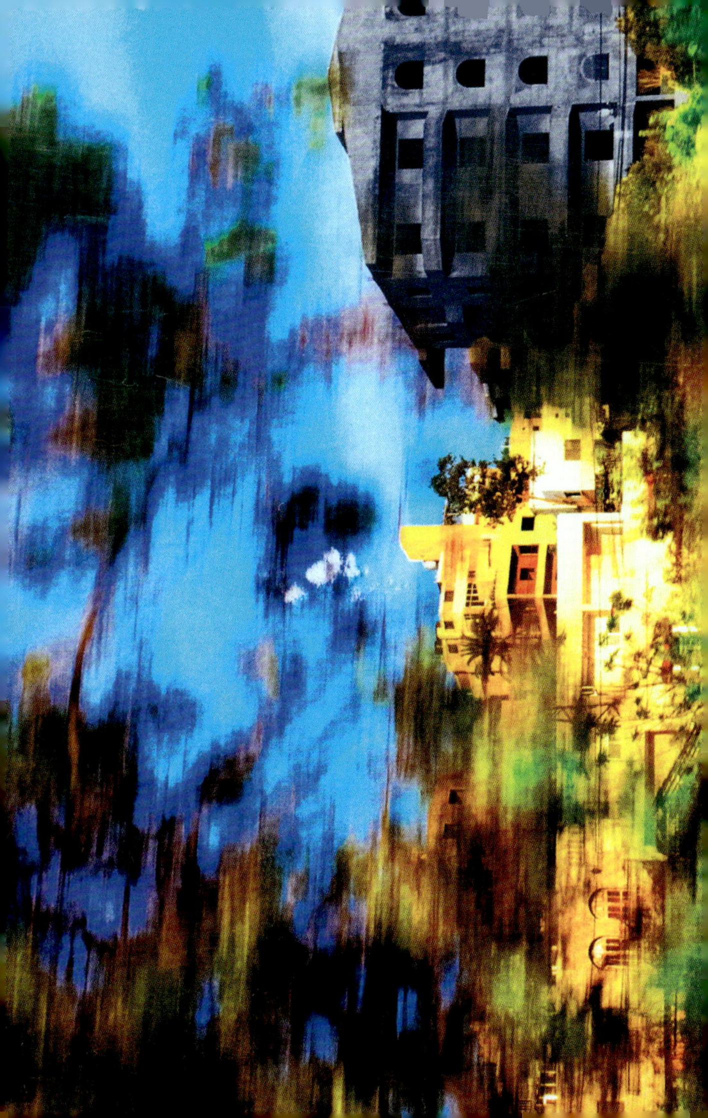

NOW THE STREET SIGN SAID RUBY AND PEARL. THE LADDER AND THE LADY IN GREENS WERE GONE.

HE PONDERED AND COMPARED DIRECTIONS, DISMISSED THE PARK, LOOKED WHERE THE MIST WAS THICKEST (DOWN "PEARL"), AND WALKED. LANYA? REMEMBERED HIS CALLING, AN ECHO IN THE DIM, AN AFTER IMAGE ON THE EAR. HERE? IN THIS CITY? HE SMILED, AND THOUGHT ABOUT HOLDING HER. HE SORTED HIS DUBIOUS RECOLLECTIONS, WONDERING WHERE HE WAS GOING. IT'S ONLY, HE THOUGHT, WHEN WE'RE STRIPPED OF PURPOSE THAT WE KNOW WHO WE ARE.

HIS MISSING NAME WAS A SUDDEN ACHE AND, SUDDENLY, HE WANTED IT, WANTED IT WITH THE SAME URGE THAT HAD MADE HIM FINALLY ACCEPT THE ONE THEY HAD GIVEN. WITHOUT IT HE COULD SEARCH, SURVIVE, MAKE WORD CONVECTIONS IN SOMEBODY ELSE'S NOTEBOOK, COMMIT FANCIFUL MURDER, STRIVE FOR SOMEONE ELSE'S SURVIVAL. WITH IT, JUST WALKING, JUST BEING MIGHT BE EASIER. A NAME, HE THOUGHT, IS WHAT OTHER PEOPLE CALL YOU AND THAT'S EXACTLY WHERE IT'S IMPORTANT AND WHERE IT'S NOT. THE KID? HE THOUGHT: I'M GOING TO BE THIRTY IN A MOUTHFUL OF WINTER AND SO HOW UNIMPORTANT THEN THAT I CAN'T REMEMBER

Return / Retour CN 15

Schützt die Natur

REGULAR MAIL

* 0 1 1 4 0 0 0 6 8 4 0 0 1 8 1 *

50 Jahre Fehmarnsundbrücke

Deutschland 75

WILLIAM DHALGREN
ARCHIVE BOOKS
DIEFFENBACHSTRAßE 31
10967 BERLIN, GERMANY

UNFINISHED

BUILDING WITH LITTLE ARC WINDOWS

BOTTOM OF THE SLOPE

ALONG THE COASTAL HIGHWAY

BAISSARIYE, LEBANON

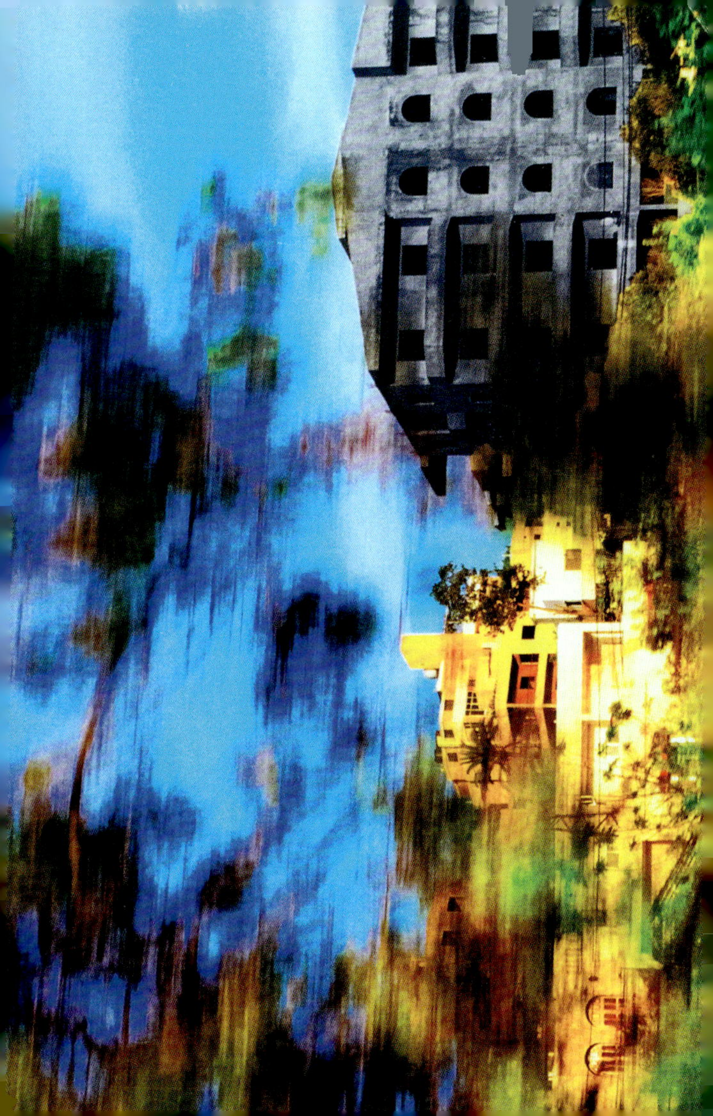

BUS ROCKED FORWARD.

AN OLD MAN SLEPT IN THE BACK SEAT, HAT DOWN, COLLAR UP.

A WOMAN IN THE FRONT SAT WITH HER HANDS CROSSED ON THE TOP OF HER POCKETBOOK. A YOUNGER WOMAN WITH A LARGE NATURAL STARED OUT THE WINDOW. A BOY WITH A SMALLER ONE SAT NERVOUSLY JUST BEHIND THE BACK DOOR, TOEING ONE SNEAKER WITH THE OTHER.

A COUPLE—HE WITH KNEES WIDE, SUNK IN THE SEAT WITH HIS ARMS FOLDED, HIS FACE SET BELLIGERENTLY, SHE WITH LEGS TOGETHER, HER FACE REGISTERING SOMETHING BETWEEN FEAR AND BOREDOM—WERE MAKING A POINT OF NOT LOOKING AT HIM.

SIMULTANEOUSLY HE REALIZED THAT THERE WAS NO SEAT FROM WHICH HE COULD WATCH EVERYBODY, AND THAT HE WAS THE ONLY NON-BLACK ON THE BUS. HE DECIDED TO GIVE UP THE OLD MAN AND TOOK THE NEXT TO THE LAST SEAT.

WHERE AM I—BUT WOULDN'T THINK: GOING. HE LOOKED OVER THE BARS ON THE SEAT BACKS TO THE BLUNT NOSE AND LIPS, THE SHARP CHIN PROFILED BELOW THE BRILLOWY BALL.

HE WATCHED THE BUILDINGS SHE WATCHED GO HEADLONG IN GOALLESS MOTION.

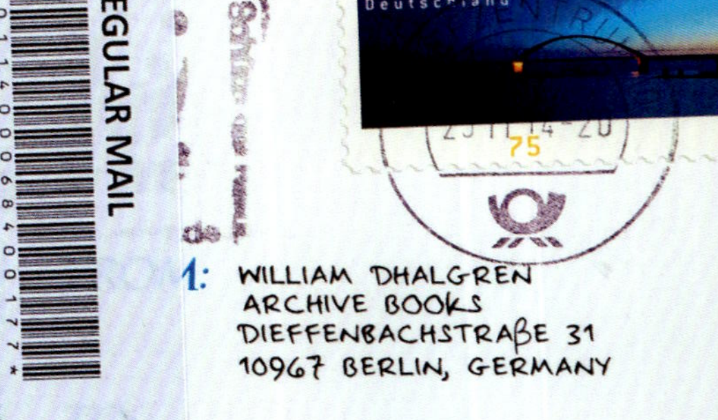

1: WILLIAM DHALGREN
ARCHIVE BOOKS
DIEFFENBACHSTRAßE 31
10967 BERLIN, GERMANY

BUILDING WITH LITTLE ARC WINDOWS

BOTTOM OF THE SLOPE

ALONG THE COASTAL HIGHWAY

BAISSARIYE, LEBANON

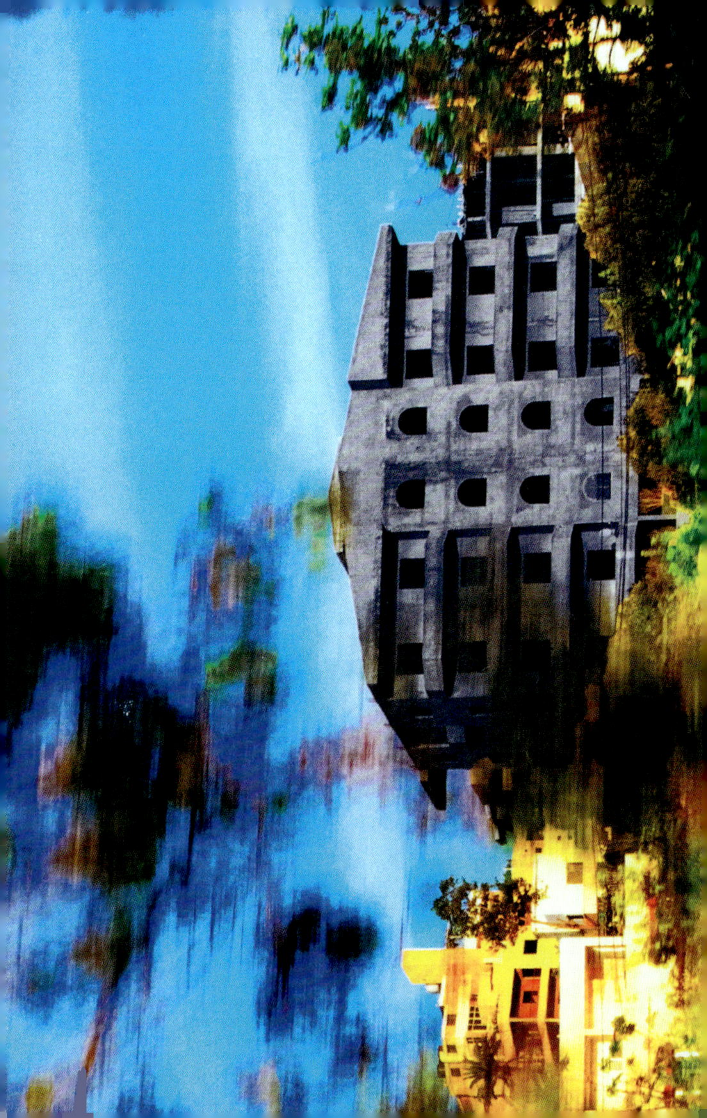

BE SOME AWFUL MISTAKES. IT'LL BE PRINTED ON SLIGHTLY BETTER PAPER THAN THAT. I'D ARGUED FOR A LARGER TYPEFACE—"

BRASS
ORCHIDS

"—BUT ROGER EXPLAINED, SOMETHING I SUPPOSE WE'RE ALL AWARE OF, THAT HERE IN BELLONA WE OFTEN HAVE TO MAKE DO."

"OH, YEAH." KID LOOKED UP AND LET THE TITLE OF HIS BOOK EMBED THAT PART OF HIS CONSCIOUSNESS RESERVED FOR REALITY, WHILE HE EXPUNGED IT FROM THE PART CALLED DREAM. THE TRANSITION CAME EASY, BUT WITH A FIRMNESS AND INEVITABILITY HE ASSOCIATED WITH COMPREHENDING VIOLENCE. HE WAS JOYOUS, AND UPSET, BUT COULD JUST DISTINGUISH THAT THE REACTIONS WERE CONTIGUOUS, NOT CONSEQUENT.

"THESE ARE THE ILLUSTRATIONS. AGAIN, WE HAVE ROGER'S SENSE OF THEATRICALITY TO CONTEND WITH. I'M NOT AT ALL SURE THEY'RE IN GOOD TASTE. FRANKLY, I DON'T THINK POETRY NEEDS ILLUSTRATION. BUT HE ASKED ME TO SHOW THEM TO YOU: THE DECISION IS YOURS, ULTIMATELY."

HE WAS ABOUT TO SAY, THEY'RE ALL BLACK,

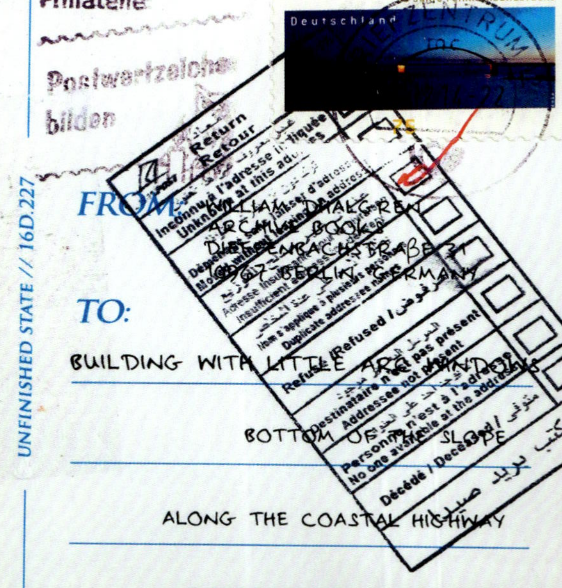

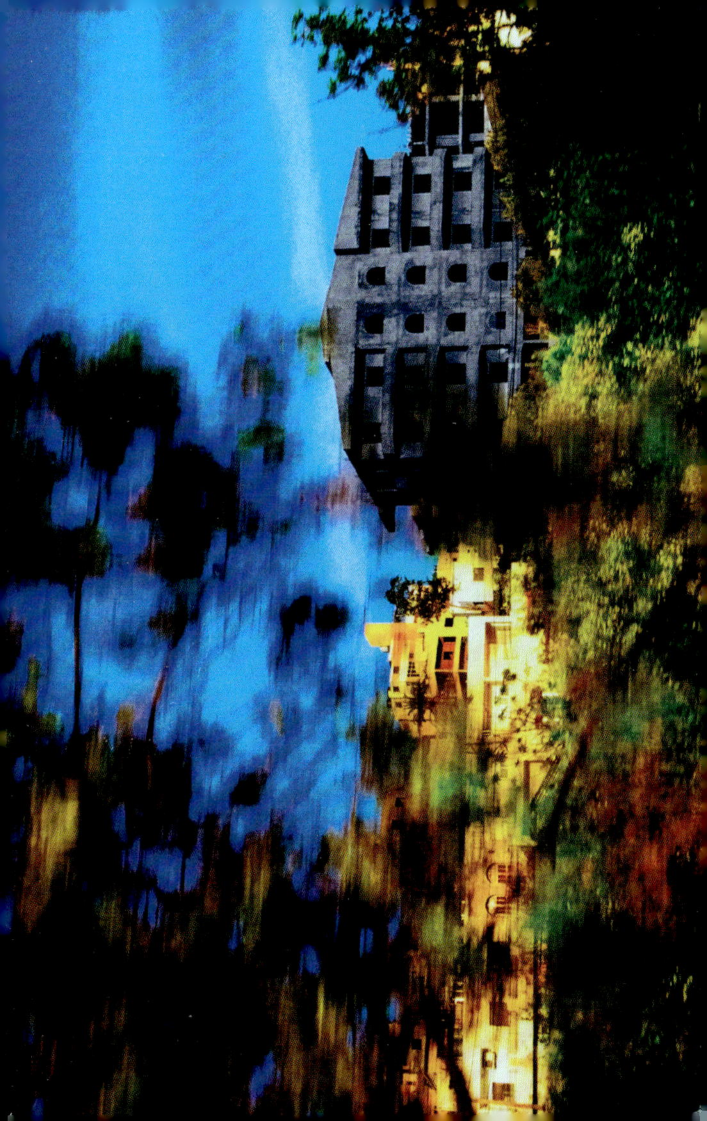

WHEN HE CAUGHT GLINTINGS IN THE MAT
STOCK.

"THEY'RE BLACK INK ON BLACK PAPER, MR NEWBOY EXPLAINED. "THE ONLY WAY Y CAN REALLY SEE THEM IS TO HOLD THEM TO THE LIGHT AND LOOK AT THEM FROM SIDE. THEN THE LIGHT CATCHES ON THE INK. ROGER FEELS THAT SINCE THE POEMS TAKE SO MUCH OF THEIR IMAGERY FROM THE CITY, HE'S USED SOME OF WHAT HE FEELS ARE THE MOST STRIKING PICTURES FROM HIS NEWSPAPER. BUT HE'S PRINTED THEM THIS WAY—I DON'T BELIEVE THERE'S BEEN ANY EFFORT TO CORRELATE PARTICULAR PICTURES WITH PARTICULAR POEMS."

KID NODDED. "THAT'S A GOOD IDEA." HE TILTED ANOTHER PICTURE TO CATCH, IN SUDDEN SILVERPOINT, BURNING BUILDINGS, PEOPLE GAPING, AND ONE CHILD, IN THE FOREGROUND, LEERING INTO THE CAMERA. "OH, YEAH!" HE LAUGHED, AND LOOKED THROUGH THE OTHERS.

"HAVE YOU ANY IDEA WHEN YOU'LL BE ABLE TO LOOK OVER THE PROOFS? THE TIMES IS NOTORIOUS FOR TYPOS. YOUR BOOK WAS SET ON THE SAME MACHINERY."

"I COULD DO IT NOW." KID PUT DOWN THE PICTURES AND PICKED UP THE GALLEYS. "HOW MANY PAGES DID YOU SAY IT WAS?"

"THIRTY-SIX. I WENT OVER IT ONCE MYSELF

REGULAR MAIL

0114000684004450

UNFINISHED STATE // 16D 228

CN 15

Retour / Return

Adresse incomplète / Incomplete address

Inconnu à l'adresse indiquée / Unknown at this address

Déménagé sans laisser d'adresse / Moved without leaving an address

Adresse insuffisante pour la livraison / Insufficient address for delivery

Le nom s'applique à plusieurs personnes / Duplicate addressee names

Refusé / Refused

Destinataire n'est pas ... / Addressee not ...

La personne n'est ... / No one available at ...

Décédé / Deceased

بريد صيدا

FROM: WILLIAM DHALGREN
ARCHIVE BOOKS
DIEFFENBACHSTRAßE 31
10967 BERLIN, GERMANY

TO:

BUILDING WITH LITTLE ARC WINDOWS

Anschrift überprüft durch Deutsche Post / BZ 10 /G

ZURÜCK:

10967

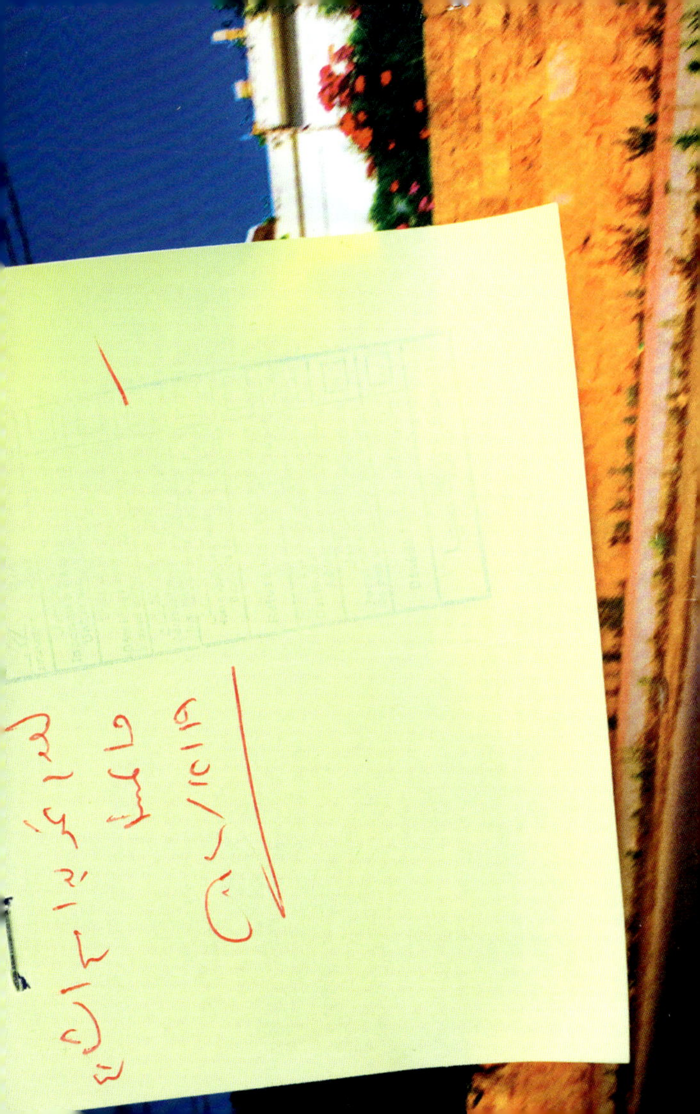

NEWBOY PURSED HIS LIPS. "ACTUALLY, I DON'T KNOW WHETHER IT'S TRUE OR NOT. BUT TRULY I DON'T SEE HOW ANY POET CAN WRITE WHO DOESN'T THINK SO."

"WHY ARE YOU GOING AWAY, MR NEWBOY?" KID HAD BEGUN THE QUESTION TO MAKE A CONNECTION: BUT NOW IT SEEMED EQUALLY APT FOR SEVERING ONE, AND NEWBOY'S EMBARRASSMENT AND HIS OWN CONFUSION SEEMED BETTER LEFT. "CAN'T YOU WORK HERE VERY WELL? BELLONA DOESN'T STIMULATE YOU?"

NEWBOY ACCEPTED THE SEVERANCE, ACKNOWLEDGING HIS ACCEPTANCE WITH ANOTHER SIP. "IN A WAY, I SUPPOSE YOU'RE RIGHT. EVERY ONCE IN A WHILE SOMETHING COMES ALONG TO REMIND ME THAT I AM—THOUGH NOT AS OFTEN AS I WOULD SOMETIMES LIKE—AFTER ALL, A POET. WHAT IS IT MR GRAVES SAYS? ALL POETRY IS ABOUT LOVE, DEATH, OR THE CHANGING OF THE SEASONS. WELL, HERE THE SEASONS DO NOT CHANGE. SO I'M LEAVING." BEHIND COILED STEAM, THE GREY EYES GLEAMED. "AFTER ALL. I'M ONLY A VISITOR. BUT CIRCUMSTANCES SEEM TO HAVE CONTRIVED TO CHANGE THAT STATUS WITH A RAPIDITY THOROUGHLY DISQUIETING." HE SHOOK HIS HEAD. "I'VE MET SOME VERY PLEASANT PEOPLE, SEEN SOME FASCINATING THINGS, HAD A WEALTH OF RICH EXPERIENCES—JUST THE WAY

50 Jahre Fehmarnsundbrücke

Deutschland 75

WILLIAM DHALGREN
ARCHIVE BOOKS
DIEFFENBACHSTRAßE 31
10967 BERLIN, GERMANY

UNFINISHED BUILDING

BEHIND THE STONE WALL WITH ROSES ON THE ROAD SOUTH OF THE STADIUM

SAIDA

LEBANON

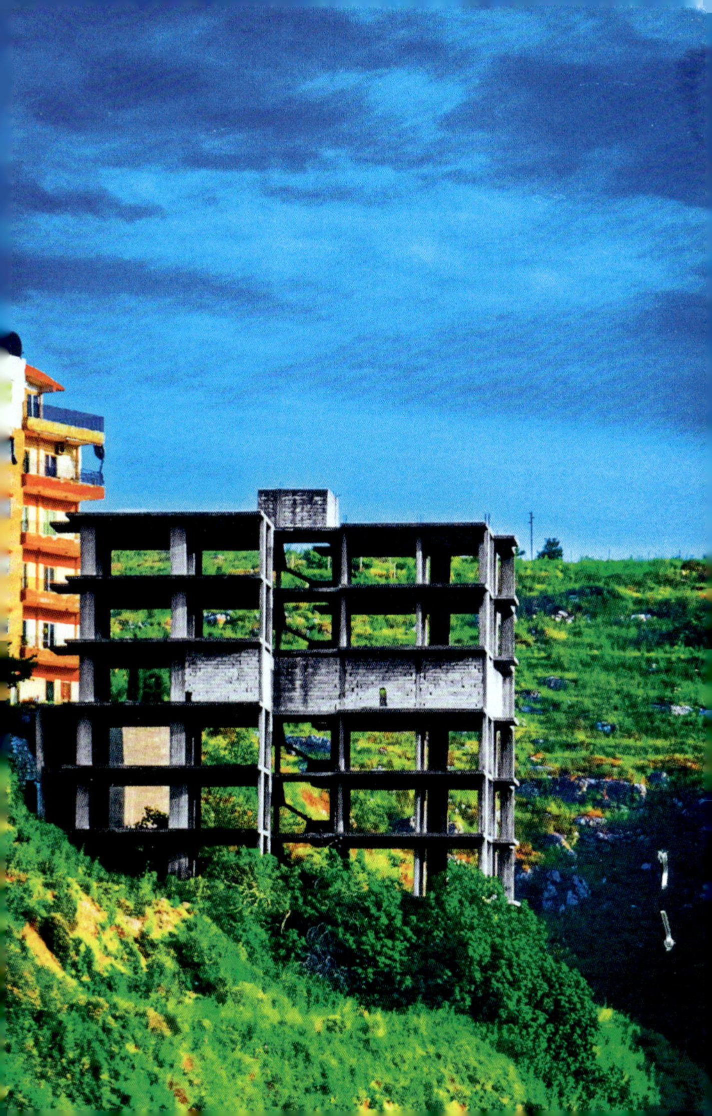

LIBANPOST ليبان بوست

RETOUR
RETURN
معاد

CN 15

غير معروف على هذا العنوان Inconnu à l'adresse indiquée Unknown at this address	☐
ترك دون أن يترك عنوانا Déménagé sans laisser d'adresse Moved without leaving an address	☐
عنوان غير صالح للتوزيع Adresse insuffisante pour la livraison Insufficient address for delivery	☒
يُطلق الإسم على عدة أشخاص Nom s'applique à plusieurs personnes Duplicate addressee names	☐
Refusé / Refused / مرفوض	☐
المرسل اليه غير موجود Destinataire n'est pas présent Addressee not present	☐
لا يوجد أحد على العنوان Personne n'est à l'adresse No one available at the address	☐
Décédé / Deceased / متوفي	☐
Others / Autres / مختلف	☐

CN 15 01/02/2011

HE FEW
RIENT—
BUT
THE
T
WHO
SOME
N HIS
AS SAY,
RTAIN
Y
TAND
SE
SION—
- ALLOW
NG,
LIZED
IS
H AS
EWER
EN THEM,
THE
GAIN
D DEAL
WARD
E
HAT
THEATRICAL SIDE OF HIS PERSONALITY OF WHICH

UNFINISHED STATE // 16D.235

Philatelie:
Postwertzeichen
bilden

Deutschland 75
50 Jahre Fehmarnsundbrücke

FROM: WILLIAM DHALGREN
ARCHIVE BOOKS
DIEFFENBACHSTRAßE 31
10967 BERLIN, GERMANY

TO:
SEE-THROUGH BUILDING
WITH NO SHEER WALLS

ON THE EDGE OF THE HILL
DIRECTLY WEST OF THE COVE

RMAILEH

LEBANON

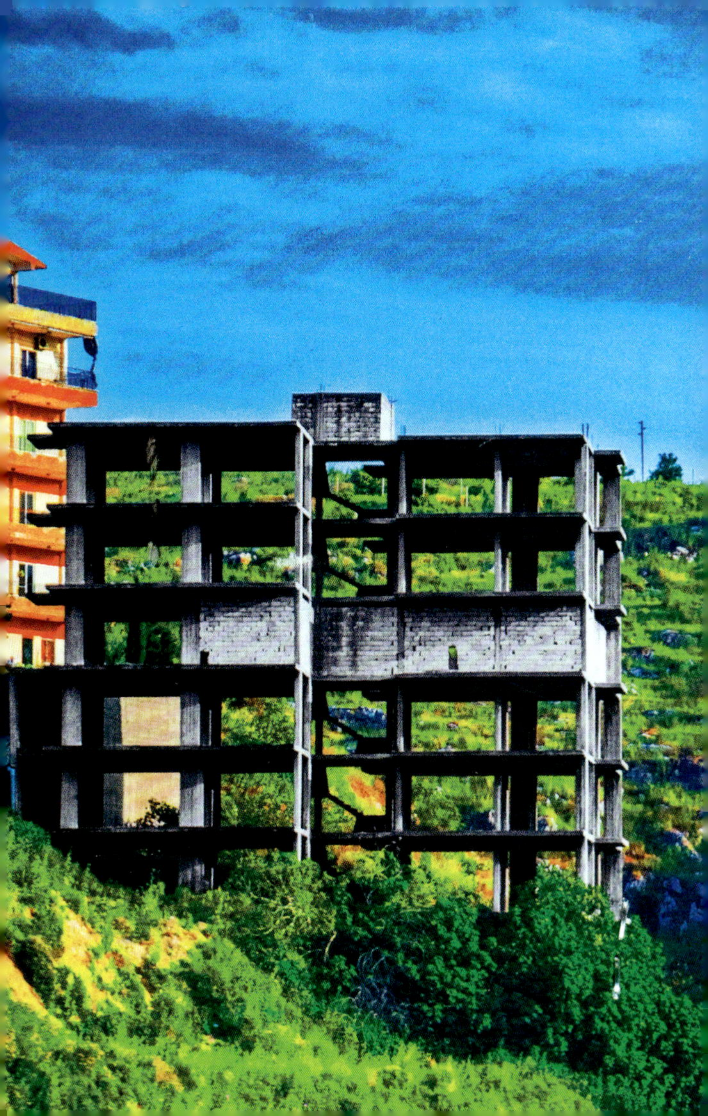

AMBITION IS ONLY A SMALL PART. HE STANDS MUCH CLOSER TO THE POOL. HE DOES NOT HURL. HE ~~DROPS.~~ ACCURACY IS AGAIN ALL-IMPORTANT: THERE ARE SOME PEOPLE WHO CAN HIT BULL'S EYE FROM A QUARTER OF A MILE WHILE OTHERS CANNOT TOUCH THE TARGET AT TEN FEET. GIVEN IT, THE PATTERNS AND RIPPLES THIS SORT OF ARTIST PRODUCES CAN BE FAR MORE INTRICATE, IF THEY LACK THE INITIAL APPEARANCE OF FORCE. HE IS MUCH MORE A VICTIM OF THE CIVILIZATION IN WHICH HE LIVES: HIS GREATEST WORKS COME FROM THE PERIODS ART HISTORIANS GROSSLY CALL 'CONDUCIVE TO AESTHETIC PRODUCTION.' I SAY HE STANDS VERY CLOSE TO THE POOLS; INDEED, HE SPENDS MOST OF HIS TIME SIMPLY GAZING INTO THEM. MYSELF, I RATHER ASPIRE TO BE THIS SECOND TYPE OF ARTIST. I CAME TO BELLONA TO EXPLORE. AND I FIND THE ENTIRE CULTURE HERE—I CANNOT BE KIND—COMPLETELY PARASITIC... SAPROPHYTIC. IT INFECTS—EVEN INSIDE ROGER'S CAREFULLY CLOSED ESTATE. IT'S NOT CONDUCIVE TO MY CONCEPT OF THE GOOD LIFE, THEREFORE, IF ONLY TERTIARILY, IT DAMAGES ALL MY IMPULSES TOWARD ART. I WOULD LIKE TO BE A GOOD PERSON. BUT IT'S TOO DIFFICULT HERE. I SUSPECT THAT'S COWARDLY, BUT IT'S TRUE."

THE COFFEE, PROMPTING A MEMORY THAT

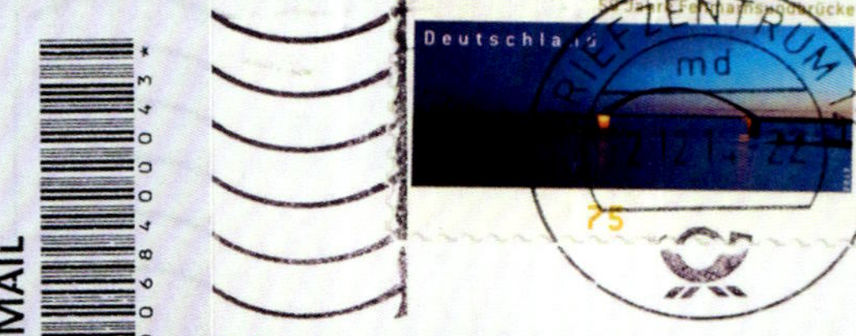

REGULAR MAIL

01140006840004 3

M: WILLIAM DHALGREN
ARCHIVE BOOKS
DIEFFENBACHSTRAßE 31
10967 BERLIN, GERMANY

Anschrift überprüft durch Deutsche Post / BZ 05
ZURÜCK:
Empfänger nicht zu ermitteln
10967

RMAILEH

LEBANON

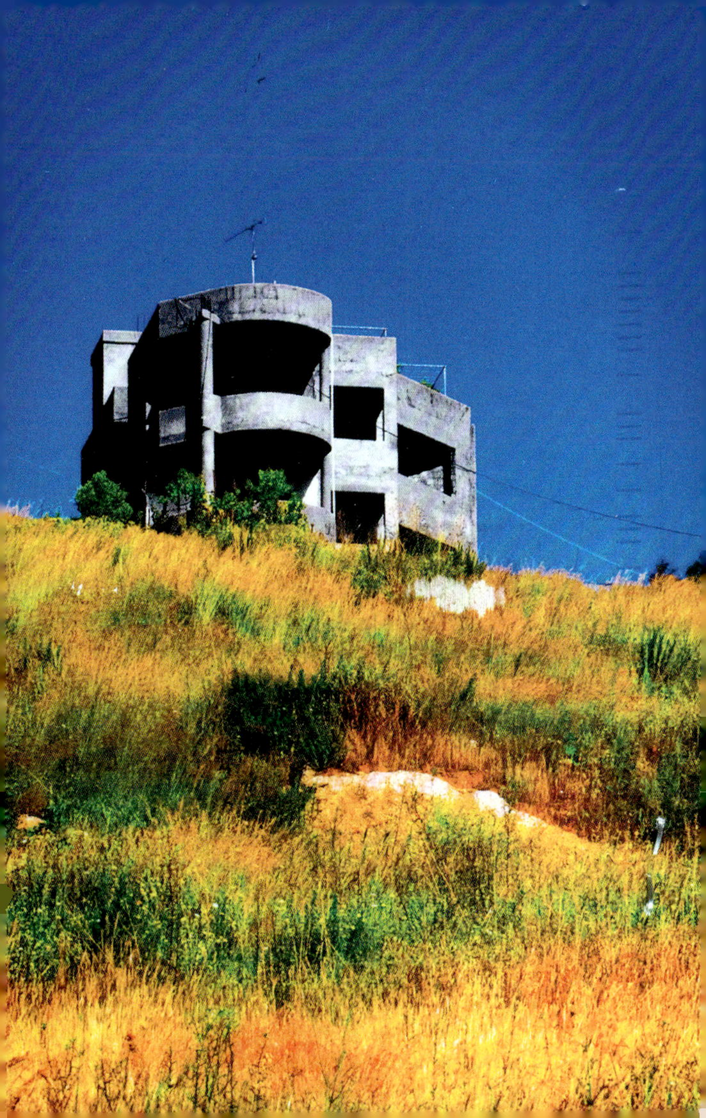

IS ABOUT THE ONLY THING THAT CAN REDEEM RELIGION, AND THE CLERICS WILL NEVER FORGIVE US THAT."

NEWBOY GLANCED AT THE CEILING AND SHOOK HIS HEAD. DULLED ORGAN MUSIC CAME FROM THE STAIR. HE LOOKED DOWN INTO HIS CASE.

"I GUESS WHAT I WANT TO KNOW, REALLY—" KID'S THUMB HAD STAINED THE GALLEY MARGIN: MOMENTARY PANIC. "DO YOU THINK THESE—" AND FOUR FINGERS MARKED THE PAPER IN A SWEEP—"THAT THESE ARE ANY GOOD?" THERE WILL BE OTHER COPIES, HE THOUGHT TO EASE HIMSELF. THERE WILL BE. "I MEAN, REALLY."

NEWBOY SUCKED HIS TEETH AND PUT THE CASE ON THE FLOOR AGAINST HIS KNEES. "YOU HAVE NO REALIZATION WHAT AN ABSURD QUESTION THAT IS. ONCE, WHEN I USED TO FIND MYSELF IN THIS SITUATION, I WOULD ALWAYS ANSWER 'NO' AUTOMATICALLY, 'I THINK THEY'RE WORTHLESS.' BUT I'M OLDER, AND I REALIZE NOW ALL I WAS DOING WAS PUNISHING PEOPLE WHO ASKED SUCH QUESTIONS FOR THEIR STUPIDITY, AND WAS ONLY BEING 'HONEST' IN THE MOST SEMANTICALLY VULGAR SENSE. I REALLY CANNOT THINK ABOUT POETRY IN SUCH ABSOLUTE TERMS AS 'GOOD' AND 'BAD', OR EVEN IN THE MORE FLEXIBLE TERMS YOU'D PROBABLY BE WILLING TO ACCEPT IN THEIR PLACE: 'WELL DONE' OR 'BADLY DONE'.

UNFINISHED STATE // 16D 239

50 Jahre Fehmarnsundbrücke
Deutschland 75
Schützt die Natur. www.wwf.de

FROM: WILLIAM DHALGREN
ARCHIVE BOOKS
DIEFFENBACHSTRAßE 31
10967 BERLIN, GERMANY

TO: UNFINISHED HOUSE WITH ROUNDED BALCONIES
ON THE HILLTOP
ABOVE THE BEACH NEAR THE PORT

JIYEH

LEBANON

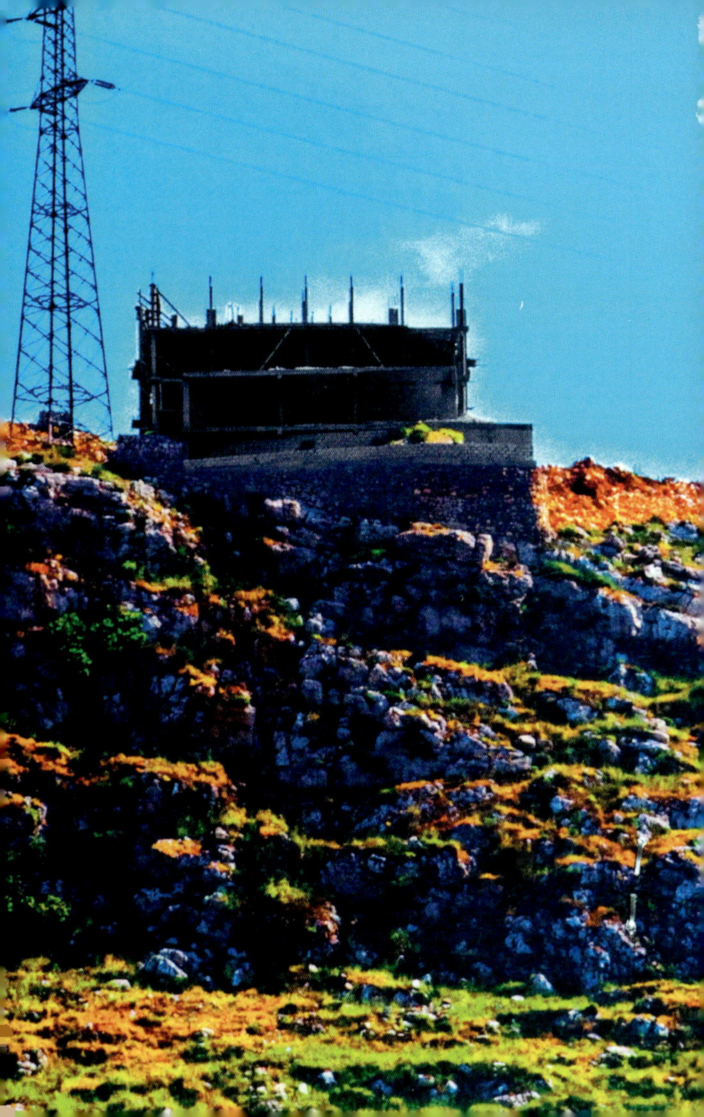

LIBANPOST ليبان بوست

RETOUR
RETURN
معاد

CN 15

غير معروف على هذا العنوان Inconnu à l'adresse indiquée Unknown at this address	☐
ترك دون أن يترك عنواناً Déménagé sans laisser d'adresse Moved without leaving an address	☐
عنوان غير صالح للتوزيع Adresse insuffisante pour la livraison Insufficient address for delivery	☒
يُطلق الإسم على عدة أشخاص Nom s'applique à plusieurs personnes Duplicate addressee names	☐
Refusé / Refused / مرفوض	☐
المرسل اليه غير موجود Destinataire n'est pas présent Addressee not present	☐
لا يوجد أحد على العنوان Personne n'est à l'adresse No one available at the address	☐
Décédé / Deceased / متوفي	☐
Others / Autres / مختلف	☐

CN 15 01/02/2011

KID LOOKED OVER

AND
IR
WO
ROM
THE
OR
AUSE
IOURS
OND,
COULD
W.
EXT
OF
RE
LINE
THE
OXES
ON
ND
PULSING
ROAT
AFTER

UNFINISHED STATE // 16D.246

50 Jahre Fehmarnsundbrücke
Deutschland
75

Schützt die Natur
WWF
www.wwf.de

FROM: WILLIAM DHALGREN
ARCHIVE BOOKS
DIEFFENBACHSTRAßE 31
10967 BERLIN, GERMANY

TO:

INCOMPLETE STRUCTURE

ON THE HILLTOP
ABOVE THE BEACH NEAR THE PORT

JIYEH

LEBANON

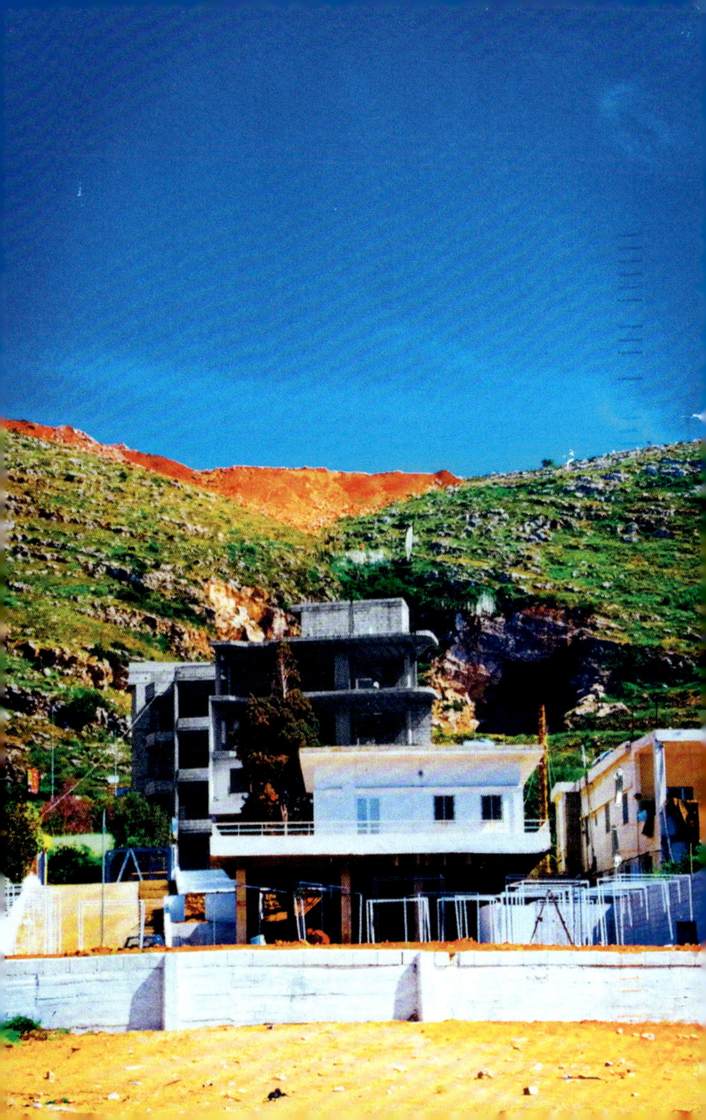

ANY—?"

BUT KID HAD FOUND ANOTHER MISTAKE.

"HERE," NEWBOY SAID. "WHY DON'T YOU LAY THE GALLEYS ON YOUR NOTEBOOK SO YOU CAN WRITE MORE EASILY."

WHILE KID PASSED THE HALFPOINT OF THE NEXT GALLEY, NEWBOY MUSED: "PERHAPS IT'S GOOD YOU'RE NOT GOING TO WRITE ANY MORE: YOU'D HAVE TO START CONSIDERING ALL THOSE DULL THINGS LIKE YOUR RELATION TO YOUR AUDIENCE, THE RELATION BETWEEN YOUR PERSONALITY AND YOUR POETRY, THE RELATION BETWEEN YOUR POETRY AND ALL THE POETRY BEFORE IT. SINCE YOU TOLD ME YOU WEREN'T RESPONSIBLE FOR THOSE NOTES, I'VE BEEN TRYING TO FIGURE OUT WHETHER IT JUST HAPPENED OR WHETHER YOU WERE MAKING A CONSCIOUS REFERENCE: YOU MANAGED TO REPRODUCE, PRACTICALLY VERBATIM, ONE OF MY FAVORITE LINES FROM GOLDING'S TRANSLATION OF THE METAMORPHOSIS."

"MMM?"

"ARE YOU FAMILIAR WITH IT?"

"IT'S A BIG GREEN AND WHITE PAPERBACK? THAT'S THE ONE SHAKESPEARE USED FOR SOME OF HIS PLAYS. I ONLY READ ABOUT THE FIRST HALF. BUT I DIDN'T TAKE ANY LINES FROM IT, AT LEAST NOT ON PURPOSE. MAYBE IT JUST HAPPENED?"

CN 15

Return

Addressee not present

No one available at the address

Décédé / Deceased / متوفى

UNFINISHED STATE // 16D.248

Schützt die Natur

WWF

www.wwf.de

50 Jahre Fehmarnsundbrücke

Deutschland

75

FROM: WILLIAM DHALGREN
ARCHIVE BOOKS
DIEFFENBACHSTRAßE 31
10967 BERLIN, GERMANY

TO: UNFINISHED HOUSE
ON THE BEACH NEAR THE PORT
JIYEH
LEBANON

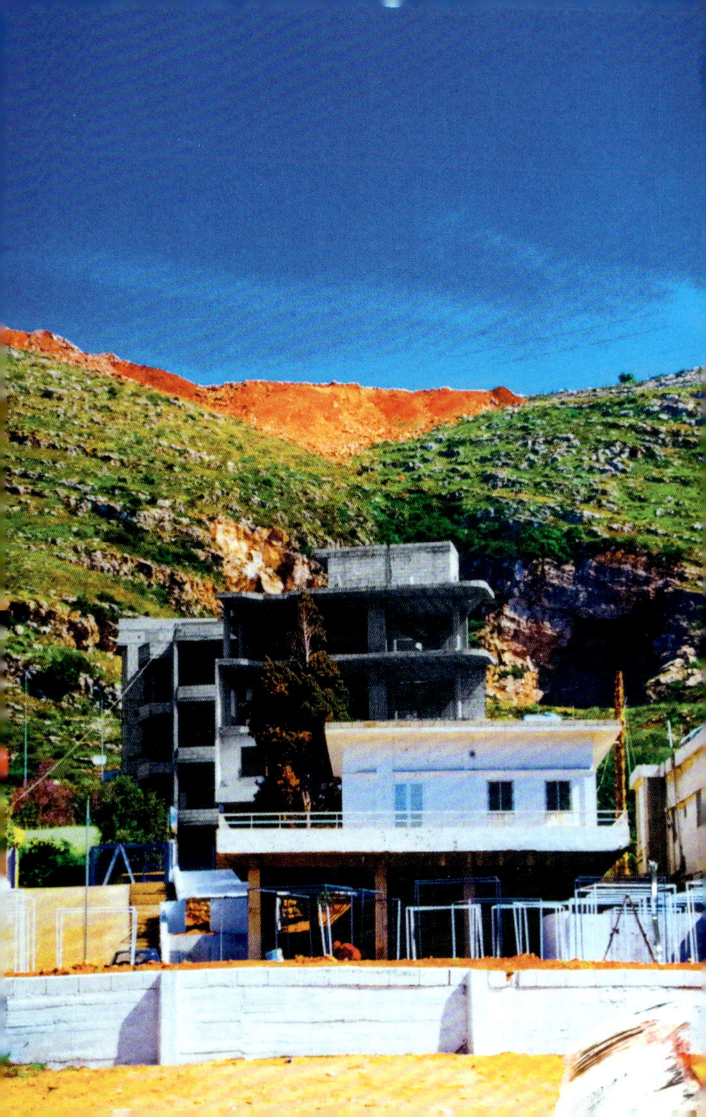

MR NEWBOY NODDED. "YOU AMAZE ME. AND WHEN YOU DO, I SUSPECT I'M RATHER A SMALLER PERSON FOR HAVING SUCH PETTY NOTIONS IN THE FIRST PLACE. WELL, THE LINE I WAS REFERRING TO WAS FROM THE LAST BOOK ANYWAY. SO YOU HADN'T GOTTEN TO THAT ONE YET. TELL ME, WHO DO YOU THINK SHOULD READ YOUR POEMS ONCE THEY'RE PUBLISHED?"

"I GUESS PEOPLE WHO... WELL, WHOEVER LIKES TO READ POETRY."

"DO YOU?"

"YEAH. I READ IT MORE THAN I READ ANYTHING ELSE, I GUESS."

"NO, THAT DOESN'T SURPRISE ME."

"YOU KNOW, IN BOOKSTORES FOR THE SCHOOLS I USED TO GO TO, OR DOWN IN THE VILLAGE IN NEW YORK, OR IN SAN FRANCISCO, THEY GOT WHOLE SECTIONS FOR POETRY. YOU CAN READ A LOT OF IT THERE."

"WHY POETRY?"

KID SHRUGGED. "MOST POEMS ARE SHORTER THAN STORIES."

NEWBOY, KID SAW, WAS SUPPRESSING A LAUGH. KID FELT EMBARRASSED.

"AND YOU'RE NOT GOING TO WRITE ANY MORE?"

"IT'S TOO HARD." KID LOOKED DOWN. "I MEAN IF I KEPT IT UP, I THINK IT WOULD KILL ME, YOU

UNFINISHED STATE // 16D.249

FROM: WILLIAM DHALGREN
ARCHIVE BOOKS
DIEFFENBACHSTRAßE 31
10967 BERLIN, GERMANY

TO:
UNFINISHED HOUSE
ON THE BEACH NEAR THE PORT
JIYEH
LEBANON

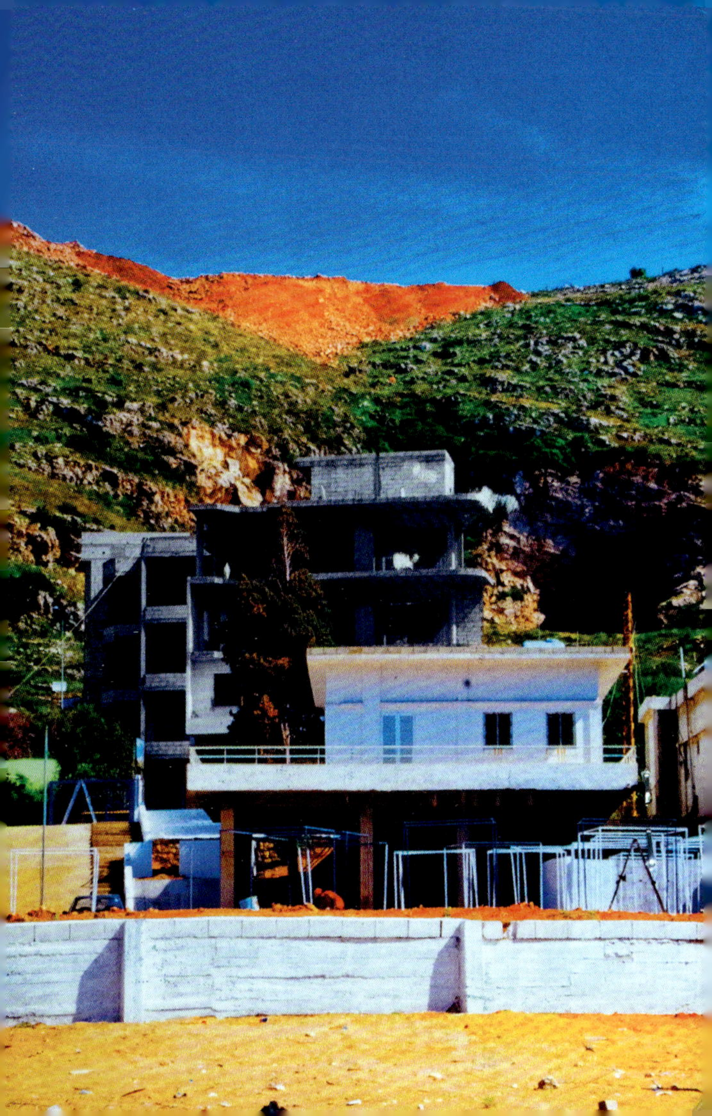

KNOW? I NEVER DID IT BEFORE, SO I JUST DIDN'T UNDERSTAND."

"THAT'S SAD—NO, I CAN BE MORE HONEST THAN THAT. IT'S FRIGHTENING FOR ONE ARTIST TO SEE ANOTHER ONE, ANY OTHER ONE TURN AWAY FROM ART."

"YEAH." KID'S EYES CAME UP. "I KNOW. I REALLY KNOW THAT. AND I WISH—I WISH I DIDN'T FRIGHTEN YOU AS MUCH AS I DO. WHAT IS IT? WHAT'S THE MATTER WITH YOU, NOW?"

"NOTHING." NEWBOY SHOOK HIS HEAD.

"I WISH I DIDN'T," KID REPEATED. "THE LAST POEM..." KID BEGAN TO TURN THROUGH THE GALLEYS. "WHAT DID YOU THINK OF THAT ONE, I MEAN COMPARED TO ALL THE REST OF THEM?"

"THE ONE IN METER? WELL, IT ISN'T FINISHED. WE PRINTED IT UP TO WHERE YOU BROKE OFF. THAT'S ANOTHER THING I WANTED TO QUERY ABOUT—"

"HOW DO YOU LIKE WHAT THERE IS?"

"FRANKLY, I DIDN'T THINK IT WAS AS STRONG AS MANY OF THE OTHERS. WHEN I WENT BACK OVER IT THE FOURTH OR FIFTH TIME, I BEGAN TO SEE THAT THE SUBSTANCE OF IT WAS PROBABLY ON ITS WAY TO A GREAT DEAL OF RICHNESS. BUT THE LANGUAGE WASN'T AS INVENTIVE. OR AS CLEAN."

KID NODDED. "THE RHYTHM OF NATURAL

UNFINISHED STATE // 16D.250

12

FROM: ~~WILLIAM DHALGREN~~
~~ARCHIVE BOOKS~~
~~DIEFFENBACHSTRAßE 31~~
~~10967 BERLIN, GERMANY~~

TO: UNFINISHED ~~HOUSE~~

ON THE BEACH NEAR THE PORT

JIYEH

LEBANON

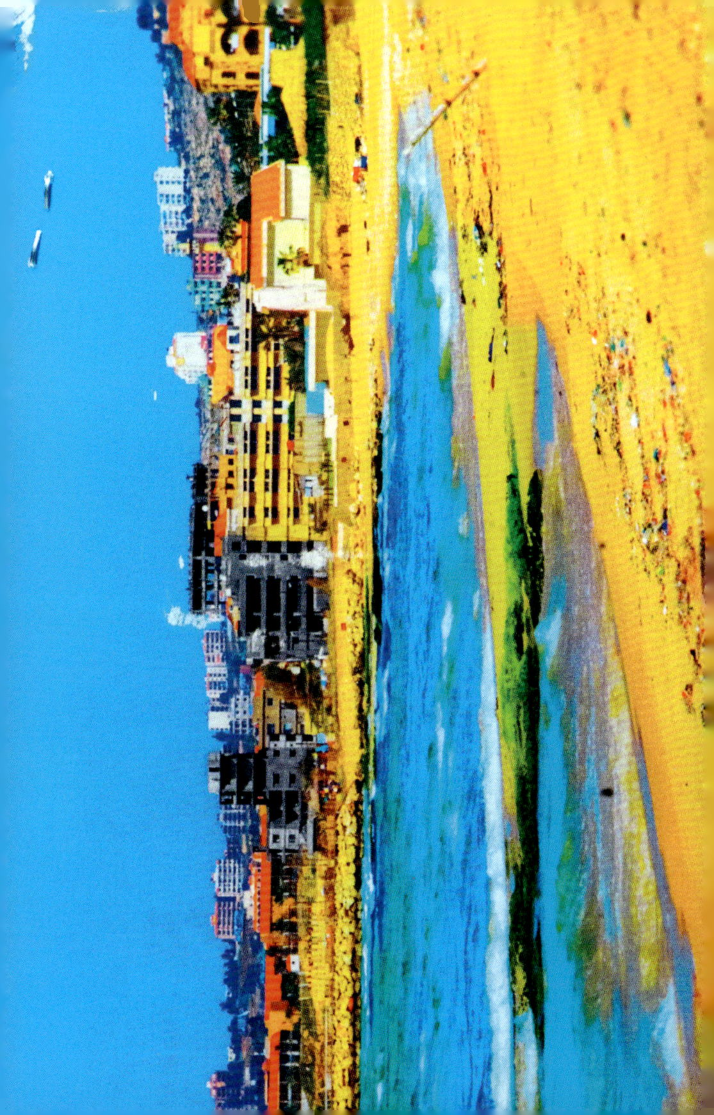

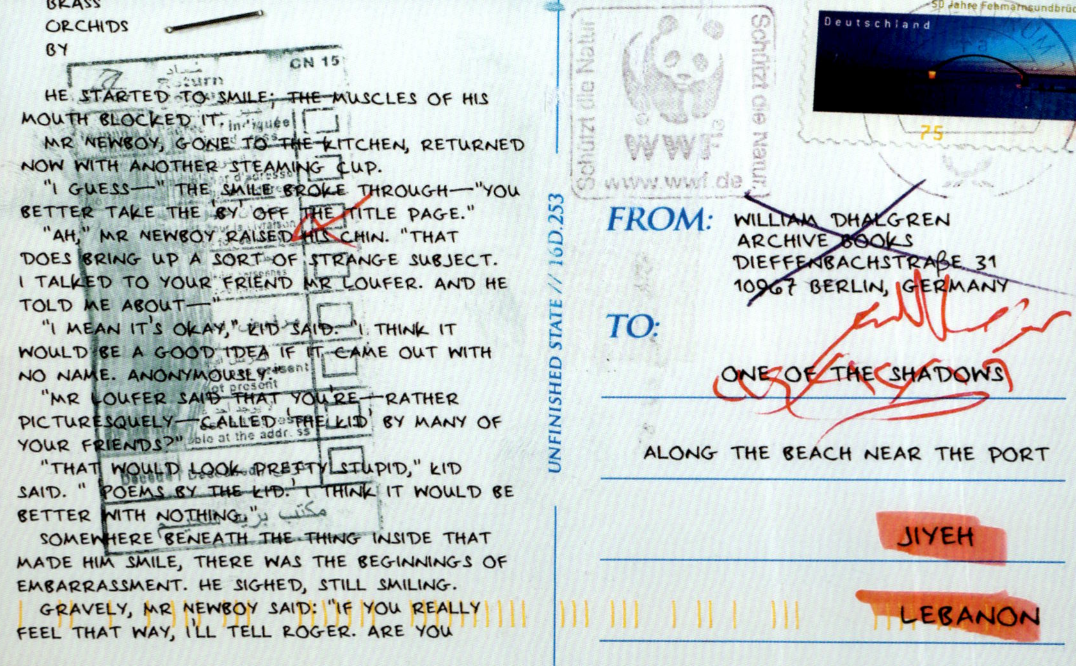
BRASS
ORCHIDS
BY
CN 15
Return
HE STARTED TO SMILE; THE MUSCLES OF HIS MOUTH BLOCKED IT.
MR NEWBOY, GONE TO THE KITCHEN, RETURNED NOW WITH ANOTHER STEAMING CUP.
"I GUESS—" THE SMILE BROKE THROUGH—"YOU BETTER TAKE THE 'BY' OFF THE TITLE PAGE."
"AH," MR NEWBOY RAISED HIS CHIN. "THAT DOES BRING UP A SORT OF STRANGE SUBJECT. I TALKED TO YOUR FRIEND MR LOUFER. AND HE TOLD ME ABOUT—"
"I MEAN IT'S OKAY," KID SAID. "I THINK IT WOULD BE A GOOD IDEA IF IT CAME OUT WITH NO NAME. ANONYMOUSLY."
"MR LOUFER SAID THAT YOU'RE—RATHER PICTURESQUELY—CALLED 'THE KID' BY MANY OF YOUR FRIENDS?"
"THAT WOULD LOOK PRETTY STUPID," KID SAID. "'POEMS BY THE KID.' I THINK IT WOULD BE BETTER WITH NOTHING."
SOMEWHERE BENEATH THE THING INSIDE THAT MADE HIM SMILE, THERE WAS THE BEGINNINGS OF EMBARRASSMENT. HE SIGHED, STILL SMILING.
GRAVELY, MR NEWBOY SAID: "IF YOU REALLY FEEL THAT WAY, I'LL TELL ROGER. ARE YOU
UNFINISHED STATE // 16D.253
Schützt die Natur
WWF
www.wwf.de
Deutschland
50 Jahre Fehmarnsundbrücke
75
FROM: WILLIAM DHALGREN
ARCHIVE BOOKS
DIEFFENBACHSTRAßE 31
10967 BERLIN, GERMANY
TO:
ONE OF THE SHADOWS
ALONG THE BEACH NEAR THE PORT
JIYEH
LEBANON

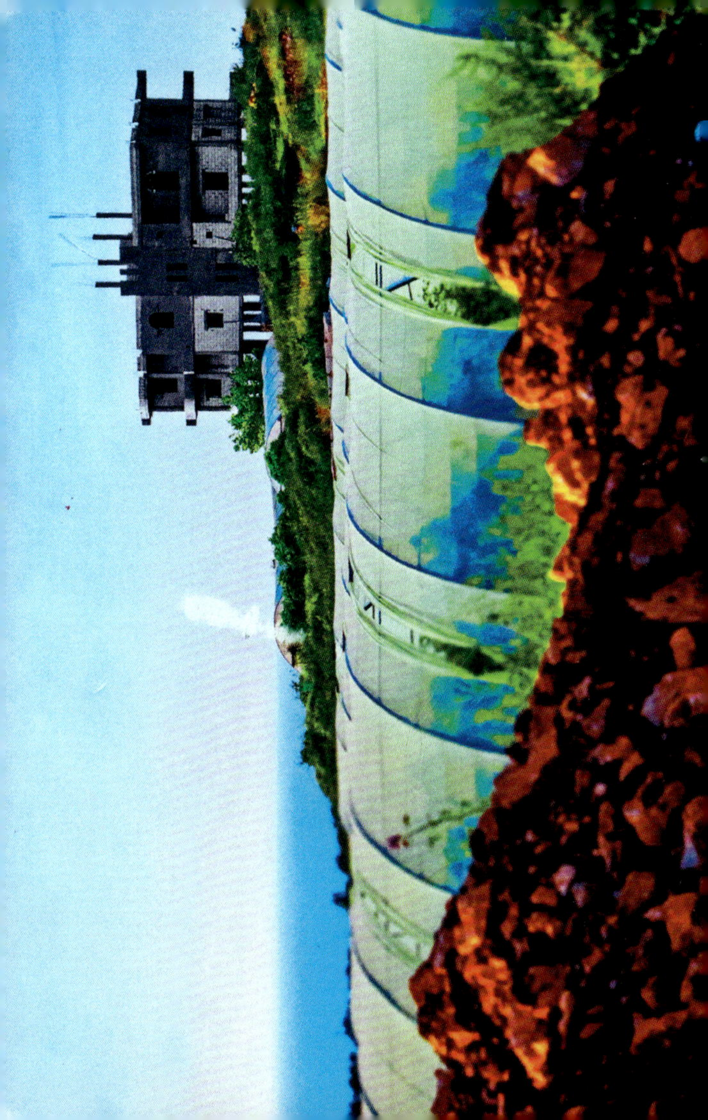

FORWARD. "I'VE REALLY ENJOYED THE TIME WE'VE SPENT TOGETHER, THE TALKS WE'VE HAD. DO SAY GOOD-BYE TO YOUR LITTLE GIRL FRIEND FOR ME?"

KID SHOOK. "YES, SIR. UM... THANK YOU VERY MUCH." THE NOTEBOOK WAS ON THE FLOOR, ONE CORNER OVER KID'S BARE FOOT.

NEWBOY WALKED TO THE STEPS.

"GOOD-BYE," KID REPEATED INTO THE SILENCE.

NEWBOY NODDED, SMILED, LEFT.

KID WAITED FOR THE DISTURBING MEMORY TO FLICKER ONCE MORE. HIS HEART QUIETED. SUDDENLY HE PICKED UP HIS AND NEWBOY'S COFFEE CUP AND WENT INTO THE KITCHEN.

SECONDS AFTER HE BEGAN TO RINSE THEM IN THE SINK, HE NOTICED HOW FIRM THE WATER PRESSURE WAS. HE RAN HIS FOREFINGER AROUND THE CROCK RIM. THE WATER HISSED ON THE ENAMEL.

SOMEBODY STRUCK A DISSONANCE ON THE PIANO.

CURIOUS, KID TURNED OFF THE WATER. THE CUPS CLINKED ON THE SIDEBOARD. AS HE CROSSED THE FLOOR, ONE OF THE BOARDS SQUEAKED: HE HAD WANTED TO BE COMPLETELY QUIET.

AT THE DARKER END OF THE AUDITORIUM, SOMEONE IN WORK CLOTHES STOOD BEFORE THE

UNFINISHED STATE // 16D.256

Return
Retour

50 Jahre Fehmarnsundbrücke
Deutschland
75

schützt die Natur.
WWF
www.wwf.de

FROM: WILLIAM DHALGREN
ARCHIVE BOOKS
DIEFFENBACHSTRAßE 31
10967 BERLIN, GERMANY

TO:

INCOMPLETE HOUSE

ON THE HILL AMONG THE GREENHOUSES
NORTH OF AL LITANI RIVER

MATARIYET AL CHOUMAR

النبطية | LEBANON

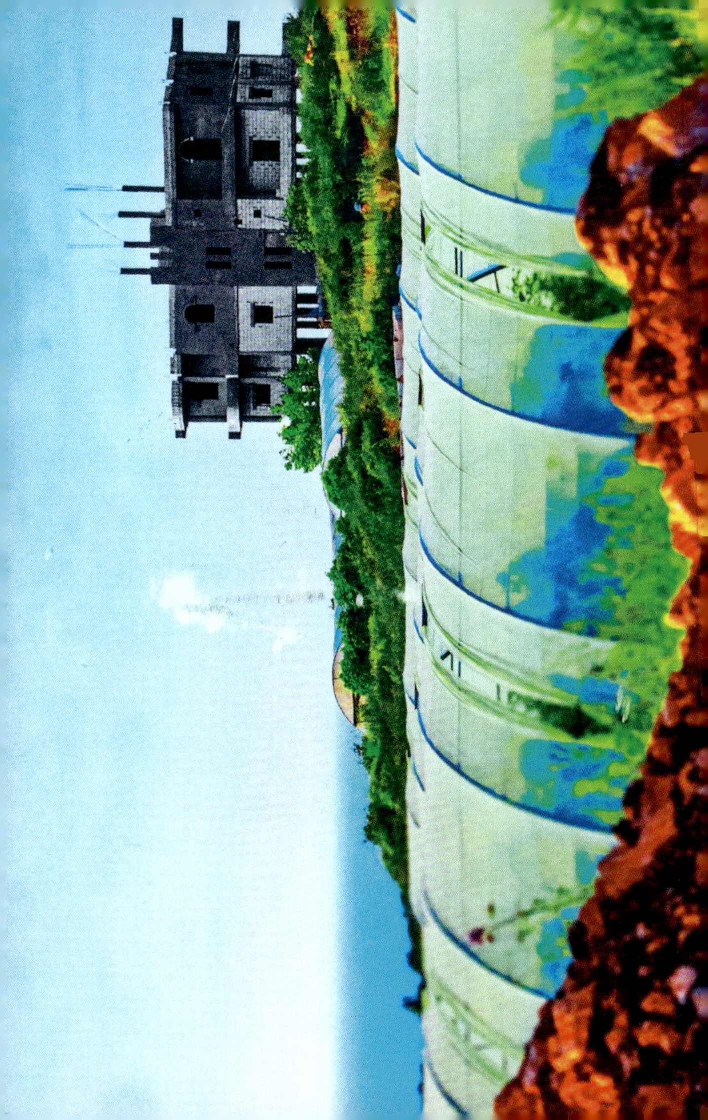

BRASS INNARDS. THE ORANGE CONSTRUCTION SHOES AND THE COVERALLS MOMENTARILY RECALLED THE WOMAN ON THE LADDER CHANGING THE STREET SIGNS.

THE FIGURE TURNED AND WALKED TO THE COUCH. " 'EY..." A HEAVY, FLATTENED VOICE, A SLIGHT NOD AND SLIGHTER SMILE. GEORGE HARRISON PICKED UP AN OLD TIMES, AND LOWERED HIMSELF TO THE COUCH, CROSSED HIS LEGS, AND OPENED THE TABLOID-SIZE PAPER.

"HELLO." KID HEARD FAINT ORGAN MUSIC.

"Y'S'POS'D BE I' 'EAH?" HARRISON LOOKED FROM BEHIND THE PAPER.

THE NATURAL RHYTHM OF ENGLISH SPEECH; NO, KID THOUGHT, IT IS IMPOSSIBLE.

"YOU SURE YOU SUPPOSED TO BE IN HERE?" GEORGE REPEATED.

"REVEREND TAYLER BROUGHT ME DOWN." (IT WOULD BE STUPID, HE DECIDED, EVEN TO TRY.)

" 'CAUSE IF YOU AIN'T SUPPOSE TO BE IN HERE, SHE GONNA GET MAD." HARRISON SMILED, A MOTTLED IVORY CRESCENT BETWEEN HIS LIPS UNEVEN PIGMENT. "SEEN YOU IN THE BAR."

"THAT'S RIGHT." KID GRINNED. "AND YOU'RE IN THOSE POSTERS ALL OVER TOWN."

"YOU SEEN THEM?" HARRISON PUT DOWN THE PAPER. "YOU KNOW, THEM FELLOWS WHAT MAKE THEM IS A LITTLE—" HE JOGGLED HIS HAND—

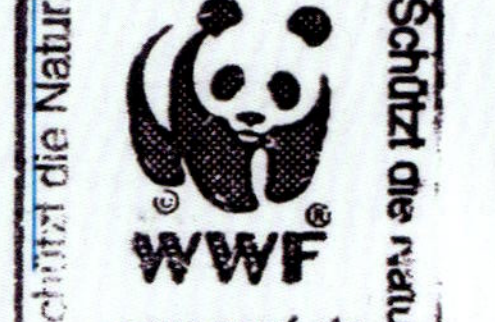

UNFINISHED STATE // 16D.257

FROM: WILLIAM DHALGREN
ARCHIVE BOOKS
DIEFFENBACHSTRAẞE 31
10967 BERLIN, GERMANY

TO:

INCOMPLETE HOUSE

ON THE HILL AMONG THE GREENHOUSES
NORTH OF AL LITANI RIVER

MATARIYET AL CHOUMAR

LEBANON

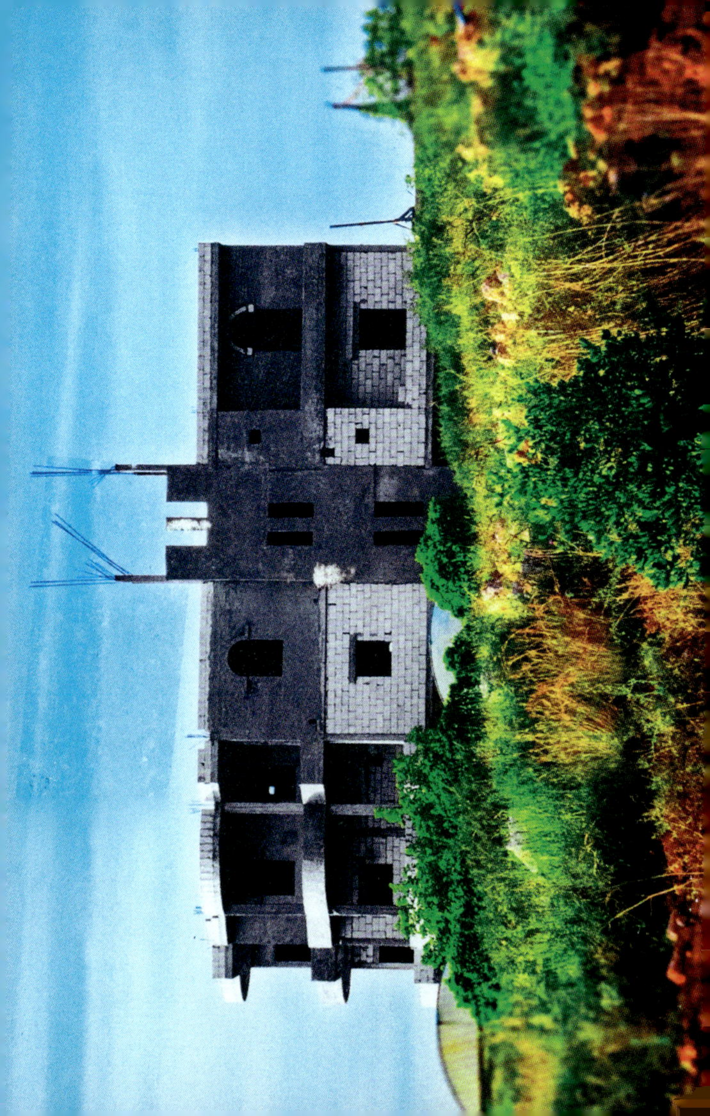

SAY?"

"IN JACKSON. YOU KNOW WHAT JACKSON IS?"

"YEAH, SURE."

BUT HARRISON WAS LAUGHING AGAIN.

HE, KID REFLECTED, IS BECOMING A GOD, TO SEE WHAT EMERGED FROM HIS TONE OF THOUGHT. KID'S INNER EYE WAS ALIVE WITH VISIONS OF JUNE.

BUT GEORGE STOOD, DROPPING HIS PAPER. WHITE LEAVES OPENED AND FELL, ONE ON THE COUCH, SEVERAL ON THE FLOOR. "YOU THE ONE THEY CALL THE KID. YEAH?"

KID WAS TERRIFIED, AND FELT STUPID FOR NOT KNOWING WHY.

"THEY TALK ABOUT YOU. I HEARD ABOUT YOU. I HEARD WHAT THEY SAID." THE FINGER SHOOK AGAIN. "YOU THE ONE THAT DON'T KNOW WHO HE IS. I HEARD THEM."

"NOBODY AROUND HERE GOT ANYTHING TO DO EXCEPT TALK," KID SAID. "YOU KNOW THAT? YOU KNOW WHAT I MEAN ABOUT THAT?"

THE BLACK HAND WENT DOWN AGAINST THE COVERALL. THE GREEN WRINKLED. "SO YOU DON'T LIKE IT HERE?"

"YEAH," KID SAID. "I LIKE IT... DON'T YOU?"

HARRISON NODDED, HIS CHEEK FILLED WITH HIS TONGUE. "YOU EVER COME OVER IN THE JACKSON?" THE TONGUE FLICKED THE LIPS.

UNFINISHED STATE // 16D 259

Return
Retour
Unknown at this address
Moved without leaving an address
Insufficient address for delivery
Duplicate addresses
Refused
Destinataire n'est pas présent
Addressee not present
Personne n'est à l'adresse
None available at the address
Deceased

schützen die Natur.
WWF
www.wwf.de

Deutschland 75
50 Jahre Fehmarnsundbrücke

FROM: WILLIAM DHALGREN
ARCHIVE BOOKS
DIEFFENBACHSTRAßE 31
10967 BERLIN, GERMANY

~~TO:~~

INCOMPLETE HOUSE

ON THE HILL AMONG THE GREENHOUSES
NORTH OF AL LITANI RIVER

MATARIYET AL CHOUMAR

البترات LEBANON

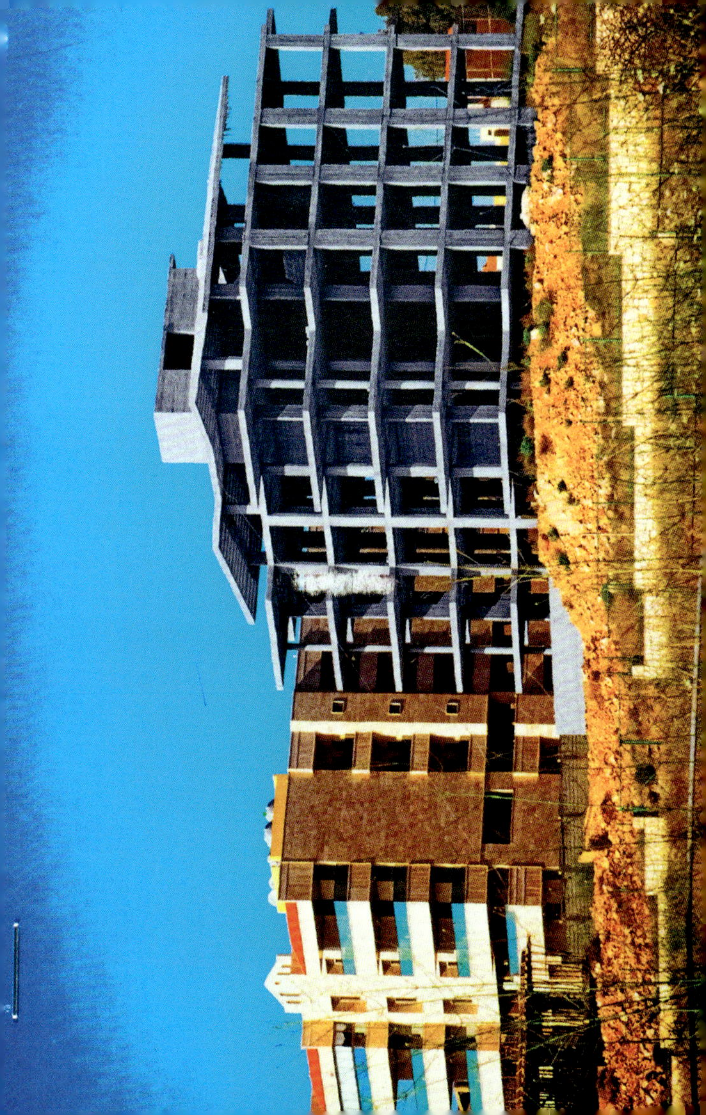

GOT SHOT. WE WERE ON THE BUS, AND HE WAS BLEEDING. AND I KEPT ON THINKING, WHAT ARE THEY GOING TO DO WITH HIM? WHERE ARE THEY GOING TO TAKE HIM? THERE ISN'T ANY DOCTOR AROUND. WE EVEN HAD HIS ARM IN A TOURNIQUET. I COULDN'T TAKE IT. SO I JUST GOT OFF THE BUS. AND CAME HERE. BECAUSE I WAS HUNGRY. I HADN'T HAD ANYTHING TO EAT ALL DAY EXCEPT A GOD-DAMN PINT OF WINE FOR BREAKFAST."

"YOU ATE HERE?" SHE LOOKED BY BOTH HIS SHOULDERS. "THAT'S GOOD."

"WHAT DID YOU DO?"

SHE WAS WEARING A WHITE BLOUSE, CLEAN BUT UNIRONED, THAT HE HAD NOT SEEN BEFORE. AS SHE WALKED BENEATH THE BULB, HE SAW HER JEANS WERE NEW ENOUGH TO SHOW THE CREASE. "YOU PICK UP SOME CLOTHES THIS AFTERNOON?" HE FOLLOWED HER INTO THE BARE AUDITORIUM.

"YESTERDAY. I FOUND THEM IN A CLOSET OF THE PLACE WHERE I'M STAYING NOW."

"YOU HAVE BEEN BUSY, HUH? YOU FOUND A HOUSE AN' ALL?"

"ABOUT THREE DAYS AGO."

"JESUS," KID SAID, "WHEN DID YOU GET TIME TO DO THAT? I DIDN'T THINK I LET YOU ALONE LONG ENOUGH TO GO TO THE DAMN BATHROOM, MUCH LESS FIND A HOUSE—"

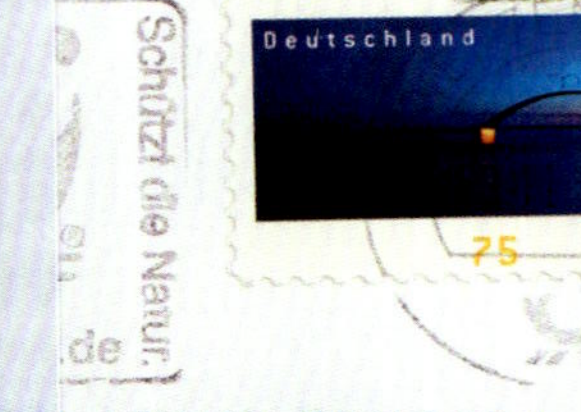

UNFINISH

WILLIAM DHALGREN
ARCHIVE BOOKS
DIEFFENBACHSTRAßE 31
10967 BERLIN, GERMANY

OPEN APARTMENTS

JUST WEST OF THE HEXAGON COMPLEX OFF THE MAIN ROAD THAT RUNS THROUGH

NABATIEH

LEBANON

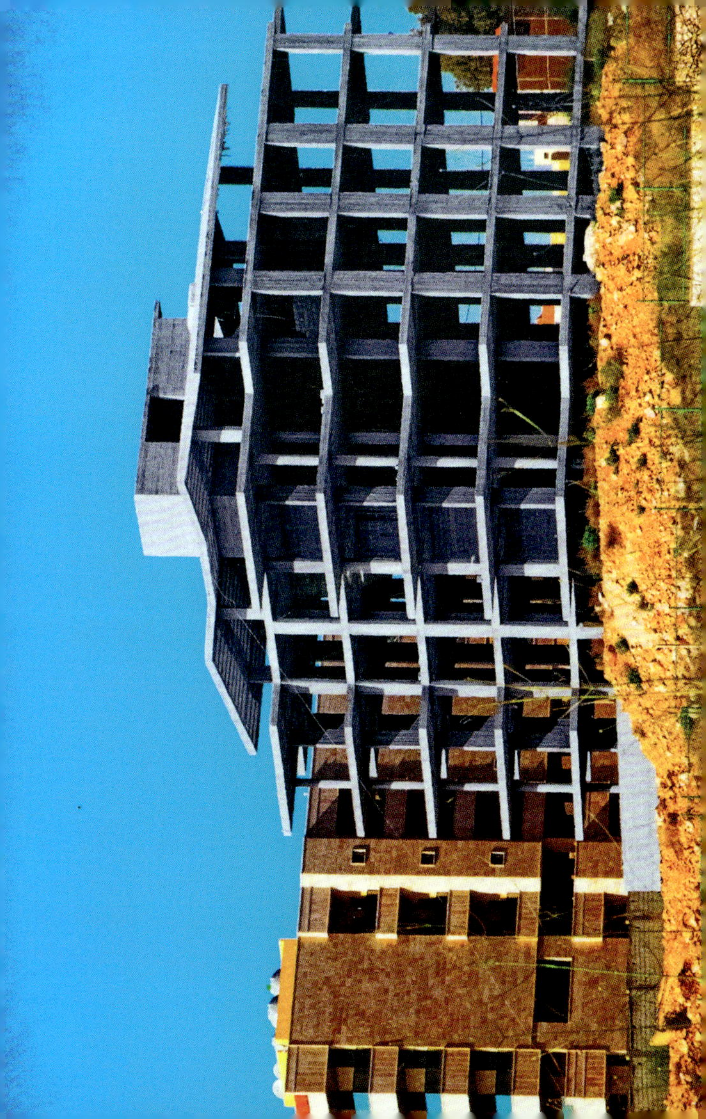

"KID..." SHE TURNED ON THE WORD TO LEAN AGAINST THE SOFA ARM. IN THE HALL, SHRILL ECHOES RETURNED. "KID," MUCH MORE SOFTLY, "I HAVEN'T SEEN YOU IN FIVE DAYS!"

"HUH?" THE HEEL ON THE FLOOR AND THE HEEL IN HIS BOOT PRICKLED. PRICKLING ROSE UP HIS LEGS, SPREAD ABOUT HIS THIGHS. "WHAT DO YOU MEAN?"

"WHAT DO YOU MEAN WHAT DO I MEAN?" SHE SPOKE CLUMSILY, BREAKING THROUGH THREE TONES OF VOICE. "WHERE HAVE YOU BEEN?" RETREATING FROM THE CLUMSINESS, HER VOICE WAS LEFT ONLY WITH HURT. "WHY DID YOU GO AWAY? WHAT DID YOU DO ALL THIS TIME?"

LITTLE THINGS CLAWED BETWEEN HIS BUTTOCKS, MOUNTED RIB BY RIB, PERCHED ON HIS SHOULDER TO NIP AT HIS NECK SO HE HAD TO DROP HIS CHIN. LINES OF PERSPIRATION SUDDENLY COOLED. "YOU'RE KIDDING WITH ME, AREN'T YOU? LIKE WITH THE MOONS?"

SHE LOOKED PUZZLED.

"THE NIGHT WHEN THE MOONS FIRST CAME OUT, AND LATER WE WERE TALKING ABOUT THEM; YOU PRETENDED THAT THERE HAD JUST BEEN ONE, AND THAT I HAD BEEN SEEING THINGS. YOU'RE FOOLING WITH ME LIKE THAT NOW?"

"NO!" SHE SHOOK HER HEAD, STOPPED IT IN THE MIDDLE OF A SHAKE. "OH, NO..."

50 Jahre Fehmarnsundbrücke
Deutschland
75

REGULAR MAIL
0114000684000140

WILLIAM DHALGREN
ARCHIVE BOOKS
DIEFFENBACHSTRAẞE 31
10967 BERLIN, GERMANY

1 9 DEC. 2014
NABATIEH

OPEN APARTMENTS

JUST WEST OF THE HEXAGON COMPLEX
OFF THE MAIN ROAD THAT RUNS THROUGH

NABATIEH

LEBANON

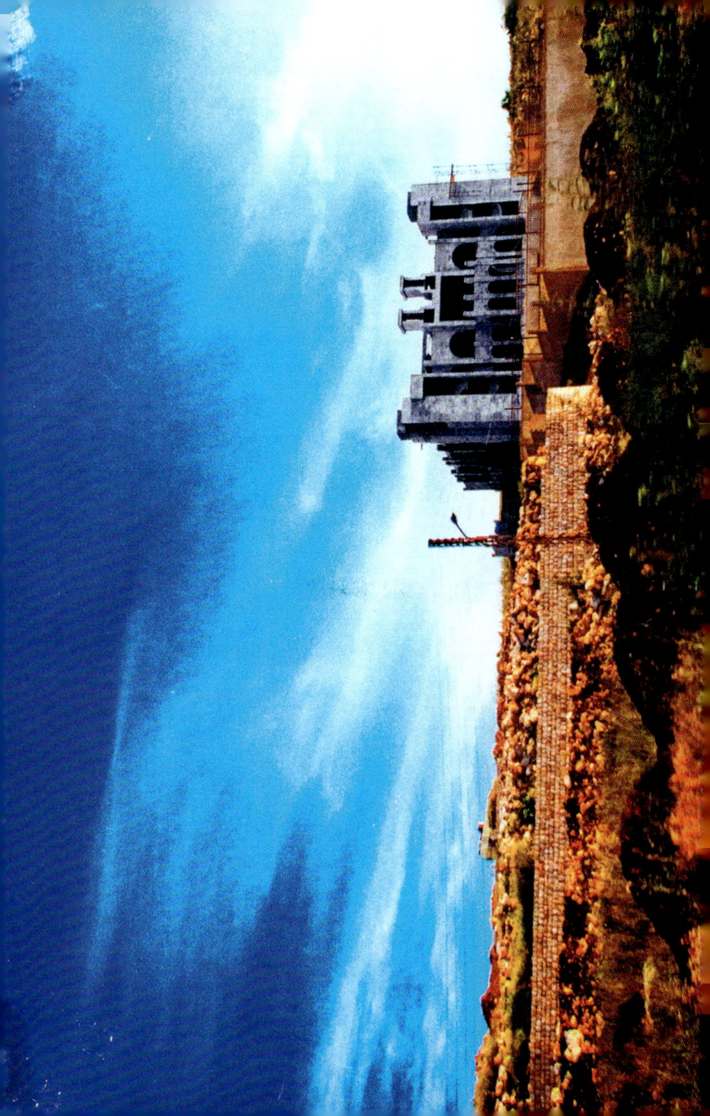

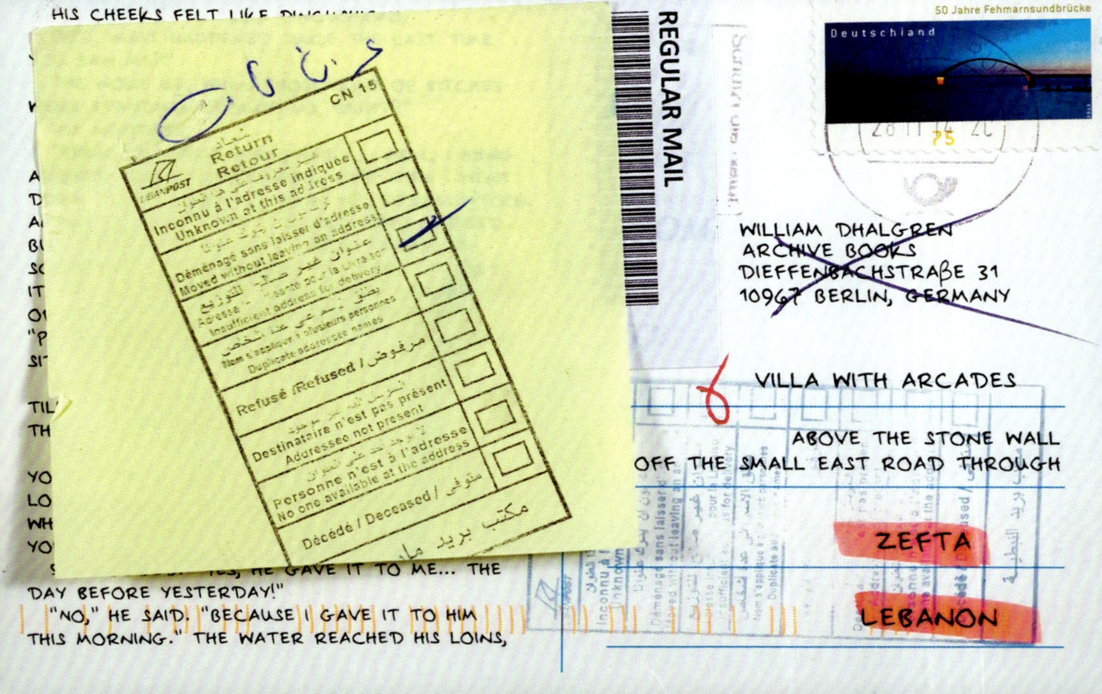
HIS CHEEKS FELT LIKE
YES, HE GAVE IT TO ME... THE
DAY BEFORE YESTERDAY!"
"NO," HE SAID. "BECAUSE I GAVE IT TO HIM
THIS MORNING." THE WATER REACHED HIS LOINS,
Return
Retour
CN 15
LIBANPOST
Inconnu à l'adresse indiquée
Unknown at this address
Déménagé sans laisser d'adresse
Moved without leaving an address
Insufficient address for delivery
Duplicate addressee names
Refusé /Refused / مرفوض
Destinataire n'est pas présent
Addressee not present
Personne n'est à l'adresse
No one available at the address
Décédé / Deceased / متوفى
مكتب بريد
REGULAR MAIL
50 Jahre Fehmarnsundbrücke
Deutschland
75
WILLIAM DHALGREN
ARCHIVE BOOKS
DIEFFENBACHSTRAẞE 31
10967 BERLIN, GERMANY
VILLA WITH ARCADES
ABOVE THE STONE WALL
OFF THE SMALL EAST ROAD THROUGH
ZEFTA
LEBANON

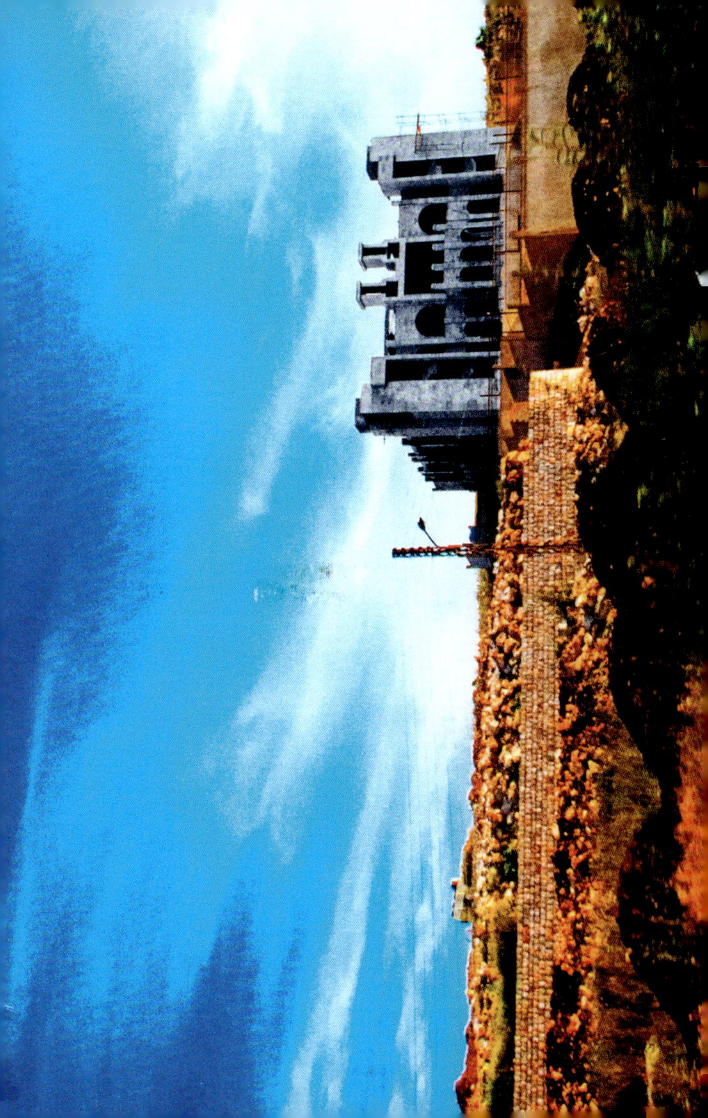

POURED INTO HIS SCROTUM; HIS SCROTUM SHRIVELED. "THEN I WENT OUT, AND ENDED UP AT THAT DEPARTMENT STORE DOWNTOWN. THAT'S WHERE I MET THE OTHER GUYS, AND WE BROKE INTO THE PLACE. THERE WERE PEOPLE LIVING IN THERE. WE GOT OUT. BUT THEY SHOT ONE OF THE GUYS. WE JUST GOT HIM OUT OF THERE, ON THE GOD-DAMN BUS THAT HAPPENED TO BE COMING ALONG!"

"THAT HAPPENED TWO NIGHTS AGO, KID! SOME OF THE SCORPIONS CAME INTO THE BAR AND WANTED TO KNOW IF ANYBODY KNEW WHERE THEY COULD GET A DOCTOR. MADAME BROWN WENT WITH THEM, BUT SHE CAME BACK IN ABOUT TEN MINUTES. EVERYBODY WAS TALKING ABOUT IT ALL YESTERDAY."

"HE WAS BLEEDING AND MOANING ON THE FLOOR OF THE BUS!" THE WATER ROARED AROUND IN KID'S CHEST, THEN FILLED THE COLUMN OF HIS NECK, FOUNTAINED INSIDE HIS HEAD. "I GOT OFF THE BUS, AND I CAME—" HE CHOKED, AND FOR A MOMENT THOUGHT HE WOULD DROWN. "—CAME HERE." THE WATER REACHED HIS EYES (AND THE WORK BULB GREW KNITTING NEEDLES OF LIGHT); HE BRUSHED IT AWAY, BEFORE MORE OF IT ROLLED DOWN HIS FACE, NO LONGER COLD, BUT HOT.

HE KEPT RUBBING AT HIS EYES WITH ONE HAND.

UNFINISHED STATE // 16D.266

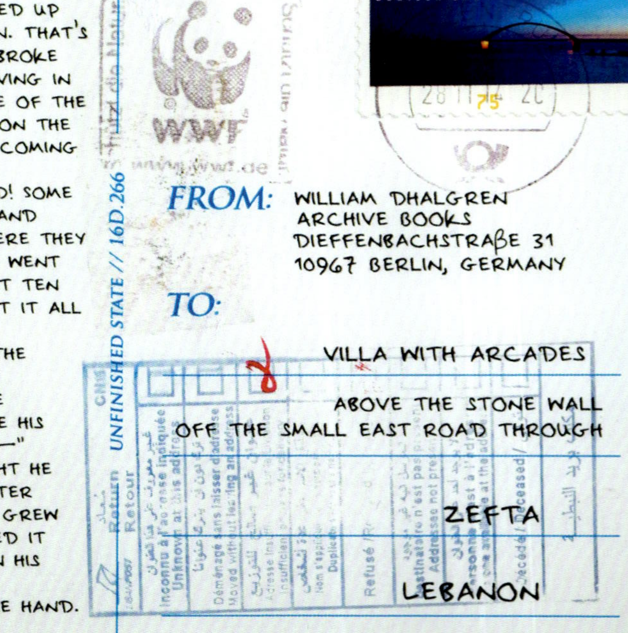

FROM: WILLIAM DHALGREN
ARCHIVE BOOKS
DIEFFENBACHSTRAßE 31
10967 BERLIN, GERMANY

TO: VILLA WITH ARCADES
ABOVE THE STONE WALL
OFF THE SMALL EAST ROAD THROUGH
ZEFTA
LEBANON

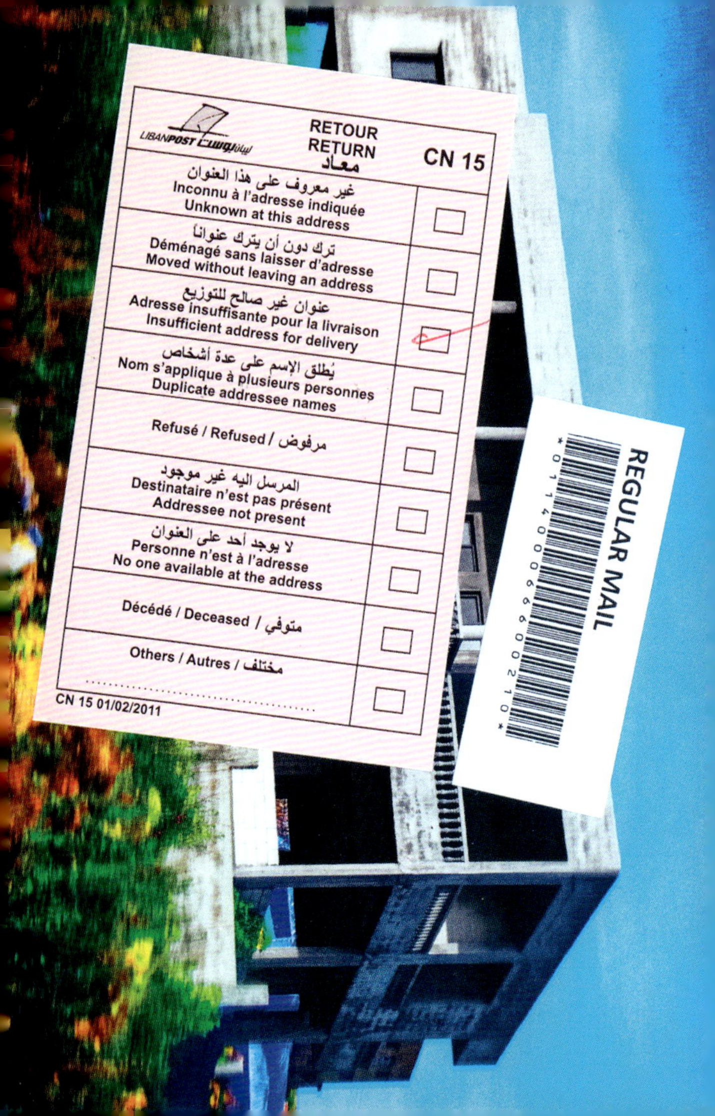

LIBANPOST ليبان بوست

RETOUR
RETURN
معاد

CN 15

غير معروف على هذا العنوان Inconnu à l'adresse indiquée Unknown at this address	☐
ترك دون أن يترك عنواناً Déménagé sans laisser d'adresse Moved without leaving an address	☐
عنوان غير صالح للتوزيع Adresse insuffisante pour la livraison Insufficient address for delivery	☑
يُطلق الإسم على عدة أشخاص Nom s'applique à plusieurs personnes Duplicate addressee names	☐
Refusé / Refused / مرفوض	☐
المرسل اليه غير موجود Destinataire n'est pas présent Addressee not present	☐
لا يوجد أحد على العنوان Personne n'est à l'adresse No one available at the address	☐
Décédé / Deceased / متوفي	☐
Others / Autres / مختلف	☐

CN 15 01/02/2011

REGULAR MAIL

0114000666600210

JUST GET A LITTLE NERVOUS WHEN I FIND MYSELF THINKING I MIGHT. THAT'S ALL."

"A WEEK." HE FELT HIS FACE TWIST. "WHAT THE HELL DID I DO FOR... FIVE DAYS? WHEN DID I..." HE REACHED FOR HER.

HER FACE CRASHED AGAINST HIS, HITTING HIS MOUTH, BUT SHE PUSHED HER TONGUE AGAINST HIS, AND WAS HOLDING TIGHT TO THE BACK OF HIS NECK. HE KEPT TRYING TO PULL HER EVEN CLOSER, LEANING AGAINST THE STAGE.

HE LOOSED ONE HAND TO DIG BETWEEN THEM, TILL HE COULD PULL THE HARMONICA FROM HER BLOUSE POCKET. IT RATTLED ON THE STAGE BEHIND THEM.

"YOU'RE NOT GOING TO HURT ANYONE," SHE SAID ONCE. "YOU'RE NOT GOING TO HURT ME. I KNOW THAT. YOU'RE NOT." THE HYSTERIA WITH WHICH SHE MADE LOVE TO HIM ON THAT DARK STAGE WAS FIRST FURIOUS, THEN FUNNY (WONDERING IF SOMEONE WAS GOING TO WALK IN, AND EXCITED BY THE IDEA); HE LAY ON HIS BACK WHILE SHE BUCKED ABOVE HIM, CLUTCHING HIS SHOULDERS, WONDERING SHOULD HE FEEL THIS WAY. BUT THE SOUND SHE WAS MAKING THAT HE'D THOUGHT WAS CRYING CLEARED TO LAUGHTER. HER BUTTOCKS FILLED HIS HANDS, AND HE DUG BETWEEN THEM.

SHE REARED TOO HIGH, AND LOST HIM TO

UNFINISHED STATE // 16D.271

Schützt die Natur
WWF
www.wwf.de

Deutschland
50 Jahre Fehmarnsundbrücke
75

FROM: WILLIAM DHALGREN
ARCHIVE BOOKS
DIEFFENBACHSTRAẞE 31
10967 BERLIN, GERMANY

TO:

VILLA WITH BALUSTRADE
NESTLED AMONG GREENHOUSES
ON THE ROAD PARALLEL TO
THE COASTAL HIGHWAY

GHAZIYE

LEBANON

LIBANPOST
12 DEC. 2014

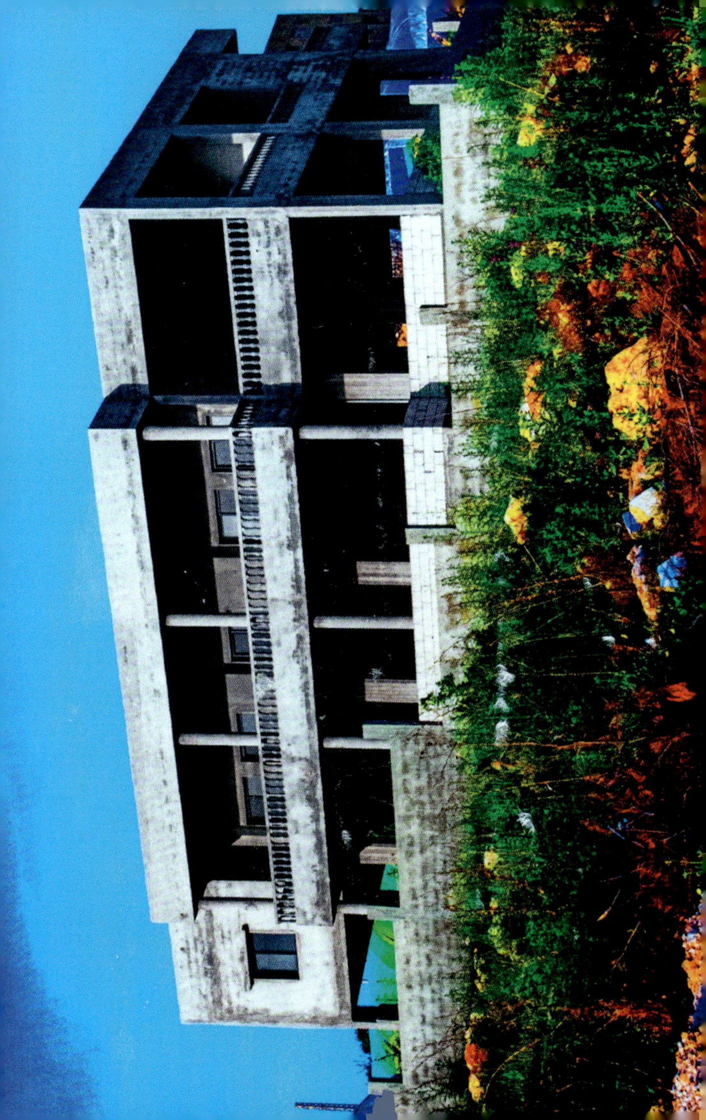

THE ANNEALING CHILL. WHILE SHE REACHED FOR HIM, HE ROLLED HER TO HER SIDE. LEGS IN THE CLUTCH OF DENIM, HE CRAWLED DOWN TO THE SWEATY CORNER OF HER BLOUSE AND PUSHED HIS TONGUE THROUGH HER SALTY HAIR. SHE LIFTED A KNEE TO LET IT FALL WIDE. AFTER SHE CAME (HE HAD WORKED HIS PANTS FREE OF ONE FOOT) HE STRADDLED HER, PUSHED HIS PENIS INTO HER AGAIN, LOWERED HIS BELLY TO HER BELLY, HIS CHEST TO HER CHEST, HIS WET FACE AGAINST THE CRUMPLED SHOULDER OF HER BLOUSE, AND BEGAN LONG FINAL STROKES, WHILE HER ARMS TIGHTENED ON HIS BACK.

COMING BURNED HIS LOINS (HE REMEMBERED THE SPILLED COFFEE) AND LEFT HIM EXHAUSTED AND STILL BURNING (HE REMEMBERED HOW IT FELT AFTER MASTURBATING WHEN ALL YOU STARTED OFF WITH WAS A PISS-ON), AND EXHAUSTION WON. LAKES OF SWEAT COOLED AROUND HIS BODY. SHE NODDED IN THE CROOK OF HIS SHOULDER, WHERE HE KNEW HIS ARM WOULD NUMB SOON, BUT DIDN'T FEEL LIKE DOING ANYTHING ABOUT IT. HE SLID HIS HAND DOWN HIS OWN CHEST, TILL HIS FINGERS CAUGHT IN THE TRANSVERSE CHAIN, BENEATH ANGULAR SHAPES.

TIME'S VOICES IN AGON? WHO WANTS TO HEAR HUNCHBACKS AND SPASTICS HAGGLE? EVEN, IF THERE ARE NO OTHERS IN CONCERT. WE SHOULD

UNFINISHED STATE // 16D.272

50 Jahre Fehmarnsundbrücke
Deutschland
75

FROM: WILLIAM DHALGREN
ARCHIVE BOOKS
DIEFFENBACHSTRAßE 31
10967 BERLIN, GERMANY

TO:

رجع

VILLA WITH BALUSTRADE
NESTLED AMONG GREENHOUSES
ON THE ROAD PARALLEL TO
THE COASTAL HIGHWAY
GHAZIYE
LEBANON

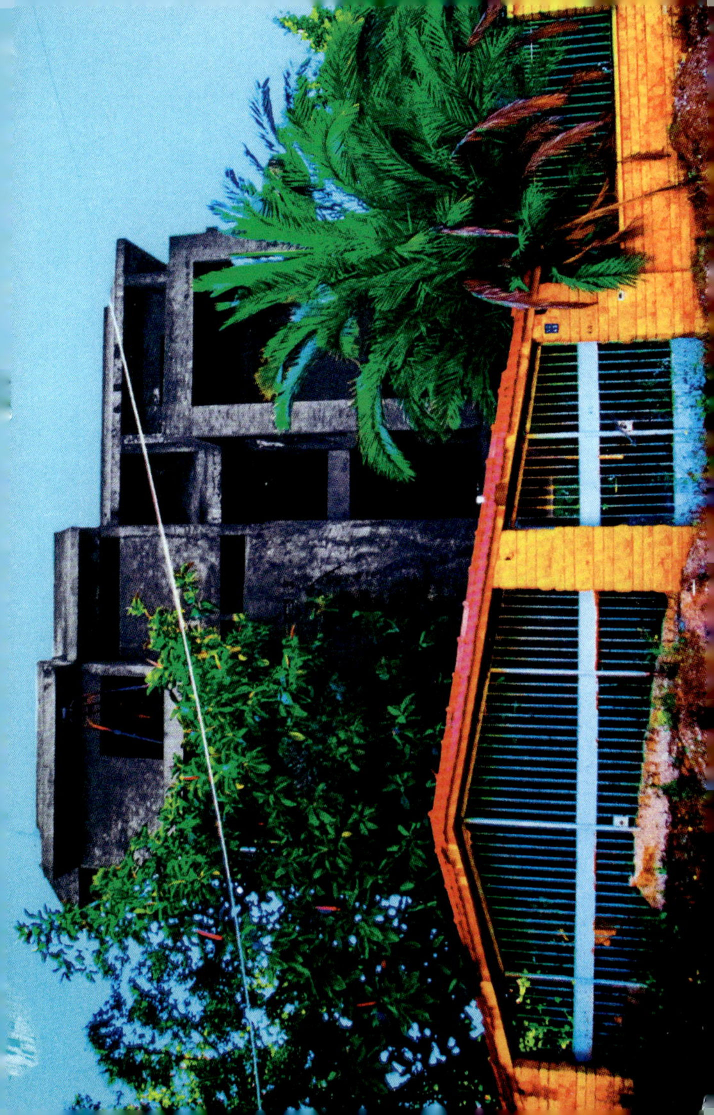

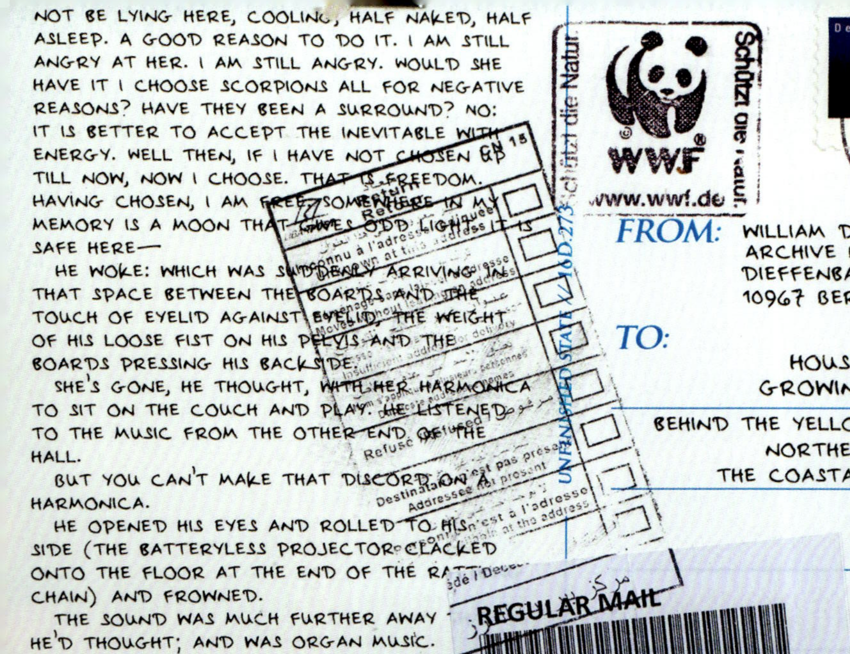

NOT BE LYING HERE, COOLING, HALF NAKED, HALF ASLEEP. A GOOD REASON TO DO IT. I AM STILL ANGRY AT HER. I AM STILL ANGRY. WOULD SHE HAVE IT I CHOOSE SCORPIONS ALL FOR NEGATIVE REASONS? HAVE THEY BEEN A SURROUND? NO: IT IS BETTER TO ACCEPT THE INEVITABLE WITH ENERGY. WELL THEN, IF I HAVE NOT CHOSEN UP TILL NOW, NOW I CHOOSE. THAT IS FREEDOM. HAVING CHOSEN, I AM FREE. SOMEWHERE IN MY MEMORY IS A MOON THAT GIVES ODD LIGHT. IT IS SAFE HERE—

HE WOKE: WHICH WAS SUDDENLY ARRIVING IN THAT SPACE BETWEEN THE BOARDS AND THE TOUCH OF EYELID AGAINST EYELID, THE WEIGHT OF HIS LOOSE FIST ON HIS PELVIS AND THE BOARDS PRESSING HIS BACKSIDE.

SHE'S GONE, HE THOUGHT, WITH HER HARMONICA TO SIT ON THE COUCH AND PLAY. HE LISTENED TO THE MUSIC FROM THE OTHER END OF THE HALL.

BUT YOU CAN'T MAKE THAT DISCORD ON A HARMONICA.

HE OPENED HIS EYES AND ROLLED TO HIS SIDE (THE BATTERYLESS PROJECTOR CLACKED ONTO THE FLOOR AT THE END OF THE RAT... CHAIN) AND FROWNED.

THE SOUND WAS MUCH FURTHER AWAY ... HE'D THOUGHT; AND WAS ORGAN MUSIC.

UNFINISHED STATE // 16D.273

FROM: WILLIAM DHALGREN
ARCHIVE BOOKS
DIEFFENBACHSTRAẞE 31
10967 BERLIN, GERMANY

TO:
HOUSE WITH TREES GROWING OUT OF IT
BEHIND THE YELLOW BRICK FENCE
NORTHERN EXIT OFF OF
THE COASTAL HIGHWAY INTO
ANSARIYEH
LEBANON

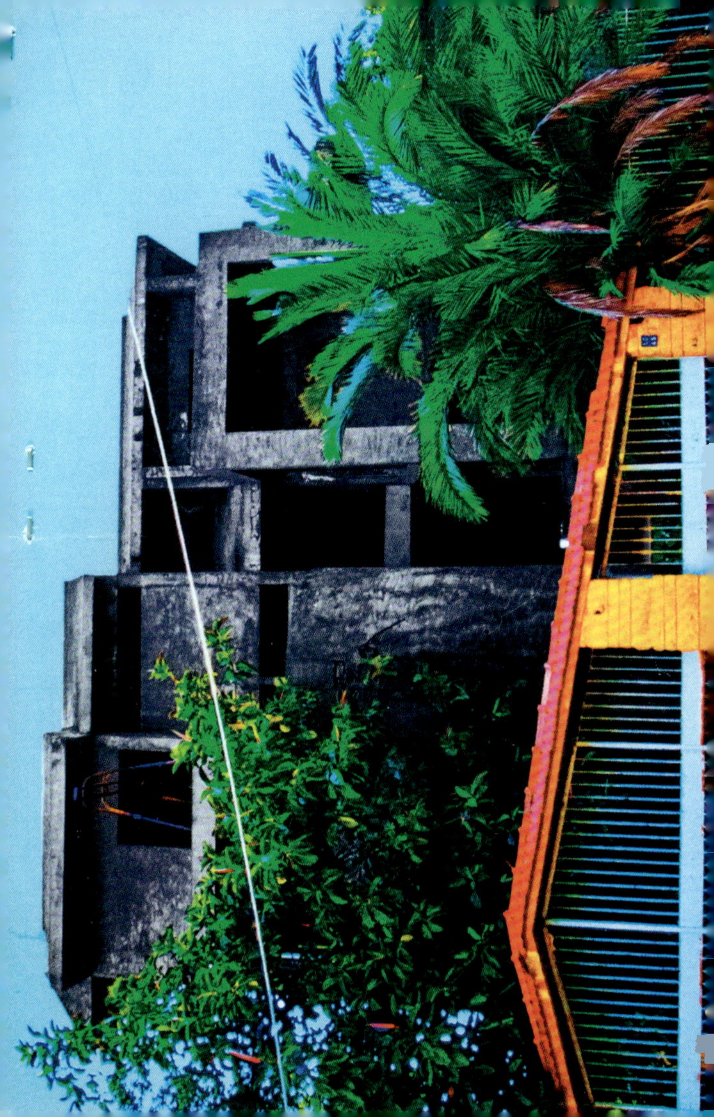

Return
Retour

…nu à l'adresse indiquée
Unknown at this address

Déménagé sans laisser d'adresse
…without leaving an address

عنوان غير صالح للتوزيع
…Insuffisant pour la Livraison

Refused / مرفوض

Destinataire n'est pas présent
…not present

Personne n'est à l'adresse
No one available at…

Décédé / Deceased

مكتب بريد صيدا

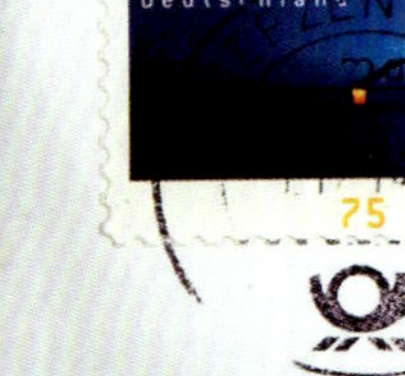

Schützt die Natur.

WILLIAM DHALGREN
ARCHIVE BOOKS
DIEFFENBACHSTRAßE 31
10967 BERLIN, GERMANY

HOUSE WITH TREES
GROWING OUT OF IT
HIND THE YELLOW BRICK FENCE
NORTHERN EXIT OFF OF
THE COASTAL HIGHWAY INTO

ANSARIYEH

LEBANON

FRIENDLY. THE VOICES TURNED AND BLURRED

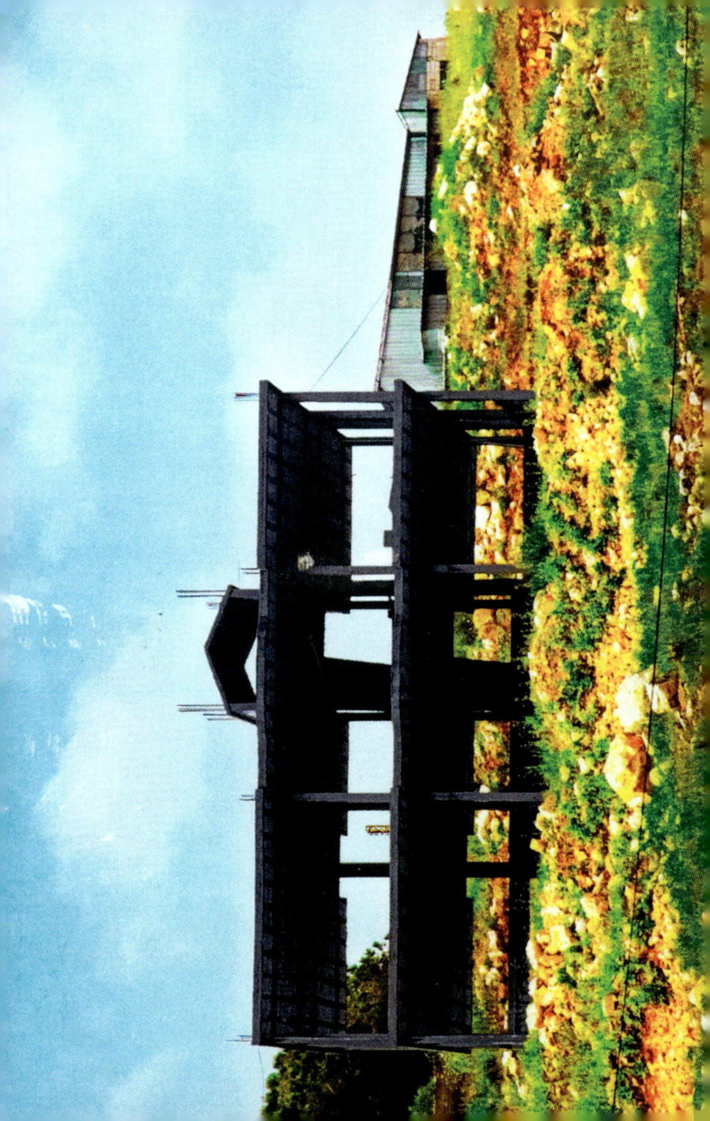

LIKE SMOKE, OR PRICKLED WITH LAUGHTER THAT MELTED WITH THE NEXT DOZEN AMBLING BY THE CLOSED OFFICE.

"LOVELY SERVICE, DON'T YOU THINK..."

"SHE AIN'T GONNA TALK ABOUT ALL THAT STUFF NEXT TIME TOO, IS SHE, 'CAUSE I..."

"DIDN'T YOU THINK IT WAS A LOVELY SERVICE..."

HE STEPPED AMONG THEM TO LEAVE. SOMEBODY KICKED HIS BARE HEEL TWICE, BUT HE RACKED IT TO ACCIDENT AND DIDN'T LOOK. OUTSIDE, THE EVENING WAS PURPLE GREY; SMOKE BLUNTED THE FACADES ACROSS THE STREET.

ONLY A FEW WHITE PEOPLE PASSED THROUGH THE TRAPEZOID OF LIGHT ACROSS THE SIDEWALK. A WOMAN WITH A FLOWERED SCARF TIED AROUND HER HEAD FOLLOWED AN OLDER MAN, TALKING EARNESTLY WITH A BLACK COMPANION; AND A HEAVY GUY, BLOND, IN A SHIRT WITH NO COLLAR THAT LOOKED AS IF IT WERE MADE OF ARMY BLANKET PLANTED HIMSELF BEFORE THE DOOR, WHILE BROWN AND DARKER FACES PASSED AROUND HIM. NOW A GAUNT GIRL, WITH FRECKLES ON HER TAN CHEEKS AND BRICK-RED HAIR, REACHED HIM. THE TWO WHISPERED TOGETHER, WALKED INTO THE DARKNESS.

KID WAITED BY THE DOOR, WATCHING THE WORSHIPPERS, LISTENING TO THE TAPE. PEOPLE

UNFINISHED STATE // 16D 275

Deutschland 75

REGULAR MAIL

0114000684001 31

FROM: WILLIAM DHALGREN
ARCHIVE BOOKS
DIEFFENBACHSTRAẞE 31
10967 BERLIN, GERMANY

SEE THROUGH HOUSE

OFF THE MAIN ROAD
GOING SOUTH THROUGH

NABATIEH

LEBANON

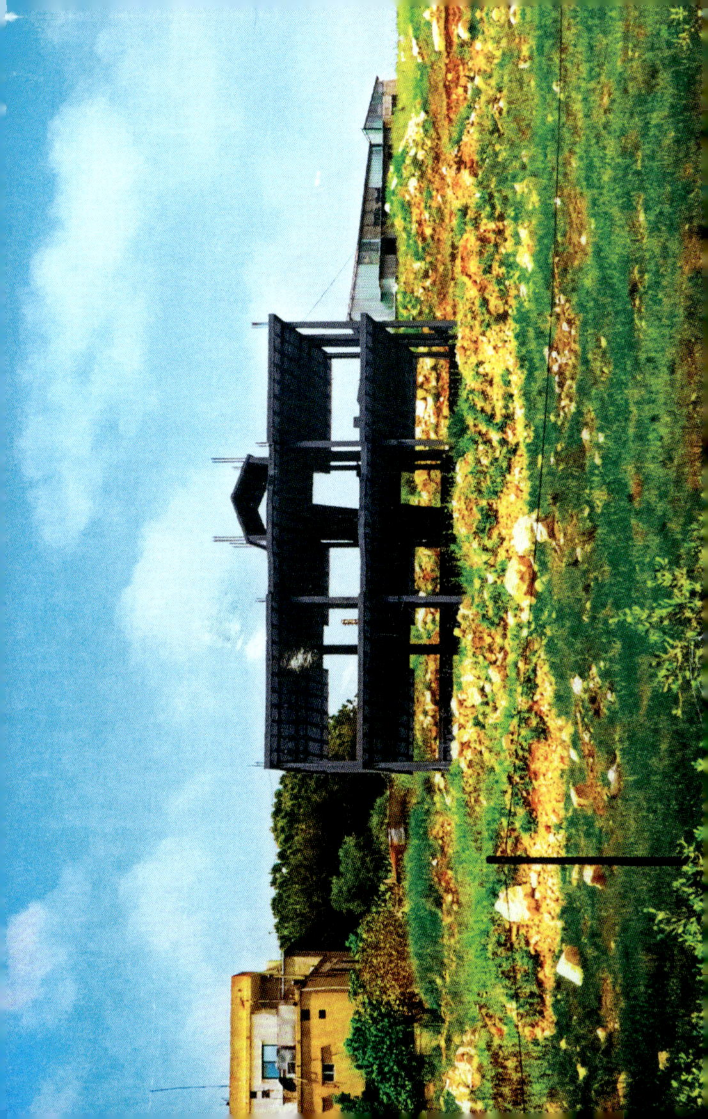

KID CAME OUT ON THE DAWN-DIM PORCH HUNG WITH HOOKS AND COILED WITH SMOKE. HE JUMPED FROM THE PLATFORM, STILL GROGGY, STILL BLINKING, STILL FILLED WITH THE TERROR FOR WHICH THERE WAS NO OTHER WAY TO DEAL WITH SAVE LAUGHTER. AFTER ALL, HE THOUGHT, AMBLING TOWARD THE CORNER, IF THIS BURNING CAN GO ON FOREVER, IF BESIDE THE MOON THERE REALLY IS A GEORGE, IF TAK KICKS ME OUT FOR A GLASS-EYED SPADE, IF DAYS CAN DISAPPEAR LIKE POCKETED DOLLARS, THEN THERE IS NO TELLING. OR ONLY THE TELLING, BUT NO REASONING. HE HOOKED HIS THUMBS IN HIS POCKETS WHERE THE MATERIAL WAS ALREADY FRAYING, AND TURNED THE CORNER.

BETWEEN THE WAREHOUSES, DEALING AND FADING IN MOVING SMOKE, THE BRIDGE ROSE AND SWUNG OUT INTO OBLIVION.

AMONG THE CONSORTED FRAGMENTS OF HIS CURIOSITY, THE THOUGHT REMAINED: I SHOULD HAVE AT LEAST MADE HIM GIVE ME A CUP OF COFFEE BEFORE I WENT. HE CLEARED HIS STICKY THROAT, AND TURNED, EXPECTING THE SUSPENSION CABLES ANY MOMENT TO FADE FOREVER, WHILE HE (FOREVER?) WANDERED THE SMELLY WATERFRONT THAT SOMEHOW NEVER ACTUALLY OPENED ON WATER.

THIS WIDE AVENUE HAD TO LEAD ONTO THE

50 Jahre Fehmarnsundbrücke
Deutschland
75

REGULAR MAIL
011400068400212

1: WILLIAM DHALGREN
ARCHIVE BOOKS
DIEFFENBACHSTRAßE 31
10967 BERLIN, GERMANY

SEE THROUGH HOUSE

OFF THE MAIN ROAD
GOING SOUTH THROUGH

NABATIEH

LEBANON

19 DEC. 2014
LIBANPOST
5665
NABATIEH

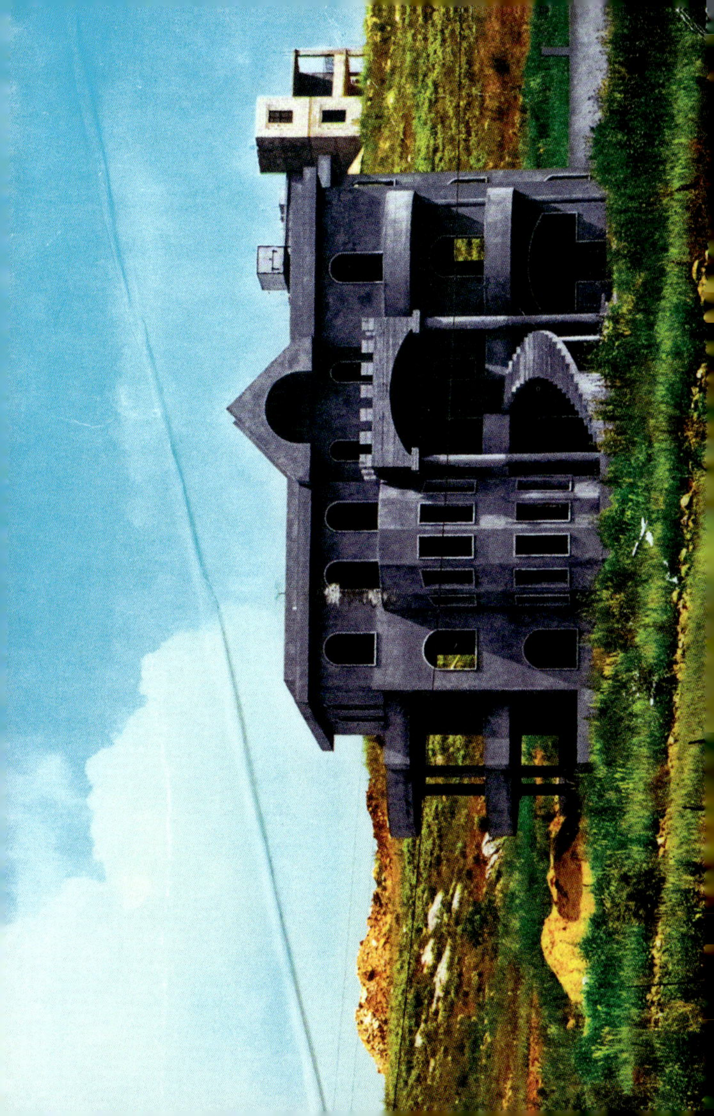

BRIDGE.

KID FOLLOWED IT FOR TWO BLOCKS AROUND A DARK, OFFICIAL BUILDING. THEN, BEYOND A TWIST OF FIGURE-EIGHTS AND CLOVER-LEAFS, THE ROAD ROLLED OUT BETWEEN THE SUSPENSORS, OVER THE RIVER.

HE COULD ONLY SEE AS FAR AS THE START OF THE SECOND SPAN. THE MIST, AMONG FOLDS AND TENDRILS, CONDENSED THE LIMITS OF VISION. FOGGY DAWNS SHOULD BE CHILL AND DAMP. THIS ONE WAS GRIT DRY, TICKLED THE BACK OF HIS ARMS AND THE SKIN BENEATH HIS NECK WITH SOMETHING ONLY A BREATH OFF BODY TEMPERATURE. HE WALKED UP THE EDGE OF THE ROAD, THINKING: THERE ARE NO CARS, I COULD RUN DOWN THE MIDDLE. SUDDENLY HE LAUGHED LOUDLY (SWALLOWING PHLEGM CAUGHT THERE IN THE NIGHT) AND RAN FORWARD, WAVING HIS ARMS, YELLING.

THE CITY ABSORBED THE SOUND, RETURNED NO ECHOES.

AFTER THIRTY YARDS HE WAS TIRED, SO HE TRUDGED AND PANTED IN THE THICK, DRY AIR. MAYBE ALL THESE ROADS JUST GO ON, HE THEORIZED, AND THE BRIDGE KEEPS HANGING THERE. HELL, I'VE ONLY BEEN GOING TEN MINUTES. HE WALKED BENEATH SEVERAL OVERPASSES. HE STARTED TO RUN AGAIN,

UNFINISHED S

WILLIAM DHALGREN
ARCHIVE BOOKS
DIEFFENBACHSTRAßE 31
10967 BERLIN, GERMANY

THE VILLA WITH A CURVED STAIRCASE

ON THE HILL OFF THE MAIN ROAD
GOING SOUTH THROUGH

NABATIEH

LEBANON

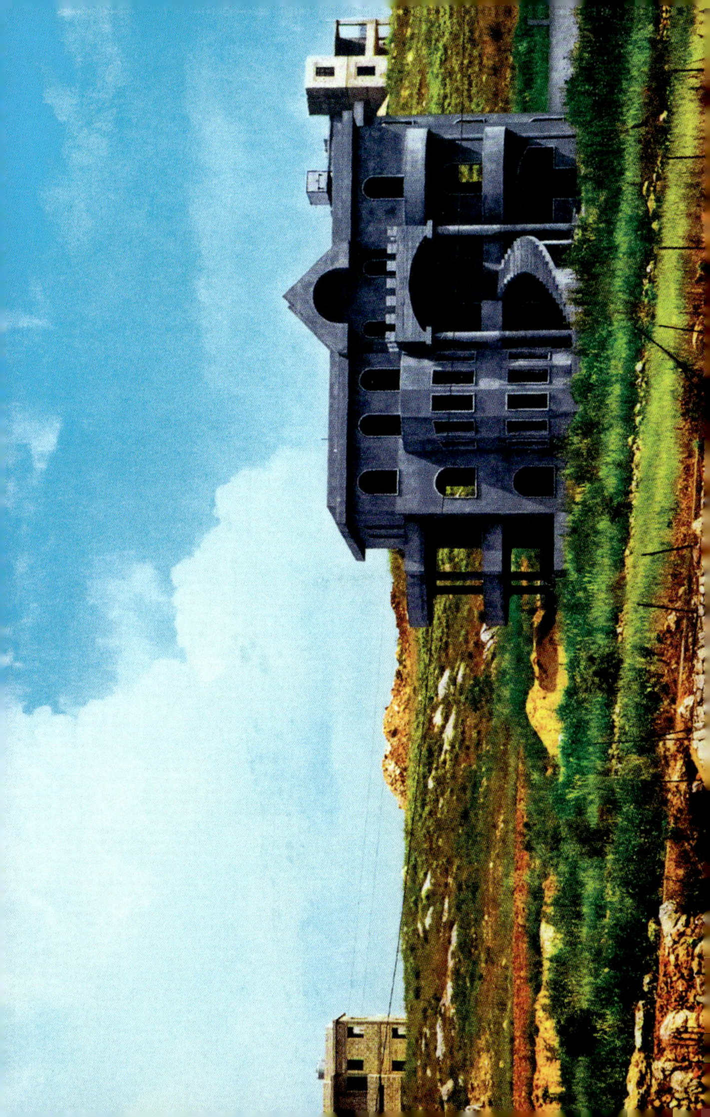

COMING AROUND A CURVE TO THE BRIDGE'S ACTUAL ENTRANCE.

THE ROADS' LINES BETWEEN THE CABLES BEGAN A DOZEN PERSPECTIVE V'S, THEIR SINGLE VERTEX LOPPED BY FOG. SLOWLY, WONDERINGLY, HE STARTED ACROSS TOWARD THE INVISIBLE SHORE. ONCE HE WENT TO THE RAIL AND LOOKED OVER THROUGH THE SMOKE TO THE WATER. HE LOOKED UP THROUGH GIRDERS AND CABLES PAST THE WALKWAY TOWARD THE STANCHION TOWER. WHAT AM I DOING HERE? HE THOUGHT, AND LOOKED AGAIN INTO THE FOG.

THE CAR WAS BACK AMONG THE UNDERPASSES HALF A MINUTE WHILE ITS MOTOR GOT LOUDER. MAROON, BLUNT, AND TWENTY YEARS OLD, IT SWUNG OUT ONTO THE GRIDDED MACADAM; AS IT GROWLED BY, A MAN IN THE BACK SEAT TURNED, SMILED, WAVED.

"HEY!" KID CALLED, AND WAVED AFTER HIM.

THE CAR DID NOT SLOW. BUT THE MAN GESTURED AGAIN THROUGH THE BACK WINDSHIELD.

"MR NEWBOY!" KID TOOK SIX RUNNING STEPS AND SHOUTED: "GOOD-BYE! GOOD-BYE, MR NEWBOY!"

THE CAR DIMINISHED BETWEEN THE GRILLS OF CABLE, HIT THE SMOKE, AND SANK LIKE A WEIGHT ON LOOSE COTTON. A MOMENT LATER—TOO

UNFINISHED STATE // 17D.278

REGULAR MAIL

* 0 1 1 4 0 0 0 6 2 9 0 2 0 1 3 *

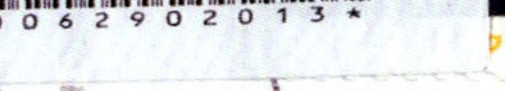

FROM: WILLIAM DHALGREN
ARCHIVE BOOKS
DIEFFENBACHSTRAßE 31
10967 BERLIN, GERMANY

TO:

THE VILLA WITH A CURVED STAIRCASE
ON THE HILL OFF THE MAIN ROAD
GOING SOUTH THROUGH
NABATIEH
LEBANON

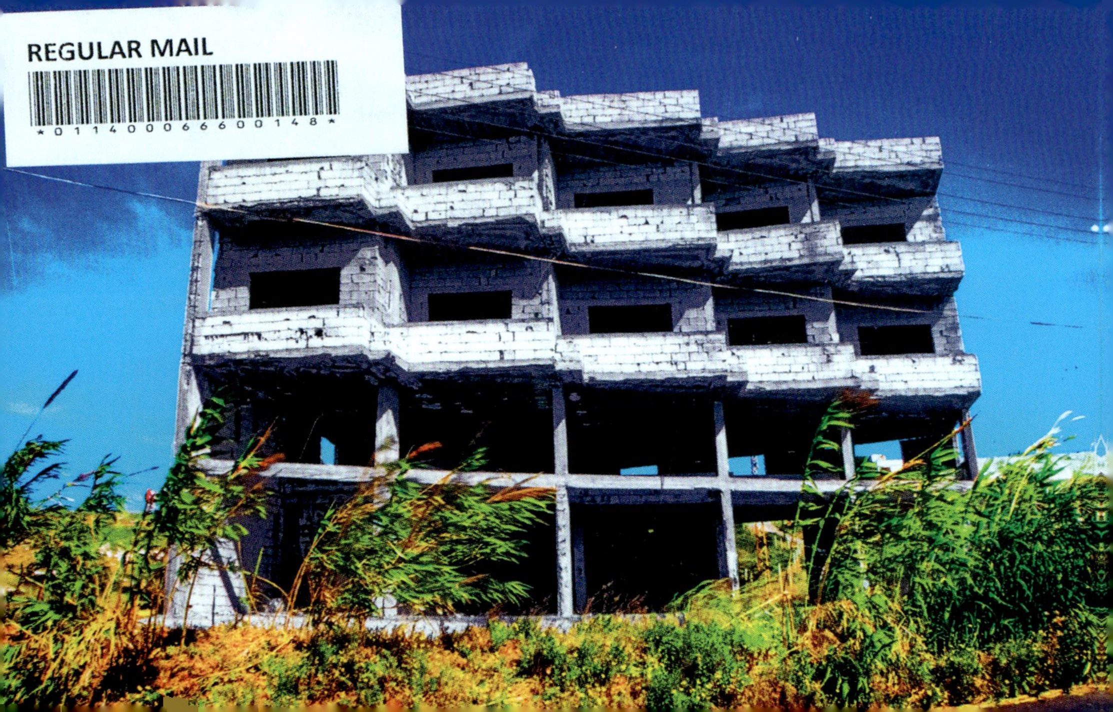
REGULAR MAIL
01140006660014 8

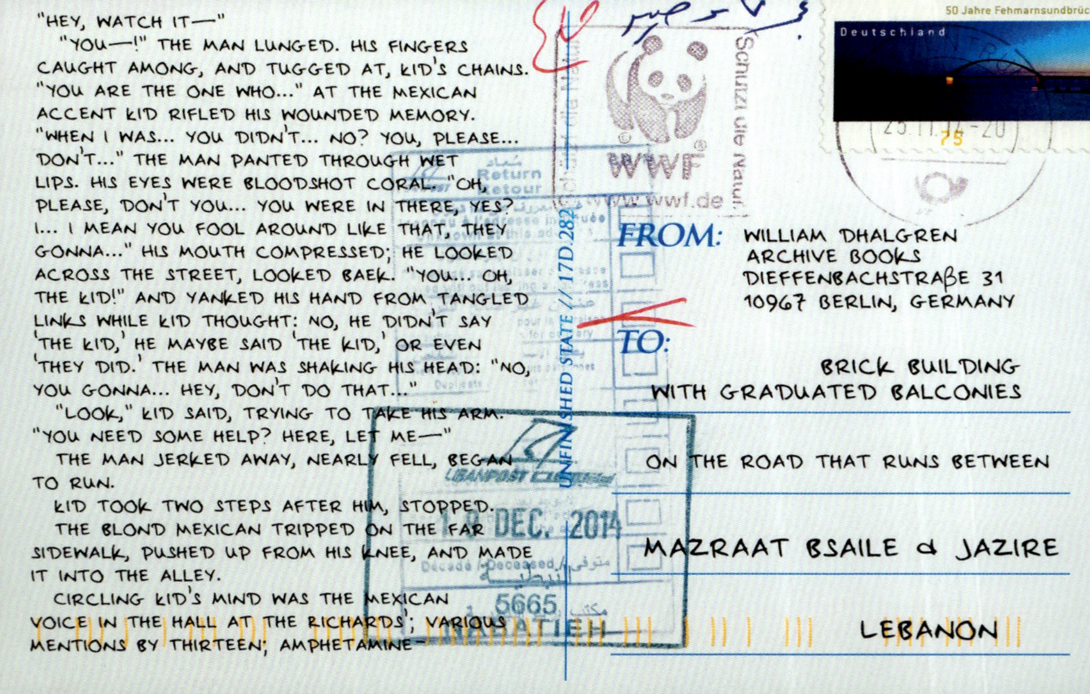
"HEY, WATCH IT—"
"YOU—!" THE MAN LUNGED. HIS FINGERS CAUGHT AMONG, AND TUGGED AT, KID'S CHAINS. "YOU ARE THE ONE WHO..." AT THE MEXICAN ACCENT KID RIFLED HIS WOUNDED MEMORY. "WHEN I WAS... YOU DIDN'T... NO? YOU, PLEASE... DON'T..." THE MAN PANTED THROUGH WET LIPS. HIS EYES WERE BLOODSHOT CORAL. "OH, PLEASE, DON'T YOU... YOU WERE IN THERE, YES? I... I MEAN YOU FOOL AROUND LIKE THAT, THEY GONNA..." HIS MOUTH COMPRESSED; HE LOOKED ACROSS THE STREET, LOOKED BAEK. "YOU... OH, THE KID!" AND YANKED HIS HAND FROM TANGLED LINKS WHILE KID THOUGHT: NO, HE DIDN'T SAY 'THE KID,' HE MAYBE SAID 'THE KID,' OR EVEN 'THEY DID.' THE MAN WAS SHAKING HIS HEAD: "NO, YOU GONNA... HEY, DON'T DO THAT..."
"LOOK," KID SAID, TRYING TO TAKE HIS ARM. "YOU NEED SOME HELP? HERE, LET ME—"
THE MAN JERKED AWAY, NEARLY FELL, BEGAN TO RUN.
KID TOOK TWO STEPS AFTER HIM, STOPPED.
THE BLOND MEXICAN TRIPPED ON THE FAR SIDEWALK, PUSHED UP FROM HIS KNEE, AND MADE IT INTO THE ALLEY.
CIRCLING KID'S MIND WAS THE MEXICAN VOICE IN THE HALL AT THE RICHARDS'; VARIOUS MENTIONS BY THIRTEEN; AMPHETAMINE–
UNFINISHED STATE // 17D.282
FROM: WILLIAM DHALGREN
ARCHIVE BOOKS
DIEFFENBACHSTRAẞE 31
10967 BERLIN, GERMANY
TO: BRICK BUILDING
WITH GRADUATED BALCONIES
ON THE ROAD THAT RUNS BETWEEN
MAZRAAT BSAILE & JAZIRE
LEBANON
50 Jahre Fehmarnsundbrücke
Deutschland
75
WWF
www.wwf.de
Schützt die Natur
Return
Retour
LIBANPOST
18 DEC. 2014
Décédé / Deceased
5665

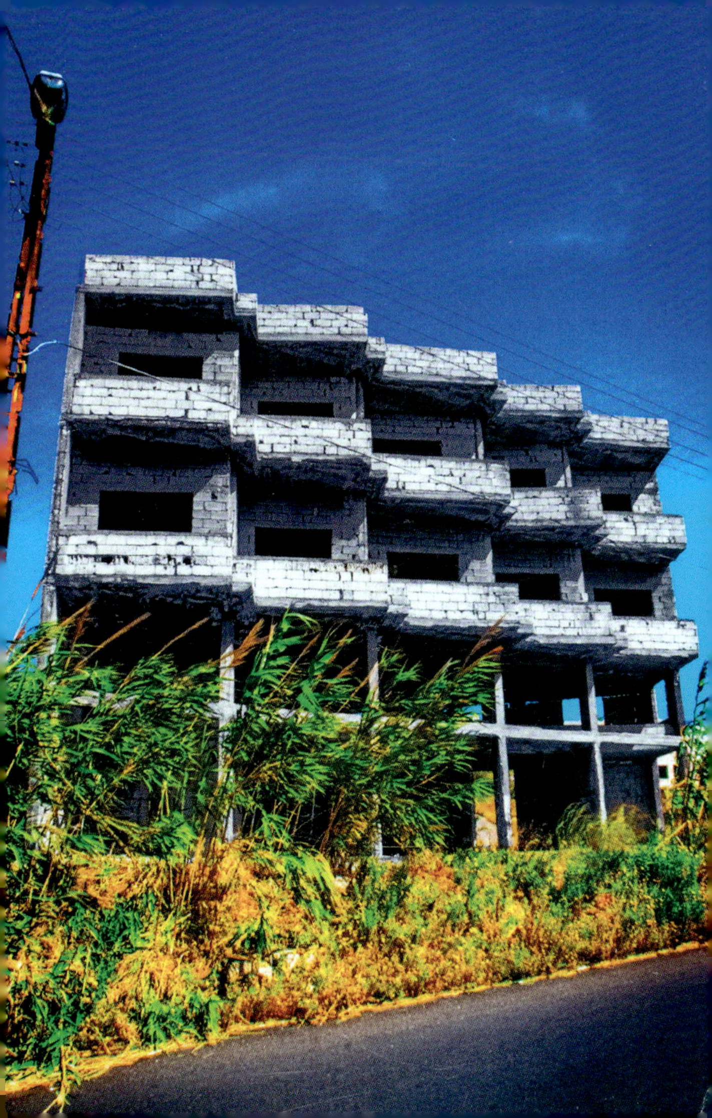

PSYCHOSIS? AND THEN THE THOUGHT, CLEAR AND OVERRIDING:

HE WAS... CRAZY!

SOMETHING CASCADED, TICKLING LIKE A LINE OF INSECTS, ACROSS HIS STOMACH. FOR A MOMENT HE MISTOOK IT FOR A CHILL OF RECOGNITION; INDEED, REAL CHILLS IGNITED A MOMENT AFTER.

BUT THE OPTIC CHAIN HAD PARTED, PROBABLY UNDER THE MAN'S TUGGING, AND FALLEN DOWN OVER HIS BELT.

KID PICKED UP THE LOOSE END, FOUND THE OTHER HANGING ACROSS HIS CHEST—IT HAD PARTED BETWEEN LENS AND PRISM—AND PULLED THE THIN BRASS TOGETHER. ON ONE END STILL HUNG A TINY, TWISTED LINK. WITH GREAT, STUBBY FINGERS, NEARLY NUMB INSIDE THEIR CALLOUS, HE TRIED TO GET IT CLOSED. HE STOOD IN THE STREET, PINCHING, TWISTING, SOMETIMES HOLDING HIS BREATH, SOMETIMES LETTING IT ALL OUT SUDDENLY WITH A MUMBLED "SHIT..." OR "FUCK..." HIS ARMPITS SLIPPED WITH THE SWEAT OF CONCENTRATION. HIS HEELS, ONE ON LEATHER, ONE ON PAVEMENT, STUNG AT DIFFERENT HEATS. HIS CHIN STAYED TUCKED INTO HIS NECK: HE SQUINTED IN THE DAWN LIGHT, TURNING ONCE SO THAT HIS OWN, EDGELESS SHADOW SLID FROM HIS FUMBLING NUBS. IT TOOK PRACTICALLY TEN

ISHED STATE // 17D.283

FROM: WILLIAM DHALGREN
ARCHIVE BOOKS
DIEFFENBACHSTRAßE 31
10967 BERLIN, GERMANY

TO: BRICK BUILDING
WITH GRADUATED BALCONIES
LEBANON

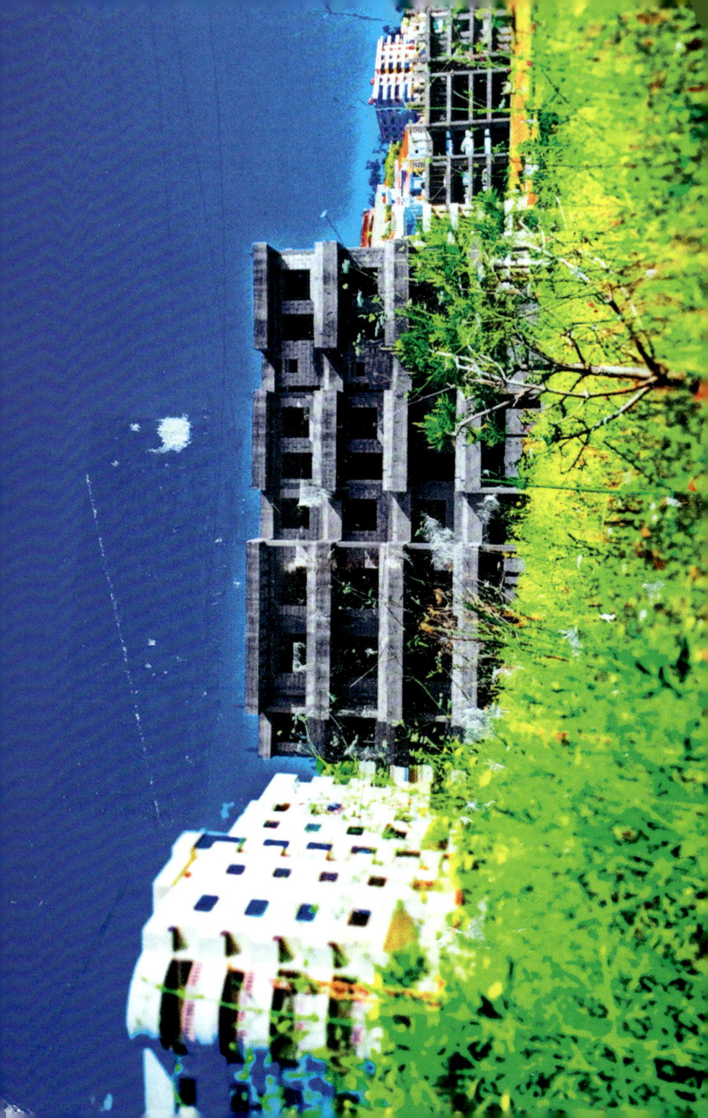

CRAMPED BENEATH HIS SIDE. HE WAS FILLED WITH THE TINGLING ONE HAS AFTER HAVING LAUGHED A LONG TIME. HE LAY, TRYING TO REMEMBER WHAT HAD JUST PASSED, GNAWING AT HIS FINGERS TILL HE TASTED BLOOD. AND KEPT GNAWING.

LANYA SHIFTED, MADE SOME SLOW, SLEEPY SOUND. KID TOOK HIS HAND FROM HIS MOUTH, CURLED HIS FINGERTIPS TIGHT AGAINST HIS PALM. "HEY," HE SAID. "ARE YOU ASLEEP...?"

LANYA STRETCHED. "MORE OR LESS..." SHE LOWERED HER CHIN AND LOOKED DOWN AT THE BLOND HEAD BETWEEN THEIR HIPS. "WHAT WAS HIS NAME?" KID LAUGHED.

DENNY'S HAND UNCURLED ON KID'S THIGH. THEN THE BLOND HEAD CAME UP. "... HUH?"

"WHAT'S YOUR NAME?" SHE PUSHED BACK CORDS OF HIS HAIR.

DENNY'S LIDS SLID CLOSED. HE SIGHED WITHOUT ANSWERING AND LAY DOWN AGAIN.

KID HELD HIS LAUGHTER IN THIS TIME. LANYA SHOOK HER HEAD; HER HAND AT KID'S FOREHEAD PUSHING AT HIS COARSER HAIR.

"HOW WAS HE?" HE WHISPERED, FROM SOMEWHERE DOWN IN HIS CHEST.

"MMMM?"

"I HEARD YOU TWO WHEN I WAS SORT OF HALF-ASLEEP." HE CUPPED HER CHEEK AND SHE

UNFINISHED STATE // 19D.304

Deutschland
75
30.11.

FROM: WILLIAM DHALGREN
ARCHIVE BOOKS
DIEFFENBACHSTRAßE 31
10967 BERLIN, GERMANY

TO:

SQUARE BRICK APARTMENTS

OFF THE HIGHWAY
NORTH OF FOAAD CHEHAB

SAIDA

LEBANON

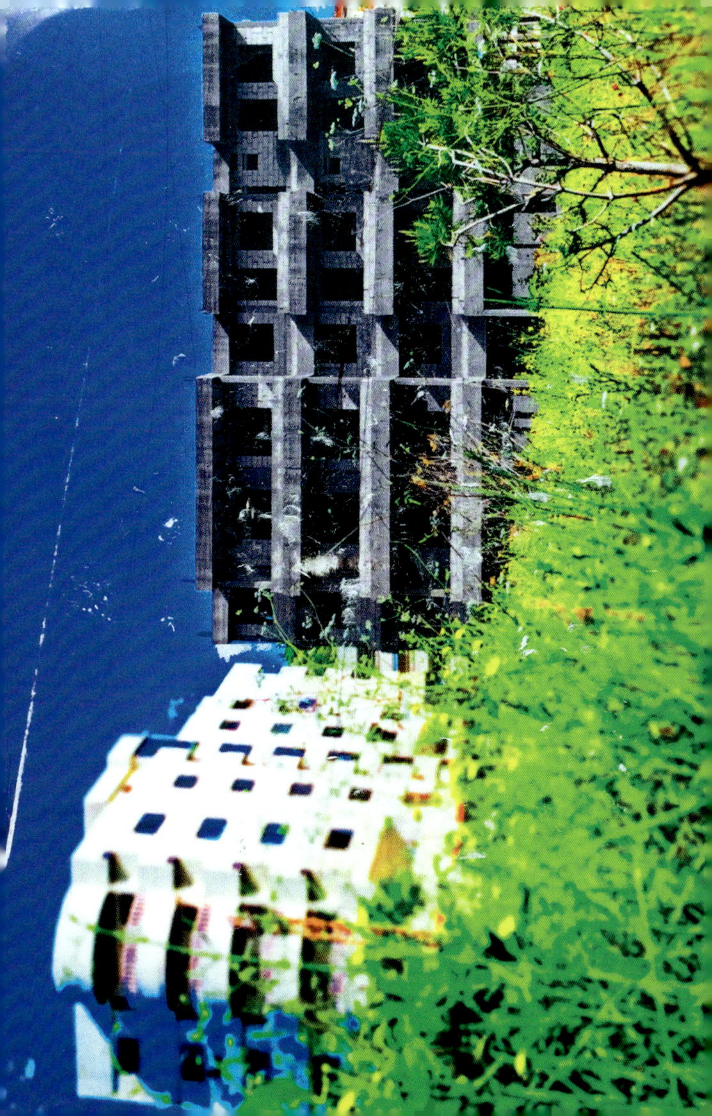

"THEN I GUESS IT WOULD BE OKAY TO ASK YOU QUESTIONS ABOUT THE MOON." KID GRINNED.

KAMP NODDED. "SOUNDS LIKE A PRETTY SAFE TOPIC."

"CAN YOU TELL ME SOMETHING ABOUT THE MOON YOU'VE NEVER TOLD ANYBODY ELSE BEFORE?"

AFTER A SECOND, KAMP LAUGHED. "NOW THAT IS A NEW ONE. I'M NOT SURE I KNOW WHAT YOU MEAN."

"YOU WERE THERE. I'D LIKE TO KNOW SOMETHING ABOUT THE MOON THAT SOMEONE COULD ONLY KNOW WHAT WAS ACTUALLY ON IT. I DON'T MEAN ANYTHING BIG. BUT JUST SOMETHING."

"THE WHOLE FLIGHT WAS BROADCAST. AND WE WERE PRETTY THOROUGH IN OUR REPORT. WE TRIED TO TAKE PICTURES OF JUST ABOUT EVERYTHING. ALSO, THAT'S A FEW YEARS AGO; AND WE WERE ONLY OUT WALKING AROUND FOR SIX AND A HALF HOURS."

"YEAH, I KNOW. I WATCHED IT."

"THEN I STILL DON'T GET YOU."

"WELL: I COULD BRING A COUPLE OF TELEVISION CAMERAS IN HERE, SAY, AND TAKE A LOT OF PICTURES, AND REPORT ON ALL THE PEOPLE, TELL HOW MANY WERE HERE OR WHAT HAVE YOU. BUT AFTERWARD, IF SOMEBODY ASKED

UNFINISHED STATE // 20D.305

50 Jahre Fehmarnsundbrücke
Deutschland
75

Schützt die Natur
WWF
www.wwf.de

FROM: WILLIAM DHALGREN
ARCHIVE BOOKS
DIEFFENBACHSTRAßE 31
10967 BERLIN, GERMANY

TO:

SQUARE BRICK APARTMENTS

OFF THE HIGHWAY
NORTH OF FOAAD CHEHAB

SAIDA

LEBANON

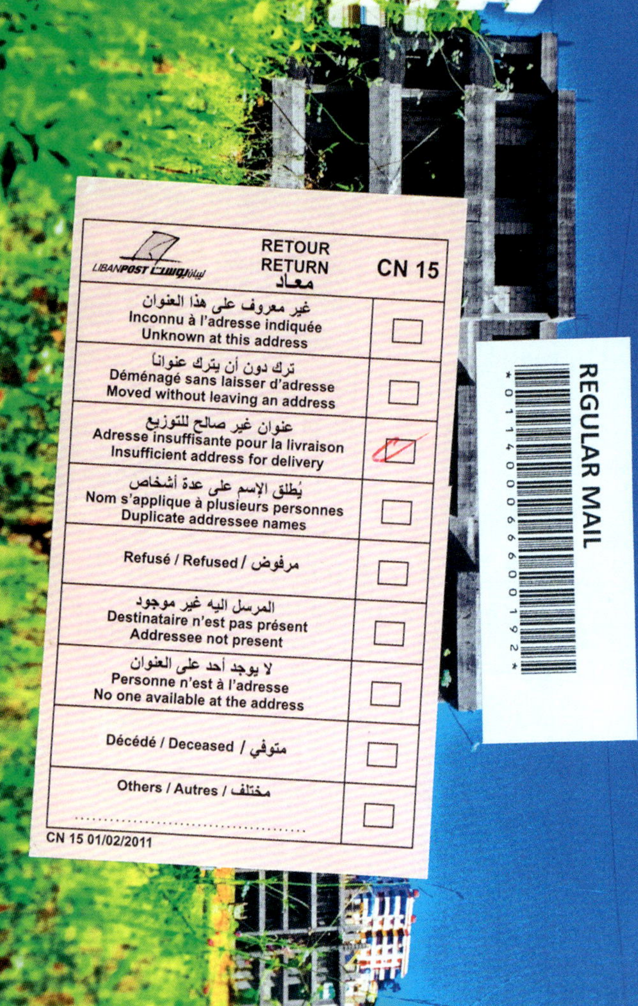

LIBANPOST ليبان بوست
RETOUR
RETURN
معاد
CN 15
غير معروف على هذا العنوان
Inconnu à l'adresse indiquée
Unknown at this address
ترك دون أن يترك عنواناً
Déménagé sans laisser d'adresse
Moved without leaving an address
عنوان غير صالح للتوزيع
Adresse insuffisante pour la livraison
Insufficient address for delivery
يُطلق الإسم على عدة أشخاص
Nom s'applique à plusieurs personnes
Duplicate addressee names
Refusé / Refused / مرفوض
المرسل اليه غير موجود
Destinataire n'est pas présent
Addressee not present
لا يوجد أحد على العنوان
Personne n'est à l'adresse
No one available at the address
Décédé / Deceased / متوفي
Others / Autres / مختلف
CN 15 01/02/2011
REGULAR MAIL
01140006660019 2

ME TO TELL THEM SOMETHING THAT WASN'T IN THE COVERAGE, I'D CLOSE MY EYES AND SORT OF PICTURE THE PLACE. THEN I MIGHT SAY, WELL, ON THE BACK OF THE COUNTER WITH THE BOTTLES, THE BOTTLE SECOND FROM THE LEFT—I DON'T REMEMBER WHAT THE LABEL WAS—BUT THE LITTLE CONE OF GLASS AT THE BOTTOM WAS JUST ABOVE THE TOP OF THE LIQUOR." KID OPENED HIS EYES. "SEE?"

KAMP RAN HIS KNUCKLES UNDER HIS CHIN. "I'M NOT USED TO THINKING LIKE THAT. BUT IT'S INTERESTING."

"TRY. JUST MENTION SOME ROCK, OR COLLECTION OF ROCKS, OR SHAPE ON THE HORIZON THAT YOU DIDN'T MENTION TO ANYONE ELSE."

"WE TOOK PHOTOGRAPHS OF ALL THREE HUNDRED AND SIXTY DEGREES OF THE HORIZON—"

"THEN SOMETHING ELSE."

"IT WOULD BE EASIER TO TELL YOU SOMETHING LIKE THAT ABOUT THE MODULE. I REMEMBER..." THEN HE COCKED HIS HEAD.

"I GUESS THAT WOULD DO," KID SAID. "BUT I'D PREFER IT WAS ABOUT THE MOON."

"HEY, HERE'S SOMETHING." KAMP LEANED FORWARD. "WHEN I GOT DOWN THE LADDER—DO YOU REMEMBER THE FOIL-COVERED FOOTPATHS

SHED STATE // 20D.306

50 Jahre Fehmarnsundbrücke
Deutschland
75

Schützt die Natur
WWF
www.wwf.de
Schützt die Natur

FROM: WILLIAM DHALGREN
ARCHIVE BOOKS
DIEFFENBACHSTRAßE 31
10967 BERLIN, GERMANY

TO:

SQUARE BRICK APARTMENTS

Anschrift überprüft durch Deutsche Post / BZ 05
ZURÜCK:
Empfänger nicht zu ermitteln
10967

LEBANON

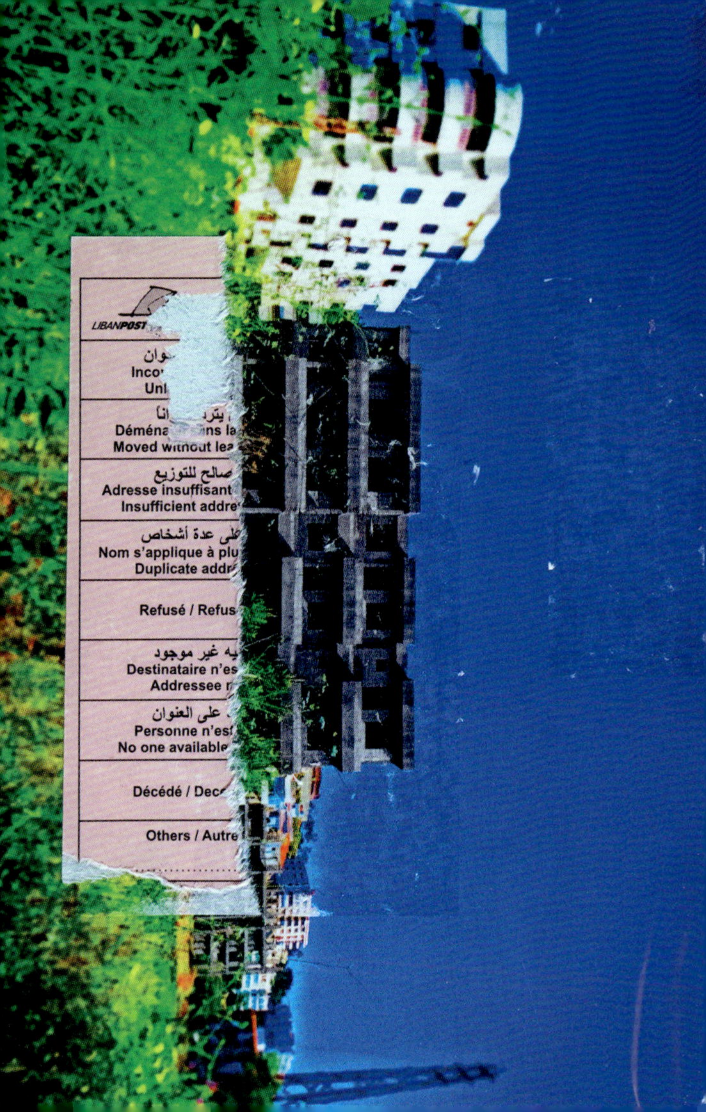

LIBANPOST
Inco
Unl
Déména ins la
Moved without lea
صالح للتوزيع
Adresse insuffisant
Insufficient addre
عدة أشخاص
Nom s'applique à plu
Duplicate addr
Refusé / Refus
غير موجود
Destinataire n'es
Addressee
على العنوان
Personne n'es
No one available
Décédé / Dec
Others / Autre

THAT THE MODULES RESTED ON? YOU SAY YOU WATCHED IT." KID NODDED.

"WELL, NOW, WHEN I WAS GETTING SOME OF THE EQUIPMENT OUT OF THE AUXILIARY COMPARTMENTS—I'D BEEN ACTUALLY ON SURFACE MAYBE A MINUTE, MAYBE NOT QUITE: A LOT OF PEOPLE, BACK BEFORE THE PROBE SHOTS, HAD THE IDEA THE MOON WAS COVERED WITH DUST. BUT IT WAS PURPLISH BROWN DIRT AND ROCK AND GRAVEL. THE FEET DIDN'T SINK AT ALL." KID THOUGHT: TRANSLATION. KID THOUGHT: TRANSITION.

"THE MODULE'S FEET WERE ON UNIVERSAL JOINTS, YOU KNOW? ANYWAY. THE ONE TO THE LEFT OF THE ENTRANCE WAS TILTED ON A SMALL ROCK, MAYBE TWO INCHES THROUGH. THE SHADOWS WERE PRETTY SHARP. I GUESS WHEN I WAS PASSING BY IT, MY SHADOW PASSED OVER THE MODULE FOOT. AND THE SHADOW FROM THE PAD, MADE BY THE ROCK IT WAS SITTING ON, AND MY SHADOW, JOINING IT, FOR JUST A SECOND MADE IT LOOK LIKE SOMETHING MOVED UNDER THERE. YOU KNOW? I WAS EXCITED, SEE, BECAUSE I WAS ON THE MOON. AND IT JUST ISN'T LIKE ANYTHING IN THE TRAINING SESSIONS AT ALL. BUT I DO REMEMBER FOR MAYBE THREE SECONDS, WHILE I WAS GOING ON DOING ALL THE THINGS I HAD TO DO, THINKING, THERE'S A MOON-MOUSE,

UNFINISHED STATE // 20D.307

Schützt die Natur
WWF
www.wwf.de

50 Jahre Fehmarnsundbrücke
Deutschland
75

FROM: WILLIAM DHALGREN
ARCHIVE BOOKS
DIEFFENBACHSTRAßE 31
10967 BERLIN, GERMANY

TO:

SQUARE BRICK APARTMENTS

OFF THE HIGHWAY
NORTH OF FOAAD CHEHAB

SAIDA

LEBANON

LIBANPOST ليبان بوست	معاد RETOUR RETURN	CN 15
غير معروف على هذا العنوان Inconnu à l'adresse Indiquée Unknow at this address		☐
ترك دون أن يترك عنواناً Déménagé sans laisser d'adresse Moved without leaving an address		☐
عنوان غير صالح للتوزيع Adresse insuffisante pour la livraison Insufficient address for delivery		☑
يُطلق الإسم على عدة أشخاص Plusieurs personnes portent le même nom Duplicate address names		☐
Refusé / Refused / مرفوض		☐
Nom réclamé / Unclaimed / لم يطلب		☐
صندوق بريد مقفل Boite postale fermée Closed P.O.Box		☐
Décédé / Deceased / متوفي		☐
Others / Autres / مختلف		☐

CN 15 31/05/2005

REGULAR MAIL

01140006660022 2

OR A MOON-BEETLE UNDER THERE.' AND FEELING SILLY THAT I COULDN'T SAY ANYTHING—I WAS BROADCASTING ALL THE TIME, DESCRIBING WHAT I SAW—BECAUSE THERE COULDN'T BE ANYTHING ALIVE ON THE MOON, RIGHT? LIKE I SAID, IT JUST TOOK ME A COUPLE OF SECONDS TO FIGURE OUT WHAT IT REALLY WAS. BUT FOR A MOMENT IT WAS PRETTY FUNNY. NOW THERE. THAT'S SOMETHING I NEVER TOLD ANYBODY... NO, I THINK I DID MENTION IT ONCE TO NEIL, WHEN I GOT BACK. BUT I DON'T THINK HE WAS LISTENING. AND I TOLD IT JUST LIKE A JOKE." FORMATION. KID THOUGHT: TRANSFORMATION. "IS THAT THE SORT OF THING YOU MEAN?" KID HAD EXPECTED KAMP TO BE SMILING AT THE END OF HIS STORY. BUT EACH FEATURE RESTED JUST WITHIN THE LIMIT OF SOBRIETY.

"YES. WHAT ARE YOU THINKING NOW?"

"I'M WONDERING WHY I TOLD YOU. BUT I GUESS BELLONA IS THE KIND OF PLACE YOU COME TO DO SOMETHING NEW, RIGHT? SEE NEW THINGS. DO NEW THINGS."

"WHAT DO PEOPLE SAY ABOUT THIS PLACE, OUTSIDE? DO PEOPLE WHO COME BACK FROM HERE TELL YOU ALL ABOUT LIFE UNDER THE FOG? WHO DID YOU TALK TO THAT MADE YOU WANT TO COME?"

"I DON'T THINK I'VE EVER MET ANYONE WHO'S

50 Jahre Fehmarnsundbrücke
Deutschland
75

Schützt die Natur
WWF
www.wwf.de

INISHED STATE // 20D.308

FROM: WILLIAM DHALGREN
ARCHIVE BOOKS
DIEFFENBACHSTRAßE 31
10967 BERLIN, GERMANY

TO:
SQUARE BRICK APARTMENTS
OFF THE HIGHWAY
LEBANON

Anschrift überprüft durch Deutsche Post / BZ 05
ZURÜCK:
Empfänger nicht zu ermitteln
10967

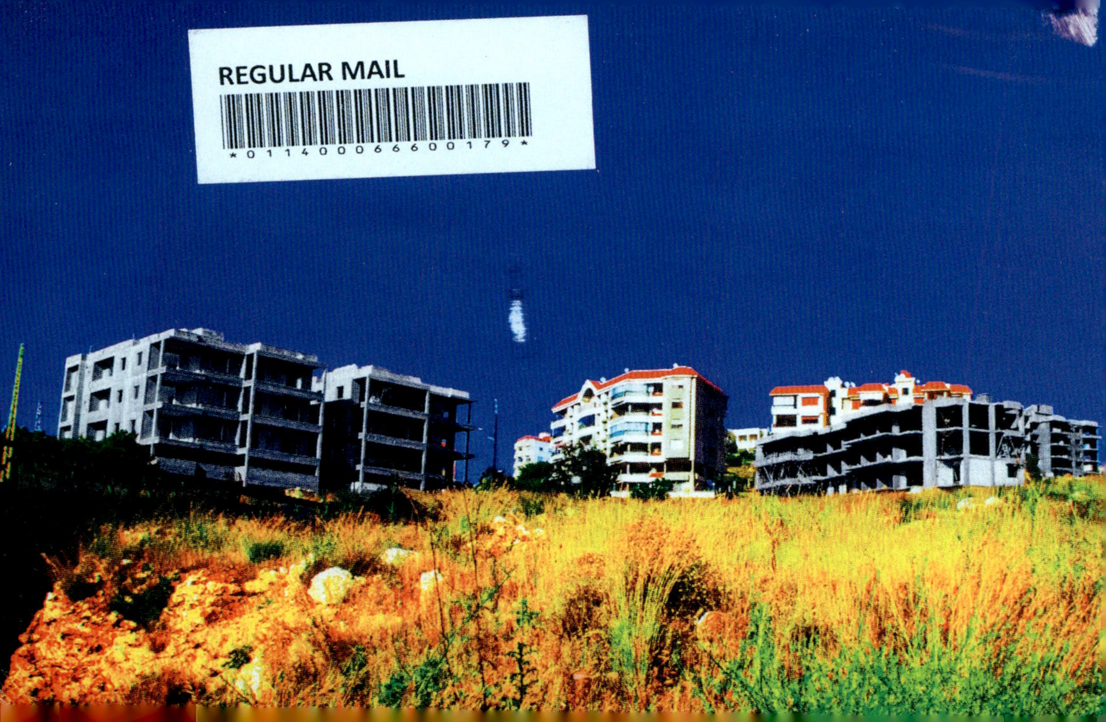

WHILE TAK TOOK THE HASP IN BOTH HANDS, GRUNTED. THE DOOR RUMBLED BACK FROM A PLANK OF BLACKNESS. TAK LOOKED AT HIS HANDS, THEIR CLEANNESS EMPHASIZED BY SWIPES OF RUSTY GREASE.

"GO ON IN." TAK HELD HIS HANDS FROM HIS HIPS TO KEEP THEM FROM HIS [illegible]

KID STEPPE[illegible] [illegible]'S TIMBRE CHANGE. IRON STEPS ROSE TO A CONCRETE PO[illegible]

"GO ON UP." [illegible]

KID DID AND STEPPED SIDEWAYS THROUGH THE DOOR AT THEIR [illegible]

THE SKYLIGHT, THREE STORIES ABOVE, MAPPED CONTINENTS IN DIRT AND LIGHT, AMONG LONGITUDINAL AND LATITUDINAL TESSELLATIONS.

"WHAT'S IN—" THE REVERBERATION HALTED HIM— "WHAT'S IN HERE?"

"GO ON," AND TAK [illegible] WITHOUT FACE. HE PASSED AHEAD OF KID. EACH FOOTFALL ON THE CONCRETE CAST BACK [illegible] ECHOES.

IT WAS VERY COOL.

BLOCKED BY EIGHT-FOOT PLANK X'S, SPOOLS BIG ENOUGH FOR UNDERGROUND ELECTRICAL CABLE SAT ABOUT THE FLOOR AMONG TWENTY- AND THIRTY-FOOT STACKS OF CARTONS. KID PASSED TWO BEFORE HE RECOGNIZED WHAT WAS WOUND ON THEM.

LATER HE TRIED TO FIGURE OUT WHAT THE

CN 15
Return
Retour
Inconnu à l'adresse indiquée
Unknown at this address
Déménagé sans laisser d'adresse
Moved without leaving an address
Adresse insuffisante pour la Livraison
Insufficient address for delivery
Nom répété sur plusieurs personnes
Duplicate address
Refusé
Destinataire n'est pas présent
Addressee not present
Personne n'est à cette adresse
No one available at the address
Décédé / Deceased /

UNFINISHED STATE // 23D. 312

Schützt die Natur
WWF
www.wwf.de
Schützt die Natur

50 Jahre Fehmarnsundbrücke
Deutschland
75

FROM: WILLIAM DHALGREN
ARCHIVE BOOKS
DIEFFENBACHSTRAßE 31
10967 BERLIN, GERMANY

TO:
THE UNFINISHED CONDOMINIUMS
BETWEEN THE COMPLEXES WITH
RED TILE ROOFS
ON THE HILL ACROSS FROM
MAJDELYOUN

AL HARA, HILLS ABOVE SAIDA

LEBANON

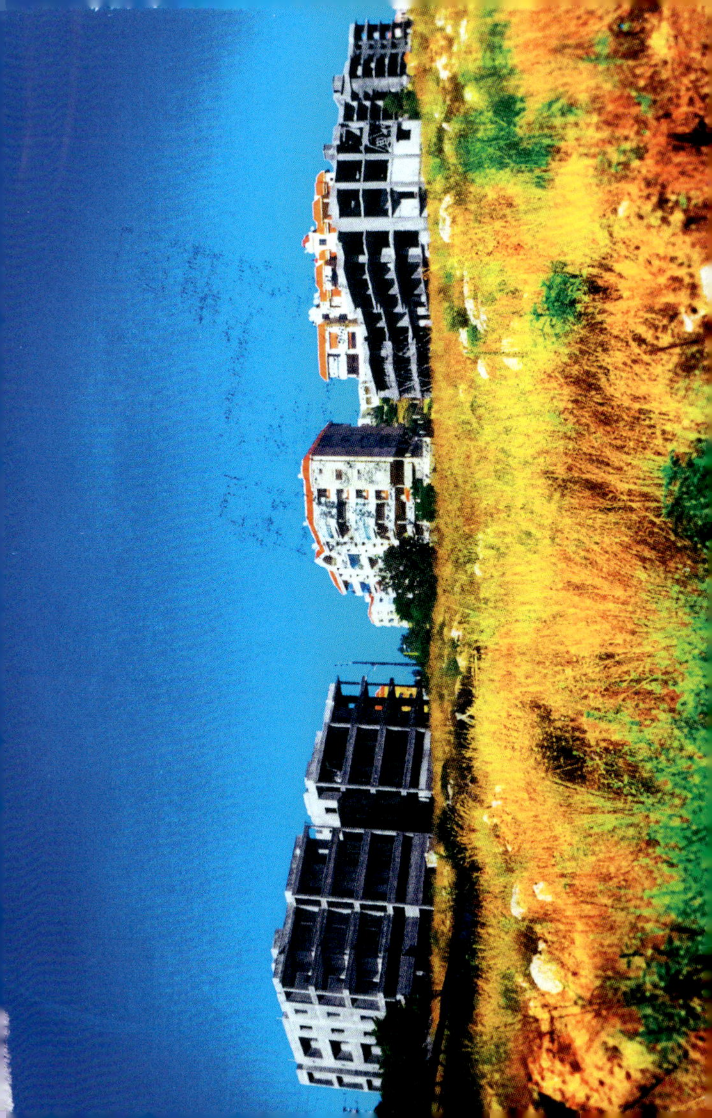

PROCESS OF RECOGNITION HAD BEEN. AT THE MOMENT OF SEEING THERE WAS A PERIOD IN WHICH ALL EMOTIONS WERE DEAD, DURING WHICH HE HAD GONE UP TO ONE—YES, HE HAD PUT OUT HIS HAND, PULLED IT BACK, AND JUST STOOD THERE A LONG WHILE.

IN HANKS, IN DRIPPING LOOPS FROM THE DRUM (HUNDREDS OF FEET? HUNDREDS OF THOUSANDS? AND HOW MANY DRUMS WERE THERE IN THE [SQUARE WAREHOUSE?]) THE BRASS CHAIN, SET WITH PRISMS, MIRRORS, LENSES, LOOPED.

HE STOOD BEFORE THE RANKED GLITTER, WAITING FOR IT TO STRIKE UP SOME EXPLANATORY THOUGHT.

THE END OF THE CHAIN HUNG TO THE FLOOR, WHERE A FEW FEET FORMED A FULL (C.300 STARS?) PLEIADES.

THERE WAS AN OPEN CARDBOARD CARTON BESIDE THE SPOOL. KID BENT DOWN, PUSHED BACK THE FLAP. THEY LOOKED LIKE COPPER BEETLES. HE PUSHED HIS HAND INTO THE METAL TABS, PICKED OUT ONE—THERE WAS A HOLE AT ONE END—AND TRIED TO READ WHAT WAS EMBOSSED ON IT. THE LIGHT WAS TOO DIM, AND THE CORNERS OF HIS EYES WERE STINGING.

ON THE CARTON, HOWEVER, STENCILED IN WHITE, WAS: PRODUCTO DO BRAZIL.

KID STOOD.

UNFINISHED STATE // 23D. 313

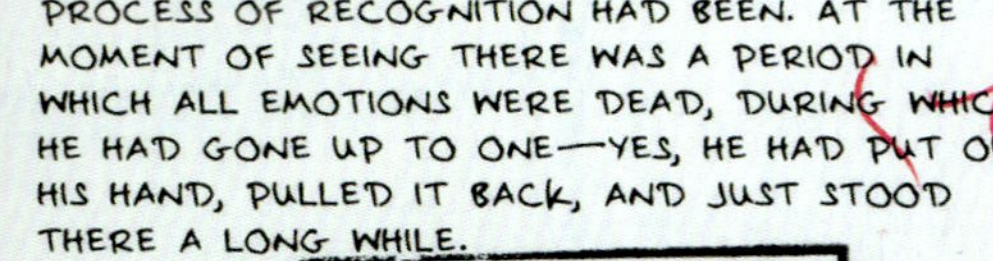

FROM: WILLIAM DHALGREN
ARCHIVE BOOKS
DIEFFENBACHSTRAßE 31
10967 BERLIN, GERMANY

TO: THE UNFINISHED CONDOMINIUMS
BETWEEN THE COMPLEXES WITH
RED TILE ROOFS
ON THE HILL ACROSS FROM
MAJDELYOUN

AL HARA, HILLS ABOVE SAIDA

LEBANON

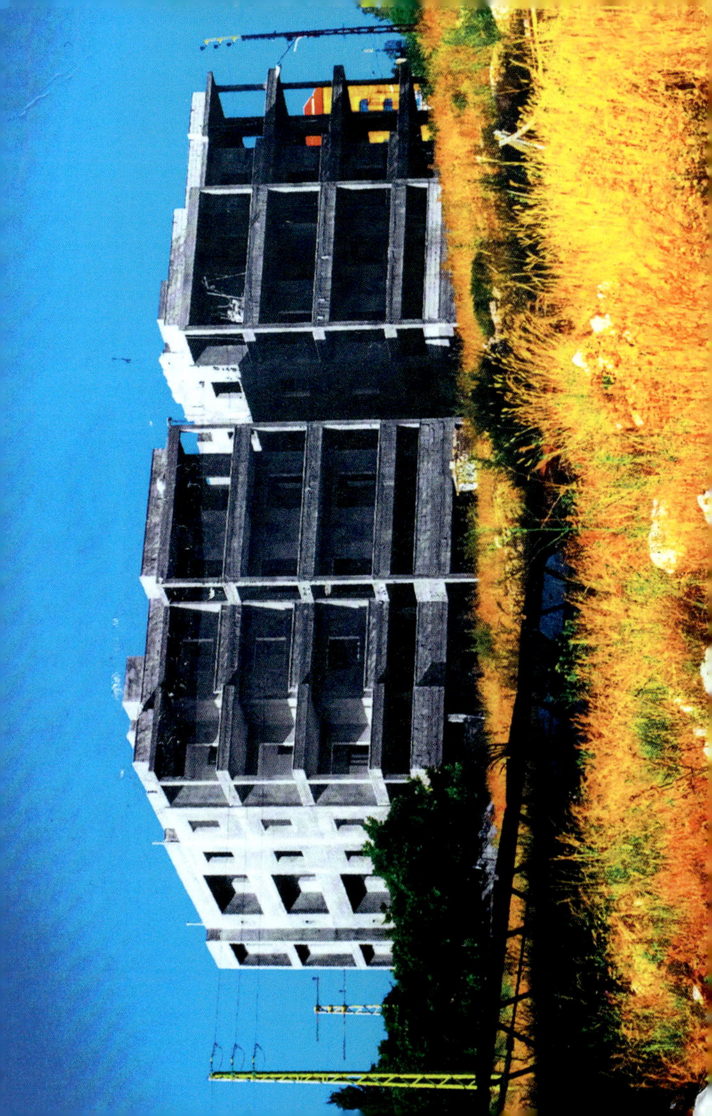

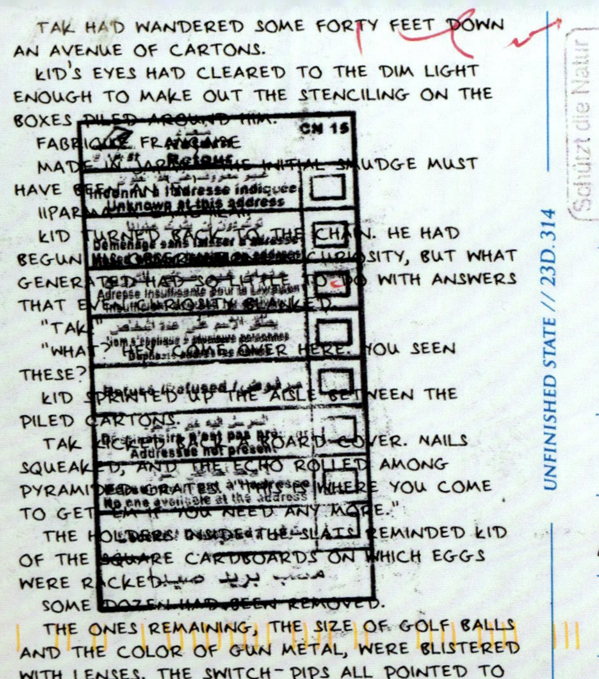

TAK HAD WANDERED SOME FORTY FEET DOWN AN AVENUE OF CARTONS.

KID'S EYES HAD CLEARED TO THE DIM LIGHT ENOUGH TO MAKE OUT THE STENCILING ON THE BOXES PILED AROUND HIM:

FABRIQUÉ FRANÇAISE

MADE IN JAPAN. THE INITIAL SMUDGE MUST HAVE BEEN AN [illegible]

IIPAR[illegible]

KID TURNED BACK TO THE CHAIN. HE HAD BEGUN [illegible] CURIOSITY, BUT WHAT GENERATED HAD SO LITTLE TO DO WITH ANSWERS THAT EVEN CURIOSITY BLANKED.

"TAK?"

"WHAT? HEY. COME OVER HERE. YOU SEEN THESE?"

KID SPRINTED UP THE AISLE BETWEEN THE PILED CARTONS.

TAK KICKED BACK A BOARD COVER. NAILS SQUEAKED, AND THE ECHO ROLLED AMONG PYRAMIDED CRATES. "THIS IS WHERE YOU COME TO GET 'EM IF YOU NEED ANY MORE."

THE HOLDERS INSIDE THE SLATS REMINDED KID OF THE SQUARE CARDBOARDS ON WHICH EGGS WERE RACKED.

SOME DOZEN HAD BEEN REMOVED.

THE ONES REMAINING, THE SIZE OF GOLF BALLS AND THE COLOR OF GUN METAL, WERE BLISTERED WITH LENSES. THE SWITCH-PIPS ALL POINTED TO

UNFINISHED STATE // 23D.314

FROM: WILLIAM DHALGREN
ARCHIVE BOOKS
DIEFFENBACHSTRAßE 31
10967 BERLIN, GERMANY

TO:
UNFINISHED CONDOMINIUM
LEFT SIDE OF THE COMPLEXES WITH
RED TILE ROOFS
ON THE HILL ACROSS FROM
MAJDELYOUN
AL HARA, HILLS ABOVE SAIDA
LEBANON

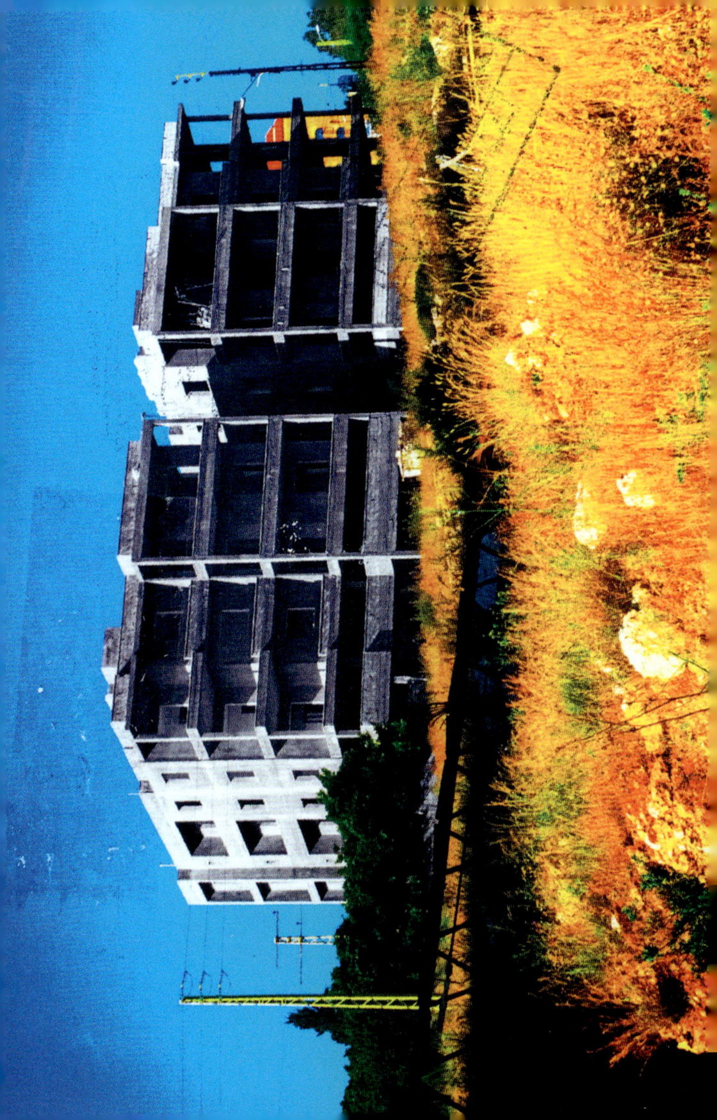

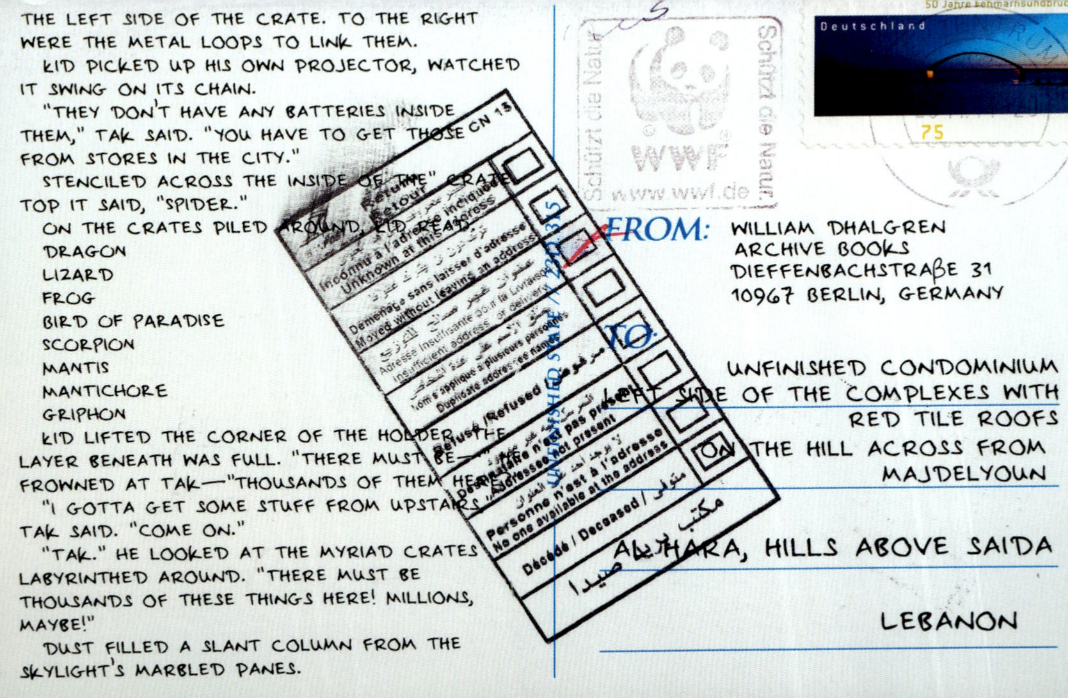
THE LEFT SIDE OF THE CRATE. TO THE RIGHT WERE THE METAL LOOPS TO LINK THEM.
KID PICKED UP HIS OWN PROJECTOR, WATCHED IT SWING ON ITS CHAIN.
"THEY DON'T HAVE ANY BATTERIES INSIDE THEM," TAK SAID. "YOU HAVE TO GET THOSE FROM STORES IN THE CITY."
STENCILED ACROSS THE INSIDE OF THE CRATE TOP IT SAID, "SPIDER."
ON THE CRATES PILED AROUND, KID READ:
DRAGON
LIZARD
FROG
BIRD OF PARADISE
SCORPION
MANTIS
MANTICHORE
GRIPHON
KID LIFTED THE CORNER OF THE HOLDER. THE LAYER BENEATH WAS FULL. "THERE MUST BE—" HE FROWNED AT TAK—"THOUSANDS OF THEM HERE!"
"I GOTTA GET SOME STUFF FROM UPSTAIRS," TAK SAID. "COME ON."
"TAK." HE LOOKED AT THE MYRIAD CRATES LABYRINTHED AROUND. "THERE MUST BE THOUSANDS OF THESE THINGS HERE! MILLIONS, MAYBE!"
DUST FILLED A SLANT COLUMN FROM THE SKYLIGHT'S MARBLED PANES.
CN 15
Retour
Inconnu à l'adresse indiquée
Unknown at this address
Déménagé sans laisser d'adresse
Moved without leaving an address
Adresse insuffisante pour la Livraison
Insufficient address for delivery
Nom s'applique à plusieurs personnes
Duplicate addressee names
Refusé / Refused
Destinataire n'est pas présent
Addressee not present
Personne n'est à l'adresse
No one available at the address
Décédé / Deceased
UNFINISHED STATE // 23D.315
Schützt die Natur
WWF
www.wwf.de
50 Jahre Fehmarnsundbrücke
Deutschland
75
FROM:
WILLIAM DHALGREN
ARCHIVE BOOKS
DIEFFENBACHSTRAßE 31
10967 BERLIN, GERMANY
TO:
UNFINISHED CONDOMINIUM
LEFT SIDE OF THE COMPLEXES WITH
RED TILE ROOFS
ON THE HILL ACROSS FROM
MAJDELYOUN
AL HARA, HILLS ABOVE SAIDA
LEBANON

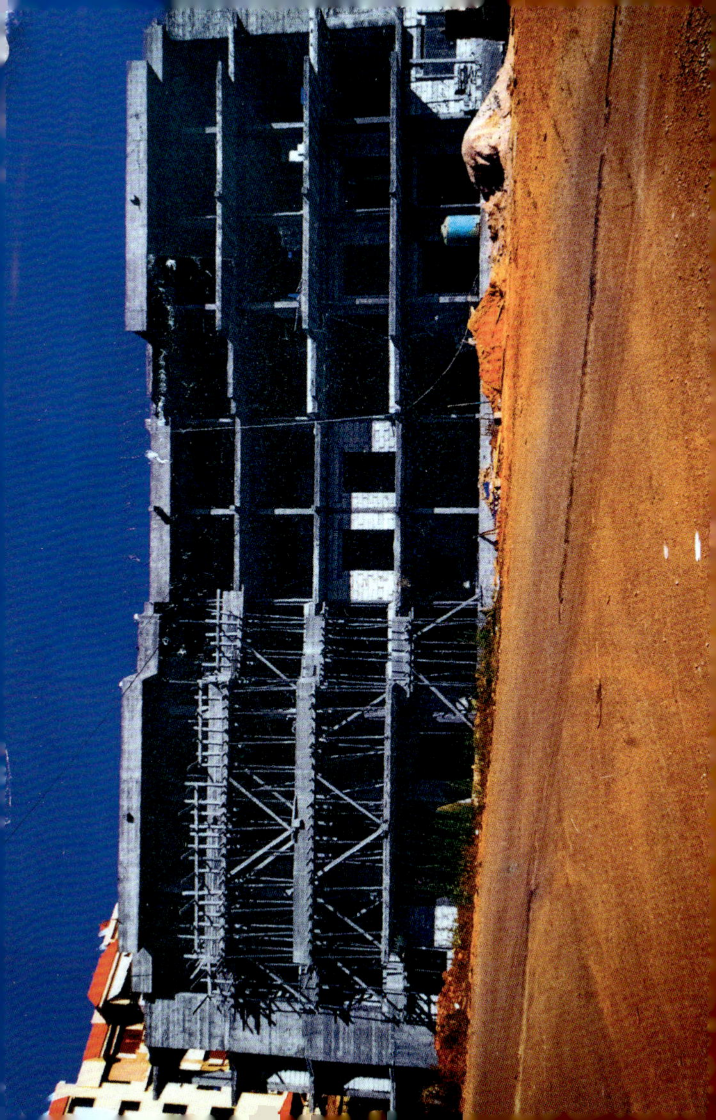

EXPLORE, IF YOU WANT. I'LL GIVE A YELL WHEN I'M LEAVING."

KID WALKED A DOZEN STEPS FURTHER, GLANCED BACK. TAK WAS STILL STRETCHING OUT YARDS OF CLOTH. THEN WALKED ON.

THE CARTONS NEAR [illegible]ALLER AND PILED HAPHAZARDLY—WERE STENCILED WITH CLUMSY REPRESENTATIONS OF [illegible]S. HE STEPPED AROUND THEM. ANOTHER, OPENED LIKE THE BOX OF TA[illegible]S, HAD BEEN LEFT IN THE MIDDLE OF THE PLATED WALKWAY.

HIS OWN STEP, EVEN HIS BARE FOOT, SET OFF A METALLIC RING. THE OPEN TOP JOGGLED WITH THE SHAKING OF THE FLOOR.

DIAGONALLY ACROSS THE CARDBOARD WAS STENCILED:

RED EYE-CAPS

HE DID NOT FROWN. ALL THE MUSCLES OF HIS FACE URGED HIM TOWARD THE EXPRESSION. BUT SOMETHING ELSE WAS PARALYZED. HE SQUATTED, PUSHED BACK THE TOP.

THEY HAD PROBABLY BEEN STACKED NEATLY TOGETHER ONCE. BUT MOVEMENT HAD JUMBLED MOST OF THEM. HE PICKED UP ONE. IT WAS LIKE A CONCAVE DISK THE SIZE OF A QUARTER, CUT FROM A PINGPONG BALL.

IT WAS RED.

HE TURNED IT IN HORNY FINGERS. BUT IT DOESN'T EXPLAIN IT, HE THOUGHT. THEN

CN 15
Return
Retour
Inconnu à l'adresse indiquée
Unknown at this address
Déménagé sans laisser d'adresse
Moved without leaving an address
Adresse insuffisante pour la Livraison
Insufficient address for delivery
Nom s'applique à plusieurs personnes
Duplicate names
Refusé /Refused /
Destinataire n'est pas présent
Addressee not present
Personne n'est à l'adresse
No one available at the address

UNFINISHED STATE // 23D. 317

Schützt die Natur
WWF
www.wwf.de

Deutschland
75
50 Jahre Fehmarnsundbrücke

FROM: WILLIAM DHALGREN
ARCHIVE BOOKS
DIEFFENBACHSTRAβE 31
10967 BERLIN, GERMANY

TO:
APARTMENT BUILDING
WITH OLD WOOD SCAFFOLDING

FROM AL JAYESH TAKE TWO RIGHTS
THEN UP THE DIRT ROAD

AL HARA, SAIDA HILLS

LEBANON

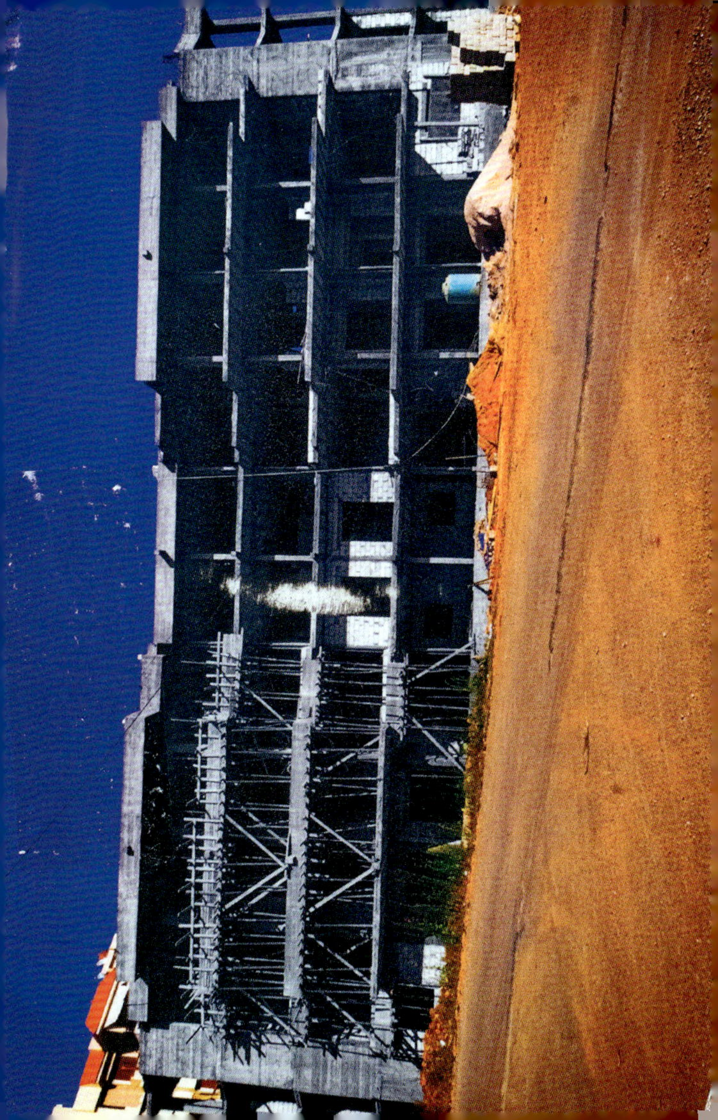

TOO SCARED TO ASK!

"HEY, ARE YOU ALL RIGHT?" TAK RAISED HIS HEAD. THE SHADOW BOBBED ON THE TOP HALF OF HIS FACE. "YOU'RE NOT GOING TO GO INTO ANOTHER ONE OF YOUR FLIP-OUTS, ARE YOU?"

KID TRIED TO SAY, I'M ALL RIGHT. ALL HE DID WA[illegible] EXPEL ANOTHER BREATH.

FROM THE CARTON TAK REMOVED SOME SQUARE PIECE OF METALLIC EQUIPMENT AND STO[illegible]HED.

HALFWAY DOWN THE STAIRS [illegible]ID MANAGED TO [illegible] IT HUNG DETACHED IN DU[illegible] ECHOES. TAK GAVE HIM A SARCASTIC GLANCE.

[illegible] ONE OF THE THINGS THAT, A MINUTE HENCE, WILL [illegible]IP FROM THE RE[illegible] TO TAKE SOME INACCESSIBLE ADDRESS BESIDE MY NAME?

(HE CLOSED HIS MOUTH, AND THE ROAR HE HAD MOVED THROUGH FOR THE LAST MINUTES CEASED [illegible] IT IS ONE OF THOSE THINGS THAT I WILL NEVER BE ABLE TO SPEAK OF, AND NEVER FORGET.

THEY WERE HALFWAY TO THE DOOR BEFORE THE FIRST VOICE PROPORTIONED WITH AMUSEMENT YAWNED SOMEWHERE AND INQUIRED, NEVER? THEN GIGGLED, TURNED OVER, AND WENT TO SLEEP.

WELL NOT FOR A HELL OF A LONG TIME.

BUT HE FELT A LITTLE BIT BETTER.

UNFINISHED STATE // 23D.319

Schützt die Natur
WWF
www.wwf.de

50 Jahre Fehmarnsundbrücke
Deutschland
75

FROM: WILLIAM DHALGREN
ARCHIVE BOOKS
DIEFFENBACHSTRAßE 31
10967 BERLIN, GERMANY

TO:
APARTMENT BUILDING
WITH OLD WOOD SCAFFOLDING

FROM AL JAYESH TAKE TWO RIGHTS
THEN UP THE DIRT ROAD

AL HARA, SAIDA HILLS

LEBANON

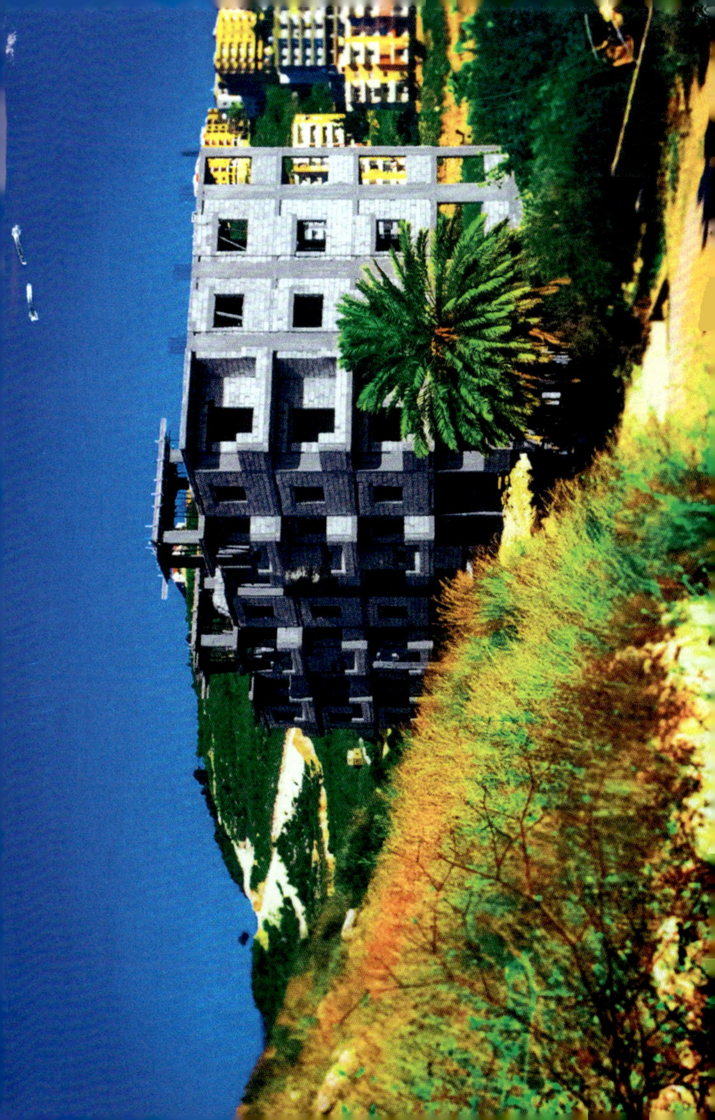

"DID YOU SEE THOSE?" TAK NODDED DOWN ANOTHER AISLE OF CRATES.

"WHAT?" KID'S HEART STILL BEAT VERY FAST. HE FELT LIGHT-HEADED.

"COME ON." TAK LED HIM ALONG.

THE ORCHIDS HUNG ON WOODEN RACKS PEGGED OVER WITH DOWELS.

KID WALKED TO ONE STAND. "THIS IS... THE FANCY KIND." HE LOOKED BACK. "LIKE YOU HAVE, ISN'T IT?"

"PLAIN ONES ARE OVER THERE." TAK STEPPED BESIDE HIM. "I REALLY THOUGHT YOU'D PROBABLY BEEN IN HERE BEFORE."

TO KID'S QUESTIONING GLANCE, TAK TOOK DOWN THE NEAREST. BENEATH IT WAS LETTERED:

BRASS ORCHIDS

KID LAUGHED. IT MADE A WEAK SOUND IN HIS "THROAT, BUT ECHO LENT IT BODY. "HERE, LET ME SEE THAT?" KID TOOK THE SCROLLED CONTRIVANCE AND TURNED IT AROUND AND AROUND. "I GUESS IT WOULD BE OKAY IF I TOOK THIS ONE... WOULDN'T IT?"

TAK SHRUGGED. "WHY NOT?"

KID FOLDED HIS FINGERS TOGETHER AND PUSHED THEM THROUGH THE WRIST BAND. "I LEFT [illegible] ONE BACK AT THE NEST. MIGHT AS

UNFINISHED STATE // 23D.320

Schützt die Natur www.wwf.de

Deutschland

50 Jahre Fehmarnsundbrücke

REGULAR MAIL

01140006840043O

FROM: WILLIAM DHALGREN
ARCHIVE BOOKS
DIEFFENBACHSTRAßE 31
10967 BERLIN, GERMANY

TO:
INCOMPLETE APARTMENTS
WITH A BIG PALM TREE

OFF THE MAIN HIGHWAY
AROUND THE CURVE OF THE HILL

RMAILEH

LEBANON

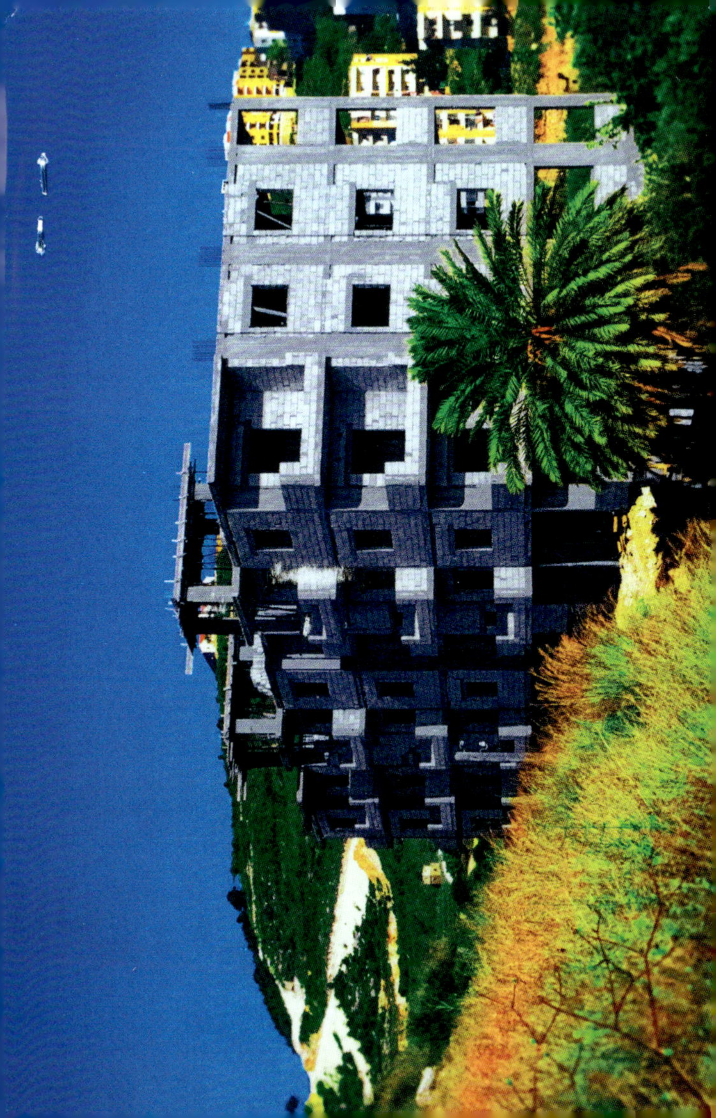

WELL HAVE TWO—ONE FOR SPECIAL OCCASIONS." HE MADE A SUDDEN FEINT AT TAK. "YOU LIKE THAT?" HE LAUGHED AGAIN.

"COME ON." TAK HAD NOT MOVED AT ALL. "LET'S GO."

THEY WERE IN SIGHT OF THE DOOR WHEN KID GOT ANOTHER ATTACK OF GOOSEFLESH. BUT THIS ONE JUST MADE HIM GRIN. HE LOOKED UP AT THE SKYLIGHT, HUNCHED HIS SHOULDERS, AND HURRIED AFTER TAK. I'LL PROBABLY NEVER BE ABLE TO FIND THIS PLACE AGAIN, HE THOUGHT. TO STEAL A SOUVENIR (HE LOOKED DOWN AT THE YELLOW BLADES ABOUT HIS HAND) SEEMED SUDDENLY THE ULTIMATE CUNNING.

OUTSIDE, TAK SMOOTHED THE FOLDED MATERIAL ACROSS HIS ARM. "SINCE THIS IS GOING TO BE YOUR GIRL FRIEND'S BALL GOWN, I SHOULDN'T SHOW YOU HOW IT WORKS. BUT IT'S SORT OF NEAT. JUST A SECOND." HE TOOK OUT OF HIS POCKET THE PIECE OF EQUIPMENT—A METAL BOX THE SIZE OF A CIGARETTE PACK WITH THREE DIALS, TWO KNOBS, AND A SMALL LIGHT ON ONE CORNER. "GIVE ME A LOAN OF THE BATTERY IN YOUR SHIELD."

"OH, SURE." KID FUMBLED THE SPHERE THROUGH THE BLADES. THE PROJECTOR CLICKED OPEN. "I ONLY GOT ONE HAND. YOU TAKE IT OUT."

"RIGHT."

UNFINISHED STATE // 23D.321

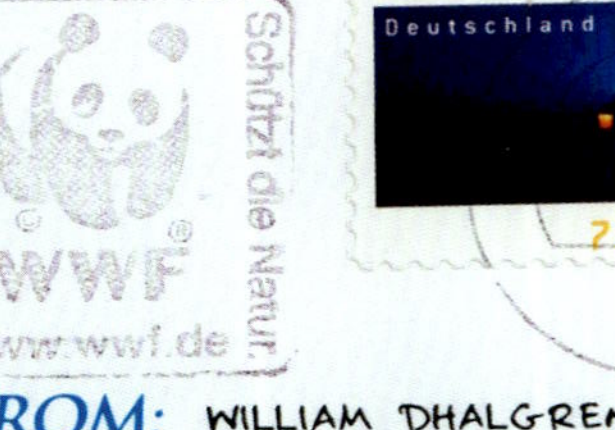

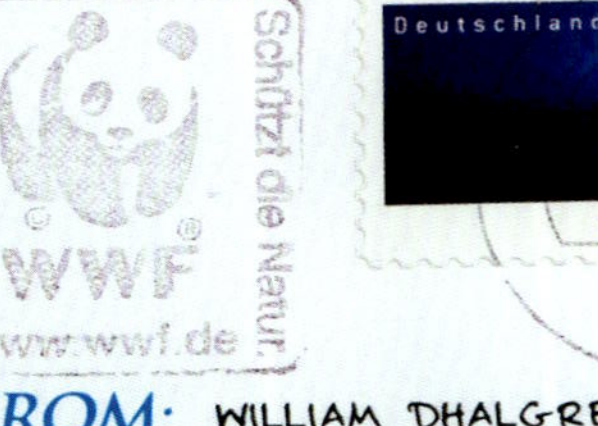

FROM: WILLIAM DHALGREN
ARCHIVE BOOKS
DIEFFENBACHSTRAßE 31
10967 BERLIN, GERMANY

TO: INCOMPLETE APARTMENTS
WITH A BIG PALM TREE

OFF THE MAIN HIGHWAY
AROUND THE CURVE OF THE HILL

RMAILEH

ION

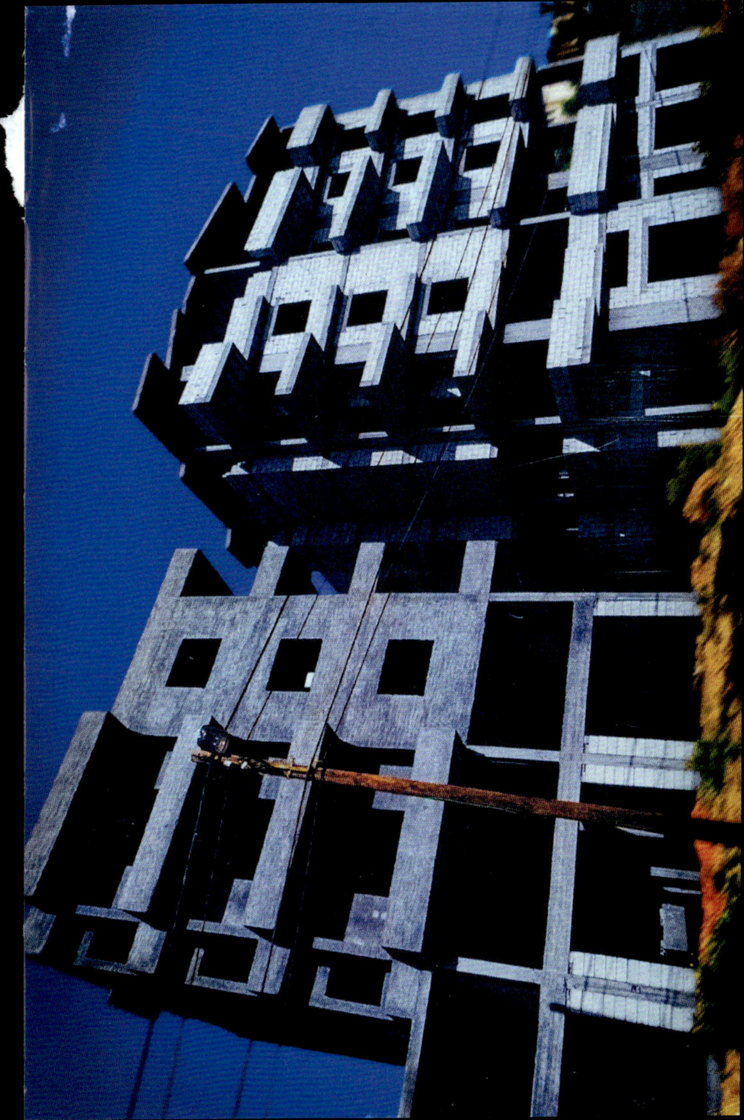

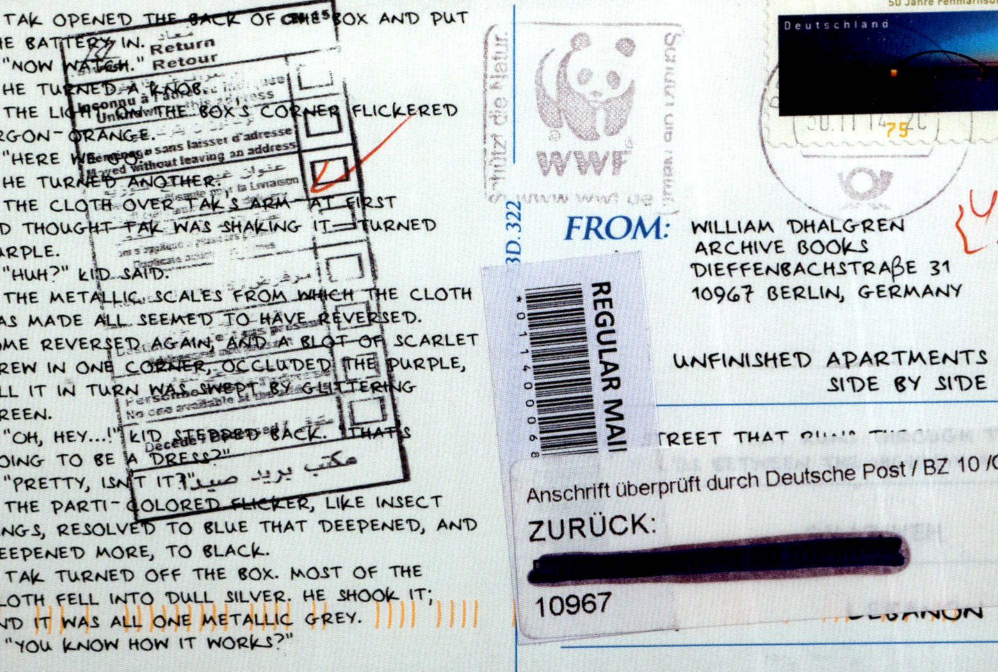
TAK OPENED THE BACK OF THE BOX AND PUT THE BATTERY IN.
"NOW WATCH."
HE TURNED A KNOB.
THE LIGHT ON THE BOX'S CORNER FLICKERED ARGON-ORANGE.
"HERE WE GO."
HE TURNED ANOTHER.
THE CLOTH OVER TAK'S ARM—AT FIRST KID THOUGHT TAK WAS SHAKING IT—TURNED PURPLE.
"HUH?" KID SAID.
THE METALLIC SCALES FROM WHICH THE CLOTH WAS MADE ALL SEEMED TO HAVE REVERSED. SOME REVERSED AGAIN, AND A BLOT OF SCARLET GREW IN ONE CORNER, OCCLUDED THE PURPLE, TILL IT IN TURN WAS SWEPT BY GLITTERING GREEN.
"OH, HEY...!" KID STEPPED BACK. "THAT'S GOING TO BE A DRESS?"
"PRETTY, ISN'T IT?"
THE PARTI-COLORED FLICKER, LIKE INSECT WINGS, RESOLVED TO BLUE THAT DEEPENED, AND DEEPENED MORE, TO BLACK.
TAK TURNED OFF THE BOX. MOST OF THE CLOTH FELL INTO DULL SILVER. HE SHOOK IT, AND IT WAS ALL ONE METALLIC GREY.
"YOU KNOW HOW IT WORKS?"
معاد Return
Retour
Inconnu à l'adresse indiquée
Unknown at this address
Déménagé sans laisser d'adresse
Moved without leaving an address
Refusé
Decédé
مكتب بريد صيدا
Schützt die Natur.
WWF
www.wwf.de
50 Jahre Fehmarnsundbrücke
Deutschland
75
3D.322
FROM:
WILLIAM DHALGREN
ARCHIVE BOOKS
DIEFFENBACHSTRAßE 31
10967 BERLIN, GERMANY
UNFINISHED APARTMENTS
SIDE BY SIDE
REGULAR MAI
0114000068
Anschrift überprüft durch Deutsche Post / BZ 10 /G
ZURÜCK:
10967

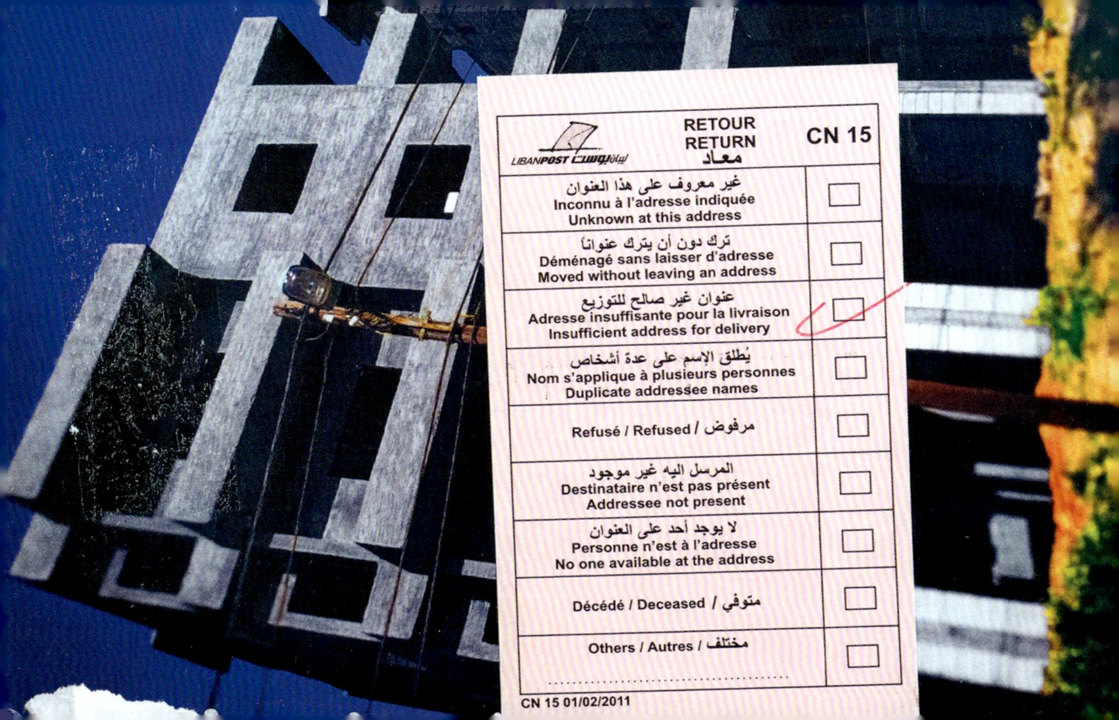

LIBANPOST ليبان بوست

RETOUR
RETURN
معاد

CN 15

غير معروف على هذا العنوان Inconnu à l'adresse indiquée Unknown at this address	☐
ترك دون أن يترك عنواناً Déménagé sans laisser d'adresse Moved without leaving an address	☐
عنوان غير صالح للتوزيع Adresse insuffisante pour la livraison Insufficient address for delivery	☐
يُطلق الإسم على عدة أشخاص Nom s'applique à plusieurs personnes Duplicate addressee names	☐
Refusé / Refused / مرفوض	☐
المرسل اليه غير موجود Destinataire n'est pas présent Addressee not present	☐
لا يوجد أحد على العنوان Personne n'est à l'adresse No one available at the address	☐
Décédé / Deceased / متوفي	☐
Others / Autres / مختلف	☐

CN 15 01/02/2011

I COME. I GO. RATHER THAN GOING, THOUGH, I'LL STAY. THIS CAGE SEEMS TOO EASY TO FLEE. IS THAT WHAT KEEPS US HERE? TO LEAVE THE CITY: THAT IS THE THOUGHT THAT MAKES ME WEAK IN THE SMALL OF THE BACK AND WATERY IN THE MIND, SO MUCH SO THAT IT IS EASIER NOT TO REMEMBER IT ONCE THE THOUGHT IS PAST. WAITING FOR A WORD TO PUSH ON THESE WALLS, WITH ITS BASS HISS, THERE IS NO WAY TO BEGIN. ADJUSTING THE FRAME TO ACCOMMODATE THE DAY, I AM SWOLLEN WITH TERROR AT MY INABILITY TO DISTINGUISH, AT ANY ACTION, WHAT DIFFERENTIATES TIME AFTER FROM TIME BEFORE.

"HI, WHAT ARE YOU PUTTING TOGETHER?" SHE ASKED.

"JUST A PIECE OF JUNK—" RAVEN SAID.

DENNY CLAPPED ESCHER CLOSED, AND ROLLED TO LEAN OVER THE EDGE. "HEY! LANYA!"

"HI, BABES. IS KID UP THERE?"

"YEAH, HE'S RIGHT HERE."

"ROOM FOR ME?" THEN HER HEAD CAME OVER THE LOFT'S EDGE, AND FROWNED. "...THIS ONE IS HARDER TO CLIMB THAN THE LADDER ON THE OTHER ONE."

KID PUSHED UP TO HIS KNEES TO GRAB HER SHOULDER. DENNY WAS ALREADY AT THE EDGE TO HELP.

"HEY, I THINK I CAN DO IT MORE EASILY MYSELF. LET'S SEE..." SHE SCRUNCHED HER

UNFINISHED STATE // 24D.323

FROM: WILLIAM DHALGREN
ARCHIVE BOOKS
DIEFFENBACHSTRAßE 31
10967 BERLIN, GERMANY

TO: UNFINISHED APARTMENTS

ON THE STREET THAT RUNS THROUGH THE FIELDS BETWEEN THE HIGHWAY AND

GHAZIYEH

LEBANON

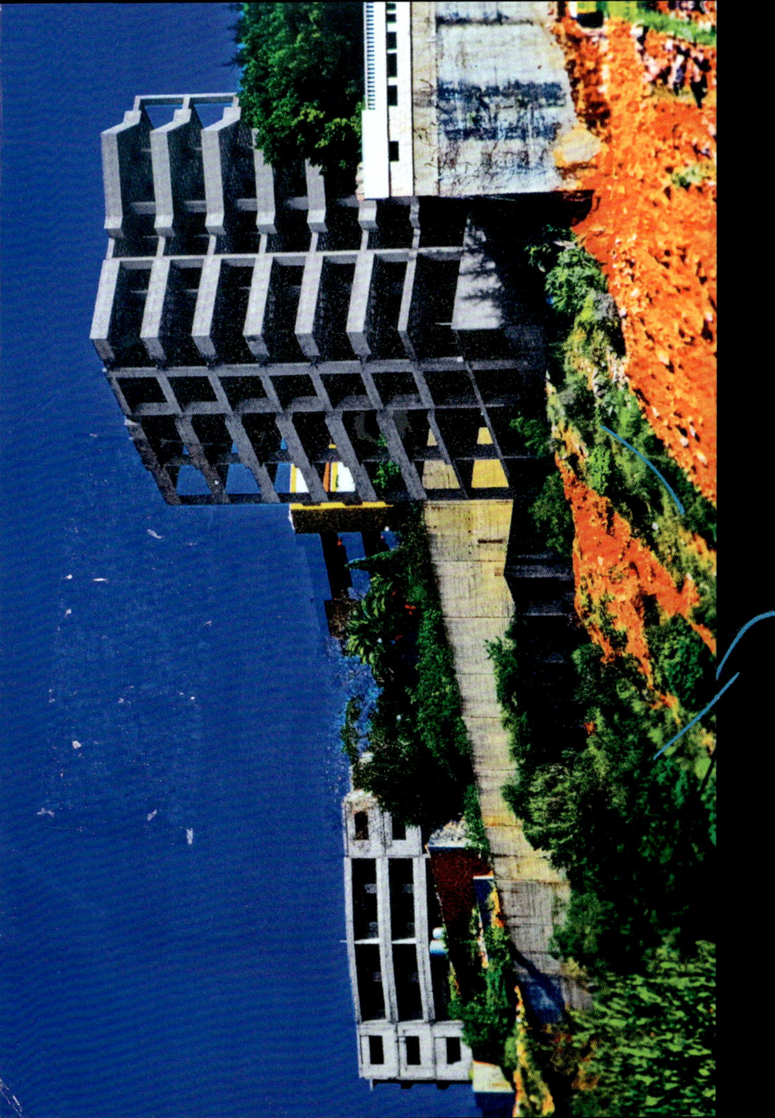

HALFWAY THROUGH A ROUND OF POCKET-POOL. SURE. I RELAXED MY STOMACH (IT HAD TIGHTENED IN THE CLIMB) AND AMBLED, BREATHING LOUDLY, OVER THE RED AND GREY FLAGS. BETWEEN DUSTY PANES, DUSTY BLURRED THE LEADED TESSELATIONS. AT THE SAME MOMENT I DECIDED THE PLACE WAS DESERTED, A MAN IN A HOOD AND ROBE STEPPED AROUND THE CORNER AND PEERED.

I TOOK MY HANDS OUT OF MY POCKETS.

HE FOLDED HIS OVER HIS LAP AND CAME FORWARD. THEY WERE BIG, AND TRANSLUCENT. THE WHITE-AND-BLACK TOES OF VERY OLD BASKETBALL SNEAKERS POKED ALTERNATELY FROM HIS HEM. HIS EYES WERE GREY. HIS SMILE LOOKED LIKE THE AMPHETAMINE FREEZE ON A PARTICULARLY PALE AIRLINE STEWARDESS. HIS HOOD WAS BACK ENOUGH TO SEE HIS SKULL WAS WHITE AS BREAD DOUGH. A SORE, MOSTLY HIDDEN, LIKE AN ECCENTRIC MAP, WAS VISIBLE UNDER THE HOOD'S EDGE: WET, RAISED, WITH PURPLE BITS CRUSTED INSIDE IT AND YELLOW FLAKING AROUND IT. "YES," HE ASKED. "CAN I HELP YOU?"

I SMILED AND SHRUGGED.

"I SAW YOU COMING UP THE STEPS AND I WAS WONDERING IF THERE WAS ANYTHING I COULD DO FOR YOU, ANYONE IN PARTICULAR YOU WANTED

CN 15

Retour
Return

Inconnu à l'adresse indiquée
Unknown at this address

Parti sans laisser d'adresse
Moved without leaving an address

Adresse insuffisante pour la Livraison
Insufficient address for delivery

Nom identique à plusieurs personnes
Duplicate addressee names

Refusé / Refused

Le destinataire n'est pas présent
Addressee not present

UNFINISHED STATE // 28D. 3-8

50 Jahre Fehmarnsundbrücke
Deutschland
75

FROM: WILLIAM DHALGREN
ARCHIVE BOOKS
DIEFFENBACHSTRAßE 31
10967 BERLIN, GERMANY

TO: INCOMPLETE CONDOMINIUMS
BUILT ALONG RETAINING WALL

HLALIYEH ROAD

HLALIYEH

LEBANON

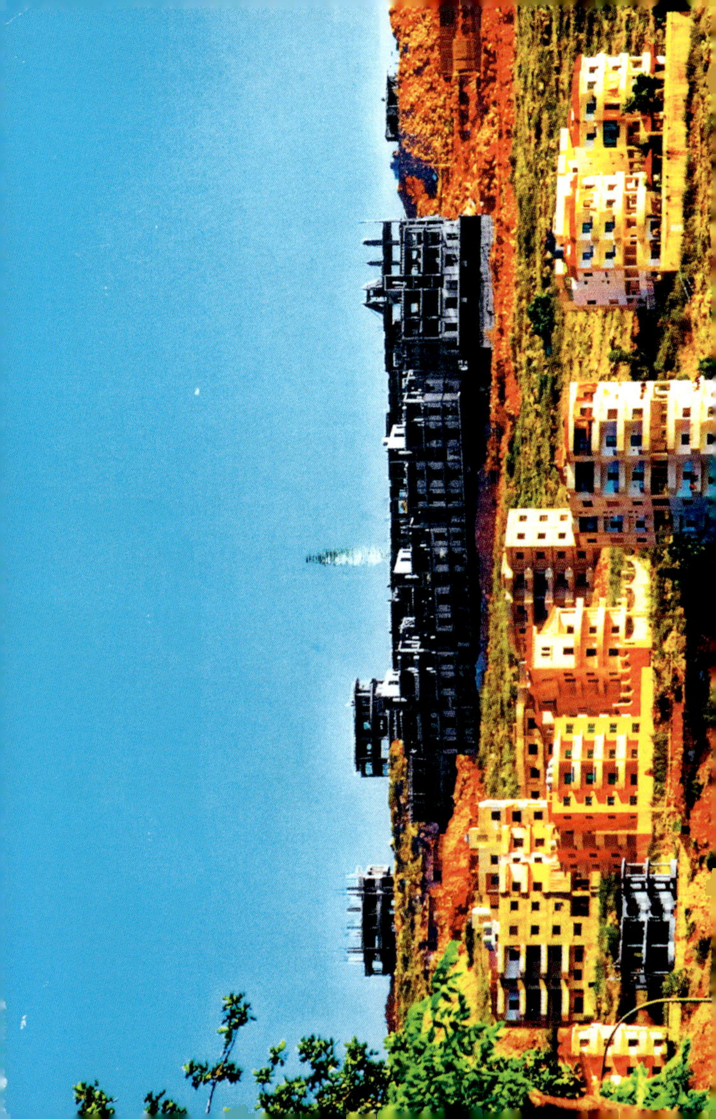

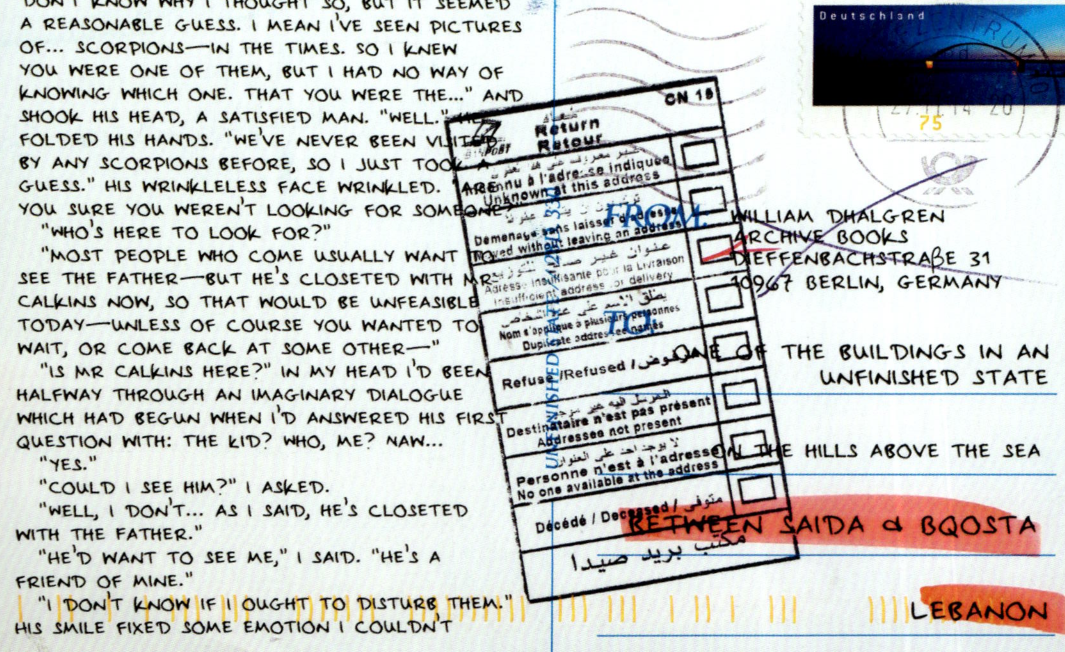

DON'T KNOW WHY I THOUGHT SO, BUT IT SEEMED A REASONABLE GUESS. I MEAN I'VE SEEN PICTURES OF... SCORPIONS—IN THE TIMES. SO I KNEW YOU WERE ONE OF THEM, BUT I HAD NO WAY OF KNOWING WHICH ONE. THAT YOU WERE THE..." AND SHOOK HIS HEAD, A SATISFIED MAN. "WELL." HE FOLDED HIS HANDS. "WE'VE NEVER BEEN VISITED BY ANY SCORPIONS BEFORE, SO I JUST TOOK A GUESS." HIS WRINKLELESS FACE WRINKLED. "ARE YOU SURE YOU WEREN'T LOOKING FOR SOMEONE?"
"WHO'S HERE TO LOOK FOR?"
"MOST PEOPLE WHO COME USUALLY WANT TO SEE THE FATHER—BUT HE'S CLOSETED WITH MR CALKINS NOW, SO THAT WOULD BE UNFEASIBLE TODAY—UNLESS OF COURSE YOU WANTED TO WAIT, OR COME BACK AT SOME OTHER—"
"IS MR CALKINS HERE?" IN MY HEAD I'D BEEN HALFWAY THROUGH AN IMAGINARY DIALOGUE WHICH HAD BEGUN WHEN I'D ANSWERED HIS FIRST QUESTION WITH: THE KID? WHO, ME? NAW...
"YES."
"COULD I SEE HIM?" I ASKED.
"WELL, I DON'T... AS I SAID, HE'S CLOSETED WITH THE FATHER."
"HE'D WANT TO SEE ME," I SAID. "HE'S A FRIEND OF MINE."
"I DON'T KNOW IF I OUGHT TO DISTURB THEM."
HIS SMILE FIXED SOME EMOTION I COULDN'T
50 Jahre Fehmarnsundbrücke
Deutschland
75
CN 15
Return
Retour
Inconnu à l'adresse indiquée
Unknown at this address
Demenagé sans laisser d'adresse
Moved without leaving an address
Adresse insuffisante pour la Livraison
Insufficient address for delivery
Nom s'applique à plusieurs personnes
Duplicate address or names
Refusé /Refused /
Destinataire n'est pas présent
Addressee not present
Personne n'est à l'adresse
No one available at the address
Décédé / Deceased /
مكتب بريد صيدا
UNFINISHED STATE / 12/11 330
FROM:
WILLIAM DHALGREN
ARCHIVE BOOKS
DIEFFENBACHSTRAßE 31
10967 BERLIN, GERMANY
TO:
ONE OF THE BUILDINGS IN AN
UNFINISHED STATE
ON THE HILLS ABOVE THE SEA
BETWEEN SAIDA & BQOSTA
LEBANON

"DON'T WORRY," I SAID, "I WON'T PRY INTO ANY SECRETS ABOUT YOUR DEVOTIONAL GAMES HERE," WISHING I SORT OF COULD.

BUT THE VOICE SAID: "NO, NOT QUESTIONS THAT HAVE ANYTHING TO DO WITH THE MONASTERY."

AND (WHILE HE CONSIDERED FURTHER EXPLANATION?) I CONSIDERED THE TOWER EXPLODING SLOWLY, THRUSTING MASONRY ON BLURRED AIR TOO THIN TO FLOAT BRICK AND BOLTS AND BELLROPE.

"I DON'T THINK THERE'S ANYTHING ABOUT THE MONASTERY YOU COULD ASK I WOULDN'T BE ALLOWED TO ANSWER—IF I KNEW THE ANSWERS. BUT PART OF THE TRAINING IS A SORT OF SELF-DISCIPLINE: ANY QUESTION THAT SPARKS CERTAIN INTERNAL REACTIONS IN ME, CAUSES ME TO THINK CERTAIN THOUGHTS, TO FEEL CERTAIN FEELINGS, RATHER THAN RUSH INTO SOME VERBAL RESPONSE THAT, INFORMATIVE OR NOT, IS STILL PUT UP MAINLY TO REPRESS THOSE THOUGHTS AND FEELINGS, I'M SUPPOSED TO EXPERIENCE THEM FULLY IN THE ANXIETY OF SILENCE."

"OH," I SAID. "WHAT SORT OF THOUGHTS AND FEELINGS?" AFTER TEN QUIET SECONDS, I LAUGHED. "I'M SORRY. I GUESS THAT'S SORT OF LIKE NOT THINKING ABOUT THE WHITE HIPPOPOTAMUS WHEN YOU'RE CHANGING THE BOILING WATER INTO GOLD."

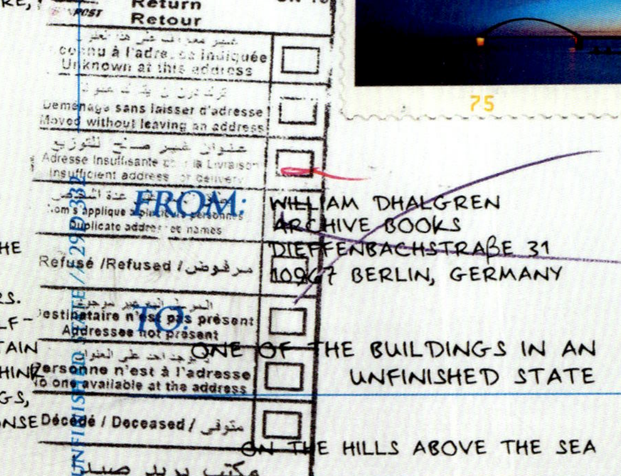

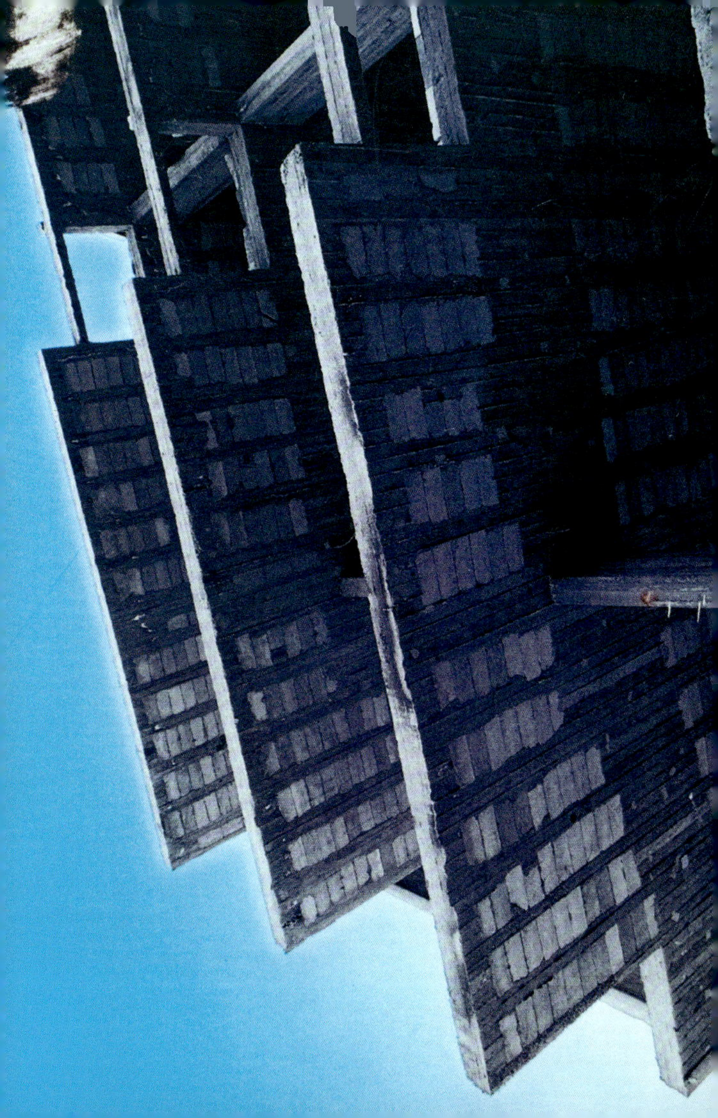

CITY OF DREADFUL

AN OCEAN OF SMOKE AND EVENING.

I TRIED TO SMELL IT, BUT MY NOSTRILS WERE NUMB OR ACCLIMATED. THE LIONS GAPED IN THE BLURR. WE NEARED THE FOGGED PEARL OF ONE FUNCTIONING LAMP, AND HER FACE GOT ALL TWISTED. SHE STOPPED, TURQUOISE, HEM TO KNEES, EXPLODING HIGH AS HER SCARLET WAIST. "SHOULD WE... KID, DO YOU KNOW WHAT THEY SAID?" "WILL YOU PLEASE..." I ASKED HER. MY THROAT HURT WITH RUNNING AND THE RAW AIR. "WILL YOU PLEASE TELL ME WHAT... WHAT THEY SAID!"

BOTH HANDS CAME UP TO CAGE HER MOUTH. SHE WAS A SHOWER OF SLIVER ON METALLIC BLACK. "SOMEONE, UP ON THE ROOF OF THE BANK: THE SECOND CITY BANK — OH, A GODT SNIPER!"

"WHO, FOR CHRIST'S SAKE?" I GRABBED HER SMALL ELBOWS AND THE HAIR SHOOK AROUNT HEAD. "WILL YOU TELL ME WHO THEY GOT?"

"PAUL," SHE WHISPERED. "PAUL FENSTER! TH SCHOOL, KID... EVERYTHING"

"IS HE DEAD?"

HER HEAD SHOOK IN A WAY THAT MEANT SHE DIDN'T KNOW. HER HANDS TWISTED SILVER CLOTH AT HER HIPS: SCARLET BLED DOWN FROM ONE; YELLOW SNAKED ACROSS HER BELLY FROM THE OTHER. "IN THE BURNING," SHE SAID VERY

CN 15
Retour
Retour
Inconnu à l'adresse indiquée
Unknown at this address
Moved without leaving an address
عنوان غير صالح للتوزيع
Adresse insuffisante pour la Livraison
Refusé / Refused / مرفوض
Destinataire n'est pas présent
Personne n'est à l'adresse
Décédé / Deceased / متوفى

Schützt die Natur

REGULAR MAIL

0114000699004 50

50 Jahre Fehmarnsundbrücke
Deutschland
75

WILLIAM DHALGREN
ARCHIVE BOOKS
DIEFFENBACHSTRAßE 31
10967 BERLIN, GERMANY

Anschrift überprüft durch Deutsche Post / BZ 05

ZURÜCK:

Empfänger nicht zu ermitteln

10967

No one available
Décédé / Dece...

LEBANON

QUICKLY. "IN THE FIRE... ALL YOUR POEMS, THE NEW ONES; THEY BURNED...!" HER LIPS KEPT TOUCHING AND PARTING, SORTING MORE WORDS, NONE OF WHICH FIT. "EVERYTHING, ALL OF THEM... I COULDN'T..."

"UNNN..." SOMETHING WENT RIGHT INTO MY STOMACH WITHOUT USING GUT OR THROAT FOR ENTRANCE, I SAID, "UNNN..." SHE LET GO HER SKIRT.

"THAT'S... GOOD I GUESS," WAS ALL I COULD SAY. "I DIDN'T LIKE THEM. SO IT'S GOOD THEY'RE... GONE."

"YOU SHOULD HAVE KEPT THEM IN YOUR NOTEBOOK! I WAS WRONG! YOU SHOULD..." SHE SHOOK HER HEAD. "OH, I'M SO SORRY!"

I STARTED TO COUGH.

"LOOK," SHE SAID, "I KNOW HALF OF THEM BY HEART ANYWAY. YOU COULD RECONSTRUCT—"

"NO," I SAID.

"—AND EVERETT FOREST MADE THAT..."

"NO. IT'S GOOD THEY'RE GONE."

"KID," SHE SAID, "WHAT ABOUT PAUL...? UP ON THE SECOND CITY BANK BUILDING. WERE YOU...? OH, PLEASE TRY TO REMEMBER!" THEN SHE STARTED AS THOUGH SHE'D SEEN SOMETHING (BEHIND ME? ABOVE ME? WERE MY LIGHTS STILL ON? I DON'T REMEMBER!), AND TURNED. AND RAN, BLAZING GOLD A MOMENT BEFORE SHADOW TOOK HER AND I RAN AFTER, INTO THE BRUSH,

UNFINISHED STATE // 30D. 335

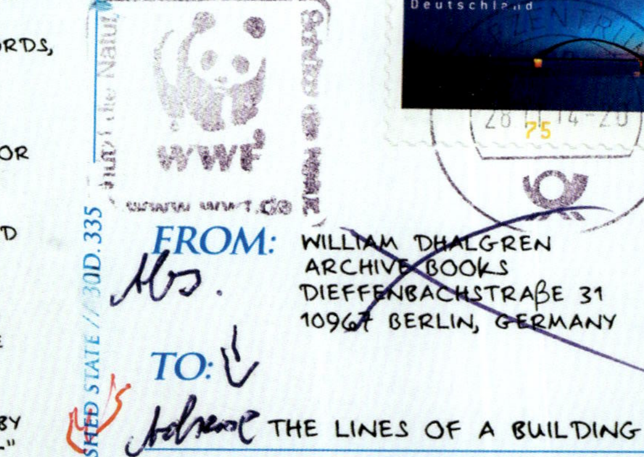

FROM: Ms. WILLIAM DHALGREN
ARCHIVE BOOKS
DIEFFENBACHSTRAẞE 31
10967 BERLIN, GERMANY

TO: Adrienne THE LINES OF A BUILDING

ABOVE THE GREENHOUSES
JUST NORTH OF

GHAZIYEH

LEBANON

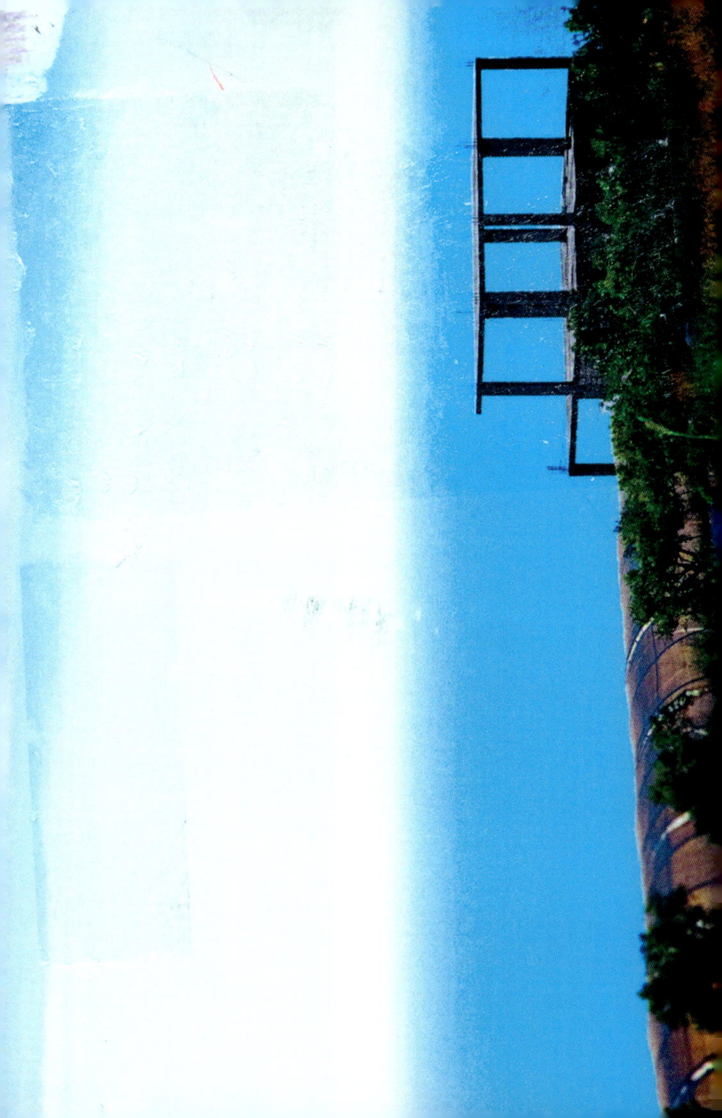

AN APPLE TO DISCOVER? STILL THEY SHOULD HAVE SAVED AROUND WHAT OR FIXED HER. EXCEPT IN THE UNDERPINNED WHITE SHELL, HERE ARE SOME SCABS IN PURPLE; EVERY BEACH BUT EFFLUVIA. AND THEY HAD BOUGHT US UP TO MIX HERE SO FEW CONCEPTS WITH THE LAZY DRINKS, HAD SAT SOBER OR REINSTATED OUR PERSONAL FIXATED INTENSITY. SOON THEY CAUTERIZED WHAT YOU, CONSTANCY AND EXEGESIS, WERE FOUND VERY LOOSE AROUND HIM THAT WE HAD EACH, WITHOUT DENNY EXPLAINING, FISHED TO FASCINATE THEM, BEAUTIFULLY OR LAZILY. THEY SHOULD HAVE ALLOWED HER LESS THAN AN ALLIGATOR HAS AN EYELID NEVER PULLED HER FROM A QUIVER; TERROR STILL FELT LESS ALIVE.

"LANYA?"

I TURNED TO FIXATIVE AMONG THE WALKINGS. BEYOND THE LEAVES, THE FIGURE MOVED SO THAT I STILL COULDN'T

THE BLUE ENVELOPE, BARRED ALONG ITS EDGE WITH RED AND NAVY, IS HELD TO THE BOTTOM OF THE ABOVE PAGE WITH YELLOW, BUBBLED SCOTCHTAPE. THERE ARE TWO, CANCELED, EIGHT-CENT STAMPS IN THE UPPER, RIGHT-HAND CORNER. THE POSTMARK IS ILLEGIBLE. THE BELLONA ADDRESS READS:

UNFINISHED STATE // 31D.336

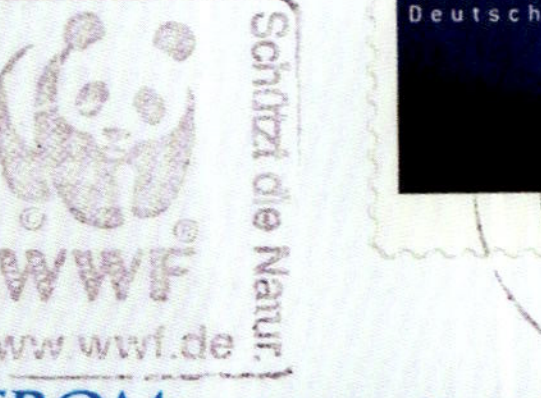

FROM: WILLIAM DHALGREN
ARCHIVE BOOKS
DIEFFENBACHSTRAßE 31
10967 BERLIN, GERMANY

TO:

THE LINES OF A BUILDING

ABOVE THE GREENHOUSES
JUST NORTH OF

GHAZIYEH

LEBANON

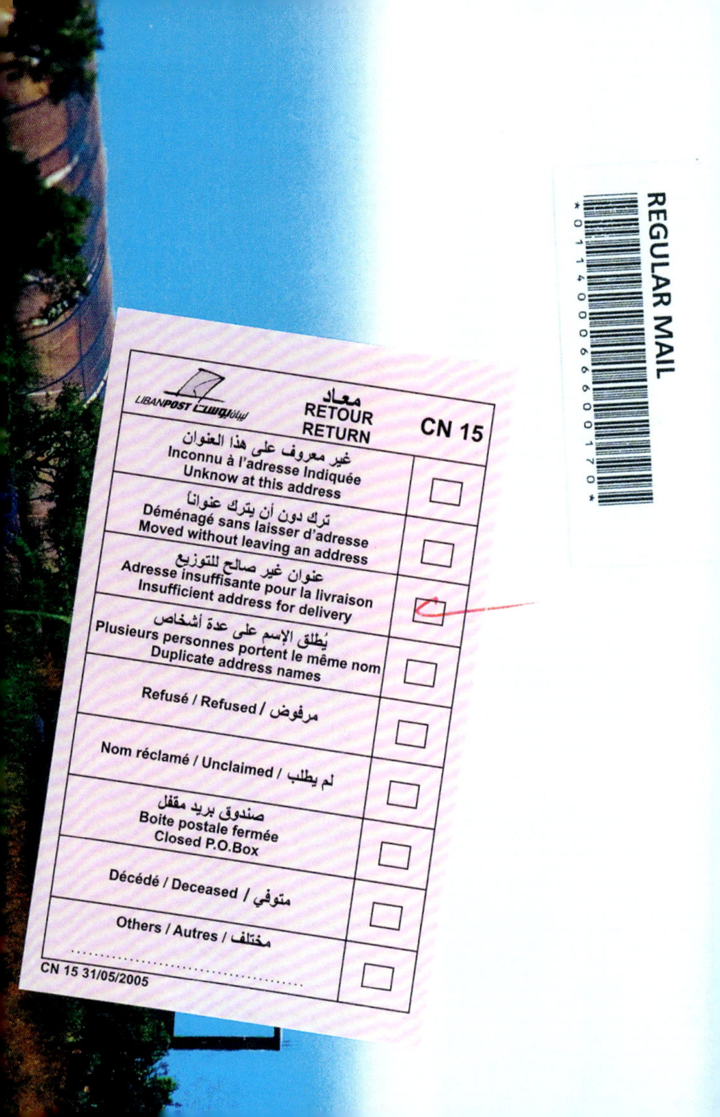

LIBANPOST ليبان بوست

معاد
RETOUR
RETURN

CN 15

غير معروف على هذا العنوان Inconnu à l'adresse Indiquée Unknow at this address	☐
ترك دون أن يترك عنواناً Déménagé sans laisser d'adresse Moved without leaving an address	☐
عنوان غير صالح للتوزيع Adresse insuffisante pour la livraison Insufficient address for delivery	☑
يُطلق الإسم على عدة أشخاص Plusieurs personnes portent le même nom Duplicate address names	☐
Refusé / Refused / مرفوض	☐
Nom réclamé / Unclaimed / لم يطلب	☐
صندوق بريد مقفل Boite postale fermée Closed P.O.Box	☐
Décédé / Deceased / متوفي	☐
Others / Autres / مختلف	☐

CN 15 31/05/2005

REGULAR MAIL

01140006600170

MRS. AUTHOR RICHARDS
THE LABRY APARTMENTS (#17-E)
400, 36TH STREET
BELLONA, U.S.A.

THE RETURN ADDRESS, WRITTEN IN THE SAME HAND (BOTH IN GREEN INK):

MS. JULIA HARRINGTON
7 LILAC VISTA
LOS ANGELES 6, CALIFORNIA

THE LETTER ITSELF HAS EITHER BEEN REMOVED, OR LOST.

WHEN I CAME UP THE STAIRS, HER OFFICE DOOR WAS CLOSED. SO I WANDERED FROM THE STUDY TO THE KITCHEN INTO LANYA'S ROOM AND BACK. FINALLY I SAT ON THE EDGE OF THE DESK IN THE HALL, TILTED THE NEWBOY VOLUMES FROM BETWEEN THE STATUETTES, PILED THEM BESIDE ME, AND BEGAN TO FLIP PAGES.

WHICH WAS FUNNY: AFTER FIVE MINUTES I STILL HADN'T READ ONE WHOLE POEM, OR ONE COMPLETE PARAGRAPH FROM THE ESSAYS OR STORIES. MY EYES COULD ONLY FOCUS BEFORE OR BEHIND THE PAGE. THAT PART OF THE BRAIN, DIRECTLY BEHIND THE EYE, THAT REFRACTS

UNFINISHED STATE // 31D.337

50 Jahre Fehmarnsundbrücke
Deutschland
75

Schützt die Natur
WWF
www.wwf.de

FROM: WILLIAM DHALGREN
ARCHIVE BOOKS
DIEFFENBACHSTRAẞE 31
10967 BERLIN, GERMANY

TO:

THE LINES OF A BUILDING

ABOVE THE GREENHOUSES
JUST NORTH OF

GHAZIYEH

LEBANON

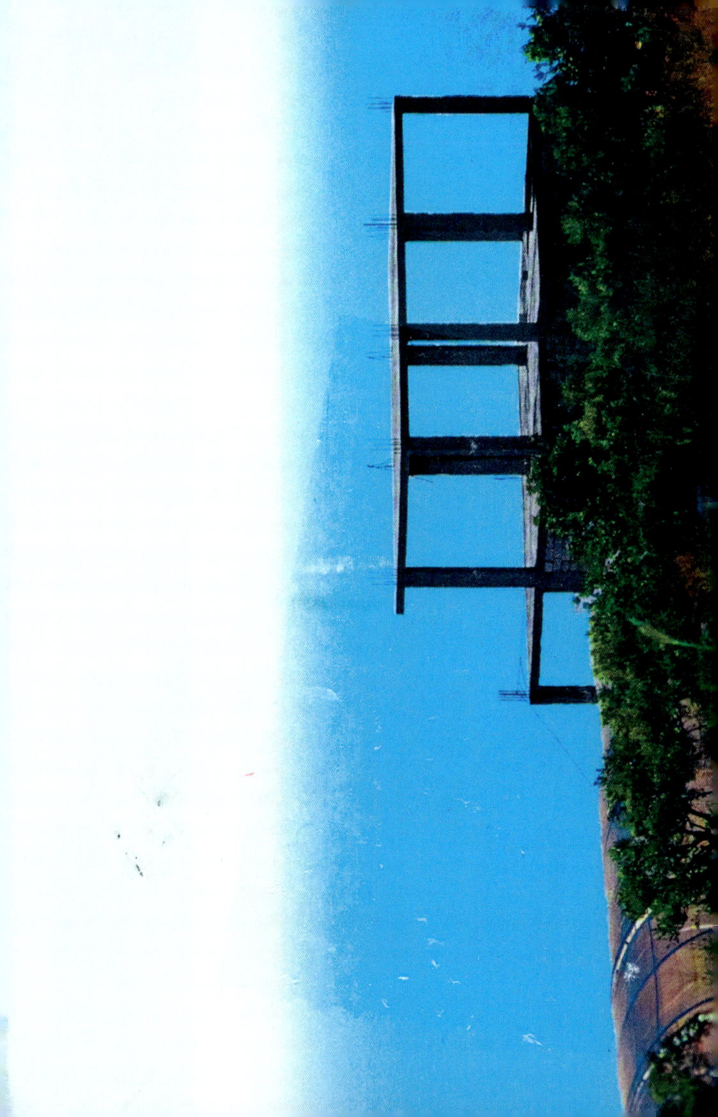

THE JEWELRY OF WORDS INTO IMAGE, IDEA, OR INFORMATION, WOULDN'T WORK. (I EVEN WONDERED A WHILE HOW MUCH OF THAT WAS BECAUSE I'D HEARD HIM SPEAK.) THE BOOKS HAD GENERATED GHOSTS OF THEMSELVES, AND I COULDN'T READ THE WORDS FOR THEIR AFTER-IMAGES. I KEPT PICKING UP DIFFERENT VOLUMES, HEFTING THEM, CLOSED, ON MY PALM, PUTTING THEM DOWN, THEN HEFTING MY EMPTIED PALM AGAIN, FEELING FOR THE GHOST'S WEIGHT.
MY STOMACH BEGAN TO HURT BECAUSE I WAS CONCENTRATING SO WIDELY. I PUT THEM ALL BACK—FIRST I ORDERED THEM BY SIZE, THEN I PULLED THEM OUT AGAIN AND REORDERED THEM BY THE DATES ON THE COPYRIGHT PAGES—AND WALKED FOR A WHILE (REMEMBER THE FOURTH DAY ON SPEED?), RETURNING TO THE DESK, PULLING THE BOOKS OUT AGAIN, LEAVING—REALLY FINDING I'D WANDERED AWAY JUST AS I'D TURN AROUND TO GO BACK.

WHAT IS IT AROUND THESE OBJECTS THAT VIBRATES SO MUCH THE OBJECTS THEMSELVES VANISH? A FIELD, CAST BY THE NAME OF A MAN, WHO, WITHOUT MY EVER HAVING READ A COMPLETE WORK OF HIS, THE HIDDEN MACHINERY OF MY CONSCIOUSNESS AT SOME POINT DECIDED WAS AN ARTIST. HOW COMICAL, SAD, EXHAUSTING. WHY AM I A VICTIM OF THIS MAGIC? BUT FOR ALL

UNFINISHED STATE // 31D. 338

50 Jahre Fehmarnsundbrücke

Deutschland

28.11.14-20

Schützt die Natur

WWF

www.wwf.de

FROM: WILLIAM DHALGREN
ARCHIVE BOOKS
DIEFFENBACHSTRAßE 31
10967 BERLIN, GERMANY

TO: غازية

THE LINES OF A BUILDING

ABOVE THE GREENHOUSES
JUST NORTH OF

GHAZIYEH

LEBANON

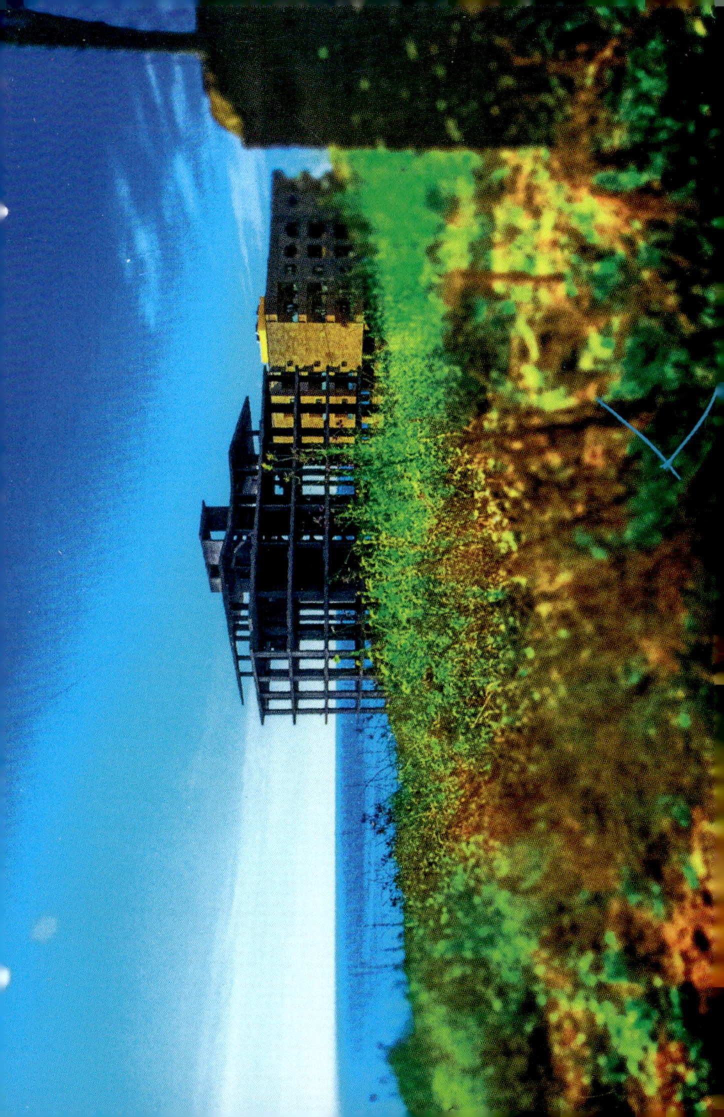

I RECOGNIZE OUT OF ME, I WONDER FURIOUSLY WHO WOULD HOLD BRASS ORCHIDS ON THEIR HAND, HEFTING FOR NOUMENAL WEIGHT?

"KID?" MADAME BROWN'S BODY AND FACE WERE SLICED BY THE DOOR. "YOU'RE HERE. GOOD."

"HELLO." I CLOSED THE THE CHARTERHOUSE OF BALLARAT. "YOU READY FOR ME TO COME IN NOW?"

SHE OPENED THE DOOR THE REST OF THE WAY; I GOT OFF THE DESK.

"YES, LET'S BEGIN. I HOPE I DIDN'T KEEP YOU WAITING...?"

"THAT'S OKAY." I WALKED INTO THE ROOM.

COMING IN TO THE DULL GREEN WALLS, DARK WOOD UP TO THE WAIST, A DAY BED WITH A GREEN CORDUROY SPREAD, THREE BIG LEATHER CHAIRS, A TALL BOOKSHELF, DARK GREEN DRAPES, I HAD TO READJUST MY SPATIAL MODEL OF THE HOUSE: IT WAS THE BIGGEST ROOM ON THE FLOOR AND I'D NEVER BEEN IN IT.

ON THE WALL WAS A SWING-OUT DISPLAY RACK, LIKE IN POSTER SHOPS. I WALKED OVER, STARTED TO OPEN IT, GLANCED AT MADAME BROWN—

"GO AHEAD."

—AND TURNED THE FIRST LEAF, EXPECTING GEORGE:

Schützt die Natur

REGULAR MAIL

0115000220109 7

50 Jahre Fehmarnsundbrücke

Deutschland

75

WILLIAM DHALGREN
ARCHIVE BOOKS
DIEFFENBACHSTRAßE 31
10967 BERLIN, GERMANY

UNFINISHED

THE SEE-THROUGH BUILDING

ON THE HILL SOUTH OF CHAMS RIVER
SECOND ROAD OFF THE HIGHWAY

DARB ES SIM

LEBANON

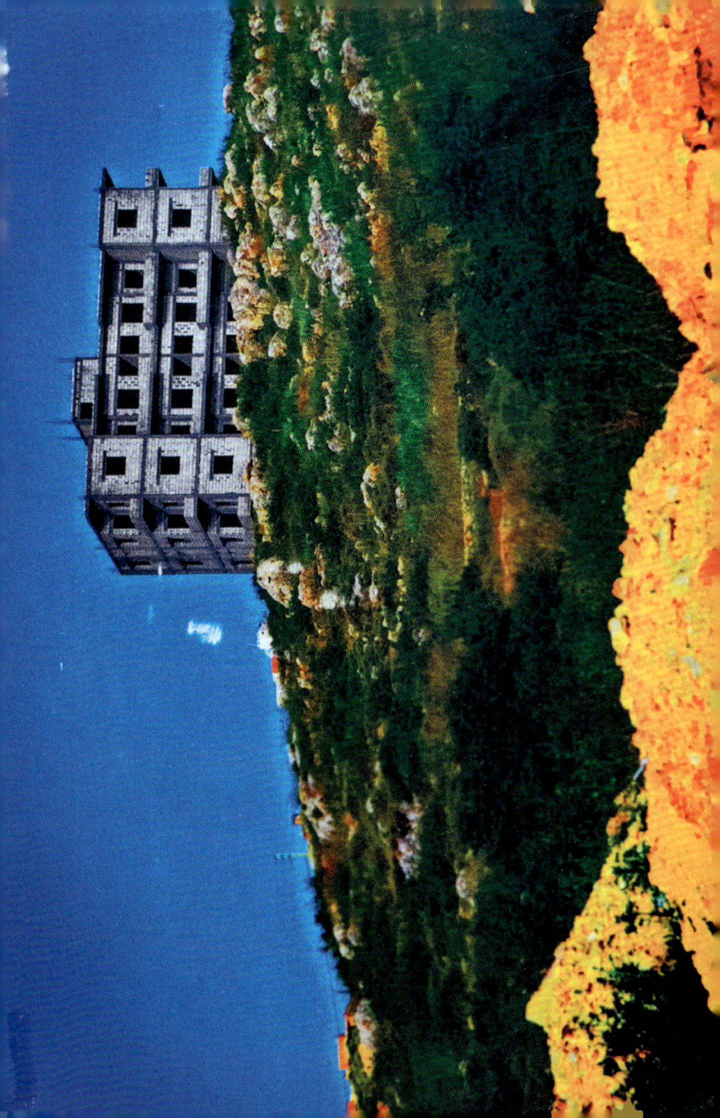

MADAME BROWN SAID; BUT LOOKED PUZZLED. "WE ALL HAVE TO GO ON FROM WHERE WE ARE. AND OF COURSE WE'VE ALL COME FROM WHERE WE'VE BEEN. CERTAINLY, AT SOME POINT, YOU MUST HAVE COME HERE. MORE IMPORTANT, THOUGH, IS NOT TO GET TRAPPED IN SOME CIRCLE OF YOUR OWN, HABITUAL—" OUTSIDE, THE DOG BARKED. "OH, THAT MUST BE MY NEXT PATIENT," MADAME BROWN INTERRUPTED HERSELF. THE DOG BARKED, KEPT BARKING.

MADAME BROWN FROWNED, HALF ROSE FROM THE CHAIR, ONE HAND AGAIN ABSENTLY AT HER BEADS. "MURIEL!" SHE CALLED; HER VOICE WAS LOUD AND LOW. "MURIEL!"

IT MUST HAVE BEEN SOMETHING IN THE JUXTAPOSITION: THE CHAINS OF LENSES AND PRISMS, OR PERHAPS THAT SHE HAD SAID THE BEADS MEANT NOTHING CONVINCED ME I WAS ABOUT TO LEARN THEIR REAL MEANING; NOT THAT I WAS THE PERSON IN THE HOSPITAL BUT THAT SOMEHOW I OR HE... OR THAT WAY SHE CALLED THE DOG MADE ME TRY TO REMEMBER SOME PLACE OR SOME TIME WHEN SHE, OR SOMEONE ELSE, HAD CALLED IT; NOT EVEN MY NAME, BUT POSSIBLY SOME OTHER, IF I COULD RECALL IT—EACH ELEMENT SEEMED ABOUT TO EXPLAIN THE OTHERS, CLEARING THE PATTERN; AND THAT SCRATCH... I GOT CHILLS. I WAS BEING NUDGED, PUSHED, ABOUT TO BE REMINDED OF...

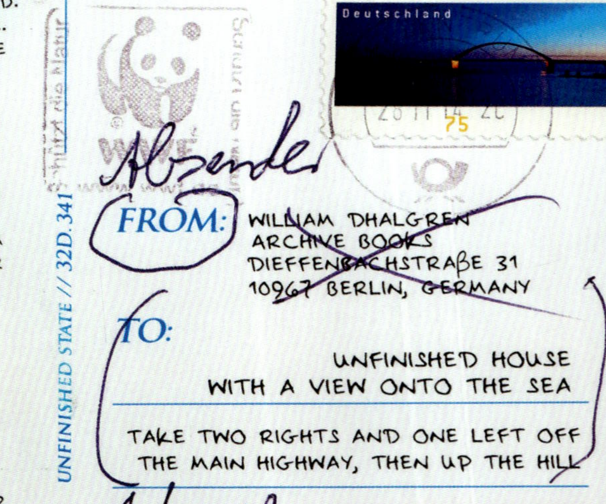